Group Psychotherapy

Interventions with Special Populations

Edited by

Milton Seligman, Ph.D.
University of Pittsburgh

Laura E. Marshak, Ph.D.
Indiana University of Pennsylvania

Allyn and Bacon
Boston   London   Sydney   Toronto

**To our mothers,
Irma Seligman and Dorothy Marshak**

Copyright © 1990 by Allyn and Bacon

A Division of Simon & Schuster, Inc.
160 Gould Street
Needham Heights, Massachusetts 02194

ISBN 0-205-12523-9

Library of Congress Cataloging-in-Publication Data not
available at press time.

Printed in the United States of America

10 9 8 7 6 5 4 3 2 1   95 94 93 92 91 90

Contents

Preface

The field of psychotherapy has become more specialized. With increasing frequency, psychotherapists are claiming specialized knowledge and experience in a variety of specific areas. This phenomenon follows on the heels of increased specialization in other fields, such as medicine, and is partially a result of burgeoning knowledge about the treatment of specific disorders and conditions, specialized training, and the increasingly segregated nature of service delivery systems. For example, persons with alcoholism are no longer chiefly treated by therapists working in community mental health settings. They are often referred to specialized settings where the staff has expertise in the area of alcoholism. Clinical settings which focus on a particular disorder are now frequently regarded as optimal for persons who experience other complex and serious conditions such as chronic pain, eating disorders, post-traumatic stress disorder, infertility, disability in the family, unemployment, or sexual victimization. A major rationale for specialized treament for specific disorders and conditions derives from the premise that extensive training and experience is a prerequisite for successful therapeutic outcome.

For the same reasons that individual psychotherapy has become more specialized, group psychotherapy has likewise increasingly sought to treat persons in groups who share a common major clinical disorder or life condition. Whereas expediency served as a major thrust for increased group activity following World War II, the chief factors for the increasing development of homogenous groups center upon certain therapeutic benefits. These include the therapeutic effects derived from a shared problem, such as a more immediate source of identification and understanding, a clearer sense of group purpose, and increased cohesiveness. Other reported benefits of homogeneous groups include a shortened period of treatment, less resistance, fewer cliques, better attendance, and quicker symptomatic relief (Furst, 1960; Yalom, 1985).

Our goal in this book is to provide the reader with an opportunity to understand the relevant group therapeutic approaches with specific client populations. In order to be maximally effective one needs to have an in-depth appreciation of the clinical population being served. Therefore, each chapter includes a profile of the clinical population to provide readers with an appreciation of treatment relevant factors, such as problems commonly experienced by the population, psychological aspects of the disorder, and demographic characteristics.

Each chapter provides a rationale for the efficacy of group therapy with the particular client population being discussed. A discussion of the factors that point to group treatment as a useful adjunct or intervention of choice highlights central features of the disorder/condition and how they may be ameliorated in group therapy.

Each chapter then elaborates on specific group therapy interventions. Embedded in this discussion are specialized interventions, clinical examples, common group themes, treatment precautions, and leadership issues. Many chapters also include resources for readers who wish more comprehensive information on particular conditions and treatment strategies.

In light of the growing role of support groups, a number of chapters refer to self-help models that serve as useful adjunct treatments. In addition, Chapter 1 explores the self-help group movement in some depth.

We recognize that research on group therapy with particular populations is not in abundance and that investigations related to specific interventions is similarly scarce. Nevertheless, where applicable and where a research base exists, relevant studies are briefly discussed.

Our society's heightened awareness of such human problems as easting disorders, AIDS, agoraphobia, and chronic mental illness, among others, has prompted therapists of various persuasions to consider interventions, such as group therapy, to help alleviate the human suffering that accompanies these conditions. With this in mind, it is our intent in this volume to address group treatment with such populations that have received short shrift in the past.

We owe a major debt of gratitude to the authors of each chapter. Their contributions reflect a major area of research and clinical interest for them. As editors, we believe that we have placed the substance of the book in capable hands. We would also like to acknowledge Mary Jane Alm and Roberta Allen for their help and support in bringing this book to fruition.

Milton Seligman
Laura E. Marshak

REFERENCES

Furst, W. (1960). Homogeneous versus heterogeneous groups. *Topical Problems in Psychotherapy, 2,* 170–173.

Yalom, I. (1985). *The theory and practice of group psychotherapy.* (3rd. Ed.). New York: Basic Books.

Contributors

Norman E. Amundson, Ph.D.
Department of Counseling Psychology, University of British Columbia
Vancouver, British Columbia

William A. Borgen, Ph.D.
Department of Counseling Psychology, University of British Columbia
Vancouver, British Columbia

Hugh Carberry, Ph.D.
Head Trauma Services, Our Lady of Lourdes Medical Center
Camden, New Jersey

William I. Cohen, M.D.
Private Practice
Pittsburgh, Pennsylvania

Lauren K. Cohn, Ph.D.
Hughes Medical Center and Miami Children's Hospital
Miami Florida

Rita G. Drapkin, Doctoral Candidate, University of Pittsburgh
Counseling and Student Center, Indiana University of Pennsylvania
Indiana, Pennsylvania

Michael Greenwald, Ph.D.
Private Practice
Pittsburgh, Pennsylvania

Patricia A. Halvorson, Ph.D.
Concordia College
Moorhead, Minnesota

Mark T. Hegel, Ph.D.
Department of Psychiatry, School of Medicine, Dartmouth University
Hanover, New Hampshire

James Huggins, Ph.D.
Persad Center, Inc.
Pittsburgh, Pennsylvania

Michael C. Hughes, M.D.
Hughes Mental Health Center and University of Miami School of Medicine
South Miami, Florida

Robert D. Kerns, Ph.D.
Department of Psychiatry, Yale University School of Medicine
Chief of Psychology Service and Director of the Comprehensive Pain Management
Center, VA Medical Center, New Haven, Connecticut

Morton A. Lieberman, Ph.D.
Aging and Mental Health Program, University of California
San Francisco, California

Laura E. Marshak, Ph.D.
Rehabilitation Program, Indiana University of Pennsylvania
Indiana, Pennsylvania

Jerome A. Motto, M.D.
University of California Medical Center
San Francisco, California

Patricia A. Neuman, Ed.S.
Moorhead State University
Moorhead, Minnesota

C. B. Scrignar, M.D.
Department of Psychiatry and Neurology, Tulane University School of Medicine
New Orleans, Louisiana

Milton Seligman, Ph.D.
Counseling Psychology Program, University of Pittsburgh
Pittsburgh, Pennsylvania

Deborah P. Valentine, Ph.D.
College of Social Work, University of South Carolina
Columbia, South Carolina

Marsha Vannicelli, Ph.D.
Appleton Outpatient Clinic, McLean Hospital and Harvard Medical School
Boston, Massachusetts

Mona Wasow, M.S.W.
School of Social Work, University of Wisconsin
Madison, Wisconsin

1
A Group Therapist Perspective on Self-Help Groups

Why would a group psychotherapist be interested in self-help groups (SHGs)? I became interested in SHGs in the early 1970s. At that point in my career, I had recently completed a major comparative study of ten "types" of encounter groups, a study undertaken in an attempt to broaden the knowledge base of group psychotherapy (Lieberman, Yalom, & Miles, 1973). One of the study's unanticipated findings was that two groups directed by a simple audiotape program had better positive outcomes than two-thirds of all the groups led by highly skilled leaders. This study stimulated questions on the nature of what leaders do in group therapy and how they contribute to the psychotherapeutic process (Lieberman, 1975, 1976, 1977).

Dissatisfied with the somewhat artificial context created by tape-led groups, I began to search for "real life groups" dealing with meaningful personal problems that did not utilize professional therapists. The obvious settings were SHGs, and I subsequently launched a series of studies on a variety of SHGs (Lieberman & Borman, 1976, 1979). My initial interest in self-help was as a researcher examining processes. Over the years, as my research and exposure to self-help broadened, other considerations of why a group therapist should be interested in SHGs came to dominate my thinking. For myself, it clearly was a laboratory for discovering processes that are relevant to how groups facilitate change in people, processes that I as a group therapist and researcher had heretofore not recognized. Beyond that, however, is the fact that such groups provide an important resource in our society for millions of people, and, as will become evident in this chapter, they are an effective alternative treatment system.

The chapter is divided into three parts. Part I outlines some of the fundamental facts we now know about SHGs—their origins, scope, magnitude, growth, and effectiveness. Part II examines some of the ways that SHGs and group psychotherapy are similar and different. Part III provides information on how group therapists have facilitated the well-being, growth, and stability of SHGs.

PART I: OVERVIEW OF SELF-HELP GROUPS

The designation "self-help group" is commonly applied to a wide variety of activities. Killilea's (1976) extensive review indicates that SHGs are described as support systems; social movements; spiritual movements and secular religions; systems of consumer participa-

This work was supported in part by a Research Scientist Award (5K05 Mh20343). Part I drew on previously published material, "Self Help Groups and Psychiatry," Chapter 35 in *APA Annual Review*, Vol. 5, 1986. This work also appears in part in the *International Journal of Group Psychotherapy* Vol. 40 (July 1990), International University Press, ©1990, American Group Psychotherapy Association, Inc. Reprinted by permission.

tion; alternative, care-giving systems adjunct to professional helping systems; intentional communities; supplementary communities; expressive-social influence groups; and organizations of the deviant and stigmatized. Of special interest to group therapists are SHGs that serve populations requiring or desiring mental health services, including individuals in emotional distress associated with physical conditions, stigmatized roles in society, and difficulties in negotiating the normal transitions of the life cycle, as well as dilemmas arising from the variety of stresses and strains that characterize modern society.

The self-help, or mutual-aid, group is an ill-defined, unbounded area, in which arbitrary judgments rather than conceptual structure are the rule. I will define self-help groups for the purposes of this chapter as being composed of members who share a common condition, situation, heritage, symptom, or experience. They are largely self-governing and self-regulating. They emphasize self-reliance and generally offer a face-to-face or phone-to-phone fellowship network that is available and accessible without charge. They tend to be self-supporting rather than dependent on external funding.

Development and Origins

Although the use of groups by mental health practitioners for aiding people in distress is of relatively recent origin, small groups have always served as improtant healing agents from the beginning of recorded history. Group forces have been used to inspire hope, increase morale, offer strong emotional support, induce serenity and confidence, or counteract psychic and bodily ills. Religious healers have always relied heavily on group forces, but when healing passed from the priestly to the medical profession, deliberate use of group forces fell into decline until post-World War II.

Although it is not difficult to find surface similarities between some SHG and professionally conducted psychotherapy groups, group psychotherapy and the vast majority of SHGs have distinctive historical roots. An examination of the published scholarship on the history of SHGs reveals a number of different perspectives, a difference in part based on the level of analyses and the scope of historical time considered. Some authors (Katz & Bender, 1976) focus on the origins of SHGs in Anglo-Saxon society, seeing the development of "friendly societies" in the eighteenth century as a parallel to the development of current SHGs. Other scholars (Hurvitz, 1974), studying such groups as Alcoholics Anonymous, Recovery Inc., and Synanon, see SHGs as developing out of a cultural context based on the interaction of the Protestant tradition in the U.S. with a secular democratic-populist philosophy.

The most common explanatory model used to account for the current development of SHGs is based on a functionalist framework, which sees new institutions arising in society when there are meaningful and recognized needs among members of that society that are not being met by existing institutions. This functionalist view accounts for the emergence of SHGs where there are unmet needs that apparently "fall between the cracks" of available services. Examples are plentiful. The inadequate professional response to the problems of alcoholism is proffered as the classic example. The recent development of SHGs for chronic medical conditions, despite the proliferation of professional rehabilitation services, is seen by some (Tracy & Gussow, 1976) as an indicator of the inadequacy of professional institutions to meet such needs.

In contrast to the functionalist view is the explanation of alternative pathways in which members of society obtain services already acknowledged in the programs of other institutions in that society. Here the emphasis is not so much on the unmet need as on the incorrectly or inadequately met need; the focus is on the form through which the service is offered.

Still another view is that the growth and development of such institutions are best explained by individual needs for affiliation and community with others in similar conditions. Here again the emphasis is on unmet needs but needs of a different kind than those addressed by the group's function. For many in modern western society, traditional affiliative bonds that might exist through professional societies, labor unions, and other such groups are limited or decreasing to a point where new foci of affiliation are required.

The Scope of Self-Help Groups

A good index of the diversity and magnitude of SHGs is provided by the information made available by a relatively new structure related to SHGs, self-help clearing houses or information exchanges. They provide for exchange among SHGs as well as information to prospective participants. Some centers provide consultation to ongoing SHGs; some are engaged in the development of new groups. The Self-Help Center of Evanston, Illinois, publishes (as do many others) a listing of active SHGs within the metropolitan area. The current directory has 320 organizations listed. They range from well-known organizations representing a number of local chapters, such as Alcoholics Anonymous, to small one- or two-chapter organizations, such as All but Dissertation Self-Help groups.

The breadth and diversity of problems these groups address is indeed astonishing—almost all chronic diseases are represented, as are psychiatric conditions such as agoraphobia, depression, epilepsy, families of suicide victims, a variety of neurological diseases, eating disorders, as well as a multitude of serious emotional crises brought on by expected as well as unexpected life events—retirement, widowhood, loss of a child, various illness or handicaps of children, unemployment, and divorce. The range of afflictions represented by SHGs is broad and appears to be increasing exponentially. Almost any definable physical and emotional problem, as well as stigmatized conditions and feelings of deviance, provides a nexus for their formation.

Results from a recent national survey permit us to be more precise about the prevalence and utilization of SHGs. Mellinger and Balter (1983) reported findings on 1-year utilization rates from a national probability sample of over 3,000 households. One-year prevalence rates for help-seeking were: 5.6% sought out mental health professionals; 5% used clergy or pastoral sources; and 5.8% participated in SHGs (groups directed toward behavioral change such as AA represented a 2.3% prevalence rate, those whose goals were to provide support such as widows' groups represented a 0.7% prevalence rate, and groups for personal development represented a 2.2% prevalence rate [Lieberman, 1986]). These findings suggest that mutual aid groups are a major and growing source of therapeutic treatment for a variety of physical and emotional difficulties, and estimates that 12 to 14 million adult Americans utilize such groups have some basis in empirical fact.

Effectiveness of SHGs

Empirical research on outcomes is limited and covers a narrow band of activities. Studies of behavioral deviations—alcoholism, overeating, and drug abuse—predominate. Less frequent are studies of groups that deal with various life transitions or crises and major mental disorders. Compared with the relative sophistication of current empirical studies on psychotherapy, the number and quality of studies available for assessing the effects of SHG resemble the status of psychotherapy research in the 1950s.

Clinical-descriptive studies are far more numerous than more rigorous quasi-experimental or experimental designs. The special dilemmas facing investigators in designing self-help outcome research probably contribute to the scarcity of well-controlled studies. The context of SHGs, in contrast to settings for psychotherapy, are not under the control of the investigator. The values inherent in SHGs and their community base frequently make it difficult to design research meeting current standards of psychotherapy evaluation. For example, the methods that SHGs use to recruit their members would make the usual design requirements for random assignment, alternate treatments, or delayed treatment controls logistically difficult. The few experimental studies that exist on SHGs (Farash, 1979; Gates, 1980; Gordon, Edmunson, Bedell, & Goldstein, 1979; Gould, Garrigues, & Scheikowitz, 1975) represent self-help in name only, since they are frequently controlled by professionals, of brief duration, and do not represent some of the essential characteristics of SHGs. At best, quality evaluative research on SHGs represents quasi-experimental designs, using contrast groups for comparisons.

These methodologic and design issues should not create in the reader's mind the view that it is not possible to evaluate the impact of SHGs. Rather, it should alert us, on one hand, to the current state of knowledge and, on the other hand, to the fact that the solutions to good empirical research will, by the very nature of the phenomena being studied, have to be somewhat different than traditional solutions to psychotherapy outcome research.

Some Representative Findings on the Effectiveness of SHGs

The most widely studied SHG is Alcoholics Anonymous. Some studies evaluate AA alone (Bohince & Orensteen, 1950; Henry & Robinson, 1978); others have examined the contribution of AA as one of several interventions (Kish & Hermann, 1970; McCance & McCance, 1969; Oakley & Holden, 1972; Pattison, Headley, Glesser, & Gottschalk, 1968; Robson, Paulus, & Clarke, 1965; Rohan, 1970; Rossi, 1970; Tomsovic, 1970). Large-scale studies based on cross-sectional surveys are represented by Bailey and Leech (1965), who obtained questionnaire responses from over 1,000 persons; Edwards, Hensman, Hawker, and Williamson (1967), who reported on 306 respondents. Such cross-sectional findings suggest that at any point in time, from one-third to a half of the members have been sober less than one year. Those studies that evaluated AA as one element in the treatment program suggest that alcoholics who attend AA in addition to other treatment modalities do better. Despite the overall positive findings, methodologic problems of measurement and sampling do not permit a definitive statement about the efficacy.

SHGs addressing eating disorders are rapidly expanding; estimates of upwards of a half a million members in the U.S. for TOPS (Take Off Pounds Sensibly) have been proposed. In a series of studies, Stunkard, Levine, and Fox (1970) suggested that the effectiveness of TOPS is limited. In contrast, a study by Grimsmo, Helgesen, and Borchgrevink (1981), reporting on a large-scale prospective study of over 10,000 people in a Norwegian SHG for weight reduction, found significant and meaningful weight reduction that was retained over 4 years among participants in SHGs. These contrasting findings eloquently address the oft-repeated caution that SHGs represent a variety of activities, processes, and conditions. Generalizations without the detailed build-up of empirical studies and conceptual analyses that address not only effectiveness but the link between the processes and effectiveness remain in the future.

Outcome studies of groups other than behavioral disorder groups are less plentiful. Much of this research was conducted by myself and my colleagues who have, over the past 7 years, examined eight different SHGs: Women's Consciousness-Raising Groups; Mended Hearts, a medical SHG concerned with individuals who have had open heart surgery; NAIM and THEOS, both of which are directed toward widows/widowers; Compassionate Friends, a SHG for parents who suffered the death of a child; Mothers Groups and Mothers of Twins Groups, both of which are directed toward addressing the emotional problems of motherhood; and Senior Actualization and Growth Explorations (SAGE), a SHG directed toward those over age 65 (Lieberman & Borman, 1979).

A variety of methods were used in the series of studies, including ethnographic observation, intensive interviews and large-scale panel surveys of members and nonmembers ($N = 5,000$). The survey questionnaires generated information about the people who join, the pathways by which people enter such organizations, alternative help-seeking behavior, and use of the SHG by members, and a variety of outcome instruments assessed indices of mental and physical health role functioning, coping strategies, and "affliction" or illness attitudes and beliefs. A follow-up strategy was utilized whereby members and controls were assessed for a minimum of two points in time separated by a year, while in the bereavement groups, a long-term follow-up 4 years later was also conducted.

Overall, the results of this research are encouraging: measurable improvement was found in levels of depression and self-esteem in women who joined consciousness-raising groups (Lieberman, Solow, Bond, & Reibstein, 1979); the spousally bereaved who participated in SHGs compared with controls showed a marked improvement in levels of depression, well-being, self-esteem, and life satisfaction (Lieberman & Videka-Sherman, 1986); among the members of Mended Hearts (Bond et al., 1979), the large subgroup who had retired as a consequence of surgery showed significantly improved scores on mental health indicators; among parents who had lost children, we found improvement, again compared with a control group, in coping strategies and in measures of existential concerns but did not find significant improvement after 1 year participation in mental health or social functioning (Videka-Sherman & Lieberman, 1985). The results for first-time mothers (Reibstein, 1981) were more ambiguous, and we could find no substantial data that participation in such groups significantly improved women's psychological or social functioning. Mothers of twins, however, showed some improvement in their social and psychological functioning (Glaser, 1981).

PART II: A COMPARISON OF GROUP PSYCHOTHERAPY AND SHG PROCESSES

This section examines the similarities and differences between group psychotherapy and SHGs using both empirical evidence and conceptual analyses. The first analysis looks at helping groups in general to determine the basis of the common grounds. Then the sources of heterogeneity in SHGs are analyzed. The section ends with a theoretical framework for comparing a variety of helping situations in order to better place the similarities and differences between SHGs and group psychotherapy in a conceptual context.

Common Ground

No matter what theoretical position is taken by professional or nonprofessional leaders, helping groups are small, face-to-face, interactive units. The fact that individuals enter such structures in a high state of personal need and are required to share with others topics and feelings that are often considered personal and private leads to important consequences for the kinds of experiences paticipants will encounter. They arrive in helping groups and find themselves faced with a number of strangers frequently dissimilar to themselves except for one critical characteristic, the shared problem. No matter whether it is a professionally led, traditional psychotherapeutic group, one of the groups promulgated in the last decade for personal growth, or a collectivity of similarly afflicted—all such groups share three basic elements: the intensity of need expressed by the individuals joining them; the requirements, no matter how banal, to share something personal; and the real or perceived similarity in their suffering. These conditions and the structure of a small, face-to-face interactive system have profound consequences for what will occur.

Foremost is the capacity of such groups to generate a sense of belonging among the participants, a shared sense of similar suffering that creates high levels of cohesiveness. It provides the motivation for participants to remain in and work with the group. Cohesive groups offer their members almost unconditional acceptance and provide a supportive atmosphere for taking risks, which in most such groups involves the sharing of personal material and the expression of emotions that may, from the participant's perspective, be difficult to do among strangers.

Another factor creating a high sense of belonging is the perception by the participants of their deviant status in society. In small groups, the feeling of being stigmatized frequently leads to the creation of a feeling of "we-ness" and a sharp boundary line between them and us, the "them" usually referring to the rest of society.

The high level of cohesiveness, perceived similarity, and the perception that they are "different" from others outside of the "refuge" influences the saliency of being a participant. In some ways, the group takes on the characteristics of a primary group; it becomes "family-like" and does, in fact, serve as a new reference group for the participants. These interrelated properties of small groups are not a product of the particular group theory or ideology, type of problem, or style of leadership, but rather are intrinsic conditions of small groups, made all the more pronounced in groups of similarly afflicted individuals by the state of need in which they enter such groups and by the requirements for certain kinds of personal sharing and banding together against a perceived hostile external world. Experiences seen by participants as helpful, in both group psychotherapy and self-help groups, uniformly cite support, acceptance, and normalizing of their perceived affliction as helpful (Lieberman, 1985).

The group's capacity to control behavior and to provide a system of rewards and punishments is closely associated with and dependent on the level of cohesiveness. As a microcosm of a larger socieety, small face-to-face groups develop their own cultures and depend on special rules or standards that they establish as they extend their lives. How much one talks, what one does or does not talk about, even "the way" one talks about certain things are aspects of behavior that the group influences. The group member is almost inevitably confronted with pressure from others to change behaviors and views. The need to be in step, to abide by the rules, is a powerful factor in inducing conformity in the group. Disregard of the rules means possible psychological punishment. The ultimate punishment available to the group is the power of exclusion, either psychological or physical. An additional strong force pulling members toward conformity is the group's most prized reward, the authenticating affirmation of one's peers. The experience of consensual validation (approval by other members who have become important) appears to be one of the most important and gratifying experiences available to members in the group.

Illustrations of this group characteristic from SHGs I have studied are abundant, for example, the emphasis in consciousness-raising (CR) groups on issues centered around being women. The interest in women's issues as important change processes is in part understandable, not necessarily because of the intrinsic needs of the participants but because of the influence of the group toward a certain kind of conformity. We found that most women joined CR groups to address emotionally distressing problems (Lieberman & Bond, 1976). However, it is probably impossible to remain a participant in a CR group without being influenced by their particular emphasis on women's issues. This is not to say that these explorations do not prove useful to the members of such groups, but rather to place such perceptions in context and see them not only as a product of ideologic issues or the nature of the affliction but also as a product of the particular characteristics of all face-to-face groups.

Another important aspect of small face-to-face groups is their capacity to induce powerful affective states in the participants. Individuals may get carried away, experiencing feelings that they later believe uncharacteristic of themselves and acting on feelings without displaying their typical controls. The group's potential to stimulate emotionality is an important characteristic that bears directly on the experiences members have in small face-to-face groups. This is particularly important in helping groups, where members arrive with high needs, are frequently in states of vulnerability, and are required to share personal matters. This group property is likely to lead to certain expressions of affect. Most notable, in the self-help groups that I have studied, are the emotional expressions of pain, anger, and profound sadness. For example, Compassionate Friends' opening ritual where members recite the loss of their child usually induces in new members strong affects that soon become shared by all in attendance.

Another common characteristic of groups is social comparisons. Because the group members are placed in a social context that expects, and often demands, that they talk about personal matters and needs relevant to the problem that brought them to the group, this social comparative process becomes all the more compelling. Individuals contrast their attitudes and feelings about things that matter, and such comparisons facilitate revision of the person's identity by suggesting new possibilities for feeling, perceiving, and behaving. The cognitive mechanism of modeling, in which individuals are able to compare their own approach to particular problems with that of others and to gain new perspectives, is a prime example of this process. Another illustration is the emphasis in Compassionate Friends on the inculcation of hope through seeing others endure. Because such groups focus around specific relevant issues in an emotionally charged setting, they provide their members with a wide variety of information about how others who are perceived as similar feel, think, believe, and behave.

Taken together, these characteristics provide the commonness for both SHGs and psychotherapy groups. They are intrinsic properties of groups and are conditions that prevail no matter what the particular ideology, affliction, or the belief system of a leader of such groups. They certainly influence what members perceive as important and, in fact, influence the actual kinds of experiences people are likely to have in such groups. They occur because individuals in high need have sought out such groups.

Specificity

Self-help groups are complex entities. They create experiences that are thought to be therapeutic in nature such as inculcation of hope, development of understanding, and the experience of being loved. Self-help groups are also cognitive restructuring systems that possess elaborate ideologies about the core cause and source of difficulty and about the way individuals need to think about their dilemmas in order to get help. Additionally, they are social linkage systems where people form relationships, and in that sense, they provide social support. We found that all types of SHGs are unified by the simple fact that all are collections of fellow sufferers in high states of personal need and that all require some aspect of the personal and often painful affliction to be shared in public. Regardless of the type of group, participants uniformly indicated that the abilities of such groups to provide for normalization (universalization) and support were central. Despite these common elements, examination of each of the nine types of SHGs studied suggests major differences in emphasis on a variety of other mechanisms. Self-help groups differ considerably, for example, with regard to their emphasis on cognitive mechanisms. Such processes—increasing understanding, putting roles into perspective, and providing insight into personal problems—are critical in women's CR groups. In contrast, Commpassionate Friends' participants emphasize the inculcation of hope and existential concerns; they view cognitive mechanisms as relatively unimportant. Mended Hearts emphasizes altruism, apparently in response to survivor guilt themes in those who have had open heart surgery. Overall, our findings suggest that despite a common core there are major differences in the mechanisms that the participants find useful (Lieberman, 1983).

Another perspective on specificity is offered by the work of Antze (1976), who suggests that each group he studied (AA, Recovery Inc., and Synanon) has a specific ideology that is closely linked to the underlying psychological problem associated with the affliction. He suggests that the common pathology found among alcoholics reflects an exaggerated sense of personal power, and that this attitude plays a central role in the psychology of compulsive drinking. His analysis of AA ideology suggests that AA provides a specific and thorough antidote to the alcoholic's way of being; its prime therapeutic function is to induce a wide range of contradictions in a member's sense of exaggerated power. To absorb the AA message is to see oneself as less the author of events in life, the active fighter and doer, and more as a person with the wisdom to accept limitations and wait for things to come. Antze's careful analysis of AA and comparison to Recovery Inc., which on superficial grounds may appear to function similarly, demonstrate each group's specific and unique characteristics.

A recent study provides empirical support to the obervation of highly specific processes (Lieberman, 1983). I chose three organizations for a test of specific "curative factors" associated with benefit. All three types of SHGs involved significant personal losses, spousal bereavement (THEOS and NAIM), and child loss by parents (Compassionate Friends). A 31-item instrument indexing change mechanisms was adminstered after 1 year of participation. Members were asked how helpful, in a three-point scale, each of the 31 items had been in their learning. The change mechanism categories used to generate the items were: Universality, Support, Self-Disclosure, Catharsis, Insight, Social Analysis, Advice-Information, Perspective, Feedback, Comparative-Vicarious Learning, Altruism, and Existential Experimentation (Lieberman & Borman, 1979).

Outcome was measured using a common central concern of bereavement—feelings of guilt and anger. Each participant was asked to indicate, on a series of scales, the ways he or she had changed. The participants studied included 491 THEOS members, 187 NAIM members, and 197 members of Compassionate Friends. Separate factor analysis of the responses to this questionnaire for each of the self-help organizations yielded a factor concerned with guilt and anger. Low significance correlations (.20-range) were found between this factor and standard depression and self-esteem scales. Decreased guilt was defined by scores 1 *SD* below the group mean; 1 *SD* above the group mean was defined as a low-change group. We asked what events or experiences judged to be helpful would maximally distinguish the high and low learners; we found that the particular sets of events distinguishing those who decreased in guilt and those who increased in guilt were unique for each type of SHG.

For the widows in NAIM the core experiences associated with guilt reduction were the sharing of troublesome feelings; normalization, not feeling out of place; the redirection of anger by externalizing it; the seeing of problems as a product of an insensitive world; and more socially acceptable reaching out to others in need. The avoidance of hostile impulses by not venting anger and by avoiding the aggressive implications of social comparison was characteristic of those who did not show guilt reduction. The conversion of feelings outside of self as well as catharsis in a setting that signifies that their feelings, behaviors, and thoughts are normal were central.

In the other type of spousal bereavement SHG, THEOS, contrasting results were observed. The normalization aspects were certainly there, but rather than emphasis on expressivity, revelation, and externalization onto objects outside of self, an emphasis on cognitive mastery and the use of the group context for experimentation was characteristic.

Among parents who have lost children, change mechanisms different from either of the two widowhood groups occur. Although normalization is common to all three, critical for guilt reduction in Compassionate Friends are existential considerations; the inculcation of hope and confrontation with the situation. Loss of a child, especially where the loss was unexpected, was uniformly accompanied by bitterness and fury at society. Many parents experienced isolation from everyone; this appeared to represent a distinct psychological state different from what we have seen among our widows and widowers. Perhaps the dilemma facing those who have lost a child and the consequent experience of acute guilt and responsibility can best be resolved through confrontation with the ultimate meaning of their lives.

Another empirical test of SHG specificity was demonstrated by two recently completed studies examining bereaved parents and widows and widowers (Lieberman & Videka-Sherman, 1986; Videka-Sherman & Lieberman, 1985). The methods for study were identical. Cohorts of bereaved who were members of SHGs (those who participated in at least three meetings) were compared with matched bereaved parents or the spousally bereaved who had access to but chose not to join such groups. All were followed for 1 year, and outcome was measured by assessments of mental health, social functioning, and physical health. Analysis of the spousally bereaved indicated that the development of new linkages with other widows or widowers in which mutual exchange occurred was the necessary condition for significant change. Those participants who experienced a diversity of therapeutic mechanisms, including abreaction, advice, and inculcation of hope, but who did not form such new social exchange relationships, did not significantly improve. However, using identical measures among the bereaved parents, those who established such relationships were no more likely to improve than those who did not establish significant exchange relationships.

Such findings suggest that detailed studies of processes are required before making the all-too-easy generalization that SHGs benefit people because they provide excellent sources of social support. In two related problem areas, spousal bereavement and bereavement due to the death of a child, we found that the psychology of each is different and that the processes by which such structures as SHGs work are distinct. These findings are particularly important because of the all too common perception equating SHGs and social support, leading some to see SHG participation as evidence for the beneficial effects of social supportive relationships. Certainly, relationships are formed in all the groups we studied. People talk to one another, often about emotionally important and sensitive issues, and share important information about the affliction. Members frequently are exposed to information about coping strategies, and often they are provided acceptance and the enhancement of self-esteem. It is thus not an issue whether certain socially supportive transactions occur both during formal meetings and in between meetings. Their occurrence, however, does not translate directly into evidence that these are the necessary and sufficient conditions for the helpfulness of SHGs.

A Framework for Comparing Group Helping Systems

Differences among the many dyadic and group settings that offer psychological help, including individual dynamic psychotherapy, intensive group therapy, SHGs, peer counseling, homogeneous group therapy, and social supports, can be usefully described by five dimensions:

The helping group as a social microcosm. All group psychotherapists, no matter what their theoretical persuasions, share, as a fundamental assumption, a view of the group as a social microcosm: a small, complete social world, reflecting in miniature all of the dimensions of real social environments. It is this aspect of the group—its reflection of the intrapersonal issues that confront individuals in a larger society—that is most highly prized as a group property linked to an individual's change. Various schools of psychotherapeutic thought differ over what transactions are most important—those between patient and therapist, or those among patients. They also differ regarding which emotional states are most conducive to positive change. But underneath all activities lies the assumption that cure or change is based on the exploration and reworking of relationships in the group. SHGs develop a rather different stance on the issue of the group as a social microcosm. Interaction among members as a vehicle for change is deemphasized. The group is a supportive environment for developing new behavior, not primarily within the group, but outside. The group may become a vehicle for cognitive restructuring, but analysis of the transaction among members is not the basic tool of change.

Technological complexity/simplicity. This concept portrays one attempt to capture the central characteristic of professional psychotherapy that distinguishes it from the help provided by peers and nonprofessionals. It defines the theoretical model delineating the nature of the problem, methods for translating information provided by the client into a diagnosis, and principles guiding interventions used to bring about change in the client. Most professional treatment models depend on complex technologies that may require many years of training for accurate and effective implementation. In contrast, help provided within the client's informal network relies on the simplest of technologies: no formal definitions of problems, no diagnoses, and "interventions" rooted in everyday social interactions.

This dimension may also be used to describe a wide range of other nonprofessional help systems. For example, Goodman's (1972) companionship therapy, where college students "counseled" high school students, grew out of the assumption that most psychologically healthy people have the capacity and know-how to be helpful. Such interventions resemble normal social exchange and are similar to help given within the informal network. However, because peer counselors encounter more defined problems and have access to training and supervision, their interventions are somewhat more complex than those offered in ordinary relationships.

SHGs offer more systematic codes of treatment than those provided by friends and relatives or peer counselors. While SHG interventions appear simple, drawing on everyday skills, their help methods follow a specific ideology that defines the problem and directs specific interventions. Through participation, members learn the ideology and incorporate principles into their thinking and interactions with others. It should be noted that professional help is not always equated with high technological complexity and nonprofessional help with low complexity. Rioch, Elkes, and Flint's (1963) classic project for training housewives to be psychotherapists relied on the induction of complex technology.

Psychological distance/closeness between helper and helpee. Located at one extreme, many professionals, through both special training and manipulation of symbols and settings attendant to professionalism, increase the psychological distance between themselves and the patient. Nonprofessional help systems assume that reducing psychological distance promotes identification and trust, which in turn facilitates productive therapy. In peer counseling, when the selected helper shares a cultural background or social position with the client, he or she would presumably convey greater understanding of certain problems and would appear less threatening to the person seeking help. Of all help systems, SHGs achieve the greatest psychological parity between the helper and those being helped. Not only are helpers frequently similar in social background, but more importantly, they share the same affliction as those seeking help. Client control of the organization also erases psychological distance between helper and helpee; often all members work together to solve problems with no formal distinctions between helper and client.

Specificity/generality of help methods. This concept portrays variations in how the methods of helping systems relate to the particular dilemma, distress, or affliction they address. High generality, in which methods do not vary with the particular dilemma, characterizes the help offered by friends and family. People offer support, warmth, understanding, and instrumental help in much the same manner regardless of whether the dilemma arose from widowhood, illness, or any one of the variety of problems and predicaments that plague the human condition. The help provided by nonprofessional therapists and peer counselors tends toward the general. Interventions rooted in normal social exchange resemble each other regardless of the nature of the particular problem.

The help methods employed by professional therapists are more specific than the generalized support offered by peer counselors, but less specific than the help offered in mutual aid or self-help groups (with few important exceptions, e.g., behavioral modification regimes). Exercises and methods used in encounter groups, although sometimes directed toward particular group members, do not necessarily respond to individual differences. Helping systems such as client-centered therapy that do not emphasize diagnosis tend to be quite general, despite codified intervention techniques. Dynamic psychotherapies assign a diagnosis and more specifically address personal problems, although considerable evidence of nonspecific therapeutic factors exists.

High specificity characterizes SHGs. Antze's (1976) study of self-help organizations demonstrates how they develop specific ideologies about the nature of the problem and tailor appropriate help methods to the specific afflictions they address. Drug abuse groups conducted by ex-addicts employed confrontive, often explosive, emotionally exhausting techniques in order to counteract the mounting anxieties and social withdrawal characteristics of certain types of drug abusers. In Mended Hearts, a self-help group for individuals who have had open-heart surgery, help methods focus on altruism in order to deal with the "survival" guilt found among such patients (Bond et al., 1979).

Differentiation versus nondifferentiation among participants. Being neurotic, having psychological difficulty, or being a patient are vague and relatively unbound identifications compared with being a widow, a parent whose child has died, an alcoholic, or someone who has undergone open heart surgery. It is easier for SHGs to stress identity with a common core problem than it is for psychotherapy groups. Although it is typical for a psychotherapeutic group to go through a period of time in which similarities are stressed, this is usually an early developmental phase and represents an attempt of the group to achieve some form of cohesiveness. It is not the raison d'etre of the group as it may be for a self-help group. In fact, there is some evidence that psychotherapeutic group participants who remain committed to a sense of similarity are less likely to experience positive change. The potency of SHGs, on the other hand, appears to stem from their continued insistence on the possession of a common problem; the members believe they derive support from their identification with a common core issue.

There is a class of group psychotherapy, however, labeled by Weiner (1986) as homogeneous group therapy, whose members are united by their struggle with a common problem. Weiner reviews the literature of such group psychotherapy for a variety of psychiatric and physical problems. This is a parallel development in group psychotherapy and, in terms of the framework presented here, represents properties and characteristics shared between more traditional group psychotherapy and SHGs. Weiner states that such homogeneous groups appear more useful than other therapeutic approaches in dealing with persons whose complaints center around a single problem or behavior or who see themselves as reacting to environmental pressures. They are also useful in treating patients for whom education, identification, and mutual support are the most important elements of therapy, and for patients who are better able to make peer identifications than to identify with the therapist.

On examining the points at which these dimensions intersect, we can see patterns emerging: most SHGs are low on complexity, use of the group context as a social microcosm, and differentiation. They are high on specificity and low on psychological distance. Traditional dynamic group psychotherapy is high on complexity and social microcosm, moderate on specificity, and high on psychological distance and differentiation. Encounter groups tend to be high on complexity, low on specificity and differentiation, moderate to low on psychological distance, and moderate on the use of the group as a social microcosm. Social support from family and friends and peer counseling are low on complexity, low on specificity, and low on psychological distance. Nonprofessional, individual therapies incorporating the training methods such as those Rioch et al. (1963) used with the housewives in their study are high on complexity, low on specificity, and moderate on psychological distance.

PART III: ROLES AND CONTRIBUTIONS OF GROUP THERAPISTS TO SHGs

As professionals with specialized knowledge, what can group therapists contribute to SHGs? This section examines four strategies for contribution, legitimization, transfer of technology, consultation, and the development of new groups. Also examined are concerns that group therapists may have about the continued development and expansion of SHGs covering an ever larger range of problem areas.

Professional Concerns

Does the spread of SHGs that resemble but are certainly not identical with psychotherapy groups pose a problem for professional practice? Are SHGs competitors in the marketplace? This concern is particularly salient given the expansion of professionals trained to provide service and the shrinking of resources among a population who may need and desire such services but lack adequate finances. Superficially, the answer to this question seems to be obvious; however, empirical findings suggest quite the contrary. In a national sample of 721 widows and widowers, composed of both participants in a SHG, THEOS, and a group of nonparticipant controls, we found that 28% of the sample had used professional mental health services for problems associated with spousal bereavement (Lieberman & Videka-Sherman, 1986). Although the sample was by no means representative of all widows, it does provide some clues regarding the utilization of services. On a national basis, only 4% of the spousally bereaved utilized professional mental health services for problems associated with spousal bereavement. The finding in our sample that somewhat over a quarter of the widows and widowers utilized psychotherapy underscores a more generalizable characteristic of self-help participants, namely, that they are users of multiple services. When compared with nonparticipants, they significantly avail themselves of professional services more often, and have better social support networks. We have in the past made similar observations on participants in SHGs for those that have experienced the death of a child (Videka-Sherman & Lieberman, 1985), as well as women who participated in women's CR groups (Lieberman & Bond, 1976). Also found was that the majority of such multiservice users perceive the services they have received in the various settings as productive.

Some mental health professionals are concerned about the harm that may be caused to the psychiatrically vulnerable by participation in SHGs. The simple fact that SHG helping processes are different from those utilized by mental health professionals is not a prima facie case for SHG inadequacy or harmfulness. Those who have written meaningfully about the potential harm of SHGs point to the possibility that some people are in need of services that can best be provided by professionals but are diverted into SHGs (Henry & Robinson, 1978). Harm in this sense is produced by not obtaining the help needed at a particular juncture in the person's life cycle. Our own studies have not permitted us to clarify this issue; certainly, all who have been students of SHGs can point to specific individuals at particular times whose problems were of such a magnitude that the group could not reasonably address them. Serious and major depressive illness precipitated by the loss of a spouse has, in my experience, not been amenable to the otherwise positive benefits of widow and widower SHGs. Beyond case examples, however, our own data suggest that most individuals who participate in SHGs ordinarily avail themselves of a variety of services.

Other investigators have pointed to the potential of the self-help "movement" to divert society from developing and funding critical services. The social criticism is a serious one and certainly should be noted; unfortunately, at this juncture no meaningful empirical evidence exists that would shed light on this issue.

Strategies Used by Group Therapist in Aiding SHG Legitimization

SHGs, like other help-providing structures, require societal legitimization. Professionals can play a critical role here. Health-care providers frequently function to transfer legitimization initially granted to them by society to SHGs. Other traditional systems, such as religious institutions sanctioned by society for serving the bereaved, are frequently the prime legitimizers of bereavement SHGs. A critical function that group therapists can play in aiding SHGs is simply to help give them legitimacy. Simple strategies such as referral to SHGs when indicated and providing back-up support for referral are common examples. Without a source of legitimacy, SHGs look inward, lack vitality, and often disappear within a few years.

The Transfer of Technology

Perhaps the most common role and the one that flows most logically from the group psychotherapist's specialized knowledge is the provision of technical skill for nonprofessionals. The transfer of technology through education, training, and supervision from professionals to nonprofessionals has a long and variable history (for general reviews see Cowen, Gardner, & Zacks, 1976; Grosser, Henry, & Kelley, 1969; Williams & Ozarin, 1968). The need to transfer technolgy reflects broad societal changes in who delivers psychotherapeutic services. Since the 1960s, help for psychological problems has been offered by a wide range of sources: high school students, middle-aged housewives, neighborhood workers, nurses, retired people, ex-addicts, ex-alcoholics, and parents who are trained to treat their own children. Conceptual ambiguity marks these efforts since the activities labeled peer therapy may have little in common with one another. Peer treatment implies that those conducting the therapy share a significant characteristic with their clients such as the presenting problem or social class.

Despite this long tradition and considerable clinical and evaluative experience, the view taken here is that the transfer of technology by the development of *self-help group leaders* educated in the helping strategies developed by professionals is not a useful direction. This conclusion is based on both a conceptual analysis and some empirical findings. Part II outlined differences between group psychotherapy and SHGs. Five dimensions were described: social microcosm, technical complexity-simplicity, specificity-generality of helping methods, degree of psychological distance between the group leader/therapist and participants, and the differentiation-nondifferentiation among participants. That analysis led to the conclusion that there are fundamental differences between the SHG model and group psychotherapy. Particularly important was the emphasis by group therapists on therapeutic strategies that were based on viewing the group as a social microcosm and their intervention styles that were rooted in a highly developed complex technology. Both are not characteristic of SHGs. Nor are they strategies that would easily be skillfully emphasized by nonprofessionals. In addition, the training of peers in professional styles increases the psychological distance between the provider of service and those who are helped (a central and critical ingredient in SHGs).

This is not to say that professionally trained peer helpers are not effective in certain settings and circumstances. However, if we accept the view that SHGs are highly specific structures with their own characteristics that make them successful, and if we believe that such groups have evolved an elaborate and intricate ideology (cognitive structure) out of the experiences of the afflicted themselves, we then need to recognize that SHGs are a fundamentally different activity for alleviating human suffering from the processes of alleviation provided by professional group therapists.

One study (Lieberman & Bliwise, 1985) provides some empirical support on the limits of technological transfer. SAGE, a group program developed for the community elderly, compared participants randomly assigned to groups led by professionals with groups led by the elderly who were trained and supervised by the SAGE professional staff. Both conditions were compared with a wait control group. A series of pre- and postmeasures in goal attainment scales and physical and mental health were used to evaluate impact. After 9 months of intervention, analysis revealed statistically significant evidence that the groups conducted by professionals had a more positive impact than those led by the peers. Differences in the group processes between professional and peer-led leaders provided some confirmatory evidence.

We know from review of outcome in Part I that SHGs can be effective; we also have evidence (Durlak, 1979) that paraprofessionals or nonprofessionals can be effective therapists. The implications of the SAGE study need to be placed in context. The efficacies of SHGs cited in Part I are those of groups that have evolved their own helping procedures. There is no reason to assume that nonprofessionals trained in professional helping procedures could do as well as professionals. If we accept the unique processes of SHGs, then there appears no rationale for a strategy based on the transfer of technology despite its obvious appeal. At best, it can only create an underclass of helpers who probably cannot operate with the skill of professionals.

Another model for the transfer of technology has recently evolved, based on new institutions developed to facilitate SHGs. These are professionally directed settings—self-help clearing houses—that provide a variety of facilitative services to established SHGs by linking people in need of such services to appropriate settings, providing legitimization, and helping to establish new SHGs. The information exchanged in these settings is, however, based on the methods of established self-help organizations, a technology that is distinct from professional therapeutics. Caution needs to be exercised, however, when using this approach. For example, new SHGs are often "spun off" from older ones. Well-established groups such as Alcoholics Anonymous are copied by people with a variety of other afflictions. This approach has had limited success. Since the ideology, strategy, and structure of AA address the special issues of alcoholism, they may have little to do with other problems. Those groups that appear to have been successful in borrowing current ideologies and structures have modified them. The group therapist can help in this transfer by aiding in the differentiation of appropriate and inappropriate "borrowing." Self-help clearing houses have helped the spread and maintenance of SHGs by providing consultation from one SHG to another. It is important, however, for professionals to constantly remind themselves that what enables most SHGs to flourish and maintain themselves over time is a set of shared ideas. Professionals must be sensitive to these ideas, which address the nature, cause, and cure of afflictions or problems. These ideas may often be diametrically opposed to a professional view of the nature of the problem and most particularly the procedures for helping.

A study of the history of many SHGs (Lieberman & Borman, 1979) clearly suggests the central role of professionals in many such organizations. The models are many, and those that have been successful recognize the distinction between professional involvement and professional direct service. It is the latter that inhibits the development of SHGs. Above all we need to be clear as to what kind of institutions we are trying to aid, and we must not make the all too frequent mistake of co-opting terms that may have current value (such as self-help) by simply relabeling traditional methods. SHGs that are useful on pragmatic grounds offer an alternative to professional service. The issue is not deciding which is better but rather recognizing the value of encouraging diversity in service.

The Consultative Approach

Our experiences and those of other group therapists are that most SHGs and organizations welcome the participation of professionals. Two straightforward problem areas encountered by many SHGs would benefit substantially by the involvement of professionals with special skills in mental health and small groups. A common, although in my experience infrequent, occurrence is precipitated in SHGs that may attract participants with serious psychopathology. Some SHGs such as Recovery, Inc., specifically address individuals with major psychopathology and have developed methods for addressing these problems. However, in settings that are not geared to such a problem area, such as bereavement groups whose group procedures are geared toward distress but not illness, people experience considerable difficulty in responding to those who may have serious psychopathology. Consulting with mental health professionals and providing alternative service settings is a welcome and meaningful contribution we can make to SHGs.

Group therapists have a variety of well-developed professional skills that include methods for developing the therapeutic aspects of a group. They also possess skills that address the management issue of bringing together a group of needy and distressed individuals and creating a functioning social system in which they can practice their therapeutic skills. Many SHGs will from time to time experience problems in how to manage the system—troublesome members, high turnover, nonparticipating people, and the like. These are common occurrences in both SHGs and group psychotherapy, and consultation on the social system aspects of groups, not the treatment model, is a meaningful contribution that a group therapist can make to self-help.

The Development of New SHGs

The most challenging and perhaps most satisfying contribution group therapists can make is the development of new SHGs that would provide ongoing services for a wide variety of conditions and problems. I have already touched on some of the ways professionals have attempted this complex task. This section describes two other strategies that have recently been used to facilitate the development of new SHGs. Perhaps the most exciting is the one developed by the California Self-help Center at U.C.L.A. The group at U.C.L.A. has developed a series of tapes (Common Concern) that provide a generic structure that leads a group of laypeople without benefit of a professional through a series of experiences and teachings about helping behavior and how to conduct a group. The tape program is capable of creating a fully functioning, independent SHG. Although it is too early for a formal test, pilot data gathered by the group at U.C.L.A. are highly encouraging that fully functioning SHGs can be developed by this method.

There are many examples of the collaborative efforts between concerned professionals and individuals who desired to develop SHGs for a particular problem area. Such collaborative arrangements, in which professionals aid in organizational issues, legitimization, and support, appear to be a successful strategy for aiding those desiring to develop SHGs. The Duke Experiment, which developed SHGs in North Carolina for caregivers of Alzheimer patients, and the development of cancer SHGs in South Carolina are but two examples of such strategies. Unfortunately, each seems to be a special and perhaps unique set of circumstances; it is still too early to provide any meaningful generalizations on the long-term success of these strategies. It is useful to remind ourselves that since the inception of self-help, professionals have been involved in the initiation and development of such groups. What is important is to recognize the distinction between these groups and professional services, and to be sensitive to the complex and often intricate and subtle ways that SHGs view the cause and cure of problems, ways that are often distinct from what we as professionals practice in group therapy. By maintaining this distinction and by providing a variety of facilitative professional activities we are likely to maximize success. Facilitation will be enhanced if we maintain the boundary between what we do as professionals and what SHGs offer.

REFERENCES

Antze, P. (1976). Role of ideologies in peer psychotherapy groups. *Journal of Applied Behavioral Sciences, 12*, 300–310.

Bailey, M. B., & Leech, B. (1965). *Alcoholics Anonymous, Pathway to recovery: A study of 1,058 members of the AA fellowship in New York City*. New York: The National Council on Alcoholism.

Bohince, E. A., & Orensteen, A. C. (1950). *An evaluation of the services and program of the Minneapolis Chapter of Alcoholics Anonymous*. Unpublished master's thesis, University of Minnesota at Minneapolis.

Bond, G. R., Borman, L. D., Bankoff, E., Lieberman, M. A., Daiter, S., & Videka, L. (1979). Mended Hearts: A self help case study. *Social Policy,* 50–57.

Borman, L., & Lieberman, M. A. (Eds.). (1976). Self-help groups [special issue]. *Journal of Applied Behavioral Science, 12*(3).

Cowen, C. L., Gardner, F. A., & Zax, M. (Eds.). (1967). *Emergent approaches to mental health problems*. New York: Appleton-Century, Crofts.

Durlak, J. A. (1979). Comparative effectiveness of paraprofessional and professional helpers. *Psychology Bulletin, 86,* 80–92.

Farash, J. L. (1979). Effect of counselling on resolution of loss and body image disturbance following a mastectomy. *Dissertation Abstracts International, 39* (8), 4027–B.

Gates, J. C. (1980). Comparison of behavior mod and self-help groups with conventional therapy of diabetes. *Dissertation Abstracts International, 40* (7), 3084–B.

Glaser, K. (1981). *Social support and mother's adjustment to the birth of twins*. Chicago: Department of Behavioral Sciences (Human Development), University of Chicago.

Goodman, G. (1972). *Companionship Therapy*. San Francisco: Jossey-Bass.

Gordon, R. E., Edmunson, E., Bedell, J., & Goldstein, N. (1979). Peer mutual aid networks reduce rehospitalization of mental patients. *Self-Help Reporter, 3* (2), 3.

Gould, E., Garrigues, C. S., & Scheikowitz, K. (1975). Interaction in hospitalized patient-led and staff-led psychotherapy groups. *American Journal of Psychotherapy, 29* (3), 383–390.

Grimsmo, A., Helgesen, G., & Borchgrevink, C. (1981). Short-term and long-term effects of lay groups on weight reduction. *British Medical Journal, 283,* 1093–1095.

Grosser, C., Henry, W., Kelly, J. G. (Eds.). (1969). *Nonprofessionals and the human service*. San Francisco: Jossey-Bass.

Henry, S., & Robinson, D. (1978). Understanding Alcoholics Anonymous. *Lancet 1* (8060), 372–375.

Hurvitz, N. (1974). Peer self-help psychotherapy groups: Psychotherapy without psychotherapists. In P. M. Roman, H. M. Trice (Eds.), *The sociology of psychotherapy*. New York: Jason Aronson.

Katz, A. H., & Bender, E. I. (1976). Self-help groups in western society: History and prospects. *The Journal of Applied Behavioral Science, 12* (3), 265–282.

Killilea, M. (1976). Mutual help organizations: Interpretations in the literature. In G. Caplan, & M. Killilea (Eds.), *Support systems and mutual help*. Philadelphia: Grune & Stratton.

Kish, G. B., & Hermann, H. T. (1971). The Fort Meade alcoholism treatment programme: A follow-up study. *Quarterly Journal of Studies on Alcohol, 32,* 628–635.

Lieberman, M. A. (1975). Group psychotherapies. In F. H. Kanfer & A. P. Goldstein (Eds.), *Helping people change: Methods and material* (pp. 433–486). New York: Pergamon.

Lieberman, M. A. (1976). Change induction in small groups. *Annual Review of Psychology, 27,* 217–250.

Lieberman, M. A. (1977). Problems in integrating traditional group therapies with new group forms. *International Journal of Group Psychotherapy, 27* (1), 19–32.

Lieberman, M. A. (1985). Comparative analyses of change mechanisms in groups. *International Journal of Group Psychotherapy, 35* (2), 155–174.

Lieberman, M. A. (1986, January 1). Self-help groups: Comparisons to group therapy. *American Psychiatric Association in Annual Review, 5,* 436–457.

Lieberman, M. A., & Bond, G. R. (1976). The problem of being a woman: A survey of 1,700 women in consciousness-raising groups. *Journal of Applied Behavioral Sciences, 12* (3), 363–379.

Lieberman, M. A., & Borman, L. (1979). *Self-help groups for coping with crises: Origins, members, processes, and impact.* San Francisco: Jossey-Bass.

Lieberman, M. A., & Bliwise, N. G. (1985). Comparisons among peer and professionally directed groups for the elderly. *International Journal of Group Therapy, 35* (2), 155–164.

Lieberman, M. A., & Gourash, N. (1979). Evaluating the effects of change groups on the elderly: The impact of SAGE. *International Journal of Group Psychotherapy, 29,* 283–304.

Lieberman, M. A., Solow, N., Bond, G. R., & Reibstein, J. (1979). The psychotherapeutic impact of women's consciousness-raising groups. *Archives of General Psychiatry, 36,* 161–168.

Lieberman, M. A., & Videka-Sherman, L. (1986). The impact of self-help groups on the mental health of widows and widowers. *Journal of Orthopsychiatry, 56,* 435–445.

Lieberman, M. A., Yalom, I. D., & Miles, M. B. (1973). *Encounter groups: First facts.* New York: Basic Books.

McCance, C., & McCance, P. F. (1969). Alcoholism in North East Scotland: Its treatment and outcome. *British Journal of Psychiatry, 115,* 189–198.

Mellinger, G., & Balter, M. (1983). *Collaborative project, GMIRSB Report.* Washington, DC: National Institute of Mental Health.

Oakley, S., & Holden, P. H. (1972). Alcoholic Rehabilitation Center: Follow-up survey 1969. Inventory, North Carolina, *20,* 2–4, 19, 1971.

Pattison, E. M., Headley, E. B., Glesser, G. C., & Gottschalk, L. A. (1968). Abstinence and abnormal drinking: An assessment of changes in drinking patterns in alcoholics after treatment. *Quarterly Journal of Studies on Alcohol, 29,* 610–633.

Reibstein, J. (1981). *Adjustment to the maternal role for mothers leaving careers: The impact of their interaction with role colleagues.* Unpublished doctoral dissertation, University of Chicago.

Rioch, M., Elkes, D., & Flint, A. (1963). *A pilot project in training mental health counselors* (DHHS Publication No. 1254). Washington, DC: U.S. Government Printing Office.

Robson, R. A. H., Paulus, I., & Clarke, G. C. (1965). An evaluation of the effect of a clinic treatment programme on the rehabilitation of alcoholic patients. *Quarterly Journal of Studies on Alcohol, 26,* 264–278.

Rohan, W. P. (1970). A follow-up study of problem drinkers. *Diseases of the Nervous System, 31,* 259–265.

Rossi, J. J. (1970). A holistic treatment programme for alcholism rehabilitation. *Medical Ecology and Clinical Research, 3,* 6–16.

Stunkard, A., Levine, H., & Fox, S. (1970). The management of obesity: Patient self-help and medical treatment. *Archives of Internal Medicine, 125,* 1067–1072.

Tomsovic. M. (1970). A follow-up study of discharged alcoholics. *Hospital and Community Psychiatry, 21,* 94–97.

Tracy, G., & Gussow, Z. (1976). Self-help groups: A grass-root response to a need for services. *Journal of Applied Behavioral Sciences, 12* (3), 381–396.

Videka-Sherman, L. (1979). Psychosocial adaption in heart surgery patients. In M. A. Lieberman & L. D. Borman (Eds.), *Self-help groups for coping with crisis: Origins, members, processes and impact.* San Francisco: Jossey-Bass.

Videka-Sherman, L., & Lieberman, M. A. (1985). The effects of self-help groups on child loss: The limits of recovery. *American Journal of Orthopsychiatry, 55,* 70–81.

Weiner, M. (1986). Homogenous groups. In *APA Annual Review* (Vol. 5) (pp. 714–728). Washington DC: American Psychological Association.

Williams, R. H., & Ozarin I. D. (Eds.). (1968). *Community mental health.* San Francisco: Jossey-Bass.

2
Experiencing Infertility: Groups for Support and Mutual Aid

Infertility is defined by most physicians as the inability to conceive a pregnancy after a year or more of regular sexual relationships without contraception or the inability to carry a pregnancy to live birth (Mazor & Simmons, 1984, p. xvi). Approximately 15 to 20% of all married couples in the United States experience infertility (Kraft, Palombo, Mitchell, Dean, Meyers, & Schmidt, 1980). Menning (1980) estimates that this represents 10 million people. She further estimates that 50 to 60% of all persons who receive expert medical care will respond to treatment and conceive. For 4 to 5 million persons, however, conceiving or carrying a pregnancy to live birth will never occur.

The causes of infertility are numerous. Physical anomalies contributing to infertility include blocked fallopian tubes, premature menopause, endometriosis, failure to ovulate, pelvic abnormalities caused by exposure to diethylstilbestrol (DES) while females were in utero, or genetic problems. Other causes of infertility include varicoceles, vein abnormalities, bacterial infections, and low sperm count and infertility due to the ingestion of drugs such as tobacco, marijuana, or alcohol ("Spotlight Swinging," 1985). The increase in infertility in recent years can be attributed to several factors. For example, fertility in both men and women appears to be maximal in their mid-twenties (Thompson, 1980). Postponement of marriage and childbearing into one's thirties or forties, for a diversity of personal, social, and economic reasons, is one factor contributing to the number of people who have or will have infertility problems. As the prevalence of sexually transmitted diseases such as chlamydia rises, so does the incidence of reproductive tract scarring that may potentially cause infertility in both men and women. Infertility may also result from the use of certain contraceptive methods such as the intrauterine device (IUD) or birth control pills. Endometriosis, the existence of endometrial tissue outside the uterine cavity, is also a common cause of infertility. Abortions may also cause damage to the cervix and result in the inability to carry a desired pregnancy to term. Other factors that contribute to the likelihood of infertility include exposure to chemicals or radiation.

As recently as 1960, it was believed that 90% of involuntarily childless marriages were caused by problems attributed to women. Medical experts now agree that female reproductive problems account for only approximately 40% of infertility cases. Male reproductive problems account for another 40% of infertility cases. Twenty percent of infertility cases are attributed to a combination of male and female reproductive problems or unknown factors.

As recently as 1963, 50% of cases of infertility were referred to as psychogenic infertility and were attributed to emotional or psychological pathology (Eisner, 1963). Psychogenic infertility was typically applied to women whose emotional characteristics were thought to cause an inability to conceive. Infertile women were described as having disturbed relationships with their mothers (Herman, 1955), ambivalence about motherhood (Rommer & Rommer, 1957), or mental tension that produced genital dysfunctioning and/or abnormal attitudes toward parenthood (Sandler, 1968). An illustration of this attitude is represented by Denber (1978), who maintained that infertility "can be seen as a defensive reaction against pregnancy that, if it occurred, would allow these conflicts to materialize and emerge into awareness, with potentially catastrophic results" (p. 25). As medical assessments and interventions improve, heretofore undetected physiological causes of infertility are identified. Only 5 to 10% of infertility cases currently have unknown etiology, that is, no physical or metabolic reason can be found to account for infertility (Speroff, Glass, & Kase, 1973). These patients are referred to as "normal infertile" by many physicians. A more recent study by Drake, Tredway, Buchanan, Takaki, and Daane (1977) indicates that, based on a study of 229 couples, the incidence of unexplained infertility is only 3.5%. Furthermore, there is no evidence for assuming the possibility that couples experiencing infertility of unknown etiology suffer from some psychologically pathological condition. Despite research to the contrary, however, the myth that infertility is caused and can be corrected by psychiatric intervention persists. In a 1984 edition of *The Female Stress Syndrome*, for example, Witkin-Lanail states: "Great-grandmothers knew a lot about this Female Stress Syndrome. They knew that tension could create temporary infertility. Their recommendation to a couple . . . would have been, 'Take a vacation together.' It is still worth a try" (p. 60).

Fortunately, increased attention is being given to the emotional impact of the infertility experience. Medical and mental health professionals are becoming increasingly aware that the sadness, anxiety, pain, and loss experienced by persons unable to conceive and bear a child are the emotional *consequences* of the infertility experience, not the *cause* of infertility.

EMOTIONAL DIMENSIONS OF THE INFERTILITY EXPERIENCE

Infertility is an emotionally multidimensional experience. A variety of factors contribute to and affect the nature, intensity, and quality of this experience, and the emotional impact varies for individual persons. Before the emotional impact of infertility is described, a discussion of the contextual factors that contribute to the stresses experienced by infertile persons will be discussed.

The Psychosocial Context of Infertility

The context in which infertility is experienced includes cultural and societal expectations toward childbearing and parenthood, the existence or lack of institutional and formal supports such as medical technology and the medical and mental health professions, and the availability and helpfulness of informal supports such as friends, family, and acquaintances.

The motivation for childbearing is a complex phenomenon that involves bio-based factors and social roles and expectations. Although voluntary childlessness has increased slightly in the last decade, childlessness, regardless of choice, is still defined in almost exclusively negative terms in our society. The veneration of motherhood as the essence of femaleness, in particular, has a long history (Rhodes, 1987). Childlessness is stigmatizing, regardless of its etiology.

As part of the first generation of persons to expect control over their reproductive abilities, infertile persons experience an inability to "plan a family." A life goal of parenthood and the typical movement of mastery of developmental tasks over the family life cycle are thwarted. Traditional goals, expected role identifications, and expectations must be postponed or abandoned in a society that sends the message that the majority of women need motherhood in order to achieve fulfillment (Friedan, 1981).

The nature of infertility also requires that the individual or couple receives medical evaluations and/or treatment. Patients frequently report that these medical processes are physically and psychologically intrusive. According to Covington (1987):

> Medical evaluation involves such procedures as physical examination of the body, particularly the genitals and reproductive organs; hormonal testing, through blood samples or radiological procedures; and investigation of sexual habits and behaviors, such as frequency of coitus, technique and orgasmic performance. Medical treatment may involve surgical repair of the genitals and reproductive organs; drug therapy; and/or physical intervention which encourages conception (p. 22).

As a result, Covington (1987) suggests that infertile patients frequently feel inadequate and defective. These feelings are reinforced by medical terminology that describes reproductive functioning as hostile (cervical mucous), incompetent (cervix), defective (luteal phase), or poor (semen).

Family, friends, and acquaintances also provide a more personal and intense relational context for the infertile couple. The couple may not expect medical or mental health professionals to be sensitive to their feelings about the inability to have a child, but insensitivity from loved ones is experienced with great disappointment. On several occasions, comments from family members, friends, and acquaintances are described by infertile persons as cruel and painful. Remarks such as "just relax" or "adopt and you'll get pregnant" are described as particularly hurtful (Valentine, 1986).

Even strangers communicate their impatience with the infertile person's distress. One gentleman writing to Dear Abby states:

> Dear Abby: I would like to comment on the many childless couples who write to you moaning about how miserable they are because they can't have children "of their own."
>
> Don't get me wrong, I'm not unsympathetic toward infertile couples. I am, however, a bit disgusted with childless couples who are so obsessed with reproducing that they speak of little else (Van Buren, 1984).

The Emotional Impact of Infertility

The emotional impact of the infertility experience has been receiving increased attention during the past 5 years. Qualitative and quantitative research investigations have been conducted, and clinical observations that have yielded remarkably consistent results have been reported.

Stress and crisis. Crisis theory may be useful in explaining emotional and behavioral reactions to infertility for some individuals. Golan (1979) maintains that "unanticipated events are the unpredictable changes that can occur to anyone, at any stage in life, with little or no advance warning. They usually involve some actual or threatened loss of a person, a capacity or a function" (p. 514). Infertility as an unanticipated event may be experienced as a threat or loss to a life goal. Goodman and Rothman (1984) suggest that "infertility crisis is a special kind of crisis. It is not just a one time hazardous event" (p. 90). The multitude of stressors associated with infertility taxes customary coping mechanisms and a period of psychological disequilibrium is reported. Additionally, the experience of infertility entails multiple sources of stress that may include intrusive and insensitive medical procedures, hurtful comments, dissatisfaction with sexual relations, miscarriages and stillbirths, or lengthy adoption studies. Infertile persons participating in Valentine's (1986) research study report experiencing anxiety, disorganization, distractibility, moodiness, unpredictability, and fatigue. These behavioral consequences are typical of persons in a state of active crisis (Caplan, 1964; Golan, 1979; Paul, 1966). Menning (1977) also describes infertility as a major crisis with accompanying feelings of surprise, denial, isolation, anger, guilt and unworthiness, depression, and grief.

Depression and loss.   Losses are multiple for the infertile couple, and the experience of loss contributes to depression and active crisis. The primary loss from infertility is obviously the loss of a biological child. This loss is experienced as sadness, depression, worry, desperation, hurt, humiliation, and disappointment (Berger, 1980; Menning, 1977; Valentine, 1986). However, many other associated losses have also been identified in the literature. These associated losses include: lost fantasies; loss of genetic continuity; loss of one's self as a fertile person; loss of control; loss of a successful pregnancy, birth, and breastfeeding experiences; loss of the opportunity to move to the next stage in the family life cycle; relationship losses; loss of the parenting experience; and losses for other family members such as potential grandparents (Conway & Valentine, 1987; Herz, 1984; Klaus & Kennell, 1976; Knapp & Peppers, 1979; Menning, 1977, 1980).

Conway and Valentine (1987) report in a qualitative study of 10 infertile couples that the intensity of grieving changes over time. Although no consensus about the duration of the grief process was suggested, the intensity of the grief experience was affected by the number and recurrence of losses common among persons experiencing infertility (miscarriage, stillbirth, and unsuccessful medical interventions). The authors also identified six emotions characteristic of the grieving process as reported by participants: shock, unfairness and envy, fear, anger, feeling different, and hurt.

Mahlstedt (1985) further supports the position that an essential feature of persons experiencing infertility is loss and grief. She argues that the experience of infertility involves all the losses in adulthood that are of greatest clinical importance as etiologic factors in depression as described by White, David, and Cantrell (1977): (1) loss of a relationship, (2) loss of health, (3) loss of status or prestige, (4) loss of self-esteem, (5) loss of self-confidence, (6) loss of security, (7) loss of a fantasy or the hope of fulfilling an important fantasy, and (8) loss of something or someone of great symbolic value. Mahlstedt (1985) states that the "grief associated with infertility has been compared with the grief caused by the death of a child. But it is the child who was never born, and there is no funeral. In most cases, the intense emotional responses are appropriate; there is a lot to cry about" (p. 341). Unfortunately, the losses associated with the infertility experience are frequently not acknowledged by friends, family, or health and mental health service providers.

Marital relationship.   The marital relationship, often a primary source of support, can also be a source of stress. The sexual relationship may be strained as preoccupations with fertility overshadow the marital relationship. Experiencing an interruption in regular sexual relations, a decline in sexual pleasure or desire, and/or a dissatisfaction with sexual functioning have been reported by infertile couples (Menning, 1977; Shapiro, 1982; Valentine, 1986). Valentine (1986) reports that the majority of female participants in her study would like to spend more time talking with their husbands about the infertility experience. Although male participants expressed a sincere desire to be supportive and available to their wives, they report that talking about infertility increases their stress level rather than decreases it.

COPING, ADAPTATION, AND DECISION-MAKING

There do appear to be factors that mediate the intensity individuals experience infertility. Based on interviews with 10 couples, Conway and Valentine (1987) suggest that at least six factors mediate the grieving process, including the following:

1. Multiple losses that increase the intensity of grieving and tend to prolong the grieving process;
2. Existing relationships (professional, family, and friends) that are perceived as supportive decrease unpleasant, painful feelings;
3. Perception of one's own and/or one's partner's role in "causing" the infertility and the ability of the marital relationship to accept shared responsibility without blame facilitates the grieving process;
4. Difference in the expression of grief between men and women—women and men both perceive women as sadder and as making more adjustments than men;
5. The identification, recognition, and acknowledgment of infertility as a significant loss by both infertile persons and their supports facilitate grieving; and
6. Cultural factors that include regional, religious, or occupational variations regarding the importance of family, or the prominence of child-oriented holidays that affect the level of stress experienced by infertile couples.

Overall, individuals and couples who cope best are those who maintain ongoing supportive relationships with family, friends, and other infertile persons. Support groups for infertile persons can be particularly important for providing opportunities for people to share experiences, gain information, and "tell their stories." A discussion of group work with persons experiencing infertility will be detailed later in this chapter.

A preoccupation with fertility is also a common coping mechanism—an effort to control the uncontrollable. This mechanism may take the form of actively participating in a local infertility organization, producing videotapes on infertility for community education purposes, writing articles for newspapers or newsletters, or reading about and participating in new medical procedures that might offer hope to the infertile person.

Infertile individuals who persist in selecting coping strategies that are isolatory (avoiding contacts with children, families, baby showers, friends with children) or who continually avoid the issue of infertility appear to be especially emotionally fragile. These persons tend to internalize or deny their grief and lose opportunities to receive support from others. Other unsuccessful coping strategies, if they persist over long periods of time, include excessive denial, anger or rage, and pathologic depression (Mahlstedt, 1985).

The point at which a couple decides the course of the future of their family is a critical time in the adaptation process. Menning (1977) suggests that there are three basic alternatives available to the infertile couple: adoption, donor insemination, and childfree living.

Medical technology has increased the number of options for infertile couples since 1977, however. Approximately 600 surrogate mothers have been fertilized through insemination with a fertile man's sperm and have then surrendered the baby to the infertile couple after birth (Quindlen, 1987). Other recent options for infertile couples include: eggs donated anonymously by another woman, which are fertilized with the husband's sperm and implanted in the wife's uterus; gamete interfallopian transfer (GIFT), in which the eggs and sperm are brought together outside the body and placed back into the fallopian tube; and a surrogate or host arrangement, in which a fertilized egg from one couple is placed in the uterus of another woman to be carried to term (Quindlen, 1987). Making a decision is a turning point for many couples. Persons describe a sense of relief and freedom from the constant stress of trying to conceive and monthly anticipation after this turning point has been successfully encountered (Valentine, 1986).

But how do persons experiencing infertility *resolve* their feelings? And do they? Menning (1977) defines resolution as "working through a difficult feeling or emotion" (p. 113). She states that there are three distinct steps in achieving resolution:

1.   The particular feeling is discovered and named;
2.   The named feeling is talked about as honestly as possible. The origins of the feeling are discovered and are talked about in depth; and
3.   The person feels relief from and subsiding of the bothersome feeling and is ready to progress to a new feeling state (Menning, 1977, pp. 113–114.).

Adoption workers and mental health professionals expect that after an appropriate period of time, persons will resolve their feelings about infertility. Yet, there is some question about whether resolution is a reasonable expectation (Fleming & Burry, 1987). Infertile persons who have adopted or persons with birth children experiencing secondary infertility describe equally intense and similar emotional reactions to secondary infertility and the postadoption period. Fleming (1984) suggests that infertility, especially infertility of an uncertain outcome (not "cured" by pregnancy or diagnosed as permanent), can be more accurately described as a chronic illness. Thus, resolution may not be the most appropriate goal of coping with infertility; perhaps *adaptation* better describes the emotional process of learning to live with infertility.

GROUP WORK WITH PERSONS EXPERIENCING INFERTILITY

Group support for persons experiencing infertility began as a discussion group on infertility in 1973 under the leadership of Barbara Eck Menning, a nurse who personally experienced infertility. These groups were sponsored by RESOLVE, Inc., a tax-exempt organization that began as a "small, free, telephone counseling service to help infertile people find information and support for their feelings" (Menning, 1976, p. 258). The discussion group quickly turned into a "peer support group" and the demand for more groups and more leaders increased. At the present time, there are 47 chapters of RESOLVE, Inc., in 40 states with over 10,000 members and at least 35 support groups being led across the nation (B. Freeman, personal communication, June 1987). There are also numerous groups offered to support persons experiencing infertility that are not under the auspices of RESOLVE, Inc. A wide variety of affiliations for these groups are represented, including sponsorship by infertility clinics or medical practices, reproductive planning organizations, private mental health practitioners, or informal, self-help groups that have been started by infertile persons on a grass roots level.

The most common group model serving persons experiencing infertility is the "support group," sometimes referred to as "mutual aid" or "mutual help" group (more on self-help groups in Chapter 1). According to Silverman (1987), "A mutual help exchange occurs when people who share a common problem or predicament come together for mutual support and constructive action to solve their shared problem" (p. 171). Although mutual aid can remain casual and informal, mutual aid groups with infertile persons are frequently formalized. Barker (1987) defines the support group as "an interrelated group of people who have regular direct contact and provide individuals with emotional, informational, material and affectional sustenance" (p. 161). Many persons across the country who are experiencing infertility find it helpful to join together on a fairly regular basis for the purpose of helping each other cope more effectively with the shared infertility experience.

The support group is concerned with relationships that join persons together so that a reliable system of helping is available. The emphasis is on the nurturance and feedback individuals give to and receive from each other. As can be concluded from the earlier discussion, the emotional impact of infertility is viewed as a "normal," expected consequence of the infertility crisis, and as such, the support group or mutual aid group framework is frequently the most appropriate method of offering emotional assistance (Abarnal & Bach, 1959; Menning, 1976).

Garbarino (1983) maintains that proponents of the support group framework look to the collective—to the social network:

> Proponents of this approach see that social resources can compensate for individual inadequacies and provide buoyancy so that individuals need not sink even if they do not know how to swim. What is more, those who emphasize social resources argue that no one can master the heaviest seas of life alone and that even those with normally adequate levels of personal resources may need to be thrown a lifeline in times of extraordinary stress (p. 20).

Individuals and couples experiencing infertility who participate in support groups or mutual aid groups discover that what seems emotionally overwhelming or unusual is common to others in a similar situation. Group members no longer feel alone with their problems. Their emotions and experiences are legitimized, and an opportunity is provided for coping with the emotional, physical, and relationship struggles that accompany the infertility experience. Not only is support, understanding, and kindness available to group members, but infertile persons are also exposed to an expanded repertoire of appropriate coping strategies.

Silverman (1987) observes that individuals undergoing transitions involving a role shift during a period of critical change are often attracted to organizations or groups offering mutual support. Persons experiencing infertility are frequently reevaluating their identities, roles, and futures as adults. Group service offers a direct and immediate alternative to the psychosocial loneliness and isolation experienced by infertile persons (Goodman & Rothman, 1984). Schwartz (1961) maintains that "the group is an enterprise in mutual aid, an alliance of individuals who need each other, in varying degrees, to work on common problems . . . The need to use each other, to create not one but many helping relationships is a vital ingredient of the group process" (p. 15). Infertile persons who participate in support groups find this experience to be a powerfully important and helpful one. B. Freeman (personal communication,

June 1987) states that "there is not a single support group that RESOLVE has offered in the last 14 years that isn't still meeting." Although most groups for infertile persons are support groups, other groups are also available. A partial list of groups for infertile persons include: "rap groups," "dinner parties" with facilitation discussing a specific issue such as coping with the holidays; preadoptive groups, psychoeducational groups, workshops for men, women's self-awareness groups, postadoption groups for infertile persons, groups for persons experiencing secondary infertility (infertility that occurs after one or more successful pregnancies); artificial insemination by donor groups, assertiveness groups, relaxation/stress reduction groups, monthly programs, therapy groups, and more traditional support groups.

Group Purpose and Goals

The purposes and goals of group work with persons experiencing infertility vary depending on the type or specific focus of the group. As can be seen, groups for persons experiencing infertility can be built around issues, experiences, themes, gender, type of infertility, critical times in the course of the infertility experience, or particular decisions or alternatives selected for family building.

Two purposes of group work with persons experiencing infertility seem to be common to most groups. These include (1) increasing an individual's knowledge about infertility and (2) reducing isolation and establishing a support system.

Increasing knowledge about infertility.   Throughout the infertility experience, individuals and couples are seeking information about infertility, their medical condition, medical options, and family-building alternatives. Frequently, information obtained by physicians and other health care professionals is neither sufficient nor available enough to meet the infertile person's almost insatiable quest for knowledge. Information gathering for persons in crisis or for people in the midst of a stressful situation is a very adaptive and helpful coping strategy. The acquisition of knowledge about one's situation has several benefits and can be accomplished efficiently and effectively in a group setting. First, information helps one explain and make sense of the experience. It is validating. It is a reminder that one's experience is not unique. Group participants can benefit from each other's inquiries and research. Secondly, additional information contributes to one's sense of control and self-determination. One becomes increasingly aware of a wide range of options for the evaluation and treatment of infertility. Assistance with the emotional impact of the infertility experience is also available. Group members observe others explore and select a wide range of options. Additionally, the group is a particularly powerful medium for providing information that dispels inaccuracies or myths and faulty attitudes among persons experiencing infertility (Abarnal & Bach, 1959).

Reducing isolation.   "We didn't have anyone going through the same problems." "I feel different." The inability of family and friends to discuss infertility is common. Persons usually counted as part of an individual's support system suddenly feel awkward and embarrassed or simply do not know how to be helpful (Mahlstedt & Johnson, 1987). Rosenfeld and Mitchell (1979) maintain that alienation and isolation are the major symptoms associated with infertility and are significant interpersonal obstacles associated with coping with infertility. Goodman and Rothman (1984) suggest that "at a time when the individual or couple most need support, they feel separate and cut off from those they believe cannot comprehend the extent of their pain" (p. 83). Issues related to infertility may be embarrassing, private, taboo, or perhaps feel "shameful" when discussed with friends, family, or acquaintances. Sharing private matters regarding infertility with others experiencing similar difficulties facilitates group therapeutic factors such as instillation of hope, universality, imparting of information, and altruism (Yalom, 1985).

Other purposes and goals of group work with persons experiencing infertility may also be to facilitate decision-making regarding future family building, decrease depression, increase self-esteem, improve the marital relationship, improve the physician-patient relationship, and/or develop coping strategies for dealing with a wide variety of topics (holidays, adoption home studies, etc.).

Group Structure

As described earlier, groups that serve infertile persons or couples vary widely. Structural and format decisions should, of course, be made based on the individual focus of the group and on the individual needs of the members. Several issues should be considered.

Recruitment. Whether affiliated with a formal support organization such as RESOLVE, Inc., an infertility clinic, or a more informal gathering, an effort to reach out to potential group members is an essential ingredient of a successful infertility support group. Distribution of information sheets in strategic locations, notice of meetings in newspaper columns announcing community activities, and personal telephone calls will increase the likelihood of reaching infertile persons who may benefit from group services but be isolated from others experiencing infertility. Enlisting the support of physicians and other health care personnel, reproductive planning services, and mental health agencies are also important recruitment sources. During the early awareness of a fertility problem, persons may deny the seriousness of the problem and a group experience may be inappropriate. Early respectful intervention by health care personnel, however, frequently is extraordinarily important during the early months of discovery (Covington, 1987). As infertility is acknowledged and various tests and medical interventions are attempted, individuals may begin to feel the intense emotional impact of infertility. Group support is particularly helpful during this phase of the infertility process and a referral from the understanding, supportive health care provider can be extraordinarily powerful. Help is anticipated and referrals are more likely to be accepted.

Location and time factors. Groups for infertile persons can be held in a variety of locations: people's homes, the group leader's office, or a physician's or clinic office. These locations tend to communicate the uniqueness and importance of the infertility experience. Less successful locations include meetings at churches, agencies whose purpose is unrelated to infertility, or library meeting rooms. Regardless of the selection of location, however, easy access and comfort are important. Infertility support groups typically meet weekly, biweekly, or monthly for 1 to 2 hours, depending on group focus and purpose.

Open versus closed groups. Open membership, closed membership, and time-limited group models have been successfully utilized with members experiencing infertility. A closed membership, time-limited group for infertile couples or individuals is typically 8 to 10 weekly sessions with a membership of 5 to 15 persons. Members frequently pay a fee (for example, $80-$100) and are asked to make a commitment to attend all sessions. Discussion regarding the advisability of allowing the continued participation of persons who become pregnant during the course of the group is addressed later. The advantages of a time-limited, closed group format are that members are helped to focus quickly and maintain purpose and direction, membership is stabilized so that group process can be facilitated through the intimacy and differentiation stage, and variability of attendance and outside factors can be held to a minimum (Indelecato & Goldberg, 1986).

Open-ended, open-enrollment groups, on the other hand, "insure the immediate availability of services, particularly to people in crisis . . . When ongoing support or therapy is required, members can remain in the group as long as necessary and departing members can be offered the option of returning as the need arises" (Schopler & Galinsky, 1984, p. 4). A support group that meets regularly, routinely, and expectably is a potent community resource for individuals in need of emotional support and mutual aid. For infertile persons, the need for affiliation, information, and support may wax and wane over a period of years or even decades. The predictable availability of a support group proves comforting.

Group Process—Themes and Issues

There are several mutual aid processes that Shulman (1986) maintains are characteristic of an effective small group. These include: "Sharing data; the dialectical process; entering taboo areas; the 'all in the same boat' phenomenon; mutual support; mutual demand; individual problem solving; rehearsal; and the strength in numbers phenomenon" (Shulman, 1986, p. 52). These mutual aid processes can be observed in infertility groups as members discuss a wide range of characteristic themes.

Managing medical treatment.   Sharing knowledge of and experience with various medical interventions is a typical theme of infertility group discussion—especially during beginning sessions. Goodman and Rothman (1984) report that repeated descriptions of medical treatments are not uncommon and an individual or couple's "periodic vacation from treatment" is also understood and accepted.

Managing grief.   Persons experiencing infertility report the deep and intense loss and grief described earlier. Frequently, infertile persons feel that they are "teetering between grieving and not grieving" (R. Berman, personal communication, June 1987) and must emotionally cope with infertility by learning how to "navigate the ups and downs" of the infertility experience (L. Miller, personal communication, June 1987). Other infertile persons sharing their experiences, feelings, and thoughts in a group setting facilitates the coping process. The group strengthens the members' ability to help each other. As group members help an individual with a specific concern, they are often also helping themselves with their own similar problems (Shulman, 1986). Unspoken secrets, guilts, and taboos can be explored and shared with others, placed in perspective, and integrated.

Marital relationship.   The impact of infertility on the marital relationship is often a common and emotionally charged group theme. The marital relationship is experienced as both a primary source of support for infertile couples, as well as a source of stress. B. Freeman (personal communication, June 1987), executive director of RESOLVE, Inc., reports that groups offering to address couples' communication are among the most popular, since men and women appear to handle the infertility crisis and express their grief differently. A group experience may meet needs that cannot be met within the marital relationship. Thus, a secondary gain of the group experience may be improved marital functioning.

Sexuality.   In addition to the change in the sexual relationship between the infertile partners, other issues pertaining to sexuality emerge during the group process. Members share their feelings of embarrassment and helplessness as they try to respond to the inquiries of friends and family about sexual matters, such as why the wife isn't pregnant, or as their physicians and health care professionals pry and probe into private behaviors. The ability to speak frankly about sexually taboo subjects is a source of support and relief for many infertile persons participating in a group.

Relationships with family and friends.   Avoiding family, friends, or acquaintances, especially those with children, may increase the isolation and aloneness reported by persons experiencing infertility. In turn, friends and relatives may feel awkward about their own children or pregnancies and avoid the infertile couple. Efforts to help or be supportive: "Don't try so hard" or "There are so many children who need homes" are unintentionally hurtful to the infertile person who struggles with the daily complexities of infertility. The group experience provides a safe and accepting place to ventilate anger and rage about the insensitivities of friends and family members, while exploring strategies for coping with the remarks of others or sadness about being left out of family-oriented activities. Members participating in support groups are reported to be extraordinarily sensitive to each other's needs (Goodman & Rothman, 1984).

Decision-making and family building alternatives.   As individuals move toward decision-making, infertility support groups tend to focus on decisions to remain childfree, to adopt, or to explore the possibility of donor insemination, surrogacy, or other family-building options. Making the difficult decision about the future of their family appears to be a major turning point in an infertile individual or couple's life. The group experience is frequently helpful as members explore their options, their feelings, and anticipated consequences. Special topic groups are frequently built around the family-building choice of infertile persons. They include artificial insemination by donor groups, both preadoption and postadoption groups, or surrogacy groups.

Special issues.   Several other special issues that may be addressed by groups serving persons experiencing infertility must also be mentioned. These may include coping with holiday seasons, dealing with a seriously depressed or potentially suicidal group member, or coping with a group member or couple who successfully achieve a pregnancy. A successful pregnancy is, of course, the desired outcome for all group members. A pregnancy is often received by other group members with mixed emotions, however: jealousy, anger, hopefulness, and joy. Many infertility groups choose not to allow pregnant members to continue in the group for the comfort of all concerned. One group model asks the pregnant member or expectant couple to return to one last group meeting to facilitate the group's processing the pregnancy and as a way of terminating the member(s)' participation (L. Miller, personal communication, June 1987).

Group Leadership

Leadership responsibilities for groups whose members are experiencing infertility vary. RESOLVE, Inc., has national guidelines for the selection and hiring of group leaders and requires that group leaders be trained at the masters level in psychology, counseling, social work, or a related field. In addition, family therapy and group work experiences are preferred (B. Freeman, personal communication, June 1987). The importance of skillful, sensitive leadership cannot be overemphasized. As discussed previously, the infertility experience impacts on many levels—intrapersonal, interpersonal, and with regard to the person's position in the community. Leaders must be aware of their own feelings about their personal struggle with infertility, perhaps their own biases, prejudices, or insensitivities to the struggles of others.

Regardless of group focus or purpose, the group leader is responsible for fostering and stimulating mutual aid attitudes and behaviors. Attention should be paid to the common experience of infertility and the consequent emotional pain. The group leader should be reminded that he or she is but one source of help to group members; the power of group members of giving as well as receiving help should not be overlooked.

The group leader may also be required to exercise the responsibility of referring an individual or a couple who are inappropriate for group membership to another more appropriate resource. The leader's expertise may also be utilized in the rare circumstance when a group member expresses extreme depression or suicidal tendencies (Young, personal communication, June 1987). Group leadership may also require participation in recruitment efforts, member selection, and/or site selection.

Knowledge and experience in grief work is also extremely important for leaders of groups serving infertile persons. As described, multiple losses accompany infertility, and skill is required to assist group members to address these multiple losses and learn coping strategies most appropriate for them.

CONCLUDING REMARKS

Infertility is an emotionally powerful and intense experience for many individuals and couples. Persons experiencing infertility report feelings of anger, guilt, unworthiness, deep sadness, depression, loss, and grief. Anxiety, disorganization, distractibility, moodiness, fatigue, and irritability are also common responses to infertility. Infertile persons also frequently feel alone and isolated—everyone around them seems to be a parent or pregnant. How can coping with the infertility experience be facilitated?

One excellent option is membership in a group designed to meet the emotional and informational needs of persons experiencing infertility. A safe opportunity is available for coping with emotional and relationship struggles that accompany the infertility experience. Group membership can offer an effective and straightforward alternative to the loneliness and emptiness experienced by infertile individuals.

REFERENCES

Abarnal, A. R., & Bach, G. (1959). Group psychotherapy for the infertile couple. *International Journal of Fertility, 4,* 151–160.

Barker, R. L. (1987). *The social work dictionary.* Silver Springs, MD: NASW.

Berger, D. M. (1980). Infertility: A psychiatrist's perspective. *Canadian Journal of Psychiatry, 25* (7), 553–558.

Conway, P., & Valentine, D. (1987). Reproductive losses and grieving. *Journal of Social Work and Human Sexuality, 6* (1), 43–64.

Caplan, G. (1964). *Principles of preventive psychiatry.* New York: Basic Books.

Covington, S. N. (1987). Psychosocial evaluation of the infertile couple: Implications for social work practice. *Journal of Social Work and Human Sexuality, 6* (1), 21–36.

Denber, H. C. B. (1978). Psychiatric aspects of infertility. *Journal of Reproductive Medicine, 20* (1), 23–29.

Drake, T., Tredway, D., Buchanan, G., Takaki, N., & Daane, T. (1977). Unexplained infertility. *Obstetrics and Gynecology, 50* (6), 644–646.

Eisner, B. (1963). Some psychological differences between fertile and infertile women. *Journal of Clinical Psychology, 19,* 391.

Fleming, J. (1984). Infertility as a chronic illness. *Resolve Newsletter,* p. 5.

Fleming, J., & Burry, K. (1987). The process of coping with the infertility experience. *Journal of Social Work and Human Sexuality, 6* (1), 37–42.

Friedan, B. (1981). *The second stage.* New York: Summit Books.

Garbarino, J. (1983). Social support networks: Rx for the helping professions. In J. K. Whittaker & J. Garbarino (Eds.), *Social support networks: Informal helping in the human services* (pp. 19–20). New York: Aldine.

Golan, N. (1979). Crisis theory. In F. J. Turner (Ed.), *Social work treatment: Interlocking theoretical approaches* (pp. 420–456). New York: Free Press.

Goodman, K., & Rothman, B. (1984). Group work in infertility treatment. *Social Work with Groups, 7,* (1), 79–89.

Herman, M. (1955). Psychoanalytic evaluation of the problem of "one child" sterility. *Fertility and Sterility, 6,* 405–414.

Herz, E. (1984). Psychological repercussions of pregnancy loss. *Psychiatric Annals, 14* (6), 454–457.

Indelecato, S., & Goldberg, P. (1986). Harrassed and alone: Parents of learning disabled children. In A. Gitterman & L. Shulman (Eds.), *Mutual aid groups and the life cycle* (pp. 195-209). Itasca, IL: F. E. Peacock.

Klaus, M. H., & Kennell, J. H. (1976). *Maternal-infant bonding.* St. Louis: C.V. Mosby.

Knapp, R. J., & Peppers, L. G. (1979). Doctor-patient relationships in fetal/infant death encounters. *Journal of Medical Education, 54,* 775–780.

Kraft, A. S., Palombo, J., Mitchell, D., Dean, C., Meyers, S., & Schmidt, A. (1980). The psychological dimensions of infertility. *American Journal of Orthopsychiatry, 50* (4), 618–628.

Mahlstedt, P. (1985). The psychological component of infertility. *Fertility and Sterility, 43* (3), 335–346.

Mahlstedt, P., & Johnson, P. (1987). Support to persons experiencing infertility: Familyand friends can help. *Journal of Social Work and Human Sexuality, 6* (1), 65–72.

Mazor, M. D., & Simons, H. F. (Eds.). (1984). *Infertility: Medical, emotional and social considerations.* New York: Human Sciences Press.

Menning, B. E. (1976). Resolve: A support group for infertile couples. *American Journal of Nursing, 76* (2), 258–259.

Menning, B. E. (1977). *Infertility: A guide for the childless couple.* Englewood Cliffs, NJ: Prentice-Hall.

Menning, B. E. (1980). The emotional needs of infertile couples. *Fertility and Sterility, 34* (4), 313–319.

Paul, L. (1966). Crisis intervention. *Mental Hygiene, 50,* 141–145.

Quindlen, A. (1987, June). Baby craving. *Life,* pp. 23–26.

Rhodes, R. (1987). Women, motherhood, and infertility: The social and historical context. *Journal of Social Work and Human Sexuality, 6* (1), 5–20.

Rommer, J. J., & Rommer, C. S. (1957). Sexual tones in marriage of the sterile and once sterile woman. *Fertility and Sterility, 9,* 309–320.

Rosenfeld, D. L., & Mitchell, E. (1979). Treating the emotional aspects of infertility: Counseling services in an infertility clinic. *American Journal of Obstetrics and Gynecology, 135* (2), 177–180.

Sandler, B. (1968). Emotional stress and infertility. *Journal of Psychosomatic Research, 12,* 51–59.

Schopler, J. H., & Galinsky, M. J. (1984). Meeting practice needs: Conceptualizing the open-ended group. *Social Work with Groups, 7* (2), 3–21.

Schwartz, W. (1961). The social worker in the group. In R. W. Klenk & R. M. Ryan (Eds.), *The practice of social work* (2nd. ed.) (pp. 208–228). Belmont, CA: Wadsworth.

Shapiro, C. H. (1982). The impact of infertility on the marital relationship. *Social Casework, 63* (7), 387–393.

Shulman, L. (1986). The dynamics of mutual aid. *Social Work with Groups, 9,* 51–61.

Silverman, P. R. (1987). Mutual help groups. In *Encyclopedia of Social Work* (pp. 171–176) (Vol. 2) (18th ed.). Silver Springs, MD: NASW.

Speroff, L., Glass, R. H., & Kase, N. G. (1973). *Clinical gynecologic endocrinology and infertility.* Baltimore: Williams & Wilkins.

Spotlight swinging from women to men in infertility issue. (1985, February 3) *The State*, p. 5E.

Thompson, I. E. (1980). The medical work-up: Female and combined problems. In M. D. Mazor & H. F. Simons (Eds.), *Infertility: Medical, emotional and social considerations* (pp. 3–13). New York: Human Sciences Press.

Valentine, D. (1986). Psychological impact of infertility: Identifying issues and needs. *Social Work and Health Care, 11* (4), 61–69.

Van Buren, A. (1984, June 1). *The State*, p. 6E.

White, R. B., David, H. K., & Cantrell, W. A. (1977). Psychodynamics of depression: Implications for treatment. In G. Usden (Ed.) *Depression: Clinical, biological and psychological perspectives* (p. 308). New York: Brunner/Mazel.

Witkin-Lanail, G. (1984). *Female stress syndrome.* New York: Newmarket Press.

Yalom, I. (1985). *The theory and practice of group psychotherapy.* New York: Basic Books.

3
Group Therapy with Victims of Post-Traumatic Stress Disorder

Post-Traumatic Stress Disorder (PTSD) has been a recognized clinical entity since its inclusion in the *Diagnostic and Statistical Manual of Mental Disorders*, third edition (DSM-III) (APA, 1980), in 1980. There has been considerable professional and public comment regarding PTSD, spurred largely by the numerous Vietnam veterans and more recently sexual assault victims with the Stress Disorder (Figley, 1978; Veronen & Kilpatrick, 1983). The revised edition of DSM-III (DSM-III-R) (APA, 1987) lists a variety of stressors that can precipitate a PTSD: rape, assault, military combat, natural disasters (e.g., floods, earthquakes), accidental disasters (e.g., car accidents with serious physical injury, airplane crashes, large fires, collapse of physical structures), or deliberately caused disasters (e.g., bombing, torture, death camps), and direct damage to the central nervous system (e.g., malnutrition, head injury). Psychotraumatologists have studied the effects of environmental trauma on children, and for the first time in DSM-III-R (1987), there are several specific references to children. PTSD, a heretofore underdiagnosed disorder, has drawn adherents from many specialties, and clinicians scramble to advance theories and propose treatment based on a variety of approaches from biologic and behavioral to psychoanalytic (Horowitz, 1974; Scrignar, 1984, 1988; van der Kolk, Greenberg, Boyd, & Krystal, 1985). Thus far enthusiasm has far exceeded scientific rigor, and one therapeutic model does not prevail over another. However, data are accumulating to support behavioral interventions (Fairbank & Brown, 1987; Keane, Zimering, & Caddell, 1985).

A homogeneity of symptoms exists among persons who develop a PTSD, and a further division into groups according to the commonality of stressors is natural. Women suffering from Rape Trauma Syndrome (Burgess, 1983), a synonym for PTSD, gather for group treatment in rape crisis centers. Group therapy is an important treatment modality for Vietnam veterans who are treated in Veterans Administration facilities or Vet Centers (Walker & Nash, 1981). Family violence can precipitate a PTSD, and it is estimated that between 5 and 6 million children, spouses, and elderly individuals are neglected, battered, and abused in the United States every year (Rosenbaum, 1986). The development of group therapy for battered spouses and abused children could do much to ameliorate suffering. The alarming increase of crime statistics parallels the growing number of criminal assault victims, many of whom develop a PTSD and could benefit from group treatment. Victims of terrorism, many of whom have been subjected to torture, and their families could benefit from group therapy (Ochberg & Soskis, 1982). A victim's psychological needs following an industrial or vehicular accident have been largely ignored by professionals. Trauma centers, which cater primarily to the physical needs of injured patients, should require supplemental assistance from the behavioral sciences to identify PTSD sufferers; thereafter therapy groups could easily be formed as an adjunct to physical treatment. The environment's potential for imposing a serious threat to an individual's life or physical integrity is almost limitless, and group treatment offers the most economic approach for the treatment of PTSD, in terms of time, effort, and money.

HISTORICAL PERSPECTIVE

No doubt, psychological abnormalities following a trauma are coeval with humanity itself. Wars provide a microcosm of trauma, and there can be no question that some soldiers throughout history have suffered emotionally, either temporarily or permanently, as a consequence of combat. The relationship between war trauma and psychological symptoms, however, received little attention until the late nineteenth century. DaCosta (1871) studied a group of young, symptomatic, yet physically unscathed Civil War veterans who complained of palpitations, increased pain in the cardiac region, tachycardia, cardiac uneasiness, headache, dimness of vision, and giddiness. Since there was no evidence of myocardial disease, DaCosta concluded that the condition was due to a disturbance of the sympathetic nervous system and labeled the disorder "Irritable Heart"; later it became known as "Soldier's Heart" or "DaCosta's Syndrome." Similar symptoms were noted in combat veterans of World War I but were labeled "Effort Syndrome" (Lewis, 1919) because of an exacerbation of symptoms on exercise. Others, more impressed with the psychoneurotic manifestations of the veterans, preferred the term "Neurocirculatory Asthenia" (Oppenheimer, 1918). Following World War I the study of the effects of trauma on living organisms proceeded in three separate but related directions: psychoanalysis (Neurosis), stress ("Fight or Flight" and the "Alarm Reaction"), and behavioral psychology (learning and conditioning).

Neurosis and Traumatic Neurosis

Sigmund Freud (1895/1962) wrote a paper entitled "On the Grounds for Detaching a Particular Syndrome from Neurasthenia Under the Description 'Anxiety Neurosis.' " The concept of Anxiety Neurosis evolved and gained acceptance; by the 1940s this new knowledge was applied to World War II veterans who "broke down emotionally" following a battle (Grinker & Spiegel, 1945). Although the soldiers' symptoms were the same as those observed by DaCosta (1871), Lewis (1919), and Oppenheimer (1918), previous diagnostic labels were abandoned in favor of "Traumatic War Neurosis" and "Combat Neurosis" (Kardiner & Spiegel, 1947).

Following World War II, the theory of Neurosis gained ascendancy and was the conceptual framework within which civilian trauma was viewed; the term "Traumatic Neurosis" came into popular usage (Kaiser, 1968). It was noted that a high percentage of persons developing a "Traumatic Neurosis" had premorbid personality problems, which raised the possibility that a latent neurotic illness was precipitated by the traumatic incident. Perplexingly, clinicians also observed that apparently healthy individuals with no neurotic predisposition also developed a "Traumatic Neurosis." This led to a subdivision of "Traumatic Neurosis" into: (1) Traumatic Neurosis and (2) Compensation or Triggered Neurosis (Round Table, 1960). This classification fitted the facts as observed by clinicians, but it fitted poorly into the nosology of Neurosis. Neurosis is generally considered to be a developmental disorder, and unresolved unconscious conflicts with parents or significant others during childhood are considered to be etiologically significant. In "Traumatic Neurosis," the disorder is precipitated by an environmental event later in life. According to the Round Table classification, only a healthy (nonneurotic) individual can become neurotic as a result of an environmental stress (trauma). Persons who are presumably neurotic or emotionally unstable can, following exposure to trauma, have their neurosis "triggered" for unconscious reasons related to compensation. This unclear and somewhat judgmental classification was perhaps one reason why "Traumatic Neurosis" was never accepted into the *Diagnostic and Statistical Manual of Mental Disorders* by the American Psychiatric Association.

Trauma and Stress

Other investigators in a different domain studied the psychophysiological effects of trauma ("emergency situations") and wrote about "homeostasis" and the "fight or flight" response (Cannon, 1929) and the "alarm reaction" as the first stage of the "General Adaptation Syndrome" (Selye, 1946). Cannon and Selye, pioneers in stress research (Selye coined the word "stress" as a physiologic concept), were laboratory scientists studying the effects of trauma on lower animals. Many years would pass before the concept of stress entered the fields of medicine and psychology. It is important to note that the observations of Cannon and Selye were strikingly similar to those described by DaCosta, Lewis, Oppenheimer, and Freud, but this is not surprising since they were all studying the response of the same physiologic system.

Behavioral Perspective

Wolpe (1958) conducted animal experiments in the late 1940s that he described as "experimental neurosis," but that could be viewed as an analogue for Traumatic Neurosis or Post-Traumatic Stress Disorder. Cats, while standing in a special cage, were made "neurotic" by a series of electrical shocks to their feet. The expected response of fear (anxiety, stress) continued long after the electric shocks were discontinued, thus in Wolpe's mind establishing an experimentally induced neurosis. The electric shock (unconditioned stimulus) elicited a response of fear (anxiety, stress) in the cats, which later became conditioned to other aspects of the experimental situation (the cage, experimental room, animal handlers, etc.). Whenever the cats were exposed to these conditioned stimuli (CS), they exhibited fear in the absence of any electrical shock. In this classic conditioning experiment, Wolpe clearly demonstrated the relationship between a traumatic stimulus (unconditioned stimulus) and the CS in producing symptoms in cats similar to anxiety in humans. This Pavlovian experiment (Pavlov, 1927) was not new, but its extrapolation of the results to humans led to a different way of conceptualizing Neurosis and, more importantly, opened a new therapeutic window—systematic desensitization or exposure treatment (Wolpe, 1958). The stimulus-response relationship between environment and anxiety following a trauma sparked a trend toward a more objective analysis of post-traumatic behavior.

Other investigators have elaborated on Wolpe's experiment and described PTSD symptoms as essentially a learned response to an antecedent traumatic conditioning event

(Keane et al., 1985; Kolb & Mutalipassi, 1982). A traumatic event (unconditioned stimulus) becomes paired with a previously neutral stimulus that then acts as a CS. Through the principles of classical conditioning, the CS may elicit adverse cognitive, physiologic, and emotional reactions in traumatized individuals. By the principles of instrumental conditioning, traumatized patients may then learn to avoid and escape traumatically conditioned CS as a means of reducing the conditioned adversive state. This learned avoidance response is viewed as critical to the maintenance of many of the symptoms of PTSD (Fairbank & Nicholson, 1987). Although a growing body of research is providing indirect empirical support for a conditioning model of arousal and avoidance in PTSD (Fairbank & Keane, 1982), critics (Saigh, 1985) have expressed concern that this model does not adequately account for the potential mediating influence of PTSD patients' cognitive response to trauma on adaptation and symptom development.

The development of cognitive behavior therapy added another dimension to the analysis and treatment of post-traumatic behavior (Beck, 1976; Foy, Donahoe, Carroll, Gallers, & Reno, 1987; Meichenbaum, 1977). Cognitive theory explains the relationship between covert mental processes and post-traumatic symptoms. Cognitions (intrusive thoughts, vivid visual recollections, flashbacks, or nightmares), the "videotapes of the mind," could now be correlated with anxiety and analyzed in terms of trauma. The sequence —traumatic event, cognitions, anxiety (stress)—explained what clinicians observed in traumatized patients. The persistence of symptoms beyond the traumatic event could now be explained in part by cognitive retraumatization; the patient, when exposed to events that symbolize or resemble an aspect of the traumatic event, relives the traumatic experience many times each day in imagination. Cognitive restructuring to control and diminish symptoms has important therapeutic significance, as will be discussed later in this chapter.

In summary, our knowledge about PTSD has evolved from several separate but related sources. Physicians, including psychiatrists, psychologists, stress researchers, and behaviorists, have studied the same phenomena but have emphasized only those aspects common to their training and experience. Like the proverbial blind men of Indostan touching the various parts of an elephant, clinicians and researchers have been studying the same elephant but drawing different conclusions when touching the trunk and then the tail. The confluence of these parallel perspectives was influenced by a historical event—the Vietnam conflict. The laboratory of war once again furnished clinicians with hapless victims to study and to treat. In response to the large number of Vietnam veterans with stress symptoms, clinicians with different professional proclivities and backgrounds converged, new theoretical and therapeutic practices emerged, and PTSD entered our nomenclature.

DIAGNOSING PTSD

Confusion concerning the definition of "stressor" and "trauma" sometimes interferes with the correct diagnosis of PTSD. "Trauma" has a generic meaning in the behavioral sciences that encompasses all insults to the personality. For example, trauma in psychodynamic formulations includes the impact of family conflicts on a developing child. Although psychologically painful, trauma in this sense does not fulfill the diagnostic criteria for a PTSD. Sociologically, poverty, racism, overpopulation, or oppression certainly are pernicious and "traumatic" but do not pose an immediate threat to life or limb. "Trauma," as a stressor that precipitates a PTSD, has a specific and precise definition as outlined in DSM-III-R.

According to DSM-III-R (1987), the stressor must be outside the range of usual human experiences and be markedly distressing to almost anyone. The stressor must pose serious threat to one's life or physical integrity. Exceptions to this criterion include a serious threat or harm to one's children, spouse, close relatives, or friends; witnessing the destruction of one's home or community; or seeing another person who has recently been seriously injured or killed. Clearly, the traumatic event must be viewed by the victim as a realistic threat to life or limb. Alternatively, through the process of identification, witnessing other people who have been seriously injured or killed or seeing the destruction of one's dwelling is sufficient stressor to qualify as a trauma that can precipitate a PTSD.

The sine qua non for PTSD is listed in the DSM-III-R (1987): "The traumatic event is persistently reexperienced." Revivification can occur by intrusive distressing recollections of the event, recurrent distressing dreams, dissociative episodes (flashbacks), or by exposure to events that symbolize or resemble an aspect of the traumatic event. Cognitions, therefore, play an important role in the furtherance of symptoms, and cognitive restructuring becomes an essential element of an effective treatment program.

Phobic behavior or avoidance of stimuli associated with the trauma is acknowledged in DSM-III-R (1987). Attempts to avoid thoughts, feelings, activities, or situations associated with the trauma characterize most PTSD patients. In my experience "psychological amnesia" is an infrequent finding; some patients may seem amnesic but in reality are reluctant to talk about the trauma because recollections evoke uncomfortable feelings of anxiety. Numbing of general responsiveness not present before the trauma is also mentioned in the DSM-III-R. Diminished interest in significant activities, feelings of detachment or estrangement from others, restricted range of affect, and a sense of a foreshortened future reflect a preoccupation with one's vulnerability and tenuous existence. Ruminations often induce speculations about more dire consequences that could have resulted from the trauma. Obsessing about more serious injury or even death does produce a numbing of general responsiveness and dysthymic mood. When negative cognitions overwhelm a person's mind, clinical depression is often the result (Beck, Rush, Shaw, & Emery, 1979).

Autonomic hyperactivity or persistent symptoms of increased arousal not present before the trauma are listed in DSM-III-R (1987). Insomnia is generally caused by ceaseless thoughts about the trauma or some aspect of it. Chronic anxiety is associated with irritability and outbursts of anger as well as difficulties in concentration. Being "on edge," hypervigilant, or easily startled are also signs of high anxiety. When victims are exposed to events that symbolize or resemble some aspect of the trauma, anxiety may lead to avoidance, further crippling the patient.

Unfortunately, in DSM-III-R (1987) the classification of acute and chronic PTSD has been abolished. PTSD, like any other illness or disorder, has a progressive course with an acute and chronic component. During the acute phase, anxiety symptoms predominate, whereas in the chronic phase disability and depression become more distinctive. The delayed subtype has also been eliminated because of the recognition that symptoms usually begin immediately or shortly after the trauma. When patients delay the reporting of symptoms or are exposed to additional stress unrelated to the original trauma, PTSD remains undiagnosed and it may appear that the onset was delayed. Close questioning usually reveals that some symptoms were present at the onset.

THE TRAUMATIC PRINCIPLE

All persons certainly do not respond to trauma identically; therefore, any attempt to predict the impact of a specific stressor on an individual is fraught with difficulty. Actually, any stressor that poses a realistic threat to life or limb could induce a PTSD in vulnerable individuals. How can this general statement help the clinician sort out the truly traumatized from others? The answer is: by application of the "Traumatic Principle."

The Traumatic Principle is: Any environmental stimulus that poses a realistic threat to life or limb, impacting on one or more likely a combination of the five sensory pathways to the brain, if perceived as a serious threat to one's life or physical integrity regardless of whether it produces physical injury, can be regarded as a trauma and precipitate a PTSD in a vulnerable individual (Scrignar, 1988). The central factor in the development of a PTSD is not necessarily the type or duration of the environmental trauma, but whether the trauma poses a realistic threat to life or limb and the person's conscious awareness and full appreciation of the trauma's potential for causing serious injury or death to self or others. Also vital, and a natural consequence of exposure to a traumatic event, is an intense activation of a person's autonomic nervous system. The sequence—realistic traumatic event, perception of potential danger to life or limb of self or others, intense activation of the autonomic nervous system—may occur before, during, or after the trauma. Sufficient time is necessary for the life-threatening nature of the trauma to be impressed on the mind, sometimes only seconds but more often longer exposure to the "dangerous situation" is required. No physical injury need occur, although one may result, but a neurophysiologic response to the trauma must eventuate before a PTSD can develop. Viewing victims of physical violence or the destruction of one's property, if considered dangerous to self, also fulfills the criteria of the "Traumatic Principle." Symptoms must persist or intensify beyond 1 month before a PTSD can be diagnosed. Clinically, the application of the "Traumatic Principle" assists in the diagnostic evaluation by eliminating those disorders that do not fulfill this basic criterion.

THEMES OF A PTSD

Misconceptions

All patients who have been exposed to a life-threatening situation, no matter what the nature of the stressor, are confronted with their own mortality. For the first time, most patients consider the prospect of death or a disabling injury and dwell in a state of uncertainty concerning their existence. Dysphoric emotions abound in the mind and often the trauma is not placed into perspective. The "videotapes of the mind" accurately record all of the frightening aspects of a trauma but usually do not include the fact of survival. Misconceptions grow around this incomplete or partial scenario, which lies embedded in the mind, and patients begin to act as if death or serious injury were imminent. Patients embroider "What if?" questions, speculating on a more dire conclusion to their trauma. Post-traumatic symptoms may not be recognized as a manifestation of a mental disorder but as a portent of future danger, and patients live life as if death were around the corner. Patients must be persuaded that perhaps a philosophical attitude toward life, buttressed by a realistic concern for self-preservation and appropriate actions for one's safety, would be in their own best interest. Misconceptions concerning post-traumatic emotions and behavior, a common theme in PTSD, must be constantly addressed and corrected during group treatment by persuasion and education.

Uncontrollable Thoughts

PTSD patients are plagued with seemingly uncontrollable thoughts that run rampant through their mind. Intrusive recollections, illusions, hallucinations, and dissociative episodes (flashbacks) seem to occur spontaneously, producing a feeling of powerlessness and a state of helplessness. To a patient, cognitive events associated with the trauma seem to explode in the mind, detonated by invisible forces outside one's control. As one patient said, "It is an awful thing to wake up each morning knowing with certainty that you will suddenly recall a terrifying event several times during the day." The theme of intrusive distressing recollections of the traumatic event (cognitive retraumatization) plays havoc with all PTSD patients. In both group and individual therapy, learning how to cope by cognitive restructuring becomes a matter of prime importance.

Avoidance

When patients begin to avoid activities or situations that resemble some aspect of the traumatic event, PTSD has assumed a central role in their lives. The theme of avoidance represents phobic behavior that wastes a person's time and energy and restricts normal living. If the trauma was work-related, avoidance often results in unemployment and a loss of income. Rape trauma may be followed by lack of sexual desire and an avoidance of sexual activity, which in turn erodes a loving relationship. A person who has been criminally assaulted may avoid the place of the crime, or if the robbery took place at home, he or she may feel uneasy or petrified with fear while in their house; some burglary victims feel compelled to change residences. Persons involved in vehicular accidents may avoid these conveyances, thereby restricting their mobility and interfering with daily activities. The theme of avoidance is present to some extent in every PTSD patient and is one of the chief concerns during therapy.

Increased Arousal

Symptoms of increased arousal related to autonomic hyperactivity cause hypervigilance, an exaggerated startle response, and increased motor tension. Difficulties in concentration, sleep disturbances, fatigue, and also reflections of abnormal arousal that interferes with interpersonal relationships produce a choleric mood. Physiologic reactivity on exposure to events that symbolize or resemble an aspect of the trauma may lead to avoidance or phobic behavior. Increased arousal really means increased anxiety, and this theme requires constant attention during group treatment.

Numbing of General Responsiveness

Obsessive preoccupation with the more frightening aspects of the traumatic event leads to feelings of detachment or estrangement from others, a markedly diminished interest in significant activities, isolation, hopelessness, and a nihilistic attitude. The sense of a foreshortened future interferes with planning and goal setting. A restricted range of affect and an inability to have loving feelings reflect a dysthymic mood. The theme of "numbing" is generally associated with depression that saps energy, lowers confidence, decreases pleasure, and disrupts group processes; it must be dealt with during group therapy.

SELECTING GROUP MEMBERS

Selecting appropriate patients, an important decision for all group therapists, is no less important when forming PTSD groups. The therapist must decide whether to mix patients suffering from heterogeneous trauma or to limit the group to individuals who have experienced a similar trauma. Circumstances and availablility of patients usually determine the types of groups that are formed. Veterans suffering from PTSD flock for treatment to Veterans Administration hospitals or Vet Centers where patients are selected for groups. Sexual assault victims filter through law enforcement agencies who refer prospective patients to rape crisis centers or to sex therapy clinics, and groups evolve from these centers. Mental health professionals rush to the site of natural or man-made disasters where group therapy is administered "in situ" to victims of a mass tragedy. At the conclusion of a hostage incident, survivors are herded into groups where they receive debriefing and therapy. Shelters for battered women provide crisis intervention and an opportunity to implement group therapy. Trauma Centers, which are beginning to emerge throughout the United States, deal primarily with accident victims' broken bones and battered bodies; liaison with these centers would certainly disclose emotionally traumatized patients who could form the nucleus of a group. As a natural consequence of their function, community institutions and administrative agencies separate persons who are involved in a trauma into unified groups ready for professional consideration and placement into therapy groups.

When organizing a group of PTSD patients, common sense indicates the selection of a homogeneously traumatized group. Combining Vietnam veterans, rape victims, and recently released hostages into one therapy group does not seem wise. Group members with similar traumatic experiences can empathize with each other and, in a collegial fashion, learn from one another. It is a good rule to select patients for group therapy based on a commonality or similarity of a trauma.

Whether to mix patients with acute cases of PTSD with patients who have become chronic is another decision that must be made. Chronic patients, especially those who have become despondent and hopeless, project a sense of futility and would seem to be poor role models for acute PTSD cases. On the other hand, heterogeneity in terms of PTSD duration allows for the discussion of a broader range of issues during group therapy. The distinction between acute and chronic may not be as important as an assessment of motivation. Prior to placement in a group, patients who complain of chronic pain, obsess about physical symptoms, exhibit symptoms of a major depression, or require daily use of a narcotic analgesic must be carefully screened and evaluated regarding a desire to change. Often secondary issues take precedence over therapy, and patients who have a different agenda may contaminate the group process. Patients displaying any of the following characteristics should be carefully evaluated: Substance Use Disorder, Somatoform Disorders, Antisocial Personality Disorder, Factitious Disorder, and Malingering. By and large, in regard to mixing acute and chronic cases when forming a PTSD group, the fewer restrictions the better. The group process creates an impetus that can overcome most obstacles brought forth by mixing acute and chronic patients.

STARTING A GROUP

Group treatment for PTSD is not complicated, but it keeps the therapist busy. Preliminary diagnostic interviews identify PTSD from other disorders that patients may experience post-traumatically. Dysthymic Disorder, Major Depressive Disorder, Panic Disorder, Organic Personality Syndrome, and Somatoform Disorders must be ruled out by a mental status examination. If the trauma resulted in head trauma and unconsciousness, a neurosurgeon must be consulted to determine the extent of Organic Mental Syndrome. When physical injury coexists with a PTSD, liaison with the treating physician(s) allows for an exchange of information related to ongoing medical treatment and prognosis. For those patients who are selected and offered an opportunity to enter group therapy, the introductory interview consists of a thorough explanation of PTSD, emphasizing the need and rationale for group treatment. An outline of therapy, consisting of PTSD themes, group therapy interventions, objectives, goals, and duration of treatment, is presented to each patient. Prior to the start of group therapy, it is a good idea to furnish each patient with a copy of the agenda, briefly summarizing the 10-session package that will be discussed shortly. A syllabus stating the objectives and goals of each session allows patients time for preparation and serves to maintain continuity. Patients' questions are answered, fees for professional services are settled, and a date is set for the first session.

The group leader(s) is an active participant and fulfills the role of empathic therapist, compassionate teacher, and pragmatic professor. The therapist, like the director of a new play, has a flexible script, the details of which may be modified as therapy progresses. The fundamental elements of group treatment consist of education, cognitive restructuring, training in relaxation, and exposure treatment. Assertiveness training (anger reduction), family interventions, and problem-solving constitute a second phalanx of stratagems. Homework assignments glue the sessions together and are an essential component of therapy. Throughout therapy, patients apply therapeutic interventions, assess progress, and reset goals. Because of the numerous tasks, inexperienced therapists are advised initially to limit the number of patients in a group to three or four. When the treatment process has been mastered, subsequent groups can include a maximum of eight patients.

Session 1: Explanation-Education

At the beginning of each session, the group leader sets the stage for therapy by delivering a short lecture (Yost, Beutler, Corbishley, & Allender, 1986). During the first session, group members receive information concerning the various themes of a PTSD. Many patients are unaware that their response to trauma is pathologic, even as symptoms become protracted. Acceptance of a Stress Disorder as "normal" or "justifiable" contravenes the necessity for change. The "bad news–good news" message of the brief lecture emphasizes that the patients are suffering from a PTSD, but it is treatable. The rationale for each treatment intervention is explained, with the imperative that a good outcome depends on cooperation and completion of all homework assignments.

Correcting misconceptions about the emotional sequelae of trauma allows patients to proceed in therapy, unencumbered by a false belief. Some common misconceptions include:

1. *"I cannot control my thoughts about the trauma."* Although intrusive thoughts seem guided by unseen forces, the truth is that all thoughts can be altered or modified to some extent by cognitive restructuring. Patients are reassured that if they follow instructions and consciously reduce thoughts about their trauma by 20 to 30%, significant positive changes will result.

2. *"I cannot influence what I dream."* While nightmares occur spontaneously during a sleeping state, what one dreams usually reflects what one thinks during the day(s) preceding sleep. When patients continue to report frequent nightmares, it indicates obsessional thinking about the trauma during the day. Persistent bad dreams therefore can signify the necessity for more assiduous attention to techniques of cognitive restructuring.

3. *"I can never return to the scene of the trauma or any place that resembles it."* This misconception may prevent patients from working, driving automobiles, flying in airplanes, or engaging in any activity related to the trauma. Exposure treatment allows patients to overcome fears related to the traumatic event. Results from numerous studies involving exposure treatment (systematic desensitization or flooding) help to rid patients of a pessimistic attitude and point the way to an effective treatment intervention (Marks, 1981).

4. *"I'll never forget the trauma."* While it is true that the traumatic event will remain embedded in memory, the emotions associated with it will diminish and recede with therapy and time. The traumatic event will be removed from the front-center stage of the mind by appropriate therapy and will be allowed to recede into the "attic of the mind," a place similar to the attic in a house where things are stored and remain unseen, sometimes forever.

5. *"My personality has been irreversibly changed by the trauma."* Everyone experiences unpleasant events during life; although the personality may become nicked and scarred, it does not basically change following a trauma. All human beings have the capacity of adapting to adversity, and group treatment will facilitate this process.

6. *"I am dead sexually."* Anxiety, anger, and pain or physical discomfort cause sexual dysfunction, but as these dysphoric emotions abate, pleasurable sexual feelings will return and a resumption of normal sexual activity can be expected.

7. *"My spouse doesn't love me anymore."* At times chronically dependent PTSD patients may not be so lovable, and disability certainly places a strain on a marriage, but in my experience divorce seldom occurs. Spouses of patients may resent the child-like dependent behavior exhibited by some PTSD patients, but positive changes can result.

8. *"I can't do anything."* Even for severely injured PTSD patients, this generalization is not true. Normal life activities may have been disrupted and patients may have to make adjustments; however, a repertoire of useful behaviors still exist or can be developed. When patients make a comparison between pre- and post-traumatic life style, dissatisfaction invariably results; patience is an attribute patients must acquire

because a resumption of pretrauma activities is slow and gradual. The importance of establishing a regular routine of eating, sleeping, and exercise "normalizes" life and precedes major changes.

After the introductory remarks and the question and answer period, patients are asked to give an account of their trauma. To ensure against repetition, patients are informed that only once will they be allowed to relate the trauma in detail. This admonition is consistent with the therapeutic philosophy of the group: concentrate on coping rather than on the trauma. Catharsis and abreaction may occur as patients tell about their trauma, and this is empathetically accepted; however, the group leader must emphasize the fact of survival. At the conclusion of each recitation, group members are encouraged to comment; the therapist assists by pointing out salient aspects of the history that can be impacted by therapeutic interventions.

During the first session, an atmosphere that encourages a positive expectation must be created in concert with the necessity of self-help. Information will be provided and therapeutic techniques will be taught, but success or failure depends on the patient's ability to carry out recommendations. Throughout treatment, the modality of explanation-education occupies a prominent position. Brief lectures furnish information and are the vehicle for instruction, but informal discussions supplement didactic presentations at each group session.

Sessions 2 and 3: Cognitive Restructuring

During the introductory lecture, the therapist presents the basic constructs of cognitive theory, explaining the relationship between intrusive thoughts and subsequent symptoms— how positive or negative thoughts influence feelings and ultimately behavior can be illustrated by examples common to everyone. Thoughts about one's achievements lead to feelings of well-being and predispose a person to further accomplishment. Sexual thoughts lead to sexual arousal and a desire for sexual fulfillment. Thoughts about a gourmet meal, especially if one has not eaten for awhile, stimulate the gastrointestinal tract, causing a feeling of hunger and a strong urge to eat. Similarly, negative emotions and behavior can be stimulated and influenced by distressing thoughts. Thinking frightening thoughts leads to a feeling of fear, which, to a varying extent, immobilizes a person. Angry feelings are always preceded by angry thoughts and followed by verbal, physical, or other manifestations of rage that are expressed directly or obliquely. For example, thinking about being wronged by a boss, friend, or relative leads to feelings of indignation, irritation, and anger, followed by a strong desire to retaliate with words or deeds. Recurrent and intrusive distressing thoughts about a trauma are associated with feelings of fear, anxiety, despair, anger, or guilt, depending on which aspect of the trauma comes to mind. These dysphoric emotions or feelings in turn stimulate negative behaviors that are usually maladaptive.

Once patients understand and accept cognitive theory, they are asked to become more introspective; recognition of one's thoughts precedes the application of cognitive restructuring. Next, patients record the frequency and duration of traumatic thoughts in a log or diary. These data direct the patient to unwanted thoughts and can serve as a baseline from which to measure progress.

Changing or modifying distressing thoughts is achieved by thought-stopping and thought-substitution techniques (Bain, 1928; Yamagami, 1971). During the group, patients are asked to close their eyes and produce distressing thoughts related to their trauma. After about 1 minute, the group leader shouts, "Stop! Get out of there!" Patients are momentarily shaken and will invariably report that their thought processes were interrupted. The procedure is repeated, but this time patients are instructed to emphatically, but silently, repeat the phrase, "Stop! Get out of there!" each time the therapist signals by a verbal command that is given every 5 seconds for about 10 repetitions. Next, patients are asked to employ the stopping procedure independently as often as necessary to control and reduce distressing thoughts. A rubber or elastic band can be worn around the wrist and snapped simultaneously when patients silently shout, "Stop! Get out of there!" (Mahoney, 1971). The momentary pain and the simultaneous phrase are most effective in stopping unwanted mental activity. Most patients are amazed and pleased with the results.

Stopping procedures effectively control thoughts like, "What if?" or "I could have . . . died . . . , been more seriously injured . . . , or it could happen again." These common covert statements of PTSD patients are usually associated with anxiety-generating images, the "videotapes of the mind," which portray danger and disaster. The therapeutic intervention of thought-substitution consists of replacing the old "videotapes of the mind" with a new one, ending happily. The title of the new "videotape" might be, "What If Everything Turns Out Alright?" The patients then have the option of thinking and visualizing scenes that generate happiness and tranquility rather than fear and anxiety. Scenes can be created from fantasy or can be retrieved from past pleasant memories. Once conceived, the new, more relaxing scenarios are practiced in the group until proficiency is achieved. Outside the group, patients are asked to substitute the new scenes immediately whenever intrusive thoughts begin. Some patients may report that they cannot think of any happy or pleasant situations. This "blind spot" usually dissolves as other group members relate pleasant thoughts and memories they used during the thought-substitution exercise.

At the third sesion group members report on homework assignments by referring to logs or diaries. Successes are verbally reinforced, failures are analyzed, suggestions are given, and patients are encouraged to keep trying. As patients report good results with cognitive restructuring, the group process not only serves as an elixir for all, but also creates a positive attitudinal change that promotes coping.

Session 4: Relaxation Training

Fear and anxiety, symptoms of increased arousal, are ameliorated by training patients in the technique of muscle relaxation (Jacobsen, 1974). During the brief lecture preceding group instruction in relaxation, patients are told that progressive muscle relaxation, hypnosis and self-hypnosis, autogenic training, transcendental meditation, and even prayer are all similar. When practiced successfully, all methods produce the same beneficial physiologic result, lowering the activity of the autonomic nervous sytem and decreasing motor tension. After this preamble, the entire group is taught progressive muscle relaxation. The technique of tensing and then relaxing various muscle groups is simple, but proficiency depends on daily practice. At the conclusion of the session, all group members invariably report a feeling of relaxation and well-being, something that they have not experienced in a long time.

There are many variations of the technique of relaxation, and the group leader should become familiar with one technique and teach it directly to all patients during a group session. The author furnishes each group member with a prerecorded audiocassette that contains not only relaxation exercises but information related to stress management, coping skills, and cognitive restructuring. If the group leader does not choose to record his or her own technique of relaxation, many tapes and records are currently on the market. Coping with symptoms of increased arousal by a relaxation procedure gives patients control over symptoms, and this leads to a positive expectation related to treatment and feelings of self-confidence.

Session 5: Exposure Treatment

PTSD patients tend to avoid activities, situations, or places reminiscent of the trauma because exposure to various elements of the trauma elicits uncomfortable feelings of anxiety. Behavior theorists postulate that the traumatic event, the unconditioned stimulus, elicits feelings of fear and anxiety that then became conditioned to stimuli associated with trauma. Following the trauma, these cues or conditioned stimuli stimulate fear and anxiety. To reduce or eliminate these uncomfortable feelings, patients tend to avoid situations that produce them. If persistent avoidance or phobic behavior results, it can be terribly debilitating.

Information about learning, conditioning, avoidance behavior, and the rationale underlying exposure treatment (systematic desensitization or flooding) is integrated during the lecture. Research studies are quoted to substantiate the efficacy of exposure treatment (Marks, 1981; Wolpe, 1958). Next, patients are asked to list all situations or activities that they currently avoid because of undue anxiety. For each item or theme, a hierarchy is constructed using quantifiable variables such as time or distance to indicate various levels of anxiety. For example, an auto accident victim who avoids riding or driving a car may identify as the lowest level of discomfort the following situation: "I am being driven around the block where I live by a trusted friend." At the top of the list evoking the highest level of discomfort: "I am driving alone on the expressway during peak traffic." Intermediate items of the hierarchy would include variables such as: time or distance away from home, city streets versus expressways, and the degree of traffic congestion. Initially, homework assignments consist of patients exposing themselves to the situation that evokes the lowest degree of discomfort. It is important that patients remain in that situation until anxiety levels subside to a comfortable or tolerable level before proceeding to the next item on the hierarchy. Systematically, patients expose themselves to more anxiety-evoking situations until they reach the top of the list. Often the place where the trauma occurred becomes a phobic stimulus. If a sexual assault took place in their apartment, rape victims may abandon autonomous living, even though it is their personal preference. Being home alone at night elicits so much anxiety that rape victims seek the shelter and security of group living, either with parents or friends. Before beginning exposure treatment, patients must be persuaded that if certain precautions are taken, living alone does not pose a serious threat to one's safety. Sometimes to ensure that a dwelling meets an acceptable standard for safety, a security specialist must be consulted to install burglar bars and an alarm system. The hierarchy that is employed during exposure treatment consists of two variables: being alone in an apartment and illumination. The lowest level of discomfort in the hierarchy might be: "I am in my apartment with a trusted friend during the daytime." The highest, most anxiety-evoking situation might be: "I am in my apartment, and it is a pitch-black night." Time spent with a trusted friend (eventually alone) is measured by a clock, and illumination is adjusted by means of a rheostat. Rape victims gradually expose themselves to situations of increasing discomfort, never moving up unless they feel reasonably comfortable in the preceding situation. At the conclusion of exposure treatment, the rape victim experiences tolerable anxiety while alone in a darkened apartment.

For a factory worker who is traumatized in an industrial accident, avoidance of the workplace means unemployment. In this case, exposure treatment must be coordinated with the plant physician and supervisor or foreman, who must understand the principles of desensitization. Time spent in the factory and proximity to the accident site are the main variables that correlate with increasing anxiety. Time is lengthened and distance shortened as exposure therapy proceeds. Following successful treatment, the factory worker experiences minimal discomfort at the accident site and can spend the full working day in the plant.

During the procedure of exposure treatment, patients are encouraged to utilize cognitive restructuring and progressive muscle relaxation to diminish fear and anxiety. Progression to a more anxiety-evoking step of the hierarchy should not take place unless the patient feels reasonably calm in the preceding step. Some clinicians (Keane & Kaloupek, 1982) advocate rapid exposure (flooding) with PTSD patients. Sometimes, however, flooding causes a worsening of symptoms and sensitization results. When a relapse occurs, future cooperation from patients is jeopardized. Gradual exposure, which offers no serious complications, is recommended, especially for novices.

At the end of the session, patients are given homework assignments and asked to assess and record the results of exposure treatment. At the next session, all patients report on the results of desensitization. Any difficulties are discussed and remedied, and, of course, progress is verbally reinforced by the group leader and usually applauded by the group members.

Session 6: Assertive Training (Anger Reduction)

PTSD patients have a tendency, especially if the trauma is of human design, to engage in periodic outbursts of anger directed toward anyone associated with the trauma. Even if overt expressions of anger do not occur, resentment smolders as patients ruminate about the negligence of others. After provocation has passed, anger, a disruptive emotion, is maladaptive. In PTSD patients, overt anger or covert resentment revivifies the trauma, causing a resurgence of symptoms.

The lecture at the beginning of the sixth session outlines the difference between aggression and assertion. Aggression is a militant act with intent of harming someone, verbally or physically. Assertion is standing up for one's rights (Alberti & Emmons, 1978; Dawley & Wenrich, 1976). Nonassertive or passive behavior, another characteristic of PTSD patients, fuels frustration as problems go unsolved. The group leader gives several examples of each type of behavior, pointing out that assertive actions make a person feel good and maximizes the achievement of objectives.

Group members are asked to air their grievances, then to engage in appropriate assertive response by behavioral rehearsal or role-playing exercises, first with the group leader and later with other group members. Any irrational outburst of anger or passive acceptance is likely to become evident to all. Following a discussion and analysis of the interaction, behavioral rehearsal is repeated using principles of assertion. Patients are told it is useless to berate employers or those believed responsible for the trauma. If negligence occurred, it usually was not intentional. However, the rightful avenue for redress is in the courts. In civilized society, retribution occurs as a result of civil legal action and is not based on Hammurabi's code of "an eye for an eye and a tooth for a tooth." Civil litigation offers victims an opportunity to receive monetary compensation for damages, both physical and emotional. If legal redress is not possible, traumatized patients must assume a philosophical attitude because harboring resentment interferes with treatment and a return to normal living.

Session 7: Family Relationships

Family life goes out of kilter when one member develops a PTSD. This is especially true when disability leads to unemployment and a role reversal occurs within the marital unit. Dysfunctional dependent behavior may be tolerated by a spouse for a short period of time, but eventually increased marital tension results in disputes and sexual dysfunction (Scrignar, 1987).

The brief lecture that begins session 7 presents information about the duties, responsibilities, and roles of the various members of a family unit. When one member becomes ill, the balance and burden of responsibility shifts to healthy members of the family. Unless one is seriously incapacitated, the lecture continues, a disabled person can usually make some contribution to the welfare of the family. Group members may protest that they can't do anything, but these complaints can be responded to by stories illustrating how others have overcome adversity. The therapist, from his or her own experiences or newspaper accounts, can relate stories about the tenacity and courage of disabled persons who learned how to cope with illness and handicaps.

Patients, hopefully motivated by inspirational stories, are asked how they can contribute more to the functioning of their family. Group process and the therapist can deal benevolently with any negative reaction, and patients are persuaded to look beyond themselves to the needs of the family. Following a trauma, it is natural for the mind's eye to turn inward, causing patients to become self-centered and oblivious to the needs of others. This tendency can be reversed by gentle, nonaccusatory, but firm persuasion, directing patients toward the acquisition of behaviors to remedy damaged family relationships. Whining and complaining, social isolation, and outbursts of anger are some negative behaviors that diminish pleasurable interaction with family members. Conversely, the addition of positive behaviors such as sharing household duties, helping manage children, increasing intimate interaction (conversation as well as sexual activity), and engaging more frequently in social and recreational activities helps to restore the family equilibrium.

Patients are asked to construct two lists. The first list consists of previously enjoyed activities and tasks. General terms such as work, exercise, or recreational activities are to be avoided in favor of specific time-limited activities. Work might include clean out garage, take out the garbage, or mow the front lawn, while exercise would consist of walking around the block, lifting light weights for 5 minutes, and jogging one-quarter mile; recreational activities would include watching a baseball game, going to a party, bowling, and so on. The second list includes the names of all significant family members. The patient is then asked how an increase in activities compiled in the first list would affect the important people in the second list. As group members come to grips with the answer, they begin to realize the reciprocal nature of relationships; you get what you give.

Homework assignments consist of a commitment to engage in three helping behaviors that impact directly on family members. The result, including the response of the family member, becomes grist for group discussion during the next session. Group members are generally surprised as they begin to reap the benefits of improved family relationships produced by seemingly small changes in their behavior. Success reported by one patient has a motivating impact on all members of the group, especially when the group leader verbally rewards positive change. Occasionally a conjoint session with patient and spouse must be arranged outside of the group in order to resolve intense marital conflicts (Stuart, 1980).

Session 8: Problem-Solving

Unresolved problems are a source of stress, and PTSD patients often develop tunnel-vision and are unable to envisage alternatives to dilemmas. Problem-solving during sessions allows patients the opportunity to widen their vision by group discussion that offers alternative solutions. The introductory lecture reviews the principles of cognitive theory mentioned during sessions 2 and 3. Thinking or worrying about unresolved problems does increase stress and anxiety, even if the thoughts are not directly related to the trauma. Patients are instructed to record in a notebook the amount of time they think about specific problems each day. By the end of 1 week data concerning worrisome subjects accumulate, and the time spent thinking about specific problems reflects the relative importance of that problem. The list is subdivided into problems that have a long-range solution and those that can be acted on immediately. Those problems that have a long-range solution are set aside, while the second list becomes the subject for sessions. The group then grapples with the most expeditious way to manage each problem. Family conferences and assertiveness training sessions resolve most problems; the remainder may only require sound counsel from the group, making it easier for the patient to decide on solutions.

The therapist and group members can help redefine the problem so that it is specific. Problems should not include symptoms of the Stress Disorder, which was addressed earlier. Inability to work, financial problems, legal difficulties, diminished involvement in social and recreational activities, and lack of exercise can be addressed and discussed by the patient and the group. Advice about budgeting, debt consolidation, or bankruptcy can resolve many problems dealing with money. When patients have legal difficulties, the names and addresses of several competent and respected lawyers may be all that is necessary to alleviate this problem.

The therapist records, as a reminder, the acceptance of the solution by the patient so that the outcome can be reported during the next session. Action, no matter what the outcome, is applauded, and patients are reminded that in life, perfect solutions occur infrequently. Partial resolution of problems, however, diminishes stress and provides the impetus for further change. Some clinicians may disparage advice-giving, but successful people in all walks of life consult outside sources for guidance and counsel as they decide on a course of action.

Problems that have no immediate solution must be placed in the "attic of the mind" to await future consideration. Placing a problem in proper perspective reduces urgency; all problems eventually are resolved or forgotten, and life moves on.

Sessions 9 and 10: Consolidation-Termination

In many ways, the termination of group treatment is the most difficult part of therapy. Time grows short for the implementation of the various therapeutic interventions. The therapist sorts out and concentrates on those patients who have made insufficient progress with their problems. A few members of the group may say, "I still don't understand why I have problems," "I can't relax," "I don't understand how I can change what I think," "Exposing myself to the traumatic situation only makes me feel more nervous," "I'm still mad as hell at those people who hurt me," or "My spouse doesn't understand me." Rather than confront patients with the obvious retort, "Where have you been for the last eight weeks?" the therapist solicits the help of group members who have done well (usually the majority) to serve as models and "trouble-shooters" for those having difficulty. Thus, the group leader avoids a nonproductive confrontation with a resisting patient and can still function to facilitate the flow of information from the "doing good" group members to the others. The benefits derived from cognitive restructuring, muscle relaxation, exposure treatment, and other therapeutic interventions are reviewed by the "doing good" group. Those patients who have had difficulties applying these therapeutic concepts and have reached an impasse are encouraged to keep trying as the principles of therapy are reviewed. The therapist's expertise and knowledge concerning group process and dynamics help to overcome resistance. The maintenance of an optimistic atmosphere within the group fosters a positive expectation that effects motivation and outcome.

All group members prepare for termination by setting post-therapy goals and assigning priorities for future action. Termination from therapy does not mean the cessation of therapeutic interventions. The necessity for the continued application of the principles and tactics learned during group treatment becomes a major issue during the last two group sessions. To keep patients motivated, plans for a 3- and 6-month follow-up are finalized, and patients are asked to keep notes and record all post-therapy progress. Setting a specific date for follow-up not only indicates the therapist's interest in the welfare of the patients, but also reminds patients to continue working on their problems. Two weeks before the follow-up date, a letter or phone call alerts each group member of the impending follow-up session. On occasion, additional therapy, either individual, group, or family, may be necessary to assist those patients with continuing problems.

THEORETICAL PERSPECTIVES

Psychodynamic Treatment

In early psychodynamic formulations, theorists postulated an energy overload. After a trauma, the ego attempts to restore homeostasis by "binding, discharging, or abreacting" the excess energy (Horowitz, 1974). More recently, psychodynamic formulations have emphasized information overload rather than energy overload, and the task confronting patients is seen as reconciling the occurrence of the traumatic event, including the various meanings associated with it and with the individuals' enduring schemata, such as their concept of self and the world around them. Within this framework, emotions are viewed as reactions to discrepancies between external and internal information and also serve as motives for defense and control (Horowitz & Kaltreider, 1980). The fundamental problem of patients with PTSD has been variably described as ideational incongruity (Horowitz, 1974), "split-off experience" (Brende & McCann, 1984), emotional blocking and "unfinished business" (Crump, 1984), or disruption of the normal course of psychosocial and personality development (Blackburn, O'Connell, & Richman, 1984). The optimal goal of psychodynamic treatment of PTSD is the integration of the traumatic experience, usually by means of therapeutic "revivification" (Brende, 1981). The particular psychodynamic techniques used to accomplish this end will vary as a function of the phase of PTSD (Horowitz & Kaltreider, 1980), the stage of therapy (Brende & McCann, 1984), and the personality style of the patient (Horowitz, 1974).

Two studies have systematically investigated the efficacy of psychodynamically oriented psychotherapy for stress response syndromes (Horowitz, Marmer, Weiss, Dewitt, & Rosenbaum, 1984; Lindy, Green, Grace, & Titchener, 1984). These studies, however, were uncontrolled and did not deal exclusively with PTSD. Although these studies represent an important first step in the evaluation of dynamic psychotherapy in the treatment of stress response syndromes, Fairbank and Nicholson (1987) have pointed out that the diagnostic heterogeneity of the treated groups and the absence of untreated controlled groups were serious limitations, and their analysis indicated that there were no differences between treated and untreated groups. Caution was urged in interpreting the finding of significant before-after change in studies, and the need for controlled outcome research was also underscored (Fairbank & Nicholson, 1987).

One must also be cautious about applying psychodynamic concepts in the treatment of patients with a PTSD. Unlike classically neurotic patients who have developed problems over a lifetime, PTSD patients become symptomatic later in life following an environmentally induced event. Therapy based on psychodynamic formulations related to psychopathologic conflicts earlier in life is therefore inappropriate. Traumatized patients see little relevance between neurotic conflicts and post-traumatic symptoms, and research does not indicate a clear-cut relationship between pre-traumatic personality and the development of a PTSD. Psychodynamically oriented groups, which focus on psychopathology rather than emphasize stratagems that help patients cope with post-traumatic symptoms and behavior, can adversely influence outcome by heightening anxiety and reinforcing negative symptoms. Traumatized patients require information to correct misconceptions, encouragement to employ therapeutic interventions, and support from group members and the therapist, and not a personality overhaul.

Psychodynamic insight involving knowledge about human motivation is important in assessing group process, but this information is best possessed by the therapist who must manage group interaction. Assessment of the pre-traumatic personality utilizing psychodynamic concepts has value, since ability to cope with the aftermaths of trauma is related to preexisting psychopathology. PTSD patients with a pre-traumatic "emotionally healthy personality" have a better prognosis.

Rap Groups

"Rap group therapy," popularized with the Vietnam veterans, refers to a highly unstructured setting where group members are encouraged to talk about traumatic war experiences and abreact with little or no interference from a therapist (Brende, 1981). There is no magic in catharsis or abreaction; in fact, by itself, unchecked emotional outbursts can be detrimental. Proponents of "rap group therapy" often confuse ranting with catharsis and abreaction. Prolonged and unchecked exchanges of traumatic combat experiences among veterans in group treatment can degenerate to "Can you top this?" Already excited veterans can be verbally flailed to a frenzy by horrible stories of war atrocities. Revivification of traumatic war experiences results in retraumatization, which exacerbates symptoms of a PTSD. Group members should, of course, have the opportunity to share their trauma with the group to promote group cohesiveness, and abreaction does alleviate some tension; however, continuous retelling is counterproductive. Advocates of "rap groups" state that camaraderie and a group identity are fostered by sharing war experiences (Parson, 1984), but group cohesiveness is present in all groups sharing a common goal. During group therapy the trauma must be placed into perspective, and patients must learn coping techniques to deal with intrusive thoughts and memories of the trauma. Unstructured groups such as a traditional "rap group" do not address the key symptoms of a PTSD in a systematic fashion.

Cognitive-Behavioral Approaches

A cognitive-behavioral approach to the treatment of PTSD impacts the hallmark symptoms: persistent, distressing, and intrusive recollections of aspects of the traumatic event (cognitive); disturbed affect (emotional); conditioned autonomic reactivity to cues associated with the trauma (physiologic); and avoidance of various stimuli that remind one of the traumatic event (behavioral) (Fairbank & Nicholson, 1987). While there is a paucity of controlled and comparative outcome research regarding the treatment of PTSD, more data on the efficacy of behavioral interventions exist than do for all other theoretical orientations. Three controlled studies regarding the treatment of Vietnam veterans suffering from PTSD are currently in progress at the Boston Veterans Administration Medical Center and at the Augusta, Georgia Veterans Administration Medical Center, and at the Eastern Pennsylvania Psychiatric Institute, a treatment research study regarding sexual assault victims is being conducted (Fairbank & Nicholson, 1987).

The effectiveness of stress inoculation training (SIT) (Pearson, Poquette, & Wasden, 1983) for sexual assault victims has been examined by a comparison of three types of group therapy for rape victims (Resick, Jordan, Girelli, Hutter, & Marhoefer-Dvorak, 1985). The three types of group therapy were: SIT ($N = 12$), assertion training ($N = 13$), and supportive psychotherapy ($N = 12$). The SIT package included Jacobsonian relaxation, diaphragmatic breathing, role-playing, covert modeling, thought-stopping, and guided self-dialogue (Pearson, Poquette, & Wasden, 1983). Group treatment consisted of six 2-hour sesions led by male-female cotherapists. All three groups were given a cognitive-behavioral explanation of the development of rape-induced fear and depression during the first session. The waiting list control group remained unchanged, while the three treatment groups evidenced significant improvement on a standardized and self-monitored measure of fear and anxiety, interpersonal sensitivity, assertiveness, and, to a lesser extent, depression. The majority of these gains were maintained at a 3- and 6-month follow-up. Although none of the three types of group therapy appeared to be a superior mode of treatment, the authors speculated that the group format or the educational component (i.e., cognitive-behavioral model) may have accounted for similar results in all three groups.

Although most research relates to Vietnam veterans and sexual assault victims, the cognitive-behavioral approaches to treatment may ultimately prove to be important in the treatment of all types of PTSD. I have advocated a number of therapeutic interventions for anxiety disorders, including PTSD, which include: explanation-education, training in relaxation, cognitive restructuring, medication, exposure treatment (systematic desensitization-flooding), assertive training for anger reduction, family participation, and problem-solving (Scrignar, 1983). These interventions, originally based on individual therapy, have been modified for groups (Scrignar, 1984). All of the symptom themes of PTSD mentioned earlier in this chapter are impacted by one or more of these therapeutic interventions. Data from controlled studies, investigating individual and group therapy, will shed more light on the cognitive-behavioral approach to the treatment of PTSD.

SUMMARY AND RECOMMENDATIONS

Over the years, psychodynamic formulations of the emotional sequelae of trauma have proved interesting, but unfortunately theoretical constructs have not undergone the scrutiny of controlled research. No consistent psychodynamic therapeutic technology has emerged for the treatment of PTSD. Data from uncontrolled studies and single case designs involving a cognitive-behavioral approach for the treatment of PTSD are proliferating, mainly with Vietnam combat veterans and sexual assault victims. Existing evidence points to a conceptual model for PTSD that involves learning and conditioning. Classic and instrumental conditioning explain the genesis and sustainment of PTSD symptoms, while behavioral techniques currently exist for the treatment of the classes of symptoms found in a PTSD: cognitive restructuring for intrusive and distressing thoughts, exposure treatment for avoidance behavior, and relaxation training for symptoms of increased arousal. This chapter enlarges the range of possible therapeutic interventions to include assertiveness training, family intervention, and problem-solving. Related issues involving work, social and recreational activities, exercise, and nutrition are interwoven into a comprehensive treatment program. It remains for future researchers to determine the efficacy of a cognitive-behavioral approach to the treatment of PTSD. In my experience, the approach discussed in this chapter has considerable merit.

REFERENCES

Alberti, R. E., & Emmons, M. L. (1978). *Your perfect right* (3rd ed.). San Luis Obispo: Impact.

American Psychiatric Association (1980). *Diagnostic and statistical manual of mental disorders* (3rd ed.). Washington, DC: American Psychiatric Association.

American Psychiatric Association (1987). *Diagnostic and statistical manual of mental disorders* (3rd ed. -revised). Washington, DC: American Psychiatric Association.

Bain, J. S. (1928). *Thought control in everyday life.* New York: Funk and Wagnalls.

Beck, A. T. (1976). *Cognitive therapy and the emotional disorders.* New York: International Universities.

Beck, A. T., Rush, A. J., Shaw, B. F., & Emery, G. (1979). *Cognitive therapy of depression.* New York: Guilford Press.

Blackburn, A. B., O'Connell, W. E., & Richman, B. W. (1984). PTSD, the Vietnam Veteran, and Adlerian Natural High Therapy. *Individual Psychology, Journal of Adlerian Theory, Research and Practice, 40,* 317–332.

Brende, J. O. (1981). Combined individual and group therapy for Vietnam Veterans. *International Journal of Group Psychotherapy, 31,* 367–378.

Brende, J. O., & McCann, I. L. (1984). Regressive experiences in Vietnam Veterans: Their relationship to war, post-traumatic symptoms and recovery. *Journal of Contemporary Psychotherapy, 14,* 57–75.

Burgess, A. W. (1983). Rape trauma syndrome. *Behavioral Science and the Law, 1,* 97–114.

Cannon, W. B. (1929). *Bodily changes in pain, hunger, fear, and rage: An account of recent researchers into the function of emotional excitement* (2nd ed.). New York: Appleton-Century-Crofts.

Crump, L. E. (1984). Gestalt therapy in the treatment of Vietnam Veterans experiencing PTSD symptomatology. *Journal of Contemporary Psychotherapy, 14,* 90–98.

DaCosta, J. M. (1871). On irritable heart: A clinical study of a form of functional cardiac disorder and its consequences. *American Journal of Medical Science, 61,* 17–52.

Dawley, H. H., & Wenrich, W. W. (1976). *Achieving assertive behavior.* California: Bricks/Cole.

Fairbank, J. A., & Brown, T. A. (1987). Current behavioral approaches to the treatment of Post-Traumatic Stress Disorder. *The Behavior Therapist, 10,* 57–64.

Fairbank, J. A., & Keane, T. M. (1982). Flooding for combat-related stress disorders: Assessment of anxiety reduction across traumatic memories. *Behavior Therapy, 13,* 499–510.

Fairbank, J. A., & Nicholson, R. T. (1987). Theoretical and empirical issues in the treatment of Post-Traumatic Stress Disorder in Vietnam Veterans. *Journal of Clinical Psychology, 43,* 44–55.

Figley, C. R. (1978). *Stress disorders among Vietnam Veterans.* New York: Brunner/Mazel.

Foy, D. W., Donahoe, C. P., Carroll, E. M., Gallers, J., & Reno, R. (1987). Post-Traumatic Stress Disorder. In L. Michelson & M. Ascher (Eds.), *Anxiety and stress disorders* (pp. 361–378). New York: Guilford.

Freud, S. (1962). On the grounds for detaching a particular syndrome from neurasthenia under the description "Anxiety Neurosis." In *Standard edition of the complete psychological works of Sigmund Freud* (Vol. 3, p. 90). London: Hogarth Press. (Original work published in 1895)

Grinker, R., & Spiegel, J. P. (1945). *Men under stress.* Philadelphia: Blakiston.

Horowitz, M. (1974). Stress response syndromes, character style, and dynamic psychotherapy. *Archives of General Psychiatry, 31*, 768–781.

Horowtiz, M. J., & Kaltreider, N. B. (1980). Brief psychotherapy of stress response syndromes. In T. B. Karasu & L. Bellak (Eds.), *Specialized techniques in individual psychotherapy.* New York: Brunner/Mazel.

Horowitz, M. J., Marmer, C., Weiss, D. S., Dewitt, K. N., & Rosenbaum, R. (1984). Brief psychotherapy of bereavement reactions: The relationship of process to outcome. *Archives of General Psychiatry, 41*, 438–448.

Jacobsen, E. (1974). *Progressive relaxation: A physiological and clinical investigation of muscular states and their significance in psychology and medical practice* (3rd ed.). Chicago: University of Chicago.

Kaiser, L. (1968). *The traumatic neurosis.* Philadelphia: Lippincott.

Kardiner, A., & Spiegel, H. (1947). *War stress and neurotic illness.* New York: Hoeber: Harper.

Keane, T. M., & Kaloupek, D. G. (1982). Brief reports: Imaginal flooding in the treatment of a Post-Traumatic Stress Disorder. *Journal of Consulting & Clinical Psychology, 50*, 138–140.

Keane, T. M., Zimering, R. T., & Caddell, J. M. (1985). A behavioral formulation of Post-Traumatic Stress Disorder in Vietnam Veterans. *Behavior Therapist, 8*, 9–12.

Kilpatrick, D. G., Veronen, L. J., & Resick, P. A. (1982). Psychological sequelae to rape: Assessment and treatment strategies. In D. M. Doleys, R. L. Meredith, & A. R. Ciminero (Eds.), *Behavioral medicine: Assessment and treatment strategies.* New York: Plenum.

Kolb, L. C., & Mutalipassi, L. R. (1982). The conditioned emotional response: A subclass of the chronic and delayed Post-Traumatic Stress Disorder. *Psychiatric Annals, 12*, 979–987.

Lewis, T. (1919). *The soldier's heart and the effort syndrome.* New York: Hoeber.

Lindy, J. D., Green, B. L., Grace, M., & Titchener, J. (1983). Psychotherapy with survivors of the Beverly Hills Supper Club Fire. *American Journal of Psychotherapy, 37*, 593–610.

Mahoney, M. J. (1971). The self-management of covert behavior: A case study. *Behavior Therapist, 2*, 575–578.

Marks, I. (1981). *Cure and care of neurosis.* New York: Wiley.

Meichenbaum, D. D. (1977). *Cognitive-behavior modification: An integrated approach.* New York: Plenum.

Ochberg, F. M., & Soskis, D. A. (1982). Planning for the future: Means and ends. In F. M. Ochberg & D.A. Soskis (Eds.), *Victims of terrorism* (pp. 173–190). Boulder, CO: Westview Press.

Oppenheimer, B. S. (1918). Report on neurocirculatory asthenia and its management. *Military Surgery, 42*, 7–11.

Parson, E. R. (1984). The role of psychodynamic group therapy in the treatment of the combat veteran. In H. J. Schwartz (Ed.), *Psychotherapy of the combat veteran* (pp. 153–220). New York: SP Medical and Scientific Books.

Pavlov, I. P. (1927). *Conditioned reflexes.* New York: Liveright.

Pearson, M. A., Poquette, B. M., & Wasden, R. E. (1983). Stress-inoculation and the treatment of post-rape trauma: A case report. *Behavior Therapist, 6*, 58–59.

Rosenbaum, A. (1986). Family violence. In W. J. Curran, A. L. McGarry, & S. A. Shah (Eds.), *Forensic psychiatry and psychology: Perspectives and standards for interdisciplinary practice* (pp. 227–246). Philadelphia: F. A. Davis.

Round Table Meeting. (1960). *Neurosis and trauma.* APA Convention, Atlantic City, NJ.

Saigh, P. A. (1985). On the nature and etiology of traumatic stress. *Behavior Therapist, 16*, 423–426.

Scrignar, C. B. (1983). *Stress strategies: The treatment of the anxiety disorders.* Basel: S. Karger.

Scrignar, C. B. (1984). *Post-Traumatic Stress Disorder: Diagnosis, treatment, and legal issues.* New York: Praeger.

Scrignar, C. B. (1987). Post-Traumatic Stress Disorder and sexual dysfunction. *Medical Aspects of Human Sexuality, 21*, 102–112.

Scrignar, C. B. (1988). Post-traumatic stress disorder: Diagnosis, treatment, and legal issues (2nd ed.). New Orleans: Bruno Press.

Selye, H. (1946). The general adaptation syndrome and the diseases of adaptation. *Journal of Clinical Endocrinology, 6*, 117–130.

Stuart, R. B. (1980). *Helping couples change*. New York: Guilford.

van der Kolk, B., Greenberg, M., Boyd, H., & Krystal, J. (1985). Inescapable shock, neurotransmitters, and addition to trauma: Toward a psychobiology of post-traumatic stress. *Biological Psychiatry, 20*, 314–325.

Veronen, L. J., & Kilpatrick, D. G. (1983). Stress management for rape victims. In D. Meichenbaum & M. E. Jaremko (Eds.), *Stress reduction and prevention* (pp. 341–374). New York: Plenum.

Walker, J. I., & Nash, J. L. (1981). Group therapy in the treatment of Vietnam combat veterans. *International Journal of Group Psychotherapy, 31*, 379–388.

Wolpe, J. (1958). *Psychotherapy by reciprocal inhibition*. Stanford: Stanford University.

Yamagami, T. (1971). The treatment of an obsession by thought-stopping. *Journal of Behavior Therapy and Experimental Psychiatry, 2*, 133–135.

Yost, E. B., Beutler, L. E., Corbishley, M. A., & Allender, J. R. (1986). *Group cognitive therapy*. New York: Pergamon.

JAMES HUGGINS
WILLIAM I. COHEN

4
A Group Approach for Working with Gay and Bisexual Men with AIDS

Acquired Immune Deficiency Syndrome (AIDS) has captured the attention of virtually every section of the population, in large part due to the dramatic way it has entered our consciousness. The Surgeon General has predicted that by 1991, there will have been 270,000 cases of this disease diagnosed in the United States and 179,000 people will have died (Koop, undated, c. 1987). Consequently, the burden placed on all facets of the health care system will be staggering.

AIDS has been and continues to be associated with gay and bisexual behavior. This association reflects the fact that this population was the first to manifest the disease in great numbers. However, AIDS is sexually transmitted, and therefore sexually active people are at risk. Indeed, the current statistics indicate that the virus has spread throughout the population. Other groups at great risk include intravenous drug users who share needles and syringes, as well as their sexual partners, the children born of infected women, and recipients of infected blood or blood products, notably men with hemophilia.

In describing group interventions for people with AIDS, we decided to limit the scope of this chapter to gay and bisexual men. Several factors led to this decision. First, gay and bisexual men have accounted for approximately 70% of the total number of persons diagnosed with AIDS (Koop, undated, c. 1987). Although great attention has been placed on the spread of this disease into the heterosexual population, the greatest percentage of individuals with AIDS will continue, for many years, to be gay and bisexual men. Therefore, the mental health community will be confronted with the need to respond to an ever-increasing demand for services from this population. Second, although many mental health professionals are skilled in treating persons with chronic and terminal illnesses, gay and bisexual men with AIDS present unique life experiences that require additional sensitivity and expertise. Lastly, our experience has been primarily with this population.

In this chapter, we briefly describe the current understanding of AIDS and its manifestations, the psychosocial issues and reactions confronting both the client and the therapist, the stages of psychological adjustment to the disease, and the ways these various factors interact in the group process.

As noted, AIDS affects all of us. Other affected individuals, such as ethnic and racial minorities, children, people in prison, and intravenous drug users, present unique challenges. It is our hope that this chapter can provide a frame of reference that can be adapted to the specific needs and sociocultural realities of those groups.

Finally, we wish to state our awareness of the fact that one brief chapter can only skim the surface of this problem. We wish to direct the interested reader to an important resource: *What To Do about AIDS: Physicians and Mental Health Professionals Discuss the Issues.*

This book, edited by McKusick (1986), provides background information in greater depth. We highly recommend it as a starting point. With the rapid changes in our understanding of the disease, health care providers must continue to update their knowledge base, especially since the person with AIDS will have many questions about recently reported advances, treatments, and speculations.

WHAT IS AIDS?

AIDS is a sexually transmitted disease, first described in 1981. It is caused by a virus, now known as human immunodeficiency virus (HIV). The virus was formerly known by a variety of other names, such as HTLV-III (human T-cell lymphotropic virus, type III), LAV (lymphadenopathy associated virus), and ARV (AIDS-related virus). These were all different names of the same virus. For simplicity, we will use the current nomenclature of HIV.

HIV is found in various body fluids. The current evidence is quite strong that the disease is transmitted by contact with infected blood and infected sexual fluids, primarily semen. Any sexual practice that exposes an individual to sexual fluids (semen or vaginal secretions) is potentially dangerous. However, it is known that the individual who is the recipient of anal or vaginal intercourse seems to be at significantly greater risk than persons who engage in other sexual practices. Therefore, if one has sex with an individual who has the virus in his body, or if one has blood-to-blood contact with such an individual via transfusion or sharing of needles and syringes, there would be a reasonable likelihood of being infected with this virus.

The HIV virus specifically attacks and destroys the T-4 lymphocyte, that part of the immune system that protects the body from microorganisms such as fungi, parasites, viruses, and unusual bacteria. The destruction of these cells leaves the individual vulnerable to infection by these microorganisms. Individuals with normal immune systems do not become ill with these conditions, so the illnesses are referred to as "opportunistic infections" because they take the opportunity of a compromised immune system to flourish. The most common condition is *Pneumocystis carinii* pneumonia. Since the normal function of the immune system is to protect the body from spontaneously occurring cancers, another manifestation of the immune system destruction is the development of relatively rare malignancies such as Kaposi's sarcoma, a kind of skin cancer.

The diagnosis of AIDS can be defined as the destruction of the immune system by HIV infection as manifested by an opportunistic infection or cancer.

There is no known cure for this disease, and once an individual has received the diagnosis of AIDS, it is expected that he or she will not recover; the illness is considered invariably fatal.

However, we know that the virus can enter the body and cause a limited infection, so that it can be detected by a specific test (for the HIV antibody), without causing the person to have any outward manifestations of illness. This asymptomatic individual, however, can transmit the virus to others, as described above. Often there appears to be a significant latency (lag time) between the exposure to the virus and the onset of overt immune deficiency. This lag time has been estimated to be approximately 5 to 12 years.

Asymptomatic individuals are probably the largest group of individuals infected by HIV. They are not ill in any way. Some have learned, by choice or by chance, that their body has been exposed to HIV. Others are unaware of the infection. At the present time, there is no way of knowing whether the asymptomatic individual will continue to remain healthy or become ill with AIDS-related Complex (ARC) or AIDS.

Those individuals with ARC represent an intermediate position. They have laboratory and clinical evidence of immune deficiency, but they do not have one of the serious opportunistic infections or a malignancy. Their symptoms may include swollen lymph glands, intermittent fevers, weight loss, fatigue, and malaise.

Manifestations of AIDS

The common characteristic of this condition is that the individual experiences a wasting process. Commonly experienced symptoms, which are similar to those experienced by a patient with ARC, include swollen lymph nodes, fever, fatigue, and malaise. The most dramatic effects relate to the various opportunistic infections such as pneumonia and meningitis. It is common for these individuals to have yeast infections (thrush) of the mouth on a chronic basis and diarrheal disease.

The central nervous system is frequently involved, as a result of opportunistic infections, such as cryptococcal meningitis. In addition, the virus has been demonstrated to directly affect the central nervous system, causing an acute neuropsychiatric syndrome of delirium and a chronic syndrome of dementia. Anxiety and depression are common concurrent occurrences.

Treatment and Course

There is no current treatment that destroys the virus and restores the immune system to its normal function. A variety of antiviral medications have had varying success in arresting the spread of the virus. However, none of them has been able to eradicate it. These drugs have extended the lives of some AIDS patients, but have not provided a cure.

However, a variety of treatments are available for the opportunistic infections; some of these work quite well. For example, *Pneumocystis carinii* pneumonia can be successfully treated, although it commonly recurs. Kaposi's sarcoma and the other malignancies may also respond to chemotherapy. The ability to treat the other infections varies. However, the lack of a functional immune system usually leads to the demise of the individual, since, as time goes on, the body weakens and is less able to respond to medical treatments.

In general, the course of the illness is manifested by periods of relative wellness alternating with periods of serious acute illness requiring intensive hospital care.

Death from this disease is unfortunately not a peaceful one. The process of wasting renders these individuals shadows of their former selves. They require extensive medical care; they may lose intellectual function and control of bladder or bowels and may experience significant discomfort. Furthermore, the burden on caretakers is enormous.

THE STIGMA OF AIDS

In dealing with people with AIDS, the health professional usually has experience with many of the issues of chronic progressive illness. Indeed, AIDS is not the first fatal illness in the history of medicine. Nevertheless, there are two issues of special importance that must be addressed at the outset: mortality and sexuality.

Regarding mortality, AIDS very much resembles cancer in that it is associated with death, with the difference being that cancer is correctly considered to be a serious but, in many instances, treatable disease. Cancer patients experience enormous fears related to the popular image of this disease as insidious, silently doing its evil business until it has spread throughout the body. This mythology of cancer has been cogently described by Susan Sontag in *Illness as Metaphor* (1978). The reality of cure and successful treatment generally palls in the face of the mythology of death, disfigurement, and pain.

In addition to the misconceptions shared with cancer, AIDS is further contaminated with the stigma of sexuality, in general, and homosexuality, in particular. In the sex-negative society of modern America, the individual with AIDS faces the stigma of a sexually transmitted disease that is uniformly fatal. Some fundamentalist religious groups consider AIDS to be punishment for homosexuality. This attitude can lead to an increase in guilt on the part of the religious individual with AIDS. Instead of receiving comfort, the person may feel judged and blamed.

Non-gay individuals (hemophilia patients, transfusion recipients) have to contend with the overtones of sexuality. Early in the history of their disease, they may be badgered repeatedly about their sexual activity.

The stigma of AIDS and the shame it induces result from the inevitable association with morality that occurs with a sexually transmitted disease (Gould, 1987). The stakes are doubled by the fact that not only is AIDS sometimes associated with activities that are considered morally wrong (sex and intravenous drug use), but specifically with homosexuality and homosexual behavior, which have been associated with mental illness (Mandel, 1986). Nowhere is this moral note sounded more clearly than in the popular concept that recipients of contaminated blood products and children infected in their mother's wombs are the "innocent victims" of AIDS. The implication of this statement is clear enough: the gay/bisexual/intravenous drug user and, to a lesser extent, their partners deserve to have this disease (Silverman, 1986).

The issue of homophobia underlies the reaction of both the person with AIDS and the health care worker. Success with this client population depends on adequately addressing this issue.

Homophobia, an irrational fear of homosexuals, needs to be understood in the context of its effects on gay and bisexual men and those who interact with them. Most gay and bisexual men remain hidden about their sexuality, fearful of disclosing this information to others outside of a chosen, trusted few. Homophobia is at the root of this fear.

In some major cities, such as New York and San Francisco, gay and bisexual men enjoy the protection of certain civil rights. However, in most areas of the country, one can be denied housing, public accommodations, credit, and employment for being gay or bisexual. Nationally, one can be prevented from entering the military, marrying a member of one's own sex, and raising one's own children simply because one is gay or bisexual. Clearly, the message to gay and bisexual individuals is to be careful and quiet about your lifestyle or you will be punished. Consequently, most gays and bisexuals lead a "double life." They are open to some and not others.

The roots of homophobia go deeper on an individual level. Most of us have been taught to view gay and bisexual men as possessing stereotypic mannerisms and characteristics. Gay and bisexual men are often assumed to be unhappy, neurotic individuals who lack a sense of morality, especially where sex is concerned. Most of us are taught to be suspicious and fearful of these men.

Unfortunately, these same stereotypes are often incorporated into an internalized homophobia that creates guilt and shame. It is difficult for the gay or bisexual man to feel good about himself while living in a culture that condemns him.

Negative injunctions about gay and bisexual men are part of the growing-up process for most Americans. Health care workers are not exempt from this socialization. It is into the hands of these people that gay and bisexual men must place themselves because of AIDS. It is no wonder that they feel so vulnerable. Their ability to choose who will know and who will not know about their sexuality has been taken from them.

Homophobia, as described above, is most often reflected in the serious dilemmas that the person with AIDS faces in terms of control of information. The diagnosis of AIDS, or even the consideration of such a diagnosis, opens up to examination some of the most private aspects of an individual's life: his sexual orientation, his sexual behavior, or both. Most gay and bisexual men maintain that part of their life outside of the knowledge of most individuals they deal with in their day-to-day activity. In general, it is irrelevant. While many gay men choose to experience a greater level of freedom by "coming out" to their families, straight friends, and coworkers, the majority do not. Those who decide to "come out" make the decision to disclose this information at a time and in a place and manner that are of their own choosing. AIDS removes that control.

Gay clients entering treatment are likely to assume that therapists and other health care providers will not understand, be sympathetic to, or be knowledgeable of their lifestyle. They might well anticipate an overtly judgmental response. Until recently, most health care providers have not had to address the issue of gay sexuality because these men were successful in their ability to maintain privacy about their sexuality. The diagnosis of AIDS removes the choice of privacy.

For the bisexual man, in particular, the lack of control of information about his sexuality may seem overwhelming. If he is married, his diagnosis of AIDS may be the first time his wife and children learn that he was engaging in sex with men.

Another dilemma is presented by the man who has had predominantly homosexual activity but does not define himself as gay. This individual may need to explore his ideas about his own sexuality in the context of having received the diagnosis of HIV infection.

Group treatment provides a forum in which clients may find support and coping mechanisms for dealing with the stigma of AIDS and homophobia. We turn now to a discussion of other reasons group treatment may be beneficial to gay and bisexual men with AIDS.

RATIONALE FOR GROUP TREATMENT

We believe that gay and bisexual men with AIDS are particularly well-suited for group interventions. These individuals start out as members of a minority culture. The diagnosis of AIDS makes them a minority within a minority. Furthermore, many of these people have difficult or conflictual relations with their families. Gay men frequently identify with their peers in the world of the gay subculture. Inasmuch as societal homophobia has intensified the suffering of persons with AIDS, it is only natural to assume that a large number of persons with AIDS would look to a group to find emotional support. This tendency has been validated in recent literature, which shows that "emotionally sustaining kinds of social support were more desirable, useful, available, and likely to be used than problem-solving types of support" (Mandel, 1986, p. 79).

A recent study of the concerns of 46 persons with AIDS revealed that their greatest concerns were centered on the future and the length and quality of their lives (Namir, 1986). Next in importance were concerns regarding work and finances, and the third and fourth concerns related to self-esteem and friendship. Health came fifth, and religious concerns were last. When compared with a group of 59 cancer patients, the concerns were similar, except that cancer patients expressed more family and health concerns.

It is in the area of self-esteem and friendship that group interventions are particularly appropriate. Namir (1986) identifies the issues of loneliness, the necessity of moving, the need to ask for assistance, social isolation, sexual dissatisfaction, self-blame, and feelings of irritability, guilt, and moodiness. Although the content of group sessions may address some of these issues directly, the group itself by its existence responds to the major themes of loneliness and social isolation.

Inasmuch as gay and bisexual men with AIDS are frequently cut off from their biological families, the role of a support group is clearly of major importance. Through a support group, an individual can find acceptance of his sexuality, as well as a place to express fears, anxieties, and frustrations. A survey of the needs of people with AIDS revealed that 81% wanted group or individual psychotherapy, but only 28% were receiving any psychological services (Wolcott, Fawzy, Landsverk, & McCombs, 1986).

Some bisexual men feel comfortable with both the heterosexual and homoexual components of their sexuality. We would anticipate that they would easily integrate into a predominantly gay group. Those bisexual men who experience the homosexual part as a source of pain and discomfort may well resist participating in such a group. Therefore, in terms of screening for inclusion in a support group, prospective members should be informed of the sexual orientations of the group members so that they can decide if they feel comfortable.

In cities where AIDS has been epidemic for the last 7 years (New York, Los Angeles, San Francisco, Chicago, etc.), massive supportive services have arisen within the gay community to meet the needs of persons with AIDS. These services have been particularly important because many of the gay residents of these cities have left the heartland of America to move to the more positive environments of large cities. Indeed, many of these individuals escaped in order to avoid the dilemma of addressing their sexuality with their families. Groups such as the Gay Men's Health Crisis in New York and the Shanti Project in San Francisco, therefore, provide a sense of "family" and community. The community frequently becomes the family for gay men. Networks of friends also provide support, but in these cities, the ability of individuals to continue to respond has been compromised by "bereavement overload," a term coined by Kastenbaum (1977) to describe the experience of an elderly individual who experiences the death of many friends in a short period of time.

In the smaller and middle-sized cities of the United States, a different phenomenon has occurred. In addition to the indigenous population of gay and bisexual men afflicted with AIDS, men who emigrated to big cities frequently return home at the time of diagnosis. Their families may then be confronted with the revelation of their sexual orientation at the same time that they learn of the fatal diagnosis. Smaller communities have not had much experience with alternative sexual orientations; therefore, the person with AIDS who returns home faces the prejudices he sought to avoid. Support groups become a validating experience, providing an environment in which this individual can find some measure of acceptance.

STAGES OF ADJUSTMENT

People with AIDS do not remain static in response to their disease; they move through a series of stages that require different adjustments and psychological tasks. Group leaders need to be aware of these stages so that they can adequately assess the group member's experience and facilitate his adjustment.

Macks and Turner (1986) describe three stages that they feel are most common to AIDS patients: (1) initial diagnosis, (2) middle phase of adjustment to chronic illness, and (3) preparation for death. Each member of a group will be experiencing the emotional and psychological reactions to his particular stage of adjustment. Part of the group process is to help each person achieve a sense of mastery and control while experiencing the emotional turmoil of accommodation to each stage and the support of others during this stressful period. A brief description of each stage will help to understand the psychological tasks that confront the individual with AIDS.

Initial Diagnosis

An initial diagnosis of AIDS is usually the culmination of a growing sense of vulnerability and fear on the part of clients. They may have already had ARC and known that they were HIV-antibody positive. They may have been experiencing a great deal of anxiety about whether they would actually develop the disease. A diagnosis of AIDS will confirm the client's worst fears and expectations.

Some clients may therefore suspect that they have the disease, whereas for others the initial diagnosis will come as a complete surprise. They may not have been tested for HIV infection or may have felt that even though they were positive for the HIV antibody they would not develop the disease. For these individuals, the initial shock of diagnosis will be particularly devastating.

A crisis is usually precipitated after the diagnosis is made. The uncertainty of the progression of the disease often leads persons with AIDS to feel that their lives will shortly be over; everything must be dealt with and decided on immediately. The shock and disbelief accompanying the initial diagnosis may lead to a series of questions about what to do: "What about my job, my family and school? How will I pay for treatment? What kind of treatment should I receive? Whom should I tell?" These urgent questions may lead to "emergency" decisions that are poorly thought out due to the great emotional stress of the situation. The group can help persons with AIDS reconsider impulsive decisions that they may later regret.

Typically, considerable anxiety is focused on future events. Often those who have been diagnosed with AIDS have known others who have already died of the disease and, therefore, have knowledge about how the disease progresses. Many fear becoming a burden to others. Some are afraid of losing their independence and mobility or fear becoming so seriously impaired that suicide is considered.

Anxiety and depression are common reactions to an initial diagnosis, and some group members may need to augment group treatment with individual psychotherapy (Holland & Tross, 1985). Insomnia is also a frequently expressed complaint, and psychotropic medications may be needed to help clients deal with their emotional reactions to the disease (Nichols, 1985; Tucker, 1986).

A number of the opportunistic infections that are manifestations of AIDS attack the central nervous system, causing meningitis and encephalitis. As noted previously, HIV can attack the central nervous system directly, resulting in neurologic impairment that is expressed as anxiety, depression, and dementia (Navia & Price, 1986). Psychiatric symptoms such as delirium may be a sign of an underlying central nervous system opportunistic infection. Dementia generally results from direct infection of the brain by HIV. This disorder may be manifested by the cognitive deficits such as short- and long-term memory deficits, confusion, and disorientation. In addition, one may find affective disorders such as rages, decreased frustration tolerance, affective lability, hostility, and so on. Frankly psychotic thought processes may also occur. Therefore, the group leader(s) need to identify psychiatric and neurologic consultants who will be able to assist in differentiating psychiatric from organic conditions so that appropriate interventions can be made.

Persons with AIDS express fear of contagion from themselves to others, and they may be concerned about their susceptibility to ordinary infections that may wreak havoc with their fragile health. Available evidence to date suggest that AIDS is *not* casually transmitted. The media, however, have been unable to present this fact cogently to the public. The person with AIDS thus anticipates the rejection of others because of the perception by outsiders that they can catch AIDS from casual contact.

Group support can be particularly helpful in demonstrating to newly diagnosed persons that there is usually a significant amount of time between the first diagnosis and death. This reduces the sense of urgency and gives them time for adjustment and preparation for the final, more debilitating phases of the disease. Group members can share how they move beyond the paralyzing fears of facing AIDS for the first time to dealing with it as a chronic disease that requires adjustment and accommodation, rational decision-making, and emotional control.

Adjustment to a Chronic Illness

As noted, the initial diagnosis of AIDS usually results from the development of an opportunistic infection. Treatment for this specific infection is likely to be successful; the person with AIDS begins to feel better, and death may not seem so imminent. For example, one of our clients commented, "I feel so well I wonder if they made a mistake with the diagnosis." Feeling good may facilitate the use of denial as a coping strategy. Denial may serve to allow afflicted individuals to distance themselves from the fear and anxiety of AIDS; decisions do not seem so immediate and urgent. There is a sense of getting on with life instead of waiting around for death. Consequently, questions arise concerning how to productively spend whatever time is left of one's life.

It is during this stage that the ongoing tasks of living can provide a sense of control and accomplishment. Decisions regarding wills, funeral arrangements, financial planning, and power of attorney can be made in a less emotionally stressful atmosphere. Plans can be made for subsequent medical treatment, as well as instructions to physicians concerning living wills and when to discontinue treatment. Group members may serve as resource persons by providing information and referral.

Unfinished business may need to be addressed in the group. Past resentments or conflicts with lovers, friends, or family members can be resolved and current relationships may be altered or strengthened. Other people may need to be told of the diagnosis, and homophobia among caregivers may need to be confronted. Some members can be encouraged to pursue pleasurable activities such as a long-postponed vacation.

Dependency issues become particularly important during this phase of adjustment. The majority of people with AIDS are in their twenties, thirties, and forties. They are generally at their peak in productivity and earning power. Caretaking responsibilities for these young adults are frequently placed on elderly parents. Previously autonomous adults may find themselves children once again within the context of their families.

Feelings of dependency at a life stage where independence is expected may be difficult to tolerate. For example, those persons with AIDS who have lovers may find it difficult to become dependent on someone who is young and healthy. Loss of the ability to work (as well as loss of job because of the stigma of AIDS) robs individuals of a major contributor to their sense of independence and self-esteem. The inability to work leaves the individual with a sole identification as a "person with AIDS." This change in social identity carries with it extensive negative emotional connotations, which explains why most of these people can benefit tremendously from an increased level of social support such as the support available in a group (Mandel, 1986; Namir, 1986).

Although living becomes the primary focus, issues around death and dying cannot be ignored. Medical treatment failures and the development of additional symptoms may precipitate emotional crises that bring illness and death into closer focus. Existential issues of what gives life meaning and what happens after death may be of prime importance. Planning creatively for losses in independence and mobility is essential, while keeping in mind the need to plan for the quality use of the time that remains.

It is during this stage that unresolved issues of self-esteem may surface. Group members at this stage may be engaged in the hard work of making sense and meaning out of their lives so that they can better prepare for eventual losses of functioning and death.

Preparation for Death

As the eventuality of death becomes imminent, individuals with AIDS may no longer be able to attend group meetings. They may be at home or in the hospital and may need group members to come to them.

The work at this stage is to facilitate the dying process, which requires that the dying person and those who are left "let go." Group members can provide support and comfort to dying persons during this final stage, but the members will also need to care for each other as they experience anticipatory grief about their own eventual deaths. This is a period of considerable emotional upheaval for the client, lover, and/or caregiver.

GROUP THEMES AND PROCESSES

Several themes emerge repeatedly as part of the group process and stimulate the emergence of other issues. Often, threatening issues may be brought up in the context of more familiar group themes. For instance, issues of sexual attraction among group members may be addressed as part of a general discussion about sexuality. The following themes are not meant to be exhaustive, but they do reflect representative issues in AIDS groups.

Dealing with AIDS as a Disease

AIDS is a relatively new disease, the progression of which is not clearly understood. Consequently, group members often receive conflicting information about symptoms, treatment progress, and treatment modalities. Many patients are well-read and informed about the latest research on AIDS; they can provide a wealth of information to other group members who are seeking answers to questions they seem unable or unwilling to ask of their physician. For example, group members with Kaposi's sarcoma can provide invaluable information about how the disease has progressed and how they have dealt with the disfiguring aspects of the illness. Those group members who have had *Pneumocystis carinii* pneumonia can share how they experienced the shortness of breath and fatigue common to this opportunistic infection. Such exchanges of information normalize the disease process and reduce anxiety by providing anecdotal insights of what to expect. However, it is incumbent on group leaders to stay abreast of the current information about AIDS so that they can help clarify misinformation or refer group members to appropriate resources.

With drug trials being conducted by the federal government, AIDS patients are often acutely aware of who is receiving the latest experimental drug and who is not. Some group members may not meet the requirements for some of the research protocols and, consequently, are not eligible for experimental drug treatments. Some of the drugs being tested have major side effects, and group members become experts on the symptoms of these side effects. Some group members may provide access to information about treatment methods that are new, unorthodox, or controversial.

Ways to strengthen the immune system are shared within the context of the group. Diet and exercise are often explored as ways to strengthen the body's defenses. Whatever information is exchanged, the goal of the group is the same. Group members are attempting to gain some element of control over their disease through information. The sharing of common experiences can help make sense of a disease process that seems unlike any other. When frightened group members are trying desperately to understand the new sensations, aches, and pains they are experiencing in their bodies, there is no better way to reduce anxiety than being told by another member, "Get over it! I obsessed about every little ache in my body for the first six months until I got bored with it and just decided to spend my time more productively."

Sexuality and Body Image

The desire to be sexual and the desire for intimacy and touching does not end with the diagnosis of AIDS. Sexuality continues to be a theme, but the discussion of sexual concerns is often frightening and confusing for clients (Spector & Conklin, 1987). Group members are aware that it was by being sexual that most of the members of the group became infected. Consequently, discussion of sexuality may be accompanied by feelings of guilt, especially for those group members who know that some of their sexual partners and lovers are also infected. For those who were relatively promiscuous, the guilt at having developed AIDS may be manifested in a belief that they deserved to get AIDS as a punishment for past behaviors. Some may feel angry at previous partners who, they assume, infected them. Others may feel burdened about the possibility of having infected their lovers.

The disfiguring and wasting process of AIDS may be particularly difficult for some of these men to deal with. Men who once prided themselves on how attractive they looked may find in the mirror someone who resembles a refugee from a concentration camp. The lesions of Kaposi's sarcoma, which frequently occur on the face, may be so obvious that these men are embarrassed to be seen, thereby reinforcing their sense of isolation.

For many people with AIDS, however, physical contact is still desired. They want to be able to touch and be touched but are not sure how to do this in a comfortable way. The same body that brought pleasure before is now viewed as a source of contagion. Some group members see their bodies as lethal and untouchable.

Group discussion can focus on meeting sexual needs in ways that are safe for partners and for oneself. Group members and facilitators can help considerably by giving frequent hugs and appropriately affectionate touches that clearly communicate that the body is not toxic. In her study of people with AIDS, Namir (1986) found that the patients were dissatisfied with "the amount of physical contact as expression of concern and caring" (p. 92).

Disclosure of Diagnosis

Family members, lovers, and some friends may have been involved with the patient in learning about the initial diagnosis of AIDS. However, many people with AIDS, especially in the early stages of the disease, do not have physical symptoms that indicate to others that they are ill. Consequently, people can hide the fact that they have AIDS, recognizing that disclosure of the information is within their control. Some may guard this information tenaciously because they do not want to be characterized as a "person with AIDS." Who will know and who won't know become issues for group discussion. Deciding not to tell someone about AIDS allows one to be treated "just like everyone else," but it also makes it more difficult to get the emotional support needed.

Disclosure is also an issue for those persons with AIDS who want to go to gay bars and attend non-AIDS-related events and organizations. Some group members feel that they have a sign on their foreheads announcing to all who can see that they are a "person with AIDS." Others fear the gossip, rumor, and innuendo that may occur in a variety of social contexts. For example, one of our clients began giving himself haircuts to avoid any possible unpleasantness that might occur if he went to his barber. Group members who have already experienced going back into the gay subculture or the community at large can help others by sharing their experiences.

Family/Significant Others

Most people with AIDS do not experience the process of illnes, dying, and death alone. Most have families, lovers, and friends who go through the process with them. These significant others have their own issues to deal with concerning AIDS and can often benefit from a support group of their own that permits them to express their thoughts and feelings concerning themselves and their dying loved one.

Some significant others respond to the person with AIDS in a very appropriate and loving manner. Others may abandon the person with AIDS completely, while still others may become so overly involved that they foster a dependency that does not permit the AIDS patient to make decisions for himself.

The group can provide a safe place to "blow off steam" about family members and loved ones and to learn how to approach them. It is here where people with AIDS can talk realistically about the secondary benefits of being ill. For example, some group members may be able to express guilt about their enjoyment of being taken care of and assuming a more dependent role. They may be able to express how angry they are at their lovers for remaining healthy while they are dying. Group members can help each other to deal with unfinished business and past hurts that need to be resolved. In the safety of the group, negative feelings about caregivers can be freely expressed before a decision is made regarding the wisdom of expressing these feelings directly.

Death and Dying

Underlying most group meetings are the issues of death and dying. There is a feeling of immediacy because most group members feel that they do not have the luxury of wasting time. Other group members feel that time is standing still; that is, they are too ill to work and too healthy to stay home. Often there are concerns about not being able to accomplish important tasks before death. The unwritten novel should be written, the painting completed, the master's degree finished. Some may just want to continue to work and have life remain as normal as possible. Each needs to mourn the loss of a future and of fulfilling goals.

Persons with AIDS know that they are almost certain to die. We all live with the myth that we will live a long and productive life. This myth has been shattered for many members of the group, so most are struggling with how to spend the time that they have remaining. Other group members may be frustrated with the constant portrayal of AIDS as a death sentence, and they may be struggling to find ways to be hopeful about a cure. Each may be waiting for a medical breakthrough, and each may be trying to make sense of life and impending death. Such concepts are frightening to many. However, the support of the group may allow these issues to be explored in a safe atmosphere.

The fears associated with death and dying may become particularly acute for the group when one of the members becomes too ill to return to the group or when a group member dies. Adaptive strategies and coping styles that have allowed fears of dying and death to remain submerged or hidden may be shattered. The support of the group is crucial during this time.

Trust and Intimacy

Basic to the group process for people with AIDS are the issues of trust and intimacy. All group members must struggle with deciding how close and intimate they want to be with people who will eventually die. In larger cities, the number of people who have died with AIDS is so great that some gay and bisexual men have felt the need to suppress their feelings in order to make the pain of loss manageable (Morin, Charles, & Malyon, 1984). To be close to someone requires an openness to share feelings; it is important for professionals to realize that this sharing can be threatening to people with AIDS.

FACILITATING A GROUP

Different group leaders will obviously have different styles of working with people with AIDS. The general knowledge acquired about leadership will apply to working with this population. Clinicians will need all of their skills at their disposal due to the stressful nature of the issues raised in AIDS groups.

The primary therapeutic focus of most groups will be to facilitate problem-solving and to help group members to regain and maintain control. Feeling out of contol can generate a great deal of anxiety and depression. AIDS puts most group members at the mercy of a myriad of agencies, health care facilities, and bureaucracies. Ill health and the dependencies it creates can lead to feelings of helplessness. Group members can use their expertise and experience to help each other learn to be active participants in their living and in their dying.

Hopelessness is frequently seen in people with AIDS. It is often an expression of shame in those individuals who believe that they were the cause of their own illness. In these people, the attribution of responsibility to themselves leads to enormous distress and suffering that frequently manifests itself in virtually untreatable anxiety, guilt, and depression. On the other hand, those individuals who attribute the disease to bad luck are frequently better able to take steps to improve their mood (Mandel, 1986).

Hopelessness may manifest itself in the form of "truthfulness" on the part of caregivers. Mandel (1986) comments that the statements in the media regarding the 100% mortality with AIDS produce devastating effects in some clients: "We must recognize that, as clinicians, [in supporting hopefulness] we are not colluding in our patients' defenses; rather we are supporting something vital to the quality, and maybe even the length of their lives" (p. 84).

Kübler-Ross (1969) has delineated the typical reactions to death, dying, and bereavement. The grief stages of denial, anger, bargaining, depression, and acceptance are familiar to most therapists. Within a group of people with AIDS, the members will be at different stages at different times. It is an important part of the group dynamic that participants will be struggling to maintain an adjustment to their own stage of grief while attempting to help others in the group adjust to the same or different stage. When a man becomes ill and has to be hospitalized, his denial is shaken. Others in the group who are using denial as a coping strategy will also confront reality when this occurs. The death of a group member brings reality into stark focus. The group facilitator can aid the process by encouraging group members to express their anger, fear, and frustration and by supporting those who need to temporarily return again to denial to reduce their level of anxiety. We see denial as a valid coping strategy and would discourage the group therapist from forcing a "breakthrough" of the denial. We stress that it is imperative to evaluate first whether the denial is functional.

Group leaders need to be sensitive to the fact that group members may not always want to deal with serious matters. Support can come through sharing funny stories, discussing plans for going back to work, or planning a vacation. However, as in other groups, the facilitator can be helpful in focusing the discussion on issues that are of importance to group members. Some balance between reality and fantasy should be considered.

It is our experience that discussions of symptoms and treatments can often be used by group members to move the group focus away from difficult and anxiety-producing topics. Sharing of information is important, but these types of discussions are usually done without much emotion. Feelings are harder to express, and there are times when the group leader needs to encourage members to express them.

Anger is an emotion that may need to be encouraged. As an individual who is healthy, the group leader may receive the brunt of this anger. Group leaders need to understand the issues that precipitate the anger and not assume that the group is turning on them. If the leader is gay, his or her health and future may be envied and resented, and he or she can also be the target of angry feelings. Lesbians and heterosexuals may be singled out for anger not only because they are healthy, but also because they are viewed as being at less risk for AIDS.

ISSUES FOR THERAPISTS

AIDS presents each of us with various issues with which we must struggle. No one who works with this population is untouched. Perhaps medical personnel, such as oncology teams who have experience working with cancer patients, may be better prepared for the emotional reactions engendered by working with people with AIDS. The average mental health therapist, however, has not had to deal with these issues and may feel unprepared to deal with the pain of losing clients in whom a great deal of time and energy has been invested.

As therapists, we are taught to search within ourselves for insight into the feelings and reactions that clients evoke in us. And yet, if our own feelings are painful or confusing, we may, however subtly, tell our clients to back off, change direction, or protect us. It is essential in working with people with AIDS that the therapist communicates that any subject is safe and appropriate to bring to the group. To feel safe, clients must sense that the therapist can handle the emotional content of the discussions. Therapists may unwittingly stifle the discussion of significant issues because of their discomfort in handling certain topics.

To achieve a level of comfort, therapists need to address their own beliefs, feelings, and values relating to AIDS. Good supervision is the essential key to that process of self-exploration. Reading will help, but consultation and training with colleagues who are experienced in working with gay and bisexual men is vital, and knowledge and experience working with persons who are confronting death are also valuable.

Fears of Disease and Disfigurement

Most gay and bisexual men with AIDS are between the ages of 20 and 50. Consequently, therapists are presented with men who are relatively young, are often quite involved and successful in their work, and would have been expected to live long and productive lives. Many men appear free from disease when they first join a group because they usually recover almost completely after the first opportunistic infection. They may not manifest any obvious signs of illness and they may begin to gain weight and may even return to work.

But AIDS is usually a fatal disease and most men will succumb within 19 to 24 months: 2-year mortality has been reported to approach 75% (Selwyn, 1986). As the wasting process of the disease progresses, more and more weight is lost; once healthy-looking men gradually become frail and weak. The lesions of Kaposi's sarcoma may disfigure a man to the degree that his face and body are covered with blue-black spots and patches.

This wasting transformation takes place before the eyes of the therapist who, most often, is accustomed to clients getting better, not worse. Most who work in mental health are not accustomed to clients dying. Working with people with AIDS forces therapists to confront their own mortality, their own sense of vulnerability, and their own fears of disease and disfigurement. If a therapist is a gay man, he may feel particularly vulnerable because he, his friends, and loved ones may be at risk.

Fears of Contagion

Fear of contagion is a normal initial reaction to working with people with AIDS. With all of the confusing reports from the news media, scientific journals, and popular magazines, most people have been inundated with conflicting information about the routes of transmission of this diseasee. The overwhelming evidence supports the notion that the disease is not spread through casual contact (Fischl et al., 1987; Friedland et al., 1986). Yet, on first contact with a person with AIDS, many therapists ask themselves, "What if they are wrong?" Feeling vulnerable, fearful, and at risk is an expected first reaction.

While it is understandable as an initial reaction, remaining fearful of infection should require a therapist to question the wisdom of working with this population. People with AIDS are often treated by others as if they were lepers. How can clients discuss their disease with a therapist who treats them in the same way?

Touch is extremely important for most people with AIDS because they have often been deprived of much of it due to irrational fears. Therapists who are normally "touchers" and "huggers" need to find ways to incorporate appropriate touching into the therapeutic process.

Sexuality

Most gay and bisexual persons have been infected by the AIDS virus through what have proven to be unsafe sexual practices (Winkelstein et al., 1987). Although this population is changing its behaviors, some may have changed their sexual practices after it was too late, that is, after they had already been infected. Others may not have changed their sexual behaviors at all before they were diagnosed with AIDS and, consequently, may have been infecting partners. Still others may continue to be involved in sexual relationships after they learned of their infection.

It is essential that therapists who treat people with AIDS are aware of their own sexual values and judgments. AIDS is a sexually transmitted disease; most gay and bisexual men contracted it through sex. Some have given it to others. The guilt associated with the means of transmission cannot be discussed with a therapist who is judgmental.

As previously discussed, the hatred and fear associated with homosexuality (homophobia) is deeply rooted within our culture; it is naive to assume that anyone, including a gay or bisexual therapist, is exempt from having to address this issue. Promiscuity has traditionally been frowned on as sexual excess engaged in by those who are out of control sexually or who have no sense of appropriate sexual boundaries. Although this may not be true for some, the majority of gay and bisexual men who have been promiscuous have found, through their sexuality, a vehicle for the expression of freedom, masculinity, and self-esteem (Hirsch & Enlow, 1984). Unfortunately, for many, AIDS has linked sexual pleasure with disease; judgment and guilt have been given free rein.

Therapists who have not addressed their personal feelings and values concerning their own sexuality, as well as the sexuality of people with AIDS, will be hampered in their ability to help clients deal with these same issues and may give implicit messages that sex is not an appropriate or comfortable topic for group discussion. Therapists burdened by their own judgmental ideas should not be working with this population.

Fears of Intimacy

Clients who are dying provide a dilemma for therapists who are seeking a balance between emotional distance, which provides for needed objectivity, and intimacy, which allows for appropriate caring, concern, and involvement. Group members die; the pain of that reality creates a bereavement process for the therapist. There is a continual sense of loss as group members become too ill to attend group meetings and finally die. Each new member who joins the group presents the therapist with the challenge of establishing active care and concern for someone who will eventually die while simultaneously being objective.

Burnout

Working with people with AIDS is not for everyone; it requires an ability to maintain a strong sense of self and a positive outlook on life in the midst of incredible suffering. Feeling happy and healthy, without guilt, may be difficult when one is helping others to adjust to the loss of functioning and eventual death. Burnout is frequently reported as an occupational hazard of working with this population (Horstman & McKusick, 1986).

To avoid burnout, therapists may need to take frequent "vacations" from working with AIDS patients, if only for an evening or a weekend. It is important to find time away from clients, colleagues, and friends who are associated with AIDS. Staff discussions and mutual support is vital. Many agencies and organizations have support groups for those who are providing services to this population. These groups allow for the free expression of anger, frustration, sorrow, and pain. Without support, burnout is likely. It is incumbent on agencies that provide services for AIDS patients to provide necessary vehicles for supportive environments for its employees.

CONCLUSION

In this chapter, we have sought to illuminate the central issues involved in group work with gay and bisexual men with AIDS. We discussed the stigma of AIDS and the devastating effect of homophobia superimposed on a deadly disease. We have described the psychosocial issues as they arise in the group process. We have delineated issues for the therapist that often parallel the issues for the client.

For us, facilitating groups for gay and bisexual men with AIDS has been rewarding, exhausting, exhilarating, growth-promoting, frustrating, depressing, and satisfying. But as a result of our work in this area, our respect and admiration for the human spirit has increased considerably. We have gotten more than we gave. We have felt the pain of loss and we have learned to value living more. More than ever, we yearn for a cure for AIDS.

REFERENCES

Fischl, M. A., Dickinson, G. M., Scott, G. B., Klimas, N., Fletcher, M. A., & Parks, W. (1987). Evaluation of heterosexual partners, children, and household contacts of adults with AIDS. *Journal of the American Medical Association, 257* (5), 640–644.

Friedland, G. H., Saltzman, B. R., Rogers, M. F., Kahl, P. A., Lesser, M. L., Mayers, M. M., & Klein, R. S. (1986). Lack of transmission of HTLV-III/LAV infection to household contacts of patients with AIDS or AIDS-related complex with oral candidiasis. *New England Journal of Medicine, 314,* 344–349.

Gould, S. J. (1987, April 19). The terrifying normalcy of AIDS. *New York Times Magazine,* p. 33.

Hirsch, D. A., & Enlow, R. W. (1984). The effects of the acquired immune deficiency syndrome on gay lifestyle and the gay individual. *Annals of the New York Academy of Sciences, 437,* 273–282.

Holland, J. C., & Tross, S. (1985). The psychosocial and neuropsychiatric sequelae of the acquired immuno-deficiency syndrome and related disorders. *Annals of Internal Medicine, 103,* 760–764.

Horstman, W., & McKusick, L. (1986). The impact of AIDS on the physician. In L. McKusick (Ed.), *What to do about AIDS: Physicians and mental health professionals discuss the issues* (pp. 63–74). Berkeley: Unviersity of California Press.

Kastenbaum, R. (1977). Death and development through the life span. In H. Feigel (Ed.), *New meanings of death* (pp. 17–45). New York: McGraw-Hill.

Koop, C. E. (undated, c. 1987). *Surgeon General's report on Acquired Immune Deficiency Syndrome.* Washington, D.C.: U.S. Public Health Service, Public Affairs Office.

Kübler-Ross, E. (1969). *On death and dying.* London: MacMillan.

Macks, J., & Turner D. (1986). Mental health issues of persons with AIDS. In L. McKusick (Ed.), *What to do about AIDS: Physicians and mental health professionals discuss the issues* (pp. 111–124). Berkeley: University of California Press.

Mandel, J. S. (1986). Psychosocial challenges of AIDS and ARC: Clinical and research obsrvations. In L. McKusick (Ed.), *What to do about AIDS: Physicians and mental health professionals discuss the issues* (pp. 75–86). Berkeley: University of California Press.

McKusick, L. (Ed.). (1986). *What to do about AIDS: Physicians and mental health professionals discuss the issues.* Berkeley: University of California Press.

Morin, S. F., Charles, K. A., & Malyon, A. K. (1984). The psychological impact of AIDS on gay men. *American Psychologist, 39,* 1288–1293.

Namir, S. (1986). Treatment issues concerning persons with AIDS. In L. McKusick (Ed.), *What to do about AIDS: Physicians and mental health professionals discuss the issues* (pp. 87–94). Berkeley: University of California Press.

Navia, B. A., & Price, R. W. (1986). Dementia complicating AIDS. *Psychiatric Annals, 16* (3), 158–166.

Nichols, S. E. (1985). Psychosocial reactions of persons with the acquired immunodeficiency syndrome. *Annals of Internal Medicine, 103,* 765–767.

Selwyn, P. A. (1986, May 15). AIDS: What is now known. *Hospital Practice,* pp. 67–82.

Silverman, M. (1986). Introduction: What we have learned. In L. McKusick (Ed.), *What to do about AIDS: Physicians and mental health professionals discuss the issues* (pp. 1–9). Berkeley: University of California Press.

Spector, I. C., & Conklin, R. (1987). AIDS group psychotherapy. *International Journal of Group Psychotherapy, 37* (3), 433–439.

Sontag, S. (1978). *Illness as metaphor.* New York: Farrar, Straus, & Giroux.

Tucker, S. (1986). The role of psychiatry: Evaluation and treatment of the altered mental status in persons with AIDS. In L. McKusick (Ed.), *What to do about AIDS: Physicians and mental health professionals discuss the issues* (pp.45–50). Berkeley: University of California Press.

Wolcott, D. L., Fawzy, F. I., Landsverk, J., & McCombs, M. (1986). AIDS patients' needs for psychosocial services and their use of community service organizations. *Journal of Psychosocial Oncology, 4,* 135–146.

Winklestein, W., Lyman, D. M., Padian, N., Grant, R., Samuel, M., Wiley, J. A., Anderson, R. E., Lang, W., Riggs, J., & Levy, J. A. (1987). Sexual practices and risk of infection by the human immunodeficiency virus. *Journal of the American Medical Association, 257* (3), 321–325.

NORMAN E. AMUNDSON
WILLIAM A. BORGEN

5
Displaced Workers: Coping with the Effects of Unemployment in Groups

Each of us is a member of many groups, for instance, a family, a work group, and a friendship group. Much of what is learned about ourselves comes from group interaction. Much of what we believe and feel about ourselves is formed from the feedback received from members of groups to which we have belonged. According to Alfred Adler (1964), humans are social beings who develop a sense of meaning within the context of the group. It is important, then, to bear in mind that when a person loses a job, he or she also loses membership in a very significant group, the work group.

Unemployment can affect the lives of people in a variety of ways. It is the purpose of this chapter to describe some of the reactions that people have to unemployment, and to suggest ways in which group counseling may be efficacious in helping them cope.

Several studies have focused on different aspects of the unemployment experience. Orwell (1975), Schumacher (1979), Kelvin (1981), and others have discussed the importance of work in defining a healthy identity. A large number of authors (Bratfisch, 1985; Brenner, 1973; Brenner & Bartell, 1983; Finley & Lee, 1981; Gurney, 1980; Hartley, 1980; Hill, 1977; Jahoda, 1982; Jones, 1979; Kaufman, 1982; Rump, 1983; Sinfield, 1981; Tiggemann & Winefield, 1984; Warr, Jackson, & Banks, 1982) have described various aspects of the psychological reactions to unemployment. Authors, such as Marsden (1982) in his book *Workless*, have delineated some of the stresses associated with job search, while others have described factors that influence people's experience of unemployment (Hepworth, 1980; Kemp & Mercer, 1983; Swinburne, 1981). All of these authors state or allude to changes in financial status, friendship patterns, family relationships, and career paths. These changes, in turn, can cause a characteristic shift in the capacity people have to meet their needs and cope on a day-to-day basis.

EMOTIONAL REACTIONS TO UNEMPLOYMENT

Human needs have been outlined by Maslow (1968) in a hierarchical fashion. The key message of Maslow's model is that lower order (physiological, safety) needs must be met before those of a higher order (love and belonging, esteem, self-actualization) can be addressed. This hierarchical model suggests that environmental order and stability needs must

The authors would like to acknowledge the contribution of Derek Swain for gathering information used in parts of this paper.

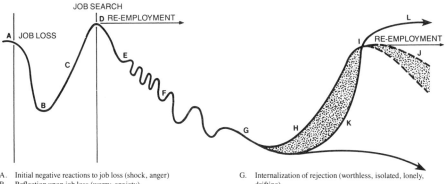

FIGURE 5-1. Dynamics of unemployment. (Reproduced with permission from Borgen, W. A., & Amundson, N. E. (1984). *The experience of unemployment.* Toronto: Nelson Canada.)

be met before achievement needs can be met. For many individuals, achievement, recognition, and personal contact needs are met through their work. The loss of a job results in the elimination of their means of satisfying higher order needs. Furthermore, the loss of employment confronts people with financial concerns that impact on their lower order needs, such as paying the mortgage or the rent, or paying for children's recreational activities. Thus, individuals who have lost their jobs often experience a series of emotional reactions as they tumble down the hierarchy. These feelings may be exacerbated by anxiety as they confront unfamiliar threats to their lower order needs.

The emotional reactions that can influence the feelings, thoughts, and behavior of unemployed people during the job loss/job search process have been described as an emotional roller coaster (Borgen & Amundson, 1984, 1987). In a study of unemployed people, we found that approximately half of those interviewed demonstrated a pattern of emotional reactions similar to that shown in Figure 5-1. The reactions often begin with shock and disbelief that unemployment will occur or has just occurred. Shock is followed by periods of sadness and sometimes anger, coupled with feelings of helplessness and despair. For most people this phase lasts for about 1 to 2 months, during which time people feel pressured to engage in job search but still feel caught up with their reactions to job loss. That is, they still feel angry and sad, lingering emotions that inhibit their ability to search for work effectively.

Near the end of this initial phase of reactions, people with sufficient psychological strength and environmental support come to an acceptance of their situations and feel a release of energy to engage in job search. This period has a positive and negative side to it. On the positive side, people may feel energized and willing to engage in job search with a constructive attitude. On the negative side, some people feel so positive that they adopt an unrealistic view of their employment prospects, find it difficult to consider "survival jobs," and may reject job opportunities that they later wish that they had accepted.

The real job search phase, following a period of loss, may begin with a sense of optimism—whether realistic or unrealistic. However, if people experience a continual lack of success in finding work, their energy begins to erode and feelings of frustration begin to take over, which are then followed by a kind of stagnation. What follows for many people is a period of erratic job search activities and changing moods. The process has been described by one unemployed person as an "emotional yo-yo" in which a person works up to a job interview with great expectations but then comes "crashing down" when he/she does not get the job. As this pattern repeats itself, people find it more difficult to muster the energy to engage in job search activities and begin to expect rejection—a form of learned helplessness. This overall process leaves people with feelings of worthlessness that make them less likely to engage in job search activities. At the end of this period of oscillating emotions, it may be difficult for these individuals to present themselves in a job interview in a way that would encourage employers to hire them.

Some unemployed people continue the downward cycle and become increasingly apathetic. Others, faced with this extremely negative situation, reevaluate their options. Often they reduce job search activities and engage in alternative activities that make them feel worthwhile. These people are typically ones who have support from their environment, such as family, friends, or employment counseling groups. People in this phase frequently describe a return of feelings of optimism and, with the optimism, a return to some job search activities. They also tend to enter educational training programs and are willing to accept survival jobs such as working in a fast food chain. For these people a strong sense of self-worth returns that is not tied so closely to paid employment. Thus, two major response styles seem to emerge from the experience of unemployment, either an active reevaluation of options and an adjustment of one's goals and activities or a passive surrender to circumstances.

The reactions to unemployment experienced by those in our study (Borgen & Amundson, 1984) seem clearly linked to the literature related to grieving reactions (Kübler-Ross, 1969) and job-related stress reactions (Baum, Singer, & Baum, 1981; Edelwich & Brodsky, 1980). The emotional reactions to loss of employment can also be understood in terms of the basic needs that were mentioned earlier. Thinking about the Maslow hierarchy, job loss is almost like falling down a flight of stairs. A person may be operating near the top of the staircase and suddenly find himself or herself near the bottom, often seemingly through no fault of his or her own. This abrupt change is then followed by a period of restricted financial reasources and social isolation. Only the most basic needs are being met at this time.

Alvin Toffler (1980) also described human needs in a way that has relevance for the experience of unemployed people. He suggested that people have three basic needs: community, meaning, and structure. From the outline of the unemployment experience just described, it is evident that the jobless period can severely threaten the ability of people to meet their needs in all three of these areas. People interviewed in our study suggested that they had lost most of their friends from their previous place of work. Furthermore, they did not view themselves as being engaged in any activities that had meaning, and they had difficulty structuring their time. One person said that he spent all day doing what used to take him half an hour, just so that he would have something to do each day.

From another theoretical perspective the concepts of victimization and attribution theory are particularly helpful in interpreting the results of our study. The term "victim" can be applied to "anyone who suffers as a result of ruthless design incidentally or accidentally"

(*Webster's Third New International Dictionary*, 1971). It can be argued that many of the "new unemployed" find themselves in a loss situation as a result of circumstances that are beyond their control. As a result, they experience psychological reactions that are similar to those of others who find themselves in the role of victim such as rape, incest, disease, and crime victims. The emotional reactions suggested by the literature on victimization include shock, confusion, helplessness, anxiety, fear, and depression (Janoff-Bulman & Frieze, 1983). Nesdale (1983) suggests that how a person reacts to being a victim depends on whether they were expecting to be victimized. He suggests that a victim who was expecting to be victimized reacts less severely and recovers more rapidly than the person who was not expecting the victimization.

Another way of conceptualizing victimization is to examine the basic assumptions people hold about themselves and their world and how these assumptions are shattered through the victimization experience. According to Janoff-Bulman and Frieze (1983), three assumptions come under attack: (1) the belief of personal invulnerability, (2) the perception of the world as meaningful, and (3) the view of self as positive. The destruction of these assumptions causes instability and as Bard and Sangrey (1979) write, victims experience a "loss of equilibrium. The world is suddenly out of whack. Things no longer work the way they used to" (p. 14). This experience is similar to that of the "victims" of unemployment.

From another perspective, a prolonged unproductive job search can be seen to lead to the experience of what Seligman (1975) has described as "learned helplessness." In this situation, an aversive stimulation is constant and seems uncontrollable, resulting in a feeling of helplessness. The extent of the learned helplessness seems to be dependent on a person's sense of personal control and power. Peterson and Seligman (1983) indicate that when people face a negative situation they invariably ask themselves "Why?" Their answer plays an important part in determining their emotional reactions. If the person attributes the cause to external factors, the loss of self-esteem will be minimal. If, however, the person adopts the internal perspective and blames himself or herself for the negative circumstances, the result will be loss of self-esteem. It would seem, then, that as an unemployed person experiences the frustrations of unsuccessful job search and the resulting lowering of self-esteem, he or she would eventually adopt a learned helplessness stance. Overcoming this sense of helplessness depends partially on helping a person realize that job loss is, for the most part, beyond his or her control. Released from a position of constant self-blame, the individual may be able to see his or her situation from a more realistic perspective, one that leads to new coping strategies.

These theoretical perspectives are consonant with the results of our research, which provides a picture of a person who has experienced prolonged unemployment as one characterized by periods of apathy alternating with anger, sadness, and sporadic optimism, few habits of regular structured activities, and few meaningful personal contacts. Dominant feelings are victimization, lack of personal power, and low self-worth. None of these characteristics coincide with a readiness or ability to engage in sustained and effective job search.

The literature also contains important implications for the design of counseling interventions for victims of unemployment. For example, Nesdale's (1983) work would seem to suggest that sufficient notice of pending unemployment would help persons better deal with the trauma of job loss. Bratfisch (1985) and Cooney and Hargest (1986) provide examples of counseling interventions designed to help "surplus" employees prepare for unemployment prior to their actual date of termination, and Jacobson (1984) provides a similar example in preparing students for the inevitability of graduation and employment search. Furthermore, counseling interventions should consider that the victims of unemployment could benefit from the same crisis coping skills that are taught to other victims (Wortman, 1983). In this regard Avedon (1986) notes that displaced workers can be effectively helped through shared understanding of the change process or emotional dynamics that they will experience, along with positive reinforcement and emotional support that emphasizes their competencies, encourages the development of coping strategies, and minimizes their deficiencies.

Given the complex nature of individuals' reactions to unemployment, it is apparent that a fairly comprehensive approach to counseling is needed when working with this population. The upheaval in ability to fulfill needs and the loneliness precipitated by the experience of unemployment would suggest that a necessary first step is client-centered listening and use of empathic skills. In addition, clients need to be helped to reframe their experience as well as the causes for it.

The provision of information, an important aspect of cognitive therapy, can help unemployed persons to look at situations differently so that they need not see negative events as being internally caused or viewed as a catastrophe. Furnham (1984) makes a similar recommendation in reference to the unemployed. He notes that if unemployed persons tend to blame themselves for their situation, they are less likely to adapt well to unemployment or to adopt effective or efficient job search strategies. Conversely, if they blame unemployment on structural or societal factors, their adaptation may be considerably better because their self-esteem is kept intact. Thus, methods to help the unemployed may involve examining their beliefs about their own joblessness and unemployment.

Finally, it is important to assist unemployed clients to consolidate their new understandings regarding their level of personal control into action. This part of the counseling process may involve a variety of behavioral approaches like skill practice, action planning, and so on.

COPING WITH UNEMPLOYMENT

Individuals caught in the emotional turmoil that characterizes unemployment have been able to identify factors that help them to cope and factors that destroy this ability (Amundson & Borgen, 1987a, 1987b). Obviously, these factors constitute significant information for counselors, whether they are designing individual or group counseling interventions. Several of the factors from our research are listed in Table 5-1.

Many of the factors identified as positive help people to meet those needs identified by Toffler (1980): needs for community (support from family and friends, a sense of being valued and respected in a group context), meaning (thinking positively, part-time or temporary work), and structure (making job contacts, part-time or temporary work, physical activity). Of particular significance in the list of positive factors is the mention of job search support groups. Nearly every subject in our study who was a member of a job search support group identified the experience as a useful one.

In looking at the list of negative factors, it becomes evident that many of these factors detract significantly from the ability of people to meet their needs for community (spouse/family problems) and meaning (job rejection, future unknown or negative, thinking negatively, financial pressures). Although a lack of structure is not specifically identified, the statements of some individuals that they isolate themselves by sitting in front of the television all day indicate how negative a lack of structure can be.

TABLE 5-1
Factors That Influence the Coping Ability of Unemployed People

Positive Factors	Negative Factors
1. Support from family	1. Job rejections
2. Support from friends	2. Financial pressure
3. Thinking positively	3. Contact with agencies
4. Career changes, plans for retraining	4. Future unknown or negative
5. Part-time or temporary work	5. Job search activities
6. Job search/support groups, vocational counseling	6. Thinking negatively
7. Initial job search, making job contacts	7. Spouse or family problems
8. Physical activity	

The identification of these positive and negative factors by victims of unemployment suggests that it is essential to consider basic human needs when developing counseling interventions. There is also a clear indication that group employment counseling can provide an excellent vehicle by which to offer service to unemployed people.

GROUP EMPLOYMENT COUNSELING FOR UNEMPLOYED PEOPLE

Group counseling can be a very effective intervention for unemployed people. The group is particularly useful in disseminating relevant information and teaching new ideas or skills. However, the group experience seems to have other very valuable features. The group provides a forum through which individuals can share their views and express their feelings. By expressing their feelings in a group, individuals may be encouraged to share them with significant others, providing them the opportunity to elicit the support and understanding of their immediate community. The group also helps to normalize the individual's experience by providing recognition that others have similar problems, worries, or concerns. Through the sharing of personal information, ideas, and skills, the group serves as a catalyst to the acknowledgment or expansion of an individual's own repertoire, as well as fostering the development of social interaction skills. Through the group, ongoing mutual support relationships may be established that may continue after the group intervention has ended. Finally, the group provides a situation whereby several people can benefit from a single leader. In fact, the leader may be varied to maximize the available resources, skills, and knowledge of the counseling agency. The employment group, then, can be a cost-effective counseling intervention with multiple benefits for both sponsors and participants.

The type of groups that are available to unemployed people varies widely. These groups have proven effective in a number of different contexts, for example, with unemployed college graduates and dropouts; physically, emotionally, and socially handicapped job seekers; and welfare recipients and others (Azrin, Flores, & Kaplan, 1975; Azrin & Philip, 1979; Azrin, Philip, Thienes-Hontos, & Besalel, 1980; Borgen, Amundson, & Biela, 1987; Carkhuff, Pierce, Friel, & Willis, 1975; Hicks & Kelvin, 1983; Keith, Engeles, & Winborn, 1977; McWhirter, Nichols, & Banks, 1984). While some groups are primarily focused on the dissemination of information and some emphasize support, the greatest number seem to have the task of career exploration or job search as their focus (Trimmer, 1984).

Career Exploration Groups

Career exploration groups are designed for those persons who are undecided about a career direction. Some of the people who can benefit from this type of exploratory group include those who are making a career shift, women returning to work, young people exploring various career directions, and displaced workers. In this type of group some common themes that are addressed include identification of transferable skills, development of an increased awareness of the labor market and organizational trends, self-exploration of interests, values, and personal style, and provision of information on various career possibilities. In addition, these groups work toward identification of various barriers to employment, evaluation of career options, and development of an action plan. As a result of participating in a career exploration group, participants are better prepared to enter a job search group.

JOB SEARCH GROUP

With a clear career direction, involvement in a job search group can be particularly helpful. The nature of job search groups seems to vary somewhat, but they also have several common components:

1. Participants identify several possible employment directions. This often involves the identification of employment barriers and transferable skills.
2. Participants gain motivation to engage in job search from the group experience. This motivation arises from the sense of community they acquire from working with other group members and from the opportunities the group affords to discuss emotional reactions to unemployment.
3. Participants are taught job search techniques such as how to obtain job leads, how to make appointments for interviews over the telephone, how to fill out application forms, how to write resumes and cover letters, interview techniques, how to answer difficult questions, and how to keep a job. People are often videotaped in an interview situation, an exercise that affords them an opportunity to observe themselves and obtain feedback from other participants and the group leader.
4. Participants are expected to treat looking for a job as a job, and regular attendance at group meetings is expected. They are also expected to apply job search techniques by developing a network of contacts, making telephone calls to potential employers, and by arranging interviews.
5. Participants are typically involved in job search groups for a 2–3-week period of time. Some groups, such as Job Club, then offer the opportunity to continue until employment is realized, while others offer a series of other follow-up services such as individual referral to other agencies.
6. Agencies offering job search groups typically offer necessary support services like access to telephone and typing and duplicating facilities.

In many respects, the prototype for this type of job search group has been the Job Club developed by Azrin and Besalel (1979). The Club functions to provide a combined effort of all group members to help each other find a job. Utilizing the techniques of behaviorism, an intensive and structured learning situation is created to provide members with direct practice in job search skills. The goal of the Club is to help the members obtain a high quality job within the shortest possible time, a task most members achieve within the first 2 weeks of the program. At the end of a 3-week period, a new Club is started and any unsuccessful members of the preceding group are automatically integrated into the new Club (Mills, 1985).

In several studies in the United States, the Job Club has been found to achieve high employment rates, varying from 62 to 95% (Azrin, Flores, & Kaplan, 1975; Azrin & Philip, 1979; Azrin, Philip, Thienes-Hontos, & Besalel, 1980). Canadian results of groups based on the Azrin model are similar, ranging from 65 to 93% (Mills, 1985). A study that attempted to separate the components of instruction and behavioral rehearsal (Azrin, Besalel, Wisotzek, McMorrow, & Bechtel, 1982) found that clients receiving both components achieved a significantly higher placement rate than those who received only instruction in job-seeking skills. In another study of Job Clubs, Chandler (1984) noted the subjective evaluations of groups by their members who "reported feeling less isolated and less stigmatized as unemployed individuals and also stated that the structure of coming to group meetings provided motivation for job-seeking activity" (p. 101). It seems from this description that, while the purpose of a job search group is to teach job search skills, there are a number of other factors that account for the success of the group. Other authors who have also addressed this area include Shifron, Dye, and Shifron (1983) and Pearson (1983), who suggest that the greatest gains from participating in a group come from sharing the experience, accompanied by reciprocal understanding, acceptance, support, respect, and caring. Although the work just cited suggests some general factors that may contribute to the success of job search groups, Trimmer (1984), in a review of the literature on group job search, concludes by saying that: "It is difficult to indicate precisely why GJS (Group Job Search) is such a highly successful approach. This analysis has examined a variety of programs, all of which seem to work quite well" (p. 115).

A STUDY OF EMPLOYMENT COUNSELING GROUPS

Our research (Amundson & Borgen, 1988) builds on the strategies just cited and outlines specifically the particular benefits of participating in various job search groups. The importance of emotional support generally and the apparent significance of job search support groups specifically led to the development of the following research questions for this study: (1) What are the factors in job search/support groups that make them effective interventions?; and (2) Are there critical times in the unemployment experience for a group intervention?

The research was conducted in the greater Vancouver area, a large metropolitan area on the west coast of Canada. The 77 subjects (41 males, 36 females) were volunteers who had participated in one of five groups. Included in these groups were people of various employment backgrounds and social status. The subjects were interviewed approximately 3 months after completing the group, using phenomenological (Colaizzi, 1978; Fischer, 1979) and critical incident (Andersson & Nilsson, 1964; Flanagan, 1954, 1978) techniques. These interviewing techniques helped subjects provide a description of the experience of unemployment along with the facilitating and hindering of incidents that may have occurred in the groups in which they had participated.

The analysis of the data from the above interviews focused primarily on facilitating and hindering incidents that reflected how subjects experienced the job search groups.

Trained graduate assistants summarized the information from the interviews and then checked their summaries through telephone contacts with the subjects. Once this had been accomplished, a classification system based on the first group analyzed was developed. The reliability and exhaustiveness of the system was then explored using the data from the other groups. The original system of 19 categories was created from 160 facilitating incidents. These incidents were successfully placed in 19 categories independently by two research assistants with over 90% agreement. The exhaustiveness of the category system was indicated when incidents from four other groups were able to be placed, almost without exception, in the already established categories.

The 77 subjects reported 619 facilitating incidents and only 51 hindering incidents. People seemed to have nothing negative to say about the job group experience. Generally speaking, it represented a very special and positive time for them and, even if they were still unemployed,* they remained enthusiastic about their group experience. They reported that the group was the best thing that had happened while they were unemployed and they only wished that it had been available to them earlier in their unemployment experience.

The factors that were identified as being helpful can be clustered using broader categories such as "support/self-esteem" and "task orientation." Perhaps the task orientation category is the easiest to define. Under this heading we would include any factor that related directly to job search skill-building. A typical illustration of the type of comments that reflects the task category follows:

> Through the activities in the group I learned how to present myself better. I learned how to knock on the door, get past the receptionist and get to the personnel manager. I also learned how to develop a resume, set up letters and do a follow-up. (From a married, 44-year-old, male shipper receiver)

In terms of support/self-esteem, we placed factors that focused on interpersonal relations and self-concept development under this broad category. The following comment illustrates this concept:

> When you have a job you work with other people. When you're looking for a job it seems that you're all alone. There aren't a lot of encouraging things built into job search, especially if your interviews don't go well as you get rejected all the time. You start to feel lousy after a while. In the group we worked together and shared the good and the bad experiences. We encouraged each other and we seemed to all have job prospects to pass on to each other. We became friends. (From a separated, 29-year-old, female bookkeeper)

The general category system is provided in Table 5-2. Of the 19 factors that were identified, 17 can be accounted for in the clusters of Task Orientation and Support/Self-Esteem. The remaining two seem to stand on their own.

Two of the factors were difficult to place in the Task Orientation or Support/Self-Esteem categories. The first factor, "Follow-up Support and Services" seemed to apply to both categories and thus was not included in either list. The second factor, "Enjoying the Job Club Routine" also seemed to stand on its own. The group routine involved regular attendance,

---

*At the time of the interviews (an average of 5 months after their job search group experience), 37 people out of 77 were working and 40 were still unemployed.

TABLE 5-2
Facilitating Factors in Job Search/Support Groups

Task Orientation	Support/Self-Esteem	Other
Job search strategies	Belonging	Job Club "routine"
Videotape feedback	Mutual support and encouragement	Follow-up support
Job leads	Absorbing others' enthusiasm	and services
Telephone techniques	and success	
Interview practice and	Social comparison	
preparation	Contribution	
Instruction in resumes and	Ventilating	
correspondence	A positive outlook	
Information	Leadership	
Goal setting		
Supplies and services		

homework assignments, and project commitments. A comment that reflects this particular factor follows:

> Being in the group was like going to work. You knew that you had to get up in the morning and be at class by a certain time. A number of hours of each day were committed to being in that class. That alone, getting a routine into your life really helps. (From a married, 54 year-old, female dry cleaner)

Organizing the 19 factors in this particular way is similar in many respects to the principles proposed by Toffler (1980), that is, needs for community, meaning, and structure. In this case, Support/Self-Esteem would be comparable to community, while task orientation would be encompassed by the concept of meaning. The structure component would refer to "Enjoying the Job Club Routine."

It is difficult to place a value on the various factors, but what does seem to dominate is the significant role of Task Orientation and Support/Self-Esteem. In fact, it probably would be more accurate to describe the groups as job search/support groups in view of the importance of the support dimension. Support was so significant that people said that they benefited from their experience in the groups regardless of whether they found employment. Those who were still unemployed at the end of the group sessions reported that they were able to maintain a more effective job search and a positive self-image as a result of their experiences in the groups.

These findings reinforce the significance of the opening statements of this chapter. When considering the predicament of the unemployed, it is important to remember that they have not only lost a job but also membership in a significant group. Furthermore, in our group research, most people indicated that a job search group would have been most helpful in the first 3 months of unemployment. This finding certainly emphasizes the need to provide a job search/support group for the unemployed at the earliest opportunity.

DESIGNING GROUPS FOR UNEMPLOYED PEOPLE

The design of a group experience should be based on the needs of the group members. According to Borgen, Pollard, Amundson, and Westwood (1987), the design for unemployment groups should include *information* that helps the members to normalize and understand their emotional experience and helps them to acknowledge alternatives and options that are available to them so that they can make better decisions, adopt more efficient coping strategies, and gain some sense of control over the next step in their career development. The design should also include opportunities for the *expression of feelings*, providing the members with a forum to ventilate their anger, frustration, fear, and so on, and, again, to experience the normalization of those feelings. In describing the benefits of an unemployment workshop involving information giving and the expression of feelings, Papalia, Dai, and Devine (1986) note that: "It was apparent from their reactions that the group process affected a positive change in attitudes, level of self-confidence, and motivation among participants. Feelings of alienation and mistrust were diminished as the group moved toward a more cohesive level" (p. 201). Furthermore, group work with unemployed people should include *job search skill development*, involving both instruction and practice in skills while in a safe environment, so that the members may gain confidence and become better equipped to engage in job search activities.

The nature, intensity, and proportion of the three components of information provision, expression of feelings, and skill development will vary with the specific needs of the group. The types of groups may range from proactive groups preparing for the probability of layoff, to reactive groups involved in the remedial work of recent or long-term unemployment. Each of these groups will be composed of people who are at different stages of emotional reaction to unemployment, so the content of the group experience should be varied accordingly. For example, in the proactive group, typically comprised of members of the same organization facing reduction in force (RIF), the provision of information regarding the financial status of the employer will show that the forthcoming RIF is due to circumstances external to the individual employee (Hayslip & Van Zandt, 1985). Both proactive and reactive groups for members having a common employer may be assisted by information on company benefits and separation packages. Other groups may be assisted by information on government or community financial aid.

As Mirabile (1985) notes, the experience of unemployment involves the intertwining of the fiscal pain of reduced income and the emotional pain of termination. Individuals need to separate the two in order to adopt effective coping mechanisms. It is particularly important that individuals work through any anger or resentment toward the former employer in order to avoid interference with the mechanics of job search. Ramey (1986) recommends that group work should adopt a coherent approach to stress reduction, with daily components built into the group design. Thus, the group counseling intervention should progress through therapeutic work to the development of job search skills.

In addition to those needs that are specific to the experience of unemployment, group participants have characteristics common to all group members. According to Johnson and Johnson (1982), as group members, unemployed people will: "(a) interact with each other, (b) be interdependent, (c) define themselves and are defined by others as belonging to the group, (d) share norms concerning matters of common interest and participate in a system of interlocking roles, (e) influence each other, (f) find the group rewarding, and (g) pursue common goals" (p. 7). They will also have needs characteristic of all group members. These needs have been described by Schutz (1958) as needs for : (1) inclusion, a sense of belonging to the group, (2) control, a sense of being able to influence what happens to them and sometimes others in the group, and (3) trust, an ability to feel close to and secure with other group members. In addition, members can be expected to progress through stages of group development. These are defined by Corey (1985) as follows: the

Initial Stage, where group members become acquainted with one another, the leader, and the goals of the group; the Transition Stage, in which members evaluate their commitment to personalizing the goals of the groups and sometimes offer some resistance; the Working Stage, where members are committed to and are working toward their goals; and the Termination Stage, in which members evaluate their gains and experience some sense of loss as they realize the group is ending.

Group Membership

Unemployment groups are for people who are functioning "normally" and who are obliged to cope with the crisis of unemployment, rather than for individuals who require special services of a psychotherapeutic nature. Because groups are particularly effective when the members share a common goal, prescreening of the membership is useful to reduce the possibility of destructive influences. Broussard and DeLargey (1979) recommend that excessively angry individuals should be dissuaded from group participation, the cliques of alumni from one small organizational unit should be separated to reduce the influence of old, unfinished business and grudges, and that extremes or contrasts in organization or management level should be avoided so that members might mix more effectively. Other screening criteria may also be used according to the nature and purposes of the group. For example, in a job-finding club in which the goal was clearly to find employment for each other, participants were screened to avoid competition by selecting people with different education or work goals and to promote success by selecting people who were the most motivated and mobile (Doyon, 1985).

Leadership

Trotzer (1977) states that leadership should be viewed on a continuum with one extreme being total control by the leader and the other extreme being total control by the group members (p. 91). In considering groups for the unemployed, a more useful position is that of Mahler (1969), who states that "the main responsibility for growth of the group rests with members but the leader does all he/she can to facilitate that process" (p. 194). The leader, at all times, guarantees the well-being of the members and ensures that group interactions are constructive. Members have a right to assume that as far as possible, the leader will not allow them to be hurt. The members must decide their own level of commitment to goals and challenges. It is useful to remember that the level of commitment will change as trust and inclusion grow.

Leadership issues that may arise in working with the unemployed are both challenging and rewarding. Of particular concern may be group hostility generated by the disparity in status between an employed leader and the unemployed group members. This hostility may be particularly exacerbated when the leader is an employee or a consultant hired by the company that is experiencing reduction in force. It is important, then, for the leader to defuse the personal antagonism by empathizing with the members and encouraging them to express their feelings and concerns through structured learning activities. In fact, it is recommended that unemployment groups should be organized as structured learning groups, involving specific components of stress or tension reduction.

Peer leaders can also be helpful in working with the unemployed. In a program designed for displaced workers, Ramey (1986) found that peer facilitators as assistants to professionals were important to the success of the program because they were able to locate and recruit participants, reduce barriers, maintain attendance and participation, and offer day-to-day support and encouragement. Peer-led self-help groups have also emerged for the unemployed, modeling the programs of Alcoholics Anonymous. The activities they foster include courses in job search skills, exchange services through which members swap labor and skills, and intercity networks so that members visiting another city to pursue employment can make local contacts and even be offered temporary housing. These groups are linked by some 27 clearing houses in the United States and three in Canada (Balthazar, 1987).

SUMMARY

What seem particularly prominent in the research and literature that has been reviewed is the important role of groups in moving unemployed people toward a more positive perspective regarding life generally and job search specifically. To understand the reasons for this impact one needs only to consider how basic needs are met through involvement in paid work. Work provides financial rewards, but is also can offer meaning in life, relationships with others, and a sense of structure and organization. When people become unemployed it becomes more difficult to meet basic needs and the outcome is a number of loss and stress reactions (an emotional roller coaster). Groups address the needs for meaning, community, and structure and thus can play an important stabilizing function.

The follow-up research on job groups documents the positive impact of groups, even after people have been away from them for several months. In instances where employment was not found, the unemployed people still reported that following participation in a group they were able to maintain a more effective job search and a positive self-image. Most people also indicated that they wished the groups had been available to them in the first 3 months of unemployment. This points to the need for offering this type of intervention at the earliest opportunity.

REFERENCES

Adler, A. (1984). *Social interest: A challenge to mankind.* New York: Capricorn Books.
Amundson, N. E., & Borgen, W. A. (1987a). *At the controls: Charting a course through unemployment.* Toronto: Nelson Canada.
Amundson, N. E., & Borgen, W. A. (1987b). Coping with unemployment: What helps and hinders. *Journal of Employment Counseling, 24*, 97–106.
Amundson, N. E., & Borgen, W. A. (1988). Factors that help and hinder in group employment counseling. *Journal of Employment Counseling, 25*, 104–114.
Andersson, B., & Nilsson, S. (1964). Studies in the reliability validity of the critical incident technique. *Journal of Applied Psychology, 48*, 398–403.
Avedon, L. (1986). Coping strategies used by victims of job loss. *Natcon, 12*, 427–444.
Azrin, N. H., Flores, T., & Kaplan, S. J. (1975). Job-finding club: A group assisted program for obtaining employment. *Behavior Research and Therapy, 13*, 17–27.
Azrin, N. H., & Besalel, V. B. (1979). *Job club counselor's manual: A behavioral approach to vocational counseling.* Baltimore: Universtiy Park Press.
Azrin, N. H., & Philip, R. A. (1979). The job club method for the handicapped: A comparative outcome

study. *Rehabilitation Counseling Bulletin, 23,* 144–155.

Azrin, N. H., Philip, R. A., Thienes-Hontos, P., & Besalel, V. B. (1980). Comparative evaluation of the job club program with welfare recipients. *Journal of Vocational Behavior, 16,* 133–145.

Azrin, N. H., & Besalel, V. A., Wisotzek, I., McMorrow, M., & Bechtel, R. (1982). Behavioral supervision versus informational counseling of job seeking in the Job Club. *Rehabilitation Counseling Bulletin, 25,* 212–218.

Balthazar, H. (1987). Self help groups for unemployment. *Natcon, 12,* 71–80.

Bard, M., & Sangrey, D. (1979). *The crime victim's book.* New York: Basic Books.

Baum, A., Singer, J. E., & Baum, C. S. (1981). Stress and the environment. *Journal of Social Issues, 37,* 4–35.

Borgen, W. A., & Amundson, N. E. (1984). *The experience of employment.* Toronto: Nelson Canada.

Borgen, W. A., Amundson, N. E., & Biela, P. M. (1987). The experience of unemployment for persons who are physically disabled. *Journal of Applied Rehabilitation Counseling, 18,* in press.

Borgen, W. A., & Amundson, N. E. (1987). The dynamics of unemployment. *Journal of Counseling and Development, 66,* 180–184.

Borgen, W. A., Pollard, D., Amundson, N. E., & Westwood, M. (1987). *Employment groups: The counseling connection.* Ottawa: Canada Employment and Immigration Commission.

Bratfisch, O. (1985). Counseling the unemployed. *Natcon, 9,* 91–102.

Brenner, M. H. (1973). *Mental illness and the economy.* Cambridge: Harvard University Press.

Brenner, S. O., & Bartell, R. (1983). The structural analysis of sectional data. *Journal of Occupational Psychology, 56,* 129–136.

Broussard, W. J., & DeLargey, R. J. (1979, December). The dynamics of the group outplacement workshop. *Personnel Journal,* pp. 855–857.

Carkhuff, R. R., Pierce, R. M., Friel, T. W., & Willis, D. G. (1985). *Get a job.* Amherst, MA: Human Resource Development Press.

Chandler, A. L. (1984). Using an abbreviated job club program in job service setting. *Journal of Employment Counseling, 21,* 98–102.

Colaizzi, P. F. (1978). Psychological research as the phenomenologist veiws it. In R. S. Valle, & M. King (Eds.), *Existential-phenomenological alternatives for psychology.* New York: Oxford University Press.

Corey, G. (1985). *Theory and practice of group counseling.* (2nd Ed.) Belmont, CA: Wadsworth.

Cooney, D., & Hargest, M. (1986). A counseling model for staff reduction. *Natcon, 13* (2), 625–640.

Doyon, D. (1985). Job finding club. *Natcon, 10,* 15–28.

Edelwich, J., & Brodsky, A. (1980). *Burn-out: Stages of disillusionment in the helping professions.* New York: Human Sciences Press.

Finley, M. H., & Lee, A. T. (1981). The terminated executive: It's like dying. *Personnel and Guidance Journal, 59,* 382–384.

Fischer, C. T. (1979). Individualized assessment and phenomenological psychology. *Journal of Personality Assessment, 43,* 115–122.

Flanagan, J. (1954). The critical incident technique. *Psychological Bulletin, 51,* 327–356.

Flanagan, J. (1978). A research approach to improving our quality of life. *American Psychologist, 33,* 138–147.

Furnham, A. (1984). Unemployment, attribution theory, and mental health. *International Journal of Mental Health, 13,* 51–67.

Gurney, R. M. (1980). The effects of unemployment on the psycho-social development of school-leavers. *Journal of Occupational Psychology, 53,* 205–213.

Hartley, J. (1980). Psychological approaches to unemployment. *Bulletin of the British Psychological Society, 32,* 309–315.

Hayslip, J. B., & Van Zandt, C. B. (1985). Dealing with reduction in force: Career guidance for state employees. *Vocational Guidance Quarterly, 33,* 256–261.

Hepworth, S. J. (1980). Moderating factors of the psychological impact of unemployment. *Journal of Occupational Psychology, 53,* 139–145.

Hicks, B., & Kelvin, C. (1983). *Job finding club: Evaluation report.* Ottawa: Canada Employment and Immigration Commission.

Hill, J. M. M. (1977). *The social and psychological impact of unemployment* (Document No. 2T74). London: Tavistock Institute of Human Relations.

Jacobson, T. J. (1984). Self-directed job search training in occupational classes. *Journal of Employment Counseling, 21*, 117–125.

Jahoda, M. (1982). *Employment and unemployment: A social-psychological analysis.* Cambridge: Cambridge University Press.

Janoff-Bulman, R., & Frieze, I. (1983). A theoretical perspective for understanding reactions to victimization. *Journal of Social Issues, 39*, 1–17.

Johnson, D., & Johnson, R. (1982). *Joining together: Group theory and group skills* (2nd ed.). Englewood Cliffs, NJ: Prentice Hall.

Jones, W. H. (1979). Grief and involuntary career change: Its implications for counseling. *The Vocational Guidance Quarterly, 27*, 196–201.

Kaufman, H. G. (1982). *Professionals in search of work.* New York: Wiley and Sons.

Keith, R. D., Engeles, J. R., & Winborn, B. B. (1977). Employment-seeking preparation and activity: An experimental job-placement training model for rehabilitation clients. *Rehabilitation Counseling Bulletin, 21*, 159–165.

Kelvin, P. (1981). Work as a source of identity: The implications of unemployment. *British Journal of Guidance and Counseling, 9*, 2–11.

Kemp, N. J., & Mercer, A. (1983). Unemployment, disability, and rehabilitation centers and their effects on mental health. *Journal of Occupational Psychology, 56*, 37–48.

Kübler-Ross, E. (1969). *On death and dying.* New York: Macmillan.

Mahler, C. A. (1969). *Group counseling in the schools.* Boston: Houghton Mifflin.

Marsden, D. (1982). *Workless.* London: Croom Helm.

Maslow, A. E. (1968). *Toward a psychology of being* (2nd ed.). Toronto: D. Van Nostrand.

McWhirter, J., Nichols, E., & Banks, N. (1984). Career awareness and self-exploration (case) groups: A self-assessment model for career decision making. *The Personnel and Guidance Journal, 62*, 580–582.

Mills, A. (1985). Job finding club program. *Natcon, 8*, 293–301.

Mirabile, R. J. (1985). Outplacement as transition counseling. *Journal of Employment Counseling, 22*, 39–45.

Nesdale, A. (1983). Effects of person and situation expectations on explanation seeking and causal attributions. *British Journal of Social Psychology, 22*, 93–99.

Orwell, G. (1975). *The road to Wigan Pier.* London: Penguin.

Papalia, A. D., Dai, S., & Devine, P. (1986). An educational and industrial partnership in the delivery of outplacement services. *Vocational Guidance Quarterly, 34*, 197–203.

Pearson, R. (1983). Support groups: A conceptualization. *The Personnel and Guidance Journal, 6*, 361–364.

Peterson, C., & Seligman, M. E. P. (1983). Learned helplessness and victimization. *Journal of Social Issues, 39*, 103–116.

Ramey, L. (1986). Reemployment training for displaced automobile workers: Program description and evaluation. *Journal of Employment Counseling, 23*, 78–86.

Rump, E. E. (1983). A comment on Dowling and O'Brien's 'employed' and 'unemployed' groups. *Australian Journal of Psychology, 35*, 89–90.

Schumacher, E. F. (1979). *Good work.* New York: Anchor Press.

Schutz, W. C. (1958). *Firo: A three dimensional theory of interpersonal behavior.* New York: Holt, Rhinehart & Winston.

Seligman, M. E. P. (1975). *Helplessness: On depression, development and death.* San Francisco: Freeman.

Shifron, R., Dye, A., & Shifron, G. (1983). Implications for counseling the unemployed in a recessionary economy. *Personnel and Guidance Journal, 61*, 527–529.

Sinfield, A. (1981). *What unemployment means.* Oxford: Martin Robertson.

Swinburne, P. (1981). The psychological impact of unemployment on managers and professional staff. *Journal of Occupational Psychology, 54*, 47–64.

Tiggemann, M., & Winefield, M. (1984). The effects of unemployment on the mood, self-esteem, locus of control, and depressive affect of school-leavers. *Journal of Occupational Psychology, 57*, 33–42.

Toffler, A. (1980). *The third wave.* New York: Bantam.

Trimmer, H. W. (1984). Group job search workshops: A concept whose time is here. *Journal of Employment Counseling, 21*, 103–116.

Trotzer, J. P. (1977). *The counsellor and group: Integrating theory, training and practice.* Monterey, CA: Brooks/Cole.

Warr, P. G., Jackson, P. R., & Banks, M. H. (1982). Deviation of unemployment and psychological well being in young men and women. *Current Psychological Research, 2*, 207–214.

Webster's Third New International Dictionary. (1971). Springfield, MA: Merriam.

Wortman, C. (1983). Coping with victimization: Conclusions for future research. *Journal of Social Issues, 39*, 195–221.

6
Outpatient Group Psychotherapy for Persons with Chronic Mental Illnesses

Depending on the manner in which it is conducted, group therapy with chronically mentally ill persons can result in significant benefit or detriment. If used judiciously, group therapy provides support and opportunities for problem resolution, intimacy, improved self-worth, and the acquisition of specific socialization skills. If therapeutic procedures and techniques are used without modification from those used in insight-oriented group psychotherapy, the end result can be deterioration. This chapter discusses the principles of effective group therapy with persons in outpatient treatment for chronic mental illness and provides an overview of specialized group models that can contribute to their psychiatric treatment and rehabilitation.

THE IMPACT OF CHRONIC MENTAL ILLNESS

There are an estimated 1.7 to 2.4 million persons with chronic mental illness in the United States (Goldman, Gatozzi, & Taube, 1981). The specific nature of an individual's psychiatric diagnosis alone does not determine whether that individual's psychiatric illness is defined as chronic. Rather, determination of chronicity is based on the degree to which the psychiatric disorder interferes with abilities in the areas of self-care, socialization, and employment or education (Goldman, Gatozzi, & Taube, 1981). Psychotic disorders predominate among the chronically mentally ill, and of these disorders, schizophrenia is the most common. Major affective disorders and organic brain syndromes are also relatively prevalent disorders that may cause chronic psychiatric disablement.

Despite significant differences in symptom profiles, persons with chronic mental illness share many salient experiences and problems; one of the foremost is the experience of uncontrollable persistent psychiatric symptomatology. For many, symptomatology involves distortions of reality such as auditory hallucinations and delusions. Frequent concomitants of these generally frightening psychotic experiences include increased dependency and a diminished trust of one's senses and judgment. Extreme reliance on another individual and a severe restriction of activities may result from attempts to avoid situations they feel would evoke additional symptomatology. Describing the experience of uncontrollable symptomatology (as reported by McGhie & Chapman, 1961), one individual commented, "Things just happen to me now and I have no control over them. I don't seem to have the same say in things any more. At times I can't even control what I want to think about" (p. 109).

Changes in affective life may be as incapacitating as psychotic intrusions. Depressive symptomatology occurs frequently and often includes feelings of worthlessness, self-reproach, and inappropriate guilt. Such symptoms are not restricted to the major affective disorders; they are also found in other psychiatric disorders including schizophrenia and organic brain syndromes. In addition to depressive symptomatology, the chronically mentally ill person may experience a pervasive apathy. These symptoms often pose significant obstacles to independent functioning and frequently preclude involvement in activities that could be pleasurable or enhance self-worth.

For many, daily life is also profoundly affected by difficulties in processing stimuli and information. Among other effects, these symptoms result in an inability to respond appropriately in social situations. This inability may be particularly painful for individuals who are aware of both their social ineptness and their considerable need for social contact.

Loneliness, caused by impaired social abilities, is greatly exacerbated by widespread stigmatization of the mentally ill. Stigmatization becomes a feature of daily life and has been considered a secondary handicap that is nearly as demoralizing as living with recurrent symptomatology, alterations of mood, and impaired thought processes. Stigmatization of the mentally ill is often present in the attitudes of the general public, family members, and other mentally ill persons. Social stigma can take forms ranging from avoidance to ridicule. Social service professionals are not immune from negative attitudes toward mentally ill persons, and their attitudes are often as negative as those of the general public (Tringo, 1970). Because mental illness is an "invisible" disability in the sense that one's body does not show outward evidence of a disease process or injury, others may regard the individual as malingering or simply lacking in self-discipline. For example, the disordered behavior that accompanies a manic episode during bipolar illness is often perceived by spouses as willful, spiteful behavior that could be controlled (De-Nour, 1980).

Attitudes toward persons with chronic rather than acute mental illnesses are particularly negative. The President's Commission on Mental Health (1978) underscored the intensely negative social standing of the chronically mentally ill:

> The chronically mentally disabled are a minority within minorities. They are the most stigmatized of the mentally ill. They are politically and economically powerless and rarely speak for themselves. Their stigma is multiplied, since disproportionate numbers among them are also elderly, poor or members of racial or ethnic minority groups. They are the totally disenfranchised among us (p. 362).

In general, relatively more support and empathy is demonstrated by family members, friends, employers, and professionals when there is a belief that the individual will recover from the psychiatric disorder; support and understanding are often withdrawn when it is apparent that the individual will not recover (Krauss & Slavinsky, 1982).

It is not surprising that the experience of living with chronic mental illness often results in an internalization of societal devaluement. This in turn undermines the individual's ability to cope with the effects of the disorder. The internalization of societal prejudice against the mentally ill may also lead the individual to avoid others with psychiatric disorders and thereby lose a potential source of social acceptance and social support.

Although with social support and vocational rehabilitation a substantial number of chronically mentally ill persons have the potential for some type of employment, many are unemployed for a variety of reasons. For these persons unemployment further contributes to a sense of isolation and diminished self-worth—especially since social identity and opportunities for socialization are generally derived to a great extent from activities related to employment. In this manner they are set even further apart from the mainstream of society.

RATIONALE FOR GROUP TREATMENT

The potential benefits of group treatment for persons with chronic mental illness are apparent when considering the extent of their isolation and social impairment. Persons with severe, chronic psychiatric illnesses such as schizophrenia are often protrayed as "loners," a description that is only partially accurate. The mentally ill person's choice to be alone does not arise from a particular sense of pleasure in a solitary existence. It arises from the belief that there is danger in closeness—because of either the real or the imagined likelihood of rejection, manipulation, or humiliation by others. Group therapy enables these individuals to learn that social interaction can be "a rewarding rather than frightening experience" (Donlon, Rada, & Knight, 1973, p. 684). The same opportunity for learning is not available consistently in individual psychotherapy, and there may be some deleterious effects in a one-to-one relationship. For example, the transference that may develop in individual psychotherapy has been viewed as too intense for chronically mentally ill clients to tolerate. As a result, group therapy has long been considered particularly useful for these clients because transference is diluted and consequently less distressing (Cutler, 1978; Spotnitz, 1957). For many chronically mentally ill persons, group therapy alleviates isolation, feelings of estrangement, and diminished self-worth. It also provides the opportunity for participants to acquire and practice interpersonal and social skills that may never have been adequately established or may have deteriorated from disuse.

Group therapy is not to be considered a substitute for ongoing individual psychiatric treatment, which generally includes medication and monitoring of psychiatric status. However, group therapy can properly be regarded as both a complementary and viable alternative to individual counseling. Several studies comparing individual and group counseling for psychiatrically disabled persons concluded that clients and therapists alike reported more positive feelings regarding their experiences with group treatment compared with individual counseling (Donlon, Rada, & Knight, 1973; Herz, Spitzer, Gibbon, Greenspan, & Reibel, 1974; O'Brien et al., 1972). Some mental health clinicians prefer the use of group interventions because clients can be observed while engaging in a broader range of behaviors than is possible within the confines of individual therapy (O'Brien, 1975). This, in turn, facilitates the assessment of psychological and social functioning and is one reason why group treatment has been viewed as a fundamental aspect of partial hopitalization programs (Hersen & Luber, 1977).

HISTORICAL OVERVIEW

For more than 60 years, group therapy has been used in the treatment of persons with psychotic disorders and other chronic mental illnesses. Lazell (1921) is credited as the first to use a group treatment modality, a didactic approach involving group lectures to persons in treatment for schizophrenia. This method of group treatment of those with severe psychiatric disorders was adopted for use by many others. Throughout the next 4 or 5 decades, group treatment of the chronically mentally ill gained in popularity and therapists frequently applied techniques traditionally used in dynamic psychoanalytic groups. During this period of time, psychotic disorders were viewed as stemming from intrapsychic conflicts. Group leaders encouraged members to work through their "conflicts" through group interaction. It was assumed that approaches that were useful with persons with neurotic disorders would work equally well with those with psychotic disorders because the difference between neurotic and psychotic disorders was viewed as one of degree (Day & Semrad, 1971). The occurrence of a member becoming psychotic during group treatment was viewed as an inevitable part of conflict resolution.

As the field of psychiatry began to recognize the etiologic role of biochemistry in severe psychiatric disorders, the utility of psychotherapy for persons with psychotic disorders was questioned. It was recognized that insight-oriented therapy would not cure disorders that had biochemical etiologies, and, as a result, the emphasis of treatment was placed on the use of psychotropic medications. Many mental health professionals concluded that psychotherapy was not useful for the chronically mentally ill. This misconception was probably fueled by the difficulty of working with this population, the newly discovered value of psychotropic medications, and disenchantment with group therapy because of the poor results demonstrated. The proverbial baby was thrown out with the bath water, and for a period of time the value of group psychotherapy was overlooked in the treatment and rehabilitation of chronically mentally ill persons. At times it still is overlooked despite its merits.

OUTCOME STUDIES

Research on the effectiveness of group therapy with mentally ill outpatients generally supports its use in conjunction with psychotropic medication (as needed). This conclusion must be qualified by noting that care must be exercised in using appropriate methods with selected clients. Kanas's (1986) review of studies of outpatient group thearpy with schizophrenics concluded that group therapy was superior to no group therapy in 80% of the studies. In addition, group therapy was found to equal or exceed individual therapy in effectiveness in each of the studies that compared the two modalities. Kanas's review also indicated that group methods that emphasized effective social interactions rather than insight resulted in more favorable outcomes.

Several studies examined the effects of group counseling on rates of rehospitalization. Studies by Purvis and Miskimins (1970) and Battegay and von Marschall (1978) found that group treatment was effective in significantly diminishing the frequency of hospital admissions for clients maintained on medication in aftercare settings. Similarly positive results were reported by Alden, Weddington, Jacobson, and Gianturco (1979). Commenting on their own finding and those of others they observed that "the weight of the present evidence in the literature indicates that group follow-up combined with neuroleptic medications is an effective treatment modality in the aftercare of a large number of schizophrenics, although it may not be a consistently superior aftercare treatment for all schizophrenics" (Alden, Weddington, Jacobson, & Gianturco, 1979, p. 12). Prince, Ackerman, Carter, and Harrison's (1977) research included clients with a broader range of psychotic disorders. Their results indicated that group treatment was more effective than individual treatment with respect to maintaining clients in the community. They speculated that the positive effects of the group treatment occurred because the group provided the clients with a sense of belonging, an aspect they considered vital to community adjustment.

Other studies on the efficacy of group methods with severely psychiatrically disabled persons primarily focused on indicators of social effectiveness and participation in therapeutic aftercare services. Donlon, Rada, and Knight (1973) investigated the effects of group counseling on persons with schizophrenia who had been considered treatment-refractory and poorly motivated. The group treatment resulted in better clinic attendance for aftercare services as well as increased socialization. The benefits of group counseling in facilitating social competence were also apparent in the results of research by O'Brien et al. (1972). They found group therapy to be superior to individual therapy with respect to remediating the social deficits of persons with schizophrenia. Research by Claghorn, Johnstone, Cook, and Itschner (1974), conducted with persons being treated for schizophrenia, used a highly structured group treatment that emphasized the resolution of problems in daily living. Although the group treatment did not alter the clients' symptomatology to an appreciable extent, it did improve the clients' abilities to relate interpersonally. Reflecting on their findings, Claghorn and his colleagues made the following observation:

> The results of this research project are seemingly at variance with some of the current nihilism concerning the value of psychotherapy in the schizophrenic patient: it appears that some may be helped to live with the chronically debilitating nature of this ailment through the oppourtunity to share experiences with others (Claghorn et al., 1974, p. 365).

SUPPORTIVE GROUP THERAPY

The concept and principles of supportive group psychotherapy are central to an understanding of effective group treatment of persons with chronic mental illness. This modification of group psychotherapy evolved during the period of deinstitutionalization. It was developed for chronic psychiatric outpatients who needed more than medication maintenance or contact with social groups but who were unable to tolerate the intensity of individual psychotherapy (Krauss & Slavinsky, 1982). A strengthening of ego functioning is regarded as the primary objective of supportive group psychotherapy. According to Krauss and Slavinsky (1982), this objective is accomplished by improvements in reality testing, identification with therapists and group members, encouragement of adaptive behaviors and increased object relations, as well as support for defensive patterns.

The belief that many defensive patterns are to be supported rather than challenged is one of the most significant differences between traditional psychotherapy and supportive group formats. Repression of disturbing feelings and memories is regarded as important in order to guard against psychotic decompensation. Krauss and Slavinsky (1982) illustrate this principle:

> The patient who is prompted to reflect upon past failures when stressed by something in the group meeting would be encouraged to focus on the stress event and ignore the ruminations. Other members might be encouraged to discuss how they push certain thoughts or feelings out of their consciousness (p. 214).

The rationale for encouraging repression is described by Torrey (1983) in his warning against the use of approaches that explore preconscious or unconscious material. Although his comments pertain to schizophrenia in particular, they apply equally well to other psychotic disorders:

Given what we know about the brains of persons with schizophrenia, it should not be surprising to find that insight-oriented psychotherapy makes them sicker. Such persons are being overwhelmed by external and internal stimuli and are trying to impose some order on the chaos. In the midst of this a psychotherapist asks them to probe their unconscious motivations, a difficult enough task even when one's brain is functioning perfectly. The inevitable consequence is to add insult to injury, unleashing a cacophony of repressed thoughts and wishes into the internal maelstrom. To do insight-oriented psychotherapy on persons with schizophrenia is analogous to directing a flood into a town already ravaged by a tornado (p. 125).

EFFECTIVE GROUP LEADERSHIP

In contrast to traditional insight-oriented group psychotherapy, supportive group psychotherapy requires that the leader assume a much more active role in a comparatively wider range of aspects of the group process. The leader frequently stimulates interaction between members, may generate topics to be discussed, facilitates verbal expression, and occasionally directly teaches adaptive social behaviors. The leader needs to reinforce the well-functioning aspects of each member's personality without losing sight of the necessity to remediate areas of deficits that lead to difficulties in daily life. Although the degree of therapist activity needs to be relatively high, the therapist must be careful not to assume group responsibilities that are within the capabilities of the members.

Referring to the work of Leopold (1976), Betcher, Rice, and Weir (1982) state that the acknowledgment of treatment progress of group members is critical and often requires therapists to "recalibrate their scales of improvement so that small gains are verbally acknowledged" (p. 236). According to Leopold (1976), group leaders must be able to accept "minimal success despite their efforts." Other qualities that are conducive to effective therapy with severely psychiatrically disturbed individuals include "being able to tolerate, with a reasonable degree of comfort, bizarre behavior and thoughts, and being sensitive to communications made in verbally oblique and nonverbal ways" (Betcher et al., 1982, p. 236).

THERAPEUTIC EXPECTATIONS

It is well known that the transmission of expectations regarding client progress is inherent in the therapeutic process and is a critical determinant of its outcome. However, this principle bears repeating in the context of this discussion of group therapy because therapists working with the chronically mentally ill sometimes lose sight of it. Friedmann, Procci, and Fenn (1980) warn against the emerging pattern of "making diagnosis synonymous with prognosis" (p. 189). The chronic nature of a disorder must be recognized and acknowledged without losing sight of the hope or expectation that some functional improvement can occur. In order to help clients cope with and adapt to the impact of their psychiatric disorders, group therapists must recognize the diversity of prognoses within diagnostic groups, must examine their own feelings about chronic mental illnesses, and must be appropriately humble about their abilities to predict with certainty the future functional abilities for any given individual.

MANAGEMENT OF ANXIETY REGARDING GROUP INVOLVEMENT

Anxiety is problematic in many chronic mental illnesses; its management within group therapy is a critical and important aspect of the therapist's responsibilities (Krauss & Slavinsky, 1982). The specific sources of anxiety are varied but often are intensified by the prospect of group involvement. Some members fear they will lose control over their impulses and fear others may also be unable to control themselves in the group setting. Fears of being controlled by members or the group leader may also be experienced, especially by clients who have Schneiderian symptoms. Schneiderian symptoms, frequently present in schizophrenia, include the delusional beliefs that one's thoughts are broadcasted to others and that others can insert thoughts into one's mind. Other fears are related to past negative social experiences involving rejection, exclusion, or humiliation and the belief that group involvement is inherently risky. These types of fears may diminish in intensity during the course of the group experience, but they often do not entirely subside. Krauss and Slavinsky (1982) provide the following advice to therapists:

> . . . err in the direction of reducing anxiety in the early stages of the group until individual tolerance is revealed and understood. The therapist may allow the group to defend against anxiety by changing the subject, breaking for coffee and snacks, or diverting attention from a "hot" topic in other ways (p. 220).

Suspicions tend to arise and paranoia is aggravated in situations that are vague or ambiguous; therefore, the use of structure is important as a means to diminish fears regarding the group process. Arieti (1975) states that a structured group experience is particularly important in order to compensate for the fragmented sense of self that is often seen in persons with a history of psychoses.

A range of methods can be used to provide beneficial structure. Structuring the therapeutic experience often begins with at least one individual orientation session prior to group involvement. Structure may also be provided through explicit statements of treatment objectives and goals and the careful establishment, explanation, and implementation of limits regarding acceptable group behaviors. Limit-setting is particularly important if the group includes members who tend toward impulsivity, disruptiveness, or intoxication. The delineation of general or specific topics for group discussion is another means of providing additional structure to the group process. Equally important (but more subtle) is the structure provided by therapist interventions that encourage, divert, or clarify particular aspects of discussions.

Whereas these methods for providing structure are sufficient in most supportive psychotherapy groups, some clients need to be provided with an even more highly structured group format in order to tolerate and benefit from the group experience. Activity groups are often useful with these individuals. They can provide a relatively comfortable retreat from anxiety-laden interactions into structured activities. This format enables the member to remain in the group, focus on concrete activities, and interact socially at whatever level is comfortable. One example of an effective, highly structured activity group is found in O'Brien's (1975) description of the use of a communal meal that is planned by group members.

HANDLING PROBLEMS IN VERBAL EXPRESSION

The following comment from a person with schizophrenia, reported by Torrey (1983), illustrates one of the difficulties in verbal expression frequently experienced because of mental illness:

My thoughts get all jumbled up, I start thinking or talking about something but I never get there. Instead, I wander off in the wrong direction and get caught up with all sorts of different things that may be connected with the things I want to say but in a way I can't explain. People listening to me get more lost than I do (p. 18).

The active, structuring role of the group leader or therapist frequently needs to extend to the domain of helping clients express their thoughts. The ability and willingness to assume this role without subtly altering the meaning of the client's comments is critical. This process requires an understanding that highly disorganized or seemingly nonsensical comments do not mean that the person does not have a meaningful point to express. Bruch (1966) writes: "One prerequisite for successful psychotherapy with schizophrenics is the possibility of establishing meaningful interpersonal communication through being able to see meaning in the distorted verbalization, bizarre behavior, and fluctuating attitudes of his patient, so as to better be able to communicate together" (p. 347). Looseness of associations between thoughts is a common difficulty. Rather than feign comprehension, as many inexperienced therapists will do for fear of jeopardizing "rapport," one should request clarification. It is important to do this in a manner that communicates an interest in understanding rather than one that underscores the group member's deficit (MacKinnon & Michels, 1971). The suggestions MacKinnon and Michels make regarding interviewing persons with schizophrenia are applicable to group therapy: "Rather than saying, 'You're not making yourself clear,' the interviewer can say, 'I'm having difficulty following what you are saying.' Similarly, 'I don't understand how we got on this subject,' is preferable to, 'Why do you keep changing the subject?'" (p. 246). Sometimes members are unable to clarify their comments further. Consequently, therapists may need to accurately translate the members' comments. Care must be taken to do this in a manner that is not misinterpreted by the client; some group members may feel they are supposed to agree with all rephrased comments and others may feel their comments are being intentionally altered. Therefore, attempts at rephrasing need to be prefaced with statements such as: "Correct me if I am wrong, it sounded as if you might have been saying. . . ." or "I don't want to put words in your mouth but. . . ." It may also be useful to ask another group member to help clarify the comment for the group.

Other problems in verbal expression that may affect group counseling involve the amount and rate of the client's speech. Flight of ideas may be problematic; this accelerated speech and abrupt jumping from topic to topic can be handled, to some extent, by a slowing down of the therapist's speech. The group therapist must not hesitate to interrupt the client repeatedly if necessary. Whereas many clients experience the problems associated with flight of ideas, other clients find communication laborious due to difficulties in synthesizing and responding to stimuli. They must be provided with an unusually long time to respond and encouragement to expand on fragmentary comments.

Within the group setting, some problems in communication can be diminished through the use of frequent summaries of the group discussion and interaction and active attempts to focus the discussion. Pekala, Siegel, and Farrar (1985) speak of the importance of "gatekeeping," the process of facilitating participation from a number of group members by limiting the more verbose ones and encouraging the more silent members. This type of regulation is particularly important in groups that are composed heterogeneously by diagnosis due to the different types of problems in communication that are often associated with various psychiatric conditions.

SOCIAL CONTACTS OUTSIDE OF GROUP SESSIONS

In contrast to traditional group psychotherapy, contact between group members outside of the confines of the group therapy sessions is generally viewed as an acceptable if not a positive occurrence (Day & Semrad, 1971; Krauss & Slavinsky, 1982). Although one of the ultimate objectives of group treatment with the chronically mentally ill is to increase and improve social contacts within the community, this objective is not always realistic for some members due to stigmatization and social impairment. If handled carefully, social contacts outside of the group can enhance rather than jeopardize the treatment objectives of support, interpersonal growth, and skill acquisition. Contacts between group members outside of the group need to be discussed within the group setting, and care needs to be exercised in order to identify situations that may damage the group (such as the formation of cliques) or that may develop into unhealthy relationships (Krauss & Slavinsky, 1982).

DELUSIONAL BELIEFS AND DECOMPENSATION

Therapists often are confused about how to handle the expression of delusional beliefs. Delusions are symptoms that are found in many of the major psychiatric illnesses, including schizophrenic disorders, the affective disorders, and organic mental disorders. The therapist's first inclinations are often to confront delusional members with the irrational natures of their beliefs. However, a confrontational approach (a firm and consistent attack on delusional beliefs) is counterproductive. Milton, Patwa, and Hafner (1978) found confrontation resulted in an increased intensity of adherence to delusional beliefs. Assisting the client to examine the evidence underlying his or her assumptions was found to be more effective. According to Kanas (1985), this approach is most effective when the group member is independently beginning to question delusional material and if other patients are able to join the therapist in supporting reality.

Increases in delusional beliefs may signify a change in the illness, increased risk of decompensation, and the need for the group leader to consult with others responsible for the client's treatment. Group members may respond to the worsening of another's symptoms by distancing themselves from the psychotic member as if there were contagious qualities to his or her symptoms. The absence or loss of a member due to psychiatric decompensation and need for rehospitalization is generally a disturbing event for the group because it reminds members of the unpredictable nature of their own symptomatology and the frightening aspects of their disorders. This issue needs to be addressed within the group and can be a fruitful way to address the critical issue of coping with recurrent illness.

GROUP COMPOSITION

Krauss and Slavinsky (1982) provide the following criteria for selecting individuals who may benefit from supportive group psychotherapy:

1. The patient who cannot face the intimacy of a one-to-one relationship with the therapist alone
2. The patient who requires a gradual transference to the group therapist in order to move on to an individual supportive psychotherapy relationship

3. The borderline patient who needs to have greater control over the development of relationships
4. The patient who can benefit from social interaction and interpersonal training (p. 216).

Clients who are floridly psychotic, are actively manic, or have fixed paranoid delusions are not appropriate for inclusion in an outpatient group because inclusion may hasten relapse (Krauss & Slavinsky, 1982). This does not mean that clients need to be entirely free of psychotic or manic symptoms because this would unrealistically and needlessly exclude a sizeable portion of the population of mentally ill. Individuals with significant symptomatology may be included if there is a reasonable degree of ego functioning and contact with reality.

Whether to compose a group with members having the same or differing psychiatric disorders is an important consideration that requires careful thought. Group composition that is homogeneous by diagnosis has become increasingly popular, particularly in inpatient settings. Kanas (1985) believes this form of group composition is the most effective one for outpatient group treatment of schizophrenia. Professionals who emphasize the importance of diagnostic homogeneity in group treatment generally cite two potential benefits. They note that shared diagnoses serve a cohesive function and enable information related to the specific disorder to be presented and discussed within the group setting. The merits of groups that are composed heterogeneously by diagnosis must not be overlooked. This approach to group composition enables a broader range of themes to be addressed. Identification through similarity of life issues, rather than shared diagnoses, also serves a cohesive function. This approach has the benefit of often minimizing the degree to which group members define their identities by their psychiatric labels. Neither diagnostic homogeneity nor heterogeneity is inherently more effective in the group treatment of the chronically mentally ill. The choice of composition should be guided by specific treatment needs and goals. This principle is illustrated throughout the remainder of this chapter, which provides descriptions of specialized groups.

HOMOGENEITY IN THE GROUP TREATMENT OF YOUNG ADULTS

The potential strengths of homogeneous group composition are apparent in Ely's (1985) description of the group treatment of young adult males, diagnosed with chronic schizophrenia. Her report of this group is also notable because it addresses a segment of the mentally ill population that has become a significant concern for mental health providers, young-adult, chronic clients. Young clients such as those treated by Ely are increasing in number and are troubling to mental health practitioners because of their strong resistance to psychiatric treatment and social service assistance.

Young-adult chronic clients present a range of symptoms and severe problems in social functioning. Common difficulties include paranoia, impaired judgment, poor impulse control, substance abuse, and depression. Most of these individuals are relatively transient with virtually no social support system and they often experience frequent conflicts with authorities. As a result of deinstitutionalization they are "the first generation of mental patients to have to cope, from the beginning and during most of their lives, with the tasks and stresses of community living" (Pepper, Kirshner, & Ryglewicz, 1981, p. 465). Although they clearly demonstrate psychiatric symptoms, they do not acknowledge the presence of these difficulties. According to Pepper, Kirshner, and Ryglewicz (1981):

> This reluctance to see themselves as different from anyone else functions as a barrier to accepting treatment. Yet, their persistent lack of success in achieving the goals that are socially appropriate to their age—education, mating, a steady job—does set them apart in their own despairing perception, not as patients or impaired people with special needs, but as social failures (p. 465).

Ely (1985) provides the following description of the young-adult chronic clients who eventually became successfully engaged in long-term group psychotherapy:

> These clients, all young men, irregularly attended their aftercare appointments but frequently, sometimes daily, sat in the center's waiting room, impatiently waiting for the intake worker. While waiting they badgered the secretary and bummed cigarettes from other clients. Their presentation could vary from aggressive, demanding behavior to pitiful despair; they were often intoxicated from alcohol or drugs. Occasionally they would be chaperoned by a police officer. They were generally "on the outs" with the clinical staff because of the inept, manipulative and annoying manner of their attempts to get their needs met (p. 6).

A primarily closed group membership of six was used in Ely's treatment; when two of the original members eventually left the group they were replaced. Group leadership remained unchanged throughout the life of the group. Attendance was initially marked by frequent absences, and group cohesion did not develop until about 6 months had passed. Considering the difficulties this population has in engaging in any form of outpatient treatment, it is significant that most of the group members remained involved in the group throughout its 6-year existence. The treatment method was primarily a mixture of support, shared experiences, and problem-solving. In addition to illustrating the value of a group composed homogeneously by diagnosis, Ely's description of this group illustrates the potential value of group treatment with clients who are traditionally very difficult to engage in treatment.

THEMES IN SUPPORTIVE THERAPY GROUPS

Before proceeding to a discussion of specialized and theme-centered groups, it is important to consider the themes that naturally emerge in supportive group psychotherapy and the type of material that is commonly introduced by group leaders. Emphasis is frequently placed on helping members cope with daily life and remain out of the hospital. Within this context, a range of problems and shared experiences are discussed. Support and advice are provided. General and idiosyncratic approaches to coping with residual symptomatology are often discussed by members. Complaints about psychiatric treatment and the necessity to take medication are often exchanged. However, if a member demonstrates an intention to terminate treatment or medication against medical advice, other members generally support the importance of adherence to prescribed treatment recommendations (O'Brien, 1975). When necessary, groups typically provide the consensual validation that is needed for the purpose of reality testing (Krauss & Slavinsky, 1982).

SPECIALIZED AND THEME-CENTERED GROUPS

Groups that focus on specific themes or objectives are used very effectively with the chronically mentally ill and have been regarded as one of the more promising approaches to group treatment. The principles and procedures of supportive group psychotherapy, which were described in the preceding sections of this chapter, provide the foundation that enables specific issues to be explored and specialized objectives to be addressed in the group. Treatment objectives include some emphasis on the acquisition of new skills; however, the degree of pressure to engage in new learning varies. Strayhorn (1982) notes that support and pressure for new learning are to be mixed proportionally according to the needs and capabilities of the members. Skill acquisition is emphasized in many treatment groups because of the needs to remediate extensive social deficits, to learn new ways to cope with residual symptoms, and to restore confidence. Groups that focus on skill development are also particularly well-suited for some persons with severe psychiatric disorders because they provide a high degree of structure and enable progress to be evaluated on circumscribed rather than more global group treatment objectives.

It is not possible to cover the range of theme-centered or specialized groups described in the clinical and research literature. Only those groups that I have personal experience with and have found especially useful in my own work are included in this discussion. These include groups based on problem-solving-skills training and those that are markedly instrumental in vocational rehabilitation.

Problem-Solving Groups

Problem-solving-skills training and support groups provide a structured yet flexible approach to group counseling. These types of groups evolved from the work of D'Zurilla and Goldfried (1971), which reduced effective problem-solving to a brief sequence of cognitive operations. The problem-solving training process involves teaching individuals this sequence, and the ultimate goal is to enable them to apply the problem-solving sequence independently to problems of daily living. The sequential components are: (1) problem recognition, (2) problem definition, (3) generation of alternative methods of problem resolution, (4) evaluation of these alternatives in order to reach a decision, and (5) verification that a solution has been effective.

Problem-solving–skills training is a valuable treatment approach because many psychiatric disorders result in specific deficits in problem-solving. For example, in addition to difficulty organizing thought processes, the problem-solving skills of schizophrenics are characterized by rigidity and a reluctance to alter strategies following unsuccessful attempts at resolution (Pishkin & Williams, 1977). Improved problem-solving abilities have been found to be facilitated by skills training (Coche & Douglas, 1977; Coche & Flick, 1975).

Training in problem-solving skills may be successfully accomplished on an individual basis, but the process seems to be enriched when undertaken in the group setting. When used in a group setting, participants collectively apply the problem-solving sequence to actual problems reported by members. Therapeutic benefits extend beyond improvement in problem-solving abilities and the resolution of specific problems. Improvements in self-esteem, impulse control, and sense of self-efficacy have been reported (Coche & Douglas, 1977). Group problem-solving is flexible enough that affective material is processed and support is provided to individual members. The considerable degree of structure inherent in this group enables quite symptomatic clients to be able to participate in group exchanges without losing the focus of the group discussion.

Modifications of the basic procedures are useful, enabling specific themes and treatment needs to be addressed. For example, I used the model to structure a group focused on work adjustment problems of outpatients who were engaged in the vocational rehabilitation process, groups for adolescents facing discharge from a psychiatric hospital, and groups with emotionally disturbed youth in a residential treatment center. At other times, I have combined problem-solving–skills training and social-skills training in a group setting. The combination of these two modalities increases the likelihood that members will have the specific social skills required to implement chosen solutions. Pekala, Siegel, and Farrar (1985) describe a modification of problem-solving groups that incorporates many of the principles of group psychotherapy advocated by Yalom (1985). This approach, termed the *problem-solving support group*, was developed specifically for use with persons with psychiatric disorders as an alternative to more traditional insight-oriented psychotherapy.

Vocational Groups

As noted previously, problems obtaining and maintaining employment are significant concerns for many chronically mentally ill persons. Groups are often the ideal modality for assisting persons with the complex transition from the role of a patient to that of an employee. They are useful in many stages of this process: acquisition of job-seeking skills, vocational and career planning, and the development of coping strategies to facilitate work adjustment.

Groups that focus on the development of prevocational or job-seeking skills are generally the most highly structured and use a curriculum that includes training in interview skills and the job search process. A detailed curriculum by Kramer (1984) appears to be particularly relevant to the needs of chronically psychiatrically disabled individuals. The nature of this type of group is not as exclusively didactic as it may first appear. Specifically, issues pertaining to self-esteem, personal identity, and stigmatization arise in the group when members are faced with the prospect of seeking employment after years of having the social identity of a "mental patient." The group process enables members to provide valuable assistance to each other to resolve dilemmas specifically related to coping with the effects of psychiatric disorders on employment. For example, a common dilemma addressed by group members is whether one should disclose the presence of a psychiatric disorder to potential employers.

Career exploration and planning groups are also specialized groups that are of significant benefit to many clients. The process of finding a viable vocation or career is difficult for many people and is considerably more complex for individuals with chronic mental illness. For all persons it requires identification of interests, realistic appraisal of abilities, and an integration of this information with knowledge of the demands and characteristics of various occupations. Several aspects of the career planning process often pose difficulty for individuals with chronic mental illness. Some are faced with discrepancies between their strong intellectual abilities and their limited capacities to cope with the stress or interpersonal demands related to specific occupations of interest. Persons with bipolar illness seem to encounter especially difficult problems because the periods of relatively effective functioning and stability between episodes contrast markedly with their capabilities at other times. Planning is also particularly frustrating for some of them because the onset of the disorder often occurs after a career has already begun to be established. The planning problems of the person with a schizophrenic disorder pose different difficulties due to the typically earlier onset of the disorder and the fact that impaired functioning persists to a significant extent between acute episodes. Individuals with schizophrenic disorders often have very limited knowledge regarding their own abilities and the world of work.

The following synopsis of the structure of the most recent career planning group co-led by myself is intended to illustrate the breadth of concerns that may be addressed within a career-planning group. This particular group was composed of women with heterogeneous diagnoses who had encountered difficulties with vocational rehabilitation. The members had diverse concerns, and many were at different stages of the vocational planning process. However, group cohesiveness developed relatively rapidly, possibly because of sex homogeneity and their mutual concerns regarding future vocational plans. Structure was introduced into the group format through the use of weekly individualized goals, and sessions were generally concluded with the identification of individual goals to be addressed between sessions. These goals, chosen by each member, ranged from continued abstinence for an alcoholic member to the completion of a resume that a member repeatedly avoided for fear that any job search efforts would result in further rejections. The discussion of efforts toward the attainment of personally important goals provided the opportunity to address problems and reinforce successful efforts.

Members were supportive as well as appropriately confrontational toward each other when necessitated by either inappropriate behavior in the group setting or patterns of self-defeating behavior outside of the sessions. A range of issues was able to be addressed in significant depth through this relatively highly structured group. These included coping with an inability to return to a prized career due to uncontrollable symptomatology, handling disincentives and motivational problems regarding a return to employment, and coping with a series of unsuccessful job interviews. Although the exchange of information related to vocational planning was an important aspect of the group, many of the most important interactions involved testing the reality of vocational choices and the providing of support for members facing difficult tasks and decisions. The value of a group setting for addressing vocational problems was underscored for me by the contrasting degree of change demonstrated during the group by several members who had previously demonstrated less progress while receiving individual vocational services from myself and my cotherapist.

Self-Help Groups

The value of self-help groups in the management of chronic mental illness tends to be overlooked by mental health practitioners, possibly due to the common misconceptions that they are intended to be a substitute for professional treatment and are antipsychiatric in nature. The most notable of these groups, Recovery, Inc., was established 50 years ago by a psychiatrist, Alexander Low. The organization is now entirely run by members who adhere very strictly to Low's original treatment methods. It is important to note that Recovery, Inc., is intended to be an adjunct to professional treatment, a perspective that is explicitly stated in the organization's literature. The term *self-help*, in this instance, refers to the organization's premise that members must take responsibility for control of their symptomatology. This self-control includes following physician advice at all times and extends to the need to be deliberate in handling specific detrimental impulses in an adaptive manner throughout each day. The major goals of involvement in Recovery, Inc., are described as the prevention of recurrences and the forestalling of chronicity (Low, 1950).

Group sessions are highly structured, primarily didactic, and frequently available in major cities on several nights throughout the week. They are primarily attended by persons with chronic mental illnesses but are open to family members, friends, and the general public. Low's writing serves as the foundation for panel and group discussions that emphasize the application of principles for coping with symptomatology and the effects of stigmatization. The panel discussions are followed by a less-structured period of casual interaction among group members.

Mental Health through Will Training (Low, 1950) is required reading for all members. The content of this book, to a large extent, parallels principles that are used by many professionals, although the terminology differs. For example, emphasis is placed on helping members learn to interpret events in a more rational fashion, a principle that is central to the cognitive therapies. Members are also instructed in how to avoid becoming overly anxious and overwhelmed when physiologic arousal occurs as a result of stress. This instruction is used to circumvent a potential vicious cycle in which the person becomes anxious about being anxious. Similar principles are incorporated by many professionals in therapies for persons with anxiety disorders.

Literature on Recovery, Inc., indicates that leaders of group sessions receive specific training in Low's approach and have their qualifications reviewed annually. They serve in the role of leading the panel and group discussions and do not provide counseling services to individual members. Recovery, Inc., has a standard policy of demonstrating their approach to small groups of persons interested in learning more about their method. This resource may be useful to mental health practitioners who are interested in this approach to group treatment for persons with chronic mental illness. It is a useful supplement to traditional professional therapies.

SUMMARY

This chapter has provided an overview of the potential value of group counseling in the outpatient treatment of persons with chronic mental illness. However, it is important to note that a group treatment modality is only effective when it is employed judiciously with an understanding of the needs of severely psychiatrically disabled clients. These needs include the preservation of psychological defenses, the minimization of anxiety, and the opportunity to acquire skills that may in turn enable client participation in a broader spectrum of life activities. The principles of supportive group psychotherapy were presented in this chapter in order to describe the elements that are conducive to a positive group treatment outcome and to provide an understanding of the foundation from which more specialized groups can be developed to address particular needs of clients.

Group treatment is not intended to be an exclusive or curative treatment for persons with chronic mental illness. The strong biological component to these psychiatric disorders precludes this and necessitates ongoing pharmacologic and psychiatric treatment. The role of group approaches is nontheless, an important one. Supportive group psychotherapy helps address the multitude of issues unrelated to biochemistry that determine the extent to which the individual copes effectively with residual symptomatology, remains in remission, and is able to participate in meaningful social and vocational activities.

REFERENCES

Alden, A. R., Weddington, W. W., Jacobson, C., & Gianturco, D. T. (1979). Group aftercare for chronic schizophrenia. *Journal of Clinical Psychiatry, 40*, 249–252.

Arieti, S. (1975). *Interpretation of schizophrenia*. New York: Basic Books.

Battegay, R. & von Marschall, R. (1978). Results of long term group psychotherapy with schizophrenics. *Comprehensive Psychiatry, 19*, 349–353.

Betcher, R. W., Rice, C. A., & Wier, D. M. (1982). The regressed inpatient group in a graded group treatment program. *American Journal of Psychotherapy, 36*, 229–239.

Bruch, H. (1966). Psychotherapy with schizophrenics. *Archives of General Psychiatry. 14*, 345–351.

Claghorn, J. L., Johnstone, E. E., Cook, T. H., & Itschner, L. (1974). Group therapy and maintenance treatment of schizophrenics. *Archives of General Psychiatry, 31*, 361–365.

Coche, E. & Douglas, A. A. (1977). Theraputic effects of problem-solving training and play-reading groups. *Journal of Clinical Psychology, 33*, 820–837.

Coche, E., & Flick, A. (1975). Problem-solving training groups for hospitalized psychiatric patients. *Journal of Psychology, 91*, 19–29.

Cutler, M. O. (1978). Symbolism and imagery in a group of chronic schizophrenics. *International Journal of Group Psychotherapy, 28*, 73–80.

Day, M., & Semrad, E. (1971). Group therapy with neurotics and psychotics. In H. I. Kaplan & B. J. Sadock (Eds.), *Comprehensive group psychotherapy*. Baltimore: Williams & Wilkins.

De-Nour, A. K. (1980). Psychosocial aspects of the management of mania. In R. H. Belmaker, & H. M. Van Praag (Eds.), *Mania—An evolving concept* (pp. 349-364). Jamaica, NY: SP Medical and Scientific Books.

Donlon, P. T., Rada, R. T., & Knight, S. W. (1973). A therapeutic aftercare setting for "refractory" chronic schizophrenic patients. *American Journal of Psychiatry, 130*, 682–684.

D'Zurilla, T. J., & Goldfried, M. R. (1971). Problem solving and behavior modification. *Journal of Abnormal Psychology, 78*, 107–126.

Ely, A. R. (1985). Long-term group treatment for young male "schizopaths." *Social Work, 30* (1), 5–10.

Friedmann, C. T., Procci, W. R., & Fenn, A. (1980). The role of expectation in treatment for psychotic patients. *American Journal of Psychiatry, 34*, 188–196.

Goldman, H. H., Gattozzi, A. A., & Taube, C. A. (1981). Defining and counting the chronically mentally ill. *Hospital and Community Psychiatry, 32*, 21–27.

Hersen, M., & Luber, R. F. (1977). Use of group psychotherapy in a partial hospitalization service: The remediation of basic skill deficits. *International Journal of Group Psychotherapy, 27*, 361–376.

Herz, M. I., Spitzer, R. L., Gibbon, M., Greenspan, K., & Reibel, S. (1974). Individual versus group aftercare treatment. *American Journal of Psychiatry, 28*, 54–64.

Kanas, N. (1985). Inpatient and outpatient group therapy for schizophrenic patients. *American Journal of Psychotherapy, 39*, 431–439.

Kanas, N. (1986). Group therapy with schizophrenics: A review of controlled studies. *International Journal of Group Psychotherapy, 36*, 339–351.

Kramer, L. W. (1984). SCORE: Solving community obstacles and restoring employment. *Occupational Therapy in Mental Health, 4*, 1–135.

Krauss, J. B., & Slavinsky, A. T. (1982). *The chronically ill psychiatric patient and the community*. Boston: Blackwell Scientific.

Lazell, E. W. (1921). The group treatment of Dementia Praecox. *Psycho-Analytic Review, 35*, 135–140.

Leopold, H. S. (1976). Selective group approaches with psychotic patients in hospital settings. *American Journal of Psychotherapy, 30*, 95–102.

Low, A. A. (1950). *Mental health through will training*. North Quincy, MA: The Christopher Publishing House.

MacKinnon, R. A., & Michels, R. (1971). *The psychiatric interview in clinical practice*. Philadelphia: W. B. Saunders.

McGhie, A., & Chapman, J. (1961). Disorders of attention and perception in early schizophrenia. *British Journal of Medical Psychology, 34*, 103–116.

Milton, F., Patwa, V. K., & Hafner, R. J. (1978). Confrontation versus belief modification in persistently deluded patients. *British Journal of Medical Psychology, 51*, 127–130.

O'Brien, C. P. (1975). Group therapy for schizophrenia: A practical approach. *Schizophrenia Bulletin, 13*, 119–130.

O'Brien, C. P., Hamm, K. B., Ray, B. A., Pierce, J. F., Luborsky, L., & Mintz, J. (1972). Group vs. individual psychotherapy with schizophrenics. *Archives of General Psychiatry, 27*, 474–478.

Pekala, R. J., Siegel, J. M., & Farrar, D. M. (1985). The problem-solving support group therapy with psychiatric inpatients. *International Journal of Group Psychotherapy, 35*, 391–407.

Pepper, B., Kirshner, M. C., & Ryglewicz, H. (1981). The young adult chronic patient: Overview of a population. *Hospital and Community Psychiatry, 32*, 463–469.

Pishkin, V., & Williams, W. V. (1977). Cognitive rigidity in information processing of chronic undiferentiated schizophrenics. *Journal of Clinical Psychology, 1*, 278–281.

President's Commission on Mental Health. (1978). *Task panel reports appendix* (Vol. 2). Washington DC: Government Printing Office.

Prince, R. M., Ackerman, R. E., Carter, N. C., & Harrison, A. (1977). Group aftercare-impact on a statewide program. *Disease of the Nervous System, 38*, 793–796.

Purvis, S. A., & Miskimins, R. W. (1970). Effects of community followup on posthospital adjustments of psychiatric patients. *Community Mental Health Journal, 6*, 374–382.

Spotnitz, H. (1957). The borderline schizophrenic in group psychotherapy: The importance of individuation. *International Journal of Group Psychotherapy, 7*, 165–174.

Strayhorn, J. M., Jr. (1982). *Foundations of clinical psychiatry*. Chicago: Year Book.

Torrey, E. F. (1983). *Surviving schizophrenia—A family manual*. New York: Harper & Row.

Tringo, J. (1970). The hierarchy of preference towards disability groups. *Journal of Special Education, 4*, 295.

Yalom, I. P. (1975). *The theory and practice of group psychotherapy* (2nd ed.). New York: Basic Books.

ROBERT D. KERNS
MARK T. HEGEL

7
Chronic Benign Pain: Cognitive-Behavioral Treatment and Support Groups

There is probably no greater source of stress and suffering for the individual than the experience of pain. Similarly, among physicians and other health care practitioners, pain represents a problem of enormous proportions. To date there is no general consensus on such central issues as what pain is or how it should be measured, let alone how it should be treated. The history of efforts to find relief from pain date to the Egyptians (circa 1550 B.C.) with the list of pharmaceutic agents used including virtually every known organic and inorganic substance (Turk, Meichenbaum, & Genest, 1983). Today, efforts continue with the development of innovative neuropharmacologic and surgical treatments and the proliferation of multidisciplinary rehabilitation programs. Unfortunately, for the most part, data supporting the clinical efficacy of these treatment approaches and programs are lacking or inconsistent, and the enormity of the problem continues.

It has been estimated that one-third of Americans suffer from persistent and recurrent pain (Bonica, 1981), with 35 million suffering from chronic low-back pain alone (Bonica, 1980). La Freniere (1979) suggested that 80% of the population are affected by back pain at some time in their lives. Of 1.25 million people in the United States who injure their backs each year, 65,000 will be permanently disabled (Beals & Hickman, 1972). The economic costs of chronic pain are enormous, including both direct health care costs, such as the purchase of prescribed and over-the-counter medications, and the indirect financial burden of unemployment, lost productivity, and disability compensation. The lifetime economic costs of rheumatoid arthritis alone have been estimated at over $20,000 per case in 1977 (Stone, 1984). As further evidence of the scope of the problem, over 1,200 multidisciplinary pain clinics have opened their doors to chronic pain sufferers in the United States alone (Holzman & Turk, 1986)!

The difficulty in defining pain and categorizing clinical pain problems has its roots in both basic and applied research, in clinical practice, and in the layman's phenomenology of the experience of pain. During the last century, two competing views of the nature of pain, termed the *specificity theory* (Mountcastle, 1974) and *pattern theory* (Crue & Carregal, 1975), have had considerable influence on basic research in the neurophysiology and neuroanatomy of pain. These theories basically propose a purely "somatic" explanation of pain, in which a linear relationship exists between the site, type, and degree of tissue damage and the intensity of pain experienced.

A third and more comprehensive model, the *gate control theory* of pain, has been proposed more recently by Melzack and Wall (1965). They postulate a neural gating system in the dorsal horn of the spinal cord (the section of the spinal cord that receives afferent impulses from the peripheral nervous system). This gate will open when a certain threshold of stimulation is reached, thus allowing the nerve impulses to reach the brain and provoke the experience of pain.

Melzack and Wall propose, however, that inhibitory mechanisms may be brought to bear on the functioning of the "gate" and thereby modulate the pain experience. These inhibitory impulses may have their origins in the periphery, such as through transcutaneous stimulation, but they have their primary origins in psychological functions, such as sensory/discriminative, motivational/affective, and cognitive/evaluative operations. These impulses travel along descending pathways from the brain and exert their inhibitory influence at the spinal cord level (keeping the "gate" closed).

According to the gate control model, then, psychological factors can inhibit or promote pain perception, thus providing a theoretical basis for the utilization of psychological approaches as a primary treatment for chronic pain. A further advantage of this model is that it provides a tenable framework for viewing the means by which cultural and learning variables may have their effect on the pain experience (Melzack, 1973).

Contributing to the difficulty in understanding the experience of pain is the wide range of physical problems that present with pain as a salient symptom. Included are a variety of degenerative disorders—headaches, trauma, and cancer, to name just a few. Exact diagnosis of many of these problems is complex and difficult, not only because of the multiplicity of etiologies, but also because the patient's history and physical descriptions are often vague and overlap physical and psychiatric boundaries. Several categorizations of clinical pain problems based on the presumed underlying pathophysiology have been developed.

In a review of the literature, Flor and Turk (1984) cited one pain categorization system with five classes for back pain only: (1) inflammatory, such as ankylosing spondylitis; (2) degenerative, including osteoarthritis; (3) structural, including congenital abnormalities of the spine; (4) traumatic; and (5) muscular/ligamentous, such as myalgia. Unfortunately, they concluded that there is little empirical validity to the direct association between these disorders and back pain. A similar conclusion could be drawn regarding virtually every effort to categorize pain problems on the grounds of their presumed physiologic bases.

The psychiatric community has similarly struggled to develop a diagnostic classification system for chronic pain patients who do not have a known physical etiology or who experience pain with greater intensity than can be expected from the underlying organic cause alone. Given the current challenge to the assumption of a direct relationship between pain and structural pathology generally, and the additional difficulty in making an organically based diagnostic determination, it is no wonder that efforts to obtain psychodiagnostic clarity have had a similar lack of success. At present the *Diagnostic and Statistical Manual of Mental Disorders*, third edition (DSM-III) (APA, 1980) includes a diagnosis of "Psychogenic Pain Disorder" that has been criticized for the stigmatizing choice of a label, as well as for its primarily exclusionary criteria. Alternatives to this classification have been offered, including the term *pain-prone personality* (Blumer & Heilbronn, 1982).

A recent National Institutes of Health Consensus Report endorsed the differentiation of three categories of clinical pain problems, namely, acute pain (e.g., post-operative pain), chronic malignant pain, and chronic benign pain (usually defined as pain lasting longer than 6 months and not related to malignancy) (NIH, 1986). In so doing, the report supported the clustering of a range of pain problems on the basis of two operational criteria: (1) the absence of malignancy and (2) the persistence of the complaint. For chronic benign pain, the consensus held that efforts at diagnosing and treating the "underlying" organic basis for the pain should be thorough, but only as a first step to be followed by attention to the multiplicity of associated disabilities and psychosocial problems. As a specific example of their emphasis on rehabilitation alternatives to continued somatic interventions, the report strongly encouraged restraint in the use of narcotic analgesics in cases of chronic benign pain.

Consistent with this view, scientific and clinical efforts have recently further encouraged the clustering of chronic pain patients with a range of known or presumed organic etiologies by demonstrating homogeneity among these patients in terms of a range of associated affective difficulties and functional disabilities. One example is the use of the term *chronic pain syndrome* to describe the frequent concurrent problems of insomnia, pain, depression, and anxiety (Black, 1975; Hendler, 1982). Thomas Szasz (1968) has similarly described the "painful person," whereas Richard Sternbach (1968) preferred the term "low back pain loser" to characterize the catastrophic disability and global suffering of these individuals.

In fact, data supporting the clinical impression of a high frequency of chronic affective disorders and other psychosocial disabilities among chronic pain patients are now available. For example, a major depressive disorder has been reported to be present in as many as 87% of the chronic pain patients examined in one published report (Lindsay & Wyckoff, 1981). A causal relationship, in one direction or the other, has not been clearly established. Another common problem is substance abuse and dependence on a range of narcotics and central nervous system depressants, including alcohol and minor tranquilizers. The range of problems includes unemployment and disability, marital and sexual dysfunction, debilitating anxiety, and stress-related disorders, among others.

Data from the Pain Management Program at the West Haven VA Medical Center can be used to further dramatize the extent and severity of these problems. Over the past 8 years, the pain program has screened a widely heteogeneous group of patients in terms of organic etiology, accepting referrals from virtually every medical speciality. The patients are largely male veterans with a mean age of 48 and a duration of pain averaging 10.3 years. Unemployment is reported by 55%, and 50% of the patients receive disability compensation. Recent analyses reveal that 65% of the patients meet the Research Diagnostic Criteria for major or minor depressive disorder based on data collected on a sample of 64 patients using the Schedule for Affective Disorders and Schizophrenia (Kerns, Haythornthwaite, & Giller, 1987). Previously published reports demonstrated that over 50% of both patients and spouses reported significant marital dysfunction (Kerns & Turk, 1983). Finally, to further demonstrate the deleterious impact of chronic pain, depression was found to be a frequent problem among spouses in this same sample. These data dramatically argue for a perspective on the problem that goes well beyond a primarily somatic model!

The range of variables that have been reported to influence pain perception and the extent of suffering and disability is equally broad. In the laboratory, scientists have identified individual differences and situational variables that appear to influence measures of pain thresholds and tolerance (e.g., Melzack, 1973). In the clinical pain literature, each month brings additional reports on predictors and correlates of pain and disability. Among the most salient issues in this literature at the present time are the relationship between pain and depression (Gershon, 1986; Romano & Turner, 1985), the influence of sex and age (Kashima & McCreary, 1987), the importance of personality attributes, the relevance of cognitive variables (Turk and Rudy, 1986), and the influence of learning.

Dissatisfaction with primarily sensory models of pain that propose a relatively direct, one-to-one relationship between structural tissue pathology and pain complaints, and the failure of purely somatic treatment efforts to relieve chronic pain (Toomey, Ghia, Mao, & Gregg, 1977; White & Sweet, 1969) have led to the consideration of alternative conceptual models to explain pain and to the proliferation of innovative treatment and rehabilitation programs. The NIH Consensus Report emphasized the need for more integrative and multidimensional approaches to understanding pain and supported multidisciplinary efforts directed at its management (NIH, 1986). The emergence of such a viewpoint has opened the door for investigators and clinicians representing nonmedical perspectives, including psychology. In fact, several primarily psychological models have been proposed that have been particularly influential. The volume of research based on these models and the range of intervention strategies proposed has been enormous.

The remainder of this chapter will be organized in four primary sections. First, general principles and issues concerned with the group treatment of chronic pain will be articulated. Following this general discussion, specific theoretical models that guide the conduct of group therapies will be described. This section is followed by a brief review of the empirical literature related to the group treatment of pain. Finally, two specific group treatment programs offered by the Pain Management Program at the West Haven VA Medical Center will be described.

GROUP TREATMENT FOR CHRONIC PAIN: RATIONALE AND CLINICAL ISSUES

With the development of multidisciplinary programs for the treatment of chronic pain, psychologists have developed roles ranging from psychodiagnosticians to supportive counselors, primary therapists, and program directors. Of these, one of the most commonly cited clinical roles is that of group therapy facilitator. Virtually no comprehensive pain program description goes without mentioning the clinical importance of group work, either as a primary therapeutic modality (Gentry & Owens, 1986; Sternbach, 1974) or as one of several components (Cairns, Thomas, Mooney, & Pace, 1976; Newman, Seres, Yospe, & Garlington, 1978). The widespread proliferation of group therapy approaches for chronic pain to a large extent supports beliefs about their clinical utility. Further contributing to beliefs about the credibility and efficacy of group treatment of chronic pain patients are the numerous clinical and anecdotal reports in the literature. These reports offer detailed descriptions of group approaches and examples of the successful rehabilitation of patients who were severely disabled and previously refractory to multiple treatment efforts.

A supportive rationale for the use of group treatment modalities can be developed by outlining several of the salient advantages and properties of groups that distinguish them from individual therapies. Most of these qualities are not specific to the management of chronic pain. In addition, the considerable overlap among these properties is readily apparent. They are enumerated below only for organizational and conceptual clarity.

First, despite the wide heterogeneity of pain patients in terms of their organic etiologies, the homogeneity of their experiences, disabilities, and associated concerns frequently overshadows their individual differences. The validity of this statement has become apparent to us despite a strongly cognitive-behavioral orientation that emphasizes pain patients' idiosyncratic beliefs regarding their pain experiences. In this regard, an understanding of the patients' unique histories of trauma, uncertain diagnosis, failed treatment, disability, and personal distress most often can be reflected to the patient in terms of global perceptions of frustration, helplessness, and hopelessness.

The recurrent observation of the relative ease with which pain groups develop a high degree of cohesion and mutual support has further reinforced our belief in their general efficacy and our understanding of the key "ingredients" for their success. Several of these factors appear to be related to the shared background, experiences, and beliefs among the group members. Gentry and Owens (1986) previously articulated most of these factors and rationales, and our own experience certainly supports their observations.

According to Gentry and Owens (1986), pain groups provide a means of (1) ameliorating a pervasive perception of social isolation and alienation, (2) obtaining credible feedback from peers, and (3) defining a new reference group for social comparison. As a function of a developing awareness of group unity in terms of shared concerns and problems and an associated identification with others in the group, patients are likely to be reinforced for their willingness to share their own ideas and feelings and conversely to listen more actively to others. Although there is an intuitive appeal to these rationales and observations, care must be taken, however, not to presume the presence or operation of these factors in a given group or the benefits for a given participant. For example, individuals who are particularly depressed may experience heightened alienation and withdrawal from a group that is behaving in an "upbeat," active problem-solving manner. Such an individual may be lost to the group or become more depressed without the support of an observant and skilled facilitator. Similarly, although many group members may make social comparisons with the group that allow for an elevation in perception of personal mastery and competence (e.g., I'm not as bad off as they are), others may have their perceptions of incompetence reinforced through a similar process of social comparison. Ultimately, it is an explicit sensitivity to, but not necessarily the verbalization of, these dynamics on the part of the therapist that can enhance their value in the group.

The economic advantage of group versus individual treatment of chronic pain almost goes without saying. In the short run, the use of groups substantially increases the number of patients that can be served given limited resources. Additionally, given the chronicity of the problem and the long-term task of rehabilitation confronting most pain patients, the use of open-ended support groups may offer a cost-effective alternative to termination of ongoing contact with a therapist and fellow patients. Such groups may serve to reduce recidivism and a return to an overreliance on other health-care professionals and, in fact, may serve to enhance long-term outcomes. Consistent with the increasing attention to health-care cost-containment, such a model for minimal but ongoing intervention and support may prove remarkably valuable in responding to chronic illnesses, generally.

A variety of clinical issues are central to a discussion of group therapy approaches for chronic pain management. These issues are important in clinical decision-making about whether to include group treatment as part of a programmatic effort, and if so, what format to use. Secondly, these issues may interact with the reasons for doing group work that were just outlined in determining their power and treatment-enhancing properties. For example, group size and group composition will clearly affect social comparison processes and the ability of the group members to develop trusting relationships that support feedback from others. Finally, articulation of these issues may be helpful in providing a framework for the critical evaluation of existing reports and data.

First, the theoretical rationale for using a group format should be thoroughly considered and defined. As will be reviewed in the next section, there are a wide range of psychological treatment approaches for chronic pain, each drawing on its own conceptual model and varying greatly in terms of applied structure, process, and goals. Although most of these treatment models theoretically may be applied in a group setting (and, in fact, many have been offered in groups), the specific conceptual framework should be important in making determinations about such issues as inclusion/exclusion criteria, group size, fixed group membership versus "revolving door" membership, use of a time-limited versus open-ended format, degree of facilitator/therapist participation, and so forth.

Choices regarding these "structural" issues in turn have critical implications for the overall functioning of the group in terms of both process and outcome. For example, the inclusion of family members may be presumed to be a strong advantage in a time-limited behaviorally oriented treatment group. In such a group, the therapist may be extremely active in providing a rationale for desired changes in family communication, teaching of active listening and assertiveness skills, and directing behavioral rehearsal of these new skills among family members. Conversely, it may be determined that spouses should not be included in a minimally structured, dynamically oriented, pain support group. In such a group, the inclusion of family members may be viewed as a challenge to group cohesion, the free expression of emotional issues, credible feedback from other pain patients, and social comparison with patients with similar problems. Discussions later in this chapter report on two types of groups offered in our Pain Management Program at the West Haven VA Medical Center. The reader will then have the opportunity to compare and contrast the structural and functional differences between a time-limited, cognitive-behavioral treatment group and an open-ended, pain support group.

Before moving on, it may be helpful to present a few thoughts regarding several particularly important structural variables that should be addressed prior to beginning a pain group. Related to the theoretical basis for the group program, articulation of goals for participants and the means for evaluating outcomes is strongly encouraged. For example, in many rehabilitation counseling groups, decreased affective distress and increased feelings of support may be the goals and outcomes desired. Alternatively, an operantly based group will likely be focused on decreasing medication usage and other pain behaviors (e.g., use of prosthetics, complaints of pain, distorted ambulation) and on increasing mobility and functional activity. Outcomes in the first case may be evaluated on the basis of the self-reports of group members and their attendance records; in the operant group, structured observation data and medication records may be desired. The extent to which these goals and outcomes are made explicit by the group facilitator may also vary among groups and is probably related somewhat to the theoretical perspective of the program or therapist. In fact, in some groups the goals and desired outcomes may be allowed to evolve and change over time as a function of group process and dynamics.

As for participant selection, our experience and that of others (e.g., Gentry & Owens, 1986) suggest that there are few clear criteria for determining group membership. Our program attempts to screen for individuals who are acutely psychotic or who manifest personality disorders that preclude social engagement. More generally, we attempt to make use of other resources for active alcoholics, acutely depressed and potentially suicidal patients, borderline patients, or patients with apparently acute medical needs. Recent analyses have suggested that depressed patients may be more likely than nondepressed pain patients to drop out of treatment, but among those completing an active treatment phase, there is no evidence of significant difference in outcome (Kerns & Haythornthwaite, in press). There are no data available to argue that such variables as gender, marital status, or employment status, or pain-related variables such as etiology, duration of pain, or compensation status are important selection criteria.

Similarly, no data are available to help in decisions regarding group size. Our own experience argues against a membership over 10 or 12, and in fact, most of our structured treatment groups have included only 4 to 6 members. Clearly, in groups designed to include skill training and cognitive and behavioral rehearsal, membership size should be limited to permit substantial individual attention and sufficient "air time" for each member. Longer-term support groups that are advanced in terms of group cohesion may accommodate a larger number of participants.

We are clear in our resolve to refrain from introducing new members to our more structured treatment groups once they have begun. This decision relates to the sequential and structured treatment model that is used. On the other hand, we continue to help new members join our ongoing support groups, although we have experienced some mixed results in this regard. The issues of group membership have become a recurrent concern among the group members reflecting issues of trust and cohesion. In addition, new members represent a challenge to the group in terms of the older member's established roles in the group, their sense of continuity, and other group dynamics. Nevertheless, the groups have continued to assert their group decision to welcome new members, despite their apparent ambivalence.

PSYCHOLOGICAL MODELS AND GROUP THERAPIES FOR CHRONIC PAIN

Counseling/Education Model

The most time-honored psychological model for work with chronic pain patients is the counseling/education model. It is perhaps the first example of the interdisciplinary relationship between psychology and rehabilitation. The basic tenet of this model is the assumption that the individual has a valid illness that is having a negative impact on that person's emotional and interpersonal life. Within this model, medical treatment and physical rehabilitation remain the primary focus of treatment. The role of the counselor is to provide emotional support and relevant information regarding the illness so that the adjustment process may proceed as smoothly as possible.

Schwartz, Marcon, and Condon (1978) describe a characteristic counseling/education group format as it is applied with rheumatoid arthritis patients. They focus their group counseling on four specific goals: (1) to encourage and support patients to communicate with their families, other patients, and their physicians; (2) to educate physicians regarding the emotional sequelae of chronic illness; (3) to educate patients about rheumatologic disease, its course, and treatment; and (4) to facilitate adjustment in order to enable patients to live with their disease more comfortably.

The authors speak to the advantages of conducting such groups with a multidisciplinary leadership. For instance, they developed an arthritis group headed by a rheumatologist, psychiatrist, and a physiatrist. The rheumatologist acted as the medical specialist, providing specific answers to patients about their condition and using information gathered in the sessions in order to better manage their individual cases. The physiatrist likewise served as a resource regarding the rehabilitative aspects of treatment. Finally, the psychiatrist's role was to observe the group dynamics, to comment on issues of group concern, and to assess coping mechanisms. The authors conclude that the efficiency of case management was improved and that the patients seemed to benefit along several clinical parameters (e.g., decreased pain, improved mood, and increased activity levels).

Henkle (1975) describes "social group work" with hospitalized rheumatoid arthritis patients. Her model also emphasizes a supportive milieu that encourages the open sharing of concerns related to their illness, their psychosocial well-being, and their hospitalization. She emphasizes the role of groups as a means of removing the patient from emotional and physical isolation. In addition, when patients begin to form a group cohesiveness, says Henkle, many practical solutions to problems of everyday living (such as labor-saving devices) are shared with other group members. An important point for Henkle is the necessity of providing a supportive but nonanalytic and nonthreatening group process. The goal of the group process, according to Henkle, is to decrease psychological tension—not to analyze unconscious conflicts by challenging defensive systems.

Finally, Gluck (1980) discusses her views regarding the counseling approach to group therapy. This approach is not so much focused on education but instead emphasizes the relationship between feelings, the perception of pain, and psychosocial consequences of a lifestyle organized around a sick role. The author states that the patients must begin by developing an awareness of negative feelings within themselves. She states that chronic pain patients tend to convert negative feeling states such as anger and frustration into pain complaints and therefore have difficulty identifying the emotion or the real-life circumstances related to them. The next step is to reduce dependent behaviors by teaching the pain patient the means of obtaining love and attention through appropriate expression of feelings rather than via passive-dependent bids based on the sick role. As pain patients abandon the sick role and develop a more mature coping style, their self-esteem improves and they evolve toward becoming functional members of the community.

Self-Help Group Model

The self-help philosophy involves the coming together of persons with chronic pain with the goal of helping one another cope with emotional and practical problems arising from chronic pain problems. Webb (1982) describes a large project in England designed to develop and assess the effectiveness of nationwide self-help groups for back pain sufferers. A survey of participants revealed that two-thirds of the sample felt that they had been helped by the group, although specifics in this regard are not reported. Webb emphasizes that the most successful groups, or the groups that were the most liked, were those led by non-specialists in back pain who allowed a "group identity" to form rather than functioning as a "professional advisor."

Lorig, Lubeck, Kraines, Selznick, and Holman (1985) evaluated a self-help education program for rheumatoid arthritis patients that was led by lay persons. Using a randomized, control group design, they found significant improvements in knowledge, use of recommended health behaviors, and reported pain severity. The differences remained significant at 16 months following the termination of the intervention.

In summary, it appears that self-help groups can have both general and specific benefits for participants. The combination of education, emotional support, and group problem-solving seem to be responsible for the observed effects, although the magnitude and specificity of the effects remain unclear.

Psychosomatic Model

A fairly common feature of a chronic pain syndrome is the presence of a dysthymic mood disorder or major depression. A related finding is that a majority of depressed patients that are not identified as chronic pain patients nonetheless complain of chronic pain. These types of findings have led some investigators to propose that a chronic pain syndrome is a manifestation of a primary depressive illness (e.g., Blumer & Heilbronn, 1982).

Some commonly shared symptoms between chronic pain patients and depressed patients are: (1) loss of interest or pleasure in all or almost all usual activities and past times; (2) insomnia; (3) a decrease in sexual drive; (4) loss of energy; and (5) fatigue. The severity of these depressive symptoms is typically great in magnitude and difficult to attribute entirely to the consequences of physical discomfort.

There is other evidence to support the notion that chronic pain syndromes are manifestations of underlying psychopathology. Chronic pain patients have a high incidence of alcoholism and depressive episodes prior to the onset of their pain (Katon, Egan, & Miller, 1985). Evidence further suggests that members of the immediate family also have a high incidence of alcoholism and chronic pain disorders (Schaffer, Donlon, & Bittle, 1980).

Evidence is mounting to document that chronic pain patients suffer from a condition known as alexithymia (Sifneos, Apfel-Savitz, & Frankel, 1977), which is an inability to recognize and verbalize one's feelings. According to a psychodynamic model, the chronic pain sufferer may be experiencing, perhaps primarily, a chronic depression, and they may defend against painful feelings associated with depression by focusing on the physical sensations of pain. This viewpoint appears to be in agreement with the counseling/education model of Gluck (1980) already discussed. This transformation process allows all of life's problems to be ascribed to the pain condition rather than explore possible psychological and interpersonal factors that are likely to carry the implication that the person is depressed (Engel, 1959).

Psychodynamic Group Psychotherapy

Pinsky (1978) describes a group approach that is designed to elicit affect expression and understanding. This is a relatively traditional psychodynamic viewpoint that emphasizes the forced dependency of the pain patient and the conflictual feelings that develop around a dependent–provider relationship (that is, security at the cost of autonomy).

Udelman and Udelman (1977) describe their model for group therapy with rheumatoid arthritis patients. Their type of group therapy was designed with four basic goals: (1) to provide education regarding rheumatoid arthritis, its course and its treatment; (2) to promote group cohesiveness and thereby allow members to develop an identity other than that of being a patient; (3) to develop a supportive atmosphere that allows members emotional expression without censorship and within a safe environment; and (4) to facilitate psychological exploration and the dynamic reorganization of conflicts and coping mechanisms. The authors functioned as a husband and wife team of therapists and report that this combination better enabled them to handle transference issues.

Hendler, Viernstein, Shallenberger, and Long (1981) describe the group therapy process as it progresses from an inpatient to an outpatient phase. The leader initially functions as a specialist and in a directive manner provides practical information regarding tests, procedures, and medical management. As the group progresses the therapist becomes more vague and elicits feelings of dependency, anger, and fear by emphasizing that the pain cannot be taken away. As therapy continues on an outpatient basis the feelings of abandonment and resentment toward the medical community are addressed and patients are redirected to look for resources within themselves and other group members. A long-term support group process serves to facilitate the emergence and maintenance of self-reliance.

In summary, the psychodynamic model of group therapy for chronic pain patients is very similar in style to traditional psychodynamic therapy. There is clearly a very strong emphasis placed on the role of dependency for the pain patient. The task of therapy is to explore the negative emotions of living a life that is overly dependent on family and medical communities and then to resolve the iatrogenic effects of being weaned away from such strong dependency. The issues of positive transference, negative transference, and affective insight and catharis stand as paramount in this form of therapy.

Family Systems Model

An alternative to focusing on the psychodynamics of the individual is to focus on the interpersonal dynamics within the context of the individual's family. A chronic pain condition has many consequences for a family's functioning. Social outings become restricted, job functioning and subsequent family income are lessened, demands on the family member with a pain problem are typically lowered, and emotional relationships and reactions are often disrupted. A rationale that emphasizes the family's role (or the family system) in the development and maintenance of the chronic pain syndrome is likely to focus on specific patterns of interaction, structural boundaries between family members, and signs of triangulation and scapegoating, as well as other signs of disturbed family functioning (Minuchin, 1974).

Operant Conditioning Model

Fordyce (1976) emphasized the role of the behavioral principles of operant conditioning in the development and maintenance of a chronic pain syndrome. This behavioral approach emphasizes that "pain behavior" represents the pain problem in that it is this behavior that limits functioning and elicits reinforcing events from the environment. As a result, the patient's social and physical environment becomes primarily organized around the expression of these behaviors.

Pain behaviors (e.g., grimacing, groaning, limping, rubbing) may have their onset as unconditioned responses to an unpleasant stimulus (i.e., pain) or as an operant response that has the effect of lessening the intensity of the noxious stimulus (e.g., rubbing a sore back). However, according to Fordyce, these behaviors will also elicit responses from others in the social environment that may reinforce their occurrence. Typical responses to pain behavior include expression of concern and affection, and the release from onerous responsibilities. Thus, what began as a respondent behavior to a noxious internal stimulus may quickly evolve into an interpersonal response repertoire under the control of complex external contingencies.

Operant Therapy

The operant therapy of chronic pain patients usually takes place in a hospital setting and includes (1) the identification and removal of environmental contingencies that may be reinforcing pain behaviors, (2) social reinforcement (attention and praise) for nonpain behaviors, (3) a gradual increase in tolerance for physical activity, and (4) the gradual decrease in, and perhaps the eventual elimination of, reliance on narcotic analgesics and other pain medications. The operant approach does not necessarily involve a group therapy component, although a convincing rationale for adopting this modality could easily be made. The group could serve as an important resource for the identification of pain behaviors and the environmental circumstances of which they are a function. In addition, the role of peers in suggesting alternative nonpain behaviors would seem to hold more integrity than if suggestions came from a therapist that has not struggled with the problem of chronic pain.

One addition to the operant approach that has not received enough attention is the possibility of training family members to act as behavior modifiers in the home environment.

Cairns and Pasino (1977) demonstrated that once the patient leaves the hospital setting they often relapse to pretreatment activity levels. The possibility of the systematic inclusion of family members in the treatment program is something that Fordyce (1976) suggested in order to promote generalization to the home environment. However, very little work has appeared in this area to date.

Cognitive-Behavioral Model

The cognitive-behavioral model views the chronic pain dilemma as the result of a combination of maladaptive belief systems and thought patterns on the one hand and the lack of more adaptive behavioral skills on the other hand. As outlined by Kerns, Turk, and Holzman (1983), the chronic pain sufferer views his or her pain only in purely physical terms. This conceptualization of the pain problem, which fails to acknowledge psychological contributions, promotes a viewpoint of the self as helpless and at the mercy of uncontrollable physical forces.

As an outgrowth of the basic premise that holds that the pain problem is outside of the individual's control, a number of maladaptive thought patterns and self-statements emerge. A representative sample includes "I can't tolerate this anymore," "This is too much for me," "When will it ever end," and so on. According to a cognitive behavioral orientation, these types of self-defeating thoughts will result in negative affective/motivational states. Ultimately, the maladaptive cognitive and affective events will increase the likelihood of the individual relinquishing his or her role as a healthy and productive member of society and accepting the sick role consistent with a chronic pain syndrome.

Cognitive-Behavior Therapy

Turk, Meichenbaum, and Genest (1983) developed a very comprehensive and thoroughly described cognitive-behavioral intervention for chronic pain. The treatment can essentially be divided into three phases; however, there is much overlap between phases. The initial phase is considered to be a conceptual phase, during which patients are helped to develop new perspectives for viewing their pain experience. This approach emphasizes the often overlooked influence of thoughts and feelings on the perceptions of pain and suffering.

In the second phase, patients are instructed in a number of behavioral and cognitive coping strategies (e.g., relaxation training, imagery, attention diversion). In addition, they are further instructed in the gate control theory (Melzack, 1973), which serves as the logical conceptualization for focusing on such coping skills.

The third phase of the cognitive-behavioral approach includes role-playing, cognitive rehearsal, and other behavioral exercises (e.g., exposure to noxious stimuli) as a means of practicing, integrating, and consolidating the newly acquired skills. Mastery and self-control over the pain experience are encouraged and reinforced throughout the treatment in order to counteract the typical feelings and attitudes of helplessness and passivity.

In contrast to the operant approach, most of the reported work in cognitive-behavior therapy has utilized a group therapy approach. The group interventions adhere rather closely to all or most of the components presented above. However, the published reports do not typically document the role of factors that are uniquely present and available for utilization in group therapy situations. These factors include the development of group identification, provision of credible feedback from "those who know," group problem-solving, conformity to group norms for pain behavior, imitation of appropriate nonpain behavior, and so forth. A more in-depth rationale for the development of cognitive-behavioral group therapy for chronic pain patients will be provided in a later section.

Transactional Analysis Model

The last major psychological model for the elucidation of the chronic pain syndrome is the transactional analysis model. Sternbach and Rusk (1973) describe the chronic pain patient as living a "pain career." This essentially means that they come to identify themselves as "pain patients" and go about living their lives in fulfillment of that role. The business of fulfilling the role involves the playing of numerous "pain games" that serve interpersonal and societal functions. According to this viewpoint, it is the pain "lifestyle" that must be altered and it may prove as difficult to alter as other chronic behavior patterns (e.g., smoking, obesity, alcoholism).

AN EMPIRICAL REVIEW OF PSYCHOLOGICAL TREATMENTS

The evaluation literature on group therapies for chronic benign pain includes investigations that range from clinical/anecdotal reports to the completely randomized control group design. For the most part, the literature from the psychosomatic, transactional analysis, family systems, and counseling/education models are comprised of descriptive reports and case studies. Similarly, reports concerning the efficacy of self-help groups are primarily descriptive in nature due to the difficulty in systematizing the procedures and developing target variables for assessment.

One of the few experimental studies of self-help groups was conducted by Lorig, Lubeck, Kraines, Selznick, and Holman (1985), who utilized a randomized design to compare a self-help group intervention with a no-treatment control condition for rheumatoid arthritis patients. The experimental group achieved significant improvements in knowledge, lessened pain, and nonpain behaviors, and the changes remained significant relative to the control group as well as relative to pretreatment levels at 20-month follow-up. The authors report that the intervention was led by a trained layperson and that it was largely based on behavioral principles as well as educational principles, but they do not provide an adequate description of the procedure. Although the results are encouraging, it is difficult to assess whether this intervention utilizes a true self-help approach as described earlier, and therefore it may not truly represent the self-help philosophy.

At this point it may be best to say that with the exception of operant conditioning and cognitive-behavioral treatments, most approaches have not been subjected to a rigorous evaluation of effectiveness. Therefore, their efficacy in the treatment of chronic benign pain, whether presented as individual or group therapy, is still an open question.

The greatest body of empirical research exists in the areas of operant conditioning and cognitive-behavioral treatments or variants thereof. The pure operant approach received early support from the work of Fordyce and colleagues (Fordyce, Fowler, & DeLateur, 1968; Fordyce, Fowler, Lehmann, DeLateur, Sand, & Trieschmann, 1973), with further support provided by Anderson, Cole, Gullickson, Hudgens, and Roberts (1977). These studies reported significant changes in such outcome variables as pain intensity, pain medication usage, and pain interference with daily activities. However, notable methodologic limitations, including the lack of adequate control or comparison groups, make the evaluation of these results problematic. In addition, a true assessment of the operant approach in a group format or a format including family members has yet to be completed.

Recently, treatment approaches employing a combination of behavioral and cognitive-behavioral approaches have incorporated substantially improved research methodology and have been performed in the context of group therapy. Turner (1982) compared a group cognitive-behavioral intervention (including relaxation, guided imagery, and positive self-coping statements) with a group relaxation therapy program and two waiting-list/attention control conditions in the treatment of patients with low-back pain. Following treatment, those treated in a cognitive-behavioral group demonstrated reduced pain perception, medication usage, interference with daily activities, and anxiety relative to the relaxation and control groups. These results held up at 1-month follow-up. This study represents the most methodologically sophisticated evaluation of a group-administered intervention to date. In addition to the multiple control conditions in this study, the groups were balanced for age, sex, and employment status.

Randich (1982) treated groups of arthritis patients using a cognitive-behavioral intervention and compared the results with those obtained with a support group and waiting-list control group. All patients reported significant reductions in pain levels at the end of treatment and at 8-week follow-up. However, only the cognitive-behavioral group reported a significant increase in activity level.

More recently, Cohen, Heinrich, Naliboff, Collins, and Bonebakker (1983) compared the effectiveness of a behavior therapy intervention with conventional physical therapy utilizing a randomized control group design. The behavior therapy group included such things as instruction in the role of cognitive-perceptual factors in the experience of pain, the development of the attitude of self-control, relaxation training, imagery, positive self-talk, goal-setting, and assertiveness training. At 10-week follow-up both interventions resulted in patient reports of lessened pain intensity and perception, less psychological distress, and less interference with daily activities. There were few treatment-specific differences.

In a subsequent study of the same type, Heinrich, Cohen, Naliboff, Collins, and Bonebakker (1985) utilized a 6-month follow-up period and included a slightly larger treatment sample. Physical therapy was found to increase patient's low-back control and back protection skills, but these skills were lost at 6-month follow-up. Behavior therapy showed a slight advantage over physical therapy in reducing patients' psychological distress, and this held up at 6-month follow-up. However, physical therapy also resulted in significant improvements in psychological distress compared with pretreatment levels. Both groups reported significant decreases in pain perception, and these results held up at follow-up.

To our knowledge, only one study has attempted to evaluate the benefits of including spouses in a group therapy intervention for chronic pain patients. Moore and Chaney (1985) assigned patients to couples group treatment, patient-only group treatment, or waiting-list control. The two active treatments were cognitive-behavioral in orientation and were similar to the treatment protocol outlined by Turk, Meichenbaum, and Genest (1983). The couples group treatment also included the discussion of operant components of chronic pain, as suggested by Fordyce (1976), and suggestions for changing spousal interaction patterns that may have been maintaining pain behaviors. The results showed significant changes for both active treatment groups, and these changes were maintained at 3- and 6-month follow-up. However, spouse involvement led to no additional effects.

In conclusion, it appears that the behavioral and cognitive-behavioral group treatments, as well as physical therapy, offer promise for the treatment of chronic pain syndromes. It appears likely that they are superior to no-treatment or single-faceted treatments such as relaxation training alone. Further analysis of the individual components of these multimodal interventions seems indicated in order to identify the essential procedures responsible for effectiveness. Also, group process variables and structural variables, including group membership and leadership characteristics, should be investigated in order to establish their role in treatment outcome.

PAIN MANAGEMENT PROGRAM AT THE WEST HAVEN VA MEDICAL CENTER

The Pain Management Program (PMP) is a comprehensive center for the study of chronic pain and for the evaluation and rehabilitation of chronic pain patients. The program is interdisciplinary in structure and function and is built on the cooperative efforts of the Psychology, Rehabilitation Medicine, Neurology, Nursing, and Psychiatry Services. Clinically, the program emphasizes a biopsychosocial model in providing a comprehensive assessment of each patient and in the collaborative development of individually tailored and goal-oriented plans for rehabilitation. Empirical support for its clinical efficacy has been published. Data demonstrate significant improvements in functional activity and reductions in perceived pain, affective distress, dependency, and overall use of the health care system among program participants (Kerns, Turk, Holzman, & Rudy, 1986).

The PMP draws heavily on a cognitive-behavioral perspective of pain and pain management (Turk, Meichenbaum, & Genest, 1983). As already noted, this perspective emphasizes the central role of patients' idiosyncratic cognitions regarding their pain, including attributions of causality and expectations of recovery, perceptions of self-control, and beliefs about the role of psychological and social factors in their experience of pain. Thus, the primary goal of the program is to collaborate with patients in developing valid attributions and more realistic expectations, improved cognitive coping and problem-solving skills and confidence, and generally, to develop overarching perceptions of personal mastery, control, and resourcefulness.

Also consistent with the cognitive-behavioral perspective is the broad-spectrum approach to evaluating the full impact of pain on the patients' lives. In this regard, the patients' associated social, financial, vocational, and marital problems are considered to be important targets for intervention. Other aspects of patients' affective distress and disability are also considered. Finally, the patients' ways of using health-care resources are also targeted, and specific goals such as decreased reliance on doctors, medications, and emergency rooms may be developed.

Given these multiple targets, it is important to note that psychological group intervention is rarely the only rehabilitation activity in which a patient is engaged. Rather, group treatment is most typically offered in the context of multiple concurrent therapeutic efforts.

The development of group therapy programs in the PMP occurred as a natural extension of a cognitive-behavioral perspective on pain management that emphasizes a therapeutic process involving collaborative problem-solving and structured skill training and practice, and goals such as increased socialization, decreased reliance on health-care resources, and long-term self-management. With these functions and goals in mind, two distinct group therapies have been developed. The first is a brief structured cognitive-behavioral treatment group that is offered as one component of an intensive and multidimensional active rehabilitation phase. The second is an open-ended, long-term pain support group that is offered to "graduates" of the initial treatment phase. These groups can be distinguished in terms of a variety of structural and functional variables and are designed with different goals in mind. Each will be discussed separately in the following sections.

Cognitive-Behavioral Treatment Group

This group therapy program was developed as an alternative to analogous individual treatment programs in an attempt to enhance the cost-effectiveness of the PMP. Besides more efficient use of therapists' time, it was thought that the group might facilitate patients' reconceptualization of their pain problem and the development of new coping skills. For example, therapist's goals are to facilitate the mutual sharing of past experiences, group problem-solving, and social reinforcement for adaptive coping efforts that support increased perceptions of self-control. Inclusion in a group was also generally presumed to enhance social skill development and socialization. Disadvantages of using a group approach, such as decreased individual attention, were thought to be outweighed by the potential advantages.

Group membership has typically been limited to four to six patients who had previously completed the comprehensive evaluation and goal-setting phase of the program. Decisions to offer group participation are always made during interdisciplinary discussions that consider personality factors and individual needs. No unequivocal selection criteria are applied, although clinical judgment is used to exclude patients who are considered to be particularly resistant and whose attendance is predicted to be a problem. Once the group has met, no new members are entered regardless of attrition of the original membership.

Therapists for the cognitive-behavioral groups have typically been senior clinicians in the program with group experience and occasionally a trainee who serves as a participant-observer. Consistent with the brief, structured, and goal-oriented focus of the program, the therapists maintain an active leadership role throughout the duration of the group. Therapist control and activity in the group peaks during structured skill training tasks (e.g., relaxation training) and considerably lessens during later sessions in which collaborative group problem-solving is encouraged. Successful groups are those that efficiently manage time and proceed through a series of tasks and goals while maintaining a spirit of active group involvement. Therapist skill in managing these competing objectives is clearly required.

Cognitive-behavioral groups to date have ranged from eight to ten sessions typically lasting 1 ½ hours per week. The therapeutic process has been described by Turk and his colleagues (Turk, Meichenbaum, & Genest, 1983) as being comprised of three interrelated phases: a reconceptualization phase, skills training and acquisition phase, and a skills practice phase. Rather than proceeding sequentially, these phases are conceptually and functionally interdependent and overlapping. For example, relaxation exercises are introduced in the context of presentation of a detailed rationale that emphasizes personal control of psychological processes and the ultimate use of cued relaxation as a coping skill. Home practice is emphasized and reinforced during group discussions of its efficacy, pitfalls to adherence, and the consideration of variations that enhance the personal relevance of the technique. Detailed discussion of the cognitive-behavioral treatment approach is readily available in multiple sources (cf. Turk, Meichenbaum, & Genest, 1983).

Table 7-1 provides an outline of an 8-week structured group cognitive-behavioral treatment program. This protocol serves as an important guideline to therapists, although the therapist maintains considerable flexibility in making decisions regarding relative emphasis in a particular group. The ability of the therapist to address the idiosyncratic beliefs, feelings,

TABLE 7-1

Cognitive-Behavioral Group Treatment Protocol

Group Meeting 1
  Introduction—presentation of a rationale for program
    1. Concomitants of pain experience
    2. Focus on self-control and coping
  Discussion of previous pain experience
    1. Set expectations for points of intervention
  Review of assessment phase
    1. Begin reconceptualization—multiple factors that affect pain experience
    2. Review existing coping strategies
  Review treatment goals
    1. Behavioral contracting—short-term behavioral goal for upcoming week, rationale for "small steps"

Group Meeting 2
  Review progress toward behavioral goal for week
    1. Focus on progress (positive); review problems
    2. Negotiate appropriate goal for next week
  Rationale for relaxation training
    1. Relationship between muscle tension and pain
    2. Review of psychophysiologic data, when appropriate
    3. Learned behavior requiring practice
  Relaxation training
    1. 16-muscle-group progressive muscle relaxation
  Home practice of relaxation
    1. Daily—duration of practice, amount
    2. "Ideal conditions"

Group Meeting 3
  Review progress toward behavioral goal for week
    1. Focus on progress (positive); review problems
    2. Negotiate appropriate goal for next week
  Review home practice of relaxation
    1. Compliance—reinforce practice if not successful
    2. Appropriate practice
    3. Problem-solving around difficulties
  Discussion of alternative modes of relaxation
    1. Multiple functions—decrease tension, distraction
  Relaxation exercise
    1. 16-muscle-group progressive muscle relaxation
  Home practice of relaxation
    1. Review solutions from review of home practice

Group Meeting 4
  Review progress toward goal for week
    1. Focus on progress (positive); review problems
    2. Negotiate appropriate goal for next week

3. Discuss importance of planning activities around limitations and incorporating of rest/relaxation

Review home practice of relaxation—emphasis on distraction

Brief discussion of gate control theory

   1. Distraction/relaxation as way of "closing gate"

   2. Situations that "open gate"

Concept of cognitive control—distractions

   1. Activities and thoughts as examples

Relaxation incorporating imagery

   1. 7-muscle-group progressive muscle relaxation

   2. Patient-generated example of relaxing image

Homework—generate ideas for "opening/closing gate"

Group Meeting 5

Review progress toward goal for week

   1. Discuss importance of working within limitations

Review home practice of relaxation with imagery

Discuss ideas on "opening/closing gate"

Expand on discussion of relationship between thoughts, emotions, activities, and pain experience

   1. Incorporate items from structured assessment

   2. Discussion of coping self-statements

Rehearsal/application of coping self-statements

Relaxation exercise with imagery (7-muscle group progressive muscle relaxation)

Home application of coping self-statements at lower levels of pain

Group Meeting 6

Review progress toward treatment goals

   1. Focus on positives, problem-solving around difficulties

   2. Set goal for upcoming week

Review use of coping self-statements at home

Incorporation of different strategies at different levels of pain—begin problem-solving

Relaxation exercise with imagery

Home application of coping strategies at varying levels of pain

   1. Relaxation/distraction

   2. Imagery

   3. Coping self-statements

   4. Mental activities for attentional control

Group Meeting 7

Review progress toward behavioral goal for week

Review home use of coping strategies

Further problem-solving around use of various coping strategies at varying levels of pain

Discussion of reinforcers of pain behaviors

   1. Medications

   2. Careful discussion of attention-eliciting behaviors and involvement of family members

Group Meeting 8

Review of reconceptualization

   1. Incorporating concrete examples from patient's experience

   2. Use of coping strategies as means of gaining or maintaining control

Problem-solving discussion around continuing problems

Review of progress of goals, formation of future goals

Review of follow-up

   1. Bimonthly "booster" sessions

   2. Posttreatment questionnaires and follow-up questionnaires

   3. Who to contact if necessary

and behaviors of each group participant is critical. At each step of the treatment, the therapist remains vigilant to each patient's understanding of the principle or skill under consideration and facilitates discussions designed to decrease resistance, improve adherence, and reinforce a developing conceptualization of pain as subject to personal mastery and control.

The efficacy of this outpatient cognitive-behavioral group program was first reported by Turk and Kerns (1982). A heterogeneous sample of 15 chronic pain patients were treated in one of three 10-week treatment groups. Evaluations were multidimensional in scope and conducted pre- and posttreatment and at 6 months following treatment. Results revealed significant reductions in pain intensity and measures of interference with productive activity, as well as increases in perceptions of self-control. As a group, patients realized a 47% reduction in the use of analgesic medication at the 6-month follow-up, and a 40% reduction in outpatient clinic visits during that period relative to the 6 months pretreatment.

Long-Term Support Group

The development of an open-ended pain support group within the PMP occurred primarily as a means of supporting "graduates" of a more structured rehabilitation program in their continuing efforts to cope with their chronic pain and disabilities. The group was designed to require a minimum of professional resources while offering continuity of care and professional contact within the broader network of resources available through the PMP and the hospital. It was hypothesized that such a group would enhance patients' continued learning of adaptive coping strategies, reinforce previously learned strategies, and prevent relapse. In addition, the group was designed to be an important social outlet for individuals with a range of socialization deficits. Improved mood was considered a likely outcome, as well. Finally, the group was conceptualized as an opportunity to continually reevaluate the functioning of the participants and to identify signs of recidivism and new problems in a timely fashion. Additional individual attention has been offered several times to patients during depressive episodes, periods of family crisis, or exacerbation of a degenerative disease underlying the pain problem, among other problems.

Membership of the groups has varied, but efforts have been made to maintain the active attendance of approximately 10 individuals. New members are introduced when previous participants have generally terminated their involvement. For example, one group that has been ongoing for 15 months typically has an attendance ranging from eight to ten from a total membership of fifteen. A core group of seven members rarely miss a meeting. Membership in the group is quite heterogeneous with regard to a number of factors. Among the group are several women and minorities, and the ages range from 40 to 80. The etiologies for the pain complaints include migraine headache, low-back pain secondary to degenerative disc disease, rheumatoid arthritis, and diabetic peripheral neuropathy, among others. Several are recovering alcoholics, and several have a history of major depressive disorder. All have previously participated in either individual or group cognitive-behavioral treatment for chronic pain, although their level of sophistication in regard to a self-management approach to pain and the degree to which they continue to practice active coping skills previously learned varies greatly among the members.

In contrast to the structured protocol for the cognitive-behavioral treatment group, the support group remains relatively unstructured. The functions and goals fluctuate with the interests of the group members and are rarely explicitly stated. Occasionally group members may ask for specific skill enhancement training, but more typically the group maintains a more casual and informal style of interacting. The degree to which the group supports open and frank discussions of members' problems of daily living also varies. Factors that determine the function and goals of the group have not been empirically evaluated. Experience suggests that a number of variables are probably contributory, namely, the size and membership of the group, the clinical skill and theoretical perspective of the therapist, the level of group cohesion, and the length of time the group has met.

Certainly the level of therapist involvement or activity in the support group is dramatically less than in a more structured treatment group. In fact, although the therapist is typically identified as the group leader, even this position has been challenged in older, more cohesive groups. The therapist is encouraged to respond openly to questions and to provide specific information to the group, even in a relatively didactic manner, when requested. However, the predominant role of the therapist is not a psychoeducational one. Instead, the therapist is encouraged to assume the role of group facilitator, encouraging group discussion and problem-solving.

The integrity of the cognitive-behavioral perspective on pain management is a primary goal of the therapist. Participants are continually cued to apply a problem-solving perspective to the discussion of problems and concerns. A Socratic style of interacting that challenges statements of helplessness and low problem-solving skill and confidence is particularly encouraged. In addition, the therapist encourages reporting on continued personal goal-directed activities. Although homework is not explicitly assigned, contingency "contracting" with the other group members for activities during the next week is common. In each of these activities and others, the therapist serves as an important model of consistent application of the cognitive-behavioral perspective, cued problem-solving, and social reinforcement for appropriate behavior.

To date, there have been no reports on the efficacy of this group approach or similar efforts. In particular, an assessment of the overall cost-effectiveness of the approach and an evaluation of specific outcomes is clearly indicated. Comparison with the more typical use of intermittent "booster" sessions as a means of relapse prevention and comparison with self-help group approaches are two future objectives.

SUMMARY AND CONCLUSIONS

It would be a gross misstatement if we were to conclude this chapter on a particularly optimistic note. Just as we began this chapter, we must in the end emphasize the immature state of our scientific understanding of pain, the imprecision of our measurement technology, and the inadequacy of modern-day treatment approaches. With specific reference to group treatment efforts, there are few empirical data to offer encouragement despite the proliferation and widespread clinical and anecdotal beliefs regarding their efficacy.

This rather discouraging state of affairs, however, has recently given way to the emergence of increasingly integrative conceptual models of pain and the development of interdisciplinary pain rehabilitation programs. As Wilbert Fordyce recently noted during an address to the Division of Rehabilitation Psychology at the American Psychological Association meeting, the rehabilitation of chronic pain patients demands that attention be shifted from pain as the primary target of intervention to the problems of suffering and disability experienced by these patients (Fordyce, 1988). In so doing Fordyce encourages an important discrimination of pain as a sensory-perceptual phenomenon, acute pain as a frequent direct response to trauma and nociceptive stimulation, and chronic pain as a behavioral syndrome maintained by multiple factors and impacting broadly on the patient and his or her social environment. Such a perspective clearly and importantly seems to build on the clinical implications of Melzack and Wall's gate control theory and opens the door for continued exploration of the efficacy of psychosocial interventions, in addition to medical efforts targeting primarily pain relief.

It is in this context that we have offered a review of psychological models of pain and its treatment, an overview of general and specific models of group treatment approaches, and a few details of the operation of the Pain Management Program at our facility. It is hoped that these efforts will enhance the decision-making of our readers as they consider the implementation of similar clinical programs and will encourage continued empirical evaluation of such efforts.

REFERENCES

Anderson, T. P., Cole, T. M., Gullickson, G., Hudgens, A., & Roberts, A. H. (1977). Behavior modification of chronic pain: A treatment program by a multidisciplinary team. *Journal of Clinical Orthopedics, 129*, 96–100.

Beals, R. K., & Hickman, N. W. (1972). Industrial injuries of back and extremities: Comprehensive evaluation—an aid in prognosis and management. *Journal of Bone and Joint Surgery, 54*, 1593–1611.

Black, R. G. (1975). The chronic pain syndrome. *Surgical Clinics of North America, 55*, 999–1011.

Blumer, D., & Heilbronn, M. (1982) Chronic pain as a variant of depressive disease: The pain-prone disorder. *Journal of Nervous and Mental Disease, 170*, 381–406.

Bonica, J. J. (1980). Pain research and therapy: Past and current status and future needs. In L. Ng and J. J. Bonica (Eds.), *Pain, discomfort, and humanitarian care* (pp. 1–46). New York: Elsevier.

Bonica, J. J. (1981). Preface. In L. K. Y. Ng (Eds.), *New approaches to the treatment of chronic pain* (pp. vii–x). Rockville, MD: Alcohol, Drug Abuse, and Mental Health Administration.

Cairns, D., Thomas, L., Mooney, V., & Pace, J. B. (1976). A comprehensive treatment approach to chronic low back pain. *Pain, 2*, 301–308.

Cairnes, D., & Pasino, J. A. (1977). Comparison of verbal reinforcement and feedback in the operant treatment of disability due to chronic low back pain. *Behavior Therapy, 8*, 621–630.

Crue, B. L., & Carregal, E. J. (1975). Pain begins in the dorsal horn with a proposed classification of the primary sensus. In B. L. Crue (Ed.), *Pain: Research and treatment*. New York: Academic Press.

Cohen, M. J., Heinrich, R. L., Naliboff, B. D., Collins, G. A., & Bonebakker, A. D. (1983). Group outpatient physical and behavioral therapy for chronic low back pain. *Journal of Clinical Psychology, 39*, 326–333.

Engel, G. L. (1959). "Psychogenic" pain and the pain-prone patient. *American Journal of Medicine, 26*, 899–918.

Flor, H., & Turk, D. C. (1984). Etiological theories and treatments for chronic low back pain: I. Somatic factors. *Pain, 19*, 105v121.

Fordyce, W. E. (1976). *Behavioral methods for chronic pain and illness*. St. Louis, MO: CV Mosby.

Fordyce, W. E. (1988). Pain and suffering: A reappraisal. *American Psychologist, 43*, 276–283.

Fordyce, W. E., Fowler, R. S., & DeLateur, B. (1968). An application of behavior modification technique to a problem to chronic pain. *Behavior Research and Therapy, 6*, 105–107.

Fordyce, W. E., Fowler, R. S., Jr., Lehmann, J. F., DeLateur, B. J., Sand, P. L., & Trieschmann, R. B. (1973). Operant conditioning in the treatment of chronic pain. *Archives of Physical Medicine and Rehabilitations, 54*, 399–408.

Gentry, W. D., & Owens, D. (1986). Pain groups. In A. D. Holzman & D. C. Turk (Eds.), *Pain management: A handbook of psychological treatment approaches*. New York: Pergamon.

Gershon, S. (1986). Chronic pain: Hypothesized mechanism and rationale for treatment. *Neuropsychobiology, 15*, 22–27.

Gluck, M. (1980). Group therapy in a pain management program. *Journal of Psychiatric Nursing, 18,* 21–25.

Heinrich, R. L., Cohen, J. C., Naliboff, B. D., Collins, G. A., & Bonebakker, A. D. (1985). Comparing physical and behavior therapy for chronic low back pain on physical abilities, psychological distress, and patient's perceptions. *Journal of Behavioral Medicine, 8,* 61–78.

Hendler, N. (1982). The anatomy and psychopharmacology of chronic pain. *Journal of Clinical Psychiatry, 43,* 15–20.

Hendler, N., Viernstein, M., Shallenberger, C., & Long, D. (1981). Group therapy with chronic pain patients. *Psychosomatics, 22,* 333–340.

Henkle, C. (1975). Social group work as a treatment modality for hospitalized people with rheumatoid arthritis. *Rehabilitation Literature, 36,* 334–341.

Holzman, A. D., & Turk, D. C. (1986). *Pain management: A handbook of psychological approaches.* New York: Pergamon.

Kashima, K. J., & McCreary, C. P. (1987, August). *Sex differences in chronic low back pain patients.* Paper presented at the annual meeting of the American Psychological Association, New York.

Katon, W., Egan, K., & Miller, D. (1985). Chronic pain: Lifetime psychiatric diagnosis and family history. *American Journal of Psychiatry, 142,* 1156–1160.

Kerns, R. D., & Haythornthwaite, J. (in press). Depression among chronic pain patients: Cognitive-behavioral analysis and effect on rehabilitation. *Journal of Consulting and Clinical Psychology.*

Kerns, R. D., Haythornthwaite, J., & Giller E. (1987, August). *Cognitive mediators of the relationship between chronic pain and depression.* Paper presented at the annual meeting of the American Psychological Association, New York.

Kerns, R. D., & Turk, D. C. (1983). Depression and chronic pain: The mediating role of the spouse. *Journal of Marriage and the Family, 46,* 845–852.

Kerns, R. D., Turk, D. C., & Holzman, A. D. (1983). Psychological treatment for chronic pain: A selective review. *Clinical Psychological Review, 3,* 15–26.

Kerns, R. D., Turk, D. C., Holzman, A. D., & Rudy, T. C. (1986). Comparison of cognitive-behavioral and behavioral approaches to the outpatient treatment of chronic pain. *Clinical Journal of Pain, 1,* 195–203.

La Freniere, J.G. (1979). *The low back patient.* New York: Masson.

Lindsay, P. G., & Wyckoff, M. (1981). The depression-pain syndrome and its response to antidepressants. *Psychosomatics, 22,* 571–577.

Lorig, K., Lubeck, D., Kraines, R. G., Selznik, M., & Holman, H. (1985). Outcomes of self-help education for patients with arthritis. *Arthritis and Rheumatism, 28,* 680–685.

Melzack, R. (1973). *The puzzle of pain.* New York: Basic Books.

Melzack, R., & Wall, P. D. (1965). Pain mechanisms: A new theory. *Science, 50,* 971–979.

Minuchin, S. (1974). *Families and family therapy.* Boston: Harvard University Press.

Moore, J. E., & Chaney, E. F. (1985). Outpatient group treatment of chronic pain: Effects of spouse involvement. *Journal of Counsulting and Clinical Psychology, 53,* 326–334.

Mountcastle, V. B. (1974). Pain and temperature sensibilities. In V. B. Mountcastle (Ed.), *Medical physiology.* St. Louis, MO: Mosby.

Newman, R. I., Seres, J. L., Yospe, L. P., & Garlington, B. (1978). Multidisciplinary treatment of chronic pain: Long-term follow-up of low-back pain patients. *Pain, 4,* 283–292.

National Institutes of Health. (1986). An integrative approach to the management of pain. *Connecticut Medicine, 50,* 677–682.

Pinsky, J. J. (1978). Chronic, intractable, benign pain: A syndrome and its treatment with intensive short-term group psychotherapy. *Journal of Human Stress, 4,* 17–21.

Randich, S. R. (1982). *Evaluation of stress inoculation training as a pain management program for rheumatoid arthritis.* Unpublished doctoral dissertation, Washington University, St. Louis, MO.

Romano, J. M., & Turner, J. A. (1985). Chronic pain and depression: Does the evidence support a relationship? *Psychological Bulletin, 97,* 18–34.

Schwartz, L., Marcon, R., & Condon, R. (1978). Multidisciplinary group therapy for rheumatoid arthritis. *Psychosomatics, 19,* 289–293.

Schaffer, C. B., Donlon, P. T., & Bittle, R. M. (1980). Chronic pain and depression: A clinical family history survey. *American Journal of Psychiatry, 137,* 118–120.

Sifneos, P., Apfel-Savitz, R., & Frankel, F. (1977). The phenomenon of "alexithymia." *Psychotherapy and Psychosomatics, 28,* 47-57.

Sternbach, R. A. (1968). *Pain: A psychophysiological analysis.* New York: Academic Press.

Sternbach, R. A. (1974). *Pain patients: Traits and treatment.* New York: Academic Press.

Sternbach, R. A., & Rusk, T. N. (1973). Alternatives to the pain career. *Psychotherapy: Theory, Research, and Practice, 10,* 321–324.

Stone, C. E. (1984). The lifetime economic costs of rheumatoid arthritis. *The Journal of Rheumatology, 11,* 819–827.

Szasz, T. (1968). The psychology of persistent pain: A portrait of l'homme douloureux. In A. Soulairac, J. Cahn, & J. Carpenter (Eds.), *Pain.* (pp. 93–113). New York: Academic Press.

Toomey, T. C., Ghia, J. N., Mao, W., & Gregg J. M. (1977). Acupuncture and chronic pain mechanisms: The moderating effects of affect, personality, and stress on response to treatment. *Pain, 3,* 137–145.

Turk, D. C., & Kerns, R. D. (1982, March). *Efficacy of a cognitive-behavioral group outpatients approach for the treatment of chronic pain.* Paper presented at the annual meeting of the Society of Behavioral Medicine, Chicago.

Turk, D. C., Meichenbaum, D., & Genest, M. (1983). *Pain and behavioral medicine: A cognitive-behavioral perspective.* New York: Guilford.

Turk, D. C., & Rudy, T. E. (1986). Assessment of cognitive factors in chronic pain: A worthwhile enterprise? *Journal of consulting and Clinical Psychology, 54,* 760–768.

Turner, J. A. (1982). Comparison of group progressive relaxation and cognitive-behavioral group therapy for chronic low back pain. *Journal of Consulting and Clinical Psychology, 50,* 757–765.

Udelman, H. D., & Udelman, D. L. (1977). Team therapy in a rheumatology unit. *Psychosomatics, 12,* 42–46.

Webb, P. (1982). Back to self care? *Physiotherapy, 68,* 295–297.

White, J. C., & Sweet, W. H. (1969). *Pain and the neurosurgeon: A forty-year experience.* Springfield, IL: Charles C. Thomas.

MICHAEL C. HUGHES
LAUREN K. COHN

8
Group Therapy with Chronically Ill Children

Chronic physical illness and handicapping conditions afflict 6 to 12% of school-age children and adolescents, according to epidemiologic studies (Pless & Pinkerton, 1975; Pless & Roghmann, 1971; Rutter, Tizard, Yule, Graham, & Whitmore, 1977). Although many adapt to their physical limitations quite successfully, others live with persistent psychological, social, and academic handicaps that are far greater than the biologic sequelae of their illness. This population of children is steadily increasing since advances in modern medicine are improving survival rates and limiting the extent of physical disability. As a result, attention needs to be paid to the special needs of this population, children who face unique threats to their adaptation and development.

Group treatment with chronically ill adults has long been demonstrated successful (Pratt, 1907). The numbers of self-help and peer support groups for chronic physical conditions are increasing markedly. Psychotherapy groups have also long been established as useful with this population, although this treatment modality remains underutilized. However, group work with chronically ill children has received even less attention and application. Nevertheless, there is evidence that group therapy offers unique therapeutic opportunities for this group of children and adolescents, opportunities that are not available in other forms of teatment and rehabilitation (Hughes, 1982; Rie, Boverman, Grossman, & Ozua, 1968).

Group therapy for hospitalized children at the time and place of physical and emotional crisis can provide a calm, soothing "holding environment" (Winnicott, 1965). Comfort, support, and clarification—emotional first-aid—can help children cope with adversity that often overwhelms them. They must face not only the realistic threats posed by illness, separation from family, and medical procedures and treatments, but also the fears and fantasies they experience in response to their condition. A supportive educational approach—to clarify realities of past experience and anticipate the future course of illness and treatment is particularly useful for children, whose fears and fantasies may be quite different and more threatening than the realities of illness and its consequences.

A group experience with other chronically ill children provides an opportunity to observe others with similar problems and attenuates feelings of being singled out. These fellow sufferers can accept that their illness, pain, fears, and fantasies are not unique to them but can be understood and shared with others; children learn that they are not different or deviant, and they can redefine themselves as normal by standards that are relevant to them. The opportunities for social interaction and constructive peer relationships are particularly important for this group of children, whose problems with self-esteem and the physical limitations of their illnesses often limit their social experiences and development. Outlets for active verbal and social expression are important in view of the enforced passivity and compliance that often attend chronic illness and its consequences. The value of developing supportive and meaningful relationships with peers and caretakers cannot be underestimated; with caring, acceptance, affection, pleasure, and gratification, the future becomes less threatening and can be faced with more hope. Children progressively rely on relationships with their peers for the development of ego skills, self-esteem, and mastery; group treatment methods with the chronically ill child can mobilize the developmental potential of group relationships to master special adversity and foster growth. Group work can also reach large numbers of children at risk for subsequent psychosocial and academic handicaps and can identify those in need of additional help (Bayrakal, 1975; Hagberg, 1969; Hughes, 1982).

This chapter will describe the clinical population of children with chronic illness and handicapping conditions and will discuss how group work highlights the commonality of special stresses that they endure and possible constructive adaptations. Particular emphasis will be placed on the needs and concerns of chronically ill children during the hospitalization period. Group work during this time of intensified stress is often particularly helpful. A special focus is placed on how the group process fosters mobilization of constructive potentials within the children themselves, their peer group, their families, and the hospital milieu for new relationships, mastery understanding, and emotional growth. Therapeutic techniques, countertransference issues, and limitations of group work with this population will also be discussed. Clinical illustrations are drawn from the senior author's experience with psychodynamically oriented group meetings with children and adolescents during their hospitalization on the pediatric convalescent ward at the Children's Hospital Medical Center in Boston (Hughes, 1982).

Prior clinical and research studies bearing on these issues will be discussed. Unfortunately, published work in this area is meager. A search of the literature between 1966 and 1987 produced few articles dealing specifically with group treatment for children with chronic physical health problems, in or out of the hospital. These works will be discussed, as well as models of group interventions that have been employed by the senior author.

CHRONIC ILLNESS IN CHILDREN

> Long-term or chronic illness refers to a condition with a protracted course which can be progressive or fatal, or may be associated with a relatively normal life-span, despite impaired physical or mental functioning. Such a disease frequently shows periods of acute exacerbation requiring intensive medical attention (Mattsson, 1972, p. 801).

The prolonged and sometimes life-threatening nature of these illnesses interferes with the child's physical and emotional growth and development. By comparison, acute short-term nonlife-threatening illnesses are of limited duration, so the resultant physical pain, dysfunction, and emotional upset are circumscribed and usually do not interfere with the child's developmental course.

The most common chronic conditions for children under the age of 18 are asthma and other allergic disorders, sensory disorders affecting vision and hearing, and nervous disorders (particularly epilepsy and cerebral palsy), as well as cardiac, orthopedic, metabolic, and other illnesses. The numbers of children (up to age 18) with some kind of chronic condition are very large. When conditions such as mental illness, visual and hearing impairments, mental retardation, speech problems, and learning disorders are considered in conjunction with chronic physical problems, it is estimated that 30 to 40% of children have at least one kind of chronic disability (Mattsson, 1972). However, the numbers of children afflicted by the more serious chronic illnesses of physical origin are reported by British and American epidemiologic surveys to be between 6 and 12% (Pless & Pinkerton, 1975; Pless & Roghmann, 1971; Rutter, Tizzard, Yule, Graham, & Whitmore, 1977).

Modern medicine is now saving the lives of many children who would simply have died in past years, as noted previously. Mortality rates have fallen dramatically for children aged 1 to 14 years; from 870 per 100,000 children in 1900 to 38 per 100,000 children in 1981 (Newacheck, Budetti, & Halfon, 1986; Newacheck, Budetti, & McManus, 1984). Since survival is now possible, many children live with persisting chronic illness and physical limitations. Data from the National Center for Health Statistics indicate that both the number and proportion of children with activity-limiting, chronic health conditions have been increasing for many years. The percentage of children with limitations of activity (e.g., limitations in ability to play and in school attendance) due to chronic illness has increased from 2% in the early 1960s to about 4% in 1981, thus doubling the proportion of children with this kind of handicap (Newacheck, Budetti, & Halfon, 1986).

Life for these children is far different from that of their physically healthy peer group. They face many real and imagined threats in response to their adversity. Hospitalization, which may be frequent and prolonged, results in separations from parents, brothers and sisters, as well as from their friends, familiar surroundings, possessions, activities, and physical outlets. Anxiety, sadness, and depression—in relationship to themes of loss—are commonplace. On hospital admission, the children encounter strangers within an unfamiliar setting with unpredictable events, as well as unusual and often frightening or painful and embarrassing procedures. When their disease process is active, it depletes the children's energy and focuses the attention of children and their caretakers on somatic sensations, bodily complaints, and concerns about physical adequacy and potential permanent damage. The uncertainty of illness and its consequences—which may be life-threatening—is reflected in considerable anxiety about physical injury, damage or disfigurement, fear of the future, and concerns about bodily integrity and death. These children's illnesses limit their activities and set them apart from their healthy peer group. Self-esteem, confidence, and acceptability are developed in school-age children and teenage children through relationships with others, where to be like others and accepted by their peers becomes most important; to be different and not measure up is devastating. Many children with chronic illness struggle with feeling unacceptable, not only by virtue of their illness and its manifest consequences but especially because of their difficulty accepting their own feelings and thoughts in response to their affliction.

Each individual chronic illness brings with it specific signs, symptoms, limitations, and treatment requirements. In specialized care centers, helping professionals also are knowledgeable about the specific conditions and problems that afflict children in their care. It is important to understand the reality of stresses that confront a child growing up with a chronic physical illness. However, as Bergmann and Freud (1965) have noted, a large dichotomy often exists between the practical, factual, and realistic problems and issues that concern parents and caretakers in contrast with the more unrealistic fears, fantasies, and behaviors of the chronically ill child—a gulf that may preclude empathic sharing and supportive relationships and may create exasperations, distress, and misunderstanding. Therefore, it is particularly important for caretakers to understand the child's inner life in response to his or her adversity. Although there are a very large number of chronic physical conditions, there are a greater number of individual responses from each child to his or her condition. Since every child is different, each will need an individualized approach. Nevertheless, group work with these children fosters commonalities that bring them together with others to see that their experiences and responses can be acknowledged, shared, understood, and accepted.

Garrard and Richmond (1963) suggest that, despite the varied nature of chronic handicapping diseases, they can be considered in relationship to their biologic outcome, which emphasizes central psychological problems faced by the child and family. These characteristics, rather than the specific disease entities, often determine the direction of efforts to help with psychological issues. The types of illlness described by these authors include (1) chronic diseases that end fatally or have an uncertain outcome, (2) chronic diseases that become inactive or improve without major biologic residuals, and (3) chronic diseases in which the biologic process remains active or major residual effects continue throughout life.

Cancer, muscular dystrophy, and nephrosis are examples of conditions with uncertain outcome that may be fatal. Adjustment to chronic illness tends to be difficult for patients and their families when the prognosis is uncertain, particularly when the illness involves recurrent threats to survival and the possibility that the child may face lifelong impairment. Adaptation may be easier for the child, family, and helping professionals when the illness has a certain course. Although outcome may be unfortunate, "a definable problem with a definitive end" (Garrard & Richmond, 1963, p. 380) can permit understanding, acceptance, and consistent adaptive mechanisms to be mobilized. When the illness is clearly fatal, a sense of hope in the initial phases is most important for families and children in order to support an active rather than a passive role in relationship to their adversity and to foster task-oriented coping strategies. It is most important for the child, parents, and caretakers to know that they have done everything possible. With the passage of time, the child's physical deterioration helps the parents to see their child's condition with increasing objectivity so that the mourning process may often be accomplished, to a large extent, by the parents even before their child's death. For the dying child, the progressive physical debility is generally associated with apathy, passivity, and resignation. The developmental level of the child is important in understanding their cognitive perception of death; after 9 to 10 years of age the child begins to comprehend the inevitability of death for all living things. Adolescents may often face considerable anxiety in relationship to this experience. The support system for the patient and family is essential here.

Garrard and Richmond (1963) also describe chronic diseases that may become inactive or improve without major biological residuals such as rheumatic fever, rheumatoid arthritis, and bronchial asthma. Biologic management of these conditions is concerned with minimizing residual physical deficits and limitations. The task for professionals concerned with the psychosocial aspects of the illness relates to prevention of residual psychosocial, academic, and emotional disabilities that may persist long after the central illness is gone. Ideally, on physical recovery, a child should be limited no more than the biologic residuals dictate. All too often, however, the active biologic disease process ends without physical handicaps, but the child's adaptation to the active physical illness and to his or her own fears and fantasies in relationship to it are incorporated permanently into the child's character structure as a psychological disability. Such intrapsychic effects may include inhibitions of intellectual potential, limited creativity, restricted means of adaptation and coping, inability to adapt to change, poor self-esteem, rigidity of behavior, and emotional conflict. Psychosocial limitations include altered relationships with parents, unnecessary physical restrictions and enforced passivity and dependency, limited play and social outlets, lack of opportunities for sublimation, and an unnecessarily limited view of future opportunities.

The final type of illness described by Garrard and Richmond (1963) includes those chronic diseases in which the biologic process remains active or major residual effects continue throughout life. Examples of such conditions are diabetes, epilepsy, amputations, and cerebral palsy. Here again, the psychosocial sequelae may result in greater impairment than that resulting from the disease process itself. Adaptation to this type of illness differs from the types of adaptation described earlier. It is not appropriate for the child and his or her parents to work toward a complete static acceptance of the illness. Rather, adaptation should be thought of as an ongoing process. As these conditions continue to exert their effects throughout life, new psychological and social adaptations are required of the child and parents. With each new developmental level, adjustments must be made according to the developmental tasks to be accomplished at that stage. With each new crisis, new adaptations are required, but also, greater understanding and more mature responses are possible. However, as developmental milestones are encountered, unresolved conflicts may be reactivated.

Cancer is one example of a chronic illness with an uncertain, potentially fatal outcome. The physical and psychosocial sequelae of this disease present numerous challenges for the child's adaptation. Children with cancer are often faced with aggressive chemotherapy. The side effects of this treatment can be as distressing and as life-threatening as the illness itself. Baldness, ulcers of the mouth and gastrointestinal tract, nausea, vomiting, and malnutrition are among the common side effects (Travis, 1976). Some forms of cancer necessitate limb amputation. It is interesting to note, however, that some adolescents find this severe disfigurement less distressing than the loss of hair (Zeltzer, LeBaron, & Zeltzer, 1984). Fears of death and separation may be manifested behaviorally through fear of going to sleep or requests to sleep with parents. The young cancer patient often misses school because of ongoing treatment or increased susceptibility to infection (Hockenberry, Herman, Schultz, & Falletta, 1985), resulting in decreased opportunities for peer interactions. Friends may not be permitted to play with the child because parents fear that the disease may be contagious. Peers may ridicule the child because of his or her changed appearance.

Cystic fibrosis is a chronic condition that used to be fatal during childhood. However, improvements in medical and psychosocial care now extend the life expectancy of these children beyond 18 years of age. This illness is characterized by an abnormality in the mucus-secreting glands and sweat glands. Thick, sticky mucus is produced, resulting in impaired function of the lungs and digestive system. Pulmonary complications include a chronic, productive cough, recurrent infections, clubbed fingers and toes, and a barrel-chest configuration. Digestive system dysfunction requires the use of enzyme supplements with each meal and snack. Additionally, the child must endure abdominal cramping, uncontrollable flatus, and foul-smelling bowel movements. Since patients with cystic fibrosis do not receive adequate nutrition from their food intake, they tend to lose weight. Small stature and delayed sexual development are also associated with this disorder (McCracken, 1984; Travis, 1976).

The psychosocial sequelae of cystic fibrosis are numerous. Delayed physical and sexual maturation result in embarrassment, and adolescent patients may tend to withdraw from social interaction. The need for daily pulmonary care and physical therapy further interfere with the patient's opportunities for peer interaction. Peer acceptance may be compromised due to the physical effects of the disease, as well as social isolation through hospitalizations and frequent absences from school. The adolescent struggle toward independence is particularly difficult for cystic fibrosis patients who need regular home care that cannot be performed independently and results in enforced dependency (McCracken, 1984). Adaptation to the chronic condition by the patient and family is a major factor in determining not only the quality but also the duration of life.

Juvenile diabetes is a progressive illness with complications such as blindness, vascular disorders, and heart disease. Diabetes results from a lack of insulin production that prevents the body from using carbohydrates for energy. Medical management of diabetes requires a carefully controlled regimen that includes daily insulin injections, urine and blood testing, dietary planning, and regular exercise. The diabetic child and his or her family must learn to recognize the symptoms of insulin shock (excess insulin and dangerously low blood sugar) and ketoacidosis (extremely high blood sugar and ketones) and must learn how to manage these medical emergencies. Travis (1976) illustrates some of the psychosocial concomitants of juvenile diabetes. Parents administer and then teach the child to be responsible for injections, blood and urine testing, and dietary restrictions. This situation can be especially difficult in the case of very young children who cannot understand the need for the regimen and who may come to view it as punishment. Older children and adolescents feel "different," which may result in lowered self-esteem. The strict regimen required for adequate diabetic control makes it difficult for the adolescent to participate in normal eating such as stopping for a milkshake after school with their peers. Resentment or denial of the illness may lead children to ignore their regimen and to put themselves at risk for serious complications.

The Isle of Wight study (Rutter, Tizard, Yule, Graham, & Whitmore, 1977) and other studies (Pless & Roghmann, 1971) have attempted to determine the incidence of psychiatric disorders among children with chronic physical illness. Estimates indicate that, for children with handicaps not involving the brain, the incidence of psychiatric disorder was about twice that of physically healthy peer groups; however, the rate of psychiatric disorder was much higher among those with definite brain dysfunction or damage such as epilepsy or cerebral palsy. About 1 child in 10 will experience one or more chronic physical illnesses by the age of 15, and about 30% of these children may be expected to be handicapped by secondary social and psychological maladjustment in excess of those anticipated by their physical limitations (Pless & Roghmann, 1971). This group clearly presents a population at risk for significant psychiatric disability.

Children's adaptations to chronic illness and its consequences have been well described by Garrard and Richmond (1963), Solnit (1977), Geist (1979), and others (Bergmann & Freud, 1965; Bullard, 1968; Josselyn, Simon, & Eells, 1955). Mattsson (1972) and Schowalter (1977) have written excellent reviews of the literature, and the senior author has discussed these issues as they present in group work with chronically ill children during their hospitalization (Hughes, 1982). The literature indicates that mental health services, particularly early in the course of prolonged illness, can effect a more constructive adaptation to adversity (Galdston & Hughes, 1972; Geist, 1979; Hughes & Brown, 1980). However, this population of chronically ill children—at risk for psychosocial handicaps—is underserved by mental health professionals. Many of these patients persist for years in seeking medical and physical explanations and treatments to account for their psychic pain; as a consequence, this greatly increases the cost of medical care and compounds physical and emotional problems by failing to address their psychosocial issues (Galdston & Hughes, 1972). The importance of providing psychological care for chronically ill children is illustrated by Walsh (1981), who found that asthmatic children involved in a psychotherapy group reduced acute office visits by an average of 69% over an 18-month period. The senior author (Hughes, 1984) has also discussed children with the complaint of recurrent abdominal pain and has noted that these children frequently undergo extensive medical evaluations and pediatric hospitalizations, as well as prolonged medical and even surgical treatments, although no demonstrable organic etiology can be determined. The presenting psychosocial and family problems go unrecognized and unattended.

RATIONALE FOR GROUP THERAPY WITH CHRONICALLY ILL CHILDREN

Despite developments in the use of group therapy with many different clinical populations, therapeutic group work and peer support groups have been used infrequently for chronically ill children and adolescents. While there are papers on the use of group therapy with acutely ill hospitalized children (Cofer & Nir, 1975; Frank, 1978) and educational groups for children facing hospitalization (Brett, 1983), few authors have specifically addressed group treatment for children with chronic physical illness. The publications that are available provide useful clinical descriptions of group process and therapy techniques; however, few provide solid empirical data regarding the effectiveness of group therapy with this population.

The available literature does describe the clinical effectiveness of group approaches with chronically ill children. For example, Schowalter and Lord (1970) discussed group work with acutely and chronically ill, hospitalized adolescents with particular reference to adaptation to terminal illness and surgery. Using a psychodynamic framework, their goal was to enhance relationships among the adolescents on the hospital ward with one another and with the staff, to encourage questions about being sick and hospitalized, and to educate, support, and inform. Defenses were respected and not confronted. The support of the group was enlisted in dealing with dilemmas. Topics for discussion included such issues as food, ward routine, complaints, and protests; underlying issues involved such questions as who controls and decides, death, helplessness, passivity, denial, and anger. The authors emphasized the importance of a nonthreatening opportunity for patients to meet and get to know one another within a context where adults set aside time to listen and foster positive relationships. The group experience served to reinforce the notion that the staff is concerned and involved. A forum for active participation and discussion is particularly important at a time and circumstance where passivity and regression are often prominent. The group sessions gave the staff an opportunity to handle some disruptive ward behavior and also to inform the staff about the patient milieu, the needs of the individuals and the group

Rie and his colleagues (Rie, Boverman, Grossman, & Ozua, 1968; Rie, Boverman, Ozua, & Grossman, 1964) presented papers with follow-up data on group work with hospitalized, latency-age children with rheumatic fever. Children participated in either educationally oriented group meetings or a psychotherapy group or were assigned to a control group. The education groups were led by a pediatrician and focused on specific information about rheumatic fever. The psychotherapy groups were led by a psychiatrist and provided a forum for the discussion of the children's concerns and fantasies about their illnesses. Pre-and posttreatment data were examined for each group; between-group comparisons were not made. Both experimental groups showed immediate gains in knowledge of the condition, although this increased knowledge was maintained at a significant level at follow-up by only the psychotherapy group. The tutorial group experienced a slight but short-lived initial reduction in anxiety, while the psychotherapy group showed no initial change. Both groups ultimately adapted better to illness and hospitalization than did control subjects who received no group meetings, as evidenced by a decreased tendency to minimize the negative effects of the disease. The authors speculate that the psychotherapy group encouraged active acknowledgment and resolution of concerns regarding the illness and facilitated retention of disease-related information.

Other recent work describes group therapy with a variety of chronically medically ill children, during their hospitalization and in other settings. A hospital-based play program was observed to facilitate children's adjustment to cancer, long-term hospitalization, and impending death (Adams, 1976). Children of varying ages were observed to use the available play materials to express and share anxieties about their illnesses. The group provided socialization and allowed children to use peer relationships to deal with their conflicts. Group therapy has been provided for chronically ill children in their schools. Bayrakal (1975) describes a psychodynamically oriented treatment group for adolescents with muscular dystrophy that was conducted in an educational facility. She reports that, although the group initially resisted active involvement, group members were eventually able to address such concerns as the depression and social isolation that often accompany a physical handicap. On termination, the participants were described by teachers and caregivers as having shown improvement in attitudes and functioning. Williams and Baeker (1983) described a school-based group for elementary students with a variety of chronic illnesses. The goals of the group were to increase the children's knowledge of their disease and those of other group members and to provide a forum for the expression of feelings and peer support. Techniques included descriptions of the illnesses and the required treatment regimens, discussions of family response to the illness, and puppet play to act out situations and feelings about the diseases. At the conclusion of the group, the children were noted to have improved self-esteem and knowledge of their illnesses, as measured by a self-esteem questionnaire and informal observation.

The importance of children's relationships with other children is discussed by Redl (1959), who notes that at certain times in development it is more important to bring the child's peer group into focus than other relationships, even parents. Consideration of the peer group provides a framework for the understanding of behavior, code of values, aspirations, or views of one's self or others. Redl's concept of the "life space interview"—a therapeutic intervention at the time of special stress within the ongoing life situation—is also particularly relevant for understanding group work with chronically ill children, in or out of the hospital. Traditional psychotherapy deals with children in an office setting, removed in time and circumstance from the experience of their problems. The life space interview allows for an opportunity for therapeutic intervention at the time and place of stress, when ego defenses are often overwhelmed and adaptation may be limited or inadequate. Interventions at that point can offer additional strength and support in facing adversity and can foster more realistic attempts to cope, before conflicts become internalized and inappropriate defenses become ossified.

GROUP THERAPY EXPERIENCE

Setting

For more than 10 years the senior author, a child and adolescent psychiatrist, worked on the psychiatric consultation liaison service at the Children's Hospital Medical Center in Boston, a pediatric teaching hospital for the Harvard Medical School. He provided patient evaluations as well as consultation to physicians and other caretakers for children and teenagers whose physical illness or somatic complaints were accompanied by psychosocial difficulties. Within the hospital was an extended care facility that housed children of diverse socioeconomic and ethnic backgrounds, all of whom suffered with a chronic physical condition. Diagnoses primarily included rheumatic fever and rheumatoid arthritis, orthopedic and neurologic problems, inflammatory bowel diseases such as ulcerative colitis and regional enteritis, asthma and other chronic respiratory problems, and bleeding disorders. Psychiatric conditions included conversion reactions, anorexia nervosa, and autoaggressive behavior. Children with acute illnesses, surgical problems, and terminal conditions were hospitalized elsewhere. The average age was about 10 years, with most of the children of elementary or junior-high school age. The usual length of stay in the hospital was 1 to 3 months.

Work on this ward allowed the senior author to see many of the patients and their families as a psychiatric consultant, to participate in ward meetings each week with the hospital staff, and to consult and collaborate with physicians and other ward personnel. In addition, he ran psychodynamically oriented group meetings twice a week for all the children to participate. This experience provided an opportunity to understand the children's day-to-day behavior, reactions, and preoccupations in light of the particular stresses they faced. With continued observation of the children's daily interactions came a progressive appreciation for the constructive adaptations that could be made as a function of their shared experiences and life together in the hospital. The hospital was charged with taking care of the children's physical illnesses; however, the children were also in need of day-to-day caretaking and emotional support in coping with their hardships. The experience of conducting these group meetings will be described to highlight application of group therapy to this population.

Group Methods and Clinical Issues

Group sessions were held in the playroom of the children's hospital ward for 1 hour twice a week. Eight to 15 children were present for the meetings and most attended 10 to 18 sessions during their hospital stay. Meetings were led by the senior author, who was assisted by a female psychiatric nurse for the first year and a female special education teacher for the second year. About 180 children were seen during the 2 years of the group meetings. Children joined the group on hospital admission and left with hospital discharge. When warranted, some children were also seen individually for psychiatric assessment and sometimes for individual psychotherapy. Children were told that the meetings were for them to get to know one another and to ask questions if they wished. They were expected to be out of bed and fully dressed, if their medical condition permitted, and in wheelchairs or on stretchers if necessary. Those on strict bed rest did not attend until permitted by their physical condition. Expectations for group behavior and function were clarified during the meetings; talking and listening were emphasized, and opportunities for eating and drawing were provided. Children were expected to sit together around a table and were provided with cookies, crayons, and paper; in actuality, they sat at various locations around the room and were allowed to come and go freely, which they sometimes did. Differences between expectations and behavior constituted issues for the group meetings.

> A 6-year-old boy with severe eczema became upset over sharing the group leaders' attention during his first group session. He interrupted the group and attracted attention to himself by crumbling up his cookies and throwing them on the floor. As he encountered disapproving stares, he said quickly, "Don't blame me I don't know what to do yet. I just got here." No direct intervention was necessary from the group leaders, since the responses of his peers established clear limits; however, the group leaders clarified that the meeting was for all the children to get to know one another, to get used to one another, and that the process took some time. Clarifying what was expected behavior within the group was very important for this boy, not

only in mastering his experience in the group but also in determining some structure and expectation for his future since the unpredictable nature of his illness and several prior hospitalizations caused him to view his future with considerable trepidation.

On hospital admission, separation concerns are the most prominent issues, particularly for preschool-aged children. Illness and its possible consequences and causes especially threaten school-age and teenage children. As they contain their initial distress, children then deal with the unfamiliar and often frightening aspects of life in the hospital. Difficulties are apparent early and seem to be most troublesome for younger children, those receiving inadequate parental support, and those with emotional problems that antedate hospitalization. Children are often unwilling or unable to become actively involved. For some, active illness leads to a depletion of energy and focuses attention on somatic processes; for most, loneliness and the real or imagined threats experienced in response to their adversity leave little available energy to establish new relationships. Psychiatric symptoms are usually transient, recurring at times of intensified stress, but they may persist. Symptomatic behaviors include anxiety reactions, depression, somatization, poor impulse control, eating and sleep disturbances, learning inhibitions, phobias, obsessions and tics, withdrawal and passivity, rigid self-control or obstinence and exaggerated independence, and a variety of dependent and regressive manifestations.

While the group meeting was in progress, a 6-year-old girl was being admitted to the ward and was heard crying down the hall. The attention of all of us was drawn to the cry. I wondered what the trouble might be. An unhappy 8-year-old boy, still new to the hospital, quickly said that she was "homesick." Another child wondered if the girl's parents could find her in the hospital. A teenaged girl wondered if anyone was with her. An 8-year-old girl, who had left the meeting when the cry began, reentered to say a nurse was talking with the girl. The crying had stopped. I wondered if anyone in the group missed their parents. A 14-year-old girl with ulcerative colitis angrily retorted, "You make kids worry. It's better not to think about your mother." An 11-year-old boy with rheumatic fever, confined to a wheelchair, added "The only people who really care about you are your mother and father." The discussion then included a number of complaints about nurses, doctors, and "rotten food." Many of the drawings from this meeting were of angry monsters with sharp teeth and prominent stomachs. The anxiety of the group, initially apparent during the crying of the new girl, became replaced by mutual expressions of loneliness, boredom, and anger directed at their caretakers and at themselves. This anger was acknowledged and accepted by the group and by the group leaders; the children could acknowledge and hear these difficult feelings and begin the process of putting these feelings in perspective.

At one meeting, the children discussed how to become "used to the hospital." One said it happened "by watching TV and listening to others talk," another interrupted to say "by complaining," and another added "by making friends." Someone else wondered if it was possible to "love the hospital but still want to go home." These children and their families generally had considerable respect for the hospital and its staff from the start. As the children's troublesome feelings were listened to, shared, and contained, they began to establish more meaningful relationships within the hospital. They began to see the hospital and the people around them more clearly. They could further develop security, confidence, dependence, and trust, becoming progressively able to move into and emotionally live in the hospital. They moved from shadowy, ill-defined figures to distinct individuals with their own needs, conflicts, and concerns about themselves, their illness, and the hospital.

Anger was most difficult for children to share with parents and hospital staff. Searching to explain their misfortune, children regularly invoke the Talion Law: when someone is sick, someone is to blame. They held themselves culpable for their plight as a consequence of their own real or imagined transgressions. They did not explicitly ascribe blame to their parents; however, the theme of inadequate care and mothering was regularly invoked but displaced to hospital staff and group leaders who sometimes became the "bad parents" for a time. Allegations of unfair treatment were commonplace. Children often felt unacceptable, not only because of their unique hardships but especially because of their difficulty accepting their own feelings and thoughts. They felt angry, damaged, guilty, and abandoned. On a number of occasions the meetings were organized as "protest meetings" resplendent with signs, banners, lists of complaints, and, on one occasion, a parade. Slogans and comments included: "The hospital is unfair," "The food stinks," "We demand more noisemaking time," and "Down with doctors and nurses." Although complaining about doctors and hospital staff, the children were greatly interested in our response to their complaints, looking for acceptance and even approval. This active assertion of their feelings and needs served a most important function for children who had passively experienced losses, pain, and suffering. We let the children know that we were interested in their feelings and their behavior, expecting them to put their feelings into words, pictures, or writing. They were not allowed to be destructive, abusive, or demeaning to themselves or others. The reality of their anger was acknowledged; however, their moving beyond anger to relationships, meaningful communication, trust, and productive involvement was expected.

Complaints continued, but they also became interspersed with overt expressions of affection. Children angrily demanded that their physicians spend more time with them, but they also discussed how much they enjoyed the time they did spend with their doctors. They discussed questions to ask the doctors and nurses. Written complaints and protest signs sometimes alternated with what were called "love signs" often referring to staff members. Love and hate sometimes appeared on the same picture. A 7-year-old boy handed the therapist a single picture containing two figures: one figure was smiling and labeled "I love you"; the other figure had an angry snarl on its face and was labeled "I hate you." The children laughed and understood this ambivalence quite well.

Outlets for active verbal and social expression are especially important with the enforced passivity and compliance attending medical care when the usual friendships, activities, and physical outlets are restricted. Complaining served a special function, not only as an outlet for anger but especially as an active attempt to share unhappiness and to master fear and helplessness through assertive self-expression. The initial use of anger and complaining was particularly impressive as a first step toward remobilizing more assertive participation in their rehabilitation and in regaining autonomy, curiosity, responsibility, and health. When care, sustenance, affection, play, pleasure, relationships, and gratification are available in the group setting, the future can be seen as less threatening and can be faced with hope.

Medical care involves giving up degrees of independence, especially in bodily matters, to the care and control of others. Complaints about restrictions of diet and activities, lack of privacy, needles, urine and stool collections, and disruptions of routine were commonplace. Many struggled mightily against passive compliance with bravado or uncooperative behavior; others succumbed, incurring a high cost through renunciation of degrees of autonomy, curiosity, and self-control. On the other hand, recuperation, which involves regaining autonomy and active self-assertion, also threatened children. Some expressed a reluctance to "grow up," which was seen as dangerous and fraught with possible further illness. For others, recuperation invoked the fear that no one would love or care for them if they were healthy and independent.

Sexuality is an issue important to all children; its meaning and relevance varies from child to child and is especially dependent on the level of development. In a group that contained children of various ages, from preschool through adolescent years in this instance, some dimensions of sexuality could not be dealt with directly in the group. However, issues relating to mature, genital-level sexual concerns were quite infrequent. More commonly, sexual concerns centered around issues such as nudity, since the children were frequently examined by physicians and nurses, and significant pleasure was gained by attention to their bodies and physical contact.

Group sanctions for the necessity of dependency on others for bodily care as well as encouragement of the acceptance of responsibility for bodily autonomy and resumption of physical activity when the condition warranted allowed for more active understanding and mastery. Issues of privacy were clarified for dressing and undressing and were related to assuming autonomous responsibility for bodily care.

Children's pictures illustrated concerns about sexual adequacy, heightened by the threat of physical illness. For example, several boys with rheumatoid arthritis together made a collage of a man in a football uniform, but with the shapely legs of a woman. In some pictures, genitalia were markedly absent or exaggerated. Denial of illness, injury, or disfigurement was sometimes prominent in pictures of beautiful and shapely women and strong and handsome men. Among teenagers, regressive concerns were common, initially relating to themes of loss and to their threatening, uncertain future. As they began to reconstitute and cope with their adversity, sexual concerns appropriate to their level of development began to emerge. Issues of boyfriends and girlfriends, questions about potential romantic involvements among hospital staff, and flirtatious and sexually competitive behaviors became more noteworthy.

The children's view of themselves as damaged included not only their sexual identity but other dimensions as well: they saw themselves as stupid, ugly, crazy, no good, and worthy of rejection. We did not allow children to demean themselves or other children, pointing out that all the children were real, acceptable, and intact.

> Donna was a withdrawn, unhappy 12-year-old girl with rheumatic fever who was just beginning to demonstrate the secondary sexual characteristics of adolescence. She had taken little initiative in several previous meetings. From her wheelchair she handed me a picture she had just completed of a strikingly ugly, hairy, deformed creature with sharp teeth. She announced quietly to the group that it was a picture of me. As the children laughed, watching me carefully, I showed it to the group, smiled, thanked her for it, but commented quizzically that I did not know any person like the one in the picture. As the meeting continued, Donna whispered to the girl next to her, "He's not mean; he's nice." She continued to whisper and bicker with the girl next to her during the meeting, proceeding to make her first friend.

As noted earlier, Winnicott (1965) described the calm, soothing, "holding" environment needed in time of crisis as a vital metaphor for the mother holding her infant in time of distress. Giving comfort, soothing, structuring and supporting children overwhelmed by their feelings and fantasies in response to their hardships was an important function for group leaders, hospital staff, and also the children themselves. Clear definition of structure, routine, and expectations by the group leaders mitigated fears of the unknown and supported active mastery in unaccustomed circumstances. Group sanctions for the temporary necessity of "being nursed" supported children's acceptance of these issues. Later, being told that they were expected to be out of bed, to be dressed in street clothes, and to attend the ward school regularly supported the expectation of regaining autonomy and health in a fashion more clearly understandable than a formal discussion of prognosis and pathogenesis.

The therapists actively encouraged involvement in available relationships and mutual engagement in the expression, acknowledgment, clarification, and reintegration of the children's feelings and concerns. Defenses were respected and not challenged; denial and reaction formation were commonplace and not interpreted. Children observed in other group members a variety of adaptations to adversity with opportunity for trial solutions within the support and sanctions of the group. New relationships with other hospitalized children and staff offer special opportunities, since parents and friends are less available and may not always understand.

These children, separated from their own families by their hospitalizations, demonstrate a remarkable capacity to construct family-like relationships from what is available in the hospital. Group meetings in particular lend themselves to such adaptation, consisting of a "hospital family" with parents and siblings. This process was facilitated by having both male and female therapists and membership consisting of children of varying ages living together on their hospital ward. The male psychiatrist group leader was often seen as the person who led the meetings, determined rules, handled problems, made decisions, and maintained control. He was generally at the center of discussions and activities with children bringing to him ideas, complaints, drawings, possessions, and even homework for his recognition and presentation to the group. Some younger children would simply sit on his lap. The female group leader was seen as nurturant and protective of the children and was in charge of supplies, specifically cookies, juice, crayons, and paper. Younger children, newcomers, or frightened and sad children especially would come to her for comfort and solace, leaning on her, sitting on her lap, and seeking physical and emotional support. Children often asked the therapists to examine or even touch their bodies for assorted complaints, bruises, and aches. Facilitation of the more withdrawn, unhappy, or physically handicapped members to achieve more active recognition and participation within the group process was a therapeutic task for the group leaders and the members. Imitation and even identification were regularly observed as girls helped the female therapist feed and comfort younger children while boys explained hospital procedures to newcomers and asserted their opinions and ideas.

The variety of ages of the children provided problems as well as advantages. Younger children would sometimes cry, hit, run out of the room, and directly express their needs and feelings. The older children observed such expressions of affect as well as the structuring, calming, and soothing provided by the group; regression was avoided for many by vicariously observing it in others and by helping others to cope. Discussions about their own brothers and sisters emerged as children of varying ages interacted, competed with, and accepted one another.

The children's own homes and families were discussed in highly favorable terms and at no time did they express direct anger, criticism, or blame toward their parents. The hospital, however, was often a focus for complaints, disappointments, and anger—with frequent unfavorable comparisons with their own home. When the group leaders can acknowledge, bear, and put into perspective the children's anger and anxiety about their separation from family and family surroundings, the children can move beyond the position of the traumatized, alienated newcomer. At this point the children can then become involved in the new relationships, experiences, and learning available to them in the hospital. Often parents and siblings were quite uncomfortable with the child's illness, which made it difficult for children to ask them questions. With group leadership by a physician or other hospital staff members, children can deal with these issues more directly and sometimes more appropriately. These "hospital parents," by virtue of their training, have more familiarity with the specifics of the illness and its treatment and may be better able to help the child deal with such difficulties.

Relationships with other children of similar ages are of growing importance during childhood and adolescence. Self-esteem and competence are tested through active participation, competition, interaction, and acceptance with other children. The loss of peer group ties or failure to attain satisfactory peer relationships constitutes major developmental failures. Through their relationships with other hospital peers, these children came to acknowledge and accept themselves and others with illness and emotional distress, not only through the public demonstrations of understanding and respect from the group leaders, but especially through the growing bond of support and acceptance developed within their peer group. These children could feel they belonged, could see that they were not different, and came to redefine themselves as normal by standards and circumstances that were appropriate to them.

Within the group setting, children can hear themselves and learn from and support one another in ways that are not available in relationships with parents and other adults. In addition, newcomers to the hospital and those whose illness is of recent onset can learn about their condition and related situations from the more experienced "old timers." Their groupmates can, in many ways, best explain the group meetings, hospital life, medical procedures, and the like. Children can try out and learn new ways of dealing with adversity and see that life can be better. Collective support within a relevant peer group—in dealing with common stress as well as with the feelings, fears, and fantasies in response to adversity—is a therapeutic hallmark of this group experience.

The group experience allows children to deal with these stresses at the time of greatest need. The group provides crisis support—"emotional first-aid" as Bergmann and Freud (1965) have described it—before maladaptive or symptomatic behavior becomes fixed. This maximizes opportunities to use what is available in the children's day-to-day life to help them cope with their adversity. The clear expression of care, concern, structure, and expectations from the group leaders and through the peer group helps children to reconstitute in time of stress and to use the support available for more constructive integration and functioning.

Since our group meetings took place on the children's hospital ward, the children were able to make constructive changes in their feelings, behaviors, and relationships that could then continue beyond the meetings, extending to their ongoing life in the hospital ward. The extended care ward allowed ample time for the children to acknowledge and share their experiences and their feelings. As a consequence, children came to accept themselves more appropriately and to develop more constructive adaptation and mastery within their special circumstances. In time, the individuality of each child emerged more distinctly with their own personality, belongings, questions, and ideas.

Group meetings on the children's hospital ward provide the group leaders with an additional and unique opportunity to understand the hospital milieu: the ongoing life on the hospital ward, relationships with staff, rules, procedures, stresses, and problems. The group leaders can consult with the ward staff to implement increased understanding and improved patient care by hospital personnel. The leaders are also able to identify those children in need of individual care or attention and to find it for them through implementation of special support from the hospital milieu or individual psychiatric consultation for the child and family.

CLINICAL ISSUES

In considering therapeutic approaches with this population, we need to consider many variables such as the nature and degree of physical and emotional problems, the setting in which the child is seen, and the goals established for the therapy. Group treatment methods are particularly appropriate for meeting the following needs of chronically ill children: provision of emotional support and hope for children experiencing physical and emotional distress; education about medical procedures, hospital life, and their illnesses; socialization for children whose illnesses result in social isolation; and clarification of their own feelings and the feelings of people around them. In addition, the therapy group, as a reconstruction of the family, allows for corrective working through of family conflicts. The degree to which individual emotional conflicts of the children can be worked through will vary with the objectives of the group and the techniques involved. However, it is often useful in the group to focus on the children's emotional responses and adaptation to illness and its consequences, since these experiences can generally be shared by peers in the group.

As noted in Chapter 1, leaderless support groups, modeled after Alcoholics Anonymous, are quite popular for adults faced with common adversities such as chronic physical illness. Such groups, of course, are not appropriate for children or adolescents. Nevertheless, parent support groups—often dealing with issues of advocacy, fund-raising, education, and mutual support—have proved useful around a variety of diseases such as cystic fibrosis, hemophilia, and the like. As noted elsewhere, groups led by mental health professionals or other healthcare providers offer the opportunity to work through anger and resentment about the illness and provide more thorough psychotherapeutic and educational opportunities than do leaderless groups. McCollum (1975) notes that parent groups take two basic forms: educational-informational groups and experiential-therapeutic groups.

Cotherapists offer a variety of advantages to groups for chronically ill children. With one male and one female therapist, the opportunity for recapitulating the family situation is more clearly presented. An additional therapist is also helpful in attending to individually disruptive members in the process of helping the group work toward more cohesion. It also provides for more easily developed transferences and real relationships for the children with group leaders.

The setting in which the group is undertaken may suggest the most appropriate type of group membership. In an inpatient hospital setting, an open-ended group has the advantage of representing ongoing life in the hospital. The commonality of illness and life together on the hospital ward does provide special opportunities. However, a heterogeneity of ages, physical and emotional problems, and length of time on the ward also presents disadvantages with such diversities.

An open group for hospital inpatients is not a free-standing entity, but rather is part of the ongoing life experience. Thus, appropriately, the group should accomodate to the reality of the clinical conditions and physical setting. Closed-group membership provides the advantage of selecting a more homogeneous population that continues without the disruption of new members arriving and old members leaving throughout the life of the group. Furthermore, children can be selected for groups according to age, sex, or diagnosis. Settings other than the inpatient hospital ward may be more appropriate for closed groups. These settings include mental health facilities, schools for ill or handicapped children, rehabilitation programs, recreational centers, or even clinic waiting rooms.

A variety of treatment approaches are available to professionals working with groups of chronically ill children and adolescents. The hospital ward playroom is often the site for play group approaches that provide children with a setting in which to work through conflicts about illness (Adams, 1976). Educational groups can be provided for hospital inpatients (Rie, Boverman, Grossman, & Ozua, 1968; Rie, Boverman, Ozua, & Grossman, 1964) or even in community settings such as schools. Classroom teaching approaches have also been used with healthy children in order to help children adjust more readily if hospitalization should be required in the future (Brett, 1983).

Psychodynamically oriented groups have been used in hospitals (Hughes, 1982; Schowalter & Lord, 1970). The goals of such groups include providing support, socialization, learning of adaptive behavior from others, education, and some degree of corrective emotional experience. Behavior modification approaches have also been used with groups of children with diagnoses such as cerebral palsy and mental retardation (Schofield & Wong, 1975). Goals of behavioral treatment approaches can include teaching appropriate social skills and decreasing inappropriate or disruptive behaviors. Our earlier overview of the research literature indicated that the variety of group approaches for this population have much in common and that the therapeutic factors inherent in group therapy are particularly beneficial for children with chronic illness.

While group work has many clear advantages for these children, it also has some limitations. Recent studies of the Post-Traumatic Stress Disorder (Terr, 1987) demonstrate a contagion effect—children can be traumatized by exposure to others who have experienced massive, unique stress and are themselves severely traumatized. It is our experience that the problems of children who are dying or are severely mutilated may add to the stress of children less severely afflicted (Hughes, 1986). Therefore, when possible, it is best for children with terminal or obviously mutilating conditions of major psychological impact to be afforded treatment more suitable to them and also to be hospitalized on a special ward when long-term care is undertaken. All children facing illness and hospitalization, and their parents, have some fears about mutilation and possible death that need to be addressed and clarified. This is much readily done, however, in circumstances where the recovering child is not in the midst of children with terminal or severely mutilating conditions. It is important to note that children with terminal illnesses face the same issues as those faced by children with other chronic illnesses, in addition to coping with progressive physical debility and impending death.

The open-ended nature of the group presented advantages and disadvantages, with new members joining and old members leaving frequently. The major advantage was that it allowed for a working and reworking of issues relating to attachment and separation, both of which are major themes for children separated from their families and encountering strangers in the hospital. A disadvantage was that it limited the extent to which ongoing themes could be worked through over time. Some chronically ill children would profit from ongoing closed-ended groups when they are out of the hospital and in a more stable living situation; however, during hospitalization, an open-ended group that is responsive to the realities of children's lives in the hospital is, in our experience, the treatment of choice.

The group membership consisted of patients who were living together on the ward. The obvious advantage was that of helping children deal with their day-to-day ongoing experiences together. A disadvantage, however, was that the children in attendance varied considerably in age, levels of development, and degrees of maturity of behaviors. Often, the group complained about the "babies." Surprisingly, the younger children also complained about the "babies," and we came to understand that this perjorative referred not to age-appropriate, developmental immaturity but to inappropriate, disruptive, or hostile behaviors. There were clear advantages in having the children in varying ages together when their behaviors were able to be managed; however, management of such discrepant behaviors as overintellectualization by some of the adolescents and hyperactive behavior of the younger children did present problems. Nevertheless, as we became more comfortable with the great variations in concerns and behaviors, the group itself helped deal with this as older members helped younger ones, and the direct expression of feelings by younger members allowed older children to avoid regression by vicariously experiencing it in others. Still, overt sexual material could not be dealt with directly during the group meetings. By the same token, some specific individual concerns and family issues were also inappropriate to explore in any kind of detail in the group setting. Specific eating problems, phobias, inhibitions, and other persistent intrapsychic concerns needed individualized attention. Family problems such as threatened or impending divorce, illness of a parent, death of a grandparent, and special concerns of parents need to be handled outside of the group.

Countertransference issues need to be monitored. Sympathy may sometimes cloud an understanding of these children and their circumstances, leading to a lowering of expectations that in turn deprives children of maximizing their potentials. For example, new therapists frequently have difficulty encouraging physically ill and unhappy children to function up to the level their physical illness allows. An all-too-familiar response is to say, in effect, "Don't make them go to school, or do their homework, or speak up or attend the group meetings because they're ill and unhappy." Children may be ill and unhappy, but many are in great need of attending those outside activities such as school that their level of illness will allow. They especially need to attend meetings and to speak up and ventilate their unhappiness and resentment over what has happened to them. The great anxiety these children experience—relating to such major concerns as abandonment, mutilation, castration, and death—is also difficult for therapists to bear and is sometimes defended against through denial, rationalization, or displacement.

Anger, in our experience, is the affect most likely to provoke counertransference: to become the object of the children's anger and blame can leave the therapist feeling guilty, inept, and culpable for the children's misfortune. When this response is understood, it affords the therapist the opportunity to help the children move from the position of blaming others toward the position of acceptance and understanding. When unrecognized, this response causes great difficulty for the therapist and may result in a more superficial approach or may cause the therapist to stop working with this population.

Supervision and consultation are most important for any group therapist, experienced or inexperienced, who chooses to work with this population. Knowledge of the medical and psychosocial aspects of chronic childhood illness is helpful; however, supervision, experience, and reference to the literature can make up for a lack of initial familiarity with these issues. Group work for this population can be undertaken outside the hospital. However, therapists must recognize the major impact that the hospital experience has in the lives of these children. Thus, knowledge and understanding of life in the hospital are important for the therapist so that these issues can be adequately addressed in treatment.

SUMMARY

Long afflicted with pulmonary tuberculosis, Robert Louis Stevenson wrote, "Life is not a matter of holding good cards, but of playing a poor hand well." Adaptation to chronic physical disorders and their consequences presents additional developmental problems when a child or adolescent is involved. Group treatment methods provide mental health professionals with an excellent opportunity to understand and help these youngsters in the process of acknowledging, understanding, and adapting to their extraordinary hardships.

The adversity experienced by children with chronic illnesses is encountered in many facets, including: the altered reality of their life experience; somatic distress through bodily sensations, dysfunctions, or disfigurements; alterations in their interpersonal experience with family, peers, caretakers, and strangers; and their intrapsychic experience of fantasies, fears, body image, self-concept, and self-esteem. The group therapy process highlights problems shared with other chronically ill children. They can see that the hardships they face and their responses to them are not unique but are acknowledged and understood by their caretakers and shared by a peer group that is relevant to them. Facing adversity with others of similar experience within a psychotherapeutic program is of major benefit for these children for whom life has truly been unfair.

The hardships these children face are clearly unique and separate them from their usual peer group. However, their fears and fantasies are not different but in fact are an accentuation of the fears that accompany growth and development for all children: fears of abandonment; fears about physical mutilation, violation of bodily integrity, and death; anxiety that they will be overwhelmed by the intensity of their own affects; and fear of the unknown and unexpected (Hughes, 1982).

This chapter has discussed some of the difficulties these children experience and has considered them in relationship to their presentation within psychotherapeutic group sessions during hospitalization. Therapeutic benefits that are available in the group treatment setting were addressed in regards to peer relationships, crisis support, adaptation and mastery, and hospital consultation. Constructive adaptation to chronic illness and its consequences can improve acceptance of and compliance with medical treatments and procedures, limitations, diets, and restrictions. This adaptation can also facilitate appropriate efforts toward active rehabilitation with resumption of autonomy and assertiveness of self-care. Such adaptation may favorably impact on the course of the physical ravages of the disease process itself and may also improve the quality of life through maximizing physical, cognitive, and psychosocial functions. Group work with this population can convert the adversities of chronic physical illness and its consequences into opportunities for support, relationships, adaptation, mastery, and emotional growth.

REFERENCES

Adams, M. A. (1976). A hospital play program: Helping children with serious illness. *American Journal of Orthopsychiatry, 46*, 416–424.

Bayrakal, S. (1975). A group experience with chronically disabled adolescents. *American Journal of Psychiatry, 132*, 1291–1299.

Bergmann, T., & Freud, A. (1965). *Children in the hospital.* New York: International Universities Press.

Brett, A. (1983). Preparing children for hospitalization: A classroom teaching approach. *Journal of School Health, 53*, 561–563.

Bullard, D., Jr. (1968). The response of the child to chronic physical disability. *Journal of the American Physical Therapy Association, 48*, 592–601.

Cofer, D. C., & Nir, T. (1975). Theme-focused group therapy on a pediatric ward. *International Journal of Psychiatry in Medicine, 6*, 541–550.

Frank, J. L. (1978). A weekly group meeting for children on a pediatric ward: Therapeutic and practical functions. *International Journal of Psychiatry in Medicine, 8*, 267–283.

Galdston, R., & Hughes, M. (1972). Pediatric hospitalization as crisis intervention. *American Journal of Psychiatry, 8,* 721–725.

Garrard, S., & Richmond, J. (1963). Psychological aspects of the management of chronic diseases and handicapping conditions in childhood. In H. I. Lief, V. F. Lief, & N. R. Lief (Eds.), *The psychological basis of medical practice.* New York: Harper and Row.

Geist, R. (1979). Onset of chronic illness in children and adolescents: Psychotherapeutic and consultative intervention. *American Journal of Orthopsychiatry, 49,* 4–23.

Hagberg, K. L. (1969). Social casework and group work methods in a children's hospital. *Children, 16,* 192–197.

Hockenberry, M. J., Herman, S. B., Schultz, W. H., & Falletta, J. M. (1985). Cancer in children. In A.N. O'Quinn (Ed.), *Management of chronic disorders of childhood.* Boston: GK Hall.

Hughes, M. C. (1982). Chronically ill children in groups: Recurrent issues and adaptations. *American Journal of Orthopsychiatry, 52,* 704–711.

Hughes, M. C. (1984). Recurrent abdominal pain and childhood depression. *American Journal of Orthopsychiatry, 54,* 146–151.

Hughes, M. C. (1986, October). *Pediatric liaison—New collaborative techniques.* Panel at American Academy of Child and Adolescent Psychiatry Annual Meeting, Los Angeles.

Hughes, M. C., & Brown, D. (1980). Psychiatry in pediatric practice. In J. Graef, & T. Cone, Jr. (Eds.), *Manual of pediatric therapeutics* (2nd ed.). Boston: Little, Brown.

Josselyn, I. M., Simon, A. J., & Eells, E. (1955). Anxiety in children convalescing from rheumatic fever. *American Journal of Orthopsychiatry, 25,* 109–122.

Mattsson, A. (1972). Long-term physical illness in childhood: A challenge to psychosocial adaptation. *Pediatrics, 50,* 801–811.

McCollum, A. T. (1975). *The chronically ill child.* New Haven: Yale University Press.

McCracken, M. J. (1984). Cystic fibrosis in adolescence. In R. W. Blum (Ed.), *Chronic illness and disabilities in childhood and adolescence.* Orlando: Grune & Stratton.

Newacheck, P. W., Budetti, P. P., & Halfon, N. (1986). Trends in activity-limiting chronic conditions among children. *American Journal of Public Health, 76,* 178–184.

Newacheck, P. W., Budetti, P. P., & McManus, P. (1984). Trends in childhood disability. *American Journal of Public Health, 74,* 232–236.

Pless, I., & Pinkerton, P. (1975). *Chronic childhood disorder: Promoting patterns of adjustment.* Chicago: Year Book Medical Publishers.

Pless, I., & Roghmann, K. (1971). Chronic illness and its consequences: Observations based on three epidemiologic surveys. *Journal of Pediatrics, 79,* 351–359.

Pratt, J. H. (1907). The class method of treating consumption in the homes of the poor. *Journal of the American Medical Association, 49,* 755–759.

Redl, F. (1959). The concept of the life space interview. *American Journal of Orthopsychiatry, 29,* 1–18.

Rie, H. E., Boverman, H., Grossman, B. J., & Ozua, N. (1968). Immediate and long-term effects of interventions early in prolonged hospitalization. *Pediatrics, 41,* 755–764.

Rie, H. E., Boverman, H., Ozua, N., & Grossman, B. J. (1964). Tutoring and ventilation: A pilot of reactions of hospitalized children. *Clinical Pediatrics, 3,* 581–586.

Rutter, M., Tizard, J., Yule, W., Graham, P., & Whitmore, K. (1977). Isle of Wight studies, 1964–1974. In S. Chess, & A. Thomas (Eds.), *Annual progress in child psychiatry and child development.* New York: Brunner/Mazel.

Schofield, L. J., & Wong, S. (1975). Operant approaches to group therapy in a school for handicapped children. *Developmental Medicine and Child Neurology, 17,* 425–433.

Schowalter, J. (1977). Psychological reactions to physical illness and hospitalization in adolescence. *Journal of the American Academy of Child Psychiatry, 16,* 500–516.

Schowalter, J., & Lord, R. (1970). Utilization of patient meetings on an adolescent ward. *Psychiatry in Medicine, 1,* 197–206.

Solnit, A. (Ed.). (1977). *Physical illness and handicaps in childhood: An anthology of the psychoanalytic study of the child.* New Haven: Yale University Press.

Terr, L. (1987, May). *The trauma-stress disorders.* Samuel G. Hibbs Lecture at the 140th Annual Meeting of the American Psychiatric Association, Chicago.

Travis, G. (1976). *Chronic illness in children: Its impact on child and family.* Stanford: Stanford University Press.

Walsh, S. (1981). Parents of asthmatic kids (PAK). *Pediatric Nursing, 7,* 28–29.

Williams, K., & Baeker, M. (1983). Use of small group with chronically ill children. *The Journal of School Health, 53,* 205–207.

Winnicott, D. (1965). *The maturational process and the facilitating environment.* New York: International Universities Press.

Zeltzer, L., LaBaron, S., & Zeltzer, D. (1984). The adolescent with cancer. In R. W. Blum (Ed.), *Chronic illness and disabilities in childhood and adolescence.* Orlando: Grune & Stratton.

9
Group Approaches for Parents of Children with Disabilities

Although parents of disabled children have achieved more visibility in certain respects, their mental health needs have largely gone unnoticed. The literature seems to be ambivalent on the issue of whether these parents are significantly stressed; some contributors assert that the mental health needs of parents are considerable, while others believe that parents do not experience more stress than parents of nondisabled children. Unfortunately, the research literature does not shed light on this issue and suggests that the answer is more complex than the question of whether a disabled child resides with the family (Seligman, 1983; Seligman & Darling, in press). Recognizing that the issue of parental mental health remains unsettled, in this chapter I will nonetheless examine the potential needs of parents of disabled children with a particular emphasis on the amelioration of psychological problems through the group process.

The term *disabled* or *exceptional* child as it is commonly used in education refers to children who suffer from physical or mental disabilities. These children may be visually impaired or hearing-impaired, mentally retarded, mentally ill, epileptic, physically disabled, or suffering from a rare condition. The severity of the condition is another variable that must be considered. A common denominator for parents of disabled children is that often these children are viewed as socially deviant and, perhaps by association, their parents may also be viewed (or may personally perceive themselves) as falling outside of the mainstream of society.

PSYCHOLOGICAL CONCERNS OF PARENTS

The coping mechanisms of parents are severely tested when parents who expect a normal child are confronted with the birth of a handicapped baby. Parents tend to be vulnerable at this point. The manner in which the handicap is communicated to the parents by the physician and the existence of support from important others is crucial. The expression of understanding and support from grandparents, other relatives, friends, and neighbors is essential to combat the feelings of loss and guilt that plague parents at this point. Both fathers and mothers are affected by the birth of their child, but it is still unclear whether they respond to the crisis in the same way.

The birth of a child with disabilities and the family's reaction to it can be viewed from a systems perspective in that the event elicits feelings and behaviors that affect all family members. Depending on the nature and severity of the handicap, the child can play an important part in the evolving roles family members assume. Farber (1962) theorized that in the case of the birth of a severely retarded child, the family does not emerge from the preadolescent stage of its life cycle (that is, the family is "stuck" with a dependent child beyond the normal parenting period), resulting in the disruption of family integration because each individual is frustrated in his or her anticipated roles. For example, the parents' normal expectation that their child will graduate from high school or college, marry, and achieve certain vocational objectives is thwarted.

Professionals working with parents need to consider the effect a child's dependency needs will have on the parents' independence. The range of a child's disability may be from mild to severe, and the extent to which the handicap constrains parental independence depends, in part, on this variable. Consider the difference between a learning-disabled child who is essentially self-sufficient and a severely retarded, blind, cerebral-palsied youngster who requires help in mobility, eating, hygiene, and learning the most rudimentary aspects of daily life. Recent views of institutionalization have led professionals to advise parents to keep their disabled children at home no matter how severe the handicap. Whenever possible, the family is expected to manage and rear the handicapped child at home.

The roles of siblings may also be affected. Parents may overburden nondisabled siblings with excessive responsibility for the disabled child and, at the same time, may withdraw needed emotional support and affection from the well child (Seligman, 1987). Under such circumstances it is easy to see how siblings might feel rejected, manipulated, angry (at both the parents and the disabled brother or sister), and guilty. Siblings can also be the targets for excessively high aspirations in order to compensate for parental disappointments and frustrations about the disabled child.

In addition to guilt, parents often experience anger—anger at the birth and at the child, anger at professionals who often treat parents poorly, anger toward other people's reactions toward them, and anger at the often meager or confusing services available in the community. The sources of anger are numerous, and the intensity of the anger exceeds that common to most parents. As a consequence of real or perceived rejection on the part of friends and acquaintances, parents may withdraw from social interaction and may become bitter about their isolation. This type of social withdrawal may have severe consequences for the family's adjustment to their circumstances.

All parents concern themselves with the future. They worry about their child's education, vocational endeavors, and marital prospects. Parents who have a disabled child, however, tend to be exceedingly future-oriented. They share the same concerns as other parents about education, vocation, and marriage, but they worry about these life events with more fervor. Parents of mentally retarded children may be concerned about educational (learning) problems, whether the child is mainstreamed or placed in a segregated setting. Parents of an epileptic, cerebral-palsied, or autistic youngster may worry about the stigma often attached to these afflictions that may pose significant social, vocational, and marital problems. Common to most families with a disabled child is the major concern about the future, especially if the child is by necessity dependent. Worries about what will happen when the parents are unable to provide for their handicapped child's needs may be particularly distressing. Such thoughts about the future are relentless.

Excessive financial expenses can add to the psychological burdens of these parents. As a consequence of their child's disability, parents may frequently have to visit doctors and hospitals, may need to purchase medicine and special equipment, and/or may require services from a physical, occupational, or speech therapist. The financial cost of these services, irrespective of psychological cost, can be devastating.

The periodical literature often portrays parents in the most negative of terms:

> In an attempt to highlight and to some extent dramatize the plight of the exceptional parents, writers tend to focus more on family problems than on assets and coping ability. Parents are rarely portrayed as adjusted and realistically optimistic, but tend to be projected as poor souls beset by frustration, anger, and depression, hardly in a position to interact comfortably and constructively with professionals and friends, much less with each other. The focus of the published literature is on pathology (what is wrong) to the virtual exclusion of ego (coping) mechanisms (Seligman, 1979, p. 63).

In working with this population it is important for professionals to be realistic about the potential problems parents may experience, but by the same token we must realize that human beings have extraordinary coping skills and resiliency that are often ignored. The birth of a handicapped child resembles other crises in that such events are usually not expected and tend to be devastating in their impact, at least initially. In time, for many people, accommodations are made to difficult situations and life continues. For others, crises create a great deal of chronic stress and family disruption.

Due to the presence of a disabled child and as a consequence of the factors noted above, some parents will find it exceedingly difficult to maintain a stable and happy marriage. Some years ago Toffler (1970) noted that human beings strain under the rapidly moving events of our time. Parents of disabled children not only are subjected to the strain from these events, but may be additionally burdened by the presence of a disabled child. The forces that pull and push at these parents test the strength of the fabric of their relationship. Their coping abilities are put to the test, and those who are not coping well may seek help outside of the family. It is at this point that professionals can be of benefit by providing opportunities for psychological intervention. For example, in his group counseling sessions, Huber (1979) observed that,

> For some parents there was the pressure of hostile feelings toward a child who demanded so much but gave so little. For other parents there was the confusion of adjusting to the reality that their child may never walk, talk, learn, or love as other children do. One couple was still numb from the recent discovery that their child may never see (p. 267).

In working with these parents it is essential to be cognizant of preexisting family problems. It is also important to consider the highly individualized ways people respond to stressful events. Therefore, an understanding of how a particular set of parents view and cope with their circumstances is preferable to the jaundiced view that parents chronically deny and distort, are often unrealistically angry, and are sometimes viewed as emotionally disturbed (Seligman & Seligman, 1980).

THE NEED FOR PSYCHOLOGICAL RESOURCES FOR PARENTS

Any of the potential concerns mentioned above may be the impetus for parents to seek psychological help. For some it may be the combination of living daily with numerous burdensome problems—being a parent of a disabled child is a chronic condition. For others, dealing with a seemingly minor condition and its consequences, for example, being the parent of a learning disabled child, may motivate parents to seek help. The parents' view of the child, the coping skills of the parents, and the existing environmental supports largely determine the conflicts parents may bring to a counselor, psychologist, or social worker. Friedlander and Watkins (1985) note that parents need to adapt to permanent problems in addition to other stressors and conflicting emotions such as guilt, hopelessness, exhaustion, real relationship strains, frustration, disappointment, failure, insularity, and isolation. These clinicians believe that the parents' need for social support and emotional relief is unequivocal.

The need for counseling for some parents is evident. However, I believe that most human service professionals are ill-prepared to work effectively with family members of children who are disabled. This view is not based on the belief that professionals lack appropriate clinical skills, but that they have insufficient, inadequate, and distorted knowledge about this population.

Essential to successful counseling with these parents is knowledge about the unique circumstances that confront families with a disabled child. It is important to have an in-depth understanding of these families, their unique problems, and their strengths. It is also important to have empathy for the parents' feelings of being "different," as well as an understanding of community and professional attitudes toward that difference. Also essential is that the professional be knowledgeable about available community resources.

The mental health needs of parents may be cumulative. That is, living with a handicapped child over many years can take its toll psychologically, physically, and financially. By the same token some parents adjust admirably over time as they become accustomed to their circumstances and in fact cope better than during the initial stages.

Troubled parents may simply need support from an empathic listener. Others may require counseling to help them cope with feelings of guilt that have not abated over time, and still others may be in the grip of a vicious guilt–anger cycle from which they are unable to become extricated without help. Management of a disabled child may become so stressful for a particular family that help is sought for that reason. The shame and loneliness that some parents experience because of the reactions of others may precipitate a psychological consultation. Furthermore, the adjustment difficulties that normal brothers and sisters can experience may motivate parents to seek help for their offspring or for the family.

Parents may simply need someone to be honest with them about their child in the context of a supportive relationship or they may need information about parent self-help groups and/or other needed services. Parents often find that books and articles can provide inspiration, hope, and needed information for them, the disabled youngster, or nondisabled siblings. Professional helpers should be knowledgeable about useful reading sources and use them wisely.

All in all, the mental health needs of parents can be substantial. As noted, parents must be able to cope with feelings of guilt, hopelessness, exhaustion, relationship problems, disappointment, and isolation. Several authors have discussed the advantages of individual counseling approaches to help parents cope with these problems (Laborde & Seligman, 1983; Opihory & Peters, 1982). However, the remainder of this chapter will explore group counseling approaches that seem to be helpful in providing parents with hope, inspiration, and skills in dealing with their own psychological needs as well as those of their disabled child and the family as a whole.

PHILOSOPHY AND MODELS OF PARENT COUNSELING GROUPS

Parent groups are generally designed to serve either educative, therapeutic, or both educative and therapeutic functions (Adamson, 1972; Kaplan & Williams, 1972; Ramsey, 1967; Samit, Nash, & Meyers, 1980). Groups that are primarily educative in purpose focus on providing parents with information about and understanding of their child's handicapping condition as well as training in effective coping and parenting skills. Parent groups that are essentially therapeutic in nature tend to stress the sharing and exploration of feelings (e.g., guilt, frustration, anger). In addition, such groups assist parents in gaining an awareness of their own attitudes and patterns of behavior that might bear on their child's problem and help them understand their attitudes and behaviors toward professionals. The vast majority of parent groups that are reported in the literature combine features of both educative/informational and therapeutic/interactional groups.

Friedlander and Watkins (1985) propose three basic models of groups for parents with a disabled child. In agreement with the above-cited authors, Friedlander and Watkins note that the *parent education* model is based on the premise that problems emerge from deficiencies in skills and information. This model assumes that family members can cope adaptively when they are provided with accurate and relevant information. The parent education model further implies that the parents' feelings about their disabled child should not cause problems when they have adequate resources (e.g., information and skill development in child management).

The *group therapy* model rests on the assumption that parents' emotional reactions are manifestations of pathologic personality processes and that adaptation would follow only if the parent(s) are willing to explore "hidden" concerns. Friedlander and Watkins (1985) note that this pathology-oriented view, prevalent in the 1950s and early 1960s, has fallen into disfavor and that contemporary views hold that family members are relatively healthy persons who are thrust into a personal crisis by the birth of a handicapped child. The focus now is more on family strengths and the restoration of adaptive capacities.

Emerging from the self-help movement, the *support group* model is a process of mutual aid between peers. Support groups typically possess three characteristics: voluntary participation, an emphasis on mutual self-help toward mutually agreed on goals, and peer leadership. Friedlander and Watkins (1985) propose a modified version of the support group model by having a relatively inactive professional leader conduct a group of persons with a shared problem. The professional leader in a support group context allows for considerable member freedom in terms of responsibility and agenda-setting and is available to occasionally guide and intervene during disruptive interactions. The value of having a professional leader conduct a support group is that he or she can help facilitate the discussion, by keeping it on track and is available to help with issues that go beyond support and mutual help.

In examining the purpose or focus of parent groups, the members can focus primarily on the handicapped child, the parents as individuals, the marital unit, the entire family, or some combination of these. For example, Barsch (1961), in his groups for mothers of brain-damaged children, encouraged discussion of day-to-day problems in child rearing while actively discouraging parents from disclosing any intrapsychic or marital conflict material. Philage, Kuna, and Becerril (1975), in their work with parents of learning disabled children, chose to explore family dynamics rather than focus specifically on the handicapped child. In their groups for parents of emotionally disturbed children, Pasnau, Meyer, Davis, Lloyd, and Kline (1976) emphasized parents' self-awareness and ability to accept "their role in the pathogenesis of their child's problem" (p. 90). In general, the group leader needs to make a decision about the goals of the group and how these are to be accomplished. It is useful if the group's purpose and processes are communicated to the parents.

The nature of the child's handicapping condition may partially determine the purpose and focus of the parent group. There is a tendency for groups whose participants are parents of children with certain disabilities to be therapeutic rather than educative in emphasis, with discussions often relating to problems of the parent(s) or entire family as well as those of the handicapped child. A broad-based exploration of parent feelings and family dynamics certainly seems appropriate when the child's disability derives in part from a problematic home environment and conversely when the child's behavior influences the family. Groups whose members are parents of mentally retarded, physically handicapped, or sensorily handicapped children generally emphasize educating the parents about the child's disability, its causation, and its prognosis. In these groups, parents may likewise be encouraged to express and explore their feelings. Although insight into family dynamics may also be important for these parents, these counseling groups typically focus on finding the best ways for families to facilitate the disabled child's development toward maximum independence using an educative or support group model.

GROUP COMPOSITION

Counseling groups for parents range from those that include only mothers (Barsch, 1961; Kaplan & Williams, 1972; Siegel, Sheridan, & Sheridan, 1971) to groups exclusively for fathers (Meyer, Vadasy, Fewell, & Schell, 1985; Strean, 1962), siblings (Meyer, Vadasy, & Fewell, 1985), and grandparents (Meyer & Vadasy, 1986), and from groups that accept only couples (Gottschalk, Brown, Bruney, Shumate, & Uliana, 1973; Loeb, 1977) to mixed groups composed of both couples and individual parents (Tracey, 1970). Until recently, the majority of groups were designed for mothers. This fact is consistent with the view that mothers are the primary if not the only caregivers of the children and that perhaps they experience more stress than other family members. The women's movement, economic necessity, and other socioeconomic factors have significantly loosened and redefined the roles of both men and women, mothers and fathers. Fathers are becoming increasingly involved in the care and management of children, and counseling, whenever possible, now includes both parents. Tracey (1970), in her work with parents, found that fathers were active and made a unique contribution to the groups. The work by Meyer and his associates (1985) at the University of Washington has expanded the focus on mothers to include other family members.

Besides couples groups, there are programs in which parents are involved in one group while their handicapped children concurrently participate in a separate group. Both parents' and children's groups focus on building healthy, supportive family environments. According to Pasnau, Meyer, Davis, Lloyd, and Kline (1976), the advantages of this "coordinated group therapy" are twofold. First, it focuses on family interaction rather than individual action, thereby avoiding an "identified patient" syndrome. Second, it adds to the traditional family model in three ways: (1) the process implies that the parents have a separate relationship from the children that may or may not need special attention but that obviously exists; (2) even though the parents are meeting separately from the children, they are meeting at the same time, sending the message that the parent–child relationship is important rather than just the parent or the child; and (3) in the group approach, the families are given increased opportunities for interaction with other families who have similar problems. Pasnau stated that the disadvantages of coordinated group therapy are: (1) it reduces the actual interactions between child and parent that the traditional family therapy model encourages; and (2) it increases the number of variables of which the therapist needs to be aware and demands greater expertise on his or her part (Pasnau, Meyer, Davis, Lloyd, & Kline, 1976, p. 102). In addition to these coordinated meetings, there are groups in which parents and their handicapped children meet together, at least part of the time (Meyer, Vadasy, Fewell, & Schell, 1985; Philage, Kuna, & Becerril, 1975).

According to Ramsey's (1967) review of counseling groups for parents of retarded children, selection criteria for membership in parent counseling groups generally have been weak, if they exist at all. Acceptance into these groups was often based on having a child who "fit" a designated category of mental retardation as well as parent availability and willingness to participate in a counseling group. When specific criteria were employed, they were frequently negative, designating who should be excluded, rather than positive, suggesting who should be included in a parent group. Even now, most parents are not thoroughly screened for suitability to a counseling group. Entrance into most groups continues to be based on parent availability, identification with a particular life circumstance, and desire to attend.

It makes good clinical sense to screen prospective participants prior to the beginning of the group experience, particularly if the group is more therapeutic than educative in purpose. A screening interview allows the leader to assess the appropriateness of the group for the parent: (1) exploring expectations that the parent has concerning the group; (2) imparting information pertaining to group processes and goals; (3) evaluating whether the parent could both benefit from and contribute to the group; and (4) seeking a commitment from the parent to attend and participate in group sessions. By interviewing each individual or couple, the therapist is most likely to achieve a group composition that will enhance the likelihood that the group will be a productive one, although generally speaking one cannot predict outcome based on group composition.

Parent groups vary widely as to the number of participants, the choice of open or closed format, and attendance requirements. Ramsey (1967) found that parent groups that consist of more than 10 members are usually educational in purpose, whereas those with 10 members or less tend to be therapeutically oriented. It seems reasonable that groups that encourage a great deal of self-disclosure and self-exploration should be smaller as well as more stringent in membership and attendance requirements. Repeated absences of one or both parents tend to be counterproductive to both the individual(s) and the entire group. Whether a particular group is open or closed to new members depends on a number of factors, including the type of group, the demands of the agency, and the predisposition of the leader on this matter.

GROUP/STRUCTURE FORMAT

Parent groups range from those that are highly structured and formal to those that are relatively unstructured and informal. The degree of structure and formality depends on the purpose and goals of the group, the theoretical orientation of the leader, the personal comfort of the leader, and so on. Ramsey (1967) found that groups with an educational/informational focus tended to be more structured and formal than therapeutic groups. Educational groups are frequently topic-oriented and limited to a predesignated number of sessions (usually fewer than 10). Therapeutic groups, on the other hand, tend to be held over a longer time span; some of these groups continue indefinitely and change in direction as the needs of the group dictate. Samit, Nash, and Meyers (1980) reported on a group of parents of autistic children who shifted focus from specific topics (such as toilet training and feeding) to an examination of parental stress.

Parent groups may meet weekly, every other week, or monthly, depending on the goals of the group. Typically, therapeutically oriented groups meet on a weekly basis, whereas educational or support groups meet less often.

GROUP METHODS

The methodology chosen for a parent group depends in part on the purpose of the group. Even more importantly, it depends on the theoretical orientation and intervention style of its leader. Many group leaders feel most effective employing a wide variety of interventions and techniques. For example, Loeb (1977) used a combination of reflection, interpretation, and reality therapy, as well as Gestalt techniques and learning-theory-based behavior modification. Gottschalk, Brown, Bruney, Shumate, and Uliana (1973), who like Loeb referred to their counseling approach as eclectic, described a "mixture of psychodynamic, flexibly didactic, expressive, and group process-oriented therapy" (p. 159). Leaders whose orientation is psychodynamic employ interpretation as a primary intervention (Hampton, 1962) and help members gain insight into themselves by symbolizing the group as a family (Strean, 1962). Friedlander and Watkins (1985) employed a nondirective approach with their parent groups that was designed to enable parents to take responsibility for the content and direction of the sessions. Reflecting their behavioral orientation, Jacks and Keller (1978) made wide use of role-playing in helping parents to learn effective interactive behaviors with their learning-disabled adolescents. Likewise, Schilling, Gilchrist, and Schinke (1984) found role-playing to be useful to help parents increase their personal coping.

A common group method with parents of disabled children is to invite lecturers to discuss a topic of importance followed by a discussion of the topic. Physicians, teachers, psychologists, physical therapists, and attorneys are examples of professionals who might be asked to come to a parent group. Regardless of which methods are chosen, it is essential that the leader is well-grounded in disability, family and group dynamics.

ISSUES AND THEMES IN PARENT GROUPS

Counseling groups provide the greatest benefit to their participants by providing a supportive environment, partially achieved by the leader's sensitivity but even more by surrounding parents with others who have experienced similar feelings and circumstances. Whether the group is primarily educational or therapuetic, parents are almost always provided with some opportunity to share with others the fears and frustrations, hopes and joys, that maybe only other parents like them can truly understand. The group can potentially provide a new set of peers with whom the threat of judgment and rejection is minimal.

Loeb (1977), in discussing parents of retarded children, stated that:

> . . . many of these parents need to talk about themselves and their own problems. They have been confronted with avoidance reactions, pity, or overcompensating tolerance. Concerns about genetic inferiority, insufficient care during pregnancy, and inadequate post-natal treatment have often been felt by parents, whether or not any of these factors was actually present in their own situations. These common stresses often result in unwarranted anxiety and guilt which call for a therapeutic response (p. 78).

Particularly early in their experience with their handicapped child, parents often feel a sense of bereavement or loss that for some can easily lead from simple sadness to depression (Solmit & Stark, 1961). As the child matures, parents frequently experience a great deal of frustration, which can derive from many sources, not the least of which are problems with ineffective management of the child (Golden, Chirlin, & Shone, 1970; Harris, 1983). It is probably most difficult for parents to acknowledge and express such feelings as anger and hostility or ambivalent feelings toward the handicapped child. The leader of a parent group may at times need to help parents feel comfortable in addressing these emotions. Within the safe confines of the group, members often experience relief and a sense of assurance that others have feelings similar to their own.

Not all parents or all groups progress rapidly toward discussion of feelings. For example, Strean (1962), in his counseling with fathers, discussed fears of having their own pathology explored. In many groups, parents cope with denial of their own personal hurts and frustrations by focusing the discussion exclusively on their disabled child and his or her problems. Even at this level of interaction, there is a lot to be gained by exploring with other parents some of the common problems in raising a disabled child. Parents of disabled children typically experience greater difficulties in matters concerning care, management, and discipline than other parents; parent groups provide a context for learning to cope and seeking constructive solutions to such problems. Although there is clearly a need for professional guidance in these areas, parents are capable of contributing an enormous amount of sound and creative advice to each other as well. In addition, group members can assist each other in allowing/encouraging their handicapped children to function as independently as possible.

Sometimes parent group discussions focus on the special forms of stress experienced by families. Parents may express concerns about the well-being of nondisabled siblings or concerns regarding their parents' coping (grandparents). In addition, various kinds of conflicts within the family—between parents, between parent(s) and either the disabled child or other children, and between siblings—may arise, just as they do in any family. Very often, frustrations in the marital relationship are expressed. Spouses can transfer hostile feelings toward their husbands or wives to their children or vice versa. In all, groups provide a supportive, threrapeutic context within which parents can express and explore their feelings and seek solutions to both chronic and acute problems.

STAGES OF GROUP DEVELOPMENT AND GROUP THEMES

Counseling groups for parents of handicapped children, just like other groups, evolve and change over time. For parents of newly diagnosed children, Linder (in Darling & Darling, 1982) observed that parent groups tend to move through three stages. During the initial stage parents describe the circumstances surrounding the diagnosis of their child. Parents tend to express considerable anger and anguish over the way the diagnoses are made and communicated. The second stage tends to be characterized less by emotional reactions as parents begin to exchange concrete information about treatment. Parents also tend to express their frustrations and share their techniques of coping with the medical bureaucracy. The final stage is characterized by a more informal exchange involving aspects of each other's families and how they are generally coping.

Darling and Darling (1982) note that as these stages evolve, professional group leaders need to be aware of changing needs and concerns. Talking about feelings may be most appropriate initially, whereas offering concrete suggestions and guidance for action is more useful in the second stage. These authors suggest that during the third stage the professional leader can relinquish the leadership role as the members assume more and more control and responsibility for the group's direction.

Friedlander and Watkins (1985), in the analysis of their professionally led support groups, observed the following group phases in groups composed of parents of young mentally retarded children. During the initial stage, parents disclosed how they first found out about their child's disability as they shared "horror" stories about insensitive hospital staff, lack of support from grandparents, dismal expectations of lifelong care of profoundly disabled persons, and so on. The parents often spoke of their love and acceptance of their child in spite of his or her disability, and yet it was felt by the group leaders that there was considerable unspoken ambivalence toward their children. The most talkative members drew out the more reticent ones. In general, during this stage, it was observed that group members felt considerably unburdened and found satisfaction in their identity with others as they told of their experiences.

The parents began to tire of retelling stories about their children during the second stage. The decision about investing in the group had been settled, but the question of what they wished from the group was not. Although the therapists assumed a relatively nondirective role in the groups (recall that these groups were considered support groups), the leader did shift to a more active role at this point. The leaders, for example, verbalized manifestations of resistance (e.g., signs of flight) as the group moved to its first crisis. Absenteeism was increasing and frustration with the group was growing. In a successful effort to stem the tide, the group leader wrote a letter to the group members expressing concern over the debilitating effects of irregular attendance.

A provisional statement of goals by the therapist characterized the third stage. These goals helped to provide some focus for the group and this effort was favorably received. According to Friedlander and Watkins, the resolution of the crisis of attendance and group direction led to significant risk-taking and personal growth. Common topics included fears about the future, current resentments over having extra responsibilities, antagonisms between husbands and wives, and so on. In one group, which eventually became a mothers only group, there emerged an emphasis on marital conflict, focusing on how the husbands appeared to have isolated themselves both from responsibility for the child and sharing the emotional pain the wives acutely experienced. Several members described marriages that were basically administrative arrangements. Another major problem that emerged was the mother's turning to her retarded child for emotional fulfillment. This encouraged overdependence in the child and accentuated the mother's estrangement from her husband.

The group terminated when the leader took another job. Friedlander and Watkins report that the parents expressed a great deal of satisfaction with the group experience. The participants felt that they had grown during the group and that their marriages had improved, and there were indications that support and friendship among the members would continue even though the support group was officially over.

Loeb's (1977) three stages of group development—(1) the "feeling out" period, (2) the "work phase," and (3) termination—quite closely approximate the stages delineated above. These stages are consistent with the stages of most counseling groups in which development of trust in both the leader and fellow group members precedes deeper exploration of one's self and one's problems, followed by active problem-solving and decision-making. Eventually group members must in some way come to terms with the group's end. It is important that parents receive an opportunity to discuss their feelings concerning separation from the group and also that they be informed of professional resources should they need additional help following the group experience.

GROUP LEADERSHIP

One of the most important determinants of success in a parent counseling group is the effectiveness of its leadership. According to Stemlicht and Sullivan (1974), "The leader should be someone who (a) has the training and experience in achieving the particular group's objectives, (b) feels comfortable with the purpose of the group and, most importantly, (c) who performs competently in it" (p. 13). As noted earlier, the leader should be knowledgeable about and sensitive to the psychological needs of the effects of disability in the family. The leader must also be adept at eliciting coping mechanisms and creative problem-solving as well as dealing with defense mechanisms and strong affect. In other words, an effective leader needs experience and training—in group process in general and with parents of disabled children in particular—that will equip him or her to help group members to help themselves.

The sex of the leader does not seem to be an important consideration, although some professionals may feel it makes sense to employ a female leader in mothers groups and a male leader in fathers groups. According to the fathers group model developed by Meyer, Vadasy, Fewell, and Schell (1985), a desirable mix is to have a professional male leader and a father co-leader. With the increasing emphasis on the necessity of involving both parents in parent groups, co-facilitation by a male and female team has become common practice. In couples groups, Gottschalk and his associates (1973) expressed that male and female co-therapists:

> serve as models for such problems of parents as decision-making, resolving different preferences or opinions, expressing affection or displeasure, learning to listen, compromising different child-rearing approaches, understanding the other sex, demonstrating the advantages of collaborative vs. adversary relationships, and so forth (p. 159).

Hornby and Murray (1983) support the co-leadership model. They believe that experienced leaders should accept less experienced people to join them so that they can gain experience and eventually conduct their own parent groups. These authors make the important point that co-leaders should meet before each session to map out the general thrust of the upcoming meeting. Postmeetings are encouraged so that the leaders have an opportunity to debrief the preceding session and to begin planning for the subsequent one.

Friedlander and Watkins (1985) believe that much is to be gained by having a professional lead a support group instead of having such a group led by a peer. Their rationale for professionally led support groups is that during the course of these sessions group members may need assistance with major family problems and emotional reactions. In addition, the professionally trained leader can help the group understand and overcome difficult transition points in the group and help them understand the nature and manifestations of resistance and other group dynamics. In general, though, Friedlander and Watkins advocate a relatively nondirective approach and tend to intervene more when the group is struggling or when members are trying to cope with major emotional or interpersonal issues.

Rapp, Arnheim, and Lavine (1975) believe that group leaders should be sufficiently flexible to assume different roles at different phases of group. As a facilitator, the leader should provide the impetus for meaningful discussion, help the group set up goals and norms, and assist members in examining alternate solutions to problems. As a resource person, the group leader must know the local educational and mental health agencies. As a teacher, he or she should be knowledgeable about the child's handicapping condition and strategies for resolving interpersonal impasses between parents and children and should not be hesitant to convey his or her expertise or to call in such expertise when needed.

The role of the leader(s) within a parent group depends heavily on the purpose or goals of the group. In groups that are primarily educational/informational in nature, leaders serve as both instructors and facilitators of discussion. Groups that are therapeutically oriented require a leader who fulfills a wide variety of roles, a leader who can elicit sharing and exploring responses, confront participant inconsistencies and psychological dynamics, and assist participants in gaining insight that will translate to healthier attitudes and more effective behavior. It is probably safe to conclude that groups with a primary therapeutic agenda require a leader that has extensive knowledge of group dynamics and experience as a group leader.

EFFECTS OF PARENT GROUPS

There are a number of positive effects that parents might hope to achieve by participating in a counseling group. In general, desirable outcomes encompass changes in parent, child, and family attitudes and behavior, which ultimately lead to the optimal functioning of all family members. In the literature, outcomes that have been reported by group leaders are frequently subjective (based on the clinical judgment of the leader or subjective reports of parent satisfaction) and only occasionally objective (based on some index of measured change). Needless to say, group leaders invariably believe that their groups have met some or most of the parents' needs successfully. This section will first examine a few studies using subjective assessment and then refer to a selection of studies that have attempted to evaluate the effects of parent groups objectively.

Philage, Kuna, and Becerril (1975), in assessing their group/family approach to therapy for learning-disabled children, reported positive results in both remediation and socialization of these children. Direct feedback from the children indicated that they were aware of changes in their own behavior. In addition, parental changes were observed in many of the families. Stream (1962), in his work with fathers of emotionally disturbed children, reported results based on his observations that no appreciable change was noted in the father's relationships with their respective families. He did, however, assess his groups positively in their ability to offer strength, understanding, and support to their participants. Meyer, Vadasy, and Fewell (1985) also reported favorable results of groups for fathers of young disabled children. In his groups for parents of emotionally disturbed children, Hampton (1962) stated that "such therapy helps parents to gain greater insight into themselves and their own motivations and conflicts, and at the same time is also conducive to establishing better relations between themselves and their children who are undergoing therapy" (p. 925).

A few researchers have investigated parental changes as a consequence of participating in a parent group. Based on postgroup questionnaires, Hornby and Murray (1983) report that parents of various disabled children experienced more confidence in their ability to parent their children, felt more knowledgeable about themselves and other resources, and appreciated the sharing and identification with other parents "in the same boat." On a rating scale designed to measure social performance of children with mental retardation, Siegel, Sheridan, and Sheridan (1971) found that mothers who received group therapy rated their children significantly higher in appearance and security following therapy than before participating in a group. In another study of parents of retarded children, Appell (1964) found several changes in parents following group counseling: (1) parents were more readily able to express feelings; (2) they were far more accepting of the diagnosis of retardation; (3) counseling contributed to more productive discussions concerning retardation between parents and the retardate's siblings; (4) counseling helped parents to understand others' reactions to their child; (5) parents moved from a short- to a long-term goal orientation in reference to their retarded child; and (6) parents experienced greater optimism relative to their child's future. Finally, Bitter's (1963) results on attitude changes, though inconclusive, indicated generally that "group discussion sessions are effective in changing the attitudes of parents of trainable mentally retarded children toward their retarded child and toward family problems occasioned by the retardation" (p. 179).

Gottschalk, Brown, Bruney, Shumate, and Uliana (1973) evaluated outcomes of a parents group from the viewpoints of both the participating therapist and an independent research team. Overall, they found both positive changes in the mothers' and fathers' parenting skills and changes in the children's functioning as far as outward manifestations of behavioral dysfunction were concerned. In a well-controlled study comparing the relative effectiveness of reflective and behavioral group counseling with parents of retarded children, Tavormina (1975) found that:

> both types of counseling had a beneficial effect relative to the controls but the behavioral method resulted in significantly greater magnitude of improvement . . . the behavioral technique . . . provided them with an understandable, consistent, and effective way to deal with the specific problems they were facing in raising their retarded children (p. 22).

When Tavormina, Hampson, and Luscomb (1976) examined participant evaluations of the effectiveness of their parent counseling groups, they found that mothers who were involved in behaviorally oriented groups expressed the greatest overall gains and satisfaction with their experience. Although behavioral groups seemed quite promising, these researchers did express the opinion that a combination of behavioral and reflective group counseling is probably the most desirable mix.

A MODEL GROUP PROGRAM

A pioneer in establishing parent groups in New Zealand and Great Britain, Garry Hornby and his colleague Ray Murray (Hornby & Murray, 1983) have elaborated on their particularly well-conceived model. Based on Tavormina, Hampson, and Luscomb's (1976) conclusion that a combination of reflective and behavioral counseling benefited parents more than by using just one approach, they set out to develop a group approach beneficial to parents of children with varying disabilities.

Based on their experiences of establishing and conducting groups with parents of mentally retarded, physically handicapped, and learning-impaired children, Hornby and Murray set out to establish a group model that was responsive to the parents' need for support, information, skill development, and emotional catharsis. These authors discovered that between six to eight weekly, 2-hour evening sessions were the most satisfactory. Less than six sessions was too short to incorporate what the groups were designed to accomplish, and more than eight sessions appeared to be too much of a commitment of time for parents. Sessions that met less often (say, every 2 weeks) would suffer in attendance, and evening sessions were preferable for parents and professionals alike.

The optimum group size was found to be between eight to ten parents representing six to eight families. The groups were co-led by a psychologist with previous group experience and another professional or student with little or no group training. Other professionals were frequently invited to lecture (e.g., speech therapists, physicians, physiotherapists) or to observe (e.g., special education teachers).

The format for each session included socializing, lecture, small group discussion, and summary. *Socializing* occurred before the lecture while refreshments were served and parents talked with each other and with the invited professional. The formal *lecture* was limited to 20 minutes, after which parents *discussed* how the lecture applied to their situation. Fifty minutes was devoted to a discussion of the lecture and to any other problems or feelings parents might have wished to share. The final 15 minutes was spent *summarizing* the major issues of the evening, after which the session was adjourned, perhaps followed by a brief social exchange. Parents were asked to evaluate the groups after the 6–8-week program. Hornby and Murray (1983) report that the groups were very well received and that attendance was encouraging (74% average over the various groups). Common parent concerns that emerged in the groups included: concerns about their disabled children as the parents grew older and died, teaching appropriate behavior and self-help skills, coping with the reactions of other people, learning how to be less overprotective, and learning to cope with children as they grow older.

Hornby and Murry (1983) provide a sound basic model that can be adapted to a professional's personal style, the needs of parents and the constraints of agency time and policies. In general, these authors, along with others cited in this chapter, tend to favor a dual approach to working with parents in groups: (1) providing information and skill development and (2) allowing parents to openly discuss their reactions and emotional responses to having a disabled child in the family.

SELF-HELP GROUPS

Professionals should be knowledgeable about the existence of community-based self-help organizations (SHOs). It is beneficial for professionals to view SHOs as efforts to augment whatever services they are providing parents and not as a threat to their livelihood.

As noted in Chapter 1 by Lieberman, self-help groups currently exist for persons with a wide array of shared problems. Such groups exist for alcoholics, cancer patients, obese persons, single parents, heart patients, former mental patients, gamblers, emphysema victims—and the list goes on. In writing about SHOs for parents of disabled children, Wirtz (1977) noted that:

> one of the most important aspects of program development in the United States in recent years has been the development of parents helping parents. The schools (and professionals) serving handicapped children should capitalize on the existence of these organizations, and if they are not there, should establish some of their own (pp. 63–65).

In an effort to provide much needed help to parents of disabled children in the Lexington, Kentucky, area, Project Cope was born, and the Parent Club was formed. The goals, operations, and functions of the Parent Club, as described by Taylor (1976), parallel to a large extent other parent self-help groups. The club had three primary objectives: (1) to provide social activities, (2) to provide educational opportunities through speakers from various professional fields, and (3) to develop projects to increase parents' identity as a group and provide some avenue for self-awareness and leadership for their children. The Parent Club was instrumental in establishing a state bureau of special education and a law permitting public schools to purchase services from private agencies. It was also active in various fund-raising projects.

In a more general sense, SHOs evolve as a consequence of the perceived needs of parents for mutual support, inspiration, education, and social action. Another important reason for their meteoric rise is the many needs to which our society has responded poorly, if at all. Self-help groups may also be of practical assistance by providing such services as babysitting arrangements and transportation for members. Because such groups can be an enormous help to parents of disabled children, it would be most advantageous for professionals to be aware of the ones in their community.

LIMITATIONS OF THE GROUP APPROACH

Group counseling is certainly helpful for many parents of disabled children, but like any other type of intervention, it is not a panacea. This chapter has attempted to explore some of the benefits of parent groups. It must be kept in mind, however, that there are some parents who might find other forms of assistance more beneficial. In addition, there are persons who for a variety of reasons have a negative effect on the group, that is, who deter or inhibit the effectiveness of the group. It is important for professionals who work with disabled children and their families to fully assess which intervention or combination of interventions best fits the needs of all involved parties. If a parent group does not seem suitable for the parent or the couple, other forms of guidance and counseling, for example, individual counseling or family therapy, should be offered as an alternative. If one is not equipped to provide for the needs of the family, it is the professional's responsibility to make an appropriate referral.

Generally speaking, as reflected in this chapter, a variety of group models and approaches seem to benefit family members. Professionals who are knowledgeable about group dynamics, family dynamics, and disability can structure group experiences that meet the various needs of family members. Groups are an important resource for persons who are dispirited, lonely and isolated, poorly supported, and misinformed about relevant information and services.

REFERENCES

Adamson, W. C. (1972) Helping parents of children with learning disabilities. *Journal of Learning Disability*, 326–330.

Appell, M. J. (1964). A residence program for retarded males in a community meeting. *American Journal of Mental Deficiency, 8*, 104–108.

Barsch, R. (1961). Counseling the parent of the brain-damaged child. *Journal Rehabilitation, 27*, 26–27.

Bitter, J. A. (1963). Attitude change by parents of trainable mentally retarded children as a result of group discussions. *Exceptional Child, 30,* 173–179.

Darling, R. B., & Darling, J. (1982). *Children who are different.* St. Louis: Mosby.

Farber, B. (1962). Effects of a severely retarded child on the family. In E. P. Trapp, & P. Himelstein (Eds.), *Readings on the exceptional child.* New York: Appleton-Century-Crofts.

Featherstone, H. A. (1980). *A difference in the family.* New York: Appleton-Century-Crofts.

Friedlander, S. R., & Watkins, E. C. (1985). Therapeutic aspects of support groups for parents of the mentally retarded. *International Journal of Group Psychotherapy, 35,* 65–78.

Golden, N., Chirlin, P., & Shone, B. (1970). Tuesday children. *Social Casework, 51,* 599–605.

Gottschalk, L. A., Brown, S. B., Bruney, E. H., Shumate, L. W., & Uliana, R. L. (1973). An evaluation of a parents' group in a child-centered clinic. *Psychiatry, 36,* 157–171.

Hampton, P. J. (1962). Group psychotherapy with parents. *American Journal of Orthopsychiatry, 32,* 818–826.

Harris, S. L. (1983). *Families of the developmentally disabled.* New York: Pergamon.

Hornby, G., & Murray, R. (1983). Group programmes for parents of children with various handicaps. *Child Care Health and Development, 9,* 185–198.

Huber, C. H. (1979). Parents of the handicapped child: Facilitating acceptance through group counseling. *Personnel and Guidance Journal, 57,* 267–269.

Jacks, K. B., & Keller, M. E. (1978). A humanistic approach to the adolescent with learning disabilities: An educational, psychological, and vocational model. *Adolescence, 13,* 59–68.

Kaplan, S., & Williams, M. J. (1972). Confrontation counseling: A new dimension in group counseling. *American Journal of Orthopsychiatry, 42,* 114–118.

Laborde, P. R., & Seligman, M. (1983). Individual counseling with parents of handicapped children: Rationale and strategies. In M. Seligman (Ed.), *The family with a handicapped child.* Philadelphia: Grune & Stratton, pp. 261–284.

Loeb, R. C. (1977). Group therapy for parents of mentally retarded children. *Journal of Marriage and Family Counseling, 3,* 77–83.

Meyer, D. J., Vadasy, P. F., Fewell, R. R., & Schell, G. C. (1985). *A handbook for a fathers program.* Seattle: University of Washington Press.

Meyer, D. J., Vadasy, P. F., & Fewell, R. R. (1985). *Sibshops.* Seattle: University of Washington Press.

Meyer, D. J., & Vadasy, P. F. (1986). *Grandparent workshop.* Seattle: University of Washington Press.

Opirhory, G., & Peters, G. A. (1982). Counseling intervention strategies for families with the less than perfect newborn. *Personnel & Guidance Journal, 60,* 451–455.

Pasnau, R. O., Meyer, M., Davis, L. J., Lloyd, R., & Kline, G., (1976). Coordinated group psychotherapy of children and parents. *International Journal of Group Psychotherapy, 26,* 89–103.

Philage, M. L., Kuna, D. J., & Becerril, G. (1975). A new family approach to therapy for the learning disabled child. *Journal of Learning Disabilities, 8,* 22–31.

Ramsey, C. V. (1967). Review of group methods with parents of the mentally retarded. *American Journal of Mental Deficiency, 71,* 857–863.

Rapp, H. M., Arnheim, D. L., & Lavine, B. J. (1975, October). The roles of a parent discussion group leader. *Personnel and Guidance Journal,* pp. 110–112.

Samit, C., Nash, K., & Meyers, J. (1980). The parents group: A therapeutic tool. *Social Casework, 61,* 215–222.

Schilling, R. F., Gilchrist, L. D., & Schinke, S. P. (1984). Coping and social support in families of developmentally disabled children. *Family Relations, 33,* 47–54.

Seligman, M. (1979). *Strategies for helping parents of exceptional children.* New York: The Free Press.

Seligman, M., & Seligman, P. A. (1980, October). The professional's dilemma: Learning to work with parents. *The Exceptional Parent,* pp. 511–513.

Seligman, M. (Ed.). (1983). *The family with a handicapped child.* Philadelphia: Grune & Stratton.

Seligman, M., & Darling, R. (in press). *Ordinary families, special children: A systems approach to childhood disability.* New York: Guilford.

Seligman, M. (1987). Adaptation of children to a chronically ill or mentally handicapped sibling. *Canadian Medical Association Journal, 136,* 1249–1251.

Siegel, B., Sheridan, K., & Sheridan, E. P. (1971). Group psychotherapy: Its effects on mothers who rate social performance of retardates. *American Journal of Psychiatry, 127*, 1215–1217.

Solmit, A. J., & Stark, M. H. (1961). Mourning and the birth of a defective child. *The psychoanalytic study of the child, 16*, 523–537.

Stenlicht, M., & Sullivan, I. (1974). Group counseling with parents of the MR: Leadership selection and functioning. *Mental Retardation, 12*, 11–13.

Strean, H. S. (1962). A means of involving fathers in family treatment: Guidance groups for fathers. *American Journal of Orthopsychiatry, 32*, 719–727.

Tavormina, J. B. (1975). Relative effectiveness of behavioral and reflective group counseling with parents of mentally retarded children. *Journal of Consulting, Clinical, in Psychology, 43*, 22–31.

Tavormina, J. B., Hampson, R. B., & Luscomb, R. L. (1976). Participant evaluations of the effectiveness of their parent counseling groups. *Mental Retardation, 14*, 8–9.

Taylor, F. C. (1976). Project cope. In E. J. Webster (Ed.), *Professional approaches with parents of handicapped children*. Springfield, IL: Charles C. Thomas.

Toffler, A. (1970). *Future shock*. New York: Random House.

Tracey, J. (1970). Journal of parent guidance groups: Is this therapy? *Journal of Psychiatric Nursing Mental Health Service, 8*, 11–12.

Wirtz, M. A. (1977). *An administrator's handbook of special education: A guide to better education for the handicapped*. Springfield, IL: Charles C. Thomas.

10
Group Therapy for
Suicidal Adolescents

Three major clinical situations link suicide with group therapy. The first, recognized from the beginnings of this treatment modality, is the inclusion of a suicidal person in the group. This situation has generally been regarded as undesirable, occurring as a result of clinical misjudgment, and as disruptive to the group process, especially if a suicide occurs (Bowers, Mullen, & Berkovitz, 1959; Horwitz, 1976). When suicidal patients have clearly benefitted by the group experience, it has tended to be reported as an unexpected outcome (Miller & Shaskan, 1963).

The second situation linking suicide and group therapy entails the group treatment of persons who have lost a close friend or family member to suicide. These "survivor" groups serve as a means of facilitating the mourning process and resolving the pain, anger, guilt, grief, and bewilderment generated by such a loss (Battle, 1984; Hatton & Valente, 1981; Saffer, 1986; Shulman & Margalit, 1985).

The third situation, which is the focus of this discussion, involves structuring the treatment group specifically for persons at risk for suicide. This approach serves to channel the intense energy associated with self-destructive impulses into a powerful force for group cohesion and bonding, rather than constituting an ever-present threat that can only distract the group and diminish the strengths inherent in group work.

BACKGROUND

Group therapy for suicidal adolescents evolved through a progressive refinement of clinical focus. In the field of suicide prevention, early progress in the 1950s and 1960s in recognizing and assessing suicide risk far outstripped the development of effective treatment methods. This progress led to experimenting with group treatment of suicidal adults by adapting well-established principles of group therapy (Alfaro, 1970; Billings, Rosen, Asimos, & Motto, 1974; Comstock & McDermott, 1975; Farberow, 1968; Indin, 1966; Lafuente, Paillisé, Pantinat, Villapana, Otin, & Sarró, 1981; Motto & Stein, 1973; Wedler & Wedler, 1978). Initial efforts were most frequently carried out with groups on hospital wards. These settings provided ready access to depressed and suicidal patients, 24-hour supervision, numerous staff resources, and an array of other treatment modalities, to which group therapy was simply added. Perhaps as one facet of the delay in providing specialized adolescent mental health services, group treatment of suicidal persons in this age group followed reports of adult groups by several years and were widely scattered.

Adolescent groups of various types have long been reported (Bates, 1975; Berkovits, 1972), but I have found only four reports of groups specifically for teenagers at risk for suicide. The first described an outpatient group at a University Hospital in Brno, Czechoslovakia (Hadlik, 1970), and the second was an inpatient group on a child psychiatry ward in Stuttgart, Germany (Ott, Geyer, & Schneemann, 1972). The third group reported was formed to meet the needs of some high-risk adolescents and young adults who found it difficult to fit into an adult outpatient group for suicidal persons (Asimos & Rosen, 1978). The fourth report (Ross & Motto, 1984) detailed an effort to explore the feasibility of a group counseling program for suicidal adolescents in a nonmedical free-standing Suicide Prevention and Crisis Center. This program was an outcome of a special suicide prevention program undertaken by the Center in 1975, using a health education approach in the public high schools that focused on early detection. So many requests for direct services were subsequently received from adolescents that the group counseling program was developed to help meet the special clinical needs of this population.

Another group effort for suicidal adolescents that deserves mention was carried out in Krakow and Lublin, Poland (Pluzek, 1978). Although not a treatment group in the traditional sense, this innovative program included a number of therapeutic group activities including a "Social Club" that provided a homelike setting for a Christmas party, birthday parties, and other social functions.

The meager number of reports in the behavioral literature is not an accurate reflection of recent and current activity in the area of group therapy for suicidal adolescents. One major reason for this is that from its inception, the field of suicide prevention has been staffed largely by nonacademic persons dedicated primarily to assisting those in crisis and in despair. Although guided and supervised by experienced professionals, the basic effort has been provision of effective service, rather than systematic evaluation and publication. Much has been reported informally at suicide prevention workshops and meetings, as well as in agency newsletters, without emphasis on methodologic concerns about controls, randomized design, or other elements of scientific rigor. This is a clear reflection of the current early stage of development of specialized adolescent services. In the area of suicide prevention there are relatively few mental health professionals engaged in investigations that find their way into the literature. However, many trained nonprofessional persons with a special interest in suicide are attempting to meet urgent needs not yet provided for by the established health-care system.

ORGANIZATION AND STRUCTURE

The resources required for a group treatment program dictate the need for at least one organizational sponsor, such as a psychiatric hospital, clinic, suicide prevention center, church, or emergency department of a general hospital. The sponsoring agency provides or arranges for therapists/counselors, space, a communications system, and emergency back-up resources that should provide 24-hour availability. Optimally, each group member also has an individual therapist, since the group serves best as an augmentation—not a replacement—of other forms of treatment. In practice, this policy is a difficult one to enforce in an outpatient group, so some flexibility may be required.

A system for referral to the group and a consistent screening procedure is necessary. Explicit goals of the group can be expressed as providing a caring setting in which group members discuss sources of pain, learn that others may have similar experiences, find ways to cope with their situation, and learn where help is available in a crisis.

Exclusion criteria for group membership are usually established, based on prior clinical experience and on the nature and goals of the specific group. It is common to specify an age range and to screen out adolescents whose clinical picture indicates a prominent role of violence, alcohol/drug abuse, or psychosis. These criteria are necessarily somewhat arbitrary and can lead to difficult subjective judgments as to how severe they must be to apply in a given case. The decision must ultimately be the screening clinician's intuitive impression as to how seriously the issue in question can disrupt the group process. Substance abuse, for example, may be recognized as a peripheral aspect of a stressful life situation or as a central issue that is generating the stresses underlying a suicidal state. The former may be seen as an excellent candidate for group work geared to suicide prevention, and the latter to a group focused more on substance abuse.

Questions asked most often by potential group members are concerns about confidentiality in regard to their family, school personnel, and community, and whether they would have to see a mental health professional. The group leader should clarify the relationship of the group to the school, if any, reassuring the youngster that there would be no influence on grades, possible transfer, or any entry in school records regarding their participation.

As for families, it has been found useful to explain that, while it could be very helpful to have families involved, the adolescent's judgment would be respected, so that they could tell their families as much or as little as they wished about the group, and that communication with parents would be encouraged but not required. State laws differ in this regard. In California, a minor who has attained the age of 12, as well as designated maturity and intellectual levels, can receive mental health treatment or counseling on an outpatient basis without the consent of a parent or guardian. The professional person providing such service has the psychotherapist–patient privilege in regard to confidentiality. The process of reassuring the adolescent provides an opportunity to develop trust and confidence that their concerns are understood and respected and to convey a clear message that experiencing emotional pain does not mean that one is abnormal.

Two or three group co-leaders are usually involved in order to minimize problems associated with necessary absence of a therapist or with emergency situations. It also helps to have more than one viewpoint in reviewing sessions and making decisions about issues that arise. Beyond this, co-therapists offer support to one another, improve continuity, allow for the young group members to model relationships with different personalities, and, with male/female co-leaders, provide parent and sibling figures. The many demands that can be put on a group leader by needy teenagers also make it desirable to share the task with at least one other person.

The qualifications and characteristics of the group leaders are important. A thorough understanding of the special developmental problems of the adolescent and a keen interest in young people are much more important than expertise about suicide. Emotional stability, a fundamental knowledge of human behavior, and at least basic training in the area of suicide prevention are invaluable. A professional identity is not necessary and may even be a temporary handicap. As in individual work with adolescents, how the group is conducted is generally more important than the specific strategies used. Terms used by teenagers to describe the "how" are: candor, simplicity, really interested, concerned, warm, natural, straightforward, like a person, understanding, honest, doesn't talk too much, available, empathetic. While there is nothing unusual in this list, as therapists generally see themselves, adolescents tend to be unforgiving of any shortcomings they perceive. More mature patients may allow moments of forgetfulness, phoniness, or other human frailties in a therapist. Teenagers are less accepting of such lapses in a person they need to see as omniscient and often use them to maintain distance or discontinue therapy. Even in the absence of such shortcomings, adolescents may attribute them to a therapist as a rationalization for dropping out of a group, reflecting the adolescent's intense ambivalence about dependency and fear of the vulnerability to painful rejection that is inherent in a dependent relationship.

OBSERVATIONS OF GROUP EXPERIENCE

First meetings can be started by the group leaders introducing and giving background information about themselves, including aspects of their personal life and their choice to work with youth because they like and value such relationships and experiences. This type of introduction clearly goes beyond traditional boundaries but sets a tone of openness that makes it easier for the group members to do the same when they introduce themselves.

The group "rules" can then be reviewed, such as being on time, letting the leaders know if they would be unable to attend, not smoking in the meeting room, not using drugs or alcohol when attending the group, and protecting confidentiality. These rules are presented not as controls but as ways of caring about each other and treating each other fairly. Agreement is solicited from each member.

Shyness and tentativeness typically mark the initial ventures, with everyone staying on safe ground. Descriptions of family fights, running away, suicide attempts, hospital experiences, drug or alcohol episodes, and other emotionally charged issues are usually deferred to later sessions, after a degree of comfort and trust in the group permits such revelations.

A major point before the first session ends is to emphasize the importance of communication and to suggest calling the leaders or other designated resource person if any need arises before the next meeting. The point is most meaningful if the leaders provide their home telephone numbers to each group member, although this is a matter of individual style, degree of availability, and the extent of backup services. For example, if a 24-hour telephone crisis service is available, some group therapists prefer that they be reached through the crisis line rather than directly. It is the perception of the group leaders' interest and availability that is the important element, rather than the details of the arrangement. This is one important aspect of the group leaders' more active participation in the therapeutic work than is traditional in group therapy.

In subsequent meetings the primary themes involve family relationships, peer relationships, loss-grief-pain-anger, suicidal impulses, and coping mechanisms when these are experienced as overwhelming. Typically, the initial issues of despair and suicidal ideas are quickly relinquished as the underlying conflicts come to the forefront. These conflicts take the form of concerns about dependent needs, independent strivings, issues of dating, thoughts of one person about another, the pain of perceiving others' thoughts about the self as negative, and the disbelief of perceiving those thoughts as positive. Anxiety and pain related to loss of peer or family relationships absorbs much group time, with the theme of suicide coming to be recognized as the kind of impulse that arises when the hurt is severe. Anger is described by group members as the predominant emotion expressed verbally, playing some part in most life situations and creating tensions with parents, school personnel, and employers.

Manifestations of these themes are numerous, as each adolescent presents his or her own version of them. For example (Ross & Motto, 1984), a 17-year-old girl from a violent family with an alcoholic father could scarcely contain her anger and had pounded her fist through a wall on several occasions, as well as attempting suicide twice by overdose. An 18-year-old boy created severe tensions with his family by his defiantly independent behavior but struggled with his girlfriend over excessive dependence on her with a serious suicide attempt with carbon monoxide when feeling alienated from both his family and girlfriend. A 17-year-old girl who had taken overdoses of aspirin or drugs six times insisted she did not want to kill herself but was angry with herself and wanted to punish her body. A 14-year-old boy fought incessantly with his alcoholic father, turning to alcohol and drugs himself to stave off depression.

The theme of dating and peer relationships takes on a special sense of immediacy when couples of group members pair off, coming early to see each other before the group or holding hands during the group meeting. This provides a useful situation in which to explore the anxiety, hopes, doubts, fears, disappointments, and the "natural high" associated with healthy peer interaction, feelings that all group members can share. The despondency and pain of losing peer relationships is an ever-recurring theme, with useful extension to the loss of family members and even of pets. A great deal of time and energy tends to be expended by the group when a crisis arises due to such losses by a group member, but the shared effort to help find a means of coping with the pain is an invaluable stimulus for emotional growth for all group members.

Sexuality is not a prominent theme, in spite of its importance to the adolescent period. Open discussion of sexual matters seems to create embarrassment in the group, and the issue of incest appears to be taboo, especially for those who have had such experiences. It is probably best to have groups specifically for youngsters with this background. There is not yet sufficient data to provide guidelines for dealing with sexuality with suicidal adolescents in the group setting.

The theme of suicide, although never very far away, tends to remain in the background as an impulse that arises when the pain of hurtful events exceeds a certain threshold. The focus is more on the means of fending it off—running away, using drugs or alcohol, arguing with key persons, or turning to resources in the group.

The most frequent issue brought up by group members involves family relationships, an area of conflict for all of them. Every possible family-related issue can be expected to surface, generally in the context of too-great or too-little limit-setting. Perceived expectations or demands are prominent, often complicated by parental emotional disorders or substance abuse.

Therapeutic approaches vary, of course, with different group leaders. The most frequent patterns tend to be primarily supportive, in which painful feelings are acknowledged and accepted, and the focus placed on what to do when they seem to become unbearable. A common emphasis is that if such feelings occur when the youngster is alone, he or she should have a clear awareness that there are people who care, who they are, how to get in touch with them, and that if given a chance to express their caring, they can help. As simple as these ideas sound, they take on special meaning as they are found to work in practice.

COMPARISON WITH OTHER GROUPS

Therapists experienced in group work may ask how depressed and suicidal adolescents differ from other categories of group members. Although each adolescent and group is unique, some generalizations can be ventured (Frederick & Farberow, 1970).

The degree of need these youngsters bring to the group is usually extreme. It can encompass emotional support not only for self-destructive impulses but for practically all aspects of their lives. The family turmoil, peer pressures, demands of parents, school, and jobs, as well as everyday needs such as temporary shelter or transportation, can combine to put remarkable demands on the group members.

A closely related element is the intensity of feeling generated by stress situations, which creates special concerns with youngsters who become self-destructive when feeling discouraged and despairing. Extremes of emotion are frequent, even over apparently minor issues.

One characteristic of adolescent groups, which is also observed in adult groups of depressed and suicidal persons, is a remarkably high level of communication and mutual support within the group. Thus, a telephone call from one member to another might be communicated to several other group members and to the group leader. A crisis tends to generate an atmosphere of intense group cohesion, as though a message to anyone in the group is a message to everyone in the group. No matter how distorted or exaggerated the message, empathic support is immediately and uncritically provided by the group members. This reaction differs from traditional groups, in which a serious suicidal state in one member tends to result in the other members becoming acutely anxious and drawing back from the one in crisis. The cohesion and empathy is probably the most important element in the stabilizing potential of the group approach to suicidal states, providing an influence no single therapist could provide, whatever skills or experience are brought to bear (Asimos, 1979; Farberow, 1972).

The reverse of this strength is that if the group feels that it has been deliberately misled by a group member in order to obtain its support, emotional withdrawal and rejection can be triggered just as abruptly and uncritically as the support previously offered. A painful sense of betrayal and of being used in a dishonest way generates a level of hostility that can be potentially destructive. For example, a 15-year-old girl with a history of sexual abuse evoked an intense, empathic response in an adolescent group by relating the particularly painful and touching events in her life. In subsequent efforts to find special help for her, it was learned that she had given a false age and had concealed pertinent information. On the basis of this, the group felt that she had "conned" them and used their feelings dishonestly, leading to a rejection toward her that was untempered by expressions of understanding or compassion. She was subsequently transferred to another resource.

CURRENT PROBLEM AREAS

In working with suicidal adolescents in groups, two problem areas are recognized at present: specifically, logistical problems and clinical problems. Although superficially separate, they can overlap a great deal in practice.

The clearest logistical hurdle is finding appropriate persons to serve as group leaders. Although interest in groups is generally high in mental health and educational circles, individuals with the needed training, experience, and availability are not easily found. Adolescents put unusual demands on a therapist, and when suicidal the pressures are intensified. Thus, the prospect of working with a group of six or eight suicidal teenagers at one time can be intimidating, even if each of them has an individual therapist as well. The problem of burnout is significant, but it can be minimized by the use of two or three therapists and the provision of an effective backup system for the group leaders. This system might include a "befriender" program and a 24-hour telephone crisis line (Ross & Motto, 1984), a 24-hour "hotline," and a psychiatric hospital for adolescents (Walters, 1987), or the emergency service of a psychiatric institute (Asimos & Rosen, 1978).

A more mundane potential hurdle is the administrative system of the sponsoring organization. Concerns about legal vulnerability and obtaining approval from professional advisors, such as the organization's professional advisory committee, may require many months of collaborative planning, consultation, letters of cooperation, and consistent reassurance (Hackel & Asimos, 1980). In some instances, the term *therapy* has to be avoided in favor of *group counseling, support group,* or *rap group.* The adjunctive role of a group must be made clear to all interested parties, both to clarify the goals of the program and to facilitate referral of participants from other health care agencies, such as adolescent community mental health resources, psychiatric hospitals, or private therapists.

A major clinical problem is how to structure the program in regard to the duration of group treatment. Various patterns have been used, but the limited data on this issue suggest that the open-ended format with indefinite duration is optimal. The intense dependent–independent conflict so prominent in this age group can be allowed to express itself in all its forms and to be responded to in the most growth-inducing way when not faced with an artificial termination date. Asimos and Rosen (1978) reported a clear improvement in group functioning, with reduced acting-out and diminished guilt about attendance, when they changed from a closed-ended to an open-ended structure. Ross and Motto (1984) also found it necessary to extend planned duration of the group due to clinical considerations. Prior experience with adults strongly supports the open-ended structure as well.

Termination is a delicate issue in any therapeutic relationship. For emotionally vulnerable adolescents with severe unresolved dependent needs, it can be critical to provide for the flexibility some require to avoid experiencing the termination process as a devastating rejection. If indefinite open-ended duration is not feasible, entry into a subsequent newly formed group can help and can even provide the adolescent with special stature and esteem as a more experienced member. Many will continue with or return to individual therapy or counseling. In any case, some form of follow-up for at least a year is indicated. This implies some informal expression of continuing interest after the group is ended.

There are no published systematic studies of the efficacy of special groups for suicidal adolescents. This lack reflects the relative newness of the endeavor as well as the serious methodologic obstacles faced by the entire field of psychotherapy research. However, several relevant observations have been reported. Billings (1974) demonstrated that high-risk persons 12 to 84 years of age who participated in special groups had significantly fewer subsequent suicides than those entering other modalities, or having no treatment. Frey, Motto, and Ritholz (1983) applied a systematic evaluation design to an outpatient group of suicidal persons, although it included no adolescents. It showed beneficial change, with most benefit demonstrated in the first five sessions. Walters (1987) provides the epidemiologic observation that in the 2 years following the initiation of a program of Suicide Prevention Support Groups for adolescents in Wilmington, Delaware, the yearly incidence of suicide in this age group dropped from a mean of 10 to a range of 5 to 7. An extensive preliminary evaluation of the efficacy of two adolescent groups has been carried out at the San Mateo (California) Suicide Prevention and Crisis Center (Ross, 1988). Although 6-month follow-up data indicate a good subjective outcome, the quantitative measures used do not provide clear confirmation of efficacy.

As with other modalities, there are ample supportive data of an anecdotal or testimonial nature. For example, the inpatient group for suicidal adolescents reported by Ott, Geyer, and Schneemann (1972) stressed a multidimensional approach for the nine suicidal youngsters aged 12 to 16. It included individual therapy, group therapy, role-playing groups, family therapy, and social functions. All components of the program were regarded as important, but the group therapy was characterized as "the nucleus of our therapeutic efforts" and "the best process for our problem" (addressing suicide risk) (Ott, Guyer, & Schneemann, 1972).

Its value was seen as facilitating bringing problems to the surface, enhancing rapport with the therapist and with other group members, and especially encouraging to the mutual support and security the group members provided for each other. Consistent with other observers, the group leader was seen as a key element. After a 4-month treatment period, an 18-month follow-up found no recurrence of suicidal behavior and evidence of stable patterns in school and work.

SURVIVING A SUICIDE

There are no published reports of the suicide of a group member in the course of an adolescent group, although the effect of such an event has been discussed in reports of some adult groups. In one group (Farberow, 1972), a flare-up of suicidal feelings occurred in other group members, but no further suicides or suicide attempts were triggered. A sense of guilt or personal failure was experienced by some group members, as well as anger toward the therapists for not having been able to save the person. In another group (Comstock & McDermott, 1975), initial denial of suicide was followed by anger and dismay, with a painful awareness of how survivors are the victims of a suicide. Group work intensified, but no worsening of depression was seen. The point is made that the therapists' personal feelings have to be expressed, since failure to react is seen as endorsing emotional isolation, which would be an undesirable model. In a third report (Motto, 1979), surviving group members were shaken but were able to express a wide range of emotional responses to the suicide and after a few weeks were able to continue as before without loss of momentum. The event generated an increased readiness in the therapists to take action subsequently with another group member, and it also served to forcefully remind them of their limitations.

The consequences of three suicide attempts in the course of an adolescent group are described by Ross and Motto (1984). These episodes demonstrated anew the intense emotionality of teenagers and evoked tearful anticipation of the pain that would ensue if anyone in the group "really did it." A useful discussion was triggered of how much it hurts to lose someone important to you, and how much anger is generated when someone close to you does something hurtful. An unspoken pact was entered into, with an exchange of phone numbers and a promise of support if any member needed to get through a night or a weekend.

SUMMARY

Group therapy for depressed and suicidal adolescents has emerged as an extension of group experience with suicidal adults. This emphasis in turn grew out of a need to expand our therapeutic approaches when increasing interest was focused on suicide prevention. It should come as no surprise that adolescents are extremely responsive to peer groups and that their affinity for the telephone could create a very active support system outside the group sessions. Thus, a variety of patterns have emerged, from teen rap groups through peer support groups, group counseling, and group psychotherapy. Much of the activity in this area is carried out in a nonmedical context, which is not able to offer "treatment"; hence, alternate terms for group therapy are used even though the content may not differ substantially. Common elements are the issues of coping with painful experience, self-confidence, empathic intimacy, the nature of relationships, dependent–independent strivings, resolution of feelings of guilt and inferiority, and—above all—learning and experiencing alternatives to self-destructive behaviors when under severe stress. The group itself becomes a coping instrument to be turned to in a crisis, much as an alternate close and caring family.

The mental health community has been slow to respond to the challenge of a group approach for suicidal adolescents; hence, the professional literature has relatively little to offer. Adolescent psychiatry, still in its early development, has left the investigation of this field largely to the nonmedical suicide prevention community. It must be granted that unusual demands are placed on group leaders, and the positive reports available to us give much credit to their remarkable energy, caring, responsiveness, patience, and unflagging determination that vulnerable young people learn constructive coping skills.

Perhaps the most positive observation that has emerged from adolescent group experience to date is that the common developmental tasks and emotionality of this age group lend themselves to the goals of group work. That is, intense group cohesion, uncritical support in times of need, and the learning of difficult skills in an encouraging and nonjudgmental environment, all provide confirmation of Berkovitz's (1972) cogent observation that, indeed, "adolescents grow in groups."

Current and projected programs of early detection of potential suicides in the schools are likely to generate a need for adolescent treatment and counseling resources far beyond those now available. Our readiness to utilize group treatment and counseling techniques can have a significant role in determining whether we will be up to that challenge.

REFERENCES

Alfaro, R. (1970). A group therapy approach to suicide prevention. *NIMH Bulletin of Suicidology, 6*, 56–59.

Asimos, C. (1979). Dynamic problem solving in a group for suicidal persons. *International Journal of Group Psychotherapy, 29*, 109–114.

Asimos, C., & Rosen, D. (1976). Group treatment of suicidal and depressed persons. *Bulletin of the Menninger Clinic, 42*, 515–516.

Bates, M. (1975) Themes in group counseling with adolescents. In I. Berkovitz (Ed.), *When Schools Care* (pp. 56–68). New York: Brunner/Mazel.

Battle, A. (1984). Group therapy for survivors of suicide. *Crisis, 5*, 45–58.

Berkovitz, I. (1972). *Adolescents grow in groups.* New York: Brunner/Mazel.

Billings, J. (1974). *The efficacy of group treatment with depressed and suicidal individuals in comparison with other treatment settings as regards the prevention of suicide.* Unpublished doctoral dissertation, California School of Professional Psychology, San Francisco, CA.

Billings, J., Rosen, D., Asimos, C., & Motto, J. (1974) Observations on long-term group psychotherapy with suicidal and depressed persons. *Life-Threatening Behavior, 4*, 160–170.

Bowers, K., Mullen, H., & Berkovitz, B. (1959). Observations on suicide occurring during group therapy. *American Journal of Psychotherapy, 13*, 93–106.

Comstock, B., & McDermott, M. (1975) Group therapy for patients who attempt suicide. *International Journal of Group Psychotherapy, 25*, 44–49.

Farberow, N. (1968). Group psychotherapy with suicidal persons. In H. Resnik (Ed.), *Suicidal behaviors* (pp. 328–340). Boston: Little, Brown.

Farberow, N. (1972). Vital process in suicide prevention: Group psychotherapy as a community of concern. *Life-Threatening Behavior, 2*, 239–251.

Frederick, C., & Farberow, N. (1970). Group therapy with suicidal persons: A comparison with standard group methods. *International Journal of Social Psychiatry, 16*, 103–111.

Frey, D., Motto, J., & Ritholz, M. (1983). Group therapy for persons at risk for suicide: An evaluation using the intense design. *Psychotherapy Theory, Research and Practice, 20*, 281–292.

Hackel, J., & Asimos, C. (1980). Resistances encountered in starting a group therapy program for suicide attempters in varied administrative settings. *Suicide and Life-Threatening Behavior, 10,* 100–105.

Hadlik, J. (1970). Group psychotherapy for adolescents following a suicide attempt. In R. Fox (Ed.), *Proceedings of the 5th International Congress for Suicide Prevention* (pp. 57–59). London: International Association for Suicide Prevention.

Hatton, C., & Valente, S. (1981). Bereavement group for parents who suffered a suicidal loss of a child. *Suicide and Life-Threatening Behavior, 11,* 141–150.

Horwitz, L. (1976). Indications and contraindications for group psychotherapy. *Bulletin of the Menninger Clinic, 40,* 515–518.

Indin, B. (1966). The crisis club: A group experience for suicidal patients. *Mental Hygiene, 50,* 280–290.

Lafuente, C., Paillisé, A., Pantinat, L., Villapana, Otin, J., & Sarró, B. (1981). Therapie de groupe dans une unite de suicidologie de l'hopital general. In J. Soubrier, & J. Vedrinne (Eds.), *Depression et suicide* (pp. 447–450). Paris: Pergamon Press.

Miller, R., & Shaskan, D. (1963). A note on the group management of a disgruntled suicidal patient. *International Journal of Group Psychotherapy, 13,* 216–218.

Motto, J. & Stein, E. (1973). A group approach to guilt in depressive and suicidal patients. *Journal of Religion and Health, 12,* 278–285.

Motto, J. (1979). Starting a therapy group in a suicide prevention and crisis center. *Suicide and Life-Threatening Behavior, 9,* 47–56.

Ott, J., Geyer, M., & Schneemann, K. (1972). Multidimensional clinical psychotherapy of a group of children and adolescents after attemptd suicide. *Psychiatrie, Neurologie und Medizinische Psychologie (Leipzig), 24,* 104–110. (In German).

Pluzek, Z. (1978). Efficacy of a treatment program for attempted suicides among youth. In A. Aalberg (Ed.), *Proceedings of the 9th International Congress of the International Association for Suicide Prevention* (pp. 114–118). Helsinki: Finnish Association for Mental Health.

Ross, C. (1988). *Evaluation of support groups for suicidal adolescents.* Report to the Cleveland Foundation, Suicide Prevention and Crisis Center of San Mateo County, California.

Ross, C., Motto, J. (1984). Group counseling for suicidal adolescents. In H. Sudak, A. Ford, N. Rushforth (Eds.), *Suicide in the young* (pp. 367–392). Boston: John Wright-PSG.

Saffer, J. (1986). Group therapy with friends of an adolescent suicide. *Adolescence, 21,* 743–745.

Shulman, S., & Margalit, M. (1985). Suicidal behavior at school. A systemic perspective. *Journal of Adolescence, 8,* 263–269.

Walters, M. (1987). *Cultural, social and behavioral effects on adolescents attending suicide prevention support groups.* Paper presented at 14th International Congress, International Association for Suicide Prevention, May 28, 1987, San Francisco.

Wedler, M., & Wedler, H. (1978). Group work experience with suicidal patients. In A. Aalberg (Ed.), *Proceedings of the 9th International Congress of the International Association for Suicide Prevention* (pp. 449–451). Helsinki: Finnish Association for Mental Health.

11
Group Treatment with Sexually Abused Children

Child sexual abuse has gained considerable attention in the past decade. The problem of sexual abuse, once rarely addressed in the mental health literature, has become an area of growing concern. Historical and cultural sanctions that previously discouraged discussions of incest and other forms of sexual abuse have loosened, contributing to a new awareness by mental health professionals of the severity of the problem and the prevalence of sexually exploited children. Along with the attention given sexual abuse by a variety of professionals (e.g., psychologists, social workers, nurses, doctors, lawyers, child protection workers), the media also have played an instrumental role in educating the public about the seriousness of this topic. Numerous books and television programs have detailed various aspects of child sexual abuse. The resulting heightened cultural awareness has contributed to a dramatic increase in reported cases of child sexual abuse.

The rise in reporting of sexual abuse has created complications for many mental health clinics. A majority of the sexually abused children that come to the attention of health-care professionals either seek or are referred for psychotherapy. Many agencies are not equipped to handle an increase in referrals or lack the funds and expertise to treat the sexual abuse victim. The large numbers of children needing treatment have forced many agencies to establish waiting lists. Delays in treatment can be detrimental to children because many victims experience an emotional crisis shortly after the abuse has been disclosed. Practitioners in mental health settings who are unaccustomed to treating sexual abuse or working with children often feel helpless when faced with the growing number of sexually abused children in their case load.

The scarcity of literature on the treatment of child sexual abuse provides another obstruction for those therapists who wish to increase their knowledge of how to intervene with sexually exploited children. Only a few empirical investigations have addressed issues related to treating the families and victims of sexual abuse (Kroth, 1979). Furthermore, most of the information concerning treatment has been gleaned from clinical case studies, brief descriptions of treatment groups for adults who were sexually abused as children, and a few clinical reports of groups for child victims.

Most of the clinical literature and empirical research has concentrated on three primary areas: (1) determining the incidence and prevalence of sexual abuse (Russell, 1983; Wyatt & Peters, 1986), (2) delineating the initial and long-term effects of child sexual abuse (Browne & Finkelhor, 1986), and (3) outlining the types of family environments that contribute to sexual abuse (Finkelhor, 1980; James & Nasjleti, 1983; Mrazek & Bentovim, 1981; Summit & Kryso, 1978). The findings from these investigations have helped to give definition to the picture of the sexually abused child. Substantial evidence suggests that large numbers of victims experience emotional trauma that continues for years after the termination of the abusive behavior. These results demonstrate the importance of developing effective methods of treatment that can be implemented shortly after the disclosure of sexual abuse.

The purpose of this chapter is to provide mental health practitioners with information on child sexual abuse* and on group treatment with this population. The chapter will begin with an overview of child sexual abuse, including a discussion of definitional problems, demographic and descriptive characteristics of victims, and the emotional impact of sexual abuse on children. The remainder of the chapter will focus on group treatment issues with sexually abused children, including a discussion of themes, membership, structure, and techniques as they relate to group formats. The majority of sexual abuse occurs within families (i.e., intrafamilial), and as a result the preponderance of children that are referred for treatment have experienced intrafamilial sexual abuse. Although the chapter will not concentrate exclusively on this type of sexual abuse, intrafamilial abuse will receive considerable attention throughout.

OVERVIEW OF CHILD SEXUAL ABUSE

Defining Child Sexual Abuse

A major problem encountered in the sexual abuse literature is one of definition. No consensus has been reached on the criteria for defining child sexual abuse. For example, the term *sexual abuse* has been used to describe a wide variety of behaviors such as exhibitionism, genital manipulation, intercourse, and child pornography (Mrazek, 1981). It also has been used interchangeably with such descriptors as molestation, victimization, rape, incest, exploitation, sexual assault, and sexual maltreatment (Russell, 1984).

The Child Abuse Prevention and Treatment Act of 1974 defined child sexual abuse as: "The obscene or pornographic photographing, filming, or depicting of children for commercial purposes, or the rape, molestation, incest, prostitution, or other such forms of sexual exploitation of children under circumstances which indicate that the child's health or welfare is harmed or threatened thereby" (National Center on Child Abuse and Neglect [NCCAN], 1979). Problems can occur using this definition in adversarial situations (e.g., court hearings) when the burden of proof is on victims to show some type of physical or emotional injury. Parents also have expressed concern with definitions that use the type of sexual contact as the major criterion, since normal physical contact such as bathing and dressing a child could be misconstrued as sexually exploitive (Mrazek, 1981).

In the most widely accepted definitions, the major focus is on the relationship between victim and perpetrator, with less emphasis given to the type of act committed. This follows from the commonly accepted premise that *all* forms of sexual contact between adults and children are considered inappropriate. Children are seen as developmentally immature and unable to fully comprehend or consent to the sexual exploitation (Mrazek, 1981). Therefore, child sexual abuse can be defined as any sexually exploitive behavior between a child (usually defined as under age 18, depending on the particular state law) and an older person (usually considered at least 5 years older than the victim; Finkelhor, 1979). This definition

---

*Throughout this chapter, the term *child* will be used to describe any minor, including adolescents (i.e., under age 18).

includes sibling incest and sexual offenses committed by adolescents, as long as a 5-year difference in age exists between the offender and the victim.

A distinction is commonly made between intrafamilial and extrafamilial sexual abuse. Intrafamilial sexual abuse or incest is defined as any exploitive sexual behavior between a child and a relative (Russell, 1983). Although this implies a genetic relationship between those involved (e.g., uncle, grandparent, mother, father), intrafamilial sexual abuse also includes other parent figures such as step-parents, foster-parents, and adoptive parents. Extrafamilial sexual abuse refers to all other perpetrators, regardless of whether they are familiar or unfamiliar to the victim such as baby-sitters, neighbors, and strangers (Wolfe & Wolfe, 1988; Wolfe, Wolfe, & Best, 1988).

Magnitude of the Problem

Attempts to estimate the true scope of child sexual abuse have been troublesome because of the various methods used to assess the problem (e.g., questionnaires, interviews, tallies of reported cases) and the definitional problems discussed above. Typically, a distinction is made between incidence and prevalence rates of child sexual abuse. Incidence refers to estimates of the number of new cases occurring within a specific time period, usually a given year. Nationwide incidence figures have been calculated by the National Center on Child Abuse and Neglect and the American Humane Association. These figures are based on actual cases reported to social service agencies across the country. Data collected since 1976 indicate a 3 to 7% annual rise in reported sexual abuse cases (Russell & Trainor, 1984), representing an estimated yearly incidence rate in the U.S. ranging from 0.7 (NCCAN, 1981) to 1.4 (American Humane Association, 1984) victims per 1,000 children in the population.

The rise in reported cases of child sexual abuse does not necessarily suggest that sexual abuse is increasing. This increase in the annual incidence rate may be a result of an increased awareness of sexual abuse and a decrease in the stigma associated with disclosing the abuse. Calculated incidence rates are commonly considered to be conservative estimates since they reflect only those abuse cases that have been detected. Numerous cases of sexual abuse go unreported or are classified as "unfounded" because of lack of evidence.

Another way to calculate the rates of sexual abuse of minors has been to determine prevalence figures. One advantage of prevalence figures is that they do not rely on disclosed cases of sexual abuse, thereby reducing the problem of underestimation that occurs in incidence reports. Prevalence studies estimate the proportion of the population that has been sexually abused during childhood. Finkelhor (1979) surveyed 795 college students and concluded that 19% of the women and 9% of the men in his sample had been sexually victimized before the age of 17. Similar results were reported in Russell's (1983) random interviews of 930 adult women in the San Francisco area; she found that 16% of the women reported at least one experience with intrafamilial sexual abuse prior to age 18.

The major criticism of prevalence data is that it is retrospective. Adults may have difficulty reporting on events that occurred during childhood, especially when detailing the number of incidents and duration of sexual abuse. Admittedly, there are many problems involved in computing the magnitude of sexual abuse; however, it is readily acknowledged that prevalence, as well as incidence reports, signals a much larger problem than was earlier assumed.

CHARACTERISTICS OF CHILD SEXUAL ABUSE

Sex, Age of Onset, and Duration

Most of the literature concerning victims of sexual abuse has focused on the female child because girls are reported to be sexually abused much more frequently than boys. Several studies report that girls comprise approximately 85% of all sexual abuse victims (American Humane Association, 1984; Conte & Berliner, 1981; Reinhart, 1987). Despite the consensus that girls are most often the target of sexual abuse, some discrepancy in reported cases may exist due to the reluctance of boys to disclose occurrences of sexual abuse. Clinical observations suggest that boys are more hesitant than girls to express their vulnerabilities. They also have more difficulty disclosing the sexual abuse because of the fear of being labeled "weak," and if the perpetrator was male, they are often concerned about the implications of homosexuality (James & Nasjleti, 1983; Nasjleti, 1980). Father–daughter incest has been the most commonly reported type of sexual abuse, yet a recent emphasis on male victims has revealed a startling number of victimized boys (Finkelhor, 1981). This new information suggests that large numbers of children of both sexes are being sexually exploited.

The onset of sexual abuse commonly begins when victims are between 4 and 12 years of age (Courtois, 1980). Based on research findings, particularly high-risk periods appear to be at ages 4 and 9 years. Reasons for these two specific ages of high risk are unclear, yet there is little dispute that between the ages of 4 and 9, children can be easily exploited by adults because of their desire to please, their need for affection, and their trust of parent figures (Gelinas, 1983). As children grow older, the risk of sexual abuse seems to taper off, especially with regard to intrafamilial abuse. During adolescence, peer contact becomes more meaningful, and the increased social contact helps reduce victims' dependence on the family. Adolescents subjected to intrafamilial sexual abuse may learn that this type of sexual behavior is not normal and does not occur in many other families. Older children are more mobile, in addition to growing larger and stronger. In order for the sexual abuse to continue, perpetrators often need to increase the use of force or the severity of verbal coercion (e.g., "If you tell, I will beat you up"). Instead of escalating the coercion, some perpetrators seek out younger victims. Typically, sexual abuse is terminated by ages 14 or 15 due to disclosure, threats by the victim of disclosure, or because the child runs away (Gelinas, 1983).

Child victims often are abused repeatedly over several years, with the type of sexual contact progressing in severity over time (Sgroi, 1982). Studies have demonstrated that chronic patterns of abuse (i.e., repeated incidents) comprise a large percentage of the sexual abuse experienced by children. Farber, Showers, Johnson, Joseph, and Oshins (1984) found that of 162 sexually abused boys and girls, almost half (43%) of the victims were abused on two or more occasions and that chronic abuse was considerably more frequent when the offender was a family member rather than a stranger. Other studies reported chronic abuse to be much more common than single incidents, with over 80% of the victims experiencing multiple incidents of abuse (Courtois, 1980; Harborview Sexual Abuse Treatment Program, 1979, cited in Gelinas, 1983).

Type of Sexual Abuse

An array of sexually exploitive behavior has been reported in the child sexual abuse literature. In Finkelhor's (1980) survey of college students, 40% of those sexually abused described being fondled in the genital area or being forced to touch the perpetrator's genitalia. Interestingly, intercourse was reported infrequently in this sample. In contrast, Russell's (1983) female community sample reported that one-fourth of the intrafamilial sexual abuse included forced or unforced penile–vaginal penetration, cunnilingus, and anal intercourse. Another third of the victims acknowledged experiences ranging from forced digital penetration of the vagina to unforced touching of unclothed breasts. These data suggest that the incidence of serious sexual coercion in the general population is substantial. It seems reasonable to expect even higher rates of intercourse and genital manipulation in those cases of sexual abuse that were reported to child protection agencies. Farber et al. (1984) reported that in their sample of children assessed at a medical facility for sexual abuse, approximately half of the male and female victims had been subjected to oral or vaginal intercourse. In a similar study, Reinhart (1987) found that half of the male victims between 8 and 17 years old had reported anal intercourse.

In adults, there is some evidence to suggest that the most intrusive forms of sexual contact (e.g., intercourse, oral and anal manipulation), in addition to the duration and the frequency of abuse, are linked to more negative effects (Russell, 1984). Therapists must be cautious in concluding that these factors alone will determine the degree of emotional trauma experienced by child victims. Many other factors, such as the response of family members at the time of disclosure, the type of threat or bribe used by the perpetrator, the relationship between victim and perpetrator, and the victim's perceptions of the sexual contact, contribute to the impact of the abuse.

Perpetrators and Their Methods of Coercion

Regardless of the method of data collection (e.g., reported cases, medical records, telephone surveys), statistics consistently show that well over 90% of the perpetrators of child sexual abuse are male (Farber et al., 1984; Finkelhor, 1984; NCCAN, 1979; Timnick, 1985). Similar results have been reported for both male and female victims. For example, 96% of the perpetrators in Reinhart's (1987) study of sexually abused boys were male.

It has been well established that the majority of child sexual abuse is perpetrated by a person familiar to the victim. Conte and Berliner (1981) found that of the 583 children seen within a 2-year period at a sexual assault clinic, 47% were abused by family members, 42% by unrelated but familiar persons, and only 8% by a stranger. The preponderance of familiar abusers holds true for both male and female victims (Reinhart, 1987). Considering the high number of offenders who are familiar to the victim, it seems reasonable that most sexual abuse occurs in the home, although compared with girls, boys are more likely to be abused outdoors (Farber et al., 1984).

In looking more closely at intrafamilial perpetrators, Russell (1983, 1984) found that of the women who had been subjected to incest with a parent-figure, the majority of offenders were biological fathers (60%) compared with stepfathers (33%), adoptive fathers (2%), foster fathers (2%), and biological mothers (2%). The author cautions that these data can be misleading if we conclude that biological fathers perpetrate sexual abuse more frequently than stepfathers. In fact, the study actually shows that 17% of the women who had a stepfather were abused by him (i.e., 1 of every 6), whereas only 2.3% of all women who resided with their biological father were abused by him (i.e., 1 of every 40). When stepfathers were sexually abusive, they were also found to use more serious types of sexual contact. These data seem to confirm the widespread belief that stepfathers, in comparison with biological fathers, are more likely to abuse their stepdaughters.

Sexual abuse often involves some form of bribery, threat, or other form of intimidation. Perpetrators have used bribes of money, food, beer, and cigarettes (Farber et al., 1984), as well as manipulative statements directed toward their victims' need for affection (e.g., "I'm showing you how much I love you"). Threats or implied threats also are frequent coercive tactics (e.g., "I will make you pay if you tell anyone"), as well as other coercive methods directed at the child's fear of abandonment (e.g., "Nobody will believe you," or "Everyone will hate you"). Some incidents of physical violence or threats involving a weapon have been reported, yet these extreme forms of intimidation are considered relatively rare (Finkelhor, 1982). Since most children are sexually abused by a familiar person whom they trust, perpetrators often rely on verbal coercion instead of physical force to ensure compliance during sexual abuse.

The Impact of Sexual Abuse

As noted earlier, for many victims the impact of sexual abuse can leave emotional scars that remain long after the abuse has stopped. Frequent initial effects of sexual abuse (manifested within 2 years after termination) include severe fears (Gomes-Schwartz, Horowitz, & Sauzier, 1985; Tufts, 1984), inappropriate sexual behavior (e.g., open masturbation, frequent exposure of genitals; Friedrich, Urquiza, & Beilke, 1986; Tufts, 1984), sleeping and eating disturbances, depression, guilt, shame, and anger (Anderson, Bach, & Griffith, cited in Browne & Finkelhor, 1986). Additionally, school problems (Peters, 1976) and running away from home have also been reported (Herman, 1981; Meiselman, 1978).

A frequently cited long-term effect of sexual abuse is depression, which shows up in adults victimized as children (Peters, 1985; Sedney & Brooks, 1984). Other symptoms reported by women who were sexually abused as children are self-abusive and suicidal behavior (Herman, 1981; Lindberg & Distad, 1985), anxiety (Sedney & Brooks, 1984), and lowered self-esteem (Courtois, 1979; Herman, 1981). Feelings of distrust, as well as fear, hostility, a sense of betrayal, and difficulty in close relationships have been reported by adults who experienced sexual abuse as children (Courtois, 1979; Meiselman, 1978). Furthermore, some reports link child sexual abuse with subsequent prostitution (James & Meyerding, 1977; Silbert & Pines, 1981) and drug abuse (Herman, 1981; Peters, 1985).

Recently, several clinical reports suggest that some women who experienced childhood sexual abuse meet the criterion for chronic and/or delayed Post-Traumatic Stress Disorder as defined by *The Diagnostic and Statistical Manual of Mental Disorders* (DSM-III-R; American Psychiatric Association, 1987). Some of the long-term symptoms reported were recurrent and intrusive recollections of the abuse, avoidance of activities that aroused memories of the abuse, and feelings of detachment or estrangement from others. Readers who are interested in a review of the empirical literature on initial and long-term effects of sexual abuse are referred to Browne and Finkelhor (1986).

Family Characteristics and Risk Factors

The clinical literature has given some indications of the dynamics of incestuous families, especially those involving father–daughter sexual abuse. These families are described as being impaired in their ability to function because of chaotic living situations and distorted generational boundaries. For example, Summit and Kryso (1978) report that often central to the incestuous pattern is a role reversal between mother and daughter. The mother is often described as a passive, obedient woman married to a man obsessed with controlling every aspect of his family. Because of the mother's inadequacies, the daughter takes on many parental responsibilities (e.g., cleaning, cooking, protecting younger siblings from abuse). Issues of dominance, fear, and secrecy keep the family isolated from the external world. Other scenarios may suggest a dominant mother married to a passive father or two immature partners unable to satisfy each other's needs, but all incestuous families are seriously impaired. Groth (1982) proposes a common view that exploitive sexual behavior signals complex underlying problems. He states that although the sexual abuse is legally a sexual offense, it is not primarily motivated by a desire to gain sexual pleasure. The sexual abuse is more indicative of a variety of unresolved problems or unmet needs in the personality of the offender, such as issues of competency, adequacy, worth, alienation, and identity.

Some research findings have supported the clinical descriptions of the incestuous family. Finkelhor (1980) found that marital conflict and family disturbance were strongly associated with sexual abuse. Child sexual abuse risk factors included children who had (1) a stepfather, (2) few friends, (3) a distant relationship to mother, and (4) little physical or emotional affection from father. The mother was, at times, absent from the home and was punitive about her child's sexual development and behavior. Gruber and Jones (1983) found that poor marital relations, a child living with a step- or foster father, and distant mother–child relationships differentiated sexually abused from nonabused delinquents.

GROUP TREATMENT FOR CHILD SEXUAL ABUSE

In working with child sexual abuse, mental health practitioners are initially concerned with reporting sexual abuse and helping victims and families deal with the immediate crisis that occurs at the time of disclosure. If the sexual abuse has not been previously reported, clinicians, as well as other professionals working with children (e.g., doctors, teachers, nurses, police), are mandated by law to report the sexual abuse to an official child protection agency. After disclosure, children need to be assured of protection from further sexual abuse. Victims and their families will also be making decisions about whether to file criminal charges against the perpetrator. At the time of disclosure, the therapist will likely need to work directly with other professionals who are also involved in the case. In treating sexual abuse, these initial considerations often consume a great deal of the practitioner's attention, yet the early concerns are typically only the beginning of the recovery process for the victim.

Rationale for Group Therapy

Children and adolescent victims generally need considerable help to cope with their feelings about the abuse, their relationships with family members, and their feelings about themselves. Many of the curative components of group therapy are especially well suited for the treatment of child sexual abuse. One of the most powerful elements of the group process for sexually abused children is the knowledge that they are not the only ones to have experienced this type of victimization. Victims often keep the abuse a secret because of the coercion exerted by perpetrators and the fear of what disclosure would do to their families. Furthermore, victims feel guilty and responsible for the abuse (e.g., "If I wasn't wearing that short nightgown it would never have happened" or "I should have been able to stop it"). These factors contribute to the decision by many children to keep the abuse hidden.

Group therapy provides an environment that encourages self-disclosure between group members. Frank and open interactions are a distinct contrast to the secrecy that surrounded the sexual abuse. In this respect, group therapy may have an advantage over individual therapy, since it does not reinforce the secrecy that individual therapy inadvertently encourages (Bergart, 1986). In discussing the risk of recreating the secrecy of the abuse in the therapy process, Steward, Farquhar, Dicharry, Glick, and Martin (1986) state, "It may well be exactly the individual attention of the therapist, especially when the therapist is the same sex as the child's violator, that forces the abused child into a mute, uncooperative, terrified stance which too often characterizes the first two or three months of individual treatment" (p. 263). Group treatment, unlike its individual therapy counterpart, also provides a setting in which one member is not constantly the center of attention (Knittle & Tuana, 1980). A child can learn and benefit from listening to other group members discuss their experiences with regard to sexual abuse, even when the victim is not yet ready to reveal his or her own abuse.

Emotional support from group members is another essential component of group treatment. When victims divulge the details of their sexual abuse, group members provide support, reassurance, and information about their own experiences as victims of abuse. This interaction creates opportunities for mutual sharing, development of trust, and group cohesion. Group support is especially important for those children who do not receive support from their own families. In the accepting environment of the group, children and adolescents have a chance to express and examine their feelings of shame, guilt, and anger. It is a powerful experience to learn that other children have similar feelings and that accounts of sexual abuse will be responded to with empathy and acceptance. This type of reassurance can help reduce the victim's sense of isolation and of feeling different, odd, or bad.

Victims need to have people believe them. Berliner and Barbieri (1984) state that it is quite rare for children to lie about sexual abuse. The most frequent source of false accusations comes from vindictive adults during adversarial situations such as custody disputes (Rosenfeld, Nadelson, & Krieger, 1979). Nevertheless, adults frequently respond to sexually abused children with disbelief and insinuations of lying.

Group treatment also provides an avenue to reestablish the ability to trust that is so often damaged as a result of sexual victimization. The friendships that develop within groups and the presence of caring, consistent adult therapists give group members opportunities to evaluate different kinds of relationships. Trust gradually develops over many weeks or months as victims see peers and therapists responding to them in nonmanipulative and nonsexual ways. The establishment of safety and trust in the group allows victims to discuss topics that were earlier thought to be "taboo" and to express feelings that may seem overwhelming. The cathartic effect of expressing pent-up anger and rage is beneficial to individual group members and also makes it permissible for other children to express similar powerful emotions in the group context.

Additionally, the group serves as a substitute family for those victims who have unstable, inconsistent homes. For children of intrafamilial sexual abuse whose family members refuse to believe that the abuse occurred, this new "family" may be their only source of comfort and acceptance. Depending on the circumstances surrounding the sexual abuse, the victim may need to be removed from the home and placed in a temporary protective environment outside of the child's familiar surroundings (e.g., foster or group home). The move also may require attendance at a different school. A group that meets on a regular basis can serve as an anchor for children who are confronted with uncertainty and confusion in several areas of their lives.

Goals and Themes of Group Treatment

For sexually abused children, the primary goal of group therapy is to provide a safe, consistent environment where victims are free to discuss their sexual abuse. Carozza and Hiersteiner (1983) point out that "the challenge of working with child incest victims is to provide treatment which paradoxically offers protection while encouraging expression and insight" (p. 174). Group objectives are also aimed at restoring self-esteem, aiding victims in regaining a feeling of power, and providing a forum where group members can learn new skills and gain information on topics that are important for healthy development (Boatman, Borkan, & Schetky, 1981). Useful topics include information on sexual behavior, court proceedings, heterosexual and homosexual relationships, and ways to protect oneself from further victimization.

During the course of group treatment with sexually abused children, several themes surface consistently. They include feelings of isolation, guilt, shame, anger, powerlessness, problems with sexuality, distrust of adults and authority figures, low self-esteem, and feelings of being damaged (Blick & Porter, 1982; Boatman, Borkan, & Schetky, 1981; Knittle & Tuana, 1980; Porter, Blick, & Sgroi, 1982; Sturkie, 1983). All of these themes reoccur at different times throughout the duration of group therapy, and they seem to follow no clear sequential order. Because of the prevalence and importance of these themes, they will be described in more detail in the following section.

Isolation.   Loneliness and isolation are common feelings for sexually abused children. Often victims feel totally alone as a result of the secrecy that surrounds the sexual abuse, a belief that no one else has ever experienced sexual abuse, and a fear that no one would understand (or like them) if they learned about it (Knittle & Tuana, 1980). As noted earlier, victims often attempt to keep the abuse a secret, while at the same time they fear that others can somehow recognize them as sexual abuse victims (Sturkie, 1986). The sense of isolation is exacerbated if, at the time of disclosure, family members or other important adults ignore or disbelieve the victim's portrayal of the abuse.

In the initial sessions of group treatment, it is important for group leaders to show acceptance and support for victims and their allegations. One commonly used procedure to reduce feelings of isolation is to encourage group members to discuss their abusive experience, increasing the sense of universality and common bond. Another method that can be used to broach the topic of isolation is to have group members discuss how it feels to be believed or not believed and to suggest reasons why some people may not believe the truth (Sturkie, 1986).

Guilt and Shame.   Almost without exception, children take responsibility for the sexual abuse. For example, one 10-year-old child confided that she "should have been able to stop him," even though the perpetrator was her 6-foot tall stepfather who threatened to begin abusing her younger sister if she told anyone. As a result of intrafamilial sexual abuse, children invariably feel considerable guilt for "participating" in the abuse and then subsequently for concealing the act from family members (Gagliano, 1987). Additionally, children may take responsibility for causing family conflict (e.g., family arguments, divorce) and other consequences (e.g., incarceration of abuser, scorn by friends and neighbors) that may occur after the abuse has been revealed. A recommended method of aiding the child who accepts responsibility for the abuse is for the group facilitator to give the explicit message that sexual contact between an adult and a child is *always* the responsibility of the adult, even if the adult refuses to acknowledge it (Finkelhor, 1979).

In redirecting blame and responsibility from victim to perpetrator, Conte (1985) offers a word of caution. Circumstances surrounding sexual abuse are unique for each victim. Children have individual feelings and thoughts about the sexual contact, as well as different ways of coping with the abuse. Care needs to be taken by practitioners to understand the attributions of responsibility held by victims, instead of assuming that their willingness to take responsibility is always negative and should be confronted immediately. Taking responsibility may be the only way a particular child can make sense of an otherwise disastrous situation. It may be more important to shore up the child's self-esteem before addressing the issue of responsibility.

Many victims experience added guilt if they find aspects of the sexual abuse pleasurable. Some abusers are coercive in what seems to be a gentle "loving" manner (e.g., "This is how daddy shows how much he cares about you"). These victims may feel special because of the extra attention they received during the sexual abuse, and for many children this contact is the only kind of nurturing they have received. For these reasons, some victims have ambivalent feelings of both love and hate for their offender (Gagliano, 1987). It is important to stress in the group that children can have several different feelings at the same time (e.g., fear, anger, concern for the offender, sadness) and that all of these emotions are normal and acceptable.

Anger. Children frequently feel intense anger as a result of being betrayed by a person they trusted. If the perpetrator was a father-figure, anger is also directed at mothers for "abandoning" them by not providing protection. So often, the chaos that surrounds the abuse during the period of disclosure compounds the anger already experienced by the child. Many victims describe the events occurring after the abuse is revealed as more traumatic than the sexual contact. Some children are shunned by their family, removed from the home, repeatedly questioned about the details of the abuse by an array of unfamiliar people (e.g., police, hospital staff, child protection workers, therapists), and undergo the stress of facing their perpetrators in court. These experiences can increase the negative reactions of the child and prolong their feelings of victimization.

The anger is displayed in several forms. Many of these children use denial as a way to mask their intense angry feelings or to minimize the significance of the abuse ("It wasn't really a problem because he was only my stepfather, not my real father"; Gelinas, 1983). Other children displace their hurt and anger onto group members, such as accusing group leaders of "not really caring about them" or arguing with members about feeling left out of group discussions. Safe group environments allow for expression of these intense emotions. In fact, Lubell and Soong (1982) discuss how vital it is for group members to both express and receive anger and then to experience its resolutions in a healthy manner. Although the victims were not able to stop the abuse, through role-playing or writing a letter to the perpetrator, victims can "confront" the offender and do or say what was impossible to communicate at the time of the sexual abuse. Some children are so fearful of expressing their anger that nonverbal techniques such as drawing or working with clay are useful (Carozza & Heirsteiner, 1982).

Low Self-Esteem.   Low self-esteem, powerlessness, and feelings of being damaged go hand in hand for sexually abused children. They often are physically overpowered, psychologically intimidated, and exploited by trusted adults. When children are mistreated to this degree, they believe that something must be wrong with them. Perceptions of being "bad," unlovable, and different contribute to feelings of depression. Disruptions such as moving out of the house and attending a different school cause victims to feel unable to control their lives. An important goal for group treatment is to help restore some power and control in the lives of these children. This can be accomplished by having group members identify areas of their lives in which they do have control (Sturkie, 1983). Another method to reduce feelings of powerlessness is to have group members take responsibility for some aspect of the group process, such as developing group rules or identifying topics they want to discuss. When children become more able to make decisions and increase their sense of power, self-esteem will also increase.

Group leaders should anticipate and allow for some resistance in the group (e.g., silence, rebelliousness against group rules). Resistance is both appropriate and therapeutic because it allows sexually abused children to experiment with their boundaries, thus gaining a sense of their own power (Carozza & Heirsteiner, 1982). This resistance also allows group members to test whether the group leader will protect them if they resist too harshly.

Additionally, group leaders need to watch for children who believe that their sexual abuse is less serious in comparison with the abuse of others in the group. These children often think that it would be wasting group time to discuss what happened to them. One helpful method of addressing this problem is for leaders to ask group members whether they are willing to listen to the concerns of these children. The discussion that ensues is often enough to help reluctant children feel a part of the group.

Sexuality.   Sexually abused children have many misconceptions about sexuality and sexual behavior. At times they may appear to be sophisticated about sexual matters because of the "seductive" behavior they often display. Clinical reports and research studies of children demonstrate what Burgess and Groth (cited in Sturkie, 1986) term as "sexually stylized behavior." Victims may engage in precocious sexual activities with friends and siblings, approach adults with flirtatious gestures, or display excessive sexual curiosity. During abusive incidents, victims are treated as sex objects, and many victims subsequently learn to relate to others in similar ways. They have no understanding of the distinction between genuine affection and sexual ploys to manipulate others.

Questions asked by abuse victims are often clear indications of their misinformation about sexual matters. Boatman, Borkan, and Schetky (1981) described a group for female preadolescent victims who were preoccupied with whether they were still virgins and whether they had committed adultery. Typically, boys who are sexually abused by male offenders wonder if they are homosexual. Increased fears of homosexuality occur when boys experience arousal in response to the sexual stimulation of their same-sex perpetrators. Boys may begin to lift weights, present a "tough guy" facade, or deny that they were sexually aroused in order to avoid concerns about their sexual identity. Because most perpetrators are male and there are some data to suggest that some proportion of male sex offenders were sexually abused as children (Groth, 1979), many young male victims wonder if they are destined to be perpetrators themselves in adulthood. No longitudinal studies have been conducted to determine the percentage of sexually abused boys who later become perpetrators, although it is likely that only a very small portion of the total number of male victims fall into this category.

Due to the naiveté of sexually abused children, sex education seems to be an essential component of group treatment (Blick & Porter, 1982; Boatman, Borkan, & Schetky, 1981; Carozza & Heirsteiner, 1983; Wayne & Weeks, 1984). The practitioner may be surprised to discover how little accurate information sexually abused children have about sex. Group sessions can provide a chance for them to ask questions, reveal misconceptions, and discover new information. Group leaders need to be knowledgeable about sexual issues and feel comfortable about addressing pointed questions by group members.

One method of working with children who feel guilty about experiencing sexual stimulation during the abuse is by using a technique devised by Rosensweig-Smith and associates (cited in Sturkie, 1983). Children are informed that sexual arousal is an automatic physical response, much like the body's response to tickling. Group members are reminded that when a person is tickled, he or she will probably laugh and react physically by jerks or twitches, even if the person does not want to respond. Because the response is automatic, children may feel stimulated even if they know that sexual activity between children and adults is not right. This discussion can be facilitated by having a group member agree to be tickled by another member, demonstrating the automatic response.

Distrust.   When children are betrayed by adults they trust and depend on for protection, a natural reaction is to blame themselves. Self-blame allows children to continue to believe that these adults are trustworthy. Most often, child sexual abuse is characterized by a chronic pattern that subjects the victim to repeated betrayal. If abuse occurs within the family, children eventually may conclude that no one will protect them. This realization reinforces the belief that adults are not worthy of trust. These children lack an ability to decide how much or who to trust. As a result, they often present themselves in group as either overly affectionate or distant and antagonistic. Both of these extremes are manifested by children who actually feel vulnerable, frightened, unprotected, and unsure of their relationships with adults. If untreated, there is a danger that these children will not learn ways to protect themselves in their later adult relationships. Some empirical findings (Fromuth, 1986; Miller et al., 1978) suggest that sexually abused girls have an increased risk of later victimization (i.e., rape, physical abuse by husbands or other adults). Whether the risk of revictimization holds true for male victims is, as yet, unknown.

An advantage of group therapy is that victims of sexual abuse are often less distrustful of children than they are of adults and will believe comments from their peers more readily than those of the group facilitators. Therefore, leaders need to encourage group members to take an active role in the group process, especially since confrontations and displays of empathy are often more potent coming from other sexually abused children. Participation by group members often expedites group cohesion, which in turn allows children to begin to establish trust in the group process and in other group members.

Preparing for court.   Concern about testifying against the perpetrator is also a common group theme. It is helpful for the group leader to understand procedures concerning child testimony in order to answer questions and provide support to victims, who undoubtedly will feel anxious and confused about their role in court. For an informative article outlining court procedures and methods of preparing victims for court, practitioners may consult Berliner and Barbieri (1984).

Group Composition

When selecting members for a sexual abuse victims group, certain areas need to be carefully considered. Groups for child sexual abuse can be quite different depending on a multitude of components, such as the severity of abuse and age and sex of the group members. The following section will discuss several areas that are important to address when attempting to form an effective group.

Age. There are some discrepancies in the literature about when a child can benefit from group therapy. Most group descriptions include sexually abused children approximately 9 to 17 years old, although some authors advocate group intervention for preschool children (Mrazek, 1981; Pescosolido & Petrella, 1986; Steward et al., 1986). The age of the children will influence the format used by the group. A discussion or cognitive format will require children who are capable of attending and verbally communicating, whereas groups using nonverbal methods (e.g., art or play therapy) can accommodate younger children. When including children in a group, a commonly accepted rule is that the lower age restriction should be determined more by the child's cognitive and emotional development than by chronological age (Blick & Porter, 1982; Sturkie, 1983).

Another consideration is the range of ages that can be accommodated in a group. It has been proposed that for children and adolescents, groups with age ranges no greater than 2 years are most desirable (Kempe & Kempe, 1984), yet it is often necessary to consider practical issues, such as the number of children needing treatment and the maturity level of the children. When working with abuse victims, a large age range may complicate treatment because members may span different developmental stages. Therefore, the goals of group therapy may be facilitated by including children of similar age and maturity.

Sex. With the preponderance of reported cases of female victims, most clinical descriptions of group therapy have been limited to all-female membership (Carozza & Heirsteiner, 1983; Gagliano, 1987; James, 1977; Lubell & Soong, 1982; Sturkie, 1983; Wayne & Weeks, 1984). One may question the advantages of a same-sex group or whether sexually abused males and females would benefit from a combined group approach. Currently, research has not investigated the effectiveness of various group compositions. As research becomes available, we should have a clearer indication of what type of group is most effective for what age and sex of victims.

A group composed of both boys and girls may facilitate the resolution of negative emotions toward the opposite sex that often develop after abusive encounters. Mixed groups may prove to be effective, although such a group composition may create problems. For example, some children are so uncomfortable with members of the opposite sex that they may be deterred from joining or fully participating in a mixed group. Also, during adolescence, peer relationships take on more importance and individuals struggle with themes of identity and sexuality. Same-sex adolescent groups may facilitate the exploration of sexual issues and encourage group cohesion because of adolescents' ability to have stronger identification with same-sex peers.

It is essential that sexually abused children learn to interact effectively with both sexes. Some authors who describe same-sex groups for sexually abused children also incorporate activities or outings in the overall treatment so that male and female victims can spend time together (Giarretto, 1982). Whatever the method of having children interact with both sexes, this component should not be ignored. Group leaders need to be aware that children often generalize their beliefs about the perpetrator to other same-sex adults. Some of these beliefs are dysfunctional for later development. For example, it is not healthy for female victims abused by male perpetrators to grow up believing that "I cannot trust any man."

Number of members. Children often enter treatment shortly after the sexual abuse has been discovered. They may be in the throes of a crisis and need extra attention. Assessing the emotional status of children referred for group treatment will help determine the number of members that can be accommodated in the group. For example, it seems reasonable to assume that more severely disturbed children will benefit from smaller groups. Another important determinant of group composition is the number and experience of group leaders. Dealing with sexual abuse can be quite draining for one leader, and therefore the size of the group should reflect this concern. Practicality and logistics also are important components in deciding the number of group members. For example, it is helpful to consider the size of the group room, the number of referrals, and the availability of practitioners who are willing to work with this population.

Blick and Porter (1982) recommend that the optimum group for sexually abused children contains between 8 and 10 participants. Others suggest anywhere from 6 to 10 members (Boatman, Borkan, & Schetky, 1981; Carozza & Heirsteiner, 1983; James, 1977; Lubell & Soong, 1982; Wayne & Weeks, 1984). As with other areas concerning treatment for child sexual abuse, research on the number of group members is unavailable for guiding the practitioner to the most advantageous group size. Decisions should be based on clinical judgment and on the considerations noted above.

Type of abuse. Most children who enter treatment have been victims of intrafamilial sexual abuse. Regardless of the perpetrator (i.e., uncle, stepfather, mother, grandfather), these cases are similar in that the victim was betrayed by a trusted relative. When sexual abuse occurs with a relative, the child is more likely to receive mixed messages about the abuse. Even when all other family members support the child, the victim will still need to cope with the sense of betrayal. The characteristics of extrafamilial sexual abuse often parallel intrafamilial abuse, especially when the perpetrator is a valued caregiver (e.g., teacher, babysitter). In both cases, the sexually abused child will have had a trusted relationship with the offender. Somewhat different are cases in which the abuser is a stranger. Typically, the families of these victims respond to the situation with outrage, which helps relieve the child of blame. This is not to suggest that these children are not traumatized or would not benefit from group treatment. Yet group leaders need to be sensitive to the fact that these children may have difficulty relating to some of the concerns of victims who were abused by a parent-figure.

Some questions remain as to whether the group should be homogeneous based on either the type of sexual contact or the relationship between perpetrator and victim. Knittle and Tuana (1980) suggest that groups for adolescents are most effective when membership is limited to victims of intrafamilial sexual abuse. Sturkie (1983), however, argues that combining intrafamilial and extrafamilial victims is not a problem because "the experiences of victims are so diverse that the differences associated with category of relationship are obscured" (p. 301). One caveat is that criteria for group composition should be reasonably flexible so as not to eliminate appropriate victims, yet at the same time ensure some similarity between group members. For example, groups composed only of victims experiencing father–daughter incest in which sexual intercourse occurred may be overly restricted. On the other hand, groups may benefit from being restricted to abuse by a known adult caretaker where some exploitive sexual contact occurred (compared with exhibitionism or voyeurism). Often the genetic relationship of the perpetrator and the type of sexual contact are not nearly as salient in forming a group as the other components surrounding the sexual abuse (e.g., trusted relationship, severity of abuse).

Group Structure

The type of structure used for group therapy typically reflects the theoretical orientation of the group facilitator, the number and severity of symptoms, and age of group members, as well as the constraints of the treatment setting. A major consideration in working with sexually abused children is length of treatment. In the general group literature, there has been a move from long-term psychodynamic groups to briefer, theme-centered approaches (Klein, 1983; Poey, 1985). Sexually abused children need both the structure and the consistency of a group format that lasts for several months. One determinant of the duration of the victim's treatment will be whether the family is also participating in treatment. Several of the groups described in the clinical literature used group therapy with child victims as only one component of the overall treatment (Giarretto, 1982). For centers specializing in treating incest, family members are often required to participate in family and individual therapy. Groups for the perpetrator, the victim, and the spouse of the perpetrator are also recommended for intrafamilial sexual abuse. In addition, nonabused siblings are sometimes involved in treatment. In mental health programs where sexual abuse is only a small portion of the problems treated, group therapy for victims may be the primary treatment component.

Considering the severity of emotional problems of many sexually abused children entering group therapy, duration of treatment should be determined by the needs of the victims and the availability of other therapeutic supports (e.g., caring family, supportive school environment). Short-term, theme-centered therapy groups (i.e., 8 to 12 weeks) are often used with women who were sexually abused as children (Cole, 1985; Goodman & Nowak-Scibelli, 1985; Gordy, 1983; Tsai & Wagner, 1978). It has not yet been determined how effective these groups are with sexually abused children.

Another decision related to the structure of group treatment is whether membership should be open-ended or closed. Open-ended groups have been recommended by some so that sexually abused children can enter a group immediately without having to wait for one to be organized (Blick & Porter, 1982: Sturkie, 1983). Another advantage of an open-ended group is that group members are at various phases of treatment; the more advanced group members can provide information, support, and modeling to new group members. Open-ended groups often use an ongoing group structure. The group continues as new members join and other members leave the group. This ongoing format allows individual members to remain in the group for varying lengths of time, depending on their individual needs.

Time-limited groups generally use a closed membership approach. This type of group allows a certain number of members to enter the group during the initial few sessions, but then membership is closed to any additonal members. An advantage of a time-limited approach is that it is often easier for leaders to plan sessions, prepare didactic material, and cover themes in a shorter length of time. Time-limited groups are especially useful for dispensing information, answering questions, and dispelling myths about sexual abuse. Short-term, time-limited groups are not recommended for children who are extremely distrustful of others, or for those who rely on the group format as their primary source of stability. In general, given the severity and length of the symptoms resulting from sexual abuse, a long-term format that allows children time to discuss their problems and develop trust is recommended. Short-term groups could be advantageous as secondary components in longer-term treatment, or as prevention tools used to educate children about the potential dangers of sexual abuse.

Groups usually meet for approximately 1 ½ hours on a weekly basis (Blick & Porter, 1982; Lubell & Soong, 1982; Sturkie, 1983). For younger children, sessions may need to be adjusted in length because of their shorter attention spans, and groups with seriously disturbed members may need to meet more frequently. During sessions, snack and exercise breaks can facilitate the group's attention span (Boatman et al., 1981). Food serves as a source of emotional nurturance for victimized children. Another way to increase group attention is to incorporate enjoyable activities in the group sessions, such as playing a game or drawing pictures (unrelated to the sexual abuse). These activities will also be therapeutic for sexually abused children, who often need to reestablish a sense of being spontaneous and having fun.

Group Leaders

Clinical descriptions of group treatment for sexually abused children most often suggest a co-leadership model (Blick & Porter, 1982; Boatman, Borkan, & Schetky, 1981; Carozza & Heirsteiner, 1983; Lubell & Soong, 1982). One advantage of co-therapy is that leaders can give each other support when dealing with the continual testing, acting out, and generally provocative behavior of group members (Wayne & Weeks, 1984). Working with sexually abused children can be both rewarding and draining. If a practitioner is facilitating the group without the support of a co-therapist, it is essential that the leader find support systems outside of the group, such as regularly discussing the group dynamics with a supervisor or colleague. This will help the leader avoid becoming enmeshed with the often intense feelings expressed by group members.

Views differ on whether co-leaders of groups for sexually abused children should include both a male and female therapist. In groups for female victims, Boatman, Borkan, and Schetky (1981) point out that the presence of a male therapist in adolescent groups can serve to elicit seductive behavior. This behavior allows male leaders to respond to victims in nonsexual ways. For many girls who were sexually abused by a father-figure, this may represent a new way to relate to the opposite sex. Another advantage of opposite-sex co-therapists is the ability to offer the group an alternate model of male–female interaction. This approach also provides stimuli for discussing heterosexual relationships. Male–female co-therapists provide examples of how adults can communicate in honest, respectful ways, allowing for disagreement and expression of anger without hostility, abandonment, or seductive behavior. The male–female combination also allows for the creation of a "new family" in the group, where the opportunity for transference to each "parent" substitute can occur.

Group facilitators need to be careful not to make assumptions about how a child feels about the sexual abuse. Some children may have enjoyed some aspect of the sexual contact or may not have been detrimentally affected by the abuse because of the support and protection received by family members prior to entering group treatment. Sometimes, therapists treat the sexual abuse as the only problem and focus on the abuse to the exclusion of other concerns or symptoms (Courtois & Watts, 1982). Victims may need to focus on their sadness, alienation, or fear before discussing the details of the sexual abuse. When victims do begin to divulge the details of the abuse, leaders should not encourage members to express their feelings prematurely; it takes time for group members to develop trust (Hurley, 1984). Forcing a child to elaborate on the facts of the sexual contact may further traumatize the victim and parallel the intrusiveness of the sexual abuse itself. The child will unravel the details of the sexual abuse as he or she develops trust in the context of the group.

Child sexual abuse is a horrifying crime that many people wish to ignore. It is understandable that practitioners often are uncomfortable discussing the topic of sexual abuse and must struggle with their rage when faced with descriptions of abuse inflicted on innocent children. Although group leaders may experience a variety of personal feelings about sexual abuse, they should "work through" these feelings outside of the group context with a supervisor, trusted colleague, or therapist.

It is important for group leaders to be comfortable discussing sexual abuse in order to encourage victims to do the same within the group. Some victims report that their therapists could not comfortably discuss the abuse, thereby increasing their trauma, humiliation, and reluctance to disclose further information (Herrington, 1985). Another important recommendation is for group leaders to be honest with children and not make promises about events that are in the hands of the legal system or the child protection domain. For example, children will ask numerous questions, such as whether the perpetrator will go to jail, if they will be able to return to live with their family, or if their perpetrator will ever admit to the sexual abuse. The leaders need to deal with these questions in a straightforward manner so as not to duplicate the deception victims have already experienced.

GROUP TREATMENT OUTCOMES

Group therapy is a commonly used treatment with sexually abused children and adolescents. In fact, several clinical reports written by practitioners recommend group therapy as the treatment of choice for this population (Carozza & Heirsteiner, 1983; Gagliano, 1987; Knittle & Tuana, 1980). Informal observations by group leaders and self-reports by group members have generally been quite encouraging about the effectiveness of group treatment. However, empirical evidence for the effectiveness of group treatment is currently not available, primarily because national and international attention on sexual abuse has only occurred in the past decade.

As mentioned previously, research has concentrated on discerning the magnitude of the problem and delineating characteristics of sexual abuse and not on treatment. Treatment studies have been complicated by problems inherent in sexual abuse. For example, the secrecy surrounding sexual abuse hampers and often discourages victims from seeking treatment. Also, sexually abused children frequently need immediate treatment, making controlled treatment studies difficult. For these reasons, few empirical studies dealing with treatment issues have been attempted.

A few initial investigations of group treatment are available, although any conclusions will need to be made cautiously because of the problems of methodology present in these studies (e.g., no control group, small sample size, assessment measures of unknown precision). James (1977) administered self-esteem measures to six sexually abused girls participating in group therapy. The author concluded that the group members felt more positively about themselves after discussing the sexual abuse with other group members. Another study of female victims aged 9 to 17 indicated differences in the pre- and postdrawings used in an art therapy treatment group (Carozza & Heirsteiner, 1983). These authors reported that comparisons of the before and after pictures reflected positive changes and growth processes of the girls. A study with a group of adults who were sexually abused during childhood suggests an interesting outcome. Bonney, Randall, and Cleveland (1986) administered a Q-sort and conducted an interview with seven group members to ascertain which of the curative factors were most important in their treatment. These authors used methods similar to Yalom's (1975) study of a successful outpatient therapy group not specific to problems of sexual abuse. When comparing the results of the sexual abuse group with those obtained from Yalom's study, the greatest difference was the high ranking accorded "self-understand-ing" and "family reenactment" in the sexual abuse group (first and third, respectively), whereas they were ranked fourth and tenth in the study by Yalom. It is important to note a male–female co-therapy team was used in the 1986 study. These results may suggest that family reenactment is a highly beneficial component of group therapy for sexual abuse victims. Obviously, much more research on all facets of group treatment for child sexual abuse is necessary.

SUMMARY

Childhood sexual abuse has become a significant mental health problem. The rapid increase in reporting of sexual abuse has revealed an alarming number of child and adolescent victims who need treatment. It has been demonstrated in empirical investigations that the impact of child sexual abuse has several serious immediate and long-range consequences for the victim. These consequences include depression, fear, self-abusive behavior (e.g., suicide, drug abuse), sleeping and eating disturbances, inappropriate sexual behavior (e.g., extreme sexual curiosity, prostitution), guilt, anger, and difficulty with close relationships because of problems in trusting others. Typically, victims of sexual abuse suffer more than one abusive encounter, resulting in children being repeatedly victimized by adults they rely on for nurturance, protection, and guidance. One unique characteristic of sexual abuse compared with other kinds of child maltreatment (i.e., physical abuse and neglect) is the energy involved in keeping the abuse a secret. This secrecy makes sexual abuse difficult to detect, since most perpetrators rely on threats and deception instead of physical force. As a result, there are generally no apparent physical signs of sexual abuse.

Practitioners are presently confronted with an overwhelming number of child sexual abuse cases, and many do not feel prepared to treat these children. Relatively few clinical case descriptions and even fewer empirical studies are available to help guide the practitioner in his or her treatment of these children. One common therapeutic recommendation in the clinical literature is that group treatment is a viable (and potentially quite effective) option for treating sexual abuse victims.

This chapter outlined the empirical findings on the characteristics of child sexual abuse and reviewed the use of group treatment with sexually abused children and adolescents. This form of treatment has many advantages, such as helping to reduce isolation, dissolving the secrecy surrounding the abuse, providing a supportive network, and allowing members to witness the expression of a variety of feelings and experiment with new behaviors. Because of the rise of reported cases of sexual abuse, practitioners can expect to encounter an increased number of sexually abused children. Clinicians, even those experienced in working with children, may find working with sexual abuse victims frustrating and, at times, overwhelming. The task of working with these children can be eased if practitioners gain an awareness of (1) the characteristics of child sexual abuse, (2) group treatment issues related to the sexually abused child, and (3) their own attitudes toward sexual abuse.

REFERENCES

American Humane Association. (1984). *Highlights of official child neglect and abuse reporting—1982.* Denver, CO: American Humane Association.

American Psychiatric Association. (1987). *Diagnostic and statistical manual of mental disorders* (3rd ed., Revised). Washington, DC: American Psychiatric Association.

Bergart, A. M. (1986). Isolation to intimacy: Incest survivors in group therapy. *Social Casework, 67,* 266–275.

Berliner, L., & Barbieri, M. K. (1984). The testimony of the child victim of sexual assault. *Journal of Social Issues, 40,* 125–137.

Blick, L. C., & Porter, F. S. (1982). Group therapy with female adolescent incest victims. In S. M. Sgroi (Ed.), *Handbook of clinical intervention in child sexual abuse* (pp. 147–175). Lexington, MA: Heath.

Boatman, B., Borkan, E. L., & Schetky, D. H. (1981). Treatment of child victims of incest. *American Journal of Family Therapy, 9,* 43–51.

Bonney, W. C., Randall, D. A., & Cleveland, J. D. (1986). An analysis of client-perceived curative factors in a therapy group of former incest victims. *Small Group Behavior, 17,* 303–321.

Browne, A., & Finkelhor, D. (1986). Impact of child sexual abuse: A review of the literature. *Psychological Bulletin, 99,* 66–77.

Carozza, P. M., & Heirsteiner, C. L. (1982). Young female incest victims in treatment: Stages of growth seen with a group art therapy model. *Clinical Social Work Journal, 10,* 165–175.

Cole, C. C. (1985). A group design for adult female survivors of childhood incest. *Women and Therapy, 4,* 71–82.

Conte, J. R. (1985). The effects of sexual abuse on children: A critique and suggestions for future research. *Victimology, 10,* 110–130.

Conte, J. R., & Berliner, L. (1981). Sexual abuse of children: Implications for practice. *Social Casework, 62,* 601–606.

Courtois, C. (1979). The incest experience and its aftermath. *Victimology: An International Journal, 4,* 337–347.

Courtois, C. A. (1980). Studying and counseling women with past incest experience. *Victimology: An International Journal, 5,* 322–334.

Courtois, C. A., & Watts, D. L. (1982). Counseling adult women who experienced incest in childhood or adolescence. *Personnel and Guidance Journal, 59,* 22–26.

Farber, E. D., Showers, J., Johnson, C. F., Joseph, J. A., & Oshins, L. (1984). The sexual abuse of children: A comparison of male and female victims. *Journal of Clinical Child Psychology, 13,* 294–297.

Finkelhor, D. (1979). What's wrong with sex between adults and children? Ethics and the problem of sexual abuse. *American Journal of Orthopsychiatry, 49,* 692–697.

Finkelhor, D. (1980). Risk factors in the sexual victimization of children. *Child Abuse and Neglect, 4,* 265–273.

Finkelhor, D. (1981). The sexual abuse of boys. *Victimology: An International Journal, 6,* 76–84.

Finkelhor, D. (1982). Sexual abuse: A sociological perspective. *Child Abuse and Neglect, 6,* 95–102.

Finkelhor, D. (1984). *Child sexual abuse: New theory and research.* New York: The Free Press.

Friedrich, W. N., Urquiza, A. J., & Beilke, R. (1986). Behavior problems in sexually abused young children. *Journal of Pediatric Psychology, 11,* 47–57.

Fromuth, M. E. (1986). The relationship of childhood sexual abuse with later psychological and sexual adjustment in a sample of college women. *Child Abuse and Neglect, 10,* 5–15.

Gagliano, C. K. (1987). Group treatment for sexually abused girls. *Social Casework, 68,* 102–108.

Gelinas, D. J. (1983). The persisting negative effects of incest. *Psychiatry, 46,* 312–332.

Giarretto, H. (1982). A comprehensive child sexual abuse treatment program. *Child Abuse and Neglect, 6,* 263–278.

Goodman, B., & Nowak-Scibelli, D. (1985). Group treatment for women incestuously abused as children. *International Journal of Group Psychotherapy, 35,* 531–544.

Gomes-Schwartz, B., Horowitz, J. M., & Sauzier, M. (1985). Severity of emotional distress among sexually abused preschool, school-age, and adolescent children. *Hospital and Community Psychiatry, 36*, 503–508.

Gordy, P. L. (1983). Group work that supports adult victims of childhood incest. *Social Casework, 64*, 300–307.

Groth, A. N. (1979). Sexual trauma in the life histories of rapists and child molesters. *Victimolgy, 4*, 10–16.

Groth, N. (1982). The incest offender. In S. Sgroi (Ed.), *Handbook of clinical intervention in child sexual abuse* (pp. 215–239). Lexington, MA: Heath.

Gruber, K. J., & Jones, R. J. (1983). Identifying determinants of risk of sexual victimization of youth: A multivariate approach. *Child Abuse and Neglect, 7*, 17–24.

Herman, J. L. (1981). *Father–daughter incest.* Cambridge, MA: Harvard University Press.

Herrington, L. H. (1985). Victims of crimes: Their plight, our response. *American Psychologist, 40*, 99–103.

Hurley, D. J. (1984). Resistance and work in adolescent groups. *Social Work with Groups, 7*, 71–81.

James, B., & Nasjleti, M. (1983). *Treating sexually abused children and their families.* Palo Alto, CA: Consulting Psychologists Press.

James, J., & Meyerding, J. (1977). Early sexual experiences and prostitution. *American Journal of Psychiatry, 134*, 1381–1385.

James, K. L. (1977). Incest: The teenager's perspective. *Psychotherapy: Theory, Research and Practice, 14*, 146–155.

Kempe, R. S., & Kempe, C. H. (1984). *The common secret: Sexual abuse of children and adolescents.* New York: Freeman.

Klein, R. H. (1983). Group treatment approaches. In M. Hersen, A. E. Kazdin, & A. S. Bellack (Eds.), *The clinical psychology handbook* (pp. 593–610). New York: Pergamon.

Knittle, B. J., & Tuana, S. J. (1980). Group therapy as primary treatment for adolescent victims of intrafamilial sexual abuse. *Clinical Social Work Journal, 8*, 236–242.

Kroth, J. A. (1979). *Child sexual abuse.* Springfield, IL: Charles C. Thomas.

Lindberg, F. H., & Distad, L. J. (1985). Survival responses to incest: Adolescents in crisis. *Child Abuse and Neglect, 9*, 521–526.

Lubell, D., & Soong, W. (1982). Group therapy with sexually abused adolescents. *Canadian Journal of Psychiatry, 27*, 311–315.

Meiselman, K. (1978). *Incest.* San Francisco: Jossey-Bass.

Miller, J., Moeller, D., Kaufman, A., Divasto, P., Fitzsimmons, P., Pather, D., & Christy, J. (1978). Recidivism among sexual assault victims. *American Journal of Psychiatry, 135*, 1103–1104.

Mrazek, P. B. (1981). Group psychotherapy with sexually abused children. In P. B. Mrazek, & C. H. Kempe (Eds.), *Sexually abused children and their families* (pp. 199–210). Elmsford, NY: Pergamon.

Mrazek, P. B., & Bentovim, A. (1981). Incest and the dysfunctional family system. In P. B. Mrazek, & C. H. Kempe (Eds.), *Sexually abused children and their families* (pp. 167–178). New York: Pergamon.

Nasjleti, M. (1980). Suffering in silence: The male incest victim. *Child Welfare, 59*, 269–275.

National Center on Child Abuse and Neglect. (1979). *Child sexual abuse: Incest, assault, and sexual exploitation* (DHEW Publication No. OHDS 79-30166). Washington, DC: Government Printing Office.

National Center on Child Abuse and Neglect. (1981). *Study findings: National study of the incidence and severity of child abuse and neglect* (DHHS Publication No. OHDS 81-30325). Washington, DC: Government Printing Office.

Pescosolido, F. J., & Petrella, D. M. (1986). The development, process, and evaluation of group psychotherapy with sexually abused preschool girls. *International Journal of Group Psychotherapy, 36*, 447–469.

Peters, J. (1976). Children who are victims of sexual assault and the psychology of offenders. *American Journal of Psychotherapy, 30*, 398–412.

Peters, S. D. (1985). The relationship between childhood sexual victimization and adult depression among Afroamerican and white women. *Dissertation Abstracts International, 45*, 3079B–3080B. (University Microfilm No. 84-28, 555).

Poey, K. (1985). Guidelines for the practice of brief, dynamic group therapy. *International Journal of Group Psychotherapy, 35*, 331–354.

Porter, F. S., Blick, L. C., & Sgroi, S. M. (1982). Treatment of the sexually abused child. In S. M. Sgroi (Ed.), *Handbook of clinical intervention in child abuse* (pp. 109-145). Lexington, MA: Heath.

Reinhart, M. A. (1987). Sexually abused boys. *Child Abuse and Neglect, 11*, 229–235.

Rosenfeld, A., Nadelson, C., & Krieger, M. (1979). Fantasy and reality in patient's reports of incest. *Journal of Clinical Psychiatry, 40*, 159–164.

Russell, A. B., & Trainor, C. M. (1984). *Trends in child abuse and neglect: A national perspective*. Denver, CO: American Humane Association.

Russell, D. E. H. (1983). The incidence and prevalence of intrafamilial and extrafamilial sexual abuse of female children. *Child Abuse and Neglect, 7*, 133–146.

Russell, D. E. H. (1984). The prevalence and seriousness of incestuous abuse: Stepfathers vs. biological fathers. *Child Abuse and Neglect, 8*, 15–22.

Sedney, M. A., & Brooks, B. (1984). Factors associated with a history of childhood sexual experience in a nonclinical female population. *Journal of the American Academy of Child Psychiatry, 23*, 215–218.

Sgroi, S. M. (1982). Handbook of clinical intervention in child sexual abuse. Lexington, MA: Heath.

Silbert, M. H., & Pines, A. M. (1981). Sexual child abuse as an antecedent to prostitution. *Child Abuse and Neglect, 5*, 407–411.

Steward, M. S., Farquhar, L. C., Dicharry, D. C., Glick, D. R., & Martin, P. W. (1986). Group therapy: A treatment of choice for young victims of child abuse. *International Journal of Group Psychotherapy, 36*, 261–277.

Sturkie, K. (1983). Structured group treatment for sexually abused children. *Health and Social Work, 8*, 299–308.

Sturkie, K. (1986). Treating incest victims and their families. In B. J. Vander Mey, & R. L. Neff (Eds.), *Incest as child abuse* (pp. 126–165). New York: Praeger.

Summit, R., & Kryso, J. (1978). Sexual abuse of children: A clinical spectrum. *American Journal of Orthopsychiatry, 48*, 237–251.

Timmick, L. (1985, August 25). 22% in survey were child abuse victims. *Los Angeles Times*, p. 1.

Tsai, M., & Wagner, N. N. (1978). Therapy groups for women sexually molested as children. *Archives of Sexual Behavior, 7*, 417–427.

Tufts' New England Medical Center, Division of Child Psychiatry. (1984). *Sexually exploited children: Service and research project*. (Contact No. 80-JN-AX0001,S-2). Washington, DC: National Institute for Juvenile Justice and Delinquency Prevention, U.S. Department of Justice.

Wayne, J., & Weeks, K. K. (1984). Groupwork with abused adolescent girls: A special challenge. *Social Work with Groups, 7*, 83–104.

Wolfe, D. A., Wolfe, V. V., & Best, C. L. (1988). Child victims of sexual abuse. In V. B. Van Hasselt, R. L. Morrison, A. S. Bellack, & M. Hersen (Eds.), *Handbook of family violence*, (pp. 157–185). New York: Plenum.

Wolfe, V. V., & Wolfe, D. A. (1988). The sexually abused child. In E. J. Mash, & L. G. Terdal (Eds.), *Behavioral assessment of childhood disorders* (2nd ed.), (pp. 670–716). New York: Guilford.

Wyatt, G. E., & Peters, S. D. (1986). Issues in the definition of child sexual abuse in prevalence research. *Child Abuse and Neglect, 10*, 231–240.

Yalom, I. D. (1975). *The theory and practice of group psychotherapy* (2nd ed.). New York: Basic Books.

12
Group Psychotherapy
With Adult Children
of Alcoholics

In recent years, more and more adult children of alcoholics (ACOAs) are finding their way into treatment having recognized that as adults, they are currently facing emotional and interpersonal difficulties that they attribute, at least in part, to the consequences of having grown up in an alcoholic family. The increase in ACOAs that are finding their way to treatment settings is due to the convergence of a number of important developments. First, there has been growing clinical literature, which, although largely impressionistic and anecdotal, addresses itself to the consequences in adulthood of having been raised by an alcoholic parent (Brown & Beletsis, 1986; Cermak & Brown, 1982; Gravitz & Bowden, 1984; Kern, 1985; Macdonald & Blume, 1986; Seixas & Levitan, 1984). Second, empirical investigations of alcoholic families are beginning to document alcoholism's effects not only on the chemically addicted family member but on the entire family system (Davis, Berenson, Steinglass, & Davis, 1974; Steinglass, 1979; Steinglass, Davis, & Berenson, 1977; Wolin, Steinglass, Sendroff, Davis, & Berenson, 1975). Finally, these clinical observations and research developments, although still in their preliminary stages, have been popularized by the proliferation of Al-Anon ACOA Groups and scores of self-help books available to the ACOA (Ackerman, 1986, 1987; Black, 1981; Cermak, 1985; Gravitz & Bowden, 1984; McConnell, 1980; Seixas & Youcha, 1985; Wegscheider-Cruse, 1985; Woititz, 1983).

In this chapter, I will briefly summarize current thinking about the nature of the stresses that many children from alcoholic families experience during the course of development, as well as popularly held notions about the effects of these stresses on the adult personality. I will then describe the dynamically oriented group psychotherapy program that we offer for ACOAs in our treatment setting and will provide our rationale for the use of group treatment with this population. Considerable attention will be devoted to themes that are frequent in ACOA groups and clinical interventions that may be useful. Finally, I will summarize the brief research literature that is available on group psychotherapy with this population and will suggest future directions for empirical studies in this area.

DEFINING THE POPULATION

There are estimated to be some 22 million people in the United States who are the grown offspring (age 18 or older) of parents who have had alcohol problems (Russell, Henderson, & Blume, 1985). These adults have had to contend to differing extents with a variety

---

I wish to acknowledge the substantial clinical and editorial contributions to this chapter by Appleton Outpatient Clinic staff, including Dale Dillavou, Ph.D., Diana Dill, Ph.D., John Rodolico, M.A., Judy Osborne, M.A., and Roberta Caplan, Ph.D.

of problems that are frequent in alcoholic families—inconsistency of parenting with un-predictable rules and limits; chaotic or tense family environments; poor communication with unclear messages and broken promises; and loneliness and isolation, as family members at-tempt to hide the family's problems and reduce the potential for shame and embarrassment. In short, for children who grow up with an alcoholic parent (as may also be true for children who live with other kinds of disabled or dysfunctional parents), the parent's illness often takes center stage and depletes the ability of the family to adequately meet the physical and emotional needs of the developing child.

Children growing up with these kinds of stresses develop coping mechanisms that allow them to adapt to an unpredictable and often chaotic childhood. Although the potential array of adaptive strategies and defenses that the child may develop is probably quite extensive and varies considerably from one child to the next, many authors (Beletsis & Brown, 1981; Black, 1981; Cermak & Brown, 1982; Gravitz & Bowden, 1984; Seixas, 1982; Wegsheider-Cruse, 1985; Woititz, 1983, 1985) have attempted to identify "typical" patterns of dysfunc-tion characteristic of the ACOA, along with personality traits that each believes typify this population. Although these lists vary considerably and cover a total range of nearly 30 characteristics,* few of which have been empirically verified, the lists are instructive at least in highlighting the tremendous range of possible problems.

The most commonly cited problems include (1) difficulty with intimate relationships (Ackerman, 1987; Black, 1981; Cermak & Brown, 1982; Gravitz & Bowden, 1984; Wegscheider-Cruse, 1985; Woititz, 1983); (2) lack of trust in others (Black, 1981; Cermak & Brown, 1982; Gravitz & Bowden, 1984; Greenleaf, 1981; Seixas, 1982; Wegscheider-Cruse, 1985); (3) fear of loss of control (Black, 1981; Cermak & Brown, 1982; Gravitz & Bowden, 1984); (4) conflicts over personal responsibility, which are characterized by superresponsible and superirresponsible behavior (Ackerman, 1987; Black, 1981; Cermak & Brown, 1982; Gravitz & Bowden, 1984; Greenleaf, 1981; Wegscheider-Cruse, 1985); (5) denial of feelings and of reality (Ackerman, 1987; Black, 1981; Cermak & Brown, 1982; Gravitz & Bowden, 1984; Greenleaf, 1981; Seixas, 1982; Wegscheider-Cruse, 1985; Woititz, 1983); (6) proclivity toward uncompromising self-criticism (Ackerman, 1987; Black, 1981; Cermak, 1985; Woititz, 1983); and (7) self-esteem issues (Black, 1981; Cermak, 1985; Gravitz & Bowden, 1984; Greenleaf, 1981; Woititz, 1983).

A number of writers have also described particular constellations of family roles ac-quired by many children of alcoholics that they propose are used to defend against painful feelings and to create some semblance of stability in the family and within the child. Wegscheider-Cruse (1985), for example, suggests that the most common childhood roles in-clude that of "hero," "scapegoat," "the lost child," and "the mascot." Similarly, Black (1981) proposes "the responsibile one," "the adjuster," "the placator," and "the acting-out child."

It is important to point out that such lists of roles and personality traits, while possibly useful in helping us to organize our thinking about ACOAs, can also lead to stereotyped thinking and a failure to attend to the diversity of circumstances and the variety of

---

*Perfectionism, difficulty finishing projects, lying unnecessarily, judging oneself unmercifully, difficulty having fun, taking self very seriously, difficulty in intimate relationships, overreaction to change, constant approval seeking, feeling "different," extreme loyality, superresponsible/irresponsible, impulsiveness, fear or avoidance of feelings, compulsive behavior, self-esteem based on views of others, denial of feelings and or reality, fear of losing control, lack of trust, ignoring/sacrificing one's own needs, stress-related medical problems, black-and-white thinking, fear of conflict, active/passive victim stance, confusion of love and pity, delayed grief, blaming/projecting, grandiosity, depression.

adaptations that are possible. As Beletsis and Brown (1981) appropriately point out, the dynamics of family life may vary considerably depending on such factors as (1) whether one or both parents are alcoholics; (2) the children's age when alcohol use becomes problematic; (3) the family's economic stability; and (4) the availability and use of external support systems. In addition, we might add the differential effects of the following on the ACOA's development: (1) the duration and severity of the alcoholism; (2) the number of generations of alcoholism in the family; (3) whether the alcoholic parent, as well as other family members, received treatment around the alcohol issues; (4) whether the alcoholic parent was successful in recovering from alcoholism; (5) whether there was other serious psychiatric illness or substance abuse in the family; (6) whether sexual or physical abuse was part of the picture; and (7) the resources and coping skills of the nonalcoholic parent. In summary, while caution must be exercised in talking about the "typical ACOA," parental substance abuse often creates serious family disruption, and the growing child must develop coping strategies to deal with it.

While to some degree we can characterize the stresses frequently present in this kind of dysfunctional family (enumerated earlier), it is harder by far to characterize the "typical" product of such a family. Substance-abusing parents will differ enormously in terms of patterns of abuse, personality strengths, psychopathology, defensive styles, and coping patterns. Increasingly, clinicians in the field of alcoholism refer to "the alcoholisms" rather than to alcoholism. This shift is intended to capture the tremendous variation in terms of the course of alcoholism and the diversity of the individuals that it affects. Similarly, it is important to recognize that children growing up in families where there is substance abuse—even if they are reacting to many of the same kinds of family disruptions—will develop different defensive structures to deal with them and that the degree to which children are able to shelter themselves from the negative impact of parental alcoholism may vary enormously. In fact, there is increasing evidence that many ACOAs may grow up to be well-adjusted (Barnard & Spoentgen, 1986a, 1986b; Jacob & Leonard, 1986), despite the difficulties they encountered in childhood (or perhaps *because* of the coping skills they developed). Other ACOAs will be less fortunate, and the coping strategies developed to sustain survival during childhood may become dysfunctional once the child becomes an adult. These ACOAs may need help undoing some of the overlearned patterns of their past.

In short, there are probably many alcoholisms and many different ways of being an ACOA. Clearly, the character structure, defenses, and personality types among ACOAs would be expected to be at least as varied as these factors would be in the alcoholic parents themselves. To paint this picture a bit more vividly, one might ask whether an ACOA who had an alcoholic father who recovered when he or she was a baby would be likely to experience the same kind of emotional dysfunction, course of treatment, or clinical outcome as an ACOA whose mother and father both drank throughout his or her childhood, or whose mom and dad drank until dad overdosed on the kitchen floor when the child was 9 years old. Similarly, one might wonder whether an alcoholic father who recovered when his child was 2 years old would produce an offspring who was more typically "ACOA" and more likely to fit the typical syndrome than a child whose mother had manic-depressive illness throughout his or her childhood. Equally interesting to consider is the degree of similarity between, for example, former President Ford's children and the quality of their lives in response to their mother's alcoholism compared with a child growing up with an alcoholic mother in a one-parent, poverty-stricken family. It is clear that there is tremendous variability *within* the ACOA population and probably considerable overlap between clinical ACOA populations and other clinical non-ACOA populations who have suffered through some of the same kinds of unpredictable and erratic parenting.

Although the "core constellation" of the adult child "syndrome" remains empirically undocumented, what does seem to be shared, at least by those ACOAs who find their way into treatment, is an awareness that their family lives were dysfunctional in significant ways that now affect their adult functioning. While such a view of oneself and one's family of origin is probably shared by many other clinical populations who have grown up in dysfunctional families, what may be special for the ACOA is that the current focus on this form of family dysfunction may provide, for the first time, a sense that his or her problems can be labeled and remediated.

The Self-Definition of the ACOA on Presentation to Treatment

The ACOA movement, and in particular the presence of ACOA groups, provide an opportunity for many adults from dysfunctional families to find a way into treatment. The sense that "something is wrong," that others may share similar problems, and that the problems of the past (in growing up in their own family of origin) are causing current problems in relating to others and living their lives fully are all brought into focus by the growing movement toward ACOA treatment. For many clients, the ACOA focus provides a comfortable entree into treatment that might otherwise not be available.

On the negative side, the presence of specialized ACOA programs and therapy groups may foster the myth that issues around being an "adult child" can be dealt with only in a specialized ACOA group. Although there are clearly advantages to having ACOAs together in a group, any dynamically oriented therapy group would have as part of its task the work of examining the ways in which the past (and clearly relationship to parents is an essential part of this) influences the present. It is important to recognize that an ACOA therapy group is a *therapy* group and that "adult child" issues are an essential part of any dynamically oriented therapy.

This principle is perhaps highlighted by an amusing case that recently came to my attention. A colleague of mine mentioned that a patient had recently come into her substance abuse clinic, posing as her presenting problem the need to "work on her adult child issues." When the clinician inquired which of her parents had had the alcohol problem, the patient responded, "Why, neither." "How is it then," the interviewer inquired, "that you have come to this clinic for help?" "Oh," responded the client, "I've read all the ACOA books, I really identify with the issues and I feel that I'm now ready to address them." This patient implicitly understood that "adult child" issues were an important part of understanding herself and the intrapsychic and interpersonal problems that she was experiencing. She was misguided only in her assumption that she would need to go to a specialized ACOA group to address them.

THE APPLETON ACOA GROUP TREATMENT PROGRAM

ACOAs entering the Appleton Outpatient Clinic begin treatment with two or three individual evaluation sessions, followed by placement in a short-term (five sessions, once weekly) ACOA therapy group. On completion of both the individual evaluation and the 5-week group experience, patients are then referred to one of our long-term, dynamically oriented ACOA therapy groups along with other supports—individual, couples, or family therapy—as indicated.

Evaluation and Triage

We consider assessment and appropriate triage to be an essential part of the preparatory work before placing patients in long-term therapy groups. As indicated earlier, for many patients the discovery that they are ACOAs provides an entree into treatment and is particularly helpful for the many who might not have entered treatment otherwise but who do, indeed, need help. We believe, however, that while the patient's "self-diagnosis" should be taken seriously, it should not get in the way of a more complete mental health assessment. This is particularly important with regard to the ACOA's own potential involvement with substance abuse, since we know that the offspring of alcoholics are at three to four times greater risk for developing alcoholism themselves than are the offspring of nonalcoholics (Bohman, Sigvardsson, & Cloninger, 1981; Goodwin, Schulsinger, Hermansen, Guze, & Winokur, 1973; Schuckit, Li, Cloninger, & Dietrich, 1985) and are also at greater risk for marrying substance-abusing partners (Black, 1981; Corder, McRee, & Rohrer, 1984; Gravitz & Bowden, 1984; Woititz, 1983).

Thus, at the beginning of the first evaluation interview, we recognize the patient's awareness of and discomfort around the "adult child" issues and confirm our interest in addressing these concerns. We also point out that we have learned from our work with ACOAs that there are two other areas that are important to pay attention to from the outset, namely, that ACOAs frequently repeat the patterns of their past by (1) marrying or settling in with a substance-abusing person, or (2) having concerns about their own substance use. Sometimes the latter occurs because there are, indeed, problems around usage; sometimes it is merely that there is a need and a wish to know more about how one's own substance use fits into the patterns and repetitions of the past.

If the evaluator has concerns about the patient's own current substance use or if it is clear that the patient is currently living with an active user, the patient is introduced to the concept of hierarchical treatment. That is, we treat the problem with highest crisis potential first, while at the same time paying careful attention to the ACOA issue. If we do find that there is a substance abuse problem, we tell the patient that we would want to treat this directly (and he or she would be referred to our substance-abuse track). We would also let the patient know that the ACOA problem would certainly not be ignored (since roughly 50% of the substance abusers in treatment in our program are also ACOAs). Similarly, if the person is currently living with a chemically addicted other, he or she would be referred to our family track—again with the knowledge that if this person enters our family program and joins one of our long-term, dynamically oriented family members' groups, 60 to 70% of the other participants will also be ACOAs.

Special Problem: Information Delay Regarding Patient's Substance Abuse

Although careful assessment is an essential part of the preparatory experience prior to joining the long-term ACOA group, occasionally patients may deny use of substances during the initial evaluation interviews; their substance problems will emerge only after they are in a long-term group* and feeling safe enough to talk about them. Since it is our position that the most

---

*It should be noted that the ACOA groups discussed in this chapter are intended specifically for nonsubstance-abusing ACOAs. This is consistent with our view that ACOA groups should not include currently active substance abusers or patients still in early stages of recovery. The focus on parental abuse may not only distract from one's own focus on sobriety but may, at times, serve as a rationale for continued drinking.

immediate alcohol-related situation needs to be addressed in their own right, at that point we would refer the patient to our outpatient substance-abuse track. For example, recently, a young woman who had been in one of our ACOA groups for some months finally brought her own considerable substance problem to the attention of the group. At that point, we referred her to our 5-week education and therapy sequence for substance abusers (and began contracting with her to give up all substances). Since she was already very attached to her ACOA group, we allowed her to continue in this group. However, after completing the 5-week substance abuse sequence, we required that she join a long-term group for substance abusers.

Pregroup Preparation: Setting the Group Contract

Prior to beginning the 5-week group experience, patients are given a handout by their intake interviewer that briefly describes the way our dynamically oriented therapy groups work and summarizes the ground rules. More specifically, patients are told that a special function of this kind of therapy group is that it provides a mirror of sorts of other important groups to which people belong and, as such, provides a setting in which to examine patterns of behavior with both individuals and groups. They are told that it is also a special setting in which new ways of relating can be tried out. The importance of intermember participation is emphasized, as well as the therapist's role in facilitating this. Ground rules include regular and timely attendance, payment for sessions missed without prior notice, timely payment of bills, and at least 3 weeks' advance notice prior to terminating. Confidentiality is stressed. Members are also told that they will be expected to "talk about important issues in their lives that cause difficulty in relating to others or in living life fully" and will also be expected to "talk about what is going on in the group itself as a way of better understanding their own interpersonal dynamics." Finally, patients are told that outside-of-group contact that exceeds occasional socializing at Al-Anon meetings needs to be brought back to the group in order to keep the energy as much as possible within the group.

When patients are referred to the long-term groups, a pregroup interview is held with the leader, and the ground rules are again reviewed. In the pregroup interview(s), the group leader also assesses whether the patient understands the ground rules and will be able to endorse them behaviorally. It is generally a good idea for the group leader to prepare the potential group member for the likelihood of resistance to treatment emerging at various points along the way—perhaps in the form of wishes not to attend on a given night, withdrawing from group in silence, and so on. Patients are told that this is a natural experience and happens to most people at one point or another once they get into the work of therapy, but that it is important to talk about these kinds of feelings, rather than acting on them. During the pregroup interview(s) it is also helpful if leaders can anticipate with new group members the ways in which they are likely to resist or pull back that are familiar to them from other aspects of their lives. The therapist and patient may then agree that when these behaviors occur they will be recognized as signals that something important is going on that needs to be talked about in the group.

THE RATIONALE FOR GROUP PSYCHOTHERAPY WITH ACOAs

The Interactional Group Therapy Model

The model that we use in both the 5-week and long-term groups is the dynamic interactional therapy model, which has been described in detail by Yalom (1975). Our group approach is similar to the Stanford ACOA approach described by Cermak and Brown (1982) and Brown and Beletsis (1986), with the exception that our leaders do not mail out written summaries to group members after each session. It is our view that leader summaries have the potential to exacerbate feelings of powerlessness among group members, since the leader (through the summary) always has the "last word." We also believe that the summary may undermine group members' trust in their own perceptions of reality (particularly when the leader's summary differs from a patient's perceptions of what transpired during the group).

The group format involves weekly 1 ½-hour meetings with eight to ten members who come together to explore their interpersonal relationships within a group. The group is seen as a special social microcosm in which basic feelings and life themes replay themselves and can be worked through. The group's task is to help members better understand and alter self-defeating ways of relating so that more meaningful relationships can be established. We view this kind of group therapy as a particularly helpful modality for ACOAs and often the treatment of choice for a number of reasons.

Reducing the sense of isolation. The grouping together of people who have identified themselves as ACOAs provides an initial sense of shared experience, thus increasing the potential for initial bonding. The group presents at least the possibility of belonging and of being understood. This is critically important to offset the feelings of isolation that are common in those who have grown up in dysfunctional families. Although this may be one of the helpful aspects of group work for any population, for ACOAs in particular, the stigma of the familial alcohol problem (and consequent feelings that family secrets should not be disclosed) increases the likelihood that little sharing has been done with others about the troublesome aspects of their family lives. Thus, the ACOA is likely to feel especially alone and different. As an ACOA patient in her individual therapy said about her boyfriend, "I've never had a normal relationship before. I don't know what it is. I feel crazy at times and really scared of letting him get close." Referral to a group with other ACOAs helped this young woman to realize that she was not crazy but was experiencing some understandable human emotions.

Instilling hope. The ACOA group provides an opportunity to see others who are getting better. Members often experience a sense of hope when others in the group talk in the past tense of problems that they are currently facing—communicating that these problems are something that they have known *in the past* but have now worked through. This is one advantage of a revolving membership group in which the various members are at different stages in their treatment. However, even in a group where all members are in the early phases of treatment, the members will work through different problems at different rates and thus can provide areas of hope for one another.

Conversely, hope can also be instilled by the opportunity to judge one's own progress against the yardstick of others who are still stuck. It is not unusual to hear a patient reflect, on listening to a newcomer in the group, "Hey, doesn't that sound familiar? Remember how I used to get stuck in that rut?"

Learning from watching others. The opportunity to watch other members in action who are struggling with similar kinds of conflicts is often useful in giving a clear view of the ways in which others get stalled at critical points. There is thus an opportunity to understand dysfunctional behavior and aborted communications by watching them being played out in the group.

Equally important, members model *useful* ways of communicating and interacting with one another. By watching others, members thus have an opportunity not only to learn what does *not* work but also to get a first-hand view of *successful* interactions. Finally, the group provides a safe arena in which members can learn more about their own feelings and those of others and how they can be most effectively communicated.

Altering distorted self-concepts.   Because of the potential in the group for examining one's own behavior in relationship to others (and getting group feedback), members have an opportunity to discover ways in which their self-images have been distorted and the myths about themselves that continue to be perpetuated from the past. In addition, as members have an opportunity to identify with others and to accept them in spite of their flaws and secrets, they may also learn to be more accepting of these characteristics in themselves. As such, the group experience provides a healthy climate for the special sense of joy that comes from seeing oneself and others in perspective.

Reparative family experience.   Group therapy also offers the possibility of a reparative family experience. Not only do the members have the opportunity to see their families and their roles in their families in greater perspective, but, as is often needed, new and healthier ways of relating are also learned. Long-term interactional group therapy provides an immediate "family context" in which to explore the past as it is recreated in the present. Particularly since many patients may experience their entry into treatment as an abandonment of their family of origin, the group serves as a substitute family that can be supportive during a process that is often experienced as difficult and painful. For the ACOA, the process of recovery involves a revision of the past. As Beletsis and Brown (1981) succinctly state,

> The facts of a childhood spent in a family with an alcoholic parent do not change. The memories remain detailed and vivid. However, the meaning attributed by the child to these events gives way to a cognitive restructuring. Based on the validation of experience and reparative therapeutic setting, this restructuring alters the belief system which mandated certain defenses as necessary to survival and allows for the development of more appropriate and adaptive defenses (p. 31).

Aspects of special appeal. Group therapy may also appeal to the ACOA for two additional reasons, which are somewhat distinct form the therapeutic value of group for this population. First, coming to an ACOA group provides a forum in which the patient may feel invited to *externalize* the source of his or her discomfort and pain by focusing on the problematic parent(s). And for people who have blamed themselves too long, this shift in focus may provide a source of initial relief. Thus, the ACOA problem may initially feel like a "circumscribed problem" and therefore manageable. It also provides what appears to be a single clear enemy—parental substance abuse—and a specific thing to blame. For many ACOAs the idea that something outside of themselves is bad and needs to be attended to is an easier focus on which to begin therapy. However, the idea of a single easy focus, "my ACOA issue," is soon dislodged because, in fact, the ACOA concerns involve all major issues that the patient faces, both present and past.

Second, ACOAs may find group therapy appealing because of the illusion that they can "hide out" in a group. Although patients may, in fact, enjoy "rest periods" during which they may feel "safe" because they are not actively grappling with their own problems, important growth may occur while processing the work of others. This paradoxical rest is especially likely when issues that are being actively defended against in the resting member are being actively processed by another, thus giving the resting (defended) member an opportunity to vicariously gain as the other works. It is often the case, in fact, that a patient who is defending against his or her own problems may eagerly engage in helping another sort out issues that are closely related—not recognizing until later the relevance to his or her own experience as well.

The Use of Conjoint Individual Therapy

At times individual therapy may be indicated along with the ACOA group. For example, when the group is moving quickly and intensely and a member of the group is in a crisis of sufficient magnitude that the once-weekly group therapy meeting cannot sufficiently process and contain it, the additional support of an individual therapist may be indicated. For brief periods (e.g., one or two crisis interventions), it may be appropriate for the ACOA group leader to meet individually with the patient (with the understanding that the group knows about it and that relevant information will be brought back into the group). However, if more extensive support is needed, we believe that it is more appropriate for the patient to see another therapist. (The one exception would be in clinical practices in which the therapist sees all group members individually as well as in the group.)

Individual therapy may also be helpful when a patient finds himself or herself repeating a problematic role that matches an important group need so well that the group finds it difficult to help the patient out of his or her dysfunctional role. For example, in one of our groups, one member thought of herself as the "star" in her family of origin and also needed to see herself as the group's shining success story. She found it extremely difficult to allow herself to truly engage as someone who needed help, even when (with the help of the group therapist) she had glimpses of things for her to work on. Since the group also needed a member to reflect the "group success," they colluded in preventing her from engaging in any serious work. Although the group, with time, did come to understand their collusion in this patient's defensive "success role" and eventually got down to work, the concomitant use of an individual therapist would have been very helpful.

Other Kinds of Group Support Availiable to ACOAs

In recent years, employee assistance programs have identified issues related to having grown up in an alcoholic family as a significant factor in many of their clients' physical and mental health problems. In such settings, peer groups (structured as self-help groups) have been used in helping adult children of alcoholics understand and learn to deal constructively with their problems (Russell, Henderson, & Blume, 1985).

By far the most popular self-help groups are the ACOA special interest groups of Al-Anon. This resource has grown rapidly in the last 6 years from only 14 registered Al-Anon ACOA groups in 1982 (Cermak, 1984) to 900 groups by 1987 (Krovitz, 1987).

The focus of these groups is on the AA/Al-Anon 12 steps and 12 traditions of recovery, as well as more specifically on the problems of alcoholism as it relates to adult children. The program offers structure and support within the framework of the principles on which Al-Anon was founded.*

SPECIAL ISSUES AND THEMES

There are a number of themes and issues that, while not *unique* to psychodynamically oriented groups with ACOAs, do seem to occur with somewhat greater frequency in these groups and may at times take on somewhat greater importance. However, before addressing these special themes, it is important to emphasize that the group work that we do with our ACOA patients is, for the most part, very similar to the work we do with other populations in our clinic and with other generic psychiatric outpatient populations.

In addition, it is important to be aware that the themes and problems that emerge in ACOA groups can and do occur in all dynamically oriented therapy groups. Moreover, an ACOA who is placed in a group that is not specifically designed for ACOAs (e.g., a group of substance abusers or a group for family members—or even a generic outpatient group) is still likely to enact many of these same themes. What does differentiate the ACOA group is not the presence of these themes, but rather the frequency with which they occur, the enthusiasm with which they may be embraced, and the group's tenacity in holding on to them. In addition, these themes are likely to take on special meaning because they will recapture the family dynamics of *several* members—with a greater number of group members lending themselves to the group enactments that emerge (and often with fewer members left to provide observing ego). It is thus especially important that the leader is prepared for these themes, understands what is occurring, and is able to provide a healthy, observing ego when necessary.

With this caveat about the nonexclusiveness of these themes, this chapter will now explore some of the more common themes that are likely to emerge in an ACOA group. As will be readily noted, most of the themes relate in one way or another to the powerful "family dynamic" that gets played out through the course of the therapy.

The powerful family transference that develops (which occurs, of course, in all dynamically oriented therapy groups) is particularly potent in these groups for a number of reasons. First, many ACOAs fear, as they first enter treatment, that in talking about family "secrets" they are in some way abandoning or betraying their families of origin. This feeling is probably complicated even further by a long-standing (and forbidden) wish to be able to separate emotionally or even physically from their families. Thus, there are conflicted feelings involving betrayal and abandonment, as well as a healthy wish to separate.

As one of Beletsis and Brown's patients put it, "I feel like I'm involved in a minuet, with intricate and specific dance steps. If I want to step out or do a different step, the whole family is threatened, and I will never get back in" (1981, p. 23).

---

*Information about self-help resources is available through the following organizations: National Association for Children of Alcoholics, 31706 Coast Highway, Suite 201, South Laguna, CA 92677; National Council on Alcoholism, 12 West 21st Street, New York, NY 10010; and Children of Alcoholics Foundation, Inc., 200 Park Avenue, 31st Floor, New York, NY 10010.

The fear that the ACOA will be abandoning (or will be abandoned by) the family of origin by starting therapy and making changes makes entry into a new "family" (the group) an even more powerfully loaded venture. Transference thus develops quickly and often intensely, as members embrace the new family that in fantasy, at least, will replace the one they are leaving behind. Along with this, the group leaders also become powerful transference figures—and often highly idealized initially. There is an understandable hope and wish that the leaders will provide the good (perhaps perfect) parenting that was absent in childhood and that the group will be the close and supportive family long yearned for. As Brown and Beletsis (1986) suggest, this conscious idealization of the family group tends to be even more prominent than in more heterogeneous therapy groups—in part because it is more likely to meet a shared and salient need of many members.

However, the power of the positive idealization (the initial cement of the group) also carries with it the seeds of its obverse—that is, negative transference and feelings of intense disappointment. In other words, the powerful, initial family wishes and fantasies that create the rapid bonding lead to greater initial investment. However, along with this there may also be greater intensity of negative feelings, including tremendous fear of disappointment—and often actual disappointment. As we shall see, this powerful initial chemistry relates substantially to most of the themes that follow.

Flight from the Group (the Wish to Leave Prematurely)

The wish to leave an ACOA group is an ever-present theme, and threats to leave or run away are frequently expressed, either in terms of wishes to flee from the session or to terminate from the group. The fantasied solutions of the past ("escape" from the pain and conflict) are thus reenacted in the ACOA group over and over again as conflict is encountered and tension levels rise. Since for many ACOAs, there was no doubt a time when the fantasy of running away was all that sustained them, it is not surprising that group members will continue to think about it (and even attempt to enact it) as a solution in the new family group as well. It is often useful for leaders to help group members understand that their wish represents a fantasied solution of the past, but it is not a solution that will help them in dealing effectively with the current family (the therapy group). While things may feel extremely intense and precarious, this is not in fact the old family, but a new one in which there are alternative, constructive options to fleeing. It may also be useful to help group members understand, more generally, about the intense "family glue" that gets aroused in these groups, along with the fears of disappointment and the ways this chemistry stirs up old impulses and wishes to flee.

It should also be noted that the wish to flee, in addition to being a familiar solution to old family conflicts and stresses, may also emerge because of new feelings that are being stirred up. Even the "positive" feelings regarding the "perfect" parents and the wonderful, close family can be powerfully frightening for those members who have had little experience regulating closeness and intimacy.

Finding (and Removing) the Identified Family Problem

Although scapegoating may occur in any group, ACOA groups are often especially inclined to pick "an identified patient" (IP) who the group may first "try to cure," ultimately decide is "too sick," and finally attempt to extrude. As in most instances of scapegoating, the chosen IP complies in some way, as he or she shares the group fantasy and lends himself or herself to its enactment. In this instance, the collective myth is that the family will finally be restored to happiness when the problem is removed. In other words, the group enacts the cherished fantasy of childhood that the idealized family will finally occur if the troubled (alcoholic) member is gone. In fact, the group may move from one patient to another, attempting to discover "who is the sickest" in order to target the identified patient so that the group can either cure or extrude him or her and thereby restore the health of the family.

The Search for Rescuer

Closely related to the group's search for an IP is the search for a grand and powerful figure who will "come to the rescue." While initially this may be projected onto the group leaders in the form of idealized transference, as the group moves on (and particularly as the group leaders come to be viewed more ambivalently) the members may look for a "rescuer" among themselves. The patient who is assigned this role (and who, often, all too willingly complies) may then become as rigidly stuck in this position as the identified patient can be in his or hers.

It falls to the group leaders in both instances (with the scapegoated IP and the assigned "hero") to help the group understand its need to have a person filling this role and to understand, also, the way in which the designated actor complies. In the instance of scapegoating it is sometimes helpful for the group leader to ask the IP if in some way he or she thinks the role playing might be serving a function for the group. If the group has difficulty, the leader may help further by proposing some possible suggestions such as, "I have a hunch that the group's view of Sam as 'the sick one'—perhaps too sick for this group—might be helpful to the group in recreating some old, familiar patterns. I wonder if it's possible that the group's wish to cure him or get rid of him might feel like a solution that could be understood from the past."

Similar questions to the group about the role of the rescuer might be as follows: "It seems as if the group has a powerful wish to see Susan as the 'rescuer' in here. I wonder if Susan's portrayal of herself as so much healthier than the other group members, (and the group's readiness to buy this) might serve some function for the group." After exploration the leaders may again share their hunches about the possibility that the group is enacting something in the present that might have seemed like a solution from the past. And again, although the entire group's involvement in the enactment will be important, the particular individual's willingness (and wish) to play a particular role should also be explored.

Rigid Role Assignments

In both of the themes illustrated above (scapegoat and rescuer), it is clear that in these groups members may find themselves solidly entrenched in specific, relatively limited roles with the collusion and support of the group. Although, this dynamic is possible to some extent in all psychodynamically oriented therapy groups, it may be exaggerated in these groups because dysfunctional families may be particularly likely to develop stereotyped and rigid roles that keep the family system in balance. A series of research studies (Davis, Berenson, & Steinglass, 1974; Steinglass, 1979; Steinglass, Davis, & Berenson, 1977) have documented that alcoholic families display a more rigid interactional style than is the case with nonalcoholic families and that family members tend to act in more rigidly coordinated patterns, particularly during alcohol-free periods. Although there is no empirical validation to date for the particular *kinds* of roles that individuals may play, there does seem to be some research suggesting at least a certain level of role constriction and stereotyping of response—perhaps in part due to a need to increase predictability in an arena where this is frequently lacking. The quest for predictability may manifest itself similarly in the ACOA group—where again people may fall into predictable roles with regard to one another and with regard to the group.

> Sue was seen as the helper and "healthy member" of the group. Because of the group's need for her to fill this role and her own need to preserve it, certain other work was avoided. It was very slow work for Sue and the group to see her stance as a protective maneuver. The group (spearheaded initially by the leaders) slowly chipped away at her "helper" role and her (as well as the group's) need to see her as healthier than the rest and a symbol of the one who had "made it" by leaving a sick family behind. The therapist began addressing this by asking, "How would it be for you, Sue, if you *weren't* in fact the healthiest member here and 'way beyond' the rest of the group?" and "What would it be like for you if you were very much like and with the other members?" (The leader was chipping away at Sue's fears of intimacy—shielded by her "I am distant because I am superior" stance.)

Resistance to "Taking a Look" at What's Going On

Because children who grow up in dysfunctional families often get messages from their parents that seem to invalidate the child's perception that something is wrong, a coping strategy is sometimes developed of "not seeing" what's happening. Children from alcoholic families may confront their parents about drinking problems and be told that there is "no problem," or they may even be given the impression that they are "bad" for noticing. Thus, for many ACOAs, the experience of feeling uncomfortable about what's going on but not feeling that they have either permission to really look at it or to give voice to their concerns may be a common experience. Sometimes this will become apparent in the group when members have difficulty actually looking at one another or at the therapists; at other times it may become apparent when an individual group member or the group as a whole appears to have difficulty taking a real look at what's going on in the group itself. At such times, it may be helpful for group leaders to suggest to the group that "members seem to feel that in some ways they do not have permission to look or to really 'see' what's happening" and to suggest that this might be something that the group might want to examine. Through the process of their group work, members thus may have an opportunity for the first time to go back and take a look at their past experiences and to see them as they really were. At the same time they have an opportunity in the group to learn to look at how things really are in the present and to trust their perceptions of reality.

> My eyes filled with tears when one of our oldest members was working on his termination and reviewing tenderly his course in the group and how much he had changed. Although most of the group was clearly engaged in the sweet sadness of the feelings that he was sharing, one of our newer members seemed very much disengaged from the process, while repeatedly taking quick little side glances at me.

When I inquired about what was going on for her, she said, "I don't know; I guess I was sort of interested in your face." I asked what it was that she saw, and she responded, "I don't know exactly; you seem to be having some feelings, but I felt as if I wasn't supposed to notice—and that I certainly wasn't supposed to look." After helping her to describe what she did, in fact, "see" in my face, I said, "I have a hunch that you, and perhaps others in the group, as well, often felt in the past as if you didn't really have permission to 'see what was going on.' In here we have a unique opportunity to work on that."

Fear of Losing Control or "Becoming Unglued" (The Riskiness of Opening Up in the Group)

For many ACOAs, *not* talking about certain important emotions and experiences has become a norm (along with not seeing important things). Along with this, ideas about the self may develop such that keeping things in is equated with keeping things in order and keeping oneself together. Thus, in the initial phases of ACOA groups, the fears of opening up present in all new therapy groups may be accompanied by fantasies of being overwhelmed or of coming unglued. As a result, in early stages of group life, concerns about keeping things in order and under control may lead group members to press for closure around group rules, norms for appropriate behavior, and, in particular the appropriate amount to reveal about oneself. As Brown and Beletsis (1986) suggest, group members often equate strong feelings (i.e., feeling too happy, too sad, too angry, or revealing too much of any of these) with being out of control and being drunk. Not only may a member feel out of control when feeling that he or she is revealing too much, but other members may have similar reactions based on their own low tolerance to the sustained emotional reactions of others. Thus, when one member becomes emotional in describing a current problem (or feelings about another group member), other group members may act quickly to control or limit the expression of feelings, particularly in early stages of group life. Group leaders can help the group with this, not only by modeling tolerance for expression of feeling, but more specifically, by helping members to appreciate that the group is a safe, contained place where feelings can be expressed. When the group attempts to abort the expression of feelings, leaders may comment, "It seems that the group is having trouble listening to Stephanie's anger. Perhaps there is a feeling that if we don't stop her, things will get out of control. But I wonder, how we will come to understand what she is feeling if we are unable to let her share what's going on."

Other attempts to abort feelings may come, not from the group, but from the member who is feeling acute pain and is reluctant to get in touch with it. For such patients there may be a fear that if they give word to the pain of their past, they may "cry forever." In this instance, the group leader might help patients to articulate their concern while also gently challenging this idea. To the patient who responds, "If I start to open up, I might cry forever," the group leader might ask, "Did that ever happen?" Patients often respond with surprise to this question, since, of course, to some extent tears and sadness are always self-limiting. When the patient responds, "No, but I did cry for a long time," the therapist might ask, "How were you able to stop?" (thus focusing on the self-limiting mechanisms inherent in the patient). That one can learn ways of managing intense feelings and that a situation that seems to feel a little out of control will not necessarily lead to total chaos and destruction are important lessons for a group member who has lived in a dysfunctional family, where periods of being out of control frequently reached an intolerable pitch.

For some members of ACOA groups, the fear of "coming unglued" (associated, perhaps, with being hospitalized) may be a very real one. With such patients, the leaders can also focus on the patients' adaptive strengths while at the same time acknowledging the intense fears by saying something like, "I suspect that these fears of coming unglued have been with you for a long time, and that alongside of these you've also developed ways of taking care of yourself. Perhaps at this moment you, as well as other group members, are having trouble remembering the ways in which you have been able to cope—even when stressed. Perhaps we need to look at what is going on here that is leading group members to lose sight of the parts of themselves that function adaptively."

In ACOA groups in which members have greater psychopathology, other kinds of structuring and "cooling out" activities on the part of the leaders may also be useful to help lower patients fears about things getting out of control. These will be discussed in a subsequent section.

The Problem is Outside of Me

As noted previously, the ACOA focus provides patients, particularly in the beginning, with a focus outside the self. For many patients, externalization is a comfortable and preferable alternative to the self-blame that they have been riddled with for years. For some, it thus appears that there is now an understandable cause for their problems. Thus, particularly in early phases of group life, there may be considerable focus on blaming the parents (both the parents of childhood and the parents of the present, who continue to perpetuate the crimes of the past. Along with this, group members may spend time focusing on attempts to change members of their families of origin and may find it difficult to focus on themselves. When this happens, it may be useful for group leaders to refocus the group with comments such as, "The family members who are not present in this group seem to get considerably more attention than those who are here. My hunch is that the troublesome family members that we are hearing so much about have always gotten more than their fair share of the attention. What would it be like for the family members who *are* here if more of the focus were to be on you?"

Another even more focused kind of externalization takes place in some patients who see alcohol *itself* as the externalized bad object. In this instance, the definition of "what's the matter" is even narrower and can also be used as a powerful defense against seeing the bigger picture.

One of our group members who had a particularly conflictual relationship with his idealized alcoholic father developed a nearly paranoid obsession regarding alcohol—viewing it as a poison to be avoided at all cost. His circumscribed and narrow view of the "toxic object" thus protected him from devaluing the family member who became addicted.

The view of alcohol as the enemy was also evident in another group of ACOAs who met in one of our clinic rooms decorated with alcoholism posters. Much group attention was paid to the offensiveness of a particular poster picturing a bottle of hard liquor, with repeated wishes expressed that the leaders might be somehow able to get rid of this noxious stimulus.

GROUP DEFENSIVE MANEUVERS

Perseverating around the ACOA Theme

It is common in the early stages of group therapy with ACOAs for family war stories to be the primary group theme. Group members establish a sense of cohesiveness by focusing on the one thing known to be held in common—the trials of living with an alcoholic parent. In addition, the group members have picked a relatively safe way of beginning their involvement in the group; the discussion is indeed relevant to part of the group task.

At times, however, a group may persist in focusing on the externalized "bad parent" theme long beyond the first few weeks of the group or may relapse to this limited form of interaction at times of stress in the group. When this happens, leaders often experience a sense of bewilderment: the group feels stuck and is usually dull, yet it appears to be doing at least part of what it is supposed to be doing. (After all, what could be more legitimate than discussions about how bad Dad's drinking was, his frequent broken promises, and so on, in a treatment group for Adult Children of Alcoholics?)

Another common example of defensive ACOA talk is the following. In the middle of an intense, affectively loaded exchange between two group members, another member interrupts to ask, "What does all this have to do with our ACOA issues?" This question is heralded by a chorus of support by other group members. The group leaders should immediately recognize that this protest is a defense against painful feelings that are being stirred up and that it expresses a wish to return to safer territory. It is, of course, the apparent legitimacy of the ACOA parental focus that makes it such a beguiling group defense against exploring deeper issues and achieving greater intimacy.

While it is often difficult to differentiate defensive talk about parents from appropriate discussions of family issues, the two can and must be differentiated. Defensive family focus is characterized by the presence of any of the following: (1) using ACOA-or family-related focus as a distraction (as in the example above); (2) recapping extensive details of past family drinking episodes; (3) detailed reporting of current family problems that engage other group members in extensive advice-giving; and (4) exclusiveness (i.e., the group seems to be stuck in their families of origin and outside of the group).

In contrast, appropriate discussion of family problems is (1) one of but many areas discussed, (2) characterized by expression and exploration of feelings, and (3) related to here-and-now interactions in the group, as family themes replay themselves in the present.

Assumption of "Sameness" Among Group Members

The assumption of sameness among group members (or between members and leaders) may also be used as a defense against exploring issues in greater depth and against tolerating differences and conflict. Thus, at times of stress in the group, members may attempt to abort further exploration with comments such as "This is a typical ACOA issue." However, assumptions about shared understanding and sameness—particularly between the leader (if he or she is an ACOA) and members—may keep leaders from exploring "the obvious." Thus, a "you-know-how-it-is" mentality may develop in the group about typical ACOAs, leading to tunnel vision and a lack of true exploration. (Some of these issues are exacerbated when the leader is an ACOA or in co-led groups when both leaders are ACOAs. This situation is discussed further in a later section.) Since the assumption of sameness may prevent the group from moving from one stage of group life to the next, it is important that leaders challenge this assumption when it emerges. An ACOA label should not be accepted as an adequate summary or explanation of what's going on, but rather, it should be understood as the patient's attempt to temporarily close the door on painful issues. Thus, when group members summarize what is going on as, "This is a typical ACOA issue" or "That was a typical ACOA reaction," leaders should ask, "How so?" The leaders should also inquire further about what specifically was going on for the patient involved and what additional kinds of feelings or reactions others in the group might have (thus furthering differentiation rather than supporting the defense of sameness).

Refusal to See the Family of Origin (or the Past) as Relevant

Although less common, an interesting defensive maneuver is sometimes used by patients who are taking active psychotropic medications and who wish to see all of their problems in terms of their own biology.

> In one of our groups a young woman who wished to defend against exploring the psychological issues related to her childhood and the impact of these on her current life, as well as wishing to avoid the intensity of emotional involvement in the group, would focus on the biologic aspects of her illness whenever things got too heated in the group.
>
> Thus, when Mary became stressed in the group, instead of looking either to the past or to present behavior and interactions to explain what was going on, she would comment, "You doctors want to make this all so complicated. It's clear to me that the reason I have been depressed for the past 2 weeks is that my medications are not appropriately adjusted. Once my appropriate lithium levels are restored, I will be fine."

Other patients may look to additional mechanisms for explaining their current pain rather than allowing themselves to look to the past, which is even more painful. In such instances, defenses that are already familiar may be invoked, including the use of other diagnoses or clinical labels, such as "My problem is that I'm an obsessive compulsive personality and that I view everything in a rigid way."

LEADER TECHNIQUES

Present versus Past Focus: The Delicate Balance

As in all dynamically oriented (individual or group) therapy, there will be a continuous movement between present and past, and important work to be accomplished in both areas. As group members explore present dysfunctional patterns that have repeatedly recurred in their lives, they will gain mastery as they understand how current patterns replicate childhood binds and outmoded solutions. While both the past and present are important, both can also be used defensively to take flight from frightening work in the other area.

> In one of our groups, in the midst of an intense here-and-now focus, with two members struggling to express their anger and competitive feelings toward one another, a third member interrupted to say, "I don't really see how Ted and Jane's dislike for one another has anything to do with the work that we're supposed to be doing here. I thought we

came here to understand what our parents did to us." This protest can be understood as a defense against fears of emotional overload and a wish to return to safer material.

In another group, when one member began to talk for the first time about her relationship with her father, she struggled through sobs to share painful memories that hinted of sexual abuse. Another member, whose traumatic history shared similar events, interrupted by saying, "You know, Carla, there is just so much you can accomplish by complaining about your parents. We have learned in here that we have to take responsibility for our own lives—reagardless of what our folks did or didn't do when we were little."

In both instances, the group used a seemingly legitimate group focus to defend against painful work. Since both past and present focuses are important and legitimate, it is the leader's job to know when to help the group move toward one or the other. The group will be most alive and engaging if leaders help it to move toward greater affect—understanding movement away from feelings as a defense. At times, the leader will simply interpret and explain the defensive maneuvers of the group by saying something like, "It seems as if Carla's memories about these painful times with her dad are hard for the group to stay with. It's a kind of pain that's very familiar to many people in here, and there may be a wish to push it away." At other times, when the leaders feel that the group can stay with the painful feelings, they may try to help the group get back to them. Here, the leader might encourage the group to look at what makes it difficult to stay with the feelings and might also explore the thoughts or feelings that others were having as Carla talked about her situation with her father. Clearly, there is a delicate balance between the present and the past, and there are times when the group defenses will simply be noted, as opposed to other times when the leaders will push for greater exploration.

In addition, at times of severe distress in the group, it may be necessary for the leaders to help the group move *away* from intense affect. This kind of modulation of affect may be necessary with more psychologically impaired populations of ACOAs, particularly in the early phases of group life when patients' fears of becoming unglued are at a peak and the safety of the group has not been adequately established.

There are several such modulation techniques. First, periods of heated affect can be neutralized by introducing a more cognitive element. For example, this might take place by asking patients about their *thoughts* (as opposed to their feelings) or by asking the group to make observations about what is currently going on in the group or what has transpired during the past few minutes. Similarly, leaders might summarize their own observations about what has transpired in the group. Second, movement from a present focus to a past focus or from a past focus to a present focus can also be used to diffuse affect in the group. In much the same manner as the leader can move the group *toward* more affect-laden material—choosing past or present focus in such a way as to elevate the feeling tone of the group—the leaders can make the same choices in order to cool things down. For example, patients involved in intense feelings about the past may be moved into a present focus by asking whether they experience any similar feelings toward current people in their lives or with people in the group (the choice, here, being to move toward the more neutral of the options). Similarly, the patient engaged in a present-focused heated exchange with another group member might be diverted, if the exchange is too intense for the group or for the particular member to handle, by asking the patient to think about what, from the past, this reaction might be hooking into.

These modulation techniques involve the selective use of distracting mechanisms by the leaders (defensive maneuvers of sorts) to lower the intensity of affect. While these mechanisms are appropriate and useful on occasion (and thus are skills that leaders should know how to use), it is also important to recognize that, at times, the leaders' feelings that the group process needs to be neutralized may simply resonate with the group's feeling of being out of control. It is thus important for the leaders to be aware of their own countertransference reactions before moving in too quickly to cool things down.

Use of a Co-Therapy Team

Co-therapy can be useful not only in helping leaders keep track of the many complicated dynamics in these groups but also for role-modeling healthy dyadic communication. Although we particularly like the use of a male–female co-therapy team because this heightens the family transference, same-sex co-therapists can also be effective in modeling adaptive communication, including effective ways in which people can clarify and "check in" with one another and adaptive ways of disagreeing.

To model mechanisms for clarifying communication, it is often helpful if the co-leaders make a somewhat self-conscious effort to pair in constructive ways in the group. For example, it may be helpful for a co-therapist to reiterate what the other leader has just said (especially if the message has been a bit confusing) by asking, "Were you saying . . . ?" and rephrasing the communication. Alternatively, the co-leaders may discuss a possible decision openly with one another in front of the group. For example, one leader may say to the co-therapist, "I was thinking that one thing we might do is suggest to Mr. X that he take a leave of absence from the group until he can arrange his work schedule to make more regular attendance at the group possible. What do you think?" The co-therapist might then respond: "Yes, I think that's a good idea, but it also occurred to me that we might give Mr. X another week to come back to hear the group's input before we implement that decision." The two co-leaders might then talk about the pros and cons with one another in front of the group, while also asking for the group's input.

Modeling effective *disagreement* can also be very useful—the co-leaders actively disagreeing with one another, either about an interpretation or about the next best strategy. For example, one leader might say to the other: "You were suggesting that Mr. X might take a leave of absence. I have a different idea that we might consider," or "Yes, I can see your thinking there, but I had a very different thought." It is most helpful if these kinds of exchanges communicate that each leader has heard the message of the other and has taken it quite seriously, but may see it from a different vantage point. If the leaders model respect for one another and genuine processing of each other's messages, they are in a particularly good position to also model for the group the ways in which people disagree without being destructive.

Clarifying the Mechanisms of Miscommunication

One of the most important leader tasks is to help clarify messages (and miscommunications) as well as partial communications that get transmitted. One technique that we have found useful is to call attention to the miscommunication by first asking the person to whom the message has been addressed how he or she understood what was being communicated. Often this will disclose to the speaker that his or her intention has been misunderstood. Next, we turn to the person who has been communicating and ask what, in fact, he or she *meant* to say. Pointing out the discrepancies between what has been *said* and what has been *heard* can be very useful in helping members understand how their communications can get scrambled. Other group members may also provide helpful input to the speaker about aspects of the communication that may have been confusing (e.g., additional messages that may have been communicated by tone of voice as well as possible distortions on the part of the listener).

SPECIAL LEADER PROBLEMS: THE ACOA GROUP LEADER

The extent to which the ACOA group leader resonates with the clinical material may be his or her greatest treasure in working with ACOA clients. This resonation, however, may also get the leader into trouble, if not adequately examined and understood. It is important that the ACOA therapist be aware that countertransference is a part of life as a therapist and that particular "buttons" may be easily pushed when they relate to issues that recapitulate the family drama. In this regard, the ACOA therapist's interest in this particular type of therapy group is both an asset and a liability. Familiarity with the issues is helpful, as long as distance and perspective are not lost. In this vein, it is important to remember that not all ACOAs are the same and that leaders should not get caught in the assumption that their experiences are so similar to that of their patients that they need not ask the patients for elaboration.

Because of the potential hazards for group leaders who are themselves ACOAs (overidentification with the population, assumptions of sameness, etc.), there may be some advantage to a co-therapy team that combines one group leader who is an ACOA and one who is not. Although this is probably the ideal combination (particularly when one is a male and one is a female), it may not always be possible. To some extent, tunnel vision will be reduced by the use of any co-leader (even if the second is also an ACOA) since, for the most part, two leaders are less likely to get caught up in the material in the same places and will be able to provide some distance and perspective for one another. Another alternative is the use of a non-ACOA supervisor who can help the ACOA group leader process the group material and will tend to be less caught up in the dysfunctional family with which the leader may be resonating while in the group. Finally, countertransference supervision groups in which several ACOA group leaders come together in a group format to process their countertransference issues around working with this population may be helpful.

In one group that I supervise, a particularly colorful instance of leader resonation with a group theme occurred.

> During the first few weeks of its formation, this group struggled to identify the most problematic patient. The ACOA leader found herself, by the end of the first session, colluding with the group—feeling, with them, that a particular problem patient did not fit in the group and she allowed the group to persuade this member that he did not belong. When the patient did not return the following week, the leader expressed relief, stating in supervision "that the group would be better off without this patient, who was too sick." The leader's own wish to "save the family" by "ridding it of its troubled member"—a dynamic that she was all too familiar with—blinded her to the realization of what the group (and she) was reenacting. Instead, she colluded with them and helped this "unfit" patient out of the group, thus recapitulating the family fantasy that everything would be fine if only the problem member were removed. When the group returned the second week, it took up the same cause anew—searching again for a problem patient to eliminate. At this point, the leader, understanding her own earlier collusion, was able to intervene more effectively, and this time helped the group retain and work with the new problem patient it had identified.

RESEARCH RELATED TO GROUP PSYCHOTHERAPY WITH ACOAs

Although group psychotherapy is currently being widely used with ACOA populations, there is very little solid data documenting its effectiveness. In an extensive review of ACOA literature through 1987 (abstract searches from the National Clearing House for Alcohol Information, Journal of Studies on Alcohol, and the National Library of Medicine's MEDLINE Data Base), only a single study (Barnard & Spoentgen, 1986a; also described in less detail in Barnard & Spoentgen, 1986b) was found on the effectiveness of group psychotherapy with this population. The study examined (1) adult children of nonalcoholic parents, (2) ACOAs who were not currently seeking treatment, and (3) ACOAs who were currently requesting to participate in an ACOA educational/supportive treatment group. The ACOAs receiving the group therapy intervention showed significantly more improvement in psychological functioning between the pretest (prior to the group intervention) and the posttest (following the eighth session of the group) than did the nontreatment-seeking ACOAs during the same time period. The areas of improvement following the group psychotherapy intervention included greater tendency toward inner-directedness, higher self-regard, greater capacity for intimate contact with others, and reduction in other-directedness. Thus, this study provides suggestive data about the effectiveness at least of short-term group interventions with ACOAs.

The Barnard and Spoentgen study (along with an excellent study by Jacob and Leonard, 1986) is also important in documenting that ACOAs cannot be uniformly assumed to be impaired people in need of treatment. Barnard and Spoentgen found, in fact, that the treatment-seeking ACOAs were significantly different from both the non-ACOA college students and the ACOA college students who were not seeking treatment. The two latter groups, non-treatment-seeking ACOAs and "normal" controls, in fact, differed on only one dimension, "capacity for intimate contact with others," with the nontreatment-seeking COAs having a *greater* capacity for intimate contact than the non-COAs. (The treatment-seeking COAs, as might be expected, showed a significantly poorer capacity for developing intimate contact with others than either of the other two groups, and on several other dimensions also scored more poorly.)

Jacob and Leonard's (1986) study carefully compared children of alcoholic, depressed, and control (social drinking, nondepressed) fathers on both teacher and parent ratings. Although children of alcoholics and depressives were rated higher on behavior problems than the children of controls, only a minority of these children received scores indicative of severe impairment. These studies, taken in combination, suggest (1) that care must be exercised in assuming that all ACOAs are damaged or in need of treatment, and (2) that greater precision is needed in defining ACOAs in the research that remains to be carried out. Certainly, a distinction between ACOAs who seek treatment and ACOAs who are not seeking treatment needs to be made. Along with this, a number of variables need to be explored to help us better understand why some ACOAs may suffer greater impairment while others (presumably more resilient to the influences of an alcoholic parent) suffer less. Such factors would include the following (1) subtype, duration, and severity of alcoholism; (2) whether one or both parents were alcoholic; (3) the effect of recovery of parent(s) from alcoholism, as opposed to temporary abstinence; (4) extent of alcoholism in the extended family network; (5) whether the alcoholic parent was the same sex or the opposite sex of the child; (6) how old the child was during the period of severe drinking problems; (7) whether other drug problems were present in the family; (8) whether there was other serious psychiatric psychopathology in the family; (9) whether there was physical or sexual abuse in the family; (10) whether there was serious neglect of the children; and (11) whether there was serious shortage in the family of resources for basic survival (adequate finances, shelter, food).

Clearly, then, research attempts to learn more about the effectiveness of group therapy with ACOAs will involve, initially, a more careful definition of the ACOA population and subgroups. Once this is done, we will be in a better position to ask how effective group psychotherapy is (as opposed to other treatment modalities) for various subgroups of ACOAs. We will need to know more about the outcome of therapy groups compared with (1) no treatment, (2) individual treatment, (3) self-help groups, and (4) therapy groups in combination with either individual treatment or self-help groups. We will also need to know more about the parameters of group treatment itself that influence its effectiveness, including (1) duration of the group (short-term versus long-term), (2) orientation of the group (psychodynamic versus psychoeducational versus supportive), (3) open groups (in which new members join as older members graduate) versus closed groups (in which membership is fixed and all members join and terminate together), (4) same versus mixed sex groups, (5) effect of single leader versus co-leader team, (6) effect of ACOA leader versus non-ACOA leader (and combination of the two), and (7) homogeneity versus heterogeneity of membership (i.e., demographic match of patient with other members with regard to sex, age, marital status, education, etc.). Finally, studies that differentiate among subgroups of ACOAs in terms of their ability to tolerate adverse conditions in the group (e.g., leader turnover, member turnover, less skilled group leader) would be instructive.

Although this chapter has suggested certain guidelines that I believe may be helpful in conducting group therapy with ACOAs, it is also important to remember that there are many differences among ACOAs and that the effectiveness of group treatment generally, as well as the specific clinical strategies and interventions proposed, is bound to vary considerably from one ACOA member to the next. Although when organizing a chapter, we are by necessity forced to think about similarities and trends, it is important not to lose sight of the diversity among the people that we label ACOAs.

REFERENCES

Ackerman, R. J. (1986). *Growing in the shadow*. Pompano Beach, FL: Health Communications.

Ackerman, R. J. (1987). *Same house different homes*. Pompano Beach, FL: Health Communications.

Barnard, C. P., & Spoentgen, P. (1986a). Children of alcoholics: Characteristics and treatment. *Alcoholism Treatment Quarterly, 3*(4), 47–65.

Barnard, C. P., & Spoentgen, P. (1986b). Are children of alcoholics different? A research report on group process. *Focus on Family*, 20–22.

Beletsis, S. G., & Brown, S. (1981). A developmental framework for understanding the adult children of alcoholics. *Journal of Addictions and Health, 2*(4), 2–33.

Black, C. (1981). *It will never happen to me!* Denver, CO: M.A.C.

Bohman, M., Sigvardsson, S., & Cloninger, R. (1981). Maternal inheritance of alcohol abuse. *Archives of General Psychiatry, 38*, 965–969.

Brown, S., & Beletsis, S. (1986). The development of family transference in groups for the adult children of alcoholics. *International Journal of Group Psychotherapy, 36*(1), 97–114.

Cermak, T. L. (1984). Children of alcoholics and the case for a new diagnostic category of codependency. *Alcohol Health and Research World, 8*(4), 38–42.

Cermak, T. L. (1985). *A primer on adult children of alcoholics*. Pompano Beach, FL: Health Communications.

Cermak, T. L. & Brown, S. (1982). Interactional group therapy with the adult children of alcoholics. *International Journal of Group Psychotherapy, 32,* 375–389.

Corder, B. F., McRee, C., & Rohrer, H. (1984). Daughters of alcoholics: A review of the literature. *North Carolina Journal of Mental Health, 10*(20), 37–43.

Davis, D. I., Berenson, D., Steinglass, P., & Davis, S. (1974). The adaptive consequences of drinking. *Psychiatry, 37,* 209–215.

Goodwin, D., Schulsinger, F., Hermansen, L., Guze, S., & Winokur, G. (1973). Alcohol problems in adoptees raised apart from biological parents. *Archives of General Psychiatry, 28,* 238–243.

Gravitz, H. L., & Bowden, J. D. (1984). Therapeutic issues of adult children of alcholics. *Alcohol Health and Research World, 8*(4), 25–36.

Greenleaf, J. (1981). *Co-alcoholic/para-alcoholic: Who's who and what's the difference.* Denver: M.A.C.

Jacob, T., & Leonard, K. (1986). Psychosocial functioning in children of alcoholic fathers, depressed fathers and control fathers. *Journal of Studies on Alcohol, 47,* 373–380.

Kern, J. C. (1985). Management of children of alcoholics. In S. Zimberg, J. Wallace, & S. B. Blume (Eds.), *Practical approaches to alcoholism psychotherapy* (2nd ed.). New York: Plenum Press.

Krovitz, D. (1987, May–June). Nuts and bolts of recovery: Realistic goals for quality support groups. *Changes,* 12–15.

Macdonald, D. I., & Blume, S. D. (1986). Children of alcoholics: Editorial Review. *American Journal of Diseases of Children, 140,* 750–754.

McConnell, P. (1980). *Adult children of alcoholics: A workbook for healing.* San Francisco: Harper & Row.

Russell, M., Henderson, C., & Blume, S. B. (1985). *Children of alcoholics: A review of the literature.* New York: Children of Alcoholics Foundation.

Schuckit, M. A., Li, T. K., Cloninger, C. R., & Deitrich, R. A. (1985). Genetics of alcoholism. *Alcoholism: Clinical and Experimental Research, 9,* 475–492.

Seixas, J. (1982). Children from alcoholic families. In N. Estes, & M. Heinemann (Eds.), *Alcoholism: Development, consequences and interventions* (pp. 193–201). St. Louis, MO: CV Mosby.

Seixas, J., & Levitan, M. (1984). A supportive counseling group for adult children of alcoholics. *Alcoholism Treatment Quarterly, 1*(4), 123–132.

Seixas, J., & Youcha, G. (1985). *Children of alcoholism: A survivor's manual.* New York: Harper & Row.

Steinglass, F., Davis, D. I., & Berenson, D. (1977). Observations of conjointly hospitalized "alcoholic couples" during sobriety and intoxication: Implications for theory and therapy. *Family Process, 16,* 1–16.

Steinglass, P. (1979). The alcoholic family in the interaction laboratory. *Journal of Nervous Mental Disorders, 167,* 428–436.

Wegscheider, S. (1984). Children of alcoholics caught in a family trap. *Focus on Alcohol and Drug Issues, 2,* 8.

Wegscheider-Cruse, S. (1985). *Choice-making for co-dependents, adult children and spirituality seekers.* Pompano Beach, FL: Health Communications.

Woititz, J. G. (1983). *Adult children of alcoholics.* Hollywood, FL: Health Communications.

Woititz, J. G. (1985). *Struggle for intimacy.* Pompano Beach, FL: Health Communications.

Wolin, S., Steinglass, P., Sendroff, P., Davis, D. I., & Berenson, D. (1975). Marital interaction during experimental intoxication and the relationship to family history. In M. Gross (Ed.), *Experimental studies of alcohol intoxication and withdrawal.* New York: Plenum.

Yalom, I. (1975). *Theory and practice of group psychotherapy* (2nd ed.). New York: Basic Books.

13
Group Treatment with Overweight Adults

Obesity poses a significant public health problem. According to current National Institutes of Health (NIH, 1985) standards, 34 million American adults are obese, a significant increase over the last 25 years (Van Itallie & Abraham, 1985). The number of overweight children and adolescents is on the rise, as well (NIH, 1985). The prevalence of obesity increases with decreasing socioeconomic status, with increasing age, and within various ethnic groups (Stunkard, 1975). Black women have a higher incidence of obesity than do Caucasian women at all ages. Among males, obesity is more common among whites than blacks for those younger than 34 and older than 55 years of age (Foreyt, 1987).

The terms *obese* and *overweight* are often used interchangeably, although there is a lack of consensus as to how overweight a person must be to be considered obese. *Obesity* refers to an excess of body fat (NIH, 1985; Rodin, 1982), whereas *overweight* refers to excessive body weight. In our culture overweight is determined in relation to the average weight of those of the same sex, age, height, and body frame as listed in various actuarial tables. Many weight loss studies use the arbitrary marker of 20% above these normative weights as the criterion for obesity. Body weight and body fat are often correlated but there are exceptions (Mahoney, Mahoney, Rogers, & Straw, 1979).

In 1985, NIH convened a panel representing various specialties within the medical and mental health fields. The purpose of this panel was to review new knowledge and attempt to reach a consensus regarding the health implications of obesity. Those conditions for which the panel recommended weight reduction include: (1) when obesity is accompanied by severe cardiopulmonary problems, and (2) when a person's body weight is 20% or more above the desirable weights according to the 1959 Metropolitan Life Insurance tables. The panel also recommended weight loss for individuals with lesser degrees of obesity who have other medical problems such as diabetes mellitus and hypertension. These experts found the evidence "overwhelming that obesity, as defined as excessive storage of energy in the form of fat, has adverse affects on health and longevity" (NIH, 1985, p. 1074).

Of considerable interest is the panel's finding that the "enormous psychological burden . . . may be the greatest adverse effect of obesity" (NIH, 1985, p. 1075). Yet psychological problems associated with obesity are not included in diagnostic manuals such as *The Diagnostic and Statistical Manual of Mental Disorders* (DSM-III; American Psychiatric Association, 1980), which states that obesity "is not generally associated with any distinct psychological or behavioral syndrome" (p. 67). Such exclusion officially rules out reimbursement by third parties, which complicates the attainment of psychological services. Wooley and Wooley (1980) suggest that the effect is to trivialize the disturbances of some obese patients "which may be comparable in form and intensity to those seen in anorexia" (p. 136). Prejudices toward overweight children and adults are well documented. From age 5 onward, heavier children are judged negatively by their peers (Lerner & Korn, 1972; Staffieri, 1967). Overweight individuals experience discrimination in applying for college admission (Canning & Mayer, 1966), employment (Larkin & Pines, 1979; Louderback, 1970; Roe &

Eickwort, 1976), and life insurance (Tucker, cited in Allon, 1982). The social consequences appear to be more serious in women then men (Wooley, Wooley, & Dyrenforth, cited in Foreyt, 1987) and greatest in those who are severely obese (Allon, 1982).

Professionals may also exhibit such prejudices. Maddox and Liederman (cited in Allon, 1982) found that physicians perceived obesity to be indicative of a lack of personal control and found obese individuals to be unasthetic; some physicians exhibited an unwillingness to treat the obese. Samples of adults, including health professionals, rated obese children as less likeable than children with various handicaps and deformities (Goodman, Dornbusch, Richardson, & Hastorf, 1963). Young (1983) examined the effect of obesity on counselors' clinical judgments and found that counselors rated obese clients more negatively on such symptoms of psychological functioning as hypochondriasis, impaired judgment, disorientation, and incoherent speech. These ratings varied depending on the counselor's gender, age, years of experience, and weight. Contrary to Young's hypothesis, female counselors were harsher in their judgments and less willing to work with the female obese client than were male counselors.

Despite this prejudice and discrimination, there is no evidence that overweight children or adults are more psychologically disturbed than nonoverweight individuals (Sallade, 1973; Wadden & Stunkard, 1985). Many overweight individuals have, however, internalized these cultural prejudices. Wooley and Wooley (1980) observed what appears to be a definable "psychology of obesity" that encompasses "the impact of obesity on the individual" (p. 136). Such an impact includes the relationship of the obese individual to significant others and to society, their feelings about themselves, and the effects of repeated weight loss efforts. Many overweight individuals have low self-esteem, blame themselves for their problems, have difficulty expressing anger at others, agree with their critics (Cahnman, 1968), and may go so far as to consider themselves lucky to have friends and spouses (Wooley, Wooley, & Dyrenforth, 1979a).

Obesity is a complex, multidetermined disorder. Rodin (1982) distinguished between two schools of thought regarding the etiology of obesity. One school postulated that obesity arises from lifestyle and eating habits, while the other proposed that obesity has biological determinants. Current research favors the influence of biological factors, although few would argue against a multicausal model. As Rodin (1982) notes, the onset of obesity "is determined by a combination of genetic, psychological, and environmental factors, and thus far it has been difficult to disentangle the relative importance of each component" (p. 32).

The multifaceted nature of obesity—the health implications, the psychological effects, and the influence of cultural values—impacts on the goals and methods of treatment. Despite extensive research into the treatment of obesity, particularly within the behavioral framework, it remains one of the most difficult and refractory problems to treat. The purpose of this chapter is to provide practitioners with a sampling of some of the group treatments for overweight adults. First, a rationale for group therapy with this population is presented, followed by a description of three treatment approaches, including specific therapeutic techniques: behavioral, feminist, and self-help. These approaches include some of the most popular formats and represent the diversity of the available group treatment modalities. Finally, special considerations are discussed, including group and therapist variables.

WHY A GROUP FORMAT?

There have been few empirical comparisons of individual versus group treatment for obesity. Kingsley and Wilson (1977) found no difference in weight loss between individual and group behavior therapy at the end of treatment. At 9- and 12-month follow-up, however, the group treatment produced significantly greater maintenance of weight losses. The authors hypothesized the group cohesiveness and pressure served to sustain group members' commitment and motivation.

Another study compared group and individual contingency contracts (Jeffery, Gerber, Rosenthal, & Lindquist, 1983). All participants were treated in a group format and deposited money with the treatment team at the first meeting. Participants in some groups received refunds based on individual weight loss while others received refunds based on group weight loss. Group contracts produced significantly more weight loss than individual contracts, a difference that was maintained over 1 year. The authors hypothesized that the group contracts provided a means for participants who were not doing well individually to contribute to the group effort; the group contracts also included an aspect of interpersonal accountability.

Interindividual variability in weight loss during treatment and follow-up is considerable (Wilson & Brownell, 1980). Some individuals lose large amounts of weight, but many lose little or none. Numerous studies have attempted to identify predictors of successful losers in order to better match individuals with treatments. To date, such matching criteria do not exist (Brownell & Wadden, 1986), which has led several authors to suggest that outcome might be improved and variability reduced if treatment was more tailored to individual needs.

In practice, individual treatment is difficult. There are not enough trained practitioners to provide services to all that are in need, and the cost of such treatment is prohibitive for many. In addition, individualized treatment would neglect the positive aspects of group support (Jeffery, Snell, & Forster, 1985). Some of these curative factors are integral to all types of group treatment. These include (1) the perception that one's problems are not unique, thereby decreasing a sense of isolation; (2) group support and understanding; and (3) an opportunity for vicarious learning. Other factors have been observed by practitioners who have worked with groups of overweight clients. Wollersheim (1982) noted that clients are more able to acknowledge their problems and view them objectively after hearing others discuss them, are reassured to know that weight loss is difficult for others, and are encouraged to see others stick with it, and that homework assignments are more often effective when suggested by the group rather than the therapist. Orbach (1978a, 1978b) pointed out that when an overweight individual can begin to see others who are overweight as having characteristics apart from their fat, they can begin to look beyond their self-definition as a fat person and can help challenge each other's unrealistic expectations, such as, "If I were thin, my life would be perfect." To this list Knauss and Jeffrey (1981) added the following: (1) clients receive reinforcement not only from the therapist but also from other group members, (2) group involvement can increase motivation to attend sessions and to perform assignments between sessions, and (3) the group provides a supportive environment, which these clients frequently lack.

Group Structure

Knauss and Jeffrey (1981) noted two basic types of interaction within group formats for obesity: didactic and group process. Didactic groups revolve around lecture material presented by the therapist who typically assumes a directive, teaching role. Group participation is usually in the form of questions directed toward the therapist. Such groups typically run for 1 hour. Groups that are more process-oriented also frequently include a lecture by the therapist. Following such a presentation, however, the therapist assumes more of a facilitative role, encouraging group members to share their thoughts and feelings with each other. These groups tend to run for 1 ½ to 2 hours. These authors recommend that group leaders should be comfortable at working in both modes.

Most group treatments for obesity utilize both interactive styles in varying degrees. Behavioral and psychoeducational groups for overweight adults typically lean toward the didactic model. The role of group dynamics is rarely discussed in behavioral reports, although there are some exceptions (Knauss & Jeffrey, 1981; Wollersheim, 1970, 1982). Self-help groups and groups with a feminist orientation tend to place more emphasis on group process and group discussion. More time may be allotted to group discussion of weight-related problems and to members' reports of their attempts to implement techniques learned in the group. There is usually more concern on the part of the therapist in developing group cohesion since this is seen to impact on therapeutic outcome (Knauss & Jeffrey, 1981). Membership interaction may be encouraged not only during group sessions but between sessions as well. Contacts between group members are a central feature of self-help groups such as Overeaters Anonymous (OA) and Take Off Pounds Sensibly (TOPS) and of some professionally led groups (Skovholt, Resnick, & Dewey, 1979).

BEHAVIORAL TREATMENT

Prior to 1960, psychological conceptualizations of obesity emphasized the role of emotional needs as the cause of overeating (Wooley, Wooley, & Dyrenforth, 1979b). Thus, psychodynamic and/or psychoanalytic treatments sought to resolve the underlying psychological problems. This approach, offered primarily through individual therapy, failed to produce significant or lasting weight loss. The time was ripe for the new approach that appeared in 1962 in the form of an article by Ferster, Nurnberger, and Levitt entitled "The Control of Eating." It was the first report of behavioral principles applied to the treatment of obesity. Utilizing similar methods, Stuart (1967) treated 10 obese patients individually and achieved the best results in an outpatient setting up to that time. Six patients lost more than 30 pounds; three of these lost more than 40 pounds. Stuart's report, which generated much optimism and excitement, was followed by a flurry of behavioral treatment studies, the majority of which utilized a group format.

Behavioral techniques have now been incorporated into the vast majority of weight loss programs. Both commercial and nonprofit self-help groups utilize behavioral principles, as do those groups that are focused more on the personal meanings and impact of overeating than on weight loss per se (Fodor, 1983; Orbach, 1978a; Roth, 1986). In 1 year up to one million people each week may participate in some form of behavioral, weight-focused treatment (Brownell, 1981). It is therefore strongly recommended that anyone who intends to lead a group for overweight individuals be familiar with behavioral principles and techniques as applied to overeating and weight reduction.*

---

*Those desiring a more detailed explanation are encouraged to read *Slim Chance in a Fat World* (Stuart & Davis, 1972) or *LEARN Program for Weight Control* (Brownell, 1987), both of which have been used as manuals for therapists and group members in various programs.

Standard Behavioral Treatment Package

The behavioral approach to weight loss views eating and exercise behaviors as learned habits that can be changed and replaced with other, more appropriate habits. Most behavioral programs focus on adjusting the balance between energy taken in (food) and energy output (exercise). The format of most behavioral programs, including Stuart's (1967) seminal work, is based on these two components—dietary management and exercise —along with the application of behavioral strategies to these components. These ingredients will be examined separately.

Dietary habits. Stuart's program utilized a food exchange system that categorized foods into groups and recommended daily allotments of each category (Stuart & Davis, 1972). Weight Watchers has adopted a similar model. Many programs do not offer specific food plans but focus on calorie goals based on an individual's height, starting weight, and age. Caloric restrictions are designed to produce a 1–2 pound weight loss per week in light of evidence that gradual loss is more conducive to maintenance (Stunkard & Mahoney, 1976). Dietary recommendations, for example, decreasing intake of foods high in simple carbohydrates and fat and increasing foods high in complex carbohydrates and fiber, are offered. Overall, a well-balanced, flexible food plan is encouraged. Most current behavioral programs suggest that clients not think of themselves as being on a diet but rather as making permanent changes in their eating habits. The danger in being "on a diet" is the implication that this is for the short term, after which one goes off the diet. Fad diets often list foods that can be eaten in limitless quantities and other foods that are forbidden. Many behavioral programs discourage the notion of forbidden foods because this is thought to lead to feelings of deprivation and binging (Abramson, 1977; Skovholt, Resnick, & Dewey, 1979). The popular diets available to consumers vary greatly in their quality and will not be discussed here.*

Increased exercise. Caloric expenditure is increased through exercise; when combined with diet or behavior modification, exercise has been found to result in greater weight loss than exercise, diet, or behavioral interventions alone (Thompson, Jarvie, Lahey, & Cureton, 1982). A number of studies found little or no effect of exercise on weight loss during treatment, but found that patients who exercised during treatment maintained their losses better (Brownell & Wadden, 1986). Most behavioral groups and self-help groups recommend walking and/or bicycling. Those exercises that are easily incorporated into an individual's lifestyle have been shown to produce greater weight losses than programmed aerobic exercise (Wing, Epstein, Nowalk, Koeske, & Hagg, 1985). Some programs have offered exercise during meetings as a means of providing modeling and social support for exercise (Wing et al., 1985).

Behavioral strategies designed to help people alter eating and exercise habits. Self-monitoring and stimulus control are the backbone of most behavioral programs. Group members are taught to record their daily food intake, including not only calories ingested but also time and location of eating and mood. Exercise may also be recorded. This information

---

*Those desiring more information are referred to Dwyer (1985) and Berland's *Rating the Diets*, which is published yearly.

helps members and therapists· identify problematic patterns. Self-monitoring is typically introduced at the first group session.

Stimulus or situational control in eating is encouraged and is distinguished from the notion of "will-power," which most dieters feel they lack. Some of the most common procedures for controlling stimuli that trigger eating are (1) changes in the act of eating, such as eating slowly, not eating what others leave on their plates, and practicing leaving food on one's plate, and (2) development of control of stimuli that trigger eating, for example, not keeping high calorie or binge foods in the house and restricting eating to one or two locations in the home. Typically, at least one group session will focus on applying these strategies at home, while another session will focus on food shopping and eating away from one's home. Recommendations may include eating before shopping for food or attending events where food is served, and avoiding conversing around the food table in social situations.

Basic learning principles such as reinforcement and shaping are woven into all components of the behavioral treatment program. Positive reinforcement from therapists is provided for weight loss and completing homework assignments. Food records are returned to group members with written feedback. Members are encouraged to self-reinforce for habit change and weight loss. Many overweight individuals are used to rewarding themselves with food and must be encouraged to devise alternative rewards, for example, buying a desired book or item of clothing or attending an event. During group sessions, members can assist one another in creating an appropriate list of such activities. Those activities that are incompatible with eating, such as taking a bubble bath or working in a garden, are particularly helpful (Brownell, 1987; Wollersheim, 1982). Some programs use not only positive but also negative reinforcement. For example, group members have been encouraged to carry an unflattering picture of themselves overweight (Stuart, 1971) or memorize a list of personally aversive consequences of overeating that they are to review in situations where they are tempted to overeat (Wollersheim, 1982). One rationale for such interventions is the need to counter the positive rewards of overeating, which are more proximal and immediate than the negative consequences (i.e., weight gain). Critics of these methods note a lack of evidence supporting shame-inducing techniques and question the rationale for their use. According to Wooley, Wooley, and Dyrenforth (1979a), "It seems doubtful that lack of shame over eating or appearance can be a cause of obesity" (p. 20).

Shaping refers to the use of gradual, incremental changes in modifying group members' eating and exercise patterns. For example, caloric expenditure may begin at 100 calories per week and gradually be increased to 1000 calories per week. Another important application of this principle is teaching participants to set realistic, short-term goals.

Additional Components of Behavioral Treatment

In contrast to earlier models, behavioral programs have become more comprehensive; in addition to the three components already discussed, cognitive and social support interventions have been frequently added (Brownell & Wadden, 1986). The role of exercise has been strengthened since it is one of the few predictors of success in weight loss programs (Brownell, 1984).

Cognitive. Mahoney and Mahoney (1976) published a primer, *Permanent Weight Control*, in which they described their cognitive component for the basic behavioral treatment package. A major element of this component is cognitive restructuring. The underlying rationale is that cognitive habits can greatly influence eating behavior (Collins, Rothblum, & Wilson, 1986). Therefore, clients are taught to replace negative thoughts and self-statements about food and dieting with positive self-statements. For example, "Eating that doughnut just proves that I have no willpower; I might as well forget the diet for today" can be replaced with "So I made a mistake; that's no reason to blow the rest of the day, and it doesn't mean that I have no self-control." Brownell and Wadden (1986) employed an expanded version of Mahoney and Mahoney's format that included goal setting, coping with mistakes, and motivation.

Social support. Behavior therapists have begun to examine the role of social support at home and at work. Active involvement of family members being treated for various illnesses has been shown to be a significant contributor to patient compliance (Becker & Maiman, 1980). However, studies on spouse and family involvement in behavioral weight loss programs have yielded mixed results. Some studies have found a significant positive effect of family or spouse support on weight loss (Mahoney & Mahoney, cited in Wilson, 1978), while others have found little or no effect (Wilson & Brownell, 1978; Zitter & Fremouw, 1978). Most spouse support training emphasizes the use of positive reinforcement, improving communication, and avoiding punitive behaviors. Teaching spouses not to sabotage weight loss efforts (Pearce, LeBow, & Orchard, 1981) and teaching clients to be aware of those who sabotage their efforts (Skovholt, Resnick, & Dewey, 1979) may be important as well. Such techniques can be learned through a combination of group discussion, role-playing, and written handouts.

Some clients do not want their spouses involved in treatment. In a survey of Weight Watchers members, it was not uncommon for women to indicate their desire that their husbands not participate in the program (Stuart & Mitchell, 1980). Issues surrounding the husband's and wife's roles, such as responsibilities for buying and preparing food, may be relevant to interventions. Group discussion, with or without direct spouse participation, can include such topics.

Current Avenues of Research in Behavioral Treatment

Reviews of behavioral treatment studies, most of which utilized a group format, reveal suprisingly stable results despite differences in subject characteristics, therapist experience, and other factors (Jeffery, Wing, & Stunkard, 1978; Wilson & Brownell, 1980). Programs that were 8 to 16 weeks in length produced average weight losses of 1–2 pounds per week with posttreatment losses averaging 8.5–11.5 pounds. These results proved superior to no-treatment, supportive psychotherapy (Penick, Filion, Fox, & Stunkard, 1971), a social pressure group, and a nonspecific therapy control group (Wollersheim, 1970). Such data seem to support the use of standard behavioral weight loss programs for individuals who are mildly overweight. For those individuals who are more than 20% overweight, however, the amount of weight lost is small relative to goal or target weights. The picture does not improve after treatment; those studies that have included follow-ups beyond 1 year have yielded disappointing results (Stunkard & Pennick, 1979). There is rarely a continuing decrease in weight during follow-up, with a few exceptions (Brownell, Heckerman, Westlake, Hayes, & Monti, 1978; Dahlkoetter, Callahan, & Linton, 1979). Recidivism rates as high as 75 to 100% regain of initial weight losses are cited (Jeffery, 1987). In light of this evidence, recent research on the behavioral treatment of obesity has focused on two goals: increasing initial weight losses during treatment and improving maintenance of these losses (Brownell & Wadden, 1986). The former has been more successful.

Increasing weight losses.   One of the problems with weight losses during treatment is that participants may not have lost enough weight either to meet their own expectations or to get sufficient reinforcement from others to motivate them to continue (Wollersheim, 1982). Methods of increasing weight loss include pharmacotherapy, very-low-calorie diets, and increasing the duration of treatment.

A number of studies have examined whether adding pharmocologic agents such as appetite suppressants enhances the results achieved with behavior therapy. Evidence suggests that weight loss during such combined treatment is greater than that achieved by behavior therapy alone, but weight gain after discontinuing the medication is more rapid (Brownell & Stunkard, 1981; Craighead, Stunkard, & O'Brien, 1981).

More promising results have been obtained with the very-low-calorie diet (VLCD). In clinical settings, these diets have produced losses of approximately 40 pounds in 24 weeks and have been associated with other physiologic changes such as lowering of blood pressure and decreased insulin requirements of individuals with Type II diabetes, previously referred to as adult onset diabetes (Wadden & Stunkard, 1986). For clients who are moderately and severely obese, the combination of the VLCD with behavior therapy may be appropriate (Wadden & Stunkard, 1986). The ultimate utility of the VLCD is dependent on finding ways to prevent weight regain.

Behavioral programs are typically limited to 6 months or less. Given the emphasis on gradual weight loss, losses achieved at the end of treatment remain modest. This has led to recommendations for longer treatment, particularly for those who are more than mildly obese (Brownell & Wadden, 1986), and to suggestions that clinicians consider and treat obesity as chronic rather than an acute condition (Jeffery, 1987). In response to such recommendations, Wing and her colleagues initiated a 1-year program in the fall of 1987 (Wing, 1987, personal communication). The first of its kind, the program offers weekly group meetings for 1 year and will compare behavior therapy with a combination of behavior therapy and the VLCD for obese patients with Type II diabetes. It is hoped that a longer program will serve both to increase the amount of weight lost and to help participants to maintain their losses.

Improving maintenance.   The problem of maintaining behavior change is a continuing challenge. It may be that some individuals cannot maintain their motivation without continued reinforcement from the group and/or therapist (Wollersheim, 1982). The most common resolution to the maintenance question has been the employment of additional or booster sessions after completion of treatment on a monthly, or less frequent, schedule. Typically, booster sessions include weigh-ins and review of material presented during treatment. Some programs use these sessions to review individual progress and to problem-solve for difficulties encountered between meetings (Collins, Rothblum, & Wilson, 1986; Knauss & Jeffrey, 1981). Booster sessions have had mixed effects on maintenance of weight loss (Wilson & Brownell, 1980). Mail and telephone follow-ups have also been studied. While such continued therapeutic contact sometimes slows the rate of regain, it does not prevent it (Jeffery, 1987).

Peer support may play an important role in maintaining weight loss. After treatment in one study, members in a "buddy group" continued to meet, monitor each other's weight, and problem-solve. At follow-up, these clients did significantly better than those in standard be-havior therapy with biweekly booster sessions (Perri, Shapiro, Ludwig, Twentyman, & McAdoo, 1984).

Relapse prevention training is another approach to the maintenance problem. Most relapse prevention programs are based on Marlatt and Gordon's (1979) cognitive-behavioral model of the relapse process. These authors describe relapse as the result of a lack of coping skills in a situation in which an individual is at high risk for resuming a particular behavior (in this case, overeating or going off a diet). Sternberg (1985) applied this model to groups of dieters utilizing self-monitoring, group discussion, and role-playing to help members recog-nize high-risk situations and develop coping skills.

Two studies found that relapse prevention training enhanced maintenance of weight loss (Abrams & Follick, 1983; Rosenthal & Marx, 1979), while another found that relapse prevention training improved maintenance only when combined with posttreatment therapist contact (Perri et al., 1984). This appears to be a promising area for future research.

Modifying Behavioral Treatment

A critical examination of the outcome of weight loss interventions, combined with growing frustration on the part of clients and therapists, has led some practitioners to ex-periment with more flexible treatment models. Additionally, there is increasing recognition of the heterogeneity of obesity and an interest in whether this heterogeneity affects treatment outcome. Differences among obese individuals may be physical, such as upper body versus lower body fat distribution, or behavioral, such as severity of binge eating (Marcus & Wing, 1987). This heterogeneity of obesity, combined with its complex etiology, presents to the group therapist the challenge of how to provide treatment in a group format without ignoring the individualistic nature of obesity and overeating.

Gormally and Hill (1977) addressed this challenge in their presentation of three alterna-tive treatments. These authors chose a treatment plan for each client after an assessment based on information collected on four variables: degree of obesity and weight; nature of eating problems; motivation, attitudes, and cognitions about dieting; and weight loss and dieting history. Treatment determinations were derived from clinical experience, not from empirical data. The three treatment options were (1) skills training in behavioral self-control techniques, (2) integrated treatment of group counseling and behavioral skills training, or (3) group/individual psychotherapy. The first option is primarily behavioral, the second com-bines behavioral and psychodynamic orientations, and the third is primarily psychodynamic. These three treatment options will be described.

Skills training group. Clients referred to the skills training group are typically in their early 30s or younger, exhibit a reactive or short-term weight problem, have eating problems that do not appear to be tied to other disturbances, and are relatively free of compulsive rituals such as secret eating or vomiting. This group is very similar to those discussed in the be-havioral section of this chapter. In this treatment group the therapist is directive and assumes a teaching role. Group discussions are task-oriented and do not focus on feelings.

Behavioral counseling group. Some overweight clients have a long history of dieting, tend to set goals that are difficult to attain, and are likely to eat for emotional reasons. In addition, they exhibit distorted or magical thinking, for example, "A month in this program and I will be a different person." These individuals would be referred to the group that combines behavioral skills training with group counseling. This group alternates between behavioral training sessions 1 week and group counseling the following week. The skills training sessions are very similar to those offered in the skills training group. The group counseling sessions are designed to help clients understand the emotional significance of weight and eating. They differ from the behavioral sessions in tone as well as content. The therapist plays more of a facilitative role, helping clients to gain insight into their eating and weight problems, which "could be construed as either a behavioral excess or symptomatic of an underlying disturbance, or both" (Gormally & Hill, 1977, p. 53).

Chronic dieters group.   Other clients have a history of repeated failure at dieting, perhaps including drastic methods such as gastric bypass or jaw-wiring. They often feel overwhelmed by their eating behavior and are frequently severely depressed. Their depression and sense of helplessness result in resistance to completing assigned tasks. These clients would be referred to a chronic dieters' group. Despite pressure from these clients for dieting advice, the therapist in this group needs to avoid providing specific techniques. Instead, the therapist encourages clients to examine their previous weight loss efforts to try and understand why these efforts failed. Clients are discouraged from another false start in a weight control program, and more attention is paid to controlling binges than losing weight. The goal of this group is to increase awareness about food and dieting and to promote changes in the client's self-concept.

Gormally and Hill's (1977) program is one example of modifying standardized group treatments to better suit the individual member. Research is needed to compare the results of such programs to those reported in the literature.

FEMINIST TREATMENT

The majority of overweight clients who seek treatment are women. Estimates of the percentage of women who comprise the subject pool of weight-loss studies range from 80 to 95% (Fodor & Thal, 1984), yet women are less affected than men in terms of health and longevity (Gubner, 1974). Why the disparity? Forster and Jeffery (1986) examined gender differences among participants in a weight-loss program and found that women were more likely to believe they were overweight. Fodor and Thal (1984) pointed to the societal myth that one must be thin to be considered attractive and socially acceptable as a woman. Roth (1982) noted that men are able to separate their fat from themselves, for example, having a "beer belly" does not make one an outcast, whereas women, "on the contrary, view their fat as an outward sign that something is wrong with their basic nature" (p. 3). The result, in addition to more attempts at weight loss by women, is that women's successes or failures in weight loss attempts are imbued with meanings that are out of proportion to their objective impact (e.g., "I failed to lose weight, therefore, I'm a failure as a person"). Wooley and Wooley (1980) hypothesized that for many women, the ability to control their weight and food intake becomes a symbol of their ability to control their life in general.

Viewed in this light, obesity does not seem so very different from anorexia nervosa. Bruch (1973), a pioneer in the field of eating disorders, was the first to note the similarities between the psychological problems of anorexic and obese patients. Wooley and Wooley (1980) suggested that weight and the eating disorders be classified along two dimensions: the extent of deviation from population body weight norms and the extent to which individuals are focused or obsessed with their inability to achieve or maintain ideal body weight.

Placing weight disorders on both a physical and psychological continuum may help to explain the range of body size of those women who do seek treatment. The majority of clients who enroll in behavioral treatment programs are mild to moderately overweight (Fodor & Thal, 1984). Within this weight range health risks are minimal for both sexes (Wooley & Wooley, 1980), with the exception of those suffering from accompanying medical conditions. Hall (cited in Wooley & Wooley, 1980) reported that half the applicants to a weight-loss program were within 10% of average weight. Bruch (1980) coined the term "thin-fat people" to describe women of normal weight who believe they are overweight.

The term *compulsive eaters* (or compulsive overeaters) has yet to be strictly defined but is used by practitioners (Gormally & Hill, 1977; Orbach, 1978a, 1978b, 1982; Roth, 1982, 1986; Wolman, 1982), self-help groups (Overeaters Anonymous, 1981), and lay persons to describe individuals who may or may not be overweight but who feel out of control in relation to food. According to Orbach (1982) and Roth (1986), these individuals eat in response to unconscious needs, desires, and conflicts and are not in touch with their bodies' signals of hunger or satiety. Overeaters Anonymous (OA, 1979) provides a list of 15 questions to help individuals determine whether they are compulsive eaters. Examples include "Do you give too much time and thought to food?" and "Do you have feelings of guilt and remorse after overeating?" Feminist-oriented groups for compulsive eaters have been offered since at least 1970 (Orbach, 1978a, 1978b), with Orbach (1978a, 1978b, 1982) and Roth (1982, 1986) being the most prolific among the feminist practitioners.

Goals of Treatment

Feminist clinicians and researchers have been critical of behavioral treatments for overweight clients, particularly women. These practitioners argue that cultural standards of beauty, as expressed by the fashion industry and the mass media, differentially impact on women. Rather than ignoring societal attitudes concerning weight and clients' feelings about these attitudes, treatment can help overweight women to deal with these pressures (Wooley, Wooley, & Dyrenforth, 1979b). Also neglected by many treatment programs is an examination of clients' obsession with thinness (Fodor & Thal, 1984). This approach seems particularly appropriate for the thin-fat people of whom Bruch (1980) speaks and for those who are only mildly overweight and repeatedly lose and regain the same 10 to 15 pounds. Research indicates that weight cycling might lower one's metabolic rate, thereby making weight control more difficult (Brownell, 1988). According to Drenick (cited in Polivy & Herman, 1985), such "yo-yoing" of weight seems to exacerbate existing ailments and may cause additional problems.

Feminist practitioners are of the opinion that behavioral programs are too narrowly focused on weight loss (Fodor, 1983; Wooley & Wooley, 1980). Thus, feminist programs do not begin with the assumption that weight reduction is the goal for all overweight clients who seek treatment. Wooley and coworkers (1979b) suggested that therapists should help patients to make a reasoned choice about if and when to lose weight. These practitioners perceive the first goal of treatment to be the maintenance of one's body weight on entering a program. During an initial phase of treatment, clients learn weight maintenance skills, study their eating habits, and weigh the anticipated benefits and costs of weight loss. At the end of this phase, clients decide whether or not to try and lose weight. According to Wooley, Wooley, and Dyrenforth (1979b), "the aim of treatment is presented as helping each patient learn to maintain, without undue effort, a body weight at which he or she can be comfortable. Successful completion of the program may or may not involve weight loss" (p. 244). These authors report that most but not all clients decide to try and lose weight, but do so with new attitudes. Support is offered to those clients who choose not to lose weight.

Fodor (1983) is more likely to recommend a behavioral program for weight reduction if there is a health hazard or if weight gain is of recent origin. From the outset, both Fodor's (1983) and Wooley, Wooley, and Dyrenforth's groups (1979b) share information with their clients about the problems associated with dieting and maintaining weight loss. Beliefs underlying the goal of weight reduction are examined, for example, that overweight is caused by overeating or that weight loss is healthy (Fodor, 1983), in order to help clients develop realistic goals and to relieve some of the shame and failure associated with past weight loss efforts (Wooley, Wooley, & Dyrenforth, 1979b). Programs that fail to help clients develop more realistic goals "may not only fail to reduce the gap between real and ideal weights, [but] they may also lower self-esteem by convincing clients that their self-control is inadequate" (Foder & Thal, 1984, p. 393). Fodor (1983) challenged behavior therarpists to help moderately overweight women break out of the "diet/self-hate/life-on-hold cycle" by encouraging them to work on self-acceptance and changing societal prejudices (p. 386).

Similarly, feminist groups for compulsive eaters do not focus on weight loss. Treatment goals include increasing members' self-acceptance and learning to trust one's internal cues to eat when hungry and stop when full (Orbach, 1978b, 1982; Roth, 1982, 1986). This approach differs from standard behavioral programs that rely heavily on external controls such as counting calories.

Overall, the feminist literature on obesity and compulsive eating is rich in theory and clinical examples but lacks a solid empirical base. For this reason, much of the material that follows is presented without supporting research.

Group Composition, Themes, and Structure

Membership in most, if not all, of the groups with a feminist orientation is restricted to women. Same-sex groups may be more desirable than mixed-sex groups (Gormally & Hill, 1977) to facilitate discussion and to lessen self-consciousness about weight-related topics. Although the rationale for same-sex groups is based primarily on clinical experience and theoretical orientation, there is some empirical support for sex-segregated groups for weight loss. Differences between men and women have been found in such areas as weight and dieting history, weight maintenance, eating behavior, self-efficacy in relation to eating, and response to treatment (Forster & Jeffery, 1986). Such differences suggest that sex-specific treatment may be beneficial.

Feminist therapy for obesity is based on the assumption that being overweight meets one or more needs of the client, often unconscious. Thus, clients are aided in understanding the role of weight in their lives, the meanings they attribute to fat, and the reasons that they have difficulty giving up their eating habits (Orbach, 1978a, 1978b, 1982; Roth, 1986). For example, some women experience their fat as giving them a sense of strength and power. For others, being fat is a way to avoid being treated as a sexual object. The notion that being overweight somehow satisfies the client's needs or that becoming thin is scary is often difficult for clients to accept. One method for increasing clients' awareness of these unconscious feelings is the use of guided fantasies (Orbach, 1978a, 1978b, 1982). Group members, with eyes closed, are guided by the leader through scenarios such as a party and are asked to imagine themselves at various weights. Afterward members share the images and feelings evoked by the exercise. Once group members are attuned to these feelings, they are then encouraged to (1) evaluate whether the fat serves its functions (i.e., does fat keep others from seeing you as sexual?) and (2) consider alternative ways of satisfying needs or resolving problems other than through one's fat.

Feminist groups allot significant time for group discussions concerning members' feelings about their weight and the role of food in their lives. Typically, the topics covered include body image, self-esteem, assertiveness, and social self-consciousness concerning weight and eating. Techniques utilized include cognitive-behavioral interventions used in standard behavioral treatment programs. Self-monitoring is taught but with a slightly different emphasis than in behavioral groups; caloric intake is usually not recorded but attention is given, instead, to recording feelings and thoughts prior to and following eating. As in behavioral groups, individual members' patterns are then examined and discussed in the group, and alternatives to eating are considered. If, for example, one member realizes that she often eats when she is angry, the group will help her to problem-solve for other ways to deal with her anger.

Group members are also taught to note their hunger, or lack of it, prior to eating and their satisfaction, or lack of it, after eating. Participants will frequently report that they eat now to avoid becoming hungry later, and they acknowledge a fear of being hungry. Roth (1986) trains members to use a hunger/satiety rating scale and to base initiating and terminating eating on these self-ratings. As group members are learning to trust their internal controls, some external controls are offered to help modify eating behaviors. Roth (1986), for example, provides numerous behavioral suggestions for handling eating in resturants and parties as well as entertaining at one's own home.

Consciousness-raising techniques developed in the women's movement are frequently used. Cultural prejudices toward overweight women and the relationship of these biases to women's preoccupation with dieting are discussed (Fodor, 1983; Fodor & Thal, 1984; Orbach, 1978b). Group members are encouraged to share their own experiences as well as bring in examples of societal messages about weight, such as magazine advertisements. Personal beliefs that women have formed, based on these prejudices, are shared and challenged, such as "Any one who is attracted to me fat isn't worth having" (Fodor, 1983).

Helping group members accept themselves is central to the feminist orientation. Fodor (1983) outlined a self-acceptance training program that includes cognitive restructuring and reeducation. The cognitive work is based on Ellis's (1962) "Rational Emotive Therapy." Maladaptive beliefs such as "If my body doesn't conform to a model's, then I'm fat" are challenged and replaced with more self-enhancing beliefs. A "bill of rights for fat clients" is presented, including such items as "I have a right to be overweight, not to have people comment on my appearance, a right to eat what I want without excusing myself" (Fodor, 1983, p. 389). Reeducation trains clients to enjoy life with their body type through the use of group discussion, role models, shopping expeditions, and trips to museums to view Ruben's and others' paintings of voluptuous women. Other interventions include mirror exercises and self-drawings to help women accept their bodies (Orbach, 1978a, 1978b, 1982). Also recommended are tasks that involve acting on desires that women have been postponing until they are thin, such as wearing a shirt tucked in, buying brightly colored clothing, or dancing (Fodor, 1983; Roth, 1982, 1986).

Fodor and Thal (1984) pointed out that many women remain overweight to avoid age-appropriate changes such as sexual intimacy or career changes. These authors suggested that a developmental perspective that addresses changes in women's bodies across the life cycle might prove beneficial.

Regarding the size and length of a group, only Orbach (1978a, 1978b, 1982) commented on these variables. She recommended a group of 5 to 8 members in order to allow for individual participation. Groups meet weekly for 2 hours and may facilitate membership interaction (Orbach, 1982) or may be organized such that individual members essentially work on a one-to-one basis with the group leader (Orbach, 1978a).

Outcome

It is difficult to quantify success in feminist-oriented programs given the diversity of acceptable outcomes (Wooley, Wooley, & Dryenforth, 1979b). Wooley and colleagues noted that (1) the drop-out rate was small and (2) termination was based on a client's decision that she had reached an acceptable stopping point, both of which were viewed as indications that the program was meeting clients' needs. Although self-discovery and acceptance are stressed more than weight reduction in the groups for compulsive eaters, both Orbach (1978b) and Roth (1982, 1986) report that participants do lose: "When you start eating out of physical hunger and stop eating when you're satisfied, you lose weight" (Roth, 1982, p. 179).

SELF-HELP GROUPS

Self-help programs clearly have a major role to play in the management of obesity .
. . . Since it is a disorder with multiple contributory causes, obesity must be controlled through changes both in eating and in activity patterns. . . . The achievement of these adjustments requires supportive contact extending through months of gradual weight reduction, encouraged by exposure to successful models who can accurately portray the experience of changing core aspects of daily living. For most mildly to moderately overweight people, the low cost of self-help groups may be the optimal format for service delivery (Stuart & Mitchell, 1980, p. 347).

Self-help is the most common weight-loss method (Jeffery, 1987). Overeaters Anonymous is a self-help organization that focuses on compulsive eating, not weight loss. Take Off Pounds Sensibly and Weight Watchers, two of the largest and better known self-help groups, have been studied more than other similar organizations and focus on weight control.

Overeaters Anonymous

OA was founded in 1960 by a woman who had attended a meeting of Gamblers Anonymous and believed that a similar group for compulsive overeaters was needed. Today the organization claims a membership of 135,000 individuals who participate in over 8,000 registered groups in 35 countries. A nonprofit organization, OA has no dues or fees and is supported by membership contributions.

OA views compulsive overeating as a threefold illness with three corresponding levels of recovery: emotional, spiritual, and physical. Overeating and excess weight are seen as symptoms of problems in daily living (OA, 1987a). This perspective is evident at OA meetings where discussion focuses not on diets and weight but rather on learning to cope with life stresses without overeating.

OA is based on the same 12 steps and traditions as Alcoholics Anonymous (AA), with the word "food" substituted for "alcohol." Central to the 12-step program is "a belief in a power outside oneself, a Higher Power of whatever form one chooses" (OA, 1981, p. 6). For some this higher power is God, for others it is their inner voice, and for some it is the OA group. Because OA views compulsive overeating as a disease of isolation, the personal support offered by members is central to each OA group. All members are encouraged to attend at least one meeting a week and to call other members frequently, particularly when having difficulty. Meetings are very participatory and usually include a sort of "round-robin" with each group member sharing his or her current successes and difficulties. Leadership of each meeting is rotated.

In addition to attending meetings and using the telephone, OA offers five other tools to aid members in their recovery from compulsive overeating: (1) having a sponsor, (2) giving service, (3) anonymity, (4) utilizing OA's literature, and (5) abstaining from compulsive overeating. In the past, OA suggested several food plans and tips for achieving abstinence. These are no longer provided, however, and it is up to the individual member to select an eating plan, define abstinence, and determine an acceptable body weight, or to consult with professionals (OA, 1987b).

In 1981 OA commissioned a group and membership survey (Wolborsky, 1981). The largest percentage of new members (23.3%) returned for a second meeting because they felt understood at their first meeting, while the smallest percentage (10.5%) returned because of weight loss evidenced at their first meeting. Approximately one-fourth of the respondents who had been overweight reported achieving normal weight, and of these, 22.5% reported maintaining that weight for an average of 2.2 years. Emotional and mental health was the area in which respondents felt they had made the most improvement. Particularly interesting were the data concerning referral sources to OA. Health professionals, including therapists and physicians, accounted for only 13.2% of the referrals despite the fact that over 70% of the membership reported seeing such professionals regarding weight or eating problems. Whether these professionals are unaware of OA, do not see it as effective, or are fearful of losing their clients is unclear. The latter may be supported by the survey's finding that membership use of medical treatment for obesity decreased by 60.5% after joining OA, while psychological treatment decreased by 19.5%.

Take Off Pounds Sensibly

TOPS is a nonprofit, noncommercial organization that claims a membership of more than 318,000 in 12,189 chapters in the U.S., Canada, and 22 other countries. TOPS was founded in 1948 by a homemaker who, along with a few friends, was trying to lose weight. There are five facets to the TOPS program. The first is its medical orientation. Members must receive diet and medical supervision from their own physicians. Second is competition. Weight loss competitions are held at chapter, area, state or provincial, and international levels. Third is recognition. Those who lose the most weight at the various levels of the organization are acknowledged through TOPS recognition days and are crowned king and queen. Recognition is also provided for other achievements such as losing 100 pounds or maintaining weight losses. When members reach goal weight they graduate to KOPS (Keep

Off Pounds Sensibly) and are encouraged to remain with the chapter for their own maintenance and to serve as role models for others. The fourth facet is obesity research. Professionals working with TOPS provide TOPS members with their findings. Fifth is weekly chapter meetings. TOPS meetings are led by nonpaid, trained volunteers who are elected by their chapters for a 1-year period. Meetings begin with a public weigh-in. Those who have lost weight since the previous meeting wear a "bravo" sign, those who have gained wear a pig, and those remaining stable wear a turtle. Meetings include games, singalongs, an occasional speaker, and discussions about problems faced in losing weight. As with OA, members are encouraged to contact each other between meetings, especially if they are tempted to binge or go off their diets.

Levitz and Stunkard (1974) compared 16 TOPS chapters that received one of four treatments: behavior modification conducted by a professional therapist, behavior modification conducted by a TOPS chapter leader, nutrition education by a TOPS leader, and the regular TOPS program. The two treatment conditions using behavior modification lost significantly more weight than the other two conditions. Within the behavior modification condition, members of the groups conducted by a professional therapist lost significantly more weight than members of groups led by a nonprofessional. Members of those groups that received the regular TOPS program gained weight during treatment and during the maintenance period.

Siderits and Fadden (1977) gathered data on ten TOPS chapters in an attempt to determine why some chapters were more effective than others. They found that the attributes of the therapist, particularly in showing an attitude of concern for others, the therapist's own progress with weight loss, and the other members' concern for each other were more important than techniques utilized or topics discussed.

Weight Watchers

Weight Watchers was started in a manner similiar to TOPS by a housewife who organized a support group of neighbors who were trying to lose weight. According to spokespersons for the organization, between 800,000 and 1,000,000 people attend more than 20,000 Weight Watchers meetings each week, totalling more than 25 million people since the group's inception in 1961. These chapters are spread out over 24 countries, with the majority of them in the U.S. To service all these members, Weight Watchers maintains a staff of 9,000, most of whom have lost weight through the organization.

Stuart and Mitchell (1980) compared the outcome of participants in a standard Weight Watchers program with those in a Weight Watchers program to which behavioral techniques were added. The latter group lost significantly more weight. To evaluate which behavioral aspects of the program were most effective, 151 members, each of whom had attended at least 26 meetings, were surveyed. The most highly valued techniques were the weekly weigh-ins and discussion of programs in behavioral self-management. The second most important was having a group leader who had graduated from the program. Many members surveyed expressed their disinclination to have the service professionalized.

After this study was completed, Weight Watchers became the first self-help group to incorporate behavior modification and cognitive restructuring into their basic program. This program now includes four components: (1) decreasing caloric intake through a balanced diet based on a food exchange plan; (2) increasing caloric output through one or more of five recommended activities, all at low-to-moderate levels: walking, walking-jogging, stationary bicyling, outdoor bicyling, and swimming; (3) changing eating and exercise habits through the use of behavioral and cognitive techniques; and (4) receiving group support through weekly meetings.

Meetings usually last 1 hour. Members pay their dues ($15 to join, then $6 per meeting) and are then weighed individually. Members are given a goal weight based on height, age, and sex. Once goal weight is attained, members receive a lifetime membership that entitles them to attend meetings free of charge as long as they stay within 2 pounds of this goal weight. Membership is restricted to individuals who are at least 10 pounds above ideal weight as determined by Weight Watchers tables, which are comparable to the revised 1983 Metropolitan height/weight tables (Metropolitan Life Insurance Company, 1984).

Meetings are led by trained group leaders who have lost weight through the Weight Watchers program. The exact nature of meetings may vary somewhat depending on the particular chapter or leader. As a rule, leaders will select a weight-related topic and initiate a discussion in which members are encouraged to share their ideas, problems, and experiences. Available to all Weight Watchers members are a wide variety of brochures that provide suggestions for handling potentially difficult situations such as holidays, parties,and dining out.

Weight Watchers At Work Program (WWAWP) provides an 8- or 10-week adaptation of the standard Weight Watchers group meeting format (Frankle, McIntosh, Bianchi, & Kane, 1986). Offered at the worksite, these meetings are geared for co-workers pursuing weight loss. Lectures follow a structured outline covering such topics as managing eating at the workplace and conquering coffee breaks (e.g., how to pass up doughnuts and other sweets typically available during the workday).

Ashwell (1979) reviewed surveys of independent researchers of weight-loss groups in the U.S., Great Britain, and Australia. Included were Weight Watchers, TOPS, Slimming Magazine Slimming Clubs, and Silhouette Slimming Clubs (the last groups do not have chapters in the U.S.). Ashwell found TOPS to be the least expensive organization to join, with their members losing less weight than members of the other groups.

The lowest attrition rate was in TOPS, while the highest was in WW of U.S. and Australia. The average length of membership for a TOPS member was 18.5 months. Those individuals who had previously participated in some form of group treatment were more likely to drop out. Conversely, those who had a high initial weight and those who achieved significant weight loss were less likely to drop out. As with professionally led groups, achieved weight losses showed much individual variability. Outcome differed significantly among different chapters or classes within one organization. Using a criterion of a 20-pound weight loss, WW (Great Britain) was the most successful with 52% of members losing more than 20 pounds. Greatest losses were more likely to be achieved by (1) women who were over 30 years of age, married, had high initial weights, and had no previous group experience, and (2) those who attended regularly and stuck to their diet. All groups offered maintenance techniques. Those who quit the program before reaching goal weight, however, invariably regained the weight.

Ashwell (1979) concluded that weight losses achieved by these groups are comparable to those achieved by medical or mental health practitioners. He saw poor maintenance and high attrition to be the major problems of the self-help groups studied. Ashwell recommended that these organizations devise maintenance tools for those who are only partially successful to prevent what he saw as the likelihood of relapse and weight regain.

As noted in Chapter 1, self-help groups represent a major mental health resource. Their usual low cost and accessibility to the general public are particularly advantageous. Practitioners might consider referring clients to these groups during or after termination of individual therapy. Group therapists might consider referring clients to these groups after treatment has ended, particularly in light of the difficulties associated with maintaining weight losses.

SPECIAL CONSIDERATIONS

The following topics, which are most applicable to the professionally led groups for overweight individuals discussed in this chapter, will be covered in this section: group composition, individual differences, group norms, therapist characteristics, and medical supervision.

Group Composition

Most practitioners concur that prescreening of clients through individual interviews is advisable. One purpose of such an interview is to exclude individuals who may not be appropriate for the group such as those with severe psychopathology or those for whom problems other than weight require more immediate attention. For example, an individual may have gained weight as a result of depression. Depending on the history and the severity of the current symptomatology, a referral for treatment of the depression might be more appropriate than admittance into the group at the time of the screening. The therapist needs to decide whether the client will be able to effectively utilize the group at this time, as well as whether the client will distract the group from its goals.

Another purpose of screening is to assess a client's motivation and expectations about group treatment. The therapist can also use this time to present a brief description of the group. In this way the screening interview can provide information to both the therapist and the client regarding the fit of the client with the particular therapist and group.

Gormally and Hill (1977) recommend that age, sex, and severity of overweightness be taken into account when planning a group. Group homogeneity, which facilitates peer identification and group cohesiveness, is probably more important for those groups that rely on group interaction. Clients can be divided into three age groups: adolescents; college-aged and young single adults; and middle-aged and/or married adults (Gormally & Hill, 1977). These divisions are based on developmental differences as well as probable differences in behavior patterns regarding food shopping, regularity of meals, eating, and food preparation.

Severity of overweightness is seen by Gormally and Hill (1977) as the most important group composition variable. Differences in this variable may lead to differing treatment and differing rates of progress and may threaten group cohesiveness as resentments may develop between group members of vastly different weights.

Individual Differences

Practicality does not always allow for homogeneous groupings. There may not be a sufficient number of clients to form all-male groups or groups composed of members who are all 35 or more pounds overweight. Such has been the case with groups I have conducted at a university counseling center. In the event of such heterogeneity, the therapist needs to be sensitive to the tensions that may arise in the group. Differences in weight are likely to be construed by group members as evidence that they are too dissimilar to learn from or understand one another. For example, a heavier member may look at a thinner member and wonder, "Why are you here? You don't have any reason to be upset about weight." Directly addressing these tensions from the onset of the group conveys to group members that their feelings are acknowledged. To broaden the focus from the most visible characteristic, that of weight, the group leader can graphically depict the differences and similarities of group members by diagramming the physical, psychological, and behavioral continuums of weight and eating problems. Avoidance of group differences does not make the tensions go away and usually results in drop-outs from the group.

It is imperative that individual differences continue to be acknowledged throughout treatment (Knauss & Jeffrey, 1981). It is up to the therapist to ensure that techniques are implemented by individual group members in a way that is conducive to their lifestyle. In practice this can prove difficult, depending on the size of the group, the amount of material to be covered in each session, and length of each session. Group discussions can serve this purpose, and group leaders can give some individual attention to each member on a regular basis. Knauss and Jeffrey (1981) suggest the use of co-therapists. While one therapist lectures the other can assess participants' reactions—agreement, disagreement, confusion—and encourage these members to share their feelings during the discussion period. Ancillary staff may also provide assistance in spending a few minutes with each individual going over food diaries or homework assignments. Weiss, Katzman, and Wolchik (1985), who lead groups for bulimic clients, scheduled two individual sessions during the course of group treatment to review each individual's progress. I have found it useful to schedule an individual session with each group member prior to the last group meeting to discuss individual progress and alternatives for follow-up treatment.

Group Norms

Some of the norms for groups for overweight clients are the same as those for other therapy groups, such as confidentiality concerning group discussions. The relative importance of this norm may depend on whether the group is more didactic and task-oriented or whether discussion of feelings is encouraged.

The manner in which the group therapist utilizes reinforcement will greatly influence the tone and the type of interactions that occur within the group. Some therapists utilize only positive reinforcement, while others encourage the use of both negative and positive reinforcement. Therapists may choose to target weight loss for reinforcement, or they may reinforce any attempts at behavior change and accord weight loss only secondary emphasis. Gormally and Hill (1977) prefer the latter because such behavior supports variable rates of change among group members and decreases competition between members. Some therapists, on the other hand, promote a competitive atmosphere through such activities as weight-loss contests, group weigh-ins, and announcements of "losers" and "gainers" (Wollersheim, 1982). Finally, therapists may not wish to be a source of external reinforcement. They may choose to respond neutrally to reported weight losses and gains, focusing instead on the client's response to weight changes. Gormally and Hill (1977) suggest that reinforcement on the part of the therapist may unduly influence the client's motivation (i.e., to please the therapist), which may not bode well for long-term change. There are some empirical data to support use of self-reinforcement rather than reinforcement by a therapist (Rozensky & Bellack, 1976).

Regular attendance should be stressed by the therapist at screening and again at the initial group meeting to prevent high drop-out rates, which are not uncommon. Behavioral treatment studies have reported less attrition than have self-help and commercial programs (Volkmar, Stunkard, Woolston, & Bailey, 1981; Wilson & Brownell, 1980). Other variables shown to reduce attrition are leadership by a professionally trained therapist (Levitz & Stunkard, 1974) and deposit-refund procedures (Hagen, Foreyt, & Durham, 1976; Wilson & Brownell, 1980). Attendance is important because the content of one meeting is built on previous meetings and because poor attendance may have a negative effect on group members who do attend as well as those who are absent (Knauss & Jeffrey, 1981). Wollersheim (1982) offered a list of suggestions for preventing drop-outs, including starting meetings on time, telephoning absentees, and encouraging group members to discuss thoughts of dropping out in the group.

Therapist Characteristics

The sex and weight of the therapist can influence group treatment (Gormally & Hill, 1977). In sex-segregated groups it is important that at least one therapist be the same sex as the clients because of the emotional and sometimes sexual issues that may be discussed in relation to weight.

It is common for overweight individuals to want their therapists to have conquered a weight problem. Bruch (1976) sees a successful coping model as important for clients. A therapist of average body weight who has coped with a higher weight, or an overweight therapist who is losing weight during treatment can serve as a positive model for clients (Gormally & Hill, 1977). Moderate amounts of self-disclosure by the therapist on this topic can enhance group cohesion and trust in the therapist (Gormally & Hill, 1977; Knauss & Jeffrey, 1981). For those who lack this personal background, Skovholt and colleagues (1979) recommend bringing in other role models such as former group members or asking them to serve as co-therapists.

Another influencing set of factors are the therapist's attitudes toward obesity and weight loss. Knaus and Jeffrey (1981) listed three attitudes that may reduce a leader's effectiveness: (1) seeing obesity as an insignificant problem and a desire to work with problems that are more "real"; (2) seeing obesity as primarily a medical or nutritional problem and therefore out of the therapist's realm of expertise; and (3) seeing obesity as a lack of willpower. These attitudes on the part of the therapist frequently reinforce some of the nonproductive attitudes that many overweight individuals have toward their own problems.

Perhaps the most crucial attribute for those who lead these groups, other than general skills in the practice of group therapy, is patience. These clients have probably tried other programs and failed. They may be feeling quite desperate and are likely to pressure the therapist for a "quick fix."

Medical Supervision

Weight loss and dieting can have their own "side-effects" or negative consequences (Polivy & Herman, 1985; Van Itallie & Abraham, 1985). Therapists who lead groups for weight loss need either to have available medical personnel who will screen and monitor the group members or to require members to have their own physician's approval before entering group treatment. This requirement is for the protection of both the client and the therapist. The need for medical services increases with more aggressive weight reduction regimens, such as the VLCD. Medical supervision is not necessary for those groups that are solely psychological in nature and are not actively encouraging weight loss, such as groups for compulsive eaters.

CONCLUSION

This chapter has presented a sampling of group treatments available for overweight adults. This range of treatment options, in itself, is an important step forward. Given the lack of predictor variables for success in treatment, the multidimensional nature of obesity, and the individual differences among those with weight problems, diversity in treatment is essential. When recommending a particular group for the overweight client, it is important that many factors be taken into account, including severity of overweightness, accompanying medical conditions, weight and diet history, obsession with thinness, motivation, and expectations. For some clients, particularly chronic dieters, a supportive group that will help them gain insight into their motivation for weight loss and become more self-accepting may be preferable to another "false start" at weight loss. Outcome measures that assess changes other than weight, such as improved body image and self-esteem, are needed. The problems of achieving and maintaining significant weight losses point to the need for longer treatment. Whether the goal of treatment is weight reduction, maintenance, or changes in self-concept, long-term supportive care appears necessary.

REFERENCES

Abrams, D. B., & Follick, M. J. (1983). Behavioral weight loss intervention at the worksite: Feasibility and maintenance. *Journal of Consulting and Clinical Psychology, 51,* 226–233.

Abramson, E. E. (1977). Clinical considerations in behavioral treatment of obesity. In E. E. Abramson (Ed.), *Behavioral approaches to weight control* (pp. 133–143). New York: Springer.

Allon, N. (1982). The stigma of overweight in everyday life. In B. B. Wolman (Ed.), *Psychological aspects of obesity: A handbook* (pp. 130–174). New York: Van Nostrand Reinhold.

American Psychiatric Association. (1980). *Diagnostic and statistical manual of mental disorders* (3rd ed.). Washington, DC: American Psychiatric Press.

Ashwell, M. (1979). Commercial weight loss groups. In G. A. Bray (Ed.), *Recent advances in obesity research: II* (pp. 266–276). Westport, CT: Technomic Publishing.

Becker, M. H., & Maiman, L. A. (1980). Strategies for enhancing compliance. *Journal of Community Health, 6,* 113–135.

Berland, T. (1984). *Rating the diets: Consumer Guide.* New York: Signet.

Brownell, K. D. (1981). Assessment of eating disorders. In D. H. Barlow (Ed.), *Behavioral assessment of adult disorders.* New York: Guilford.

Brownell, K. D. (1984). Behavioral, psychological, and environmental predictors of obesity and success at weight reduction. *International Journal of Obesity, 8,* 543–550.

Brownell, K. D. (1987). *The LEARN program for weight control* (2nd ed.). Philadelphia: University of Pennsylvania School of Medicine.

Brownell, K. D. (1988, January). Minding your health: Yo-Yo dieting. *Psychology Today,* pp. 20–23.

Brownell, K. D., Heckerman, C. L., Westlkake, R. I., Hayes, S. C., & Monti, P. M. (1978). The effect of couples training and partner cooperativenes in the behavioral treatment of obesity. *Behaviour*

Research and Therapy, 16, 323–334.

Brownell, K. D., & Stunkard, A. J. (1981). Couples training, pharmacotherapy, and behavior therapy in the treatment of obesity. *Archives of General Psychiatry, 38,* 1224–1229.

Brownell, K. D., & Wadden, T. A. (1986). Behavior therapy for obesity: Modern approaches and better results. In K. B. Brownell, & J. P. Foreyt (Eds.), *Handbook of eating disorders: Physiology, psychology and treatment of obesity, anorexia and bulimia* (pp. 180–197). New York: Basic Books.

Bruch, H. (1973). *Eating disorders: Obesity, anorexia, and the person within.* New York: Basic Books.

Bruch, H. (1980). Thin fat people. In J. R. Kaplan (Ed.), *A woman's conflict: The special relationship between women and food* (pp. 29–42). Englewood Cliffs, NJ: Prentice-Hall.

Bruch, M. A. (1976). Coping model treatments: Unresolved issues and needed research. *Behavior Therapy, 7,* 711–713.

Cahnman, W. J. (1968). The stigma of obesity. *Sociological Quarterly, 9,* 283–299.

Canning, H., & Mayer, J. (1966). Obesity—Its possible effect on college acceptance. *New England Journal of Medicine, 275,* 1172–1174.

Collins, R. L., Rothblum, E. D., & Wilson, G. T. (1986). The comparative efficacy of cognitive and behavioral approaches to the treatment of obesity. *Cognitive Therapy and Research, 10*(3), 299–318.

Craighead, L. W., Stunkard, A. J., & O'Brien, R. M. (1981). Behavior therapy and pharmacotherapy for obesity. *Archives of General Psychiatry, 38,* 763–768.

Dahlkoetter, J., Callahan, E. J., & Linton, J. (1979). Obesity and the unbalanced energy equation: Exercise vs. eating habit change. *Journal of Consulting and Clinical Psychology, 47,* 898–905.

Dwyer, J. (1985). Classifying current popular and fad diets. In J. Hirsch, & B. Van Itallie (Eds.), *Recent advances in obesity research: IV* (pp. 179–191). London: John Libbey.

Ellis, A. (1962). *Reason and emotion in psychotherapy.* New York: Lyce Stuart.

Ferster, C. B., Nurnberger, J. I., & Levitt, E. B. (1962). The control of eating. *Journal of Mathetics, 1,* 87–109.

Fodor, I. E. (1983). Behavior therapy for the overweight woman: A time for reappraisal. In M. Rosenbaum, C. M. Franks, & Y. Jaffe (Eds.), *Perspectives on behavioral therapy in the eighties* (pp. 378–394). New York: Spring.

Fodor, I. E., & Thal, J. (1984). Weight disorders: Overweight and anorexia. In E. A. Blechman (Ed.), *Behavior modification with women* (pp. 373–398). New York: Guilford.

Foreyt, J. P. (1987). Issues in the assessment and treatment of obesity. *Journal of Consulting and Clinical Psychology, 55*(5), 677–684.

Forster, J. L., & Jeffery, R. W. (1986). Gender differences related to weight history, eating patterns, efficacy expectations, self-esteem, and weight loss among participants in a weight reduction program. *Addictive Behaviors, 11,* 141–147.

Frankle, R. T., McIntosh, J., Bianchi, M., & Kane, E. J. (1986). The Weight Watchers® at Work program. *Journal of Nutrition Education, 18,* (1, suppl), 44–46.

Goodman, N., Dornbusch, S. M., Richardson, S. A., & Hastorf, A. H. (1963). Variant reactions to physical disabilities. *American Sociological Review, 28,* 429–435.

Gormally, J., & Hill, C. E. (1977). Treatment of overweight and eating disorders. In G. G. Harris (Ed.), *The group treatment of human problems: A social learning approach* (pp. 33–57). New York: Grune & Stratton.

Gubner, R. (1974). Overweight and health: Prognostic realities and therapeutic possibilities. In L. Lasagna (Ed.), *Obesity: Causes, consequences, and treatment.* New York: Medcom.

Hagen, R. L., Foreyt, J. P., & Durham, T. W. (1976). The dropout problem: Reducing attrition in obesity research. *Behavior Therapy, 7,* 463–471.

Jeffery, R. W. (1987). Behvioral treatment of obesity. *Annals of Behavioral Medicine, 9*(1), 20–24.

Jeffery, R. W., Gerber, W. M., Rosenthal, B. S., & Lindquist, R. A. (1983). Monetary contracts in weight control: Effectiveness of group and individual contracts of varying sizes. *Journal of Consulting and Clinical Psychology, 51*(2), 242–248.

Jeffery, R. W., Snell, M. K., & Forster, J. L. (1985). Group composition in the treatment of obesity: Does increasing group homogeneity improve treatment results? *Behavior Research and Therapy, 23*(3), 371–373.

Jeffery, R. W., Wing, R. R., Stunkard, A. J. (1978). Behavioral treatment of obesity: The state of the art 1976. *Behavior Therapy, 9*, 189–199.

Kingsley, R. G., & Wilson, G. T. (1977). Behavior therapy for obesity: A comparative investigation of long-term efficacy. *Journal of Consulting and Clinical Psychology, 45*(2), 288–298.

Knauss, M. R., & Jeffrey, D. B. (1981). Group behavior therapy for the treatment of obesity: Issues and suggestions, In D. Upper, & S. M. Ross (Eds.), *Behavioral Group Therapy, 1981: An Annual Review* (pp. 279–307). Champaign, IL.

Larkin, J. C., & Pines, H. A. (1979). No fat persons need apply: Experimental studies of the overweight stereotype and hiring preference. *Sociology of Work and Occupations, 6*, 312–227.

Lerner, R. M., & Korn, S. J. (1972). The development of body-build stereotypes in males. *Child Development, 43*, 908–920.

Levitz, L. S. & Stunkard, A. J. (1974). A therapeutic coalition for obesity: Behavior modification and patient self-help. *American Journal of Psychiatry, 131*(4), 423–427.

Louderback, L. (1970). *Fat power: Whatever you weigh is right.* New York: Hawthorn.

Mahoney, K., & Mahoney, M. J. (1976). *Permanent weight control.* New York: W.W. Norton.

Mahoney, M. J., Mahoney, B. K., Rogers, T., & Straw, M. K. (1979). Assessment of human obesity: The measurement of body composition. *Journal of Behavioral Assessment, 1*, 327–349.

Marcus, M. D., & Wing, R. R. (1987). Binge eating among the obese. *Annals of Behavioral Medicine, 9*(4), 23–27.

Marlatt, G. A., & Gordon, J. R. (1979). Determinants of relapse: Implications for the maintenance of behavior change. In P. O. Davidson, & S. M. Davidson (Eds.), *Behavioral medicine: Changing health lifestyles* (pp. 410–452). New York: Bruner/Mazel.

Metropolitan Life Insurance Company. (1984). 1983 Metropolitan height and weight tables. *Statistical Bulletin of the Metropolitan Life Insurance Company, 64*, 2–9.

National Institutes of Health Consensus Development Panel on the Health Implications of Obesity. (1985). National Institutes of Health Consensus Development Statement. *Annals of Internal Medicine, 103*, 1073–1077.

Orbach, S. (1978a). *Fat is a feminist issue.* New York: Berkley.

Orbach, S. (1978b). Social dimensions in compulsive eating in women. *Psychotherapy: Theory, Research and Practice, 15*(2), 180–189.

Orbach, S. (1982). *Fat is a feminist issue II.* New York: Berkley.

Overeaters Anonymous. (1979). *A program of recovery.* Torrance, CA: Overeaters Anonymous.

Overeaters Anonymous. (1981). *Compulsive overeating and the OA recovery program.* Torrance, CA: Overeaters Anonymous.

Overeaters Anonymous. (1987a). *OA is not a diet club.* Torrance, CA: Overeaters Anonymous.

Overeaters Anonymous. (1987b). *To the newcomer.* Torrance, CA: Overeaters Anonymous.

Pearce, J. W., LeBow, M. D., & Orchard, J. (1981). Role of spouse involvement in the behavioral treatment of overweight women. *Journal of Consulting and Clinical Psychology, 49*(2), 236–244.

Penick, S. B., Filion, R., Fox, S., & Stunkard, A. J. (1971). Behavior modification in the treatment of obesity. *Psychosomatic Medicine, 33*, 49–55.

Perri, M. G., Shapiro, R. M., Ludwig, W. W., Twentyman, C. T., & McAdoo, W. G. (1984). Maintenance strategies for the treatment of obesity: An evaluation of relapse prevention training and post-treatment contact by mail and telephone. *Journal of Consulting and Clinical Psychology, 52*, 404–413.

Polivy, J., & Herman, C. P. (1985). Dieting as a problem in behavioral medicine. In E. S. Katkin, & S. B. Manuck (Eds.), *Advances in behavioral medicine* (Vol. 1, pp. 1–37).

Rodin, J. (1982). Obesity: Why the losing battle? In B. B. Wolman (Ed.), *Psychological aspects of obesity: A handbook* (pp. 30–87). New York: Van Nostrand Reinhold.

Roe, D. A., & Eickwort, K. R. (1976). Relationships between obesity and associated health factors with unemployment among low income women. *Journal of the American Medical Women's Association, 31*, 193–204.

Rosenthal, B. S., & Marx, R. D., (1979, December). *A comparison of standard behavioral and relapse prevention weight reduction program.* Paper presented at the meeting of the Association for Advancement of Behavior Therapy, Chicago.

Roth, G. (1982). *Feeding the hungry heart: The experience of compulsive eating.* New York: Bobbs-Merrill.

Roth, G. (1986). *Breaking free from compulsive eating.* New York: Signet.

Rozensky, R. H., & Bellack, A. S. (1976). Individual differences in self-reinforcement style and performance in self- and therapist-controlled weight reduction programs. *Behavior Research and Therapy, 14,* 357–364.

Sallade, J. (1973). A comparison of the psychological adjustment of obese vs. non-obese children. *Journal of Psychosomatic Research, 17,* 89–96.

Siderits, M. A. & Fadden, T. F. (1977). Differential effectiveness of informal group procedures in weight control. *Journal of Clinical Psychology. 33*(2), 351–355.

Skovholt, T. M., Resnick, J. L., & Dewey, C. R. (1979). Weight treatment: A group approach to weight control. *Psychotherapy: Theory, Research and Practice, 16*(1), 118–123.

Staffieri, J. R. (1967). A study of social stereotype of body image in children. *Journal of Personality and Social Psychology, 7,* 101–104.

Sternberg, B. (1985). Relapse in weight control: Definitions, problems and prevention strategies. In G. A. Marlatt, & J. R. Gordon (Eds.), *Relapse prevention: Maintenance strategies in the treatment of addictive behaviors* (pp. 521–545). New York: Guilford.

Stuart, R. B. (1967). Behavioral control of overeating. *Behaviour Research and Therapy, 5,* 357–365.

Stuart, R. B. (1971). A three-dimensional program for the treatment of obesity. *Behaviour Research and Therapy, 9,* 177–186.

Stuart, R. B., & Davis, B. (1972). *Slim chance in a fat world: Behavioral control of obesity.* Champaign, IL: Research Press.

Stuart, R. B., & Mitchell, C. (1980). Self-help groups in the control of body weight. In A. J. Stunkard (Ed.), *Obesity* (pp. 345–354). Philadelphia: W. B. Saunders.

Stunkard, A. J. (1975). From explanation to action in psychosomatic medicine: The case of obesity. *Psychosomatic Medicine, 37,* 195–236.

Stunkard, A. J., & Mahoney, M. J. (1976). Behavioral treatment of the eating disorders. In H. Leitenberg (Ed.), *Handbook of behavior modification and behavior therapy* (pp. 45–73). Englewood Cliffs, NJ: Prentice-Hall.

Stunkard, A. J., & Penick, S. B. (1979). Behavior modification in the treatment of obesity: The problem of maintaining weight loss. *Archives of General Psychiatry, 36,* 810–816.

Thompson, J. K., Jarvie, G. J., Lahey, B. B., & Cureton, K. J. (1982). Exercise and obesity: Etiology, physiology and intervention. *Psychological Bulletin, 91,* 55–79.

Van Itallie, T. B., & Abraham, S. (1985). Some hazards of obesity and its treatment. In J. Hirsch, & T. B. Van Itallie (Eds.), *Recent advances in obesity research: IV* (pp. 1–19). Bondway, London: John Libbey.

Volkmar, F. R., Stunkard, A. J., Woolston, J., & Bailey, R. A. (1981). High attrition rates in commercial weight reduction programs. *Archives of Internal Medicine, 141,* 426–428.

Wadden, T. A., & Stunkard, A. J. (1985). Social and psychological consequences of obesity. *Annals of Internal Medicine, 103,* 1062–1067.

Wadden, T. A., & Stunkard, A. J. (1986). Controlled trial of very low calorie diet, behavior therapy, and their combination in the treatment of obesity. *Journal of Consulting and Clinical Psychology, 54,* 482–488.

Weiss, L., Katzman, M., & Wolchik, S. (1985). *Treating bulimia: A psychoeducational approach.* New York: Pergamon.

Wilson, G. T. (1978). Methodological considerations in treatment outcome research on obesity. *Journal of Consulting and Clinical Psychology, 46*(4), 687–702.

Wilson, G. T., & Brownell, K. G. (1978). Behavior therapy for obesity: Including family members in the treatment process. *Behavior Therapy, 9,* 943–945.

Wilson, G. T., & Brownell, K. B. (1980). Behavior therapy for obesity: An evaluation of treatment outcome. *Advances in Behavior Research and Therapy, 3,* 49–86.

Wing, R. R., Epstein, L. H., Nowalk, M. P., Koeske, R., & Hagg, S. (1985). Behavior change, weight loss, and physiological improvements in Type II diabetic patients. *Journal of Consulting and Clinical Psychology, 53*(1), 111–122.

Wolborsky, B. (1981). *A survey of Overeaters Anonymous groups and membership in North America.* (Research Report). Los Angeles: Overeaters Anonymous Inc.

Wollersheim, J. P. (1970). Effectiveness of group therapy based upon learning principles in the treatment of overweight women. *Journal of Abnormal Psychology, 76*(3), 462–474.

Wollersheim, J. P. (1982). Group therapy in the treatment of obesity. In B. B. Wolman (Ed.), *Psychological aspects of obesity: A handbook* (pp. 241–267). New York: Van Nostrand Reinhold.

Wolman, B. B. (1982). Interactional psychotherapy of obesity. In B. B. Wolman (Ed.), *Psychological aspects of obesity* (pp. 192–206). New York: Van Nostrand Reinhold.

Wooley, S. C., & Wooley, O. W. (1980). Eating disorders: Obesity and anorexia. In A. M. Brodsky, & R. T. Hare-Mustin (Eds.), *Women and psychotherapy: An assessment of research and practice* (pp. 135–158). New York: Guilford.

Wooley, S. G., Wooley, O. W., & Dyrenforth, S. R. (1979a). Theoretical, practical, and social issues in behavioral treatments of obesity. *Journal of Applied Behavior Analysis, 12*(1), 3–25.

Wooley, S. C., Wooley, O. W., & Dyrenforth, S. R. (1979b). Obesity treatment reexamined: The case for a more tentative and experimental approach. In N. A. Krasnegor (Ed.), *Behavioral analysis and treatment of substance abuse* (pp. 238–250). Rockville, MD: Department of Health, Education, and Welfare.

Young, L. M. (1983). The effects of client obesity on counselor clinical judgments. *Dissertation Abstracts International, 44*(2), 393A.

Zitter, R. E., & Fremouw, W. J. (1978). Individual versus partner consequation for weight loss. *Behavior Therapy, 9*, 808–813.

PATRICIA A. HALVORSON
PATRICIA A. NEUMAN

14
A Structured Group Therapy Approach for Clients with Bulimia

In this chapter, we discuss group treatment of bulimia nervosa from the perspective of our experience treating females on a college campus. Our focus on female college students is not meant to indicate that males or clientele in other settings cannot benefit from this type of group—we have simply never had enough males interested at a given time to form a group. The chapter addresses the use of the structured therapy group for the treatment of bulimia. Some of the areas addressed include philosophy of treatment, screening, group structure, ground rules, stages of recovery in group, and relapse and related problems in conducting groups with this population. An outline of components of a treatment plan for bulimia is included at the end of the chapter.

DESCRIPTION OF BULIMIA NERVOSA

Bulimia nervosa, a sister ailment of anorexia nervosa, is an eating disorder characterized by compulsive binge eating, a feeling of loss of control during the binge, persistent overconcern with weight, and usually purging (self-induced vomiting, laxative abuse, use of diuretics, etc.). The typical pattern of alternating binge behavior and strict dieting or fasting may lead to frequent weight fluctuations. Vigorous exercise may also be employed for weight control. A complete description of bulimia nervosa can be found in the Diagnostic and Statistical Manual of Mental Disorders, third edition revised (DSM-III-R) (APA, 1987). Most individuals with bulimia nervosa are of normal weight, although some may be either over- or underweight. If weight is extremely low and anorexia nervosa is present, dual diagnoses of anorexia nervosa and bulimia nervosa are given (DSM-III-R). Bulimia nervosa tends to run a chronic and intermittent course, with periods of temporary improvement followed by repeated relapse during the course of the illness.

For many victims of bulimia, the binge/purge behavior becomes a compulsive ritual that consumes their lives (Neuman & Halvorson, 1983, p. 57). The guilt associated with this disorder can be overwhelming and can lead to increased bulimic behavior. When guilt and embarrassment are present, as they often are, secrecy is a necessity, leading to a great deal of dishonesty even in otherwise open and honest people.

The binge eating that is a primary component of bulimia may be planned or unplanned. The food chosen during the binge is otherwise avoided. The texture of the food may also be a consideration. Usually the food chosen is of a texture that can be easily and quickly consumed as well as easily vomited. It may even be an odd concoction in the form of gruel. The binge is generally terminated by extreme physical discomfort, sleep, self-induced vomiting, or a social interruption of some kind. Vomiting is most often utilized to counteract the consequences of the binge. However, in some cases binging is carried out in order to vomit. In these instances, the goal is vomiting itself, which has been noted to have reinforcing aspects (e.g., providing a discharge of tension and/or a feeling of being cleansed). Individuals who are not bulimic also occasionally engage in binge eating and vomiting. It has been suggested that this behavior is becoming a new norm for college women in particular (Polivey & Herman, 1987). To meet the newly revised criteria for a diagnosis of bulimia nervosa, the person must average at least two binges per week for at least 3 months.

Bulimia generally begins in the teen years or early twenties. Some victims of the disorder have a history of anorexia nervosa, others develop anorexia at a later date, and still others remain free of anorexia nervosa. Young women are disproportionately affected, with approximately 10 females affected for every male (Pyle et al., 1983). Two recent studies of college freshmen in the midwest (Pyle, Halvorson, Neuman, & Mitchell, 1986; Pyle et al., 1983), conducted 3 years apart, indicate a rapidly increasing incidence of the disorder. In the 3-year interval between studies, there was a threefold increase in the number of college freshmen reporting symptoms of bulimia. Furthermore, the students in the second study reported more severe symptomatology such as more frequent binge/purge behavior and a greater fear of being fat (Pyle et al., 1986). Thus, in our society not only is the incidence of this disorder increasing, but the symptomatology is also becoming more severe.

The physical complications that can occur from bulimic behaviors are numerous. Some of these include:

1. Damage to colon (laxative abuse)
2. Esophogeal tear/hiatal hernia
3. Chronic indigestion
4. Facial puffiness
5. Swollen glands/sore throat
6. Irregular menstrual period
7. Dental problems
8. Fluid and electrolyte abnormalities
9. Dry skin
10. Bloodshot eyes

A deficiency in potassium can produce muscle weakness, abdominal distention, nervous irritability, apathy, drowsiness, mental confusion, and irregular heartbeat. Death from kidney and heart failure may occur.

The psychological complications of bulimia nervosa are also numerous and are discussed in the following sections.

Preoccupation with food, dieting, weight, and shape.   This preoccupation interferes with all aspects of life: relationships, concentration, school, work, sleep, and social activities. Clients report discomfort with social situations because food is so often involved. Thoughts of food intrude during other activities and can make sleep difficult. Maintaining interest in a simple conversation can become a losing battle. When a person is so preoccupied, it becomes impossible to fully experience anything else in life.

Increasing social isolation.   Feeling "fat" can lead to an increase in isolation due to the fear of possible negative evaluation by others. People may also be avoided to ensure the opportunity to binge and purge in private. Furthermore, the shame and depression associated with bulimia tend to result in withdrawal.

Feelings of shame and demoralization due to binge/purge behaviors. Typically there is a great deal of shame surrounding bulimic behavior. The consequence of shame is secrecy, a psychological distancing in relationships, and lowered self-esteem. The heightened tension in turn contributes to increased binge/purge behavior. The increasing loss of control leads to demoralization and a loss of hope in recovery.

Relationship difficulties. Clearly, personal relationships cannot escape being affected by the presence of bulimia. In addition to the aforementioned factors, victims of bulimia also tend to lack assertion and conflict resolution skills, which further contributes to relationship difficulties.

Presence of other addictive behaviors (e.g., laxative abuse, chemical abuse, kleptomania). Addictive behaviors accompanying bulimia are further addressed later in this chapter.

Anxiety symptoms. Anxiety symptoms occur in conjunction with bulimia and must be assessed to determine if an accompanying anxiety disorder exists.

Depression. Depression commonly accompanies bulimia. There appears to be a strong relationship between affective disorders and bulimia. Specific attention is devoted later in this chapter to the role of depression in bulimia.

Sexual dysfunction. Sexual dysfunction is not uncommon among individuals with bulimia, which is often related to a history of sexual abuse. Sexual addiction may also occur in conjunction with the eating disorder.

Use of binge/purge behavior to deal with other stresses. As bulimia becomes entrenched, the victim increasingly turns to bulimic behavior as a stress reduction measure. While the original source of the stress is not affected (i.e., the actual problem is not solved), tension is temporarily reduced. This reinforcement is immediate and powerful, contributing to a further exacerbation of symptoms.

Irritability. Irritability is a symptom common to both the depression and anxiety disorder that frequently accompany bulimia. Irritability may also be related to intrusions of barriers to bulimic activity. Physiologic changes are also implicated in the development of irritability.

Lability of mood. Mood swings may be related to physiologic factors (e.g., an "insulin dump" resulting from binging), reactions to external circumstance (e.g., all-or-none thinking), a co-existing personality disorder that is extremely common within the eating disorder population, or another co-existing mental disorder.

Impaired concentration. Loss of concentration can be another symptom of depression or an anxiety disorder accompanying bulimia. Physiologic changes resulting from bulimic behavior can also affect concentration as does the preoccupation with food, dieting, and body image.

Dishonesty and guilt. The dishonesty of keeping bulimic habits hidden can cause guilt in the affected person.

Causes

The causes of bulimia nervosa remain unclear. Dieting and weight loss appear to be the most apparent precursors to bulimia (Pyle, Mitchell, & Eckert, 1981). However, there is consensus within the professional community that eating disorders are multidetermined problems with biological, social, psychological, and cultural roots. As Mitchell and Eckert (1987) observe, it is interesting to note that eating disorders are the only common form of psychopathology for which culture has been shown to be a primary determining variable.

TREATMENT OUTCOME STUDIES AND RATIONALE FOR GROUP TREATMENT

The most successful bulimia treatment programs utilize a combination of treatment strategies. Keeping in mind that treatment outcome studies are plagued with methodological problems (e.g., uncontrolled trials, use of self-report measures, lack of long-term follow-up, small numbers of subjects) the most promising individual treatments have incorporated one or more of the following: (1) cognitive restructuring (Fairburn, 1981); (2) eating habit control (Fairburn, 1981); and (3) exposure to binge foods with response prevention (Rosen & Leitenberg, 1982). These techniques are employed *in conjuction* with process-oriented psychotherapy, behavioral contracting, self-monitoring, education, and frequently medication (most notably, antidepressant medication).*

Group therapy is quickly becoming a highly popular mode of treatment for bulimia. The reasons for this are: (1) a need for economic treatment procedures; (2) the chemical dependency and overeating treatment models that indicate that a group approach may be appropriate for treatment of bulimia; (3) the effectiveness of individual therapy techniques for bulimia such as Fairburn's cognitive behavioral approach in the context of group work (Schneider & Agras, 1985); (4) the effectiveness of cognitive group therapy for patients with depression (Hollon & Shaw 1979) that commonly afflicts individuals with bulimia; and (5) the success of groups as a *primary* mode of treatment for bulimia (Mitchell & Eckert, 1987). Group therapy has been shown to be particularly effective when combined with individual therapy (Lacey, 1983) and a structured eating program (Mitchell & Eckert, 1987).

There is general agreement that group intervention provides particular advantages for the bulimic client. The advantages usually cited are a decreasing isolation and secrecy, sharing of information, providing role models, instilling hope, reality testing for irrational beliefs and self-perceptions, increasing self-worth through group cohesion, promoting healthy attitudes, and an interpersonal context through which the links between emotions, behavior, and relationships become clear. Additionally, feedback in the group setting is believed to be particularly effective because it comes from others who are similarly afflicted. While these advantages remain untested, at this point they are common and reasonable working assumptions.

Group treatment methods for bulimia nervosa typically emphasize a combination of psychodynamic, cognitive-behavioral, behavioral, and feminist approaches. A dual focus on

---

*Antidepressant medications have been shown to be effective for some clients in eliminating binge/purge behavior (Hughes, Wells, Cunningham, & Ilstrup, 1986; Pope, Gladis, & Glassman, 1984). Although predictors for a positive response to medication have not yet been identified, it is reasonable to consider antidepressants, including monoamine oxidase inhibitors, in treatment planning for bulimia (Stewart et al.,1984; Walsh et al, 1982).

behavioral symptoms as well as feelings is maintained. Homework assignments, journal-writing, short-term, incremental goal-setting, self-recording of behavior, cognitive restructuring, affective sharing, and, in some cases, an emphasis on mutual support among group members between therapy sessions can be used. Training in assertiveness and relaxation skills is commonly incorporated, although it is reported by group members to be less valuable than other program elements in at least one study (Johnson, Connors, & Stuckey, 1983). Closed groups are more advisable due to a lower dropout rate than are open groups (Roy-Byrne, Lee-Benner, & Yager, 1984). Furthermore, it is recommended that group therapy continue after symptom reduction in order to foster a more complete integration of healthy behaviors (Stevens & Salisbury, 1984).

If bulimic individuals must wait before treatment can begin, it is vital that they be provided with some type of immediate support. The purpose of this is to prevent a loss of motivation, a critical element in the recovery process. While patients are waiting for treatment, they can be asked to list advantages and disadvantages of bulimia, an exercise that provides an additional boost to motivation; to record bulimic behavior (self-monitoring); and to attend an introductory or preparatory group. Dietary information can be provided as well as education regarding the nature of the disorder and the recovery process.

As noted above, the effectiveness of group therapy compared with other treatment modalities remains to be tested (Pyle & Mitchell, 1985). There are few, if any, adequate studies comparing the effectiveness of group therapy with individual therapy, and the assessment of group treatment is further complicated by the frequent use of concurrent treatment modalities. It must also be kept in mind that group treatment is not appropriate for all bulimics (Connors, Johnson, & Stuckey, 1984). We have yet to identify the most appropriate clients, optimal timing for a group experience, treatment format, number and gender of therapists, and other variables. The bulk of clinical evidence available at this point, however, supports a major role for group therapy in the treatment for bulimia.

Clearly, therapists working in the area of eating disorders need to be familiar with various theoretical orientations and interventions. Supervised experience and considerable clinical exposure to bulimia nervosa are essential for a therapist to be effective.

GROUP THERAPY

There are generally three types of groups employed with bulimic clients: the self-help group, the structured education group, and the therapy group. This chapter addresses primarily the third type of group; however, a brief overview of the other two types appears at the end of the chapter.

Therapy groups are often "organized for the purpose of correcting a specific emotional or behavioral disorder that impedes a person's function. In group therapy attention is given to unconscious factors and one's past as well as personality change" (Corey & Corey, 1987, p. 10). These objectives fit well with the recovery needs of the bulimic client. Our approach is a combination of cognitive, behavioral, and insight-oriented therapy.

The goals of group therapy for bulimia include (1) uncovering the underlying thoughts and feelings that trigger the starving, binging, and purging behaviors (e.g., identifying anger as a trigger for the binging and learning how to express anger in ways other than starving, binging, or purging); (2) identifying the nonfunctional behavior patterns that the client has developed in the course of the bulimia; (e.g., identifying behavior patterns and particular danger times such as late-night binging even in the absence of negative feelings); (3)

developing alternative coping behaviors; (4) instituting cognitive restructuring regarding maladaptive attitudes; and (5) preventing relapse.

We view group therapy as only part of the recovery work for bulimic clients. In addition to group therapy, individual counseling with a mental health professional who understands the eating disorder recovery process and is supportive of the group therapy experience is important. It is also essential to have medical back-up from a physician who is aware of the individual's eating disorder and supplies medical evaluation and consultation when necessary. This team approach is especially essential when the client is at a particularly difficult point in recovery or is on medication for depression. Additionally, the team approach reduces the chances of "splitting," that is, pitting one professional against another, a common hazard when more than one professional is involved with the eating disorder client. We require the client to sign release of information forms for the physician and any mental health or dietary professional with whom the client is also working. The release form should not be necessary if the professionals are all part of the same agency. Communication between the professionals can be accomplished through regularly scheduled meetings (which are very time-consuming and done only during crises times or very serious cases) or by telephone if there is an issue to discuss. The case manager or primary therapist needs to be clearly identified.

Philosophy of Group

Our philosophy regarding group therapy for bulimic clients has four main components. First, we believe that co-leadership is essential to effective management of the group process. Several factors support this thinking. First, group work in the area of eating disorders is unusually stressful, and the support, feedback, and reinforcement from another professional is vital for self-care. Co-leaders should meet weekly outside of the group to discuss concerns and progress of individual members, general group issues, and co-leader issues. We believe this weekly meeting is necessary to enable the leaders to work effectively together in group. Since no two people are alike, co-leaders also provide different reactions, backgrounds, and expertise for the group. Another benefit to co-leadership is the ability of the group to continue if one leader must miss a group meeting.

Our bias is that at least one of the co-leaders be female because healthy female modeling can have a powerful influence in recovery work. When there is a male co-leader in an all-female group, the female members tend to be much more hesitant to talk about issues of sexuality, a topic of great importance in the recovery work for bulimia. Furthermore, the group processing changes with the presence of a male. The male leader is viewed as "knowing all the answers" by virtue of being male. A female member often gives up her personal power to the male co-leader by openly agreeing with whatever he says and minimizing or completely negating any differing view she may have. Members in our groups have expressed the importance of the male co-leader liking, respecting, and accepting them. They often will mirror whatever reactions they think the male co-leader is looking for and thus slow down their own recovery work. However, using a male co-leader can enable female members to learn to relate more effectively to males in general. Therefore, if a male co-leader is present, we recommend that male co-leaders be knowledgeable and comfortable with sexuality issues and have an understanding of how and why females give up their personal power to males. This understanding needs to be based on the knowledge of the socialization of men and women.

Due to cost and time issues, therapists frequently are unable to have a co-leader. We have found it helpful to recruit as co-leaders graduate students in counseling, psychology, or social work programs as part of practicum or internship experiences. Not only are we provided with a co-leader, but we are training future professionals to work in the eating disorder area.

The second component in our philosophy, as mentioned earlier, is our preference that group therapy be combined with individual therapy, structured eating work, and medical back-up. Family or marital therapy may also be components of the recovery program. We require continued work with an individual therapist throughout group membership. The structured eating work can be undertaken with a dietition in an educational eating class or with an organization such as Overeaters Anonymous. When these services are not available, they may be included as part of the individual therapy work. Medical back-up is also required for the duration of the group experience.

Third, the leaders need to be flexible to meet the varied needs of each group member. For example, if several members are on antidepressant medication, there may be a major focus on how to cope with depression. If there are several members who are adult children of alcoholics (ACOAs), group work at times focuses on the dynamics of the alcoholic family and its influence on the group member. Additionally, some issues may need to be dealt with by using behavioral strategies, while others require insight therapy.

One of the primary reasons group therapy is effective for bulimics is because their participation in sharing similar issues and experiences is so powerful. When members realize that they are not the only ones with bulimia, they come to a point of greater self-acceptance, a potent factor for recovery work. Along with this, the group experience reinforces the members' identity development and the establishment of healthy boundaries.

The fourth component of our philosophy is a belief that group therapy is a long-term process with bulimic clients. Members are generally in group from 1 to 2 years for the necessary cognitive restructuring and identity work to be effective.

Screening

Screening of potential group members is essential. We meet individually with each potential member for the following reasons:

1. Getting acquainted with the client in this way provides at least two familiar faces for the client at the first group meeting. This tends to lessen the anxiety the new group member typically experiences.
2. The screening allows the co-leaders a chance to confirm a diagnosis. Occasionally the prospective group member does not have bulimia and needs to be appropriately referred or reassured.
3. Ground rules and general orientation issues of the group can be discussed to help create an effective understanding of the group, especially the importance of confidentiality.
4. The co-leaders can answer questions and allay fears of the group experience expressed by the potential member.
5. The co-leaders can evaluate the person's expectations of group therapy, whether these expectations are realistic and compatible with the goals of the group. If, for example, the client believes the "group will cure me," her disappointment will be great and she will probably leave the group because "it didn't work." Group members need to understand that they are expected to actively participate in a meaningful fashion.

6. The co-leaders can determine if the person is motivated and willing to make a commitment to attend group. Comments like "I can come every other time" or "whenever I don't have to work," or "my counselor told me to come" are warning signs regarding the client's commitment to actively engage in therapeutic work. In such instances the commitment issues are discussed further. If the person being interviewed does not think she will be able to commit to the group experience, other therapy options can be explored. Also the option of reinterviewing for the group in the future can be offered.

7. The co-leaders can screen out inappropriate individuals such as those who are too psychologically ill to profit from a group experience (e.g., exhibiting active psychosis, severe major depression, or extreme character pathology), excessively shy, excessively hostile, exhibiting borderline personality disorder characteristics that are extremely disruptive in a group, or those with an inability to maintain minimal weight.

Structure

The following group structure for clients with bulimia was developed for the university setting. However, this structure can be easily adapted to other settings.

The meetings are held weekly for 2 hours. The size of the group is typically between six and eight members to ensure enough time for each member to work on her problems. We keep a very short waiting list and refer other interested individuals to alternative groups in the community if we cannot accommodate them. Since we view group therapy as long term, our group is ongoing. However, four times a year, corresponding with the college quarter system, members are given the opportunity either to recommit to the group or leave. If there are vacancies, we open the group for new members. We have found the recommitment process in long-term group work to be advantageous. Without periodic recommitment the members may become complacent and group work can become stale.

If there are new members the first group meeting of each quarter, it is structured in the following manner. First, there are introductions consisting of first names and anything else the person wants to add about herself. Next, the ground rules are reviewed and additions or changes are discussed. The ground rules are presented by the members and not the leaders since these are the members' rules. Then, each member shares what she is presently working on in group and her goal(s) for the coming quarter in group. The new member(s) would also share goals.

After the first group meeting, the format of each session is as follows. First, any announcements are made. Then the clients who want time to work are identified. This is helpful in two ways: (1) the members know how many group members will be working and how much time to allow and (2) this procedure requires thought prior to the group meeting regarding "Do I want to work today?" It also fosters the development of assertiveness, a major problem of bulimics, by requiring them to ask for time to work on their own problems. This process does not preclude problems that arise spontaneously and are discussed by the group.

New members often question what the term "work" means in the group and what kinds of issues are appropriate to bring into group. We let them know that anything that has to do with their recovery is appropriate. Some examples of "work" are: (1) checking in ("I'm doing okay" and "I had a good week"); (2) an update ("Remember last week when I decided to talk to my mother? Well, I did and . . ."); (3) a problem that the member wants to work on in group such as "I have decided to go home for Thanksgiving vacation and I would like to talk about my fears";

and (4) good news! We stress the importance of sharing something positive that has happened with the group. Bulimic clients have a tendency to look at the negative areas of their recovery and often negate their positive work. This tendency is part of a common perfectionistic pattern characteristic of bulimics ("all or nothing" thinking). Each member that requests time to work is provided this time.

The next exercise is what we call "separating away." This exercise, which is done at the end of each group session, was initiated years ago when a need for separateness became apparent. For example, one of the members at that time was suicidal and shared her feelings about her suicidal thoughts with the group. By the end of group session, two other members admitted to having suicidal thoughts. We interpreted the situation as weak identity boundaries because members would easily take on another's feelings and experiences as their own. Thus the "separating away" exercise was created as a means of (1) separating one's own identity from that of the other members in the group and (2) separating one's own feelings from other members' feelings. In our groups we talk often about identity development, identity issues, and emotional boundaries in the group, and we ask members to visualize or conceptualize their own unique identity and the boundaries necessary to maintain this identity in some way.

"Separating away" is led by one of the co-leaders. The members are asked to get comfortable, close their eyes, and relax. A short, deep muscle relaxation exercise follows. Then, still with eyes closed, the members are asked to separate their own identity and feelings from those of the others and to feel their wholeness as individuals. The co-leader uses imagery and deep breathing to enhance the exercise. The other co-leader participates with the group in "separating away." (We find this exercise useful for the leaders also.) If a member must leave early we ask that she individually "separate away" in a way that will be helpful to her. She might do this by taking a moment to sit, relax, and define her own identity, or as she is walking to her next destination, experience herself in a positive way.

Since the bulimic group member is generally a passive perfectionist who wishes to please the leaders, leadership needs to be nonauthoritative (except when life-threatening). It is very important that the leaders do not become an authoritative parent replacement. It is important to give the members permission to be themselves, which gradually allows them to crystallize their identity. In an effort to depend on an authority figure, they will want the leaders to tell them what to do. It is helpful to ask the question "What do you think?" to help members become accustomed to independent thinking. "You know what is best for you. Go to your wisdom inside yourself."

Group Ground Rules

The basic rules we utilize are discussed in the following sections.

Confidentiality. Members are allowed to inform others that they are in the group and of their progress but are not allowed to identify other members or share content discussed in group.

Attendance. Since sporadic attendance is very disruptive to the group, members are allowed only two absences per 10-week quarter. If someone is going to miss a session, she is asked to call another group member to inform the group of her absence. This contact is vital for two reasons. First, if attending members don't have prior notice of an absence they become worried because bulimic clients often skip sessions when they are not doing well. Secondly, regular attendance emphasizes the importance of commitment to the group. If a member does miss more than two meetings and still wishes to belong, the group decides about the retention of the absent member. Usually the member is allowed to remain if there is a good reason given for the absences or if a pledge of greater commitment is expressed.

Group focus on the individual.   When a member asks for time to work and her time arrives, the focus of the group shifts to her. The group can react, question, respond, and share during this time but in such a way that the focus remains on the member who is working. This approach avoids "scattering," which occurs when the focus jumps from one person to another and the individual's work is left unfinished.

Naming foods.   Members do not name specific foods during group meetings. Some members have found talking about specific foods disturbing, and the discussion may even trigger a binge. Members will instead say "a certain food" or something very general.

Telephoning.   Members have a list of the first names and telephone numbers of all group members, including the co-leaders. Calling each other is highly recommended. The ground rule is specific in that these calls are to be used for individual support but are not to be used to talk about group issues. Any issues pertaining to the group need to be addressed in the group. We have found it difficult to get members to telephone regularly until they have been in group awhile and have begun to bond with each other.

Goodbyes.   Saying goodbye is usually extremely difficult for clients with bulimia. At the termination of group therapy, avoidance of saying goodbye often occurs unless structured closure is a ground rule. When a member decides to leave the group, either at the quarter break or prematurely during the quarter, she is asked to engage in "closure." Closure involves saying goodbye in a structured manner so that group members get a chance to express what it has meant to each of them to have this person in group. Closure also allows the person leaving to express her feelings about each of the other group members, the group experience, and her future plans. Finally, the closure experience minimizes discomfort for members who see each other following the group experience.

Other Rules.   Occasionally members develop additional group rules to fit a specific situation such as no telephone calls after 11:00 p.m. unless it is a crisis situation.

Stages of the Recovery Process in Group

Since group membership is generally long term (over 1 year), we have observed the stages groups traverse over this period of time. Certainly the passage through these stages is unique to each member, but we have seen general group patterns.

Stage 1: acceptance/inclusion.   The beginning stage of group is the most tenuous because the established members have not bonded with the new member(s). New members generally feel isolated from the rest of the group as they report thoughts such as: "They'll never like me," "I'll never be like them. They are so 'together,'" or "I'm not far enough in my recovery to be an acceptable group member." Their desire to be liked and accepted may be overridden by their feelings of inadequacy. Consequently they may not come to the next meeting. These initial feelings and tendencies are discussed during the first two meetings. An open discussion of these initial feelings lets members know that they are natural reactions and that they tend to change over time. We ask them to commit themselves especially to attending the first four meetings in order to get past this difficult time. We ask other members to relate how scary it was for them when they started and how they coped with this admittedly difficult stage of group membership.

Emphasis also needs to be placed on the uniqueness of each person's experience with bulimia. At times a new member may have difficulties relating to another member's more severe problems. She may feel like she doesn't fit because she doesn't have bulimia "bad enough." For example, she may not abuse laxatives and may think that she needs to start taking laxatives in order to fit in. Discussion of these concerns during screening and during the initial group meetings is vital to her continued commitment to group treatment.

The positive part of this first stage is that new members have an opportunity to see and hear others' experiences with bulimia. New members witness that group therapy is helpful and experience a sense of hope for their recovery. According to one client:

> When I started group I was very ready so I was excited, but at the same time scared to death. I asked myself a million questions like "What will they be like?" "Will they all be weird?" "Will they all be recovered and I'll be way behind?" "Will they like me?" "Will they think I'm fat?" "What if I don't fit in?" "Will they make me talk?" I was having a lot of positive thoughts and was yearning to be close to the group members. I knew I needed to talk to someone and was hoping group would be my lifesaver! And it was. Someone warned me that the group couldn't replace the friendships I needed and wanted but . . . it has taught me how to be a friend and how to reach out so I can develop friendships. I've gotten lots of practice there. For me, the beginning stage of group was scary, exciting and fun. I felt after the first group that I could make it work for me.

Stage 2: regression. The second stage is also generally a difficult time for the new member. During group, the members work on identifying feelings, expressing feelings, and self-understanding. As the new member begins this process she may feel bombarded by feelings that were previously numbed by the bulimia. This is a frightening experience and usually includes depression or feelings of anger and anxiety. Thus, new members experience a time of "feeling worse" than they did before they started group therapy. It is important for group members to be prepared for this and to discuss feeling worse as a natural part of the recovery process. They discover from the group that it will pass and that they can expect to feel better in time. Stage 2 is a time of caution for the co-leaders, since the new member occasionally will begin to have suicidal thoughts or become depressed and need antidepressant medication. It is a time when support from other group members is important both in group and outside of group. Also, communication between the group leader, the individual therapist, and the physician is advised. One member described the experience as follows:

> Part of me expected that group would solve everything. Suddenly I'd have a zillion friends, be assertive, eat perfectly with no binging and have a wonderful relationship with my husband. Boy—did I have a surprise coming. I always worked hard in individual therapy but I thought group was the easy way out. Wrong! It was work.

Along with that shock and the shock of finally talking about things I'd stuffed for so long . . . my transition stage started about the third week of group. I was very depressed, my eating was *terrible* and I cried all the time. And they told me group was good for me?!! I thought someone lied. It would have been real easy to quit at this point but . . . I had an inner feeling that group could work. I remembered well enough how sick I used to be and knew group was the only way to not be back there. It got pretty bad for a while but I knew it wasn't as bad as before. I also trusted my individual therapist a great deal and she told me it could work.

Another thing I really remember from my earlier stage is not wanting to get better. I knew who I was as a bulimic—I knew how that felt. And, the chaos and turmoil of being a bulimic was familiar. Who would I be if I got better? That scared me more than anything. Would I run out of things to work on and be real bored with life? The bulimia made my life exciting—now I realize it's all negative excitement and the positive stuff is 100 times better.

Sometimes I'd almost have a terrible week on purpose so I could go to group and talk about how bad it was. I was competing with everyone else to see who could have the worst things happen during the week. If my struggles weren't as dramatic, then they weren't worth talking about.

I don't know if this is normal for all bulimics or if the "fear of getting better" came from my Adult Children of Alcoholic issues.

Stage 3: working.   This stage is the one the member is engaged in for most of her group experience. It is a time when she has begun to feel better about herself, is able to experience progress toward recovery, and is feeling more and more an integral part of the therapy group. This may well be the first time she has experienced real emotional closeness and support from other women. The co-leader responsibilities here are to maintain motivation and an optimum level of work in the group. For example, since membership usually is long term, a member or the whole group can lapse into nonworking conversations. When this occurs, we discuss what is happening in the group and how members can get back to the working level needed. One member's description of this stage was as follows:

That's where I am now! I started working in group even during the time when I was just starting to feel really a part of the group but . . . my real turning point came the first time I called a group member. And, it hasn't even been a year ago! It seems like a lot longer than that.

Working has been very good for me. Sometimes I feel like I'm just spinning my wheels and then suddenly I jump ahead a mile. I guess all the time I'm spinning my wheels I'm building up skills to take the jump. And, I have lots of ups and downs. There are more of them than I'd like but the down times are getting shorter and not as bad as they used to be. I sometimes need someone to remind me of that. When I can see the progress it feels good.

The two major things I've worked on throughout are my eating and relationships.

The first time I called a group member and asked for help really started me working on relationships. That's when I really felt bonded to the group and felt like they cared about me more than 2 hours a week. And . . . I stopped competing with them and being jealous when they talked to each other during the week and not to me.

Group is great for learning how to have relationships. I practiced being a friend there—in a safe place. Then it's not so hard in the real world. The one thing that's still very hard is talking about my feelings outside of group. Sometimes I think it's because I have group that's such a safe place to share so I don't need to share outside. And, if that's true it's a negative thing about group. But . . . I don't really think that's true. I'm still practicing and when I'm ready—look out world . . . my feelings will come pouring out. Also . . . I'm still learning to trust myself. I can't let my feelings pour out to anyone and everyone. I have to learn how to choose the people it's okay to do that with. I don't really trust my inner voice yet!

I've grown tremendously since I started group. I like myself more of the time, my eating has improved, I feel more comfortable around people at school, I'm starting to develop some friendships again, I can relax. And my relationship with my husband is about 200% better.

I have a long way to go before I'm where I want to be and I hope I keep upping my expectations so I never get there. I always want to have something else to reach for. I don't want to get boring!

I know I'd never be where I am now without group. It has been my lifesaver.

Stage 4: questioning.   After a member has been in the group for at least a year, a "questioning stage" typically emerges. She will begin to look at her recovery, where she presently is in her therapy, and what work remains to be done. During group, she will frequently verbalize thoughts such as, "I wonder if it's time to leave group?" She may wrestle with the fears of leaving the safety of the group. The group usually tries to reinforce its faith in her individual wisdom to choose her own life course. If group members believe the leaving is premature they will typically verbalize this. Once the member has made the decision to leave the group, the fifth stage begins. As one member explained:

Members were leaving group after successfully working on their recovery in group. I started questioning should I leave now? Is it time for me? I felt scared and confused because I really wanted to stay and I had work I wanted to continue with, namely male relationships, and my continued work with my relationship with my parents. My eating had been going well. I haven't binged for 5½ months. What should I do? I asked the group for feedback. One member's response really hit home. She said "Don't leave because someone else is leaving. Leave when it's time for you to go." She's right. I'll continue the next 10 weeks and see how I feel then.

Stage 5: termination.   Termination is the fifth stage and is generally addressed the last several weeks before the end of the 10-week quarter. Termination ends with the closure process discussed earlier. Termination is an emotional time for all members, involving (1) current feelings such as caring, appreciation, and admiration and (2) the anticipation of feelings such as loneliness and the fear of the void created after the group experience is over.

After termination we recommend that group members develop an aftercare plan (Pyle, Halvorson, & Goff, 1986). Defining a support system is an essential component of such a plan. Some recommended activities include joining a women's support group, working as a volunteer in a bulimia therapy program, joining Bulimics Anonymous or Overeaters Anonymous, and continuing individual counseling for issues such as intimacy, assertiveness, or sexuality.

Another component of the aftercare plan is an individually generated list of coping techniques for stressful situations. A final component of the aftercare plan is that of relapse prevention. A specific, individualized, written, and memorized plan is suggested that would include high-risk situations and ways to cope with these situations as well as important reminders that have been helpful in past relapse situations.

The following is a note received by one group from a former group member:

> This note comes to you all as Mother's Day approaches. Each year I think of group at this time. Mother's Day is an extra special day for me because it marks the anniversary date of my abstinence from binging, and this year is my 6th anniversary. I am so grateful for the freedom I have found.

Relapse

Relapse is a common and frustrating pattern in the treatment process and one for which both the counselor and client need to prepare. When an individual has abstained, for example, from binging and purging for a period of time, it can be extremely frustrating and demoralizing to experience a relapse into old behaviors. When this happens, the tendency for the client is to slip into all-or-none thinking with thoughts such as, "I'm a failure" or "I'll never be able to do this so why try?" When this happens, it becomes especially important to keep the client engaged in the group.

We have found the work of Marlatt and George (1984) helpful in putting relapse behaviors into a useful perspective. They view relapse as a *part* of the recovery process and as a means of practicing or developing new coping skills. They identify two factors that play an important role in precipitating a relapse. One factor in relapse is the interplay between negative emotional states and behaviors that the client is attempting to eliminate. In the past a negative emotional state such as anger may have triggered a binge. If alternative coping skills have not been learned (such as expressing anger to an appropriate person), relapse is likely to occur. The second precipitating factor identified by Marlatt and George is overstepping the skill level. As clients work to develop new coping skills, they will likely encounter situations that they are not yet able to handle successfully. For instance, a client with bulimia may be doing well in terms of eating enough each day and not focusing on weight loss. But if a friend comes up and says "Hey, it looks like you're putting on a few pounds," the client is likely to be bombarded with bulimic thoughts. If she has not yet sufficiently developed the ability to counter these thoughts, a relapse is likely to occur.

Once relapse occurs, the individual develops extremely negative thoughts about herself. In this stage the client does not give herself any credit for the progress that she *has* made, but rather focuses on the relapse as proof of her unworthiness and her inability to recover. From here the client begins to play down the importance of recovery. She contends that the behavior is not that destructive and recovery is not important or probable. If we can teach clients to view relapse constructively, it is possible to turn it into helpful rather than a detrimental step in the recovery process. Relapse must be reinterpreted as part of positive skill development, and preferably this should be done early in treatment to prepare the client. An apt analogy of Marlatt and George's (1984) is learning to ride a bike—it requires a few falls in order to learn how to maintain balance. Likewise, relapse can be an opportunity to learn more about what leads one into difficulty and what kinds of skill-building are necessary for eventual recovery.

RELATED PROBLEMS

There are three other significant problems that frequently accompany an eating disorder: depression, history of sexual abuse, and other impulse control disorders. We include these here because they are issues that are regularly dealt with in the context of group therapy for bulimia.

Depression

There are indications that eating disorders, particularly bulimia, may be part of a depressive syndrome (Pope & Hudson, 1984); however, further investigation is necessary to clarify the association between bulimia and affective disorders. The available research identifies a high incidence of depression, eating disorders, chemical dependency, and obesity in the family histories of victims of eating disorders (Anderson, 1985; Hudson et al., 1983a, 1983b; Pyle, Mitchell, & Eckert, 1981). Because of this strong link with depression and the positive results of treatment with antidepressants even in those who do not evidence depressive symptomalogy, medication is assuming greater importance in the treatment of eating disorders (Agras, Dorian, Kirkley, Arrow, & Bachman, 1987; Pope & Hudson, 1984; Walsh, Stuart, Roose, Gladis, & Glassman, 1984).

Practitioners should also consider the possibility that the bulimic behavior may be causing the depression since (1) inadequate nutrition can result in depression and (2) guilt and depression are common after effects of binging and purging. As with any depression, one must always be alert to suicidal ideation and suicidal attempts.

Our practice is to evaluate a client for depression and, if appropriate, to refer the client to a psychiatrist or physician for a trial run of antidepressant medication. The rationale for this is not to treat the eating disorder per se, but rather to respond directly to the depression. If an individual is indeed suffering from an endogenous depression, there is a good chance he or she will respond positively to the medication. However, the choice of medication should be carefully considered because an increase in appetite is one of the side effects of certain antidepressants and stimulating of the appetite should be avoided in the treatment of bulimia. We find that when the depression is alleviated individuals naturally have more energy and inner resources at their disposal for dealing effectively with the eating problem. It should be again noted that there is some evidence that antidepressants can be effective in counteracting bulimia even in those individuals who do not show symptoms of depression (Pope & Hudson, 1984; Walsh, Stuart, Roose, Gladis, & Glassman, 1984).

History of Sexual Abuse

When bulimia victims have been in group for a while and have developed feelings of trust, they may start to share a history of sexual abuse. When this happens, the support of the group is critical. Acknowledging and dealing with sexual abuse issues is exceptionally difficult and painful work. When the individual is prepared to discuss the abuse, we recommend specialized therapy in a sexual abuse treatment program. In fact, we encourage clients to initiate individual therapy for sexual abuse in conjunction with group therapy for bulimia. The group member can continue the eating disorder work and begin the sexual abuse therapy. Generally we have found that when a bulimic client has been sexually abused, little progress is attained with the eating disorder until the abuse work is begun. In our experience some of the individuals with eating disorders who are labeled as chronic are in fact victims of sexual abuse who have not yet begun therapy in this area.

Impulse Control Disorder

Substance abuse is one of the impulse control problems related to eating disorders. Not only is it present in many family histories, but also in approximately half of the cases substance abuse actively accompanies bulimia (Pyle, Mitchell, & Eckert, 1981). Unfortunately, in most chemical dependency treatment programs, the bulimia is not addressed—or individuals are told that once their chemical use is under control, the bulimia will disappear, which is seldom the case. It may well be that the bulimia is the *primary* addiction, with chemicals being used as a substitute for eating or as a means to assuage the guilt and depression associated with the binge/purge behaviors. In any case, both the chemical dependency and eating disorder must be directly addressed in treatment lest the individual retreat further into one or the other.

Kleptomania is another impulsive behavior that frequently accompanies binge behavior whether it is in the context of anorexia or bulimia (Pyle, Mitchell, & Eckhert, 1981). Since victims of these disorders are by and large highly principled people, therapists often do not check out the possibility that kleptomania may be present. The reasons for stealing are varied. For some it is food-oriented; that is, food items are stolen or money is stolen to buy food. But often the stealing is unrelated to food and involves taking items that are not needed. The stealing is rarely planned in advance and appears to be impulsive. Kleptomania is an issue therapists need to address during assessment and treatment.

Compulsive shopping and spending is a third impulse control behavior. Group members define this experience as similar to a binge, but it is a binge that involves shopping for clothing, jewelry, and so on instead of food. The spending spree is followed by guilt and leaves the person financially strapped and often more dependent on the family from whom he or she is attempting to disengage.

Promiscuity is a fourth impulse control behavior that is sometimes associated with bulimia. Group members express considerable self-hatred arising from casual sexual activity or alternating sexual activity with several partners. They express concern that they really wanted to "just be held" or that they "really didn't like the person but did not want to hurt his feelings." For many, learning assertiveness skills, being more in touch with their own feelings, and learning how to develop fulfilling relationships help reduce promiscuous behavior.

The impulse control issues are often difficult to address in group because the members feel these behaviors are too shameful and embarrassing to discuss in group. It can be helpful if the leaders occasionally address these issues and allow a general discussion in group, emphasizing that these are issues commonly encountered by individuals with bulimia.

In the next section other types of groups for clients with bulimia are discussed.

Structured Education Groups

Education groups are time-limited groups usually between 8 and 14 weeks in length. The primary goal is to impart information about bulimia and to instruct the members in ways to stop the binge/purge pattern. These groups are closed and usually have one teacher/leader. We have found this type of group extremely beneficial for clients with bulimia. The structured learning environment and the support from the members and leader to stop the binge/

purge pattern can be a helpful adjunct to individual and group therapy. Usually the group is behaviorally oriented and includes recording food consumed and any form of bulimic behavior.

Self-Help Groups

Self-help groups such as Overeaters Anonymous and Bulimics Anonymous are structured after Alcoholics Anonymous. There are no professional leaders; members are the leaders and organizers of the meetings. These and other self-help groups are generally open to anyone with an eating disorder and can provide a supportive environment for working on recovery. Some individuals with bulimia find these group meetings to be an integral part of their recovery; others choose not to attend because the groups are open, membership can vary from week to week, and the person may not reach a point of feeling safe enough to share in the group.

CONCLUSION

Group therapy is clearly a viable and perhaps preferential mode of treatment for bulimia nervosa. The indirect advantages of group treatment combined with its cost-effectiveness have made group therapy highly popular. However, research on the treatment of bulimia is still in its infancy. Further studies are needed to identify subtypes and etiologic factors and to determine optimal treatment approaches. As these studies give us more information, continued refinement and improvement needs to occur in group therapy for bulimia nervosa.

APPENDIX: COMPONENTS OF A TREATMENT PLAN FOR BULIMIA

We have included this appendix as an overview of the treatment for bulimia nervosa. These components encompass the entire treatment process for bulimia, of which group therapy is one component.

1. Provide physical assessment and treatment of medical symptoms if present (e.g., gastrointestinal problems, low potassium).
2. Prescribe antidepressant medication (if appropriate).
3. Provide education regarding eating disorders, nutrition, and process of recovery.
4. Establish a reasonable weight range and activity level.
5. Institute monitoring: recording food intake and purges (can include feelings, thoughts, time, etc.).
6. Provide treatment for other existing emotional problems including chemical dependency.
7. Implement eating habit control measures such as:
   a. Eat regularly (3–5 times/day).
   b. Delay vomiting—substitute other behaviors.
   c. Increase the variety of foods consumed gradually, including "forbidden" foods (foods that trigger binging).

d. Eat slowly, at a table, doing nothing else and without rituals.

e. Interject change into vomiting pattern such as a delay or cognitive rehearsal focusing on negative consequences.

f. Utilize relaxation techniques as a stress reduction measure.

g. Practice having meals in a safe (nonbinge/purge) setting, possibly including forbidden food (e.g., with the therapist, another group member, or supportive friend).

h. Utilize the service of dietitian.

i. No dieting. After bulimic behavior is under control, the client may be given help in choosing a "healthy" reduction diet if appropriate.

j. Structure the environment through time management, food availability, and other kinds of planning.

k. Think about what you *really* want and then exert control and choice.

l. Give thought to the process of eating and be discriminating regarding choice of food. Evaluate the kind of taste and texture desired (e.g., sweet or salty, crunchy or spongy). Imagine beforehand how it will feel to eat the food, how it tastes, and how you will feel afterward.

m. Make binges a *decision* if they happen—write out the choice.

n. Develop meal plans to reduce impulsive decisions. These plans may need to include place and companions.

8. Utilization of cognitive-behavioral principles to deal with distorted thinking.

9. Stimulus identification and response control measures, including identification of emotions and possible alternatives to binge eating.

10. Development of other coping skills such as appropriate expression of feelings, initiation of social contacts, journal-writing, relaxation techniques, assertion, and problem-solving.

11. Examination of societal influences on bulimia. Identify ways in which the client has given power and control to society and the fashion industry to determine her worth as a person and as a female.

12. Attend to maintaining motivation.

13. Initiate relapse work.

14. Expect long-term therapy, usually a minimum of 1 year. It is vital not to terminate prematurely. Group therapy has particular advantages and is most often utilized.

15. Include self-help/support groups as adjunct to individual and group therapy.

REFERENCES

Agras, W. S., Dorian, B., Kirkley, B. G., Arnow, B., & Bachman, J. (1987). Imipramine and the treatment of bulimia: A double-blind controlled study. *International Journal of Eating Orders, 6*, 29–38.

American Psychiatric Association. (1987). *Diagnostic and statistical manual of mental disorders* (3rd ed., revised). Washington DC: American Psychiatric Association.

Anderson, A. E. (1985). *Practical comprehensive treatment of anorexia and bulimia*. Baltimore, MD: John Hopkins Press.

Connors, M., Johnson, C., & Stuckey, M. (1984). Treatment of bulimia with brief psychoeducational group therapy. *American Journal of Psychiatry, 141*, 1512–1516.

Corey, M. S., & Corey, G. (1987). *Group process and practice* (4th ed.). Monterey, CA: Brooks/Cole.

Fairburn, C. (1981). A cognitive behavioral approach to the treatment of bulimia. *Psychological Medicine, 11*, 707–711.

Hollon, S. D., & Shaw, B. F. (1979). Group cognitive therapy for depressed patients. In A. T. Beck, A. J. Rush, B. F. Shaw, & G. Emery et al. (Eds.), *Cognitive therapy for depression: A treatment manual* (pp. 328–353). New York, NY: Guilford.

Hudson, J. I., Pope, H. G., Jr., Jonas, J. M., & Yurgelun-Todd, D. (1983a). Family history study of anorexia nervosa and bulimia. *British Journal of Psychiatry, 142*, 133–138.

Hudson, J. I., Pope, H. G., Jr., Jonas, J. M., & Yurgelun-Todd, D. (1983b). Phenomenologic relationship of eating disorders to major affective disorder. *Psychiatry Research, 9*, 345–354.

Hughes, P. L., Wells, L. A., Cunningham, C. J., & Ilstrup, D. M. (1986). Treating bulimia with desipramine. *Archives of General Psychiatry, 43*, 182–186.

Johnson, C., Connors, M., & Stuckey, M. (1983). Short-term group treatment of bulimia: A preliminary report. *International Journal of Eating Disorders, 2*, 199–208.

Lacey, J. H. (1983). Bulimia nervosa, binge-eating and psychogenic vomiting: A controlled treatment study and long-term outcome. *British Medical Journal, 286*, 1609–1613.

Marlatt, A. G., & George, W. H. (1984). Relapse prevention: Introduction and overview of model. *British Journal of Addiction, 79*, 261–273.

Mitchell, J. E., & Eckert, E. D. (1987). Scope and significance of eating disorders. *Journal of Consulting and Clinical Psychology, 55*(5), 628–634.

Neuman, P. A., & Halvorson, P. A. (1983). *Anorexia nervosa and bulimia: A handbook for counselors and therapists*. New York: Van Nostrand Reinhold.

Polivey, J., & Herman, C. P. (1987). Diagnosis and treatment of normal eating. *Journal of Consulting and Clinical Psychology, 55*(5), 635–644.

Pope, H. G., Jr. & Hudson, J. I. (1984). *New hope for binge eaters*. New York: Harper & Row.

Pope, H. G., Jr., Hudson, J. I., Jonas, J. M., & Yorgelun-Todd, D. (1983). Bulimia treated with Imiprimine: A placebo-controlled, double-blind study. *American Journal of Psychiatry, 140*, 554–558.

Pyle, R. L., Halvorson, P. A., & Goff, G. M. (1986). The successful maintenance of treatment gains for bulimic clients. *Journal of Counseling and Development, 64*, 445–448.

Pyle, R. L., Halvorson, P., Neuman, P., & Mitchell, J. (1986). The increasing prevalence of bulimia in freshman college students. *International Journal of Eating Disorders, 5*(4), 631–647.

Pyle, R. L., Mitchell, J. E. (1985). Psychotherapy of bulimia: The role of groups in psychotherapy of bulimia. In W. H. Kaye, & H. E. Gwirtsman (Eds.), *The treatment of normal weight bulimia* (pp. 78–100). Washington, DC: American Psychiatric Press.

Pyle, R. L., Mitchell, J. E., & Eckert, E. D. (1981). Bulimia: A report of 34 cases. *Journal of Clinical Psychiatry, 42*, 60–64.

Pyle, R. L., Mitchell, J. E., Eckert, E. D., Halvorson, P. A., Neuman, P. A., & Goff, G. M. (1983). The incidence of bulimia in freshman college students. *International Journal of Eating Disorders, 2*, 75–85.

Rosen, J. C., & Leitenburg, H. (1982). Bulimia nervosa: Treatment with exposure and response prevention. *Behavior Therapy, 13*, 117–124.

Roy-Byrne, R., Lee-Benner, K., & Yager, J. (1984). Group therapy for bulimia: A year's experience. *International Journal of Eating Disorders, 3*, 97–116.

Schneider, J. A., & Agras, W. S. (1985). A cognitive behavioral group treatment of bulimia. *British Journal of Psychiatry, 146*, 66–69.

Stevens, E. V., & Salisbury, J. D. (1984). Group therapy for bulimic adults. *American Journal of Orthopsychiatry, 54*, 156–161.

Stewart, J. W., Walsh, B. T., Wright, L., Roose, S. P., & Glassman, A. H. (1984). An open trial of MAOI's in bulimia. *Journal of Clinical Psychiatry, 45*, 217–219.

Walsh, B. T., Stuart, J. W., Roose, S. P., Gladis, M., & Glassman, A. H. (1984). Treatment of bulimia with phenelzine: A double-blind, placebo-controlled study. *Archives of General Psychiatry, 41*, 1105–1109.

Walsh, B. T., Stewart, J. W., Wright, L., Harrison, W., Roose, S. P., & Glassman, A. H. (1982). Treatment of bulimia with monoamine oxidase inhibitors. *American Journal of Psychiatry, 139,* 1629–1630.

15
Group Cognitive and Behavioral Treatment of Agoraphobia

This chapter is concerned with group treatment of agoraphobia—in particular, with group cognitive and behavioral treatment of the disorder. During the past 10 years, there has been a strong interest in behavioral group treatment for agoraphobia, as witnessed by a wealth of clinical reports detailing the merit of a variety of behavioral treatments administered in a group format. Nonetheless, little has been written that might guide the practicing clinician in applying these procedures, in terms of selection of clients, group structure, typical concerns and themes, and specific suggestions for helping clients master and generalize cognitive and behavioral skills. This chapter will begin with a brief description of the syndrome, a discussion of the appropriateness of group interventions for agoraphobia, and a review of pertinent clinical outcome research. Next, general recommendations for treatment will be made together with suggestions for applying psychoeducational treatment for agoraphobia in a group setting. Specialized behavioral interventions will be discussed in light of the characteristics of the disorder. Some common group themes and issues in treatment will be discussed, and typical problems and suggestions for resolution will be offered. Finally, ideas for sequencing and combining interventions will be considered.

THE SYNDROME

Agoraphobia is the most common and most distressing phobic disorder encountered in adult clients, comprising 60% of clients seen in a clinic sample by Marks (1969). It occurs at an incidence rate of 6.3 per 1000 (Agras, Sylvester, & Oliveau, 1969), and recent estimates suggest that 5 to 11 million Americans suffer from some form of the disorder (Myers et. al., 1984). According to the *Diagnostic and Statistical Manual of Mental Disorders* (DSM-III) (APA, 1980),*

---

*The revised edition, DSM-III-R (APA, 1987), presently classifies agoraphobia with panic attacks as a species of panic disorder (Panic Disorder with agoraphobia). Under this definition, clients must meet criteria for Panic Disorder and demonstrate fear of being in places or situations from which escape might be difficult or embarrassing or in which help might not be available in the event of a panic attack. In connection with this fear is the associated fear or avoidance of "agoraphobic" situations specified in the text of this chapter. "Agoraphobia without history of Panic Disorder" involves similar fear and avoidance, but lacks history of panic; in this case, patients fear a "limited symptom attack" (developing a single or small number of symptoms, such as falling, dizziness, depersonalization, loss of bowel or bladder control, vomiting, or cardiac distress). As prevalence of the latter is rare in clinical samples, and definitions of agoraphobia with panic attacks and Panic Disorder with agoraphobia are quite similar, the former DSM-III (APA, 1980) definition will be employed for the purpose of this chapter.

agoraphobia is characterized by a marked fear and avoidance of being alone or in public places from which escape might be difficult or help not available in case of sudden incapacitation (APA, 1980). While the DSM-III definition is straightforward, Goldstein (1982) notes that it reflects only the tip of the iceberg. Individuals who suffer from this complaint fear being away from circumstances (home, familiar surroundings, family or trusted companions) that provide psychological security, and they fear and typically avoid situations in which immediate rescue or retreat to safe territory is not possible (Chambless, 1982). Thus, circumstances of *physical delay* (e.g., traffic jams, elevators, limited-access highways), *social constraint* (awaiting a meal in a crowded restaurant, waiting in a supermarket checkout line, riding public transportation, attending a party or church service), or *isolation* (traveling beyond a fixed "safety radius" or remaining alone) constitute threats to perceived safety and risk recurrence of panic attacks (episodes of terror with associated levels of physiologic and psychological arousal). A number of writers (Chambless, 1982; Goldstein & Chambless, 1978; Weekes, 1979) have observed that individuals with agoraphobia seek escape when these attacks occur because sufferers believe these attacks presage death, "insanity," fainting, or loss of control resulting in public humiliation. In addition, they suggest that since these attacks are so noxious and avoidance is often so great, the disorder should be regarded as a "fear of fear." As a result, people with this disorder often experience considerable constriction in travel and normal activities, ranging from limited travel within a safety radius with concomitant anxiety to complete restriction to home or even a single room.

Beyond the diagnosis of agoraphobia, some authorities (Goldstein & Chambless, 1978) have suggested that clinicians conduct a careful behavioral analysis of the phobia to determine the extent to which a given client can be said to possess a "simple" or "complex" agoraphobic pattern. In the first instance, clients present with agoraphobic symptoms of fear and avoidance precipitated by panic attacks that occurred subsequent to drug experiences (such as an upsetting response to experimenting with hallucinogens) or physical disorder (e.g., allergic reaction). In the case of complex agoraphobia, the more common of the two categories, the entire syndrome is present, with fear of fear as a central phobic element, low levels of self-sufficiency due to anxiety, skill deficit, or both, a tendency to misapprehend the casual antecedents of uncomfortable feelings, and onset of symptoms in a climate of interpersonal conflict. Thus, the majority of "complex" agoraphobic clients are held to be nonassertive, pervasively fearful individuals who perceive themselves to be incapable of functioning independently and who evince marked fears of responsibility and social anxiety and the apparent inability to connect emotional responses to causative events (e.g., attacks following interpersonal conflict appear to "come out of nowhere"). While some critics take issue with the simple/complex distinction, and there is a considerable range of intrapersonal characteristics among clients with this diagnosis, it is nonetheless important to recognize that agoraphobia is rarely an isolated set of phobias that exist in an otherwise well-functioning person. The majority of agoraphobic clients possess marked difficulties that predate or follow from their phobic symptoms (Chambless, 1982). Thus, the clinician conducting group interventions for this disorder would do well to be familiar with various theoretical models of the disorder, regularly occurring associated problems, common cognitive features, and underlying beliefs. Furthermore, the clinician should be familiar with a range of treatment interventions that take into account the breadth of manifest and subtle client difficulties.

Concomitant problems may include marital distress, generalized anxiety, simple or social phobia, depression, and characterologic disorders, which may interact with the agoraphobic symptoms (Barlow, 1985; Goldstein, 1982). In addition, clients may experience psychophysiological complaints (e.g., chronic gastric complaints), respiratory difficulties (hyperventilation syndrome), disorders of balance or disequilibrium (vestibular dysfunction), neuromuscular complaints (headache), or myocardial problems (e.g., mitral valve prolapse) concomitant with agoraphobia. Common cognitive, behavioral, and physiologic features associated with the disorder will be reviewed first, followed by discussion of developmental themes frequently manifested by these clients. This section will conclude with a summary of clinical features to be addressed in treatment. The interested reader is directed to Burns and Thorpe (1977), Chambless and Goldstein (1982), Marks (1969, 1970), Marks and Lader (1973), and Michelson (1987) for more detailed information concerning the syndrome.

Cognitive, Behavioral, and Physiological Features

Agoraphobia has well-known cognitive features. Clients complain of anxiety-producing thoughts, ideation, and phobic imagery. In fact, a number of authors (Chambless & Goldstein, 1982; Coleman, 1981; Goldstein & Chambless, 1978; Marks, 1969) note that a key feature of agoraphobia is the fear of the experience of anxiety and what it can or might do. Cognition (mental processing of phobic thoughts and imagery) alone will bring about marked levels of subjective distress (Marks, 1969), and there are a number of ways in which cognition contributes to distress in agoraphobia. The first, noted above, is a *preoccupation with the recurrence of panic feelings and their hypothesized impact.* Frequently, agoraphobic clients fear dying, losing control, going "crazy," or humiliating themselves (e.g., Marks, 1970). This "fear of fear" contributes to avoidance of circumstances in which panic has been experienced in the past or situations where anxiety might conceivably be experienced, and results in anticipatory anxiety (rumination about the possibility of the return of anxiety), which tends to increase distress prior to entering phobic situations. In fact, the anticipation of panic often has an anxiety-producing effect of its own (see Beck & Emery, 1985). Second, agoraphobic individuals become hypersensitive to the physical symptoms of anxiety, and as a result *physical arousal of almost any kind is frequently misconstrued as a precursor of panic* (Goldstein, 1982). Thus, excessive self-monitoring of bodily sensations and their significance contributes to increased arousal and avoidance. Third, rapid spiral of *anxiety ensues when somatic responses are catastrophically appraised* (e.g., "I'm having a heart attack!" versus "I'm nervous and my heart is beating rapidly") (Beck, 1976). In this case, the feared response, panic, is produced by faulty appraisal of physical arousal. Fourth, additional *second-order dysfunctional attitudes and beliefs are likely to arise,* such as the belief that one must avoid arousal, excitement, and strong emotion lest intolerable panic or other disastrous consequences of anxiety result (Beck & Emery, 1985; Coleman, 1981). Individuals often experience an inability to tolerate being alone (Goldstein, 1982), insist on immediate and absolute relief (Salzman, 1982), and are frequently unwilling to endure distress (Ellis, 1979). A range of precautionary ideas may develop, including dysfunctional attitudes and beliefs concerning "safety people" (e.g., that one can travel safely only in the company of certain trusted companions), elaborate planning and precautions for travel or conducting daily activities, development of rituals (e.g., scrupulously monitoring of weather and traffic reports to avoid traffic congestion), and beliefs about the necessity for various "props" or "safeguards" (carrying medication in case of panic, liquids in the event of dry throat) to mitigate against the onset of anxiety. Finally, in addition to catastrophic thoughts concerning the possible occurrence of anxiety, the misinterpretation of normal arousal, and the development of faulty beliefs concerning fear, *subsequent appraisal of one's own avoidant or phobic behavior can lead to a view of oneself as "sick," "weak," or "crazy" with subsequent loss of self-esteem and increased dependence* (e.g., Brehony & Geller, 1981). Thus, a variety of cognitive features operate at different levels in this disorder.

The principal behavioral feature of agoraphobia is avoidance or constriction of normal activities due to severe and continuous anxiety across a range of phobic situations (or the belief that the individual will experience these symptoms in such situations). This constriction may be more or less overt and may range from severe behavioral limitations (e.g., individuals who are housebound and who will not venture anywhere even with a trusted companion) to moderate limitations (those who appear to function relatively independently within a large radius, but who experience high levels of phobic anxiety). Careful questioning may reveal, among those in the latter category, a well-orchestrated array of overt and covert mechanisms for avoiding situations in which they might feel isolated from help or might not readily escape should they wish to do so immediately. Overt avoidance includes eschewing situations such as walking or driving unaccompanied, using public transportation, avoiding crowds, long lines, shopping malls, concerts, movies, elevators, tall buildings, heights, tunnels, bridges, social gatherings, open spaces, enclosed spaces, eating in restaurants, or traffic jams. Individuals may enter phobic situations but leave rapidly, as in the case of the shopper who will park close to the market, run in, buy 2 or 3 items, and use the "fast" check-out line so as not to be detained in the store any longer than absolutely necessary.

Hidden phobic behavior may include the use of safety signals (Rachman, 1984), such as keeping near one's car, carrying one's keys in hand, traveling only a single route to work or shopping, and using only familiar stores, or the establishment of a safety network (such that the client always knows where a safety person is, so that he or she can be reached instantly). Individuals may travel only under certain conditions (e.g., avoiding limited access roads, roads requiring driving beyond a certain speed, roads passing through apparently "isolated" areas, or areas that, due to road repairs, might lead to traffic delays). They may employ "props" or talismans or carry items to help them contend with symptoms of anxiety. One woman carried two large satchels containing tobacco, liquor, change of underwear, and other supplies so as to prepare for the possible onslaught of panic. More commonly, clients will carry gum, mints, keep beverages handy "in case of" anxiety, or carry tranquilizers or a paper bag (in case of hyperventilation). The specific pattern of behavioral avoidance for each client should be identified and articulated during assessment (see relevant section below) as goals of treatment, since these precautions tend to support avoidance and dysfunctional thinking.

With respect to physiologic features, agoraphobic clients have been reported to function at generally high levels of sympathetic nervous system arousal (Marks, 1969; Marks & Lader, 1973), and the level of physical arousal appears related to severity of phobic symptoms. Clients are routinely preoccupied with the implications of upsetting physical symptoms, because they might either presage panic or imply some other hitherto undiagnosed problem. Fried (1987) suggests that certain individuals, due to an underlying pathophysiology, are vulnerable to developing hyperventilation syndrome, which produces physiologic symptoms that lead to certain features of anxiety of overbreathing at one level and panic attacks at another level. This is a promising notion, especially in view of the fact that hyperventilation is common in clients with agoraphobia and has been shown to precede panic, and breathing retraining has been useful in treatment. This model accounts for a portion of the clinical features of the disorder, and to the extent hyperventilation features are present, these should be addressed (see below). Certain physiologic features associated with overbreathing are commonly observed in agoraphobic clients. These include: dyspnea, palpitations, chest pain or discomfort, choking or smothering sensations, dizziness or unsteady feelings, feeling of unreality, paresthesia, hot and cold flashes, sweating, fainting, tremor, and fear of dying. These items, taken from the DSM-III "diagnostic criteria for panic disorders," represent "an incomplete but not incorrect set of criteria for the hyperventilation syndrome" (Fried, 1987, p. 62).

COMMON THEMES IN AGORAPHOBIA

A number of writers have suggested that various themes or issues underly or co-exist in agoraphobic clients. The astute clinician, like the seasoned traveler, is well-advised to anticipate common features and variations in climate and in the territory to be explored, and to be prepared to respond to them.

For example, Salzman (1982) contends that phobic disorders are best construed from the standpoint of defense—the common agoraphobic fear of loss of control is served by the function of phobic avoidance as an absolute injunction that prevents the client from confronting any situation in which he or she might feel humiliated or worthless due to his or her "weakness." Salzman argues that high levels of obsessionality are involved in agoraphobia, and he believes treatment must address the basis for excessive feelings of insecurity that require absolute guarantees before action is pursued. This approach involves repeated encouragement to action in order that the client discover that such guarantees not only are unnecessary but also interfere with living. This understanding can be achieved only when the client can acknowledge that anxiety is universal and omnipresent and cannot be expunged from living. Therefore, the client must be supportively encouraged to enter and reexperience areas of living that have been phobically avoided. The understanding that needs to be uncovered is that the phobic behavior is a product of a character structure that requires absolute certainty in a world in which this is not possible.

Guidano (1987) and Guidano and Liotti (1983) view the cognitive organization of phobic individuals as a dynamic balance between two opposite emotional polarities: the need for protection from a world perceived as dangerous and a concurrent need to be free and independent in the same world. Thus there is a marked tendency for these clients to respond with anxiety to alterations in affectional relationships (e.g., where "protection" or loss of support is perceived) and/or changes in circumstances, interpersonal and otherwise, where freedom or loss of independence is seen to be threatened. Patterns of early development characterized by anxious attachment, involving indirect interference with the child's autonomous exploratory behavior, are held to bring about this type of personal cognitive organization.

Changing client belief systems involves a gradual and collaborative exploration and revision of each client's tacit beliefs concerning self and others and proceeds in stages. The first stage involves classic behavioral and cognitive techniques for helping clients to disprove their superficial beliefs and expectations concerning anxiety. (This aspect of treatment lends itself readily to the early stages of group treatment as described later in the present chapter.) As the first stage of group work proceeds, deeper belief structures (i.e., view of self and others) emerge. These are the grist for a second stage of treatment (which may also be addressed in group work). In this stage, tacit beliefs about the self are uncovered and jointly reviewed in the context of developmental factors—how these beliefs correspond to the client's first-hand learning experiences of self and parents. Bowlby's (1985) approach is consistent with this model. Bowlby holds that current models of perceiving and construing situations (with ensuing associated feelings and actions) are determined in large measure by tacit, emotionally significant events and experiences that are "shut away" or disallowed from cognitive processing. His approach involves helping individuals from within a highly supportive interpersonal environment (e.g., the "safe harbor" of the therapeutic relationship) to discover significant previous events or experiences and to reappraise and restructure inappropriate responses. Of particular importance is permitting, encouraging, and reviewing forbidden thoughts, feelings, and experiences that may not have been sanctioned by parents. In a letter to Guidano (Guidano, 1987), Bowlby suggests the following steps for revising the client's cognitive model of self and reality: encouraging and enabling the exploration of beliefs, helping clients to recognize the cognitive models they are employing, helping clients recall firsthand experience of how they have come to acquire these views, and reviewing sanctions parents used to insist that clients adopt as their model. Change involves many repetitions of this process.

Goldstein (1982) discusses a number of hypothesized "person variables" that predate the onset of agoraphobia and may account for the stance clients assume toward anxiety. He suggests that a hypersensitivity to aloneness-separation experiences is the core problem or issue in this disorder, and he posits that this antedates rather than follows from the occurrence of panic (although this sensitivity may be heightened following the onset of panic attacks). Based on the high incidence of phobic, alcoholic, or psychotic parents among agoraphobes (Munjack & Moss, 1981), these clients may have had early experiences in which they experienced early environmental stress far in excess of their ability to cope. They may have been exposed to an impoverished climate of care-giving or one that involved the risk of abandonment or separation. While speculative, these suggestions concerning developmental "learning" concerning relationships do nonetheless speak to the phenomenon of "anxious attachment" described by Bowlby (1971, as cited in Goldstein, 1982), in which agoraphobic clients equate the experience of aloneness with not having some "strong" other available to care for them. This sensitivity to lack of such an attachment is often chronic and is experienced with powerful affect and associations to death, nonexistence, total helplessness, and an overwhelming sense of being unable to cope independently with life's demands.

Another characteristic of agoraphobic clients described by Goldstein (1982), and a recurrent theme in treatment, is their apparent inability to appreciate the casual antecedents of emotional distress. Strong feelings of anxiety seem to arise spontaneously, "out of the blue."* Coupled with this difficulty in associating internal emotional states with appropriate causes is the tendency to label almost any state of arousal or strong emotion as anxiety or fear. Goldstein notes that it is as though they have never learned to recognize subtle distinctions in feeling states, especially interpersonal ones. These two features act in concert—thus, "panic" appears to erupt from nowhere, and little connection is made to such likely causes for emotional upset as an argument with the spouse that occurred briefly before the onset of distress. As Chambless and Goldstein (1982) note, this pattern can be described as part of an avoidant or "hysterical" style for dealing with stress, which in one sense can be seen as a coping mechanism but which in general leads to excessive restriction. Agoraphobic

---

*Often, the experience of anxiety appearing "spontaneously" is the result of subtle cuing. Thus, visceral sensations, such as arousal associated with exertion, strong emotion, or symptoms of mild illness, external stimuli previously associated with phobic cues, or external stimuli (e.g., news accounts of mental disorder) that trigger rumination about loss of control, or external cues (e.g., open space) that trigger associations to isolation, may evoke strong anxiety, the source of which may be difficult to pinpoint. There is significant value in aiding clients to identify such "triggers" in reducing the mysterious or uncontrollable sense of their symptoms.

clients go to great lengths to avoid not only physical arousal, but interpersonal unpleasantness, conflict, anger, and even strong positive emotions such as humor, excitement, or even sexuality. There is a strong tendency to deny conflict feelings both internally and in relationships and to avoid "rocking the boat," which may be related to a desire to avoid the recurrence of overwhelming or distressing affect. Resolution of these difficulties involves aiding the client to make more appropriate emotional distinctions. These include learning to appropriately label affect, to discover the cause-and-effect sequence between events and emotional response, and to discover through group and individual experiences that it is possible, "normal," and ultimately desirable to experience appropriate and gradually increased levels of affect, which does not lead to loss of control. Effective cognitive restructuring and a carefully graduated sequence of experiences, over a prolonged treatment period, is usually necessary to help individuals begin to challenge their avoidant style and beliefs concerning the necessity of control over feelings. The following sections describe how various treatment strategies are applied within a group context.

RATIONALE FOR GROUP TREATMENT

There are a number of reasons for considering group therapy approaches to agoraphobia. The first relates to clinical research experience. Over the past 10 years, numerous research investigations have demonstrated the efficacy and utility of small group behavioral treatments for this disorder (For detailed reviews, see Brehony & Geller, 1981; Jansson & Ost, 1982). Second, from a clinical perspective, many of these clients feel socially isolated, misunderstood by significant others, and different from others in general. Small group experiences provide an excellent opportunity for finding support from other individuals who share similar difficulties and for reducing isolation. Third, small groups provide encouragement, support, and mutual recognition for small steps in progress. Since the disorder typically requires many months of work to remediate and the typical treatment course features ups and downs in recovery, the group can help to maintain morale and promote continued attempts to surmount difficulties. In addition, the progress of others can inspire recalcitrant clients to take more risks in approaching feared situations. Fourth, certain procedures lend themselves to a small group approach for reasons of social modeling and cost. For example, few therapists could spend 90 to 120 minutes of prolonged in-vivo exposure in a variety of challenging phobic situations with clients seen singly. Not only would clients and therapists find the costs and time demands prohibitive, the availability of a group for such outings permits opportunities for clients to benefit from observing other clients coping and taking gradual risks in approaching and mastering anxiety. A degree of competition may even emerge that can help motivate clients to complete assignments. Fifth, during sessions in which the group focuses on individual themes, difficulties, or perspectives, other members gain from observing the therapist and a single client work together. In watching the therapist interact with an individual client on cognitive or behavioral difficulties, clients have the opportunity to learn about similar concerns of their own from a detached point of view. Sixth, group treatment permits mutual coaching and allows clients to learn coping skills from the standpoint of coach as well as consumer (see Barlow & Waddell, 1985; Meichenbaum & Genest, 1977; Rose, 1977; Suinn, 1977, for examples).

Educational Models of Group Treatment

Instructional approaches for the group treatment of agoraphobia are sensible for both psychological as well as practical reasons. Many individuals with this disorder have considerable fear of strong emotion (e.g., Guidano & Liotti, 1983) and might avoid therapies that could be viewed as highly affective or unstructured. Since loss of control is such a prominent concern among these clients, and since many experience social fears, a systematic, supportive, class-like group format is less threatening, and clients may find it to be more accessible and be more willing to participate.

Many behavioral procedures for effective anxiety management are skills, and these are best trained in a systematic, structured sequence involving information, demonstration, and practice with feedback and assignment of homework. A comprehensive approach to clients who are impaired in a number of systems (cognitive, behavioral, physiologic), requires careful monitoring and appraisal throughout, which involves considerable organization insofar as time, structure, and flow of information. A carefully thought-out group format, with an agenda for each session, and careful monitoring of each individual throughout permit clients to be effectively coached. Effective behavioral group therapy for agoraphobia requires the instigation of new behavior—primarily, graduated, self-initiated exposure of phobic situations in the client's own environment, mastery of cognitive-behavioral coping skills, and revision of beliefs concerning anxiety and identity. A number of precedents exist for use of systematic application of training cognitive-behavioral skills in groups (e.g., Rose, 1977; Sank & Schaffer, 1984; Yost, Beutler, Corbishley, & Allender, 1986), for treating anxiety specifically (Meichenbaum & Genest, 1977; Suinn, 1977; Rose, 1977), and agoraphobia in particular (Barlow, 1988; Barlow & Waddell, 1985; Michelson, 1987; Michelson, Mavissakalian, & Marchione, 1985; Michelson, Mavissakalian, Marchione, Dancu, & Greenwald, 1986).

There are limitations with psychoeducational approaches to the treatment of agoraphobia. Chambless (1982) notes that problem-focused phobia treatments are proliferating. While these are often highly useful and cost-effective, many agoraphobic clients experience a range of problems and merit a broad-spectrum intervention. Individual clients may require additional dosage and length of treatments that go beyond a 16-week program. While there are likely to be subgroups highly responsive to didactic exposure-based treatments, others, whose symptoms may be maintained by intrapsychic or interpersonal factors, will require more intensive treatment.

This chapter presumes the reader will implement group interventions in which exposure to phobic situations is but one item on a menu that includes additional treatment interventions addressing multiple problem domains (e.g., behavioral, physiologic, cognitive). It is anticipated that therapists will provide ancillary treatments, (supportive, marital, even pharmacologic) in accordance with client needs.

The following sections will describe common treatment elements that may be employed in group cognitive-behavioral treatment of agoraphobia.

Group Exposure Treatments

Exposure treatment refers to procedures involving a graduated, therapist-directed client approach to anxiety-eliciting stimuli. Generally, a distinction is made between in-vivo exposure (also referred to as flooding, in which clients approach *actual* phobic situations) and imaginal exposure (in which clients approach phobic stimuli made in *imagination*). In general, in-vivo exposure is preferred for a number of reasons (Michelson, 1987) and exposure to phobic situations is seen to be an acceptable and valid treatment by consumers (Norton, Allen, & Hilton, 1983).

Exposure treatments are undoubtedly useful and often necessary treatments for agoraphobia, as noted in recent reviews by Michelson (1987), Brehony and Geller (1981),

Jansson and Ost (1982), and Goldstein and Chambless (1978). As Michelson (1987) notes, exposure treatments are often misunderstood and mistakenly associated with implosion therapy, in which horrific or frightening cues are used to maximize arousal of anxiety. Implosion therapy is presumed by its proponents to promote rapid extinction of phobic anxiety. Clinical research with agoraphobic clients favors a gradual, carefully paced exposure to clients' unique sets of phobic situations in a slowly ascending hierarchy. Clinically, clients are given specific individual assignments on group outings that are appropriate to their level of competence (ability to cope with anxiety, readiness, and mastery of previous challenges). In this way, specific outings and assignments are tailored to client needs and capacities. Client control and choice should be maximized, given clients' cognitive structures and sensitivity to control issues. A gradual pace is sensible to minimize drop-out, noncompliance and resistance as well. The client should be actively involved in choosing the level of difficulty of assigned homework tasks in tandem with the therapist in order to minimize threat, level of anticipatory fear, and arousal during the actual tasks.

Massed, prolonged (e.g., 90 minutes or longer) in-vivo exposure to phobic situations is favored in the clinical research literature (Michelson, 1987). As Jansson and Ost (1982) notes in their comprehensive review of behavioral treatments for agoraphobia, "the more in vivo exposure that was involved in the treatment, the better the results" (p. 330).

Exposure may be self-directed (assigned by therapist for between-visit practice and reviewed together with the group) or administered in therapist-directed group outings, in which a group accompanies the therapist to a given location and members are assigned individual exposure tasks in the setting according to their readiness and particular patterns of avoidance. In practice, some combination of both forms of exposure is preferable, so as to maximize generalization and to ensure proper client exposure to phobic situations (Greenwald, 1987).

While graduated exposure appears to be an essential aspect of treatment, it is not without its difficulties. Drop-out rates between 8 and 40% have been reported (Michelson, 1987) and a median improvement rate across studies reviewed by Jansson and Ost (1982) was 62%. Mavissakalian and Michelson (1986) determined, by means of an outcome study that compared therapist-assisted, in-vivo exposure, self-directed exposure, imipramine and placebo, that clients receiving self-directed exposure (programmed practice) alone had significantly inferior outcome. Michelson (1987) concludes that "although self-directed exposure can be an effective and cost-effective strategy for reducing phobic avoidance, the majority of clients appear to require additional *therapist-assisted in vivo exposure* and or concomitant cognitive-behavioral treatments" (p. 248). In recent years, adjunctive treatments have been examined to broaden the effects of treatment and mitigate against relapse and premature termination.

Treatments Involving the Addition of Coping Skills Training

A number of research studies have investigated the merits of training clients in cognitive and behavioral skills to augment graded exposure. While exposure is a useful procedure, it may be limited in that it addresses only one aspect of the disorder, behavioral avoidance and conditioned fear. The general aim of additional procedures involves teaching clients to control physiologic arousal and to cope with phobic cognitions. Emmelkamp (1982) observed that agoraphobic clients could engage in exposure without changing their basic ideas concerning danger, vulnerability, and the like. They would involve themselves in outings but maintain control of their fear by thinking about the proximity of hospitals, identifying friends they might call should they get really nervous, and so forth. Thus, they could demonstrate behavioral accomplishments without sustaining a corrective emotional experience (involving a revision of faulty agoraphobic beliefs and views of the self). While cognitive-behavioral procedures have received endorsement in the clinical literature (Beck & Emery, 1985; Coleman, 1981; Guidano & Liotti, 1983), relatively few controlled clinical trials examining various coping skills procedures for agoraphobia have been undertaken.*

Mavissakalian, Michelson, Greenwald, Kornblith, and Greenwald (1983) examined the utility of self-statement training (SST, a procedure similar to cognitive restructuring) and paradoxical intention (PI) in a clinical trial with 26 severe agoraphobics. Both groups received instructions for self-directed programmed practice. Clients were seen in weekly 90-minute groups for a period of 3 months, with clinically and statistically significant gains for both conditions. While these findings are encouraging and clearly add to the benefit of exposure treatments, further work over the past several years has demonstrated superior benefits for cognitive therapy (e.g., Beck & Emery, 1985) as an adjunct to exposure treatment. Clients receiving sixteen weekly 2-hour group visits of cognitive therapy plus therapist-assisted graded exposure and individual programmed practice showed significant clinical gains of much greater magnitude than those achieved with SST or PI.

Progressive deep muscle relaxation training (PDMR) has also been shown to be a useful treatment adjunct in the treatment of agoraphobia (Michelson, Mavissakalian, & Marchione, 1985; Michelson, Mavissakalian, Marchione, Dancu, & Greenwald, 1986). In the first study cited, clients in 4–5-person small groups received twelve 2-hour weekly sessions of PDMR, in combination with instructions for programmed practice, the same amount of training in PI, or instruction and coaching in programmed practice together with therapist-assisted, in-vivo exposure. Clients who were trained in coping skills markedly increased the amount of time they spent in independent self-directed exposure. Relaxation training appears to have served as a self-control strategy for decreasing physiologic arousal and anxiety symptoms before, during, and after exposure to phobic situations. PDMR led to the most consistent pattern of self-directed practice (Michelson et al., 1986). The increase in practice for those receiving PDMR was closely followed by decreases in self-reported anxiety in vivo. Preliminary findings (Michelson, Mavissakalian, Marchione, Dancu, & Greenwald, 1987) indicate that PDMR significantly reduced clients' arousal, eliminated spontaneous panic attacks in over 60% of subjects, and led to normal levels of physiological arousal by the end of the 12-week study. Clients increased physiological self-control, habituated to phobic cues more readily, and increased self-directed exposure to phobic cues.

Controlled breathing procedures have been shown to be successful in treating panic attacks (Clark, Salkovskis, & Chalkley, 1985), and since hyperventilation has been argued to be implicated in the etiology of panic (Fried, 1987; Ley, 1987), breathing retraining may be included as a treatment component. Details and resources for further information will be provided in the next section.

---

*Cognitive-behavioral strategies have been effectively used in the treatment of phobias, anxiety, and depression over the past decade (see reviews by Miller & Berman, 1983; Rachman & Wilson, 1980) and have shown themselves to be superior to untreated controls and, in some cases, other therapies. Meta-analytic studies of treatment outcome (e.g., Dushe, Hirt, & Schroeder, 1983) offer support for the value of a variety of cognitive and behavioral treatments for anxiety disorders in general. But until recently, few well-controlled clinical trials had been conducted with agoraphobics.

GENERAL RECOMMENDATIONS

Diagnosis

Many agoraphobic clients have had a variety of contacts with the medical and perhaps the psychiatric community prior to appearing for treatment. Some will have had a variety of diagnoses to account for their psychiatric symptoms, as well as a range of putative causes for their physical symptoms, including hypoglycemia, vestibular dysfunction, and mitral valve prolapse. Typically, there is an absence of specific or definitive physical findings and often much misinformation concerning their symptoms. Even in the case of a proper diagnosis of agoraphobia, clients are uninformed as to what proper treatment should entail.

Agoraphobic clients are quite sensitive to the issue of diagnosis. Commonly, they have spent months attempting to pinpoint the cause of their mysterious malady and have consulted with a range of specialists from internist to cardiologist to endocrinologist, with ambiguous findings at best. Throughout this time, upsetting physical sensations and anxiety have persisted and no definitive diagnosis has been made, or if one has been advanced, pharmacologic or psychotherapeutic treatment has been unsuccessful. Not surprisingly, clients may harbor doubts about "yet another doctor" appraising them. Even so, they may hope that a specific physical disorder will be found that could account for their incapacitation. To many clients, the presence of a specific physical cause would save them face with significant others and would offer hope that their distressing symptoms could be brought under control. It is little wonder that they harbor reservations about whether their disorder isn't really more physical than psychological. A psychological disorder can be seen as less open to change, less acceptable, and less understandable by clients and significant others. In fact, physicians, friends, and family members may have been less than supportive and occasionally rather critical concerning a client's "inability" to function independently in the absence of a clear reason for why they cannot do so. In addition, the variations in impairment that occur, rendering certain activities difficult one day and less so on another, are exasperating for clients and significant others. Thus, it is understandable that individuals with agoraphobia are often attracted to physical explanations of their disorder.

In addition, media coverage of phobic disorders and recent publications that suggest that this disorder is secondary to inner ear disturbance, cardiovascular abnormality, or best viewed as an anxiety "disease" fuel doubts concerning diagnosis and commitment to and involvement in treatment. Therefore, it is wise for the clinician to be informed concerning popular accounts of anxiety disorder in order to explore with clients what they have read concerning their difficulty and to discuss their "theory" of what is wrong with them at the outset of treatment. While much of this can and should be addressed during the pretherapy treatment rationale with the group (see below), questions concerning appropriate diagnosis are best handled during screening. This approach minimizes drop-out and needless or prolonged group speculation about underlying medical problems. Naturally, careful assessment includes a thorough medical screening to rule out biological disorders.

Occasionally, concomitant difficulties such as vestibular dysfunction* are identified and may be treated concurrently. In this case, it is essential to help the client understand the interactive relationship between physical disorder and anxiety disorder: how upsetting sen-

---

*Vestibular dysfunction pertains to medical conditions affecting the organs of the inner ear that are associated with balance. Not only are the symptoms of dizziness and unsteadiness associated with these complaints upsetting to the clients who suffer them, but the symptoms are also misappraised as signs of impending incapacitation.

sations and their faulty appraisal lead to subsequent anxiety and avoidance behavior. Before proceeding, the client and therapist should share the perspective that there is a need to intervene both physically (in the case of any actual physical malady) *and* psychologically to change the pattern of distressing beliefs, emotional reactions, and avoidance that comprise the agoraphobic pattern. Unless this perspective is shared, it would be better to postpone participation in group treatment, if clients have strong reservations about the "cause" of their difficulties, until they have had the chance to complete indicated medical assessments or to discover the value of a physical remedy (e.g., for inner ear disturbance). Otherwise, the "couldn't this really be physical" concern can lead to passive participation or premature disengagement in treatment if it is not addressed. As Coleman (1981) observes, clear communication with the client concerning his or her diagnosis is imperative if a strong sense of collaboration is to be secured. As treatment proceeds, theoretical discussions about the physical versus mental cause of the problem are best avoided in favor of joint examination of data concerning relationships among each client's thoughts, circumstances, and sensations (Guidano & Liotti, 1983). This joint appraisal takes place both at the outset of and throughout treatment. Naturally, the group offers an excellent context for examining the evidence concerning the physical basis of symptoms.

Thus, careful and detailed discussion of symptoms with comments about how these relate to anxiety (e.g., see Ley, 1987 for a discussion of how breathing changes operate during anxiety to generate a range of panic symptoms), inspection of thoughts and ideas in phobic situations, and their associations with specific symptoms of arousal and phobic avoidance (Beck & Emery, 1985; Guidano & Liotti, 1983) represent an important part of the diagnostic assessment, the discussion and rationale that introduces group work, and a focus of attention throughout treatment.

Concurrent Diagnoses and Treatment Implications

This chapter addresses its recommendations principally to homogeneous groups of individuals with the primary DSM-III diagnosis of agoraphobia with panic attacks. The research investigations on which many of the recommendations are made excluded individuals with primary diagnoses of substance abuse, primary affective disorder, organic brain syndrome, psychosis, or antisocial or borderline personality disorders.

Secondary depression is common among agoraphobic clients (Barlow, 1985) and is not considered a basis for exclusion from treatment for agoraphobia. It should, however, be monitored throughout treatment and addressed with adjunctive treatment if severe. In the case of primary affective disorder, it may be wise to treat the depression with psychotherapy or medication prior to involving clients in the group.

No hard and fast guidelines are available for including or excluding individuals from psychoeducational group treatment for agoraphobia on the basis of personality features. Certain individuals may exclude themselves from a psychoeducational treatment, considering its group format, requirements for a fair amount of compliance with homework, and therapist-directed activities as incompatible with their perceived needs, expectations, or typical style or posture in therapy. Likewise, certain individuals may require or seek excessive therapist attention or support or may wish for more "air time" or interpersonal engagement than this format typically allows—this would make them less ideal candidates for this type of group treatment. While such "poor fits" for this format are uncommon, early appraisal of client needs and frank discussion of the aims, format, and activities of the group during the screening process can help both client and therapist determine whether this type of intervention makes the most sense for a given individual. Naturally, group therapists operating in a private setting may choose to broaden inclusion criteria or loosen the format or pace of the group in accord with group composition.

The psychoeducational treatment approach described in this chapter may be implemented as a time-limited, first stage of therapy (one that, incidentally, may be a sufficient intervention for a number of clients) with an optional second stage or a less structured group or individual therapy targeted at more persistent or idiosyncratic themes or issues. More focus on intrapersonal themes and interpersonal issues can be more beneficially pursued later in the course of treatment, after anxiety symptoms and avoidance are reduced and clients have both the skills and disposition to address these.

In any case, focused and aggressive treatment leading to rapid and effective symptom relief is held to be of highest priority and greatest long-term benefit in keeping individuals on the road to recovery and mitigating against pessimism and premature termination. Some symptoms such as secondary depression are likely to abate during treatment. Other issues may await specific attention until a second phase of treatment. It is unlikely that any therapy can address all complaints concurrently: participation in a highly organized agoraphobia group implies that therapists and clients share a priority for ameliorating agoraphobic symptoms.

Assessment

In general, it is useful to have preliminary measures of phobic anxiety and avoidance. Specifically, ratings of self-reported anxiety and avoidance should be collected for each individual for a wide variety of activities and situations. The list should be as exhaustive as possible and include activities that are avoided and those that are not avoided but nonetheless elicit phobic anxiety. Also important is a version of the same list rated with respect to whether an individual will attempt the activity alone or with a significant other. For example, some individuals will travel anywhere as long as they are with a trusted companion, and a client's need for accompaniment is likely to vary idiosyncratically according to task and distance from home. Thus, detailed data concerning phobic situations and anxiety ratings, alone and accompanied, should be gathered. These data represent a baseline for subsequent assessment and help to define areas for practice.

During treatment, detailed records of practice in phobic situations should be kept by each client. Length of outing, length of time in each phobic situation, peak level of self-reported anxiety, length of time until anxiety abates to a 3 or less on a 0–8 scale of self-reported severity, and final leval of anxiety, whether alone or accompanied, represent extremely useful data. Records of each client's practice are reviewed in group as data to be employed in assessing progress and setting further practice goals, examples of difficult situations for which suggestions may be made to enhance coping, and "evidence" demonstrating a client's ability to apply new skills (see "Programmed Practice"). In addition, periodic assessments of number of panic attacks per week and their duration and intensity, constellation and range of anxiety symptoms and their intensity, and level of depression ("Beck Depression Inventory"; Beck, Ward, Mendelson, Mock, & Erbaugh, 1961) are useful as well in monitoring symptoms during treatment. Attention to new achievements or accomplishments, reduction in degree and intensity of anticipatory fear, and increases in energy level and improved sleep are additional indices of improvement, noted informally, that are useful in helping clients realistically gauge their progress. An excellent discussion of assessment issues and measures for behavioral assessment is available in Barlow and Waddell (1985).

Pretherapy Orientation to Group Psychoeducational Treatment

Pretherapy preparation improves appropriate client involvement during treatment, is likely to aid attendance, and enhances outcome (Mayerson, 1984). Subsequent to assessment, individual contact that is aimed at preparing the individual for the group experience can help to increase rapport, provide assurance about the group experience, establish role expectations and reasonable outcome expectations, and secure an individual commitment to the treatment process (Yost, Beutler, Corbishley, & Alender; 1986). Individual and group orientation regarding the nature and goals of treatment is continued throughout the course of the therapy. Initially, clients are introduced to how psychoeducational treatment is distinguished from other forms of treatment they may have received in the past. Clients are first helped to better understand the syndrome and how it operates with respect to their sensations, thoughts, feelings, and actions. The approach to overcoming agoraphobia pursued with the help and support of the group is training in specific skills for facing and coping with fear. The importance of practice, taking a graduated approach to mastering difficult situations, and using available coaching, support and group problem-solving are emphasized.

Later in therapy, orientation takes the form of structuring specific expectations for treatment course, and anticipating problems that may arise, including generalization and maintenance issues (Greenwald, 1987).

Treatment Rationale

A detailed rationale featuring extensive information about the disorder is a critical part of treatment and is offered in the first group session. It should cover symptoms, known etiology, treatment course, treatment procedures to be employed, and the relationship of these to specific aspects of the disorder. The rationale serves several important functions. First, it helps to allay unanswered questions about diagnosis and puzzling symptoms that have previously defied explanation. Second, it promotes identity among group members (especially as members are invited to comment on shared features of the disorder, reactions to symptoms, and course of the syndrome). Third, it helps to provide necessary structure for the form of the group (e.g., educational, task-oriented, supportive) and the nature of the task to be shared (learning and applying skills for overcoming anxiety). Fourth, it promotes maintenance and generalization effects of treatment (Greenwald, 1987).

In general, the treatment rationale should include information about the disorder, its typical course and natural history, demographics, and frequent cognitive, physiological, and behavioral symptoms. A detailed discussion of etiological factors (biological, social learning, conditioning) should be provided, so that individuals may recognize developmental features and earlier learning experiences that may contribute to their developing the disorder (e.g., Chambless & Goldstein, 1982; Guidano & Liotti, 1983). The influence of precipitating factors such as stressful life events (loss, interpersonal conflict, etc.) preceeding onset of panic attacks can be described.

An important aspect of the rationale is a discussion of conditioning factors that lead to the cuing of phobic anxiety to places where panic has occurred as well as to symptoms of physical arousal. Both *classical conditioning* and *operant conditioning* appear to be involved in the development of the disorder: thus, individuals learn to fear situations in which they have experienced panic (and those situations that are similar), and they learn to rapidly leave situations that elicit fear since escape brings relief. Overcoming this strong behavioral response involves deconditioning, and group members need a framework involving the concepts of habituation,* deconditioning, and the value of gradual, prolonged, repeated, in-vivo exposure to phobic cues as a major treatment strategy for unlearning fear and avoidance (see Michelson, Mavissakalian, & Marchione, 1985).

Related to information concerning conditioning aspects of the disorder is material concerning the nature of anxiety and panic. Specifically, the significance of anxiety symptoms is described as part of the body's mechanism for responding to conditions of threat. Symptoms of sympathetic nervous system arousal and recovery and the way these are evoked by certain physical, environmental, or psychological cues are described (Beck & Emery, 1985: Michelson, Mavissakalian, & Marchione, 1985). The relationship between hyperventilation and panic may be described (cf. Fried, 1987; Ley, 1987). Hyperventilation leads to panic-eliciting, physiological symptoms. Information about the physiology of respiration, the effects of respiration, and instruction in breathing can be a highly useful therapy for panic attacks (Clark, Salkovskis, & Chalkley, 1985). Clearly distinguishing the symptoms of hyperventilation, sympathetic arousal, and panic from loss of control, heart attack, or "going crazy" (psychosis) is very important. Clients need to recognize that as upsetting and distressing as these symptoms may be, they are not the same as symptoms of heart attack or psychosis, present no danger in and of themselves, and will abate with time.

The role of cognitive factors needs to be made clear during the rationale. *Faulty beliefs* concerning the nature and implications of symptoms, especially panic attacks, lead to greatly magnified estimates of danger and vulnerability. *Anticipatory anxiety* (catastrophic thoughts and images concerning panic associated with and preceding entry into phobic situations) results in increased anxiety and avoidance. *Highly upsetting appraisal* of one's circumstances leads to increased arousal (production of physical symptoms of anxiety)—and consequent expanded appraisal of threat, leading to more symptoms. As a result of anxiety and avoidance, individuals develop or engage in *faulty beliefs about the self* (weakness, incapacity, helplessness, demoralization, fragility) that derive from this seemingly inexplicable limitation. The rationale should provide a discussion of how normal individuals develop arbitrary, pejorative, and upsetting attributions about phenomena (e.g., anxiety) that are difficult to change (see Levine & Sandeen, 1985, discussion of "blank trials law"), when they are confronted with upsetting phenomena that defy explanation.

In short, individuals should be exposed to didactic information and group discussion about the disorder, etiologic theory, information concerning how their disorder was learned and maintained (via avoidance), and the ways physiological, behavioral, and cognitive factors interrelate.

Specific treatment procedures to be employed are each given detailed introduction and rationale at their point of introduction in treatment. Each procedure to be introduced to the group (e.g., graded exposure, programmed practice, diaphragmatic breathing, Socratic questioning) should be introduced with its purpose, previous applications (how it has been

---

*Habituation refers to the decay in level of fear during exposure to a given task.

applied in the past to treat similar problems), a preview of typical steps in learning, acquisition, and application of the skill, and opportunity for questions.*

The rationale as described above serves as the foundation on which further interventions are built. Following the rationale, treatment that incorporates specialized interventions proceed.

SPECIALIZED BEHAVIORAL INTERVENTIONS— ASSEMBLING A TREATMENT PACKAGE

Group treatment for agoraphobia may be seen as a composite of four general elements: orientation to the disorder and the manner in which different aspects of treatment will address the problem, training in anxiety management skills, instigation of clients' approach to phobic situations (via therapist-assisted group exposure or therapist-directed independent exposure), and the restructuring of phobic beliefs. These elements interrelate with one another and require orchestration throughout treatment. Presently, there is no "best" treatment for agoraphobia, but there is increasing consensus among behavioral practitioners regarding the value of these components.

Space limitations prevent complete descriptions of the various components and their application. This section will describe requisite treatment ingredients, offer general clinical comments regarding their implementation in group treatment, and suggest references for clinicians interested in further details.

Graduated In-Vivo Exposure

In general, graduated in-vivo exposure requires considerable planning and organization before being undertaken, in terms of therapist preparation, client preparedness, integration of the procedure into the group process, construction of a suitable hierarchy of graded tasks, transportation to and from practice sites, management of clients on site, and review and integration of the exposure experience following practice. In the clinical research trials described by Mavissakalian and Michelson and colleagues, flooding commenced early in treatment, following an extensive rationale† that included a detailed description of anxiety, principles of habituation, and a description of how to cope with anxiety. This strategy of beginning early in treatment and gradually enabling clients to approach feared situations promotes rapid

---

*Modeling and coaching of approximation steps for acquiring the skill would then proceed over a sequence of sessions. A review of this general approach to training clients in cognitive-behavioral skills may be found in Cormier and Cormier (1985). Examples of specific rationales pertinent to the use of specific procedures employed in group clinical research trials with agoraphobic clients can be found in Michelson, Mavissakalian, Greenwld, Kornblith, and Greenwald (1983)—rationales for self-statement training and paradoxical intention; Michelson, Mavissakalian, Marchione, Dancu, and Greenwald (1986)—rationales for exposure, relaxation training, and programmed practice; and treatment rationales for cognitive therapy with agoraphobia can be seen in Beck and Emery (1985) and Guidano and Liotti (1983).

†Rationale, method, and procedures for conducting graduated in-vivo exposure are described in Michelson (1985); Michelson, Mavissakalian, Marchione, Dancu, and Greenwald (1986); and Mavissakalian and Michelson (1986). A discussion of issues concerning generalizing effects of in-vivo exposure can be found in Greenwald (1987).

changes in behavioral avoidance. Furthermore, as the weeks progress, therapist-assisted group outings permit an opportunity for in-vivo modeling and coaching of coping skills. The aforementioned clinical trials provided intensive treatment: approximately 90 minutes of group meetings reviewing progress or training in anxiety management skills followed by an equal period of therapist-assisted exposure. The dictates of clinical practice may preclude a similar intervention pattern. Therefore, the clinician may elect to embark on a course of alternating exposure outings and in-office group therapy visits (focused on training, problem-solving, or psychotherapeutic issues) that follow an initial series of preparatory office meetings. As noted above, prolonged exposure is desirable, and outings should be scheduled for 90 minutes or more.

A hierarchy of destinations should be constructed well in advance of outings so as to provide clients with a carefully sequenced gradient of phobic situations. Quiet, relatively uncrowded destinations such as museums or small, enclosed shopping malls at off-peak hours might be good locations for initial outings. As time progresses and clients can tolerate more challenging environments, larger shopping areas and facilities involving more crowds and similar challenges are suitable. Ideally, sites should offer an array of challenges to meet a variety of individual client needs for practice. A large mall offers opportunities for waiting in lines, separating for increased time periods and greater distances from the therapist, having a meal in a small restaurant, trying on clothes, and using elevators, as well as offering a range of environmental stimulation from crowds, depending on the hour chosen for practice. Naturally, destinations are constrained by office location and travel times. Travel to and from destinations may also be an aspect of exposure (as well as a rich source of clinical material), since some clients dread travel to seemingly remote areas (e.g., open spaces suggestive of isolation). In addition, mode of travel to practice destinations can be varied for the group over outings, from group travel in a van in early stages to group travel employing public transportation in latter outings. With the use of an assistant, individuals can be put on a bus by one therapist at one location and met by a second therapist as they arrive at their destination. Naturally, careful preparation and gradual increases in the level of task difficulty and timing are involved in helping select appropriately challenging assignments.

Outings should address the range of circumstances that are commonly threatening to agoraphobic clients and that represent circumstances that if routinely avoided, may lead to significant impairment of social or occupational functioning, for example, shopping malls, stores, long lines, crowds, use of public transportation, and travel to and from congested urban areas. During early outings, the group would travel together to a particular location and be assigned individual tasks in the mall or store consistent with their current limitations and capacity for independent functioning (e.g., a client may be directed to enter a store and try on clothing or get change for a dollar in a crowded bank).

Over the course of graduated exposure outings, therapist availability and contact are faded as clients increase their capacity for independent functioning. At the onset, the therapist or co-therapist may accompany individual clients nearly continuously, joining them in difficult situations as needed, or they may make brief assignments that require each client to expose himself or herself to a list of specific difficult situations for specified periods of time while the therapist waits outside ("I'd like you to practice standing in line at the bank for 5 minutes and change a ten dollar bill"). As clients increase their ability to tolerate anxiety, longer assignments are offered. With tasks of longer duration, the client may be more likely to experience habituation. Tasks that offer a moderate (versus overwhelming) level of fear and represent a small approximation toward the goal of overcoming specific areas of phobic avoidance are selected. The smaller the objective, especially in early stages of treatment, the more likely the client will be successful (e.g., complete the assignment, tolerate anxiety, or experience habituation). The therapist can increase the difficulty of assigned tasks (e.g., time or distance involved) and eventually their own availability. Early in the series of outings, the therapist or assistant may simply wait at a fixed location while clients carry out separate assignments. Later on, therapists may choose to wait at one of two locations during the outing. Additional fading steps include waiting at a given location at specified times and increasing the time between periods of therapist availability. Ultimately, clients are helped to venture independently to assigned destinations, such as riding a bus while carrying a telephone number where the therapist may be reached.

Support, encouragement, trust, patience, and careful pacing are important considerations in helping clients face, tolerate, and eventually overcome their fears of panic in situations that they have scrupulously avoided. Foa, Steckett, Grayson, and Doppett (1983) note that exposure treatments require a good patient-therapist working relationship, combining warmth, support, empathy, firmness, and insistence.

Client reactions to their experiences during exposure should be elicited and participants should be extensively debriefed after each exposure outing in group to ensure that individuals accurately appraise their performance, receive recognition from each other, address any concerns or problems, and maintain appropriate expectations for progress.* A final aspect of group discussion following each outing relates to assignment of homework (programmed practice). Individuals are encouraged to expose themselves, with or without the assistance of a significant other, to the situations encountered during the group outings. Group exposure is linked to individual programmed practice in several ways: tasks practiced together may often be more easily undertaken alone after they have been completed with group or therapist support and likewise, tasks that have been difficult to approach independently can be approximated during group outings.

Programmed Practice

Clients should be helped to understand that programmed practice, that is, systematically overcoming avoidance in a number of areas that affect work and social functioning, is one of the major elements of treatment and will require time, effort, and patience. A conditioning model of phobic avoidance and fear is presented during treatment rationale,† and clients learn that in order to overcome fear and avoidance, it is necessary to enter and remain in phobic situations gradually and in a controlled fashion and to remain until anxiety decreases and the urge to escape declines. This will require gradual and repeated exposure across many

---

*A discussion of issues to address in helping clients evaluate treatment impact is in Greenwald (1987).

†Excellent rationales for the use of programmed practice can be found in the sources listed above under "Graduated Exposure." A procedural description of this treatment component can be found in Greenwald (1985). Barlow and Waddell (1985) provide a detailed description of group couples treatment of agoraphobia in which programmed practice is employed. The chapter includes an outline of treatment, assessment materials, and sample transcripts of sessions. In addition, Matthew, Geider, and Johnson (1981) contains excellent rationale sections and two treatment manuals appended to the text, both for applying programmed practice. One manual is written for clients and the second for significant others who might be aiding them in approaching phobic situations. Typical questions and answers, suggestions for goal-setting, and instructions for coping with phobic anxiety are included. Wilson (1986) also provides an excellent client manual for panic disorder.

occasions and in many settings and is best achieved through regular, daily practice over a period of several months. It is not necessary to practice under conditions of extremely high anxiety. In fact, a major therapist role in monitoring programmed practice is to help clients select practice objectives that will afford a *moderate* level of fear, so that clients will choose to remain in phobic situations, apply their coping skills, and habituate successfully.

Prefatory instructions for how to view anxiety and how to respond to phobic symptoms must be provided, together with details about how habituation occurs. For example, clients should expect that their anxiety will not disappear immediately on exposure but will rise and fall as they remain in the phobic situation until it reaches a lower level after a prolonged period. This period may be 30 minutes or more at first, but as time goes on, they may find that they will habituate more rapidly. In addition, level of fear in a given situation may vary over time, sometimes for reasons that are hard to pinpoint, but in general, programmed practice can help clients recover. Over many outings to a given situation, level and duration of fear will, on the average, decline (Matthew, Gelder, & Johnston, 1981). In the early stages of programmed practice, clients are encouraged to remain in situations, perhaps with accompaniment by a trusted companion, for brief periods to help them increase their tolerance for anxiety. When they are able to remain for 20 to 30 minutes or more, they are likely to notice habituation will and does occur. They will then be ready for increasingly challenging outings (e.g., traveling further, more crowded situations, more separation from safety cues).

Each group meeting can set aside a period for reviewing each client's records of practice experiences from the previous week and providing group and therapist support, encouragement, and suggestions for objectives for the following week's practice. Programmed practice can be integrated with therapist-assisted exposure: following a review of a given client's difficulties during solo practice, he or she can be coached individually on a similar situation by the therapist during the group outing.

Symptom Evocation Exercises

Controlled hyperventilation (see Clark, Salkovskis, & Chalkley, 1985; Ley, 1987), together with practice in remedial or controlled breathing, can be employed with careful preparation and debriefing to help clients appropriately appraise and remediate signs of physical changes associated with altered breathing. In this way, highly upsetting and "mysterious" symptoms, seemingly arising from nowhere, can be seen to be explainable and controllable.*

An extension of these exercises (which may be seen as a form of graded exposure to interoceptive cues) involves helping subjects, in the protected setting of the group, gradually expose themselves to hyperventilation and other visceral sensations, which may have come to be associated with anxiety and avoidance. A variety of tasks can be constructed, again within the structure of a graded hierarchy, to help clients approach increasing levels of idiosyncratic phobic cues: spinning in place to generate dizzy and unsteady feelings, jumping jacks to increase cardiac and respiratory activity, sensations of dry mouth and so on. These exercises may be initiated early in treatment and continued weekly with the group until visceral sensations no longer trigger high levels of fear and clients no longer avoid activities associated with their likely occurrence.

---

*Excellent discussion of hyperventilation phenomena together with specific instructions for implementing this treatment can be found in Fried (1987), Ley (1987), and Clark, Salkovskis, and Chalkley (1985).

Following a rationale describing individual "experiments" to be conducted that will help clients learn more about how their difficulty operates, clients are asked, one at a time, to enact the various tasks that elicit visceral cues evocative of anxiety. By conducting exercises within the safety of the group in which clients can turn their anxiety "on and off," their perception of control is heightened. With evocation of visceral sensations connected with panic, clients can be helped to identify faulty interpretations of normal bodily sensations (which can be addressed with cognitive interventions) or to practice reducing unpleasant physical sensations with controlled breathing or relaxation skills. Note that programmed practice assignments that encourage clients to expose themselves to these cues (jogging, practicing brief periods of hyperventilation at home and reversing it with controlled breathing) can be made.

Relaxation Training (PDMR)

Following a rationale that describes the utility of learning progressive deep muscle relaxation (PDMR) for increasing self-control of physiologic arousal, coping with phobic symptoms, applying other coping skills more effectively (e.g., cognitive procedures), and enhancing one's ability to habituate to and remain in phobic situations, clients are given an overview of the procedure, how they will learn it, and how they might be expected to apply the procedures over the weeks to come.*

Specifically, they are told that a portion of each session will be spent mastering a skill for controlling level of physical arousal. They first learn a long form of procedure, in group, to be practiced at home during nonphobic situations, requiring use of a comfortable chair or bed. This assignment involves about 20 minutes of practice per occasion, learning to tense and relax muscles in order to induce a feeling of comfort and calm that is incompatible with anxiety. As the weeks progress, they learn a variety of relaxation skills, and the procedure itself is shortened. With practice, what initially required 20 minutes of practice in a quiet and nonthreatening situation will be transformed into a brief yet equally effective method for inducing calm and reducing anxiety. The procedure can be used before, subsequent to, and, ultimately, in situations where they are likely to experience anxiety.

Portions of the weekly group meeting are set aside for training and review of practice of the entire sequence of relaxation skills. PDMR can be initiated employing 17 muscle groups, tensing each muscle group twice, and faded over a period of 6 or 7 weeks (with assigned daily practice) to whole-body relaxation cued to imagery or diaphragmatic breathing, requiring less than a minute and applied in vivo. Relaxation skills are offered in a modeling and coaching format: the therapist first describes the procedure, models it for the group, conducts practice with coaching on the skill, debriefs the group, and makes assignments for home practice (which are reviewed at the outset of the next visit). In addition, when clients attain competence in the use of relaxation skills, they receive coaching in applying them gradually to phobic situations of increasing difficulty. They are supervised in applying the relaxation skills during exposure outings and are encouraged, depending on their level of ability to apply their relaxation skills to problematic situations.

---

*A description and rationale for PDMR as employed in group treatment with agoraphobia is contained in Michelson et al. (1985, 1986, in press). Details of the PDMR procedure can be seen in Bernstein and Borkovec (1983) and Cormier and Cormier (1985).

Cognitive Therapy

As noted above, limitations do not permit a detailed exposition or treatment guide for cognitive therapy (CT). Beck and Emery's (1985) text addresses that need.* It should be noted as well that there is no substitute for training or supervision in CT if one hopes to be maximally effective in treating this severe and often chronic disorder. Barring an exhaustive treatment description for applying CT to agoraphobia, there are nonetheless aspects of cognitive treatment that might be described to orient the clinician to group treatment of the disorder.

As noted earlier in this chapter, agoraphobia presents a number of cognitive features that merit attention in treatment. These include misattribution of physical signs of arousal and fears of incapacitation, embarrassment or humiliation, loss of emotional or behavioral control, or susceptibility to other adversities, such as choking, fainting, seizure, or death. There is widespread anticipation of panic coupled with a view of the world and of others in terms of danger or threat and a pervasive view of the self as weak, vulnerable, or inadequate.

Beck and Emery (1985) suggest that as an agoraphobic person approaches a phobic situation, he or she engages a mode of thinking associated with extreme vulnerability—perhaps based on the notion that when alone, the client feels vulnerable to immediate medical or emotional incapacitation, which can be remedied if and only if safety (home, doctor, significant other) can be achieved. If such remedies are distant or obstructed, they experience normal physiologic response to threat, for example, symptoms of arousal, which are interpreted catastrophically as a sign that the worst is about to happen. This rapidly escalates further somatic symptoms and anxiety. At sufficiently high levels of anxiety, the client cannot employ normal powers of reasoning to refute exaggerated fears.† At one level, CT must address the distorted beliefs concerning physical symptoms and their interpretation that lead to anxiety (e.g.,

---

*Beck and Emery (1985) and Guidano and Liotti (1983) provide detailed overviews of CT and its application to agoraphobia. Yost, Beutler, Corbishley, and Allender (1986) provide a detailed discussion of group cognitive therapy and its applications, and although their target population is depressed rather than anxious clients, the mechanics of group CT are well described. Coleman (1981) provides an excellent discussion of CT with agoraphobia, together with a discussion of clinical issues, sample transcripts, and self-monitoring forms. A discussion of cognitive issues and relation to behavioral change and generalization in anxiety disorder can be found in Greenwald (1987). Finally, Michelson et al. (1986, in press) provide examples of rationale and treatment overview for the group cognitive treatment of agoraphobia.

Adjunctive bibliographic materials that may be employed include Beck (1976), McDay, Davis and Fanning (1983), and Burns (1979), the last of which, although aimed principally at depression, offers a detailed introduction to CT and presents chapters that relate to a number of common issues among clients with agoraphobia. Yost, Beutler, Corbishley, and Allender (1986) provide a detailed discussion of group cognitive therapy and its applications, and although their target population is depressed (versus anxious) clients, the mechanics of group CT are well described. Coleman (1981) provides an excellent discussion of CT with agoraphobia, together with a discussion of clinical issues, sample transcripts, and self-monitoring forms. Finally, Michelson, Mavissakalian, Marchione, Dancu, and Greenwald (1986) provide examples of rationale and treatment overview for the group cognitive treatment of agoraphobia. Adjunctive bibliographic materials that may be employed include Beck (1976), McKay, Davis, and Fanning (1983), and Burns (1979).

†Thus it is important to recognize, when integrating CT and exposure, that clients are helped to gradually apply these skills in situations of mild, moderate, and severe threat. Furthermore, it may be necessary to help clients choose to lower arousal by means of controlled breathing or PDMR under conditions of high anxiety prior to employing cognitive procedures. See Wilson (1986) for additonal descriptions of anxiety management skills.

does heart pounding mean heart attack?). A second level of cognitive psychotherapeutic work aimed at changing beliefs such as "I must be able to reach help immediately in order to be safe," "I can't tolerate these feelings," "These feelings will escalate into disaster" is warranted. In addition, less explicit beliefs, related to dependency, autonomy, and control, need to be modified (Beck & Emery, 1985).

Guidano and Liotti (1983) suggest that CT proceed in a series of graded steps that approach these various levels of client cognitive organization sequentially. This strategy recognizes clients' high levels of threat associated with tacit emotional material and is respectful of their strong need for control. Early stages of treatment concentrate on more superficial levels of cognitive organization. This approach includes helping clients to appreciate the relationship between ongoing thoughts, emotions, and phobic symptoms and to detach from ongoing thoughts—learning to see ideas as hypotheses that may contain distortions rather than absolute facts about the world. As therapy proceeds, clients are helped to identify deeper cognitive structures, such as basic assumptions or underlying beliefs implied by ongoing cognitions. Ultimately, issues such as those addressed in the "Common Themes" section above may be addressed, including tacit beliefs about others and about the self such as an examination of the developmental circumstances under which such views were acquired.

Thus, therapists are respectful of the client's exaggerated need for control and involve clients actively and collaboratively in learning and applying coping skills in phobic situations in order to achieve success in helping them see themselves as able to deal with situations that were previously avoided. Next, clients are helped to identify underlying beliefs concerning anxiety and to test these through "behavioral experiments" (see Beck & Emery, 1985) accomplished in vivo with the therapist on outings with the group, and during programmed practice. Symptom evocation exercises can be seen as a form of experiment in which clients can test their assumption that, for example, symptoms will invariably escalate out of control. Ultimately, basic assumptions concerning control, constriction, weakness, and related notions about the self and others are elicited and addressed.

CT sessions in the Michelson et al. (1986) and Mavissakaian and Marchione (1987) trials involved this basic approach, and weekly cognitive treatment was readily amalgamated with flooding and programmed practice. Group sessions involved programmed practice review, evocation, CT, and exposure, and sessions continued over a period of 4 months. Early CT sessions acquainted clients with a cognitive model of anxiety and panic and trained clients in identifying cognitive errors, recording their automatic thoughts in phobic or anxiety-related situations, and responding (via Socratic self-questioning) effectively to their automatic thoughts. Responding to automatic thoughts was first modeled by the therapist, and clients received individual weekly attention from the therapist in the presence of the group, focusing on cognitive distortions from the patient's weekly thought record (written log of thoughts that accompanied episodes of anxiety). At this time, the therapist focused carefully on each client's problematic thinking, acting as an alterego and addressing client cognitions via Socratic questioning. Group members had the benefit of witnessing effective CT, participating as the recipient, and serving as an assistant to the therapist in helping other clients challenge their ideas. Toward the midpoint of the therapy, sessions involved aiding clients to identify underlying beliefs and to conduct behavioral experiments to test individual beliefs, such as those concerning their ability to tolerate anxiety, during outings and independent practice experiences. Latter sessions involved uncovering and challenging underlying assumptions and beliefs about the self. Such beliefs may involve control, social disapproval or abandonment, incompetence, and vulnerability or weakness and are likely to involve themes described above.

COMMON ISSUES AND PROBLEMS: GROUP CONCERNS AND SUGGESTIONS

This section offers suggestions for structuring group expectations during the treatment course of agoraphobia, taking into account common client concerns and typical problems. Specific suggestions for structuring client expectations for the course of their recovery and expectations associated with programmed practice for therapist-assisted group graduated exposure and for application of selected cognitive strategies for change will be included.

Graduated Exposure

An important exposure issue involves fear of loss of control or of being forced to do something that a client may believe he or she is incapable of tolerating. Preliminary discussion of overall treatment objectives, coupled with the secure understanding that clients will have complete choice and control in declining any step, is often helpful in allaying fears anticipating the first outing or two. It is also helpful to set appropriate expectations concerning the amount of distress clients may be expected to tolerate. Exposure to high levels of fear for prolonged periods is not necessary for recovery, nor are immediate behavioral forays into highly threatening and strongly avoided circumstances. Clients should be informed that progress will involve many small steps and a gradual approach to situations that involve a moderate or tolerable level of fear.

A first objective involves tolerating increasing periods of uncomfortable (but not overwhelming) feelings, which helps clients to recognize that they can tolerate anxiety and approach difficult situations more capably than they might have predicted. The next objective involves remaining in phobic situations for longer periods to the point of habituation, where phobic anxiety begins to decay, leading to the client's recognition that repeated and prolonged exposure will lead to a relatively predictable and gradual decline of level and duration of phobic anxiety for given situations. The final objective involves seeking out increasingly challenging exposure goals, in a gradual way and in collaboration with the therapist and group, to decrease the social and occupational limitations brought about by phobic avoidance and to test out faulty beliefs about anxiety (what they typically predict will happen as a result of anxiety).

Thus, it is important to normalize and help clients to permit a certain level of anxiety while attempting activities that have been greatly eschewed and to help them see their anxiety in relative terms, for example, "Last week, going into a grocery store was an 8, today it is no more than a 3." Furthermore, clients can help each other to notice measurable gains in distance, diminshed requirements for accompaniment, ability to tolerate distress for increasing periods of time, reductions in time required for anxiety to abate, successful approximations for applying coping skills, and decreases in anticipatory anxiety. Group encouragement can be a valuable assest in helping individuals to recognize their accomplishments. It is important to note that anticipatory fear is the last aspect of the disorder to disappear and tends to persist for a considerable period after in-vivo anxiety declines. Therefore, clients must be encouraged to "push through" their anticipatory fear and determine for themselves the truth of the priciple that "Actual fear is almost never as bad as anticipated fear."

In-vivo exposure is also facilitated by prior practice of coping skills under nonphobic conditions in fantasy and in response to evoked anxiety in group sessions. Discussion of safety factors such as the presence of the therapist, review of mechanisms for coping with anxiety, and availability or help and client choice is likely to be helpful, especially during early outings (e.g., Rachman, 1983).

A final note pertains to therapist response to client symptoms and related distress during outings. Therapists should be sympathetic to a client's distress, but matter of fact, and act patiently to encourage use of coping skills, and assist the client to re-enter the phobic situation, with accompaniment if necessary. Excessive attention to symptoms is counter-therapeutic. Clients should be encouraged to avoid focusing on upsetting ideas, thoughts, catastrophic imagery, or unpleasant physical sensations during exposure and should be gently but persistently directed to remain in the present, involved in current tasks, and asked to apply previously learned skills. Skills can be applied together with the therapist as appropriate. Prolonged discussion of reluctance to enter a given phobic situation is to be avoided. Positive connotation and praise for any approximation to a given goal is essential, and virtually any approach or response should be reinforced. A personal, empathic approach, recognition that a given task is difficult and challenging for the individual, and mutual collaboration for achieving some tiny approximation to approaching a feared situation will often produce a successful outing for a given individual. The therapist should anticipate and expect to respond to patients' strong sense of discouragement and self-blame for difficulty in approaching feared situations and tendency to minimize accomplishments. A careful review of accomplishments following the outing with group discussion directed by the therapist may emphasize individual achievements and minimize "discounting." The group can further encourage members for willingness to enter phobic situations.

Programmed Practice

There are a number of common concerns related to programmed practice. Increases in anxiety and fatigue at onset of programmed practice are frequently seen; these feelings are transient and typically resolve as clients become accustomed to approaching feared circumstances and experiencing anxiety. Clients often ask how to handle spontaneous attacks—they should be instructed in principles for coping with anxiety (see Matthew, Gelder, & Johnston, 1981; Michelson, Mavissakalian, & Marchione, 1985; Michelson, Mavissakalian, Marchione, Dancu, & Greenwald, 1986; Michelson, Marchione, Dancu, Mavissakalian, & Greenwald, 1987). Finally, clients frequently worry about problems with habituation and treatment course. Setbacks, occasional demoralization, and fluctuations in phobic anxiety and avoidance over the course of treatment should be anticipated and discussed with patience and mutual support as these arise.

Many of the same management issues associated with in-vivo graded exposure apply to programmed practice, as both are forms of exposure. A cardinal principle involved in the selection of practice objectives for any form of graded exposure is to select with each client specific objectives that are relatively low in threat at first and that represent a small effort toward exposure that goes just beyond the current level of functioning. An appropriate goal is one the client is maximally likely to succeed at with a minimum of distress. Agoraphobic clients are highly susceptible to discouragement in the face of nonsuccess and must be helped to recognize the necessity of small approximations as a means to build confidence, to attempt small enough steps that are likely to be successful, to credit themselves for their achievements, and to view nonsuccess as a problem to be addressed through smaller approximations rather than as a sign of personal limitation and failure. Thus, if a client has avoided walking unaccompanied for any distance near their home, they might be first invited to walk to a distance of two or three houses away and remain outside for 10 minutes. If this is not attainable, they might be asked to repeat this assignment with a trusted companion or to remain out for the same period at half the distance, while keeping their house in sight.

Sometimes clients experience problems with habituation—they continue to experience severe and continuous anxiety during outings or programmed practice. This is usually associated with inappropriate choices for practice goals (e.g., trying to drive too far during the first week of practice), misguided attempts to "fight" their anxiety, preoccupation with catastrophic thoughts or ideas, difficulty applying coping skills, or extensive focusing on physiologic cues. Individuals experiencing this type of difficulty may be accompanied by the therapist into phobic situations for assessment and coaching during the outings.

Setbacks are commonly a part of recovery and can be minimized by anticipating their potential occurrence and helping clients realize that minor setbacks do not need to influence eventual course and outcome. Severity of symptoms over the course of treatment is likely to vary for a variety of reasons—some connected with individual's psychological themes of life events as described above—and changes in level of fear and avoidance should be examined for precipitating psychological or physiological precursors. From a behavioral standpoint, clients should be helped to continue programmed practice, perhaps at a temporarily reduced level with group and therapist support and pacing, and helped to recover lost territory as rapidly as possible. Loss of morale, pessimism about the future, frustration, and feelings of hopelessness should be patiently addressed with cognitive/psychotherapeutic procedures.

Cognitive Therapy

A precondition for success in CT is understanding the cognitive model and appreciating the connection between thoughts and feelings. If clients cannot recognize automatic thoughts or ideas and their association with anxiety and avoidance, or if their view of their disorder is such that they are unwilling to lend themselves to the treatment (e.g., they believe they have an anxiety "disease"), they are unlikely to become actively enough involved in cognitive treatment to benefit from it. CT relies on an active collaboration for its effectiveness. Thus, client understanding and identification with the model of the disorder as presented during the rationale is important. One way to increase the group's awareness of connections between sensations, thoughts, feelings, and behavioral predispositions involves careful questioning of clients about each of these spheres for a given anxiety experience—either a recent one or a highly salient one. For example, clients may be asked on an outing to describe their sensations, what they are imagining or thinking, how they are appraising their physical sensations, what they are predicting will happen, and what they feel impelled to do. Another method involves the use of imagination and invites clients to describe a phobic experience aloud before the group as an "instant replay" (see Beck & Emery, 1985). The evocation exercises are a rich source of information about the experience of physical sensations, their interpretation, and associated affect and behavioral inclinations. In these exercises, clients are asked to briefly hyperventilate (for example) and describe their thoughts, feelings, and the action(s) that they feel they should take. Automatic thoughts do not appear in well-formed sentences—they may take the form of images, fragments of ideas, or vague inclinations that require further probing from the therapist for further elaboration. Beck and Emery (1985) provide a variety of methods for eliciting automatic thoughts (as well as detailed treatment recommendations).

Clients must be helped to distinguish effective cognitive coping responses from bald reassurance. Cognitive therapy is neither simple positive thinking, urgently telling oneself that one will be OK, nor scolding oneself for being irrational. Effective adaptive responding to anxiety-eliciting automatic thoughts involves thinking like a scientist: adopting an objective stance and patiently examining one's thoughts for distortions, faulty perspective, or arbitrary inference and seeking an alternative view that best fits the facts of the situation. It should be emphasized that this is a skill that requires many hours of practice.

In addition to a stance toward one's ideas that sets out to be objective and problem-focused rather than feeling-focused, the production of effective adaptive responses requires an attitude toward oneself that might be likened to that assumed by a highly supportive, caring friend. When a person is operating from this perspective he or she patiently questions his or her perspective until the situation is examined as accurately as possible. Many patients respond to their automatic thoughts critically and externally and require gentle and persistent encouragement in order to avoid lecturing themselves as a scolding parent would admonish an errant child. The desired "cognitive posture" involves reasoning with oneself, not talking at oneself. It involves examining beliefs and ultimately testing the accuracy of one's own beliefs. Modeling, role-reversal, and role-play before the group are helpful here.

Improvement is experienced in challenging upsetting ideas in the form of an affective shift—a felt shift in the level of emotion associated with the upsetting cognitions. Therefore, self-ratings of level of feeling before and after challenging an automatic thought or series of thoughts may help clients appreciate progress. Clients should not expect to obliterate upsetting feelings by responding to one upsetting idea with one highly effective response. This is by far the exception rather than the rule. Rather, they may do better to anticipate a flurry of automatic thoughts, to respond to these sequentially, and to expect others to arise as they successfully challenge them—as if they could expect to encounter a series of rebuttals (see Burns, 1980). Furthermore, not all upsetting ideas are readily addressed: some involve long-overlearned or deep-seated ideas or beliefs and, in order to resolve them, may require persistent disputation, coupled with extensive behavioral disconfirmation (disproof by behavioral experiment). Others may not be well-enough formed for effective refutation, or the client may not be skilled enough at his or her given stage of treatment to dispute the ideas. In any of these instances, clients should be directed to expect occasional difficulties in coping with upsetting ideas and to utilize the group and the therapist for assistance.

Another issue involves application of skills in phobic situations. Clients need to be prepared to encounter difficulties in applying their CT skills in vivo and to take these in stride as a developmental aspect of therapy. One would not expect highly anxious individuals, who had not been used to thinking adaptively in hundreds of phobic situations, to readily implement effective cognitive strategies flawlessly in highly phobic situations. Human beings simply do not think clearly at extremely high levels of anxiety. Gradual practice in increasingly challenging situations in group and on outings, plus therapist modeling and coaching in vivo, may be helpful. Furthermore, effective coping may require the use of a calming strategy (e.g., PDMR or controlled breathing) *prior* to applying CT in highly upsetting situations.

Morale and attitude toward treatment should be assessed throughout, and client cognitions and attitudes about practicing and applying skills ("Why do I have to do this?" "Why can't I be normal like everyone else?") or attitudes toward treatment ("Treatment is not working" or "will not work," "I'll never change") need to be addressed with cognitive procedures, together with information about treatment course and recovery.

IDEAS FOR SEQUENCING AND COMBINING INTERVENTIONS

The foregoing sections described a number of interventions applicable to the group treatment of agoraphobia. The breadth and scope of a group cognitive-behavioral intervention may seem intimidating to the reader, insofar as orchestration and timing are concerned. This section will offer some brief general recommendations. Although based in part on formats employed in clinical research trials, these suggestions are nonetheless preliminary and are open to adjustment by individual clinicians. The dictates of agency or office practice will impose their own limitations on time and scope of treatment.

Foremost in the treatment package is a detailed rationale presented to the group as described above. Following the pretherapy assessment and orientation, a detailed overview of the disorder and its treatment may be accomplished in one or two meetings of 2 hours duration. Bibliographic materials (e.g., Matthew, Gelder, & Johnston, 1981) may be given out after the first visit and questions addressed at the time of the second rationale visit.

At the time of second visit, clients may be instructed in programmed practice and given detailed assignments to be reviewed within a designated period (e.g., the first 15 minutes) during each of the succeeding sessions. This exercise permits rapid acclimatization to practice and sets the stage for collaboration and goal-setting. Programmed practice and its review should be a consistent element throughout any iteration of treatment.

At this point, treatment may branch in several directions, depending on the predilections and resources of the therapist and available group time: One option would be to initiate group training in CT or CT and PDMR simultaneously, dividing sessions into two halves and training group members in the basics of these skills over a period of approximately eight 2-hour sessions. This approach has proven feasible in clinical research trials, and training in both skills might make sense if the group composition favors individuals who have a strong "loading" on physiologic features of anxiety. After eight visits, training in PDMR would be complete (although it would need to be generalized to phobic situations via coaching during in-vivo exposure), and the treatment program could pursue a course of alternating 90-minute sessions of group outings (in-vivo exposure) and in-office sessions (CT). Once behavioral avoidance is significantly reduced and the therapist is assured that clients are capable of implementing coping skills in vivo (roughly 12 to 16 exposure visits), the group could continue on a CT plus programmed practice basis, with the emphasis in CT on underlying assumptions, themes, and tacit beliefs about the self.

A second option involves treating panic first. This approach divides sessions between evocation exercises (including training in controlled and/or diaphragmatic breathing) and CT and programmed practice review and instructions. Once panic symptoms are well under control, programmed practice assignments may be employed to address behavioral avoidance and CT is continued. Evocation exercises and training in controlled breathing are likely to require 8 to 10 1-hour sessions, and a 2-hour group meeting format could conceivably house all three procedures. A second stage of treatment transpires when panic is effectively treated, with the group sessions divided between CT and programmed practice. Periodic therapist-assisted in-vivo exposure outings would be recommended to ensure that clients can in fact apply their coping skills and are indeed refraining from phobic avoidance.

These are by no means the only permutations of the treatment elements possible. CT and programmed practice alone could be employed as a minimal and arguably sufficient treatment. In any case, the above scenarios provide a range of treatment options.

SUMMARY

Agoraphobia is a chronic and debilitating disorder with an array of complex behavioral, physiologic, and cognitive features. In recent years, clinical research has augmented more traditional therapies with behavioral and cognitive procedures, which lend themselves to administration in small psychoeducationally oriented groups that address the various dimensions of the disorder. Psychological and physiologic procedures for treating panic, achieving reduced visceral arousal, and changing negative expectancies, cognitive distortions, misattributions concerning physical sensations, and underlying beliefs concerning control and other beliefs have been shown to enhance overall outcome in agoraphobia and are described with recommendations for implementation and management.

REFERENCES

Agras, S., Sylvester, D., & Oliveau, D. (1969). The epidemiology of common fears and phobias. *Comprehensive Psychiatry, 10*, 151–156.

Barlow, D. H. (1985). The dimensions of anxiety disorders. In A. H. Tuma, & J. D. Maser (Eds.), *Anxiety and the anxiety disorders*. Hillsdale, NJ: Erlbaum.

Barlow, D. H. (1988). *Anxiety and its disorders: the nature and treatment of anxiety and panic*. New York: Guilford.

Barlow, D. H., & Waddell, M. T. (1985). Agoraphobia. In D. Barlow (Ed.), *Clinical handbook of psychological disorders*. New York: Guilford.

Beck, A. (1976). *Cognitive therapy and the emotional disorders*. New York: International Universities Press.

Beck, A. T. (1976). *Cognitive therapy and emotional disorders*. New York: New American Library.

Beck, A. T., & Emery, G. (1985). *Anxiety disorders and phobias: A cognitive perspective*. New York: Basic Books.

Beck, A. T., Ward, C. H., Mendelson, M., Mock, J., & Erbaugh, J. (1961). An inventory for measuring depression. *Archives of General Psychiatry, 4*, 561–571.

Bernstein, D. A., & Borkovec, T. D. (1973). *Progressive relaxation training*. Champaign, IL: Research Press.

Bowlby, J. (1985). Childhood experience in cognitive experience, In M. J. Mahoney, & A. Freeman (Eds.), *Cognition and psychotherapy*. New York: Plenum.

Brehony, K., & Geller, E. S. (1981). Agoraphobia: Appraisal of research and a proposal for an integrative model. In M. Hersen, R. Eisler, & P. Miller (Eds.), *Progress in behavior modification* (Vol. 12). New York: Academic Press.

Burns, D. D. (1980). *Feeling good*. New York: William Morrow.

Burns, L. E., & Thorpe, G. L. (1979). The epidemiology of fears and phobias with special reference to the rational privacy of agoraphobics. *Journal of International Medical Research, 5*, 1–7.

Chambless, D. L. (1982). Characteristics of agoraphobics. In D. L. Chambless, & A. J. Goldstein (Eds.), *Agoraphobia: Multiple perspectives on theory and treatment*. New York: Wiley.

Chambless, D., & Goldstein, A. (Eds.). (1982). *Agoraphobia: Multiple perspectives on theory and treatment*. New York: Wiley.

Clark, D., Salkovskis, P., & Chalkley, A. (1985) Respiratory control as a treatment for panic attacks. *Journal of Behavioral Therapy and Experimental Psychiatry, 16*, 23–30.

Coleman, R. E. (1981). Cognitive-behavioral treatment of agoraphobia. In G. Emery, S. Hollon, & R. Bedrosian (Eds.), *New directions in cognitive therapy: A casebook*. New York: Guilford Press.

Cormier, W. H., & Cormier, L. S. (1985). *Interviewing strategies for helpers: Fundamental skills and cognitive behavioral interventions* (2nd ed.). Belmont, CA: Brooks/Cole.

Covi, L., Roth, D., & Lipman, R. S. (1982). Cognitive group psychotherapy of depression: The close-ended group. *American Journal of Psychotherapy, 36*, 459–469.

Dushe, D. M., Hirt, M. L., & Schroeder, H. (1983). Self-statement modification with adults: A meta-analysis. *Psychological Bulletin, 94*, 408–442.

Ellis, A. (1979). A note on the treatment of agoraphobics with prolonged exposure in vivo. *Behavior Research & Therapy, 17*, 162–164.

Emmelkamp, P. (1982). *Phobic and obsessive-compulsive disorders.* New York: Plenum Press.

Foa, E. B., Stekett, G., Grayson, J. B., & Doppett, H. G. (1983). Treatment of obsessive-compulsives: When do we fail? In E. B. Foa, & P. M. G. Emmelkamp (Eds.), *Failures in behavior therapy.* New York: Wiley.

Fried, R. (1987). *The hyperventilation syndrome.* Baltimore: Johns Hopkins University Press.

Goldstein, A. (1987). *Overcoming agoraphobia.* New York: Viking.

Goldstein, A. (1982). Agoraphobia: Treatment successes, treatment failures and theoretical implications. In D. Chambless & A. Goldstein (Eds.), *Agoraphobia: Multiple perspectives on theory and treatment.* New York: Wiley.

Goldstein, A. J., & Chambless, D. (1978). A reanalysis of agoraphobia. *Behavior Therapy, 9*, 47–56.

Greenwald, M. (1985). Programmed practice. In A. S. Bellack, & M. Hersen (Eds.), *Dictionary of behavior therapy techniques.* New York: Pergammon.

Greenwald, M. (1987). Programming treatment generalization. In L. Michelson, & L. Ascher (Eds.), *Anxiety and stress disorders: Cognitive-behavioral assessment and treatment.* New York: Guilford.

Guidano, V. F. (1987). *Complexity of the self—A developmental approach to psychopathology and therapy.* New York: Guilford.

Guidano, V. F., & Liotti, G. (1983). *Cognitive processes and emotional disorders—A structural approach to psychotherapy.* New York: Guilford Press.

Jansson, L., & Ost, L. (1982). Behavioral treatments for agoraphobia: An evaluative review. *Clinical Psychology Review, 2*, 311–336.

Levine, F. M., & Sandeen, E. (1985). *Conceptualization in psychotherapy: The models approach.* Hillsdale, NJ: Erlbaum.

Ley, R. (1987). Panic disorder: A hyperventilation interpretation. In L. Michelson, & L. Ascher (Eds.), *Anxiety and stress disorders: Cognitive-behavioral assessment and treatment.* New York: Guilford.

Marks, I. M. (1970). Agoraphobic syndrome (Phobic Anxiety State). *Archives of General Psychiatry, 23*, 538–553.

Marks, I. (1969). *Fears and phobias.* London: Heineman.

Marks, I., & Lader, M. (1973). Anxiety states (anxiety neurosis): A review. *Journal of Nervous and Mental Disease, 156* (1), 3–18.

Matthew, A. M., Gelder, M. G., & Johnston, D. W. (1981). *Agoraphobia: Nature and treatment.* New York: Guilford.

Mavissakalian, M., & Michelson, L. (1986). Agoraphobia: Relative and combined effectiveness of therapist-assisted in vivo exposure and imipramine. *Journal of Clinical Psychiatry, 47*, 117–122.

Mavissakalian, M., Michelson, L., Greenwald, D., Kornblith, S., & Greenwald, M. (1983). Cognitive-behavioral treatments of agoraphobia: Short- and long-term efficacy of paradoxical intention vs. self-statement training. *Behaviour Research and Therapy, 21*, 75–86.

Mayerson, N. H. (1984). Preparing clients for group therapy: A critical review and theoretical formulation. *Clinical Psychology Review, 4*, 191–213.

McKay, M., Davis, M., & Fanning, P. (1983). *Thoughts and feelings: The art of cognitive stress intervention.* Oakland. CA: New Harbinger.

Meichenbaum, D., & Genest, M. (1977). Treatment of anxiety. In G. Harris (Ed.), *The group treatment of human problems: A social learning approach.* New York: Grune & Stratton.

Michelson, L. (1987). Cognitive-behavioral assessment and treatment of agoraphobia. In L. Michelson, & L. Ascher (Eds.), *Anxiety and stress disorders: Cognitive-behavioral assessment and treatment.* New York: Guilford.

Michelson, L. (1985). Flooding. In A. S. Bellack, & M. Hersen (Eds.), *Dictionary of behavior therapy techniques.* New York: Pergammon.

Michelson, L. M., & Ascher, L. M. (1987). *Anxiety and stress disorders: Cognitive-behavioral assessment and treatment.* New York: Guilford.

Michelson, L., Marchione, D., Dancu, C., Mavissakalian, M., & Greenwald, M. (1987). Cognitive-behavioral treatments of agoraphobia: Tripartite outcome of cognitive therapy plus exposure vs. relaxation training plus exposure vs. exposure alone. *Behaviour Reserach and Therapy, 25*(5), 319–328.

Michelson, L. M., Mavissakelian, M., Greenwold, D., Kornblith S. & Greenwald, M. (1983). *Cognitive-behavioral treatment of agoraphobia: Paradoxical intention vs. self-statement training.* Paper presented at the Annual Meeting of the Association for the Advancement of Behavior Therapy, Los Angeles.

Michelson, L., Mavissakalian, M., & Marchione, K. (1985). Cognitive-behavioral treatments of agoraphobia: Clinical, behavioral and psychophysiological outcome. *Journal of Clinical and Consulting Psychology, 53*, 913–925.

Michelson, L., Mavissakalian, M., Marchione, K., Dancu, C., & Greenwald, M. (1986). The role of self-directed in vivo exposure practice in cognitive, behavioral and physiological treatments of agoraphobia. *Behavior Therapy, 17*, 91–108.

Miller, R. C., & Berman, J. S. (1983). The efficacy of cognitive-behavior therapies: A qualitative review of the research evidence. *Psychological Bulletin, 94*, 39–53.

Munjack, D. J. & Moss, H. B. (1981). Affective disorder and alcoholism in families of agoraphobics. *Archives of General Psychiatry 38*, 869–871.

Myers, J. K., Weissman, M. M., Tischler, G. L., Holzer, C. E., Leaf, P. J., Orvaschel, H., Anthony, J., Boyd, J. H., Burke, J. D., Kramer, M., & Stolzman, R. (1984). Six month prevalence of psychiatric disorders in three communities: 1980-1982. *Archives of General Psychiatry, 41*, 959–967.

Norton, G. R., Allen, G. E., & Hilton, J. (1983). The social validity of treatments for agoraphobia. *Behavior Research & Therapy, 21*, 393–399.

Rachman, S. (1983). The modification of agoraphobic avoidance behavior: Some fresh possibilities. *Behaviour Research and Therapy, 21*(5), 567–574.

Rachman, S. (1984). Agoraphobia: a safety-signal perspective. *Behaviour Research and Therapy, 22*, 59–70.

Rachman, S., & Wilson, G. T. (1980). *The effects of psychological therapy.* Oxford: Pergammon.

Rose, S. (1977). *Group therapy: A behavioral approach.* New York: Prentice-Hall.

Salzman, L. (1982). Obsessions and agoraphobia. In D. Chambless, & A. Goldstein (Eds.), *Agoraphobia: Multiple perspectives on theory and treatment.* New York: Wiley.

Sank, L. I., & Shaffer, C. S. (1984). *A therapist's manual for cognitive behavior therapy.* New York: Plenum.

Suinn, R. M. (1977). Treatment of phobias. In G. Harris (Eds.), *The group treatment of human problems: A social learning approach.* New York: Grune & Stratton.

Weekes, C. (1979). *Simple, effective treatment of agoraphobia.* New York: Bantam.

Wilson, R. R. (1986). *Don't panic: Taking control of anxiety attacks.* New York: Harper & Row.

Yost, Y. B., Beutler, L. E., Corbishley, M. A., & Allender, J. R. (1986). *Group cognitive therapy: A treatment approach for older depressed adults.* New York: Pergammon.

16
Group Interventions with Traumatically Head-Injured Adults

Traumatic head injury is an insult to the brain, not of a degenerative or congenital nature, but caused by an external physical force, that may produce a diminished or altered state of consciousness, which results in impairment of cognitive abilities or physical functioning. It can also result in the disturbance of behavioral or emotional functioning. These impairments may be either temporary or permanent and cause partial or total functional disability or psychological maladjustment (National Head Injury Foundation, 1986, p. 3).

The incidence of head injury victims in the United States has reached epidemic proportions. The National Head Injury Foundation in 1983 reported that there are 50,000 new cases of head injury each year contributing to a "silent epidemic." Paul Chance (1986) notes that 300,000 Americans survive injuries that cause significant brain damage and states that a conservative estimate is that 15% of these patients enter rehabilitation programs that are specifically designed to meet their many needs. As a consequence, the rehabilitation community is faced with a tremendous challenge in meeting the needs of this population.

Life may be permanently and substantially altered for the individual who has sustained an injury and for the patient's family members. The specific effects of traumatic head injury are numerous and varied and affect physical, cognitive, and social functioning. Following the acute phase of recovery from injury, during which time the question of survival is the primary issue, concern over the future quality of life of the survivor becomes paramount. It is during this period that the magnitude of potential problems from the brain injury becomes apparent.

The patient may demonstrate a range of deficits depending on the specific nature of the injury and the portion of the brain injured. Deficits in physical functioning may include paralysis, deafness, visual problems, impaired coordination, and the loss of senses such as taste and smell.

The most significant changes in the person who has experienced a head injury are those that affect cognitive and social functioning. Almost all brain injuries result in deficits in concentration and memory; in addition, impaired attention, thinking, oral and written communication skills, and psychological adjustment frequently occur. Cognitive deficits are not generally apparent from intelligence test scores. For example, a person with an IQ of 120 may not be able to remember what happened the previous day in a college course.

Very often, a patient who may be 1 or 2 years postaccident can be found to be at home leading an isolated and unproductive life if he or she has not had adequate rehabilitation. Family concerns and stress can be very high as the patient's problems mount. Furthermore, the patient may not be ready to work or to attend an academic program due to residual cognitive and social deficits. Deficits in the cognitive areas mentioned above, as well as dramatic losses in confidence and self-esteem due to changes in life circumstances and functional abilities, may still exist. Social skill deficiencies such as impulsivity, passivity, aggressiveness, egocentricity, and lack of empathy, tact, and sensitivity may also be present. The social skill problems, when combined with the cognitive deficits, create many problems in everyday functioning and the attainment of vocational goals.

The duration of the rehabilitation process generally ranges from 2 to 5 years. The rehabilitation process consists of a goal-oriented, interdisciplinary approach designed to reinforce individual patient strengths and deficits. The approach emphasizes the systematic development of new skills and the use of existing skills. There is an emphasis on the development of new, compensatory strategies that lead to greater independence of functioning.

During the assessment phase in a rehabilitation program, the scale that is most often used to measure the cognitive status of the patient is the Ranchos Los Amigos Scale (Hagan, Malkmus, Durham, & Bowman, 1979). This scale measures from "Level I," where the patient is comatose, to "Level VIII," where the patient is totally alert and generally independent in functioning. A summary of the functions corresponding to each level is presented in Table 16–1 and is used as a reference point in this chapter.

Cognitive rehabilitation begins at the trauma center with basic sensory stimulation experiences, such as showing the patient photographs of friends and family and playing music, at Levels I through III. Inpatient rehabilitation activities occur at Levels IV through VII, while outpatient cognitive rehabilitation occurs at Levels VI through VIII.

RATIONALE FOR GROUP TREATMENT

There are certain advantages to group approaches as opposed to individual retraining and therapy with brain-injured adults, especially in the areas of social behavior and cognitive functioning. The group setting provides support, a decreased sense of isolation, and a source of identification. As noted (after the trauma and acute phase), most head trauma patients are not working and are home-bound. Very often, old friends and extended family members have stopped visiting and the patient is leading a very narrow and restricted life. Immediate family members are still adjusting to changes in the head trauma victim, and there is usually considerable tension in the home. Since the inception of the injury, hospitalization and changes in life status lead to a prevailing sense of anomie and isolation. The group experience often results in a sense of relief and support in finding a commonality of experience with similarly traumatized patients. As group members realize that they share much in common with others, their sense of being burdened with head trauma dissipates, and they find courage in not being the "only one."

Groups can be very helpful in allowing head-injured patients, who are typically young adults, to resume previous social roles with each other and in providing a platform to try out cognitive and social skills in a supportive environment. Hollahan, Marshall, and Lloyd (1981) demonstrated that group instruction is more effective than one-on-one instruction with learning-disabled children and that marked improvements were seen in the students' ability to attend to tasks and to concentrate. The benefits of group interaction are also reflected in work with head-injured populations.

Understanding when certain behavior is inappropriate is valuable feedback that the impulsive head-injured patient can receive. Getting a sense of how one comes across socially

TABLE 16–1
Ranchos Los Amigos Hospital: Scale of Cognitive Functioning

Level	Cognitive Functions
I	No response—Patient unresponsive to stimuli.
II	Generalized response—Patient reacts inconsistently and nonpurposefully to stimuli. Responses are limited and often delayed.
III	Localized response—Patient reacts specifically but inconsistently to stimuli. Responses are related to type of stimulus presented, such as focusing on an object visually or responding to sounds.
IV	Confused, agitated—Patient is extremely agitated and in a high state of confusion. Shows nonpurposeful and aggressive behavior. Unable to fully cooperate with treatments due to short attention span. Maximal assistance with self-care skills is needed.
V	Confused, Inappropriate, nonagitated—Patient is alert and can respond to simple commands on a more consistent basis. Highly distractible and needs constant cuing to attend to an activity. Memory is impaired with confusion regarding past and present. The patient can perform self-care activities with assistance. May wander and needs to be watched carefully.
VI	Confused, appropriate—Patient shows goal-directed behavior but still needs direction from staff. Follows simple tasks consistently and shows carryover for relearned tasks. The patient is more aware of deficits and has increased awareness of self, family, and basic needs.
VII	Automatic appropriate—Patient appears oriented in home and hospital and goes through daily routine automatically. Shows carryover for new learning but still requires structure and supervision to ensure safety and good judgment. Able to initiate tasks of interest.
VIII	Purposeful Appropriate—Patient is totally alert and oriented and shows good recall of past and recent events. Independent in the home and in the community. Shows a decreased ability in certain areas but has learned to compensate.

can lead to behavior change. An increased sense of personal confidence and security is achieved as group members try out various behaviors. The group can be used as a stage to attempt various roles and to get immediate feedback from other members, as well as support for trying out new behavior.

OVERVIEW OF GROUP APPROACHES

There are a variety of types of groups used with head-injured patients. These include psychotherapy groups, occupational therapy groups, recreational groups, self-help groups, and cognitive and social retraining groups.

Usually, psychotherapy groups are open-ended in that patients may enter as inpatients, continue as outpatients, and use the group as long as needed. These groups usually meet weekly for 1 to 1½ hours and the patients involved are typically moderately to mildly impaired (Levels VI, VII, and VIII of the Ranchos Scale). Psychological adjustment problems are the focus of psychotherapy groups. Personal problems ranging from marriage difficulties, sexual problems, and suicidal feelings are all part of group discussion. Overcoming problems and making progress becomes a source of inspiration for group members. Prigatano (1985) suggests that it is useful to prepare a list of topics to be discussed in group psychotherapy with brain-injured patients, and he lists 24 topics that provide both stimulation and structure, such as conflict resolution between family members, family members' perceptions of the patient before and after the head injury, and ways to handle a job interview.

Occupational therapy groups usually have a task-oriented focus in order to integrate daily functional skills such as meal-planning, decision-making, financial budgeting and balancing, and use of maps and public transportation. Patients can help define functional goals related to living at home and work, such as balancing the checkbook and filling out job application forms correctly. Developing compensatory techniques for a poor short-term memory through the use of a "memory book," "weekly scheduling book," or countercheck methods can also be developed in the occupational therapy groups. Group members exchange ideas and techniques they have found helpful to improve deficit areas.

Recreational therapy groups provide structured and purposeful recreational activities that enhance the development of both cognitive and social skills. The recreational activities themselves provide a format for learning appropriate social skills. These groups include such activities as playing games, going out to dinner, shopping trips to malls, and sporting events. Planning and organization, decision-making, and enjoyment of simple pleasures are part of the cognitive and social gains.

Cognitive Rehabilitation

In the last decade the rehabilitation of the brain-injured person has gone through major changes, moving from a simple model that typically consisted of physical, occupational, and speech therapies to a more sophisticated model that deals with cognitive and affective deficits. In the 1970s a number of rehabilitation programs began to address the higher cortical dysfunctions. The Institute of Rehabilitation Medicine at New York University Medical Center, The Brain Injury Rehabilitation Unit at Veterans Administration Medical Center (Palo, Alto, California), the Community Hospital of Indianapolis, Braintree Hospital (Braintree, Massachusetts), and the Greenery in Boston are but a few of the dozens of programs now in existence (Lynch, 1987).

The introduction of group therapy as a modality is primarily attributed to Ben-Yishay's and colleagues' work at New York University (Ben-Yishay, Diller, Gerstman, & Gordon, 1979). Today, group therapy as a modality for cognitive retraining is part of all major rehabilitation efforts in medical centers and private practices with brain-injured adults.

Cognitive rehabilitation is the process of remediation and reteaching of intellectual and social skills to traumatically brain-injured adults. This process begins with a diagnosis performed by multidisciplinary team members in order to determine the strengths and weaknesses of each patient following the assault to the brain. A common pattern of deficits would include problems in variable attention and concentration, decreased speed of information processing, long- and short-term memory (visual and auditory), impaired abstract reasoning ability, slower reaction time, lack of attention to details, problem-solving deficits, poor organizational skills, and sequencing difficulties. In addition, there are often specific academic deficits in the areas of reading, spelling, and mathematics and an overall impairment in rote memory and capacity for new learning. In terms of social protocols the patient may reflect a tendency to be impulsive, rigid in thinking, perseverent in discussion with themes being repeated, egocentric in orientation, lacking in empathy, and illogical in thinking. Some patients may be very labile emotionally, anxious or depressed. Irritability and low frustration to tolerance are typical. Impulsive behavior is a particular problem that readily becomes manifest in a group setting; people interrupt each other, start up separate conversations, talk of the topic in an egocentric manner, or become totally irrelevant. Other patients may be overly aggressive or too passive in their interaction.

Cognitive rehabilitation is a systematic attempt by mulitidisciplinary team members to remediate these deficits and to capitalize on patient's strengths and skills. Much of the training is aimed at teaching compensations for the deficit areas. Teaching compensation techniques is the most expeditious way of helping brain-injured adults (Prigatano, 1985). The overall goal is to return the patient to a functioning level in terms of everyday activities and eventually to return to productive work, school, or further vocational training.

In the acute phase of rehabilitation of the traumatically brain-injured adult, the team has a diagnostic picture of the patient's strengths and weaknesses and a plan aimed at remediating deficit areas. For example, if a patient has a short-term memory problem, each team member would expect the patient to know his or her name and discipline, assignments given the previous day, their daily schedule, and other events of the hospital day. If the patient acted impulsively by interrupting others, the team member would focus on this and reward noninterruptive behavior. Cognitive and social retraining on an individual basis permeates each activity in which the patient is involved.

Cognitive and Social Retraining Groups

The use of groups to facilitate the rehabilitation process can occur at both the acute and the outpatient phases of recovery. Most often, cognitive and social retraining groups are utilized after discharge from the inpatient unit. The patient may continue as an outpatient in physical, occupational, and speech therapy and enter a group for cognitive and social retraining. The introduction of group therapy as a modality for interaction is coordinated with and complements individual therapy. Once the acute phase of recovery is over, the patient typically is ready for group work. He or she has usually made enough progress to profit from a group reference.

Cognitive retraining is most effective in a group setting because it provides a format that is both secure and competitive (Carberry & Burd, 1984). The natural competitiveness between people is capitalized on to provide an incentive for the achievement of goals. The group leaders encourage competition by statements such as, "Let's see who can remember the most facts from yesterday's session" or "Who will take the risk of going first in this task?"

The openness of the group members about their deficits allows other members to be open in a way not possible in a one-on-one session with a team member. The group members also provide immediate feedback about performance. Comments like "You're rambling," "You really expressed that clearly," or "You're missing the main idea" serve as an impetus for self-improvement. Videotaping of the group is also an excellent form of feedback. Patient's are asked to make a formal presentation of a short article on effective listening. Their presentations are videotaped and critiques are then offered. At other times, an hour of group interaction may be taped and group members will be asked to critique their participation and behavior. A criterion for the critique is developed by group members and a grade is given.

Group cognitive and social rehabilitation most often occur concomitant with individual occupational, language, and physical therapy. The multidisciplinary team approach in rehabilitation settings is closely coordinated, and the total approach is one of a group of professionals working toward the recovery of functions of the traumatically brain-injured adult.

The cognitive and social retraining group developed at Our Lady of Lourdes Medical Center runs for 6 months, and the group meets from 9 to 12 hours per week. Two occupational therapists meet with the group for 4 weeks, and therapists from the psychology department conduct the group sessions for the remaining 5 months. Remedial reading and math specialists, as well as vocational counselors, are consulted as needed. As noted, patients typically are also having individual occupational, language, and physical therapy. Group treatment is also supplemented with individual and family counseling.

GROUP FORMAT AND LEADERSHIP

Cognitive and social retraining on an outpatient basis usually occurs 6 months to 1½ years postinjury. As noted, the typical patient begins the recovery process in a trauma center and, after emerging from coma (Levels I and II), is transferred to a hospital inpatient rehabilitation setting when stabilized. Inpatient hospitalization may last between 10 and 12 weeks. The patient very often enters the group cognitive and social retraining immediately after discharge from the inpatient rehabilitation program.

Typically, a cognitive and social retraining group includes a maximum of eight patients and two co-therapists. The patients are required to have a measured intelligence quotient of at least 80 and need to have language skills. A number of the patients have ongoing physical problems and some use wheelchairs. Reading skills need to be at least at the fourth-grade level, although exceptions have been made to this rule if other strengths exist (e.g., good verbal ability and a high level of motivation).

The atmosphere established in the group is one of a quasiacademic setting where the members are seen as students rather than patients. After a long period of hospitalization, it is important that patients begin to see themselves as persons with handicaps rather than as handicapped patients. Ideally, the physical setting should be out of the hospital in order to deemphasize the "patient" role.

Many of the group members have low self-esteem as a result of the trauma and changes that have occurred. Many of the patients are depressed and negative about entering the group either because they do not see themselves as having problems or because they feel totally overwhelmed and helpless about their problems. Depression is common. An atmosphere of unity and cohesion soon emerges among group members with an existential, philosophical position that strongly suggests, "We are all in this together; let us see what we can do." The creation of this type of atmosphere is remarkably effective in lowering defenses and creating an open, warm atmosphere that allows for positive and constructive criticism.

A considerable amount of time is devoted to creating this atmosphere. The spirit that hard work and struggle will pay off in the future is encouraged by the group leaders. A common goal is the patient's return to work or college and the skills necessary to achieve these goals. Patients are asked early in the program to list those skills that they need to perform in order to return to work. Initially, this list is simple in format, but as the group continues, a more sophisticated job analysis is done. For example, if one group member is a claims adjustor for an insurance company, he would list ordinary and special skills required, that is, telephone conversation, remembering details of policies, filing, simple mathematics using a calculator, organizing the work day, and so on. This type of analysis increases individual motivation and makes the group program more relevant.

Group issues including confidentiality, trust, dominance, resistance, withdrawal by a group member, attendance, lateness, and inappropriate and egocentric behavior are all grist for the dialogue that ensues. Time is also taken for group counseling sessions that deal with personal issues ranging from assertiveness to sexual problems. Flexibility must be extended so that affective and personal concerns are processed as they emerge in the group, and yet limits need to be set since it is not primarily a counseling group but a retraining group.

Patients in the group learn simple elements of theories such as rationale-emotive theory, behavior modification, assertiveness training, communication skills, and effective listening, which lend themselves to a self-exploration and discussion of personal problems. For example, if a group member is a perfectionist that does not allow risk-taking, Ellis' approach can be most helpful (Ellis & Harper, 1961). If a patient has a child whose behavior is disruptive, he or she can learn techniques to change this "undesirable" behavior by applying the principles of behavior modification. If a patient has a problem with confidence and is either too passive or too aggressive in interpersonal relationships, the curriculum dealing with assertiveness training can be most helpful.

Cognitive and social retraining is most usefully implemented with co-therapists. Considerable structure is needed in the program, and each day needs to be well planned and organized in order to help the patients who tend to be impulsive and disorganized. The patients also need to be confronted with their deficits and strengths since, initially, there is a great deal of denial.

Denial of deficits with brain-injured adults seems to have both an organic and psychological etiology. During the period of coma and the pre- and postamnesia, the patient's experiences also seem to contribute to denial of changes. The denial often takes the form of "My memory was never good" or "The only problem I see is my balance and coordination." The trauma of loss and differences is often so great that major vocational and social changes are inevitable. This inevitability seems to cause the defense of denial. In the group, denial is dealt with by slowly building on strengths and self-confidence and by slowly presenting evidence when tasks cannot be accomplished. There is a constant weaving back and forth between confrontation and support.

The patients also need to have a great deal of support in coping with their immediate life experience, as well as support in learning new material and facing the changes that have occurred and will continue to occur in their lives. They feel guilt about what caused the accident or events in their past lives for which they feel they are being punished. They may be angry at God because they feel they didn't deserve this accident. Also, someone may have been killed in the car when the accident occurred and friends may have deserted them because they are now different. Sexual and social problems may have emerged. Issues about body image and feelings that they are less attractive are common topics in the group. These are typical concerns of many of the patients who are typically young (average age 23) and just beginning their adult lives.

Many patients report that friends and family treat them like children, attitudes that generate feelings of resentment. At times patients report being impulsive and make inappropriate comments. The embarrassment of losing the thread of their own or others' conversation is also a relevant theme.

The therapist's ability to remain within the structure of cognitive and social retraining, and yet help patients work through their personal adjustment problems, takes considerable skill. The majority of patients in the group are also in individual counseling. In the course of a 9-hour week (3 hours per day; 3 days per week), at least 1 ½ hours is spent discussing the concerns mentioned above within the group. At times this is planned and structured; at other times the issues develop spontaneously.

Family involvement is critical in attending to the many needs and problems that surface during this period of rehabilitation. Families are seen on a regular basis as a supplement to the cognitive retraining program. The traumatic injury cannot be forgotten, and the therapist needs to expect that periods of depression, sometimes accompanied by suicidal ideation, intense frustration, and anxiety are natural consequences of the upheaval of the patient's life.

In the cognitive and social retraining group, it seems to be effective if one therapist acts in a more directive, structured manner with high expectations of group members. The co-therapist can then be the more supportive, understanding, and caring person who is more in tune with the emotional needs of the patient. The dual role of cognitive trainer and emotionally supportive therapist is extremely difficult for one therapist and leads to considerable stress.

Regular consultation between the co-therapists is essential to the smooth running of the group and in increasing the awareness of each in terms of patient needs and performance. The norm is to formally consult with the co-therapist for at least 1 ½ hours per week. Typically, the co-therapists meet at the half-hour break to discuss the direction the group is taking and the focus needed for the second hour.

Establishment of a Therapeutic Atmosphere

The therapist's initial task is to create a secure, accepting environment that allows for the relaxation of the patient's defenses in order to help overcome the denial of cognitive and social deficits. As noted above, brain-injured patients characteristically deny that anything is wrong with them cognitively, although there is an easier acceptance of visible physical disabilities. Attempts to cover up memory problems or to see little difference in problem-solving or reasoning ability are not unusual. Personality changes such as temper outbursts, a tendency to perseverate on the same theme, and impulsivity are also difficult for the patients to see in themselves. Unless patients look at their differences, they will not successfully come to grips with the changes necessary for growth. Hope becomes the prevailing atmosphere of the group, and hope can be contagious.

The therapist's primary task is to develop an atmosphere that is empathetic to the patient's life situation and feelings of vulnerability and, at the same time, to be confrontive enough to reduce the denial so that change can take place.

Patients need a secure format where they have an opportunity to model, practice, and refine behaviors necessary for effective functioning. They need to learn and practice these skills without feeling that they are a failure. The fear of embarrassment or loss of self-esteem are critical considerations. The ability to laugh at oneself seems to be a useful part of the group atmosphere. The therapist can model humor with his or her own behavior. Working with brain-injured patients is not suitable for the perfectionistic, defensive, or humorless therapist. The therapist needs to create an atmosphere of experimentation in which nothing is lost by making a mistake, but something may be lost by not trying.

Trauma can be totally overwhelming, but even the trauma of a changed life can be seen in perspective and new life and values can emerge.

An atmosphere of reality testing and feedback should also be provided. The group format provides an opportunity to test how one is perceived by others. There are many opportunities for feedback that occur within the 6-month period the group is together. The individual deficits and strengths of group members are recognized; agendas are set to work on different factors such as attention/concentration, perseverent rambling, rigidity of thought, confusion in thinking, memory problems, and lack of persistence at a task. The group members themselves become adept at giving feedback once this is modeled by the co-therapist. Feedback from group members is strongly encouraged and seems to have considerable meaning because of shared experiences. Manipulative group members, who are using their handicap to avoid responsibility, are easily confronted by other group members. Group members have a potency that the therapist does not. The therapist can facilitate the sharing of these experiences at a deep empathic level that eventually leads to group cohesiveness. Therapeutic strength can often come directly from the energy that the group emits in its interactions with each other, facilitated by the therapist. Too often we, as therapists, overlook this. The group can be both rewarding and confrontive, and inter-action breaks down rigid stances and encourages more flexible modes of thinking and the idea that there may be more than one answer.

The feedback is given in the spirit of both competition and caring that helps the patient overcome the egocentricity, sadness, and feelings of helplessness and hopelessness. This feedback is sought in daily sessions, and definite criteria and guidelines are sug-gested. Most exercises, presentations, and summaries made by group members are then critiqued by the group. The process is one that establishes ongoing goals of progress and achievement interspersed with definite appreciation for the difficulty of achieving the tasks involved.

Group Curriculum and Methods

The group experience is broken up into segments or modules, and the group members' tasks are to achieve goals in each module. The use of modules is modeled after the work of Ben-Yishay who along with Leonard Diller is a pioneer in the field of cognitive retraining (Ben-Yishay & Diller, 1983). There is certainly overlap from module to module, but for purposes of teaching in a more systematic manner, modules are introduced.

Patients are distractible and need intensive training in attention and concentration to auditory and visual material. Great emphasis is placed on this module, which is presented early in the program and continually reinforced. Short-term memory is also reinforced throughout the group process, as will be seen later in the chapter.

To train attention and concentration, notebooks are required and daily note-taking is strongly encouraged. A midterm and final exam are given as motivation to take extensive notes. A course manual that breaks the program down into weeks and goals is given to each group member. This manual also contains reading material on the information covered. The material covered is presented in a highly structured, step-by-step, outlined fashion that is often repeated. Information presented one week is reviewed the following week, and group members are responsible for this. A cumulative collection of facts and ideas is developed over time. For example, on any one day, a group member may be asked the name of any other group member along with three or four informational facts about the person that have been presented in the first week of class. An example of this type of information would be "I'm John Smith. I am 22 years old, a lab technician, and I live in Beverly, New Jersey." As the group progresses, each group member systematically adds and compiles factual information about every other group member and is accountable for this information at any time during the 25-week process and on the midterm and final examinations.

Cognitive and social retraining also involves training for generalization from the group experience to real life situations. Generalization is achieved primarily through the medium of homework. One homework assignment might be to have the group member recall as many of the details of a dinnertime conversation and to report on it the following day in the group. Members may also be given phone calls to make at certain times to reinforce their sense of accountability. For example, they may be asked to call the group leader just to say hello at 9:00 a.m.

A master chart for all the theories and ideas is developed by group members to use as a summary of course content. Group members fill in this chart as they proceed in the program. As each new concept and theory is introduced, the patient's task is to summarize key words and phrases and to enter this material in the master chart in preparation for course exams and future personal reference.

In the "attention/concentration" module, which obviously includes short-term memory, one of the group leaders presents a chronological history of his or her life, including information such as date of birth, name and date of high school, college and graduate school attended, date of marriage, ages and names of children, spouse's name, and perhaps work history. A compilation of approximately 50 to 70 facts are listed, depending on the level of the group, and the task for the patients is to remember as many as possible. Midway through the program, group members make up their own historical chronologies and present them for memorization. Mnemonic devices, connecting themes, visual associations, grouping according to categories, sequential dates, and logic are all used as memory aids. Suggestions as to how to improve memory are explored.

As noted, patients who are in the cognitive and social retraining group are outpatients who have already reached a certain cognitive level in their rehabilitation (Levels VII and VIII). Lower-level groups receive the same material, but the presentation is simpler and the process is considerably slower. I have found that the basic model and content being presented can be used with groups at a variety of levels, but modifications need to be made constantly to meet each group's need, and there may be a greater need for one-on-one instruction in occupational and speech/language therapy with lower-level groups.

The primary goal of group work with brain-injured adults is retraining and remediation of cognitive and social skills as well as processing the affective concerns of the patients. In order to integrate these goals, the subject matter for the group sessions is very important. I have found, through experimentation over the past 5 years, that the use of psychological theory as content is effective because the material lends itself to the discussion of affective concerns as well as interpersonal exploration (Carberry & Burd, 1985).

One of the primary problems with existing remediation techniques for adult head-injured patients is the childlike quality of some of the content used in cognitive remediation, as well as the saturation effect of continued and tedious practice to develop increased skills in attention/concentration, abstract reasoning, problem-solving, and memory tasks. Computer programs are also used in the program as a supplement to the group training. Individuals in the group often have one-on-one training on the computer with their occupational therapist. However, the group experience with the emphasis on interaction and verbal skills is seen as the most effective learning modality because it most accurately reflects real life situations and the generalization effect is much easier to train in a group.

Group Strategies and Techniques

Strategies and techniques that may be used by the group therapist to remediate cognitive and social skills are discussed in the following sections.

Role-playing.   In this simple psychological technique, patients are asked to play a variety of roles. Examples of role-playing situations are listed below:

1. An interview with a potential member for the cognitive and social retraining program to assess eligibility for membership
2. A job interview
3. Self-assertion in a visit with a medical practitioner who does not provide enough time to ask questions
4. Playing the role of a "teacher"

The list of worthwhile role-playing situations is endless, but it is important that they be relevant to group member concerns.

Teaching.   After reading, outlining, and digesting various short articles on listening, behavior modification, and improving memory, students are required to teach what they have learned to the rest of the group. The expectation is that the "teacher" will be able to handle questions, differences of opinion, and criticisms. This technique has obvious and valuable cognitive retraining components and requires social skills such as being sensitive and empathetic to others, relating to intellectual and social differences between the group members, and being the center of attention in a comfortable way. These skills can all be learned through practice, behavioral rehearsal, and cuing. Generalization to other group and social situations is emphasized as much as possible.

Presentation of self to group.   With this technique, the patient is either given or develops a guideline for a particular topic and presents this to the group for feedback. For example, topics may include "My Strengths and Weaknesses" or "My Vocational Goals." Again, a full array of cognitive and social skills are involved in such a presentation.

Storytelling techniques.   With this technique, the students are shown an ambiguous photo (e.g., a small boy sitting on a step) and asked to tell a story using an organizational guideline that is journalistic in nature (e.g., who, what, where, when, how, and why). Each group member's story must be different. Creativity is stressed to avoid rigidity of thinking as well as to build the ability to entertain different hypotheses. Again, following each story, a critique by other group members is offered. This technique can be enhanced by having group members deal with interruptive tasks during the exercise or by remembering previously given lists of digits, words, or abstract categories, depending on what the previous cognitive tasks were. Organizational skill development is the primary focus of this exercise.

Empathy-building tasks.   Throughout the program, members are queried as to what other group members might be feeling when they are discussing group issues, problems, or concerns. These queries are done systematically in an attempt to break down egocentric behavior. In addition to this basic and natural technique, the students are read paragraphs dealing with emotional situations and are asked to identify the feeling components involved. In the "Storytelling Technique," the feelings of the hero are explored.

There is a great deal of emphasis placed on developing empathy, which is emphasized in a number of problem-solving tasks such as "preparing and going for a job interview." Students are asked to empathize with both the interviewer and the interviewee. Daily events from newspaper accounts may be utilized. The group members are asked to discuss the feelings that could be experienced by the principal persons of the news report and various type of readers.

Counseling. In this technique, the members attempt to role-play a counselor. Another member role-plays a patient with a problem. The task of the counselor is to apply his or her "theory" in a sensitive and helping way in his or her interaction with the counselee. Advanced group members are expected to make an attempt to apply the different theories that have been taught in the program.

Task analysis points to a wide array of relevant social skills that are involved, such as the ability to listen, empathize, give support, and display sensitivity, tact, and warmth. At the same time, the patient must utilize many complex and high-level cognitive skills. This technique is attempted at the end of the 25-week program and is seen as the culmination of the social skills module.

Group curriculum. The remainder of this chapter discusses how a variety of psychological theories and ideas can be used in cognitive and social retraining as part of the 25-week curriculum.

Attention and concentration. In the early phase of training of auditory and visual attention and concentration, an article on effective listening is used by having the patients first commit the ten points of how to be a good listener to memory, review them as a group, present them individually in the role of "teacher" to the group, and then practice with each other. Each step of this process is first modeled by leaders.

The group listens to presentations of members and then offers feedback using the following guidelines:

1. Was it relevant? Did the person stick to the topic?
2. Were all points covered?
3. Did the person present in an appropriate and interesting manner?
4. Was the presentation clear?
5. Were examples used to illustrate ideas and concepts?
6. Was rapport between the groups and the speaker established?

At a later point in the 25-week program, this listening exercise is amplified by introducing a brief article on obstacles to effective listening and going through the same procedural steps as outlined above. Amplification is also made in terms of sensitivity to body language as another form of communication. At a later point, a Rogerian listening exercise is introduced emphasizing empathy, asking questions, clarifying through reflection, and nonjudgmental acceptance of the listener. This exercise is particularly effective in modifying social behavior.

The basic model for (1) attending to the material, (2) memorizing the material, (3) discussing the implications, (4) teaching the material with group feedback, and (5) applying the material in role-playing with other group members is followed with each of the content areas included in the program. A number of cognitive and social skills are involved in the critical aspect of information processing and generalization that occurs in the group setting. Homework assignments (e.g., listening to a family member for 5 minutes using techniques of questioning, clarification, and empathy) are given and reported on in the follow-up group sessions. This approach is helpful in teaching the patients to generalize.

The group leader facilitates generalization of cognitive and social skills by having group members talk about their difficulties in listening, how it feels not to be listened to, why being listened to makes you feel valuable and important, and how being a good listener can help you in a variety of life situations and interpersonal relationships. Specific problems in listening are explored with the group, along with ways of compensating if someone has problems in attending and concentrating. For example, if a group member mentions that he or she has difficulty in attending and concentrating on a speaker, it might be suggested that that patient actively ask questions as opposed to passively trying to concentrate. Another group member could paraphrase what the speaker was saying as a way of intensifying concentration.

Opportunities are provided for group members to be group leaders. Material on guidelines for leaders of small groups is used as a model. In this didactic presentation, which is accompanied by a handout on the role of the leader, attitudes of the group leader and goals are discussed. The patients are exposed to the concept of facilitating attitudes such as accurate empathy, nonauthoritarianism, warmth/acceptance, and responsible confrontation.

To help with the organization of thoughts, a criterion for critiquing the patient who plays the role of the group leader is given to the members. After each role-play of a group leader, feedback is offered such as:

1. Did the group leader clarify the problem?
2. Did the group leader get people to listen to each other?
3. Did the group leader have people respond to each other?
4. Did the group leader have everyone participate equally?
5. Did the group leader ensure that group member contributions were relevant to the problem?
6. Did the group leader get patients to summarize and reach a consensus?

During these exercises, the emotional reactions of the group members are discussed openly. For example, members are asked how they felt about playing the role of group leader and how they felt about the feedback, their fears, and anxieties. They are also asked how similar experiences could occur in their everyday home or work situation and the value of seeking feedback from others.

Abstract reasoning and problem-solving. This area receives a great deal of emphasis in the cognitive and social retraining group, and remediation of deficits in the area begins with relatively simple exercises that require members to categorize, analyze, and interpret proverbs. The group might be given the proverb "Strike while the iron is hot" and be asked to interpret it. Patients with difficulty in abstract thinking might interpret the proverb quite literally by saying, "If you have a hot iron, it will bend easier than if it is cold" or "Hot irons are easier to mold." A more abstract answer would be "Take advantage of a situation when it presents itself."

Categorization exercises are also introduced to promote abstract reasoning. Examples of a categorization exercise would be:

A.   What would the best category for Book-Professor be?
B.   Add another item that is like "A" _____.
C.   Add an item that is similar but unlike "A" _____.

Group members may also be asked to develop a category system for movies, videocassettes, sports, or music. The goal of these exercises, again, is to train the group members in conceptual thinking and the ability to distinguish between concrete/literal and abstract thinking.

In the presentation of Rational-Emotive Theory (Ellis & Harper, 1961), the basic premise is that our perceptions or interpretations of events determine our emotional reaction to them. This concept provides much opportunity for discussion and encourages flexibility of thinking, empathy, logical thinking, and abstraction skills. Application of this theory to specific case situations involves flexibility in going from concrete to abstract levels of thinking. The ability to understand how people's emotional reactions to the same event can vary is a level of thinking that is difficult for many brain-injured patients.

Once the group has mastered the basic concepts in Rational-Emotive Theory, they are introduced to the idea of distorted styles of thinking. This concept is explained as an illogical and unreasonable habitual mode of thinking that human beings develop in the process of being exposed to their environment. Fifteen styles of distorted thinking (McKay, Davis, & Fanning, 1981) are presented in a handout and explained in class. Examples of these illogical modes of thinking are as follows:

1.   Filtering: Taking the negative details and magnifying them "while filtering out all positive aspects of the situation."
2.   Shoulds: Having a list of ironclad rules about how people should act. "People who break the rules anger you, and you feel guilty if you violate the rules."
3.   Global labeling: Generalizing one or two qualities in "a negative or positive global judgment."

The dovetailing of cognitive and personal problems may be explored in almost any of the fifteen listed styles of distorted or illogical thinking. An example would be "Should." In this distortion, one operates from a list of inflexible rules about how people should act. The rules are right and indisputable. Any deviation from a particular standard is bad. Since many of the patients are struggling with increased rigidity of thinking, this "style" has particular relevance. Psychologically, this reaction seems to be related to an increased defensiveness concerning diminished intellectual skills. There is a clinging inflexibility to certain values like "people shouldn't act that way," "I should be totally self-reliant," or "I should never get angry."

When the theory of behavior modification is introduced, a simple model of antecedents and consequences for the undesirable behavior is explained. It is pointed out to the group members that rewards are most effective if given immediately following a desirable behavior. Behavior needs to be seen as changing step-by-step over time with each step being rewarded. The idea of a continuum is used to explain how behavior can be shaped.

The value of presenting this simple model of behavior modification theory is that it provides a systematic model for thinking and analyzing problems and changing behavior. Typically, when a problem is presented, group members give immediate, impulsive solutions to the problem. The group is encouraged to do a step-by-step detailed interview analysis to obtain all the pertinent information and then make recommendations within the context of the behavior modification theory. Most of the members are fairly impulsive or rigid in their thinking, and this exercise of systematic behavioral analysis demands a slow, well thought-out process. Considerable time is spent on this theory for the problem-solving aspect inherent in behavior modification as well as for the personal self-discipline involved.

Generalization of what is learned in the group in respect to the patient's life at home is critical if the group program is going to be a success. Consequently, patients are asked to present problems from their own lives. Each patient is requested to present a problem that could be handled using the behavior modification approach and to do a detailed analysis to discuss with the group.

Other aspects of the curriculum presented in the cognitive and social retraining program are as follows.

The SQ3R study method. This study method is aimed at increasing reading comprehension. The student is asked to survey a chapter, turn the chapter headings into questions, and then read to answer the question, close the book, recite the answers, and finally review the entire chapter. The mnemonic device of SQ3R is explained and used as a memory aid.

This material is helpful to the group members in learning an approach to studying as well as enhancing and developing organizational skills. The structure of the SQ3R approach is helpful in allowing the patient to select the main idea from irrelevant details, a task that is difficult for many traumatically brain-injured adults.

Progressive relaxation. In addition to the cognitive skills involved in this task, the patient is learning the technique that is used to reduce his or her own anxiety level and muscle tension. Individual relaxation tapes are given to each group member for home practice. Following the mastery of progressive relaxation, the group is introduced to the concept of visual imagery as a means of enhancing and deepening their state of relaxation.

Jacobson's method of progressive relaxation is given in a condensed form as a homework assignment to read (McKay, Davis, & Fanning, 1981) and present in class. This is followed by playing a relaxation tape to which the group listens and experiences. The final step with this material is to teach it via role-play and have the group practice the relaxation procedure themselves.

Assertiveness training. Assertiveness training is also included in the curriculum. The concepts of the aggressive-assertive and passive personality are presented both verbally and with printed handouts. Definitions of each are given, and the desirability of assertiveness is the focus. The passive and aggressive personalities are seen as individuals who have difficulty when others are critical of theme. Techniques to deal with criticism are also presented (McKay, Davis, & Fanning, 1981).

Role-playing is used extensively in this part of the curriculum. The group is asked to make discriminations between valid and invalid criticisms and appropriate techniques to use. How to be assertive in social and sales situations are role-played and practiced, and the group norm becomes an expectation that assertive behavior is healthy and appropriate. As group members master this material, they are then asked to role-play counselors at the "Assertiveness Training Clinic."

Family styles. A section of the curriculum enjoyed by the group members is a taxonomy of family styles (Parnell, Hill, Carberry, & Burd, 1982). Four family styles are presented:

1. Overprotective: The family that does too much for the patient and doesn't allow for development of individuality. Too much protection results in feelings of anger and resentment as well as feelings of inadequacy.
2. Underprotective: The family that tends to deny problems and issues. They overlook dangers and allow too much freedom and too few limits.
3. Disorganized: The family that has very little structure and no definite rules or role for family members. The results can be chaos and lack of stability.
4. Scapegoating: The family that tends to resolve conflicts by blaming each other. Nothing is resolved by blaming and problems are actually avoided, thus serving a purpose.

The effect on personality development given these stereotyped family styles is discussed, and the group is asked to speculate on what makes up a healthy family. The group's task is to learn the material and then present it to the other group members in a lecture format. Group discussion revolves around the style of their family and how this style has helped or hindered their rehabilitation. Group members are also asked to discuss their family of origin and how this has had an effect on personality development.

Curriculum, of course, needs to be flexible enough to meet the needs of a particular group. The therapist needs to be creative and flexible and to develop new material to meet the goals of the individual's rehabilitation needs. Time spent on any one part of the curriculum is related to group mastery and, as always, the level of the group itself.

SUMMARY

This chapter on group interventions with traumatically head-injured adults emphasizes the high incidence of brain-injured patients in the U.S. and the need for treatment modalities including cognitive and social group retraining. The effect of traumatic brain injury is devastating to the patient and family; the patient's life is changed and is never the same again. An injury to the brain most often results in a disruption of the functioning of the brain and in the consequent behavior and intellectual processes. Part of the brain can be damaged and destroyed; connections between the brain, senses, muscles, speech, memory, and thinking can be mildly to severely disturbed.

Cognitive rehabilitation through the group method is the means and process through which a person with brain injury is taught to relearn some of the skills lost as a result of the head injury. "Cognitive" refers to those aspects of intelligence such as attention, concentration, memory, complex thinking, planning, judgment, problem-solving, and the ability to attend to ideas and tasks simultaneously.

Cognitive retraining consists of a number of tasks and exercises aimed at improving the above-mentioned deficit areas. Short-term memory is a common deficit. Cognitive retraining asks the question, "How can we improve this person's memory so that he or she can function better than at present?" Teaching the person to use a daily journal and using different sensory modalities and repetitious memory task training are but a few of the techniques that can be systematically taught. Teaching patients how to compensate for their memory problems is a major emphasis.

The advantages and use of group work with traumatically brain-injured adults is discussed in detail with focus on support, a secure environment, a competitive/confrontive atmosphere, and an opportunity that provides reality testing and personal feedback. The use of groups with a traumatically head-injured patient population is discussed with emphasis on level of the patients, the type and kind of groups available, and development in this relatively new field.

Specialized interventions in group work are discussed with an emphasis on the use of psychological theories as content that serves the purpose of cognitive retraining, social retraining, self-exploration, and behavioral change. The structure of the cognitive and social retraining group is highlighted, as is the group format, use, and dynamics of co-therapists and leadership skills. Specific examples of curriculum content, purposes, and goals are discussed with an emphasis on flexibility and creativity to meet individual patient needs. A guide is provided for the readers to borrow from this structure to develop their own programs.

In conclusion, group work with traumatically brain-injured adults is seen as a field of expertise that is relatively new. Cognitive and social retraining in groups is seen as an approach with a great need for professional exploration, experimentation, and research.

REFERENCES

Ben-Yishay, Y., Diller, L., Gerstman, L., & Gordon, W. (1979). Working approaches to remediation of cognitive deficits in brain damage. Supplement to *Seventh Annual Workshop for Rehabilitation Professionals*, New York University, Institute of Rehabilitation Medicine.

Ben-Yishay, Y., & Diller, L. (1983). Cognitive remediation. In M. Rosenthal, E. Griffith, M. Bond, & J. D. Miller (Eds.), *Rehabilitating the head injured adult* (pp. 367–380). Philadelphia: F. A. Davis.

Carberry, H., & Burd, B. (1984). Social aspects of cognitive retraining in outpatient group setting for head trauma patients. *Cognitive Rehabilitation, 2*(5), 5–7.

Carberry, H., & Burd, B. (1985). The use of psychological theory and content as a media in the cognitive and social retraining of head injured patients. *Cognitive Rehabilitation, 3*(4), 8–10.

Chance, P. (1986, October). Life after head injury. *Psychology Today*, p. 62.

Ellis, A., & Harper, R. (1961). *A guide to rational living.* Hollywood, CA: Wilshire.

Hagan, C., Malkmus, D., Durham, R., & Bowman, K. (1979). Levels of cognitive functioning. In *Rehabilitation of the head-injured adult: Comprehensive physical management.* Downey, CA: Rancho Los Amigos Publications.

Hollahan, D. P., Marshall, K. J., & Lloyd, J. W. (1981). Self-recording during group instruction: Effects on attention to task. *Learning Disability Quarterly, 4*, 407–413.

Lynch, W. J. (1987). Neuropsychological rehabilitation: Description of an established program. In B. Caplan (Ed.), *Rehabilitation psychology desk reference* (pp. 299–321). Aspen Publication.

McGonagle, E., Carper, M., & Balicki, M. (1983). Greenery: An integrated approach to cognitive rehabilitation of the head injured patient. *Cognitive Rehabilitation, 1*(4), 8–12.

McKay, M., Davis, M., & Fanning, P. (1981). *Thoughts and feelings.* New Harbinger Publications.

National Head Injury Foundation. (1986). *The silent epidemic.*

Parnell, S., Hill S., Carberry, H., & Burd, B. (1982). *Head trauma family guide.* Camden, NJ: Lourdes Press.

Prigatano, G. P. (1985). *Psychotherapy after brain injury for neuropsychological rehabilitation after brain injury.* Baltimore: John Hopkins University Press.

17
Caring for the Body While the Brain Dies: Group Experiences for Caregivers of Alzheimer's Disease

This chapter will briefly review some dominant themes and values in our culture that influence caregivers. In addition, it will describe the topics that tend to come up in groups of caregivers and will suggest some of the taboo subjects that perhaps we should be gently raising. Recent findings will then be presented based on the literature, my experiences conducting such groups, and experiences of other group leaders in this field. Finally, some questions about what we are currently doing in groups will be raised, as well as the political and policy implications of conducting groups for caregivers of persons with Alzheimer's disease. Suggestions will be made for other possible models of group intervention for this population.

It is our brains that makes us so distinctly human. When the brain of a loved one goes seriously awry, most people are more devastated by this than when any other part of the body malfunctions. This fact alone makes group therapy with Alzheimer's disease (AD) patients quite unique. If a person becomes paraplegic but still has normal brain functions, we can attempt our usual emotional and intellectual contact and have some promise of connecting with the person we know. But in dementias or other serious brain diseases, we lose touch with the person we knew, which is massively upsetting to all concerned. We see this in the painful reactions of family members, and we see it reflected in our society as a whole.

It goes without saying that family caregivers of AD victims often come into therapy groups having undergone dreadful, long-term, and unyielding stress. It is not surprising, then, that group sessions are often painful and difficult. It is hard to extract comfort from a comfortless situation.

Because of the high levels of sadness and anxiety caused by caring for people whose brains are dying and whose bodies will inevitably follow, group leaders also feel frequent stress. Their stress is surely not as painful as that of the caregivers, but it is a force to be reckoned with. What sometimes happens to us as group leaders is that in attempting to handle our own anxieties about loss, grief, and dying, we look for neat packages or stages of coping. We want the comfort of known or predictable patterns of behavior, but we may have to give up the notion of finding any such thing.

The single most important thing I have gleaned from both experience with groups and the literature is that we run the risk of not listening well the minute we believe we "know" the answers. As one caregiver stated: "Professionals don't have to listen to us. They learned all the answers in school." If we can drop the idea of stages or predictability, we can then concentrate on what is being said and perhaps not being said. Usually the most helpful experience that can result from human contact is the feeling of truly being heard and under-stood—even when there are no solutions. To feel less lonely and isolated, connected and un-derstood by someone else is probably the most important variable in any group.

CULTURAL THEMES

In order to help caregivers within a group setting, we need to understand some of the dominant cultural themes that may intensify their burdens. For example, gerontologists in the U.S. seem to favor a positive view of family behavior, a "Norman Rockwell" idealization of the family, with the end result that family conflicts over the care of the elderly tend to be seen as individual psychological problems, rather than as deficiencies in our culture and in our government's policy of nonhelp. While individual psychological problems do of course exist, we have a culture that says the family is sacred and that we should lovingly care for the aged, but at the same time the government withholds services that would be helpful in making this possible. The main concern of governmental programs now is cost containment and efficiency. That is clearly not enough.

Caregiving for an AD patient can be a lesson in experiencing powerlessness and failure through the inability to save a loved one. It is also a reminder of one's own helplessness to eventually save oneself. In addition to our North American idealization of the family, we place a very high priority on affection. Jarrett (1985) wrote a very useful article (for both professionals and family members) called "Caregiving Within Kinship Systems: Is Affection Really Necessary?" In this article he recommends a caring that is given from motives of kin-ship obligations rather than affection. You do not have to necessarily feel affection, too, he says.

The implication here is that an overemphasis on affection has led American society to expect that closeness can and should form a basis for caregiving. The problem here, however, is that closeness dissipates under the strain of intensive long-term care. Shifts in life circumstances and different developmental stages may also require rebalancing or shifts in relationships. Just as *intense* bonding is good during infancy but is dysfunctional as a child grows older, so it may be that closeness and deep affection between caregiver and spouse or parent may be problematic rather than helpful toward the end stages of life. Perhaps a certain emotional distancing on the part of the caregiver helps him or her to last longer in the caring role.

Another cultural theme is that loving closeness is always a good emotion to feel. But Cantor's (1983) findings show that high stress diminishes closeness. Attempts by caregiving children to create psychological distance between themselves and their frail parents helped them to meet the instrumental demands involved. When Cantor looked at caregiver strain, she found that several variables played a role and that by far the most important one was the relationship to the carereceiver: the closer the bond, the greater the strain. Spouses of AD victims were the group at greatest risk, followed by children. The other variables were the degree to which the caregiver worries, attitudes about family, and the sex of the caregiver—females had a harder time and were less able to set caregiving limits than males. The more caregivers feel that family is sacred, the higher the strain.

It is a mistake to believe, as many caregivers are taught to do, that the progress of the patient depends on the caregiver's behavior. Caregivers can and should set limits on how

much of themselves they will give to their family member. These limits refer to the behaviors they will tolerate, the time and energy they will invest, and the extent to which they
are willing to suppress their own needs. Given our cultural theme about the virtues of closeness and love, however, limit-setting often evokes guilt in caregivers.

Caregivers need to shed a rescue fantasy that in part has been nurtured by professionals. It is
grandiose for family caregivers to believe they can alter a phenomenon as awesome as AD. They
need to try and make life more comfortable for themselves as well as the AD victim.

Brody (1985) asks: "Why the persistence of the myth that adult children nowadays do
not take care of their elderly, as in 'the good old days?'" (despite repeated research to the
contrary). It is very important to understand the myth because of its power to inhibit constructive practice and policy approaches—as well as induce guilt in caregivers. Its vitality,
the myth, lies at a deep level related to the dependence/independence issue. At some level,
says Brody, we all harbor an expectation that the devotion and care given by the young
parent to the infant and child should be reciprocated at the end of life's spectrum. But this is
impossible. An incontinent, toothless 90-year-old is not the same as a cute, toothless incontinent infant!

The myth persists because the guilt persists. That may be one reason, says Brody, so
many adult children are overwhelmed with guilt at nursing home placement—it is experienced as the ultimate failure to meet the parent's needs as that parent met the child's
needs in the "good old days." And the myth persists because at its heart is a fundamental
truth: adult children cannot and do not provide the same total care to their elderly parents
that those parents gave to them in their infancy and childhood. The roles of parent and child
cannot be reversed in that sense. Over and over again we hear from adult children, "I know
I'm doing everything I can for my mother, but somehow I still feel guilty." The fantasy is
that "somehow" one should do more.

We have a culture that says the family is sacred, and affection and devotion are the
necessary concomitants with which to achieve this sacred family. Combining this with caring
for an AD victim for years frequently makes for serious psychological troubles. Many
caregivers feel anger, fear, helplessness, frustration, grief, exhaustion, and isolation. These
emotions seldom go hand-in-hand with feelings of affection and devotion. At best, they can
exist side-by-side and with conflict. Consequently, we have a pretty impossible situation
built in for caregivers. In some ways it is our cultural norms that need to be taken into consideration when we work with caregivers.

Given these cultural themes, what can we do to be helpful in group counseling? This
helping can be done in a very straightforward manner by opening up to discussion the various themes of idealization of the family, the high priority put on affection and unending love,
and the myth that we do not take care of our loved ones as in the "good old days." Group
members surely do understand this and seem eager to hear about what research has to say
about these topics. The research findings of Cantor (1983), Brody (1985), and Jarrett (1985)
legitimize some of their negative feelings, thereby diminishing some of their guilt. More
about this is discussed in this chapter.

GROUP THEMES

There are themes or topics that tend to come up frequently in groups of caregivers of
Alzheimer's disease. The number one theme always centers around information about the disease
and its treatment, so education is the number one need in groups. Interestingly, a question often

asked is: "Do you know a good attorney?" While the main concern of group psychotherapy from the leader's point of view may be emotional support and insight, we must always keep in mind that caregivers need education, information, and good legal advice.

Other themes also surface quite frequently. For example, people want management techniques for their patient. Group members come up with an infinite variety of coping and management skills for night-wandering, bathing, getting lost, eating in a restaurant, social situations, removing car keys, and so on. Equally important, group members exchange different ideas for coping with the unending frustrations, fatigue, grief, resentment, exhaustion, and fears that go along with caring for AD patients. Not only is there a wonderful exchange of coping ideas, but there is also great comfort in feeling less alone and in feeling understood.

Social isolation is a theme that arises frequently in groups. People vary a great deal in their social circumstances, all the way from those who are totally isolated except for the group meetings to those having a large supportive network of people. The more isolated a person, of course, the harder it is for that person in most cases.

Guilt—the feeling that one can never do enough—is a topic always on the surface, as well as all layers in between. Closely tied to this is the recurrent theme of nursing home placement. For many, this step represents the ultimate failure in caregiving and is described as a very traumatic event. Again, the variation in how people deal with this is enormous and is tied to so many variables: finances, religion, number of available people to help, values, past relationships, availability of good nursing homes, and so forth. Each person has to struggle through this one. Ideally, the group can provide comfort, support, and different options to explore during this long and often arduous process.

Legal and financial issues are major concerns for many, for example, how to handle money, write out wills, and provide for the future. Another issue is whether to use all available medical technology to keep a person alive when it looks as if he or she might die without medical intervention.

Genetic fears are often expressed: "Will this happen to me?" or "my children?" It is helpful to mention what available statistical data we do have at our disposal, since the statistics are not bad in most cases. If a person has a 10% chance of developing AD, it still leaves him or her the option of focusing on the 90%.

Relationship concerns are a constant theme in group sessions. Generally speaking, the worse their relationship to the AD patient was prior to the diagnosis, the harder the time they are having now. Relationships to other family members and friends can also get quite complicated under the stresses of long-term caring. Philosophical issues are brought up. "Why me?" is often expressed. The meaning of life is questioned. Deeply religious people appear to have less trouble with this.

There are a few other problems that, if not unique, are very common to caregivers of AD patients. One of the worst is being in a situation of unending and one-sided giving. This situation tends to set up a vicious circle of guilt, because one can seemingly never give enough—followed by resentment and anger, which spirals into more guilt, and so on ad infinitum. Social isolation exacerbates this situation. In fact, all of these issues interact with each other. Caregivers of AD patients have a terribly difficult time of it.

TABOO THEMES

Before discussing some of the best ways of handling these painful subjects as they come up in group, brief mention will be made of a few themes that seem to be taboo for many and do *not* come up easily—if at all. When *gently* mentioned by the leader, however, these taboo areas create considerable discussion. Hepurn and Wasow (1986) state:

> Some areas of concern seldom appear in the literature. (That does not mean they are never discussed in groups, nor does it imply that they should be.) Are we overlooking some key stress points for caregivers because they are taboos in our culture? If so, should we respect these taboos or gently open up some of them for discussion? (p. 89)

Five issues particularly come to mind: sexuality, preparation for the caregiver's life after the death of the victim, permission for divorce for financial reasons for those who may wish to do so, encouragement to give up care before becoming emotionally, physically, and financially depleted, and the right to death and issues of resuscitation.

Sexuality

What happens in the sexual arena during those months or years before diagnosis and after diagnosis? Just as problems in many areas of functioning that eventually lead families to seek answers and diagnoses occur, we assume that problems also arise around sexuality. We do not really know if these problems have left damaging scars on caregivers, or if opening up the issue of sexuality for discussion might help people to feel less alone, less freakish, and perhaps relieved. Similarly, we do not know whether and to what extent sexuality between caregiver and victim remains a viable and important source of comfort and intimacy, at least in the early stages of the disease.

Preparation for the Caregiver's Life
After Death of the Victim

We know very little about what a widow or a widower of an AD victim has to cope with after the spouse's death. Such knowledge might give professionals direction in helping caregivers plan ahead in their lives. The National Hospice Care Organization recognizes the difficulties people experience after the death of a loved one, particularly the troubles that can be anticipated with seriously unresolved grief or guilt. For this reason, the organization stays in contact with families for a minimum of 1 year after the death of a relative. In many ways, a loved one's dementia is worse for caregivers than a loved one's death. Perhaps groups for AD caregivers should offer continuing support after the death, as well as before. In either case, bringing up the subject of "What will you do after (the relative) dies?" seems to be important. Some people feel awkward about broaching the subject but join in on the discussion once someone else raises it.

Permission for Divorce

The financial drain on families with dementia victims is dreadful. In many cases, divorce could prevent this because a divorced spouse can hold onto personal savings. Should we gently offer this as an option for those who are interested? I think this can be sensitively done without offending people or their values.

One could say, for example: "There is a way to avoid losing all your savings. The law is sure strange, but if you got a divorce, then you do not have to spend all of your savings on (the spouse's) care. A divorce does not have to alter your feelings or behaviors—it is merely a way of hanging onto your savings. It's peculiar, isn't it!? Well, if the idea appalls you, forget it; if it has some interest, we can discuss it further." This is a gentle approach that offers people the option of looking at both ends of the continuum.

Encouragement to Give Up Care

As one writer put it: "The vow 'till death do us part' is a promise, not a life sentence. There is a need to organize, advocate and educate so that [spouses] can have rights as well as duties and a life of fulfillment for their own remaining years" (Colman, Sommers, & Leonard, 1982, p. 4). This issue raises a dilemma of cultural values: who is more important, the dementia victim or the caregiver? We need to find a better balance between victim's and caregiver's needs. Some caregivers need help to give up total care before they themselves become victims of total depletion and exhaustion.

The Right to Death

This issue is now beginning to be raised in our culture, and it brings with it a host of anxieties, conflicts, and strong beliefs. Few people feel neutral about this subject. The reality is that the need to resuscitate often arises with dementia victims. We are aware of the legal complexities surrounding this issue, complexities that vary from state to state. Whatever the issues of a particular jurisdiction, it will be easier (both emotionally and legally) for caregivers to deal with this issue early in the disease process than it would be during an emergency. Groups can provide excellent information and support for caregivers facing this issue. Unspoken words so often carry with them a terrible burden; by creating a safe environment in which to discuss these issues, perhaps we can diminish their negative power.

One helpful approach to this topic is to invite a guest speaker, usually a lawyer or medical ethicist, who can describe the state laws. The general approach can be: "Here is what the hospital policy (or state law) says. The ultimate decision is yours, however, and for some it is not an easy one. Still, it might be easier for you to give it some thought in the relative calm of this group meeting, rather than have to cope with it in an emergency room at 3:00 a.m."

THE EFFICACY OF GROUP PSYCHOTHERAPY FOR AD CAREGIVERS—SOME FINDINGS

Serious emotional stress tends to develop when grief is intense, prolonged, and largely unresolved. This is particularly true when caring for someone dying of AD. AD creates dreadful burdens for caregivers, the grief tends to be compounded with anger and guilt, and our culture gives no formal recognition that the caregivers are grieving. There are no rituals or opportunities to grieve "normally" during this long, devastating illness. If nothing else, groups can provide a legitimate place to grieve: a place where people are among their own and know they are understood. This in and of itself is therapeutic.

The literature, my direct experience, and the experiences of other group leaders confirm the therapeutic importance of being with others who share a similar experience, the value of sharing coping skills, and the helpfulness of the educational component of groups. Understanding what the disease is, how it progresses, and how it affects the behavior of both AD victim and caregiver is critically important for caregivers. It reduces panic, stigma, and self-blame, and it usually enhances coping skills for all concerned.

One of the more interesting dichotomies surrounding group therapy is the issue of therapy versus support; they are two separate phenomena that often get mixed in conducting groups for caregivers. We need to understand more clearly when to use which one and why. Under what circumstances is it best to provide unconditional emotional support, and when is it better to focus on psychological insights into feelings and behaviors? When should we step back and respect resistances to negative feelings, and when should we gently try to understand and move beyond them?

There is a difference of opinion among group leaders regarding these issues. Some group leaders (Barnes, Riskind, Scott, & Murphy, 1981; Lazarus, 1981; Schmidt & Keyes, 1985; Wasow, 1986) contend that an understandable resistance to negative feelings arises: "They described a group defense against individual expression of anger and grief" (Wasow, 1986, p. 94). To shatter that defense might overwhelm the group. In some ways this makes sense, for what is to be gained, after a certain point, from acknowledging negative feelings about a terrible, unremitting situation with no solution? The other side of the picture is that ignoring these feelings may deprive all members of the opportunity to rage, grieve, and grow in the process of struggling (Schmidt & Keyes, 1985).

In 1985 Schmidt and Keyes tested the previously held notion that the expression of anger and grief was potentially dangerous. Their approach (encouraging the expression of strong negative feelings) did not appeal to everyone and there was some resistance, but many others benefitted. However, this group therapy was offered in conjuction with individual therapy. It may be that the individual therapy is a very important variable here. They suggested that a therapeutic approach in which the therapist encouraged expression of painful emotion, in addition to helping the caregiver develop problem-solving approaches, was superior to a group-only approach. They reported improvement in terms of reduction of psychiatric symptomatology and positive changes in caregiver–relative relationships.

Winogrond, Fisk, Kirsling, and Keyes (1987) found that as caregivers shared their stresses and gained acceptance of their negative feelings, they became better able to separate feelings of burden and low morale from their upset over patient behavior. However, they also reported resistance to therapy and insight, particularly around the stressful impact of too much information about the horrors of the illness before they were ready for it. (When is anyone ever "ready" for such information?) As Winogrond et al. (1987) note: "Perhaps separate programs for more and less functional patients and their caregivers is an option to be explored" (p. 339). If we could have separate groups for caregivers of beginning and more advanced stages of the illness, we could deal with the information that is most appropriate for each group.

So what conclusion can we draw from these conflicting reports about therapy versus support, all based on small group samples? Two thoughts come to mind. First, the obvious: group members are different, leaders are different, and you never know what the mix will be. The second thought is the importance of proceeding with *caution*. A respectful, competent, kind leader can and probably should gently push toward insights even when they are terribly painful. If the leader is gentle and skillful, he or she will know when to back off. A group will not deal with that which they cannot handle. Unless people are inappropriately forced to grapple with painful emotions, they have pretty good protective skills at denying and avoiding—and these defenses should be respected.

There are some interesting issues concerning group composition that need to be considered in therapy. At present, most groups are composed of both men and women. Brody (1985) suggests that men and women have internalized different models of caregiving based on their different life experiences. Females have an internalized model based on the parent-infant roles, which permits very little satisfaction in caring for an AD victim. Males might have a different model, derived from the work setting, where they learn skills of delegation of responsibility and recognition of limitations. Male involvement may be more discretionary, perhaps making their life somewhat less stressful regarding caretaking.

In the few general surveys that explored male–female caregiving differences, women have reported greater stress than men (Miller, 1987). They also reported higher levels of depression and mental deterioration of their own. The results of the study by Fitting, Rabins, Lucas, and Eastham (1986) were similar. Once again, since most family caregivers are women, we are talking about relatively small numbers of men.

Sex is by no means the only variable that needs to be considered in group composition. Age, relationship between patient and caregiver, amount of support available, living arrangements, religion, educational level—all need to be considered. The importance of heterogeneity among caregivers is being increasingly recognized. We must constantly be on guard against categorizing people and keep uppermost in our minds that individuals are different.

There are at least three major dilemmas with respect to group composition: (1) Is it better to mix spouses, siblings, and children together in one group or to keep them in separate groups? (2) At present, most groups have members whose relatives have just begun to deteriorate, whose relatives are at the end stages of the disease, and whose relatives are at every stage in between. Is it helpful to have this degree of diversity or does it unnecessarily complicate groups? (3) Should newcomers and experienced group members be mixed or separated?

On the issue of mixing spouses, siblings, and children together, it is my sense that it would be more effective to keep them separate. First, losing a parent is very different from losing a spouse or a sibling. For example, we expect to lose our parents eventually, but not our children and often not our siblings or spouses. Spouses may be more dependent on each other than siblings are, and so forth. Second, some caregivers—usually spouses—are responsible for primary care and are with the AD victim full time. Siblings and children often are not primary caregivers. The implication here is that the discrepancy in terms of the degree of emotional involvement, love, and dependency between three groups may be so huge that it is inappropriate to handle the situation in a group as if it were the same for everybody. To lose a sibling might be sad but not terribly disruptive to one member's life, whereas losing a spouse may feel like the end of the world to another. These differences are apparent to group members and often lead to feelings of resentment or apology.

Mixing caregivers whose relatives are at different stages of deterioration from AD raises other issues. Those who have relatives in the beginning stages of the disease may be frightened as they hear tales of what lies ahead for them. Those whose relatives are in the end stages may feel envy, boredom, or even contempt as they listen to those who they believe have it much easier than they do. As mentioned earlier, separate groups for caregivers of beginning and more advanced stages of AD would be the logical solution here.

Finally, we must recognize that caregivers' feelings change over time. There are the years of deterioration and upset before diagnosis, the crises of diagnosis, and the years of coping with progressive deterioration, institutionalization, and death. With group members, all in different stages of this lengthy process, it does make for very different needs and problems among the caregivers.

An ideal would be to separate out some of these variables; that is, separate groups for men and women; separate groups for beginning, middle, and end stages of the disease; or separate groups for siblings, spouses, and children. The reality of the situation, however, is that except in cities with very large populations, this is unlikely to occur. The aim, then, should be to enhance learning and comfort between group members. People can get a lot of satisfaction by giving to others and by exchanging ideas from different perspectives. However, a critical factor in more heterogenous groups is that the leader needs to be cognizant of the differences noted above.

POSSIBLE NEGATIVE EFFECTS OF CAREGIVER GROUPS

Are there possible negative outcomes in group therapy for caregivers? As Steuer says, "While we know little about the positive effects of these groups, we know almost nothing about the negative effects of these groups" (Steuer, 1984, p. 57) When Steuer collected data, she found that some members reported they felt more depressed, anxious, and hopeless after meetings, while others said they felt increased anger and confusion after meetings. This was also my clinical observation (Wasow, 1986). It is conceivable that constant focusing on the problems of AD, in addition to living with it day in and day out, is counterproductive. Perhaps it would be more therapeutic to have some kind of recreation on a regular basis. As one caregiver put it: "I live with this problem 24 hours a day. Then on Mondays I go through the bother of getting a sitter to get out of the house for a few hours, and what do we discuss here: AD! I'm sick of it."

Are there limits to focusing on problems of this magnitude? We assume that focusing on and ventilating one's feelings usually facilitates coping and that catharsis is helpful. But do we know if it might sometimes create just the opposite effect? How about the possible differences in the immediate and long-term effects of focusing on problems? We have all had the experience of feeling much better after a total escape from problems—and the realization that there is more to life than the major problems on which we have been focusing. It is not clear that we know exactly when and under what circumstances focusing on problems is helpful, and when it may not be.

We also need to do a better job of screening individuals who join therapy groups. Some people do not benefit from groups. An individual with a severe hearing loss does not function well in a group and creates frustrations for everyone else in the room. Some people get too easily lost in a group or do not have the strengths or skills to operate in one. A person who is not very intelligent, mixed in with brighter people—what happens to him or her in such a group? We need to offer alternative treatments for those individuals who are not appropriate for the group.

MODELS OF GROUP PSYCHOTHERAPY

I do not question the beneficial effects of good psychotherapy in the form of support, education, emotional insight, and growth. These are life-enhancing, comforting, and sometimes even life-saving aids. In addition, we can consider other models of group therapy. I will briefly discuss four different models that can be envisioned as separate models or as part of a more integrated model of group psychotherapy.

The Alcoholics Anonymous Model

This model has proven to be the most helpful model to date in helping alcoholics and their families. In most cities AA meetings are conducted daily in recognition of the need for ongoing peer support and friendship. This model can be adapted to AD groups. Family members of AD, like family members of alcoholics, are dealing with a disease that is out of their control. They stand helplessly by, unable to change the course of the illness, and they frequently ignore their own needs in the process. In both diseases caregivers are also dealing with stigma, shame, social isolation, and unpredictable crises.

This model has other advantages—the groups usually meet every day, thus providing both ongoing social support and a recognition that problems occur on a daily basis, not just at 5 p.m. on Mondays. The leaderless aspect of an AA model also has some advantages, given the present shortage of professional resources. The disadvantage of this model is that it does not offer the important professional, trained objectivity. Additionally, the skills of good group leadership may be missing. The trained professional's objectivity and skills are important.

The Recreational Model

This model could emphasize recreational activities of the members' own choosing. Recreation is therapeutic in and of itself, and it is the greatest missing part of most caregivers' lives. To have a good time with friends is to be reminded that life does go on—a very important focus for people under severe stress. For some, the recreational model might meet most of their needs and be sufficient.

The Seminar Model

This model is an extension of current educational formats. As mentioned earlier in this chapter, knowledge about an illness, its course, treatments, behavior management, and community resources is always helpful. It has been my experience that group members are very eager to hear the latest research both on AD and on caregivers. They are able to make use of this information by increasing their understanding and tolerance of both the AD patient and themselves. The research findings seem to legitimize many of their negative feelings, thereby making it easier for them to accept feelings with less guilt. For example, when caregivers see that researchers are reporting that negative feelings are normal, not sinful or bad, then painful insights can be reinterpreted in helpful ways. Much of the research does show just that (Brody, 1985; Cantor, 1983; Jarret, 1985), and caregivers are both interested and comforted by the findings.

The Political Advocacy Model

The Alzheimer's Disease and Related Disorder (ADARD) groups are for advocacy, and perhaps what we should do is make referrals to ADARD for those group members who wish to become so involved. In addition, it might be therapeutic to point out the inequities of a system that places such an unfair burden on caregivers. The government provides more services and money for most other serious disabilities than it does for AD. According to Hepurn and Wasow, "the government has defined itself as a kind of watchdog. It acts to restrain costs . . . or it serves as a provider of last resort through medical assistance programs" (1986, p. 89). Family caregivers contribute to the government's efforts to contain health costs. Hepurn and Wasow (1986) go on to ask, does the running of support and therapy groups promote this policy "and reinforce an environment of expectations in which members go past the limits of what they can do, even to their own detriment and to that of the patient?" (p. 90).

Lest the mix of political advocacy and psychotherapy seem farfetched, Pratt, Schmall, and Wright (1987) studied 240 family caregivers of AD. When asked what their primary concerns were, 116 of them expressed ethical issues that had to do with how much "obligation" they owed to their AD patient, conflicts between caregiving and taking care of other family members as well as themselves, and their overwhelming financial burdens. It seems as if the psychological and political or policy issues go very much hand in hand.

POLITICAL AND POLICY IMPLICATIONS

What are the policy and political implications of running therapy groups for caregivers? Let me make an extreme analogy: We would not try to pacify angry minorities only by running therapy groups to help them adjust to the miseries of prejudice. Hopefully, we would also encourage them to organize and put their energies into fighting prejudice. Again and again we have seen the positive psychological and political effects of such groups. Examples of this are the black power movement, the gay liberation movement, and the woman's movement. Look what happened when parents of mentally retarded children got together and advocated for better care of their loved ones. For years parents of mentally ill children were in therapy groups to discuss their problems. Today we are witnessing the phenomenal growth of the National Alliance of the Mentally Ill (NAMI), an organization of family members that is very active in political advocacy, pushing for research money and better housing and governmental help on all levels.

While I fully appreciate that political activism and group psychotherapy are two different phenomena, by no means mutually exclusive, and that political activism is not only not for everybody but is usually only for a minority—I worry that we may be missing something very important. By supporting group psychotherapy for caregivers of AD to the exclusion of activism, we may be inadvertently supporting a disgraceful governmental system of noncare. Maybe we should be directing some of the anger toward advocacy for better care. This will not alleviate the pain of losing a loved one to a dread disease, but it could alleviate some of the economic and physical stresses for caregivers.

There is certainly a great need for support and therapy for people going through the multiple stresses of caring for AD patients. In addition, we could be giving consideration to political advocacy for those people who are interested and might benefit directly (by improved services) and indirectly (by emotional satisfaction) by the work.

SUMMARY AND RECOMMENDATIONS

Caring for a family member with AD is a devastating experience, and caregivers should be given all the help we can possibly offer. Psychotherapy groups, in the broadest sense, could encompass everything from psychological insight to political advocacy. There are many factors that play into the burdens for caregivers.

First and foremost of these factors is the pain of loss: caring for a loved one whose brain is dying. Then we have a culture in which expectations of love and devotion go beyond what many can give. These expectations tend to set up an unending cycle of resentment, exhaustion, guilt, trying harder, failure, and frustration. These subjects come up in psychotherapy groups, as do the more practical concerns about legal issues, financial issues, behavior management techniques, and the need for information about AD and community resources for help.

It is also noted that some seemingly taboo subjects do not come up easily, but when mentioned by group leaders tend to stir up a lot of interest. We know relatively little about these: sexuality, thoughts about divorce for financial or other reasons, preparation for the caregiver's life after the death of their family member, the right to death, and issues around giving up care before the caregiver is completely worn out.

No one questions the help and comfort derived from being in a group among "one's own"—nor in the good of a sound educational program to give caregivers the information they need about AD and all of its many ramifications. Most of our findings to date indicate that emotional support, education, and psychological insight prove helpful to caregivers.

Questions have been raised in this chapter about group composition, when insight might be harmful, possible negative effects of focusing on AD too much, and the political implications of going along with a system that placates caregivers rather than stirring them toward political advocacy.

All of this points toward the need to be highly creative in offering different models of therapy groups, in recognition of the very different needs of caregivers. There are no neat and predictable stages of grieving and coping with AD, and we do not have any neat packages for care or therapy either. So we need to be creative in our attempts to help and, above all, to *listen carefully* to what the caregivers are telling us. We must listen with our heads and with our hearts.

REFERENCES

Barnes, R. F., Riskind, M. A., Scott, M., & Murphy, C. (1981). Problems of families caring for Alzheimer patients: The use of a support group. *Journal of the American Geriatrics Society, 29*, 80–85.

Brody, E. (1985). Parent care as normative family stress. *The Gerontologist, 25*, 19–28.

Cantor, M. (1983). Strain among caregivers: A study of experience in the U.S. *The Gerontologist, 23*, 597–604.

Colman, V., Sommers, T., & Leonard, F. (1982). *Till death do us part: Caregivers of severely disabled husbands*. Gray Paper No. 7, Issues for Action. Oakland, CA: Older Women's League.

Fitting, M., Rabins, P., Lucas, M. J., & Eastham, J. (1986). Caregivers for dementia patients: A comparison of husband and wives. *The Gerontologist, 26*, 248–252.

Hepurn, K., & Wasow, M. (1986). Support groups for family caregivers of dementia victims: Questions, directions, and future research. In N. S. Abramson, J. K. Quam, & M. Wasow (Eds.), *New directions for mental health services* (vol. 29, pp. 83–92). San Francisco: Jossey-Bass.

Jarrett, W. H. (1985). Caregiving within kinship systems: Is affection really necessary? *The Gerontologist, 25*, 5–10.

Lazarus, L. W. (1981). A pilot study of an Alzheimer patients relatives discussion group. *The Gerontologist, 21*(4), 355.

Miller, B. (1987). Gender and control among spouses of the cognitively impaired: A research note. *The*

Gerontologist, 27, 447–453.

Pratt, C., Schmall, V. & Wright, S. (1987). Ethical concerns of family caregivers to dementia patients. *The Gerontologist, 27*(5).

Schmidt, G., & Keyes, B. (1985). Group psychotherapy with family caregivers of demented patients. *The Gerontologist, 25*, 347–350.

Steuer, J. L. (1984). Caring for the caregiver. *Generations, 2*, 56–58.

Wasow, M. (1986). Support groups for family caregivers of patients with Alzheimer's disease. *Social Work, 31*(2), 93–97.

Winogrond, I., Fisk, A. A., Kirsling, R. A., & Keyes, B. (1987). The relationship of caregiver burden and morale to Alzheimer's disease patient function in a therapeutic setting. *The Gerontologist, 27*(33), 336–339.

Index